# Through our eyes

150 years of history
as seen through the eyes
of the writers and editors
of the Deseret News

**Title page photo:** A three-story adobe building on South Temple housed a church store, a post office and the Deseret News, which was at home there for 41 years. Well-known Utah photographer Charles R. Savage captured a typical day in the life of the building. Eventually the Hotel Utah was built on that corner.

# Deseret News

ISBN: 1-57345-660-8

# Through our eyes

150 years of history
as seen through the eyes
of the writers and editors
of the Deseret News

Edited by Don C. Woodward

Designed by Robert R. Noyce

Written by Twila Van Leer
and Carma Wadley
and the staff of the Deseret News,
1850-1999.

Deseret News
Salt Lake City, Utah

Publisher Wm. James Mortimer

Editor and Chief Operating Officer
John Hughes

**Photo:** The Oregon Short Line
Building, later known as the
Union Pacific Building, was
home to Deseret News for
nearly a quarter of a century.

# Publisher's letter

**By Wm. James Mortimer**
Publisher, Deseret News

One hundred and fifty years strong! That is the enviable position of the Deseret News as we move into a new millennium. We are 150 years wiser and better. We're poised to continue to grow and serve the journalistic needs of one of America's fastest-growing regions.

When the first issue of the Deseret News came out on June 15, 1850, it was not the first newspaper published by The Church of Jesus Christ of Latter-day Saints. Several, serving specific areas of church population, preceded it. None endured once the members, who had been driven out of New York, Ohio, Missouri and Illinois, found a permanent home in the Great Basin of the West where none would "come to hurt or make afraid."

Brigham Young and his hardy band of pioneers chose isolation in the barren deserts of the West, and with determination, hard work, and faith founded an empire that is still growing in world-wide importance. The church was the only organized institution in the new territory, and chose as the name of its new homeland "Deseret," taken from the Book of Mormon, a word that denoted the industriousness and hard work of the honeybee. Although the territory ultimately became known as Utah the state is still widely known as the "Beehive State."

Communication and the dissemination of information was very important to Brigham Young. He went to extraordinary efforts to bring a printing press to the territory, along with type, paper, inks, glue, and other printing supplies. While the survival of the church members in their new surroundings was of primary importance, as homes were built and crops harvested, the newspaper came into being. Dr. Willard Richards was its first editor.

From the outset the Deseret News has striven to be more than a religious newspaper. It is a rarity for a church-supported paper to deal with general news and seek a non-denominational audience, but in the estimation of Dr. Frank Luther Mott, the dean of American journalism historians, the Deseret News not only attempted, but has succeeded in its dual role as a religious and secular newspaper. He says the Deseret News has the distinction of being the first successful religious daily in the English language. (See American Journalism, p. 288.)

Today, one can only speculate as to what Brigham Young and Willard Richards envisioned for the future of the Deseret News. Surely they must have dreamed that it would survive through many difficulties and grow in its journalistic mission, both for the church and for its readers.

Those of us who now occupy the positions they once held are keenly aware of the history and traditions of this venerable institution. We have pledged our professional lives to maintaining the best of the past and to building for the future, so that we, too, can pass on to future generations of journalists a strong and vibrant newspaper.

As its first editor, Willard Richards set forth lofty goals for the Deseret News. He wrote a prospectus prior to publication and then printed it in the first edition after he had finally gained the 300 subscriptions necessary to publish.

At the top of the prospectus were the words TRUTH and LIBERTY.

Although driven from their original homelands, the members of the church maintained a strong belief in the Constitution of the United States and defended its promises of liberty. They had learned through sad experiences what it was like to be without liberty.

There is no deviation today from that sacred motto of truth and liberty. It burns within us as strongly now as it did 150 years ago.

The balance of Dr. Richards' prospectus dealt with subscription prices and costs for advertising. The six-month price was $2.50, with a single copy price of 15 cents. This has changed a little, but the next phrase in the prospectus is still good advice: "Invariably in advance."

Thus were the hopes of Dr. Richards and his small staff 150 years ago. We continue to espouse these desires and purposes, and pledge to preserve the newspaper far into the future so that those ahead may look back to us even as we look to our founders, and say that while much has been done and the foundation is secure, the best is still to come!

# Editor's letter

**By John Hughes**
Editor and Chief Operating Officer, Deseret News

Let me tell a little anecdote that underlines the pace of change in our lives.

I was born in a little Welsh town called Neath. My father was born there before me. Although this may seem incredible to today's readers, when my father was a young man there was not a single automobile in the little town of Neath. He and his brother rode the family horse about 30 miles away to the city of Cardiff to acquire the town's first car.

They traded the horse for it. But the early cars were unreliable, and on the way home it broke down. So they trudged back to Cardiff, borrowed back the horse, and used it to tow the car home. That's how the first car came, ignominiously, to the little Welsh town of Neath.

What a change we've seen in one generation, from the first car in town to a world of space ships, satellites and the Internet. Nobody understands this better than people who live in, or are familiar with, Utah, a state that in a hundred fifty years has been transformed from inhospitable desert to booming cities, a center for medical research and advanced technology, and a place where dance, music and the arts flourish.

No industry has felt the impact of this technological change more significantly than the communications industry.

As the Deseret News has chronicled these changes in Utah, so it too has been transformed from a newspaper for the early settlers, printed on a rickety, sheet-fed press, to a metropolitan newspaper in a soaring new building, which visitors declare to be equipped with the most modern technology in journalism. Our syndicated news services arrive by satellite. Our photographers use digital cameras that use no film, but send pictures back by digital signal over cell phones in seconds from anywhere in the world. Our reporters type their stories on laptop computers and transmit them from wherever news is breaking. It is a communications miracle.

But what makes a newspaper is not computers, and cameras, and presses, but the creativity and integrity of the people behind them. For 150 years, the Deseret News has been blessed by editors and reporters and other staffers of great talent. Building on that foundation, the newspaper has today assembled a staff of editors, reporters, artists, photographers and supporting personnel who are united in their dedication to their craft, and in their loyalty to the newspaper that displays it 365 days a year.

The book you hold in your hands, produced by this staff, is at once the story of Utah, and the story of the Deseret News.

We hope you will find it a volume of lasting enjoyment.

# Contents

**Photo:** In the 1920s, a line of trucks was poised and waiting for the papers to roll off the press. Most downtown papers were sold by newsboys on street corners, but copies of the paper were trucked to outlying areas.

# Foreword

Since 1850, just three years after the first pioneers jolted down Emigration Canyon into the Valley of the Great Salt Lake, the Deseret News has been part of the fabric of Utah. It was, in every sense, a pioneer newspaper when it started. Reading it over the years is like peering through a window into the past.

In that spirit, this book is offered as an affectionate look at some of the events that shaped Utah and our world over the past 150 years, as told or compiled by the staff of the state's oldest newspaper. During that time the Deseret News faithfully recorded the news, both great and small, historic and mundane, foreign and domestic, as it occurred.

You'll find those stories here, retold just as they appeared on the day they were first printed.

The book, however, is not a comprehensive history. Those people did their jobs well, turning out thousands and thousands of stories over the past century and a half. Choosing which to retell was a formidable task, and we are the first to acknowledge that a great many important stories are not included. Many significant events may be recalled with just a passing mention, even if they once occupied our attention for days or months. Others, because they are the first draft of history, are incomplete, although we've tried to provide some background and explanation for them. Our simple goal was to try to recapture the flavor of the times so that you, the reader, would have a clearer insight into the past. We hope you'll be charmed by their writing and moved by the immediacy of those events, many of which are now long-forgotten.

At the same time, the book commemorates our own 150th anniversary on June 15, 2000. By compiling these stories we pay tribute to the hundreds of talented people over the years who dedicated themselves to the newspaper and to their communities. Most of them did their work anonymously — bylines are a fairly recent practice. All kinds of skills are needed to bring a newspaper to the doorstep — writers, editors, photographers, artists, couriers, accountants, salesmen, printers, distributors, paper carriers and many more. Some of those skills (linotype operators come to mind) have since vanished only to be replaced by others (Internet editors come to mind). All of them share the common goal of bringing the most accurate news possible to the community.

This book is a tribute to their labors. It is also a tribute to the newsmakers themselves, for whom we were at once an observer, a critic and a companion.

Don Woodward, Carma Wadley, Twila Van Leer and Robert Noyce spent months digging through photo archives and microfilm files to find stories the Deseret News told during its 150 years of history.

# Settlement Era

## 1850-1860

In July 1847, when 147 members of the Vanguard company of Latter-day Saint pioneers entered the Salt Lake Valley, they opened a period of Western colonization unparalleled in the history of the United States. From then until May 1869, when the eastern and western railway lines linked together and effectively ended the "pioneer" era, approximately 60,000 people plied the Mormon trail from the banks of the Missouri River to Great Salt Lake City.

They came to escape persecution in the east. But what they found in their new home was a totally unfamiliar desert wilderness. They had to learn how to grow crops in an arid country, lay out new communities, establish a system of governance, take care of new pioneers arriving by the hundreds, find sources of raw materials and figure out a thousand other details.

Into this era of frenetic activity and significant challenge was born the Deseret News. Willard Richards, the first editor, wrote:

**DESERET NEWS,** *June 15, 1850: We propose to publish a small weekly sheet, as large as our local circumstances will permit, to be* called 'Deseret News,' designed originally to record the passing events of our State and in connection, refer to the arts and sciences, embracing general education, medicine, law, divinity, domestic and political economy and everything that may fall under our observation, which may tend to promote the best interest, welfare, pleasure and amusement of our fellow citizens.

He stressed that actual publishing would have to wait on the "action of 300 subscribers" who could get six months of the News for

$2.50 *"Invariably in advance. Single copies 15 cents."*

On June 15, 1850, the first edition came off the simple Ramage press, located in the small log territorial mint building. Eight pages of 7 1/4 by 9 3/4 inches were filled, primarily with reports from the U.S. Congress, where questions of slavery were dividing a nation. (One observer was quoted as saying that he was "confident blood will be spilt on the floor of the House before the session closes.") A message from President Zachary Taylor to the House, given five months earlier, also got space in the first issue, as did news of a San Francisco fire that had been out for six months.

If the news was stale by modern standards, it was welcomed by pioneering

Immigrants in Echo Canyon, 1866, by Charles R. Savage.

In the first decade of the Deseret News, Utahns were well under way in creating a culture and society. It was a period of intense immigration, with people arriving by the wagonloads, often speaking other languages, while settlers tried to figure out how to grow crops and create the structures of government. They founded a university (of Deseret, now Utah), were named a territory of the United States and started building. They created a dramatic society, built a Social Hall and experimented with a phonetic alphabet. But they also found themselves at war, at times with Indians in the Walker War, but also with the federal government, which sent troops to march through the city in what proved to be a misguided and embarrassing excursion for the president.

## PIONEER Immigration

| YEAR | IMMIGRANTS |
|---|---|
| 1847 | 1,637 |
| 1848 | 2,444 |
| 1849 | 1,598 |
| 1850 | 3,760 |
| 1851 | 1,735 |
| 1852 | 5,543 |
| 1853 | 3,037 |
| 1854 | 3,005 |
| 1855 | 2,046 |
| 1856 | 3,466 |
| 1857 | 1,373 |
| 1858 | 285 |
| 1859 | 1,639 |
| 1860 | 2,061 |
| TOTAL | 33,344 |

Where exact numbers were not recorded, statistics are estimates based on the usual number of people per wagon.
Provided by LDS Church Historical Department.

Utahns as a link with the outside world from which they were far removed.

The Deseret News soon became an integral part of pioneer life, bringing not only news from the larger world but also printing practical advice to a people who were adjusting to a new land, a new climate and a new life. Messages of church leaders and news of pioneers still on the trail or arriving by boat from Europe mingled with such practical items as instructions on how to grow crops, maintain health and rear children.

Brigham Young, the great pioneer leader and president of The Church of Jesus Christ of Latter-day Saints, had, in fact, led them out of the United States entirely in 1847. The Great Basin was part of the vast territory claimed by Mexico. Within a year, however, with the signing of the Treaty of Guadalupe-Hidalgo on Feb. 1, 1848, the pioneers were once again in American territory.

While international political issues resolved themselves, Young continued his colonizing ways. He envisioned a huge theo-democracy from the Rocky Mountains to the Pacific Ocean. Within months of the arrival of the first pioneer companies, his scouts fanned out from the Salt Lake Valley in all directions, finding sites suitable for colonization. His purpose was to make "every nook and cranny from here to the Bay of San

Francisco known to the Mormons."

Within a few years, Mormon pioneers were building dozens of communities radiating out from the center settlement as far afield as present-day California, Nevada, Idaho and Arizona.

Almost immediately, the settlers petitioned Congress to authorize the State of Deseret. It would have comprised a sixth of the land mass of the United States, encompassing parts of eastern California, Arizona, Colorado, New Mexico, Idaho and Wyoming as well as the entirety of what became Utah. But historic realities quickly began to erode the dimensions of Young's dreams. The Organic Act of Jan. 21, 1850, created Utah Territory, a huge tract but much smaller than the scope of his ambitions. Over the next few decades, the territory was further trimmed back to give land to surrounding states.

All of this was noted in the new newspaper. Those early pages are full of stories, great and small, that offer insights into the settlement period. Even if no one reporter took the time to write an overall story about the epic struggle they were in, the cumulative impact of those early pages is a vivid portrayal of life in early Utah.

As a unique voice on the frontier, the Deseret News became messenger, educator, arbiter, advocate and entertainer — a role it has fulfilled for 150 years.

**Ramage press that printed the first edition of the Deseret News on June 15, 1850, was hauled across the plains by wagon.**

LDS Church Museum

# Brigham Young

T he unique colonization of the Great Basin in the mid-19th century involved tens of thousands of people but bore the specific imprint of one man — Brigham Young.

Through three decades, from the arrival of the first pioneers in Salt Lake Valley in July 1847 to his death in August 1877, "Brother Brigham" was the religious inspiration, the political arbiter and the creative genius behind all aspects of a settlement story unparalleled in American history. Recognized by historians today as one of the great figures of the 19th century, the sobriquets "American Moses" and "Lion of the Lord" were well and naturally applied.

More than 100 communities dotted Utah Territory under his direction. Some remained a part of the Utah scene; others earned only passing mention in the state's history. Although the pioneer leader's schemes for self-sufficiency were not invariably successful, they indelibly colored the settlement era.

In an amazingly short time, given the challenges, Utah Territory had well-organized government structures, commerce and manufacturing, a comprehensive education system, communication networks that included transcontinental railroads and telegraph, precedent-setting irrigation systems to support desert agriculture and a relatively self-maintaining, well-ordered society.

In the period from 1847 to 1869, when the arrival of the railroad quickly supplanted overland migration, the colonies he established absorbed an estimated 60,000 newcomers. He personally oversaw the mechanics of much of the migration from the eastern United States and European countries. Although the coming of the

LDS Church Archives

**Brigham Young in 1850, photographed by Marcena Cannon.**

rails ended the Mormons' "pioneering era," massive immigration continued well into the 20th century following the pattern established by Young.

Despite his undisputed leadership of the LDS migration, Young gave the credit to another source: "I do not wish men to understand that I had anything to do with our being moved here; that was the providence of the Almighty. It was the power of God that wrought out salvation for this people. I never could have devised such a plan." He was, first and foremost, a prophet and spiritual leader for his people.

Non-LDS Church historian Herbert E. Bolton described Young as "a devout believer, but more especially, he was a lion-hearted man of iron will, an organizer and the founder of a commonwealth."

He was born June 1, 1801, in Whittingham, Windham County, Vermont, into an austere and God-fearing family of little means. As a young man, he moved to New York and lived the life of a typical New England carpenter/farmer. The pivotal events in his life came in the early 1830s when he became acquainted with the fledgling Church of Jesus Christ of Latter-day Saints. His was not a compulsive conversion. "I weighed the matter for a year and a half. I looked at it on all sides. I reasoned on it month after month until I came to a certain knowledge of its truth," he later said.

On Feb. 14, 1835, he was ordained to the Quorum of the Twelve and eventually became its president. Upon the assassination of Joseph Smith and his brother Hyrum on June 27, 1844, Young assumed leadership of the troubled church.

For some time before the martyrdom of Joseph and Hyrum Smith, church leaders studied the possibility of a move to the then-unpeopled West to escape the persecutions that had hounded the Saints from community to community through the Midwest. It fell upon Young to fulfill this mandate.

He became both the founder of Salt Lake City and governor of Utah Territory. He was the undisputed spiritual guide in what the LDS hoped would become a self-sufficient and exclusive Western state. History dictated otherwise when the inevitable settlement of the entire West began in earnest.

And if some thought his leadership over all aspects of pioneer life was heavy-handed, he made no excuses. After the church publicly acknowledged the practice of polygamy in 1852, Brigham Young became known throughout the world not only for his colonizing skills but also for the number of wives he had. He staunchly championed the doctrine all of his life. The practice placed the state at odds with the federal government for three decades, with increasingly hostile actions directed by Congress.

Although Brigham Young's approach to governance was strict, hundreds of anecdotes attest to his love, charity and long-suffering toward those he led. If he demanded a high standard of them, he applied the same to himself. In retrospect, if he had taken a less undeviating course, Utah would have evolved differently.

A New York reporter sent to Utah Territory to look at this national curiosity, the Mormons, attended a July 24 picnic party at Brighton, hosted by the pioneer leader. At the end of a busy day, the reporter wrote, he saw a lone man wandering through the campground cleaning up the debris of the celebration and seeing that all the fires were out. That man was Brigham Young, leader and servant.

Pioneer Memorial Museum

# Quotes
## OF BRIGHAM YOUNG

**Selected from thousands, these words give an insight into the founder of Utah.**

**DESERET NEWS,** *Sept. 14, 1852:*
*Permit me to say that I am proud of my religion. It is the only thing I pride myself in, on the earth. I may heap up gold and silver like the mountains; I may gather around me property, goods and chattels, but I could have no glory in that, compared with my religion ...*

**DESERET NEWS,** *June 7, 1863:*
*Will you do me the kindness to cease paying Tithing from this time forth, unless you pay it in a different manner than heretofore? They pile up wheat in Cache county, in Utah county, in Sanpete and in every other county distant from this city, in bins and houses where much of it becomes musty and good for nothing.*
**(He wanted communities to sell their goods for cash.)**

**DESERET NEWS,** *July 9, 1856:*
*Glancing at the past, perhaps we as a people have more reason to respect, honor, love and cherish the government of the United States, her Constitution and free institutions than any other people on the face of the earth; but it is lamentable that professed statesmen should so far deviate from wise and correct principles of republican government as to fail of being entitled to that respect and confidence which ought to be deserved by those entrusted with its administration.*

**DESERET NEWS,** *June 7, 1857:*
*Those whom the government sends here are a most miserable set, and, as a general rule, they do not know enough to tell a decent lie ... It is hard for them to tell a man who has got brains in his head from one who is filled with pudding. The President and his Cabinet know nothing about the*

**Brigham Young painted in the uniform of the Nauvoo Legion.**

*characters whom they send here; if they did, many who have come here never would have been sent.*

**DESERET NEWS,** *Sept. 18, 1862:*
*Do not any of you suffer the thought to enter your minds that you must go to the gold mines in search for riches. That is no place for the saints. Some have gone there and returned; they keep coming and going, but their garments are spotted, almost universally ... This world is only to be used as an apartment, in which the children of men may be prepared for their eternal redemption and exaltation in the presence of their Savior.*

**DESERET NEWS,** *Aug. 8, 1869:*
*One thing is very true and we believe it, and that is that a woman is the glory of the man; but she was not made to be worshipped by him ... A man is not made to be worshipped by his family; but he is to be their head and to be good and upright before them... and the woman is to be his helpmeet.*

**DESERET NEWS,** *April 7, 1861:*
*I am ashamed, not only in my own family, but others, to see the gewgaws that are so often put upon children, when an antelope skin or a piece of blue factory would make much more suitable clothing for them. Dress them in strong, durable cloth, and that, too, made by your own hands. But, no, the finest fabrics must be put upon them to play in. Some, if they could, would put fifty dollars' worth on a child, and send him into the street to ride upon the rails, climb trees, Etc.*

**DESERET NEWS,** *Oct. 30, 1870:*
*You come to the rich, that is, those who are best off, for we cannot boast that anybody is rich in our community, but those who have the most means, as a general thing, do the least. Our tithes and offerings are neglected; the poor are needy, they want bread, a little of something to make them comfortable.*

**DESERET NEWS,** *July 28, 1856:*
*As we have here an assemblage of the people from other settlements, I wish to impress them with the necessity of treating the Indians with kindness and to refrain from harboring that revengeful, vindictive feeling that many indulge in. I am convinced that as long as we harbor in us such feelings towards them, so long they will be our enemies and the Lord will suffer them to afflict us.*

# DESERET NEWS.

BY W. RICHARDS　　　　　　　　　　　　　　　　G. S. L. CITY, DESERET

In the 1850s, Deseret News offered sermons and advice from LDS Church leaders, immigration and settlement news, advertisements about the availability of scarce "import" goods, information on how to exist in Utah Territory's desert climate and all kinds of current events, usually days or even weeks after they occurred. A selection follows, reproduced as close as possible to the original versions:

**June, 1850**

## POETRY

### TO MY FRIENDS IN THE VALLEY

Let all who would have a good paper,
Their talents, and time ne'er abuse;
Since 'tis said, by the wise and the humored,
That the best in the world is the "NEWS."

Then ye who so long have been thinking
What paper this year you will choose,
Come trip gaily up to the office,
And subscribe for the "Deseret News.'

And now, dearest friends, I will leave you;
This counsel, I pray you, don't lose;
The best of advice I can give you
Is, pay in advance for the "News."
　　　　　　　　　　B.

G.S.L. City, May 27, 1850

This is the first poetic offering we have received, and, for aught we know, friend B's. first attempt. Try again.

**June 22, 1850**

**COUNTERFEITS** — On Tuesdy, a brass, gold piece, a poor imitation of the English Sovereign, was passed at our office, by an imigrant. Other counterfeit boguses have been offered, in various places. We would caution the brethren to be on the lookout. We advise all travellers who deal in bogus money to preserve it carefully till they get beyond Deseret, as they will find it in better demand elsewhere. We are able to furnish all we need for home consumption, and neither want to BUY or SELL; therefore, take the advice of a friend, and keep your bogus out of sight and it will speed you on your journey.

**July 20, 1850**

☞ AN ORDINANCE CREATING AN OFFICE FOR THE RECORDING OF 'MARKS AND BRANDS' on horses, mules, cattles and all other stock, passed by the Legislative Council Saturday, Dec. 19, 1849, No. 130.

It shall be the duty of the Recorder to keep exposed in his office or at some public place near the Temple Block a faithful copy of all marks or brands, recorded by him, and the names of the owners of said brands...

That William Clayton be appointed the Recorder of brands, according to the provisions of this ordinance.

**July 19, 1850**

## THE GOLDEN PASS!
## OR
## NEW ROAD THROUGH MOUNTAINS

Travellers between the States and California are respectfully informed that a new road will be opened on and after the 4th of July, between the Weber River and Great Salt Lake Valley, distance about 40 miles, avoiding the two great mountains and most of the Kanyons so troublesome on the old route.

The road is somewhat rough and unfinished, but is being made better every day. Several thousand dollars are already expended by the proprietor, who only solicits the patronage of the public at the moderate charge of

50 cents per conveyance drawn by one animal.
75 cents per conveyance drawn by two animals.
10 cents per each additional draught, pack or saddle animal.
5 cents per head for loose stock.
1 cent per head for sheep.

If a road worked by the most persevering industry, an open country, good feed and fuel, beautifully romantic and sublime scenery are any inducement, take the new road and thus encourage public improvement.
　　　　　　　　　　P. P. Pratt,
　　　　　　　　　　Proprietor

**Parley's Canyon road is now Interstate 80.**

**Feb. 20, 1851**

As I am leaving for the States about the first day of March, I take this method being the second and last time, to notify all who are indebted to me either by note or book account, to call immediately, in order to settle the same.

Any person not responding to the above request may rest assured that necessity will compel me (however reluctant) to enter my accounts for compulsory collection.

Permit me further to notify any person remitting money to the States, for the purchase and importation of any article or articles, that I will transact the business with precision and dispatch, upon as reasonable terms as the nature of the case will admit.
　　　　　　　　　　T.S. Williams

**April 8, 1851**

## DESERET BATHING HOUSE!

The inhabitants of Deseret are hereby respectfully informed that the Baths are now open and printed tickets ready for issue to accommodate families by the quarter, half year, or year. The following are the terms for privilege of the Baths, vis:

| | |
|---|---|
| For single person per quarter | $0.50 |
| Families of from 2 to 4 persons, per quarter | 1.00 |
| 5 to 8 persons per quarter | 2.00 |
| 8 to 16 persons, per quarter | 3.00 |
| 16 to 24 persons, per quarter | 3.50 |

Families to furnish their own towels.
Tickets for sale at the Tithing Office and also at the Bath House.

　　　　　　　　　　JAMES HENDRICKS, Proprietor

**May 17, 1851**

☞ RUMORS, concerning the Indians, thicker than mountain crickets, and of a greater variety of colors, waft on every breeze, but who knows where they come from, or whither gone or how much truth there is in them? Tell us, and "faith, we'll print it."

**Sept. 14, 1850**

☞ United States Mail arrived on Tuesday, direct from Independence, Mo. We gather no news of general interest from the mail, though it is reported by the carrier that President Zachary Taylor died on the 9th of July. The question has been repeatedly asked, who killed him? Rumors say, CHOLERA! We remember the short career of Pres't. Harrison and wait patiently for particulars. From the further representations of the carrier, in future we may expect a monthly mail; the next on the 1st of October, or 15 days hence.

**June 22, 1851**

The public works are progressing well, considering the circumstances which surround us. If the brethren would be more prompt with their labor tithing, and the farmers in the country would bring forward their butter, cheese, eggs, vegetables, etc., as fast as they receive it, it would be a great blessing to themselves and the workmen and expedite business.

The walls of the blacksmith shop on the Temple Block are completed; the storehouse on State House Lot, designed for the occupancy of Messrs. Livingston and Kinkead, are ready for the timbers and the brick are now being laid for the church storehouse and store, east of the Bowery. The floors are being placed in the State House and the best of slate is now quarrying at Utah for the roof. The aqueduct to the Bath House is nearly completed.

**July 19, 1851**

## THE CELEBRATION
## OF THE FOURTH OF JULY

On Friday morning, at day break, a salute of three round of cannon ushered in, to the sleeping inhabitants of Great Salt Lake City, the glorious Fourth of July; and whose peaceful slumbers were disturbed by the reverberating sound of the roaring artillery, commissioning them to prepare themselves for their chivalrous march to the shores of the Great Salt Lake — the world's ninth wonder. A response from Black Rock on the Lake at the same time (though twenty miles from the city) gave the assurance that it was prepared to receive its numerous and distinguished guests. At 7 o'clock the city began to be in motion and the busy throng to assemble. The rattling of carriages, the rumbling of wagons, the tramp of horse, the floating of banners, the swelling tones of the brass band, the elegance, beauty and smiles of the fair and the smiling heavens above, gave an enchantment to the scene and bespoke the occasion a nation's birth-day.

**July 2, 1856**

## Prospects

In addition to the drouth and destruction by insects last season, to the severity of the past winter and consequent heavy loss of stock, and to the destitution we are still suffering, the long continued dry weather, the scant supply of water at command for irrigation, the entire destruction of crops by grasshoppers in Cache county and the like destruction in portions of Box Elder and Utah counties, the general ravages of tobacco and other worms upon potatoes and corn, and the parching of whole fields of grain before the heads are filled are far from promising a surplus of food for the Saints now here and the thousands already on their way to the mountains.

Strong faith in the wisdom of the providences of the Almighty, great skill, strict obedience to the commandments of the Lord and the counsels of his servants, the most rigid economy and untiring well-directed industry may enable us to escape starvation until a harvest in 1857.

And until the elapse of at least another year, emigrants and others will fail in their dependence upon Utah for sustenance and will run great risk of starving unless they bring their supplies with them, and that, too, not in gold, silver and merchandize with a view to exchange advantageously, but in such an amount of provisions as they may need until August 1857 and for how much longer we are not informed.

**July 2, 1856**

☞ **SAVING CHOICE SEEDS** — The fact that we can get superior breeds of animals only from the very best and most perfect specimens, is so well established that no one now doubts it and thousands pay large amounts for the use or ownership of these superior breeders. Why should not the case be analagous in the raising of vegetables? Experience says it is analagous — that superior vegetables can be raised only from the most mature and perfect seeds.

**July 16, 1856**

## More of the Drowned Mail

It will be remembered that the carriers lost a portion of the May 1st mail in Weber river on the 30th of May; that they brought in several sacks on the 4th of June, the contents of many of them being much damaged; and that one sack was recovered from the water and brought in on the 7th of June, all of its contents being thoroughly soaked …

How many are still in and near that stream the Indians will probably inform us, as fast as they may casually discover them while roaming in quest of berries, roots and game.

**July 30, 1856**

On the morning of the 23rd inst., Prests. Brigham Young, Heber C. Kimball and Jedediah M. Grant and many citizens from Great Salt Lake City and surrounding country, with wives and children, entered the mouth of Big Cottonwood Kanyon on their way to the headwaters of that stream, to spend the ninth anniversary of the entrance of the Pioneers into the Valley of Great Salt Lake…

At the head of the bowery is a large pine one hundred feet high, to the top of which br. John Bagley, assisted by Patriarch John Smith, son of Hyrum Smith, who was martyred for his religion in Carthage jail, fastened the flag of the United States.

Nature seems to have exerted herself to out-vie art in forming this enchantingly beautiful place …Every heart that could feel, every mind that could appreciate the skillful blending of the sublime and picturesque and realize the deep silent peace that all nature seemed bathed in, could not entertain an angry thought, a jealous feeling, an unvirtuous desire, and hardly a willingness to ever again mingle with the ungodly world.

**Oct. 5, 1856**

## Are Our Schools Injuring the Bodies of Our Children?

There is not a more important interest in the State than the Common School. Occupying the exclusive attention of those who are to be the men and women of the next generation, for many hours of each day, its influence upon society can scarcely be over rated and any error of physical training that by implication or by constitution it circulates becomes a serious wrong.

Now, 5 1/2 hours would not be too much for any healthful child, if with the ringing of the dismissal bell there came a season of relaxation until 9 of the next day. But when we meet our boy of ten years old returning from school, we find him always loaded down with books — geography, astronomy, physiology and a half a score of the sort beside — in several of which he assures us that he must get a lesson before morning. And upon farther inquiry, we find that except for exercises in arithmetic, reading, spelling and writing, all his studying is to be done out of school hours…

Coming home from school, he is jaded and weary. He loathes the sight of a book. He longs to put his old "trowsers" on and kneel in the gutter or on the crossing to have one good game of marbles, or he agonizes for a game at ball or "tag." He wants to expand his lungs and stretch his legs and shake himself unhampered by a nice coat and out of the sight of grumbling teachers or guardians.

If (parents) sound the alarm and unite in protest against any evil of the sort, there is no question that the authorities will soon interfere to protect the suffering of the children and save the next generation from its threatened impotence.

**(American Medical Monthly)**

**Oct. 8, 1856**

## The First Deseret State Fair

Was held in this city on the 2nd, 3rd, and 4th inst. and was highly creditable to the skill and industry of our infant settlements.

The articles on exhibition filled most of the spacious rooms in the building known as the Deseret Store. In the basement were large squashes, beets and carrots; various samples of wheat, corn, flour, garden seeds, etc.; garden implements, large hens from Land's End, England, Etc…

On the 2nd, a spirited plowing match came off in one of the Governor's fields adjacent to the city. On the 3rd, there was a highly creditable exhibition of stock.

This fair will operate as a great incentive to the development of home resources, by showing the people how much has already been done, and how they can readily do far more and better.

**Aug. 12, 1857**

## SMALL POX

The small pox has been brought into Great Salt Lake County by a company which lately came in from the states with Benjamin Matthews, and who, contrary to all rules of propriety, fellow feeling or even common decency, most carefully kept to themselves the knowledge of their having imported a disease so contagious and dreaded. Through such an unwarranted course many lives have been wickedly jeopardized, with a word of warning, to an extent impossible to determine at present…

Matthews' company is camped on Big Cottonwood about a quarter of a mile northeast of br. Robert Pierce's; and all in that company who have the small pox or are liable to have it, are hereby cautioned and warned to at once remove from the road into some uninhabited and unfrequented spot and to cease traveling or mingling with those who have not had the small pox and all inhabitants liable to be infected are cautioned to keep entirely aloof from that company…

**July 22, 1857** *(excerpted from a letter by B.F. Matthews)*

I saw a notice in (a non-Mormon newspaper) stating that a train of emigrants on their way to California picked up a bead near an Indian camp, which was stuffed with cotton impregnated with smallpox virus and had been put there by the 'Mormons' to introduce that disease among the Indians, and thereby effect their destruction. This is a lie of the blackest dye, and is one of the contemptible and abominable methods by which our enemies are seeking to create excitement about and embitter the feelings of the people towards us and thereby arouse them to hostility against this people. I perceive that they have a great deal to say about the people of Utah, and a great many stories are circulated about the mistreatment of the California emigrants in the Salt Lake Valley, which I know to be false.

**Oct. 16, 1857**

## TO THE BISHOPS AND SAINTS

You are well aware that many of the brethren and sisters who annually arrive are destitute of teams, wagons, goods, cash and almost everything except what they have on. This is more particularly the case with those who have and will soon come in with hand carts, and calls for general and prompt philanthropic action on our part, that the time and skill of the new comers be not wasted, and that they may not needlessly suffer …

Suffer not people to run from Ward to Ward without a recommendation from their Bishop, that you may not be imposed upon by idlers or loafers.

While these steps are taken by the faithful and liberal, that the new comers may not be discouraged or suffer hardships uncalled for, it will be wisdom in the new comers to reflect that they have come to a new and strange country, where comforts and conveniences have to be wrested from the rude elements with much patience and labor; that they have not come here to sing themselves

(nor to be sung) away to everlasting bliss; but that useful occupation is honorable in all.

**Nov. 18, 1857**

**DROWNED** — On Saturday last, Nov. 14, while William and Samuel Frier Smith, brothers, were crossing the lower ford of Big Cottonwood Creek, the wagon upset, the box entirely covering William and resting upon Samuel F. just below his shoulders. In this position they lay some 5 hours, being unable to extricate themselves, when they were discovered by their grandmother, who went to the creek for water. They were taken out of the water lifeless, brought home to their bereaved mother, Mary Smith, who lives in the 11th Ward, G.S.L. City and buried on Mondy. William, the eldest, was aged 11 years and 9 months. Samuel F., the younger, 10 years and 2 months. Their father, W. J. Smith, is in England on a mission.

**Dec. 28, 1858**

## Another Shooting Affray

On Sunday afternoon, shortly after the close of the services at the Tabernacle, there was one of the most disgusting and disgraceful affrays that ever transpired in this city, the origin of which we have been unable to ascertain.

Some report as many as fifty shots fired by both parties, one of which was seemingly led by Lot Huntington and the other by W.A. Hickman, both of whom were wounded, the latter severly.

The shooting was commenced near Townsend's Hotel, and a running street fire kept up from thence up the street about one fourth of a mile. Huntington, who was on the retreat, then taking shelter in a house, the further effusion of blood was prevented by the interference of Gen. Grant and other citizens.

There were some eight or ten persons engaged in the combat, several of whom were closely visited with leaden balls, but none badly hurt excepting the two leaders and a man named Butcher, who, as reported, was either wounded in the affray or by the accidental discharge of his own pistol after it had ended.

Dr. D. DANIEL will phrenologise on any person's head who will come to Mr. Baylis' house in this city, for the price of one dollar. Dr. Daniel is from Texas. He will leave this city on Tuesday, July 23.

**July 16, 1856**

## THE WALL

Around the Temple Block was finished on the 15th inst., and much of the stone coping is already cut, and preparing for hoisting to its position for receiving the iron railing.

Iron masters, of Iron County, will you have the railing ready by the time the coping is laid?

**Nov. 30, 1850**

Mr. Edward Cooper of New York has been appointed Indian Agent to supply the vacancy occasioned by the resignation of Genl. John Wilson, who, we understand, is digging gold.

**April 16, 1851**

Several swarms of bees that have been brought from the States are doing well in the Valley, and it is very desirable for the brethren to bring all the bees they can; for it is believed they will flourish here; and so far as honey can be produced, it will supersede the necessity of making sugar; and if there were ever so much sugar, honey is needed as a medicine, as well as a luxury.

**March 5, 1853**

## PROFANITY

It is lamentable to what an extent profanity prevails among the youth of our country. This vice seems to be contagious. Little boys who are but just learning the use of language, whose parents give them religious instruction and advantage of the Sabbath schools, mouth oaths which would put an old sailor to the blush.

Profanity is not only wicked, but it is vulgar, low, ungentlemanly and disgusting. We hope none of our youthful readers are guilty of using profane language. If you are, quit at once, and you will never be a gentleman or a fit companion for decent persons of either sex.

**July 23, 1856**

## IRON COUNTY
### (From Elder James H. Mattheau to Lt. Gen. Wells)

Not long since Tintick's band stoled Samuel Lewis' horse; a few of the brethren went after it, surprised the Indians and retook the horse without much difficulty and no bloodshed, though the Indians were very mad.

Our corn, potatoes, beets, etc., are nearly used up by the worms, and much of the late wheat is covered with a kind of lice, though there is a considerable almost ready to cut. Some rye has been already harvested. We are not cast down, for we know it is the Lord's business to provide for his Saints, and he will do so. General health and peace prevail.

**Aug. 6, 1856**

☞ THE EASTERN MAIL arrived about 9 p.m. of the 30th ult., bringing all it started with from Independence, for a wonder, but none of the numerous sacks previously left on the route, as that would have been too much of a reformation.

It is reported the carriers lay at Hatch's, 12 miles east of this city, during most of the afternoon of the 30th and were more or less intoxicated with liquor they had bought of an emigrant train which they passed.

**June 29, 1859**

☞ DEPARTURE — Fifteen of the children that survived the "Mountain Meadows Massacre" left this city yesterday for Fort Smith, Arkansas. They went in carriages, having everything necessary provided for their comfort during their journey.

Deseret News files

**Horace Greeley**

**July 20, 1859**

(Horace Greeley, noted editor of the New York Herald, whose comment "Go West, young man," became a part of the American vernacular, finally came west himself. During his visit to Salt Lake City, the Deseret News informed him that he had three letters waiting for him in the local post office.)

## Reception of Hon. Horace Greeley

On Saturday evening last, 16th inst., the members of the Deseret Typographical Union and Press Association met at the Typographical Hall, Council House, and were entertained by speeches, songs, music, etc.

After music by Ballo's brass band, Mr. Greeley arose and in his peculiarly plain style, addressed the assembly for the space of about half an hour — alluding to the progress that had been made during his own recollection, how extraordinary had been the increase of facilities for the spread of knowledge through the press and by means of the electric telegraph; but that he yet looked forward to a day when still greater improvements would be made — when the daily newspaper, printed from continuous rolls, cut and folded by steam, would be thrown off, ready for distribution at a rate far exceeding that of the rapid eight and ten cylinder presses now in use — and when the telegraph would connect, through one grand electric current, continent with continent and island with island, till every corner of the earth shall be illumined with telegraphic communication.

Union and good feelings prevailed throughout and doubtless in years hence, Mr. Greeley will look back with pleasure on his happy interview with the printers of Great Salt Lake City.

**April 18, 1855**

## WAGONS, WAGONS!

WE HAVE for sale a number of excellent wagons suitable for general use. Also Ox yokes, chains, &c., which we offer low for flour, wheat, oats and lumber, &c.

5-4t        T.S. WILLIAMS, &Co.

## ATTENTION CAVALRY.

THE SUBSCRIBER wishes to inform the citizens of Utah Territory that he is manufacturing six-shooting Pistols on the most improved style, to which he invites inspection at his shop in the 19th ward.

5-3t        DAVIS SABINS

## HO! EVERYBODY.
### *WM. NIXON, COUNCIL HOUSE ST.*

THOSE Holding my Due Bills, please Present them for payment. All to whom I am indebted call and be paid. All who owe me please come and settle immediately.

5tf

## TO EMIGRANTS.

CHRISTOPHER ARTHUR, SEN., bread and Cracker baker, will have on hand, or make to order, Bread and Crackers, which emigrants, traveling south to California, will find advantageous and economical in their store of provisions.

Cedar City, Iron County.        3-3m

## DR. WILLIAMS,

HAS now resumed the practice of medicine and surgery, and may be found at his new residence, northeast corner of Temple block. He will attend promptly to all calls in the line of his profession.

N.B. In case of ready pay, 25 per cent will be discounted. Those indebted will please call and settle.

3-tf

## NOTICE.

The highest price paid for Bark and Sumac. Information given to those who desire it, when to cut, and how to cure the Sumac for tanning purposes.

34-6m

## GEORGE GODDARD

WILL Supply Pedlars, Country Storekeepers, &c. with Merchandise on very advantageous terms.

5-4t

**May 17, 1851**

## REMOVAL

C. SMITH, Watchmaker, has removed from his residence in the 9th ward to the 17th ward, a little west of the north west corner of the Temple block, where he is prepared to attend to the repairing of watches, clocks, jewelry, &c. Jewelry made to order.

Nov. 26, 1850.-21tf

MRS A. SMITH, late of St. Louis, invites the Ladies of Great Salt Lake City and vicinity to the inspection of a superior assortment of Velvet, Silk, Satin and Straw Bonnets, and a variety of Millenery and Fancy Goods, two lots south of Elder J. Taylor's house, in the 14th ward.

19tf

## McVICAR & BARLOW,

Watch Makers and Jewellers.

ALL kinds of jewelry, silver, tea and table spoons, and all other articles in their line of business manufactured to order.

A superior article of Gold Pens for sale.

Also, all kinds of clocks, watches, etc., repaired and warranted.

The highest cash price paid for gold dust and old silver.

Wheat taken in exchange for work. Shop in 14th ward, at Jesse Turpin's residence.

Nov. 13, 1850.-20tf

**March 5, 1853**

## G.D. WATT, REPORTER

Is on hand when called for, to make verbatim reports of the blessings of children, Confirmations, Sermons, Lectures, &c , and may be found in the Presidents Office, north west corner of the Counsel House upstairs.

P.S. When any of the Wards call a meeting for the blessing of children, it may be found for the benefit to have G.D.W. present on such occasions.

feb19 7tf

## LOOK HERE

Came into my yard about the 1st of February last, a three year old Heifer, white hind legs and belly, also some white on her back, and white star on her face, no brand. The owner can have her by proving property and paying charges.

march5.-tf        JOHN GAILY, 4th Ward.

## WILLIAM NIXON

Would respectfully inform the citizens of this valley that he is prepared to do to order, all kinds of small, fancy turning, in Brass, Horn, Bone of hard Wood, at reasonable charges... .

dec11-2-8 t

# Statehood:
## A 48-year quest

The residents of Great Salt Lake Valley were still living in rudimentary housing and gaining a tenuous toehold on their new surroundings when the fight for statehood began. Its first efforts antedated even the Deseret News. The process would require 48 years.

Gaining statehood was a priority for leaders of The Church of Jesus Christ of Latter-day Saints. That prize would ensure that the pioneering saints could make their own laws and select their own leaders. Being named a territory would open the way for heavy-handed government out of Washington, D.C., and bring unwanted "gentile" appointees to rule the Mormon colonies, they thought.

In December 1848, the pioneers penned the first of seven Utah petitions. It asked Congress to recognize the Territory of Deseret. The petition carried only 2,270 signatures and it was never actually presented to Congress, although the provisional Deseret Legislature had appointed John M. Bernhisel to make such a presentation. Before Bernhisel had the chance, the Utah legislators sent Almon W. Babbitt with a second petition aimed at statehood.

These first attempts became tangled in the slavery questions then brewing in America, issues that were addressed in the Missouri Compromise of 1850. Later in Utah's struggle for statehood, the issue of polygamy, openly announced and accepted by the church in 1852, would become the major stumbling block.

On Sept. 9, 1850, Congress pre-empted Utah's statehood attempts by setting boundaries for Utah Territory. The people most affected by the action, those then living in the new territory, didn't learn of the Organic Act until days later. Two days after the bill passed, in fact, on Sept. 11, 1850, the Utah legislature met and, according to the News of Sept. 14:

*... presented a series of resolutions to our delegates in Washington ... instructing them to press our claims to be admitted as a State into the Union ...*

A week later, a letter from the Legislature to Bernhisel and Babbitt was printed:

**DESERET NEWS,** *Sept. 21, 1850: If Congress has passed, at the present session, an act for the organization of a Territory called Utah Territory, which they design for us, regardless of all our feelings in the matter, then we have only to yield our quiet acquiescence there, for the time being ... If, on the contrary, they have adjourned and no action had upon the subject, you will only urge our claims for admission as a state ...*

**DESERET NEWS,** *Oct. 1, 1850: The Eastern Mail arrived on Tuesday evening, by which we received no newspapers, but through the politeness of our friends and perusal of the New York Herald of Aug. 11, we learn that "A Bill to establish a territorial government for Utah," has passed.*

On Nov. 30, the paper printed the Organic Act in its entirety.

Despite Bernhisel's pleas that Young be more circumspect in his relations with the "outsiders," the doughty pioneer leader, even when threatened with imminent invasion by federal troops, made such comments as:

**DESERET NEWS,** *Aug. 10, 1857: Do you wonder that they are angry? Five years ago I told them that I would be Governor as long as the Lord wanted me to be, and that all hell could not remove me. They have tried during those five years to remove me, and I have had to appoint a secretary for this territory three times in that period, for the ones appointed by the president absconded from the Territory. And the prospect now is that I shall still have to be the Governor, that I shall again have to preside over the Legislature ...*

**John Milton Bernhisel:**
Born June 23, 1799, Sandy Hills, Pa. Early convert to Mormonism, close friend of church founder Joseph Smith. Came to Utah Sept. 24, 1848, in Heber C. Kimball party. Spokesman to Congress during statehood debate, served five terms as Utah Territory representative. Studied medicine, University of Pennsylvania, expert in "bleeding." Retired from public service in 1863. First vice president, ZCMI. selected books for the first Utah library, served on first State Board of Regents for University of Deseret. Died Sept. 28, 1881.

**Almon W. Babbitt:**
Born Oct. 9, 1813, Cheshire, Mass. Early LDS convert. Studied law at State University of Cincinnati, licensed to practice in six states. Newspaper publisher. Participated in Zion's Camp. Occasionally at odds with church leaders because of strong, independent nature. Chosen delegate to promote cause of statehood with Congress in early 1850s. Named territorial secretary by President Franklin Pierce. Murdered by tomahawk-wielding Cheyenne Indians on return trip to Utah Territory, Aug. 25, 1856, at age 43, though he "fought like a grizzly bear."

Again in 1856, territory residents petitioned Congress for admission as a state. Again, the measure failed. Feeling thoroughly rebuffed by then, some Utahns wrote such doggerel as this verse of an eight-stanza song, addressed to the "Father of the Union."

**DESERET NEWS,** *Aug. 20, 1856:*
*My sisters all may be more pert, and sassier than me,*
*But, Dad, you know I'm as I am, just as the others be.*
*And why should they all flout around, turn up their nose and rage*
*I guess I'll be as smart as them, now that I am of age.*
*Stop that knocking. Let me in! (etc.)*

In 1856, the time was not opportune. President James Buchanan was preparing to send an Army to Utah, supposedly to quell rebellion. Statehood seemed more remote than ever. The struggle stretched over the decades.

# Handcart
## pioneers

**Before the first companies of LDS pioneers set foot on the Mormon Trail in 1847, church leaders had pledged that all who wanted to take part in the "gathering" would be assisted, particularly the poor who faced the greatest challenges in outfitting for the 1,000-plus-mile trek.**

**A**s the flood of immigrants, particularly those from Europe, began to exhaust the ability of the church to keep them moving over the trail in wagon trains, the idea of handcarts was born. They were cheaper to make and greatly reduced the number of animals required to make the trip. And, as Brigham Young noted in a talk reported in the Deseret News of Oct. 8, 1856, many people walked in their normal activities a distance equal to what would be required of the handcart participants.
*"Count the steps that a woman takes when she is doing her work; let them be measured and it will be found that in many instances she had taken steps enough to have traveled from 15 to 20 miles a day ...*
From 1856 to 1860, 10 companies of handcart pioneers — a total of 2,962 people — walked the distance from a staging center in Iowa City, Iowa, to the Salt Lake Valley. The majority traveled without serious problems.
When the Ellsworth Company, first in the experiment, arrived in the valley, Brigham Young and other leaders went to the mouth of Emigration Canyon to accompany them into their new home. A week after the company arrived, the Deseret News reported:

**DESERET NEWS,** *Oct. 1, 1856: Presidents Brigham Young and Heber C. Kimball, Lieut. Gen. D.H. Wells and many other citizens, in carriages, and several*

*A typical handcart owned by the William Stiff family.*

*gentlemen and ladies on horseback, with a part of Capt. H.B. Clawson's company of Lancers and the Brass Bands under Capt. William Pitt, left the governor's office at 9 a.m. with the view of meeting and escorting them into the city... Ere long, the anxiously expected train came in sight, led by Capt. Ellsworth on foot and with two aged veterans pulling the front cart, followed by a long line of carts attended by the old, middle aged and young of both sexes.*

Those already in the city turned out in a welcome until:
*a living tide lined and thronged South Temple Street... This journey has been performed with less than the average amount of mortality usually attending ox trains and all, though somewhat fatigued, stepped out with alacrity to the last, and appeared buoyant and cheerful.*

In his next address in the Bowery, Young commented:

**DESERET NEWS,** *Oct. 8, 1856: I think it is now proven to a certainty that men, women and children can cross the plains from the settlements on the Missouri River to this place on foot, and*

Handcart Pioneers in the Snow, print engraving by an unknown artist.

*draw handcarts loaded with a good portion of the articles needed to sustain them on the way. To me, this is no more a matter of fact this morning, after seeing the companies that have crossed the plains, than it was years ago... It has been a matter of doubt with many of our elders.*

The second and third companies also made the crossing without incident, but the fourth and fifth companies, led by James Willie and Edward Martin, respectively, encountered great difficulties. They started late in the season, having been held up by delays in the ocean crossings that many of the pioneers had to make to get to Iowa City initially. Unseasonal snowstorms and cold weather in Wyoming caught the two companies ill-prepared and vulnerable. Of the 500-member Willie Company, 67 died. The Martin Company suffered even more serious losses, with from 135 to 150 of the 576-member party dead before assistance could reach them.
When travelers notified President Young of the plight of the handcart groups, immediate steps were taken to send aid north. In the October semiannual conference of the church, the president's message centered on the beleaguered Saints in Wyoming.

**DESERET NEWS,** *Oct. 15, 1856: I will now give this people the subject and the text for the Elders who may speak today and during the conference. It is this. On the 5th day of October, 1856, many of our brethren and sisters are on the plains with handcarts and probably many are now 700 miles from this place and they must be brought here; we must send assistance to them. The text will be to get them here. This is my religion; this is the dictation of the Holy Ghost that I possess; it is to save the people. We must bring them in from the plains and when we get them here we will try to keep the same spirit that we have had and teach them the way of life and salvation.... I shall call upon the bishops this day, I shall not wait until tomorrow nor until the next day.*

He then asked for good horses and mules, 12 tons of flour and 40 good teamsters. His plea for immediate succor was repeated by other conference speakers.

**DESERET NEWS,** *Nov. 12, 1856:* The News printed two somewhat contradictory reports. Elder Joseph A. Young told an audience in the Tabernacle that he had been to Devil's Gate and on into Wyoming.

*The brethren and sisters appeared to be in good health and spirits... . We found plenty of teams at Fort Bridger, and by this time the handcarts have all the assistance necessary to take them up and bring them in within nine days from tomorrow.*

But George D. Grant, who had been named to head the rescue party, painted a darker picture.

*You can imagine between five and six hundred men, women and children, worn down by drawing handcarts through snow and mud; fainting by the wayside, falling, chilled by the cold; children crying, their limbs stiffened by the cold, their feet bleeding and some of them bare to snow and frost. The sight is almost too much for the stoutest of us; but we go on doing all we can, not doubting or despairing.*

*Our company is too small to help much, it is only a drop to a bucket, as it were, in comparison to what is needed. I think that not over one third of br. Martin's company is able to walk. This you may think is extravagant, but it is nevertheless true.... We will move every day toward the Valley, if we shovel snow to do it.*

Criticism of church leaders who endorsed the use of handcarts surfaced and the News printed defenses given by several officials, including Jedediah M. Grant, who was also mayor of Salt Lake City:

**DESERET NEWS,** *Nov. 12, 1856: I do not suppose that the thinking part of the community anticipated any censure being placed upon the First Presidency of this church in consequence of the sufferings of the people now upon the plains. Still there is a certain class of people whose brains never reach above the calves of their legs, and they never will know anything about the general policy of the church, about what is written, what is desired, counseled or asked for.*

The Willie Company arrived in Salt Lake City Nov. 9, and the Martin group followed on Nov. 30. They were immediately taken in by the residents who nurtured and nursed them. Although their sufferings were not typical of the handcart experience overall, the Martin and Willie companies became a symbol of the pioneer era.

**DESERET NEWS,** *Dec. 12, 1856:* Bishop L. W. Hardy reports the new arrivals to be in fine spirits, *notwithstanding their late hardships, and those who so liberally turned out to their relief report themselves ready to start out again, were it necessary... O, World, what have you to say and do about the works coupled with faith manifested by those who have gladly faced winter on the Wasatch Mountains to rescue fellow beings, most of whom they had never seen . . . Or again, what about that Spirit which causes so many to operate as one, upon the side of truth and humanity?*

# Deseret Alphabet

**DESERET NEWS,** *June 29, 1859: We present to the people the Deseret Alphabet, but have not adopted any rules to bind the taste, judgment or preference of any. Such as it is, you have it, and we are sanguine that the more it is practised and the more intimately the people become acquainted with it, the more useful and beneficial it will appear.*

The introduction of the 38-character Deseret Alphabet, (a 39th was being considered to represent the sound "ew") followed years of work by church scholars who believed its phonetic approach would correct many of the problems common to the English alphabet. One character simply stood, invariably, for one sound, eliminating silent letters and combinations of letters needed to make a single sound.

Earlier, in 1854, the News had predicted that a person trained in the new system, adopted that year by the University of Deseret regents but not yet made available to everyone, could easily write "one hundred words a minute with ease and consequently report the speech of a common speaker without much difficulty." For instance, the article said, the word "eight" would be much more easily written when it was reduced to "at." Brigham Young felt the phonetic alphabet would reduce the time children spent in school and enhance communication among adults. It also was a means of further separating the pioneer Mormons from the practices of the American population they were trying to escape.

For some time after it was formally introduced to Utah settlers in the News, the paper printed at least one article per edition in the new alphabet, often choosing scripture as a text. The church spent a considerable sum having fonts cast in type in New York, and several books were printed in the new type. However, the alphabet never caught on. Territory residents favored what they were familiar with, despite its many blemishes, to the new system. After President Young's death in 1877, the alphabet gradually dropped out of view.

# Salt Lake Temple

The vanguard company of pioneers had been in Salt Lake Valley only a few days when, on July 28, 1847, Brigham Young and other leaders walked to a section of land between two creeks in what became the north end of Great Salt Lake City. Young declared, "Here is the 40 acres for the Temple. The city can be laid out perfectly square north and south, east and west." Subsequently, the size of the temple plot was reduced to 10 acres.

Ground-breaking for the Salt Lake Temple in 1853.

**Above, Orson Pratt's Theodolite. Below, temple specs were published.**

| | To end of rock-work. | To top of spires. |
|---|---|---|
| Height of central east tower...210 ft. | | 200½ ft. |
| Height of central west tower...204 ft. | | 219 ft. |
| Height of side east towers......188 ft. | | 200 ft. |
| Height of side west towers.....182 ft. | | 194 ft. |
| Height of walls............1t.7½ ft. | | |
| Thickness of walls at bottom... 9 ft. | | |
| Thickness of walls at top....... 6 ft. | | |
| Thickness of buttresses........ 7 ft. | | |

No Deseret News then existed to announce the church leaders' decision. But when the newspaper was founded in June 1850, periodic reports on the progress being made on temple construction were important reading for pioneers.

**DESERET NEWS,** *April 19, 1851: The motion to build a Temple to the name of the Lord our God in GSL (Great Salt Lake) City was carried by acclamation. A committee of one, viz. Daniel H. Wells, was appointed to superintend the building of the Temple and the public works."*

In the same conference report, Elder E.T. Benson urged the pioneers to contribute unselfishly by tithing their time and means to make the temple a reality:

**DESERET NEWS,** *April 19, 1851: This morning you all voted to build a Temple; you appointed a committee to superintend the public works; you are aware that they cannot progress without your assistance; you are aware we are the Latter-day Saints and are the bone and sinew to roll forth the work. It is required of the presidents and quorums in this church that they pay their tithing and you know this has not been lived up*

*to; I consider it a command on this people ... This church will not come of age until we all pay our tithing."*

Within weeks, the newspaper was printing regular schedules of "labor tithing" — one day in 10 to be devoted to church projects.

**DESERET NEWS,** *May 17, 1851: Team work is much needed. Laborers to bring tools to work with.*

The News printed lists assigning days for members of the city's 19 LDS wards. Through the spring of 1853, the official survey of the temple site, the groundbreaking and cornerstone laying were all causes for celebration.

**DESERET NEWS,** *Feb. 19, 1853:*
*Agreeably to previous notice, the people, men, women and children, began to assemble on the Temple Block, about 10 a.m., Monday, February 14th, 1853, as clear and lovely a day as the sun ever shone on G. S. L. City, with from one to three inches of snow on the ground, in some places, and others quite bare; with some six inches of frost in the earth, though the thaw was mild through the day. While the people were assembling, they were cheered with the sweetest strains from the Brass and Capt. Ballo's Bands.*

*President Young arrived at 10 1/2, and with his council and the assembly, witnessed the survey of the site of the Temple …*

*The Presidency soon repaired to the South East corner of the Temple site, where they soon succeeded in picking around a piece of earth, about one foot square…*

*The President then addressed the multitude, and declared the ground broken for the Temple, blessed the people in the name of the Lord, and dismissed the assembly, and all said amen … much earth was removed that afternoon, for it was a general turnout of the saints, and those who could, had their tools ready.*

As church and civil dignitaries witnessed surveying of the property by architect Truman O. Angell and surveyor Jesse W. Fox, a $1 silver piece fell on the southeast corner. The News noted: *No one knowing from whence it came. President (Heber C.) Kimball prophecied that it was a good token and means would not be wanted to build the Temple.*

The big news was the laying of the cornerstones. Salt Lake Stake President John Young, standing atop the northwest stone, orated:

**DESERET NEWS,** *April 16, 1853:*
*"I am greatly blessed … that I am permitted to live to see the present day and to stand upon the rock which is the North West Corner Stone of a temple which is to be built upon this ground… I hope we shall see the Cap Stone brought on with shouts of joy. I believe we shall, if we remain faithful in the cause of truth."*

On Aug. 17, 1854, the News proudly printed a detailed outline of the temple plans, as provided by the architect. Angell told News readers that if they wanted even more detail they should *"Wait until the house is done, then come and see it."*

The pressures of supporting the ongoing migration of thousands of pioneers, several years of niggardly harvests and the general concentration on establishing a society in Utah Territory slowed the work on the temple. During 1855-56, Angell was sent on an "architectural" mission to Europe. He brought back some ideas that were incorporated into his design.

Then the Utah War of 1857-58 again brought a halt to work on the temple. Rather than expose another temple to the potential depredations of "outsiders," Brigham Young ordered on March 23, 1858, that the temple site be buried. When Col. Albert Sidney Johnston's troops marched through Salt Lake City in June 1858, the site resembled nothing more than "a freshly plowed field," Young wrote.

When the immediate difficulties with the federal government had been resolved, workmen unearthed the building and once again began the labor of erecting the temple walls.

Several efforts were made to expedite the flow of granite, timber and other building materials to the downtown site. On Feb. 1, 1855, the News reported that "Brigham Young, Isaac Chase and Feramorz Little and their associates and successors (had been granted) the right to make a canal from Big Cottonwood Canyon to Great Salt Lake City … " Wards were directed to provide labor tithing for the completion of the canal. In the end, it was discovered that water coursing down the waterway was absorbed by the surrounding soil so fast it was not feasible. No building materials ever traveled via the canal to the city. The expensive project was abandoned. Such obstacles, met and overcome or evaluated and abandoned, dotted the 40-year history of the temple's construction.

Quarrying stone for the temple.

## The world of the 1850s
### A TIMELINE

**1850**–Millard Filmore sworn in as president.

**1850**– Australia given self-government by British Parliament.

**1850**– California becomes the 31st state.

**1850**– Nathaniel Hawthorne publishes *The Scarlet Letter.*

**1851**– Wildlife painter James Audubon dies.

**1851**– Herman Melville publishes *Moby Dick.*

**1852**– Wells Fargo founded.

**1853**– Verdi's opera *Il Trovatore* first performed.

**1853**– Commodore Matthew Perry opens Japan to outside trade.

**1853**– India's first railway.

**1853**– Steinway factory opens in New York City.

**1853**– Levi Strauss makes first jeans.

**1854**– Crimean War.

**1854**– Kansas and Nebraska admitted to the union.

**1854**– Quinine first used for malaria.

**1854**– New York bans sale and production of alcoholic beverages.

**1855**– David Livingston discovers Victoria Falls.

**1856**– Louis Pasteur discovers bacteria.

**1856**– James Buchanan elected president.

**1857**– First passenger elevators operating.

**1857**– Opium War starts between China and Britain.

**1857**– Benito Juarez sworn in as president of Mexico.

**1858**– Minnesota becomes the 32nd state.

**1858**– First trans-Atlantic telegram.

**1858**– Queen Victoria proclaimed ruler of India.

**1859**– Oregon becomes the 33rd state.

**1859**– Suez Canal construction begins.

**1859**– Charles Darwin publishes *The Origin of Species by Natural Selection.*

LDS Church Archives

{ 255 }

NOTICE TO BISHOPS.
The following are the days set apart for the several wards to work their labor tithing, commencing Monday, May 5, 1851.
Wards 15 & 19, Monday, May 5.
" 16 & 18, Tuesday, " 6.
" 1 & 8, Wednesday, " 7.
" 2 & 7, Thursday, " 8.
" 3 4 & 6, Friday, " 9.
" 9 & 17, Saturday, " 10.
" 10 & 11, Monday, " 12.
" 12, Tuesday, " 13.
" 13, Wednesday, " 14.
" 14, Thursday, " 15.
" 15 & 19, Friday, " 16.
" 16 & 18, Saturday, " 17.
Team work much needed. Laborers to bring tools to work with.
EDWARD HUNTER,
E. D. WOOLLEY.

May 3, 1851.
☞ It is the duty of the brethren to attend to their labor tithing, in their respective specified in the above

# Utah War

**No event in the early history of Utah Territory caused more consternation for LDS settlers than the "Utah War" of 1857-58. U.S. President James Buchanan, goaded by former non-LDS territorial officials whose tenure in Utah Territory was mutually unhappy for themselves and the people they were sent to govern, ordered troops to the territory. He acted on their false reports that rebellion was brewing in the Great Basin.**

LDS Church Museum

No banner headlines in the fledgling Deseret News heralded the ongoing events of the conflict. From the time Buchanan commissioned the Utah Expedition in 1857 to the peaceful conclusion of the difficulty, the newspaper's accounts were in keeping with the times: oblique at times but full of rhetoric and passion.

Brigham Young learned on July 24, 1857, that soldiers were en route to Utah Territory. With other pioneers, he was celebrating the 10th anniversary of the Mormon arrival in Salt Lake Valley at a gala campout in Big Cottonwood Canyon. Bearers of bad news, including colorful Mormon strongman Orrin Porter Rockwell, rode into the canyon to inform Young and the other revelers of the impending invasion.

In an address in the Salt Lake Bowery the following week, Young bitterly commented:

**DESERET NEWS,** *July 29, 1857: How much better it would be, even solely in a political point of view, for the Government of the United States to grant lands and extend aid and encouragement to those hardy settlers who are turning her barren wastes into smiling fields, than to harass a portion of her citizens who are patriotic and loyal above all others, who have withdrawn themselves far from other settlements and have joyfully unfurled the stars and stripes, the insignia of equal rights, in the tops of the mountain fastnesses. But, no, priestcraft is in danger, politicians are hungry for office and spoils, editors must print spicy articles to increase the circulation of their papers and all hell must be stirred up for the extermination of the Latter Day Saints and the reversion of smiling fields and happy homes to dreary wastes and the habitations of buzzards and wolves…*

For two years — part of the time from Fillmore — the News printed developments about the conflict, usually long after they happened and frequently out of sequence. There was no need to advise the pioneers of details and decisions. They knew them. Reprints from other newspapers, including vitriolic criticism of the Mormons, were common in the paper, along with the rebuttals of territory leaders.

The ill-advised decision to send troops against the Mormon settlers in Utah Territory proved to be politically costly for Buchanan. He was increasingly criticized for his poorly founded and hasty decision and there were growing demands that he justify the action, such as this one, reprinted from a Jan. 28, 1858, article in the New York Times:

**DESERET NEWS:** *We are glad to learn that a resolution was adopted yesterday in Congress… calling on the president for information in relation to the difficulty with the Mormons, as to the causes for the Utah Expedition and whether Brigham Young is actually in a state of rebellion or resistance to the United States authorities.*

*We have had an abundance of reports of Mormon outrages and we are bound to believe that there are satisfactory reasons for the military expedition to Utah; but all the information that has been given to the public has been of a rather vague character, and much of it has come through channels which justify a suspicion that it has been considerably exaggerated.*

*… there should be the greatest caution against the perpetration of any unauthorized acts of violence towards these deluded and fanatical disciples of the Mormon Prophet, for it would be sure*

**Military band from Johnston's Army**

LDS Church Archives

to produce a sympathy for them and a reaction in their favor in the popular mind, which would infallibly tend to strengthen their hands and make them more formidable and the difficulty of dealing with them greater than ever.

On April 6, 1858, with Col. Albert Sidney Johnston's Army already poised in what was to become Wyoming, Buchanan issued a proclamation explaining his call for the Utah Expedition and offering "pardons" to all Mormons who would give up their supposed opposition to the federal government. The News reprinted the proclamation, including these excerpts:

**DESERET NEWS,**
June 16, 1858: Whereas the Territory of Utah was settled by certain emigrants from the States and from foreign countries, who have for several years past manifested a spirit of insubordination to the constitution and laws of the United States. The great mass of these settlers, acting under the influence of leaders to whom they seem to have surrendered their judgment, refuse to be controlled by any other

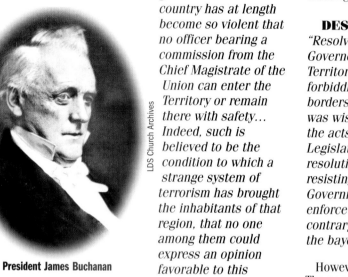
**President James Buchanan**

authority. They have been often advised to obedience and these friendly counsels have been answered with defiance. Officers of the federal government have been driven from the territory... Their (Mormon) hostility to the lawful government of the country has at length become so violent that no officer bearing a commission from the Chief Magistrate of the Union can enter the Territory or remain there with safety... Indeed, such is believed to be the condition to which a strange system of terrorism has brought the inhabitants of that region, that no one among them could express an opinion favorable to this government, or even propose to obey its laws, without exposing his life and property to peril. I accordingly ordered a detachment of the army to march for the City of Salt Lake, or within reach of that place, and to act, in case of need, as a posse for the enforcement of the laws ...

News that federal troops were en route to

the territory evoked memories of conflicts the Mormons had traveled more than a thousand miles to escape. The initial reaction among some pioneer groups was to stand and fight rather than submit to further government intrusion into their lives. For example, this report on a mass meeting in Harmony, Washington County:

**DESERET NEWS,** March 24, 1858: "Resolved, that the policy adopted by Governor Brigham Young in placing this Territory under martial law and forbidding all armed forces to enter our borders under any pretence whatever was wise, humane and just... We approve the acts of the late (territorial) Legislative Assembly in drafting resolutions to sustain Gov. Young in resisting the present force sent by the Government of the United States to enforce upon us corrupt officials, contrary to our wishes, at the point of the bayonet..."

However, through the auspices of Thomas L. Kane, a non-Mormon friendly to the saints, Young already was promoting meetings between territorial leaders and federal government representatives to try to avoid bloodshed. Ultimately, Buchanan appointed a commission consisting of Lazarus Powell and Ben McCulloch to negotiate with pioneer leaders for a peaceful resolution.

**Albert Sidney Johnston, hand tinted from Harper's Weekly.**

**Johnston's Army wintering at Fort Bridger. (Harper's Weekly)**

Deseret News files

**Lot Smith**

# THE Utah Militia

The Utah Militia, organized in January 1857, prior to the threat of federal invasion, was instrumental in resolving the Utah War even though no actual combat ever took place. Typically, the Deseret News never reported directly on the militia's activities.

General Daniel Wells appointed Lot Smith, who had served in the Mormon Battalion as a teenager, to "turn back the (wagon) trains that were on the road and burn them ... I replied that I thought I could do just what he told me to," Smith wrote in a memoir.

With a band of just over 40 men, Smith spent the fall and winter of 1857-58 harassing the federal troops — and praying for snow so deep the army would be unable to move forward. The marauders burned several supply wagons and appropriated cattle and mules, causing losses valued by the government at $80,000.

Those losses, combined with severe winter weather, kept the federal troops in Camp Scott, northern Utah Territory (now Wyoming) for the winter, allowing Brigham Young to work out diplomatic solutions to the confrontation.

Ironically, the only wounds suffered by humans in the war occurred when Smith accidentally discharged his pistol in a Utah Militia camp, shattering Orson P. Arnold's thigh "in a fearful manner." Arnold survived, but was permanently lamed.

LDS Church Museum

Still, in the spring of 1858, Johnston's troops were ready to march through Salt Lake City and a sense of unease prevailed.

Salt Lake City and others of the most populous cities of northern Utah were emptied and preparations made to burn them should Johnston's troops turn nasty. Most of the exiles relocated temporarily in Utah County and farther south until there was a full resolution of the situation.

Even the Deseret News relocated, publishing from Fillmore as a precaution against the pending arrival of the army. It reported:

**DESERET NEWS:** *June 23, 1858; Ex-Governor Powell and Major McCulloch, commissioners appointed by President Buchanan to visit Utah, and Dr. Forney, Utah Superintendent of Indian Affairs, arrived in GSL (Great Salt Lake) City on the 7th of June… On the 10th of June, Presidents Brigham Young, Heber C. Kimball and Daniel H. Wells, the majority of the Quorum of the Twelve and several other citizens visited GSL City.*

Alfred Cumming, who had been sent by Buchanan with Johnston's Army to become the new head of state in Utah Territory, was ready to make a peaceful entry into Salt Lake City, preceding the army. A true diplomat who was tolerant of the LDS Church and its practices, he became one of the more popular governors in the territory's early history. In a letter to the U.S. Secretary of State dated May 2, 1858, reported later by the newspaper he said:

**DESERET NEWS,** *July 28, 1858; I was escorted from Bear River Valley to the western end of Echo Kanyon. The journey through the kanyon being performed, for the most part, after night, it was about 11 o'clock p.m. when I arrived at Weber Station. I have been everywhere recognized as Governor of Utah; and so far from having encountered insults or indignities, I am gratified in being able to state to you that, in passing through the settlements I have been universally greeted with such respectful attentions as are due to the representative of the Executive authority of the United States… Near the Warm Springs, at the line dividing Great Salt Lake and Davis counties, I was honored with a formal and respectful reception by many gentlemen, including the Mayor and other municipal officers of the city, and by them escorted to lodgings previously provided, the Mayor occupying a seat in my carrriage.*

*I met parties of armed men at Lost and Yellow creeks as well as Echo Kanyon. At every point, however, I was recognized as the Governor of Utah and received with a military salute. When it was arranged with the Mormon officers in command of my escort that I should pass through Echo Kanyon at night, I inferred that it was with the object of concealing the barricades and other defences. I was therefore agreeably surprised by an illumination in honor of me. The bonfires kindled by the soldiers from the base to the summits of the walls of the kanyon completely illuminated the valley and disclosed the snow-covered mountains which surrounded us…*

**DESERET NEWS,** *July 7, 1858:* The News printed Cumming's official declaration to the Territory:

*Peace is restored to our Territory … Those citizens who have left their homes I invite to return, as soon as they can do so with propriety and convenience. To all I announce my determination to enforce obedience to the laws, both federal and territorial…*

In a conciliatory meeting in the Provo Bowery on June 16, as reported in the News, Commissioner Powell rejoiced that:

**DESERET NEWS,** *June 16, 1858: Only a few days ago a dark cloud hung over the inhabitants of this Territory which threatened the most direful calamity that can befall a free people… It is pleasant to me and to you and will be to all liberty-loving men throughout the Union that that cloud has been dispelled…*

Having marched through a deserted Great Salt Lake City without event, Johnston's troops established Camp Floyd in present-day Utah County. Soon, they were called back east to participate in the Civil War. Johnston himself fought for the South and lost his life at Shiloh.

The Utah War was over, but its effects were lasting. Any lingering thought Mormon leaders harbored that their people could live in their new home isolated and unsullied by outside influences were dashed forever. The outside world had arrived in earnest with Johnston's Army.

**Government troops stationed at Camp Floyd.**

LDS Church Archives

Richard Egan, left, was 18 when he carried the first Pony Express mail out of Salt Lake City to Rush Valley on his mare, "Miss Lightning." His brother, Howard, also was a rider.

*Pioneer Memorial Museum*

# The Pony Express

**The prospect of getting mail from the eastern and western reaches of the United States in "less than ten days" was big news for pioneering Utahns. They eagerly awaited the initiation of the Pony Express.**

**W**hen the Deseret News announced that riders from both directions had made it to Great Salt Lake City, one of the most colorful chapters in Western lore had begun.

**DESERET NEWS,** *April 11, 1860:*
*The first Pony Express from the West left Sacramento City, Cal., at 12 p.m. on the night of the 3d, and arrived in this city at*

*11:45 p.m. of the 7th, inside of the prospectus time. The roads were heavy and the weather stormy. The last 75 miles were made in 5 hours, 15 minutes, in a heavy rain.*

*The Express from the East left St. Joseph, Missouri, at 6:30 p.m. on the evening of the 3d and arrived in this city at 6:25 p.m. on the evening of the 9th. The difference in time between St. Joseph and this city is something like 1 hour and 15 minutes, bringing us within six days communication with the frontier and seven days from Washington — a result which we Utonians, accustomed to receive news three months after date, can well appreciate.*

*The weather has been disagreeable and stormy for the past week and in every way calculated to retard the operations of the company, and we are informed the Express eastward from this place was five hours in going to Snyder's Mill, a distance of twenty-five miles…*

*The probability is, the Express will be a little behind time in reaching Sacramento this trip, but when the weather becomes settled, and the roads good, we have no doubt they will be able to make the trip in less than ten days.*

For the next 18 months, Deseret News stories frequently bore the notation: "By the Pony Express." Newspapers printed in the Midwest especially for settlers in the West became a source of relatively fresh news.

The Express route entered Utah roughly in the corner where present-day Wyoming tucks into Utah's eastern angle. Twenty-four relief stations were strung across Utah at about 10-mile intervals to support the riders. Whipping across country as fast as possible, each rider had two minutes at a station to change horses

and be on his way again. At first, little horns were used to alert station personnel that a rider was coming in, but the horns were dropped in favor of the famed "coyote yell" that became the standard announcement. On average, each rider covered 190 miles per day. The fastest run was made in seven days, 17 hours and brought news from St. Joseph to Sacramento of President Abraham Lincoln's inaugural address and the president's hopes that civil strife could be avoided.

Riders signed a pledge to avoid liquor and to abide by company rules, and each received a specially engraved Bible. The pay for braving Indians, weather, gopher holes and the other risks of the trail was $50 per month. The average age of riders was 19, but at least one was only 13. Buffalo Bill Cody signed up when he was 15.

The Pony Express was short-lived. On Oct. 18, 1861, when the last transcontinental telegraph pole was set in downtown Salt Lake City, the need for the service ended. Letters dribbled in on Express ponies for a short while, but they had been effectively pre-empted by the marvel of telegraphy.

# Civil War
## and linkage 1860-1870

The 1860s brought an end to Utah's relative isolation from the rest of the country. The Pony Express came, then the telegraph and the railroad met in the desolate regions of the state and linked the nation from coast to coast. Utah became a crossroads, and immigrants no longer had to travel by wagon train to reach Salt Lake City. Towns throughout the region were still being settled, however, and it was by no means the end of pioneering. Many died in the Black Hawk Indian War. For the nation, it was a period of intense agony and bloodshed, with the Civil War claiming a generation of youth and laying waste to the South. For the most part, Utahns were not involved in it, although they followed the battles in great detail thanks to the daily telegraph reports.

Howard Egan

*Pioneer Memorial Museum*

John Dawson

# The sad story of
# John
# Dawson...

**John W. Dawson, third governor of Utah Territory, arrived in Salt Lake City Dec. 7, 1861, took the oath of office Dec. 10 and on Dec. 31 was headed out of town disgraced and, according to the Deseret News, "distressingly insane."**

**D**awson's short tenure epitomized the relationships pioneering Utahns tended to have with the officials sent by Washington to govern the territory.

An Indianian appointed by President Abraham Lincoln, Dawson immediately drove a wedge upon his arrival in Great Salt Lake City by asking the Saints for $40,000 to help pay for the Civil War, although it is likely there was not that much ready cash in the territory. He further antagonized the pioneers by vetoing the Legislative Assembly's petition that Congress should consider statehood. He might have survived these political stands, but when he insulted Tom Williams' widow with an indecent proposal, the end was at hand.

**DESERET NEWS,** *Jan. 1, 1862: (The governor is) on his return to Indiana, under circumstances somewhat novel and peculiar…*

*For the last eight or ten days previous to his leaving, he was confined to his room and reported to have been very sick and what was worse, in a state of mental derangement… . This report of his physician, not a very popular man in this community, was at first disbelieved, but it was subsequently ascertained to be verily true, and his affliction of a very serious character, so much so that he imagined that he had committed a heinous offense, no less than offering a gross insult to a respectable lady of this city, to whom he requested his physician to offer a large sum as hush money… .*

The News also reported that "four noted individuals" had been assigned as body guards to the departing official, to see him safely to the eastern boundary of the territory *"to wit, Lott Huntington, Jason and William Luce and Moroni Clawson."* The governor's safety, however, was not assured, as the following news item showed:

**DESERET NEWS,** *Jan. 9, 1862: Disgraceful Outrage … It is made to appear that the unfortunate and retiring representative of Federal Power fell in with a gang of thieves, who, at Hanks' Station beat him in a most cowardly and dastardly manner and robbed him and other passengers of the clothes, blankets and other things necessary to the comfort of persons in crossing the plains at this season..*

Dawson's official report of the incident followed:

**DESERET NEWS,** *Jan. 22, 1862: On reaching the coach, we found that the ruffians had taken my blankets, Chambers' blankets and an elegant beaver robe and three pairs of elegant blankets belonging to Mr. Martin. While sitting in the coach… Wood Reynolds, the driver, accosted me insolently, when I at once jumped out and started for the house. Between the coach and the house, he struck me and on reaching the house Jason Luce and Reynolds, assisted by others, began and continued a most serious violence to me, wounding my head badly in many places, kicking me in the loins and right breast until I was exhausted, when they desisted and staid 'till morning, carrying on their orgies for many hours in the night.*

He named as his attackers the four who accompanied him as "guards," in addition to John M. Luce, Reynolds and Ike (Isaac) Neibaur. He demanded that the citizens of Great Salt Lake City apprehend and punish his assailants.

In the same issue, the News, under the headline *"Exciting and Terrifying Occurrences,"* told the rest of the story:

The Luces, Reynolds and Neibaur were arrested and hauled into the local courthouse for questioning. Huntington and Clawson could not be found. In addition, the police were looking for robbers who had taken $800 from a local stable. They thought Huntington and Clawson were involved, along with John P. Smith. Reportedly headed south, Huntington and Smith were seen at Jordan Mills, where they stole a horse. Residents of Draperville in south Salt Lake Valley reported that Clawson had joined the two. Orrin Porter Rockwell, one of the sheriff's deputies, was put on the trail. He found them at Faust's Station, another stop on the trail.

Rockwell confronted the band of outlaws and in the process, Huntington bolted and was shot dead. Smith and Clawson were put in a stage with their partner's body and brought back to Great Salt Lake City and put in charge of the local policemen to be taken to jail.

**DESERET NEWS,** *Jan. 22, 1862: But before they had proceeded far, the prisoners, supposing probably that the policemen were unarmed, started to run, and were shot at and both killed before getting far away…*

*The thanks of the community are most certainly due Mr. Rockwell and those who were with him.*

Dawson's short tenure as governor began in mutual distrust, flowered in rancor and infamy and ended in violence.

**Orrin Porter Rockwell**

IN MEMORY of JOHN QUAYLE who was KILLED by INDIANS August 17th 1855 Aged 20 Years.

# ...and a grave robber

**The hurried departure of Gov. John Dawson from Utah Territory led in a roundabout way to the discovery of one of the most bizarre crimes in the history of the territory.**

Deseret News files

**M**oroni Clawson, one of the young men who attacked Dawson and who subsequently was gunned down by a Salt Lake policeman, was buried in the city cemetery, since his family did not claim the body. Officer Henry Heath saw to it himself that the young man was suitably dressed and interred. Later, Moroni's brother, George, decided to bring the body home for burial in the family plot at Willow Creek (now Draper). When "Rone's" coffin was opened, he was found to be stark naked.

Greatly agitated, the Clawsons laid into the Salt Lake Police Department. A baffled Heath was told to investigate further. Sexton J.C. Little was also nonplussed and together, the two went to the home of Jean Baptiste, the local gravedigger. They found his Avenues home filled with boxes containing burial clothing and other items.

The two men returned to the cemetery where they found Baptiste at work. Heath, so the story goes, grabbed the miscreant gravedigger by the throat and "shook him like a rat." Heath had recently buried a small daughter in the cemetery. Only when Baptiste assured him that the little girl's grave had not been desecrated did he let go.

Great Salt Lake City was in an uproar. Outraged citizens sifted through the clothing that was brought from Baptiste's home to the county courthouse. Law officers estimated that about 300 graves had been robbed. When those who could identify burial items had claimed them, the next question was what to do with Baptiste, who had been sequestered in the farthest corner of the local jail for his own protection.

Then Salt Lakers did what they always did in an emergency: Asked Brother Brigham what to do. His response, given in a meeting in the Tabernacle:

**DESERET NEWS,** *Feb. 9, 1862: It appears that a man named John Baptiste has practised robbing the dead of their clothing in our grave*

*yard during some five years… I am unable to think so low as to fully get at such a mean, contemptible, damnable trick. To hang a man for such a deed would not begin to satisfy my feelings. What should we do with him? Shoot him? No, that would do no good to anybody but himself … If it was left to me, I would make him a fugitive and a vagabond upon the earth…*

*Many are anxious to know what effect it will have upon their dead who have been robbed … A thief may dig up dead bodies and sell them for the dissecting knife or may take their raiment from them, but when the resurrection takes place, the Saints will come forth with all the glory, beauty and excellency of resurrected Saints, clothed as they were when they were laid away … Do as you please with regard to taking up your friends. If I should undertake to do anything of the kind, I should clothe them completely and then lay them away again. And if you are afraid of their being robbed again, put them into your gardens where you can watch them by day and night until you are pretty sure that the clothing is rotted, and then lay them away in the burying ground …*

The law did the best it could, under the circumstances, to make Baptiste a

"fugitive and a vagabond." Officers first took him to Antelope Island, then fearing the water was so shallow that he could walk back to the mainland, they relocated him to Fremont Island where there was a little shed for shelter and some pioneer livestock for company.

Awhile later, when they returned to check on him, the shed had been dismantled and the remains of a slaughtered heifer were nearby. The assumption was that Baptiste had made a raft and escaped the island. Although stories circulated for years that he had been seen here or there, the grave robber never was found.

---

SEXTON'S REPORT.

G. S. L. City Sexton's Report for the months of April and May, 1865.

| Total No. of interments, | | 46 |
| --- | --- | --- |
| Adults | - | 15 |
| Children | - | 31 | 46 |

DIED OF THE FOLLOWING CAUSES AS REPORTED.

| Scarlet Fever | - | 10 |
| --- | --- | --- |
| Consumption | - | 5 |
| Putrid sore throat | - | 4 |
| Inflammation lungs & bowels | - | 4 |
| Stillborn | - | 4 |
| Died at birth | - | 4 |
| Cancer | - | 3 |
| Canker | - | 2 |
| Liver complaint | - | 2 |
| Dropsy | - | 2 |
| General debility | - | 2 |
| Conjestive chills | - | 2 |
| Pleurisy | - | 1 |
| Typhoid fever | - | 1 |
| Old age | - | 1 | 46 |

| Brought from country places for interment | - | 10 |
| --- | --- | --- |
| Transient Residents | - | 2 |
| Resident citizens | - | 34 | 46 |

JOSEPH E. TAYLOR, Sexton.

—The Sandusky Register says

# The Telegraph

## Electric bands link a nation

**The telegraph, technological marvel of the era, had a technical glitch on its first application in Salt Lake City.**

Telegraph key was used in the first telegraph system in Utah.

LDS Musuem

**DESERET NEWS,** *Oct. 23, 1861: On Thursday afternoon, the "operator" connected with the Eastern portion of the telegraph line informed the visitors who had gathered around his table to witness the first operations in communicating with the Eastern States that the "line was built," but for some reason, there was no "through message" either sent or received till the following day.*

Although the system wasn't in operation until Oct. 24, Brigham Young sent the first "message by wire" out of Salt Lake City dated Oct. 18, 1861, the day that the last pole was set in downtown Salt Lake City near the present ZCMI Building. It was addressed to J.H. Wade, president of the Pacific Telegraph Co., Cleveland, Ohio. After congratulating Wade on the *"energy displayed by yourself and associates in the rapid and successful prosecution of a work so beneficial,"* Young assured him that *"Utah has not seceeded, but is firm for the*

Salt Lake's telegraph office was located on Main Street in the early 1860s.

LDS Church Archives

*Constitution and laws of our once happy country."*

Young's reference was to the beginning of the Civil War on April 12, 1861, when Southerners fired on Fort Sumter, N.C., triggering the dissolution of the Union.

Wade responded by joining in the *"hope that this enterprise may tend to promote the welfare and happiness of all concerned, and that the annihilation of time in our means of communication may also tend to annihilate prejudice, cultivate brotherly love, facilitate commerce and strengthen the bonds of our once and again-to-be happy union."*

Frank Fuller, acting governor of Utah Territory, also made use of the newly connected telegraph to wire President Abraham Lincoln. His message avowed loyalty from Utah Territory:

**DESERET NEWS:** *Utah, whose citizens strenuously resist all imputations of disloyalty, congratulates the President upon the completion of an enterprise which spans a continent, unites two oceans and connects with nerves of iron the remote extremities of the body politic with the great Governmental heart. May the whole system speedily thrill with the quickened pulsations of that heart as the parricide hand is palsied, treason is punished and the entire sisterhood of States join hands in glad re-union around the National fireside.*

Ironically, Lincoln had been one of the detractors of the proposed transcontinental telegraph, predicting it would be impossible to get poles and equipment across the vast expanses of prairie between centers of civilization. Indians would not leave them in place anyway, he glumly predicted.

Nonetheless, he took advantage of the new marvel to wire Fuller back: *"The completion of the telegraph is auspicious of the stability and union of the Republic. The Government reciprocates your congratulations."*

For Utah Territory, the joining of the electric wires running east from Carson City, Nev., and west from Omaha, Neb., spelled the end of relative isolation and the halting communications of earlier eras — when things went well. They didn't always go well:

**DESERET NEWS,** *July 23, 1862: That portion of the Telegraphic line extending eastward from Great Salt Lake City, has been*

*an ineffective, crippled, diseased, dilapidated crazy concern for a long time, so much so that it has been a very uncertain medium for the transmission of intelligence. It has been dumb defacto to that extent that fears are entertained, if some potent curative be not speedily applied it will become a confirmed mute.*

*Questions are daily asked relative to the cause of the apparent inefficiency of the*

Workmen used the railroad lines to build a telegraph line in Weber Canyon.

Utah State Historical Society

*institution, and why the poles are prostrate and the wires severed, or so efflected that they have been speechless … The most probable reasons that we have heard assigned for its imbecility are that the construction was too hurried and the work not done in a proper manner, or that there are and have been more secessionists along the line than reported…*

Nevertheless, as the Oct. 23, 1861, Deseret News article rejoiced:
*"… the inhabitants of the Pacific and Atlantic States will be united in electric bands."*

# The Railroad
## Ribbons of iron

On May 10, 1869, a terse telegraph message to U.S. President Ulysses S. Grant notified him that "The last rail is laid, the last spike is driven. The Pacific Railroad is finished." Soon, Americans from ocean to ocean were aware that unbroken ribbons of iron now tied the United States into a neat package from Atlantic to Pacific.

C̄owcatcher-to-cowcatcher on Utah Territory's Promontory Summit, Central Pacific's engine Jupiter and Union Pacific's No. 119 proved the skeptics had been wrong. Almost 1,700 miles of prairie, mountains and desert had not been enough to defeat man's ingenuity and determination.

The following day, the Deseret News reported on "The Proceedings at Promontory Summit" in eloquent terms:

Utah State Historical Society

*DESERET NEWS, May 11, 1869: The meridian hour has come and on the expansive and lofty plateau at the summit of the Promontory, a scene is disclosed in the conception of which every exultant element of humanity is revivified. Never before has this continent disclosed anything bearing comparison with it...*

*A thousand throbbing hearts impulsively beat to the motion of the trains as the front locomotives of each Company led on majestically up to the very verge of the narrow break between the lines, where, in a few moments, was to be consummated the nuptial rites uniting the gorgeous east and the imperial west of America, with the indissoluble seal of inter-oceanic commerce.*

There followed a long list of the dignitaries, including railroad officials, political leaders and the governors of California, Arizona and Nevada.

California's Gov. Leland Stanford set the tone for eloquence, the News suggested, when he stated:

*"Never since history commenced her record of human events has man been called upon to meet the completion of a work so magnificent in contemplation and so marvelous in execution."*

With great ceremony, railroad officials then placed the final tie, a handsome specimen of California laurel wood, with a silver plate noting the historic date. Then, Stanford, who also was a CP official, stood on one side wielding a silver maul and UP president T.C. Durant on the other and, at a given signal, they drove the ceremonial golden spike completing the link.

*"Instantaneously, the electric current flashed the tidings east and west, that the work was done, and the same electric flash sent the reverberating discharge of 220 guns from the batteries of San Francisco,"* the News reported.

Notably missing from the list of distinguished guests at the ceremonies was the name of Brigham Young, Utah Territory's most prominent figure. He had opposed the route selected by Congress for the rail line, hoping for something closer to Salt Lake City than the selected site through Promontory.

Nevertheless, Salt Lakers waited for the telegraph signal set off by the electric wires attached to the mauls that drove the final spike.

*Upon announcement by telegram that the connecting rail is laid, a salute will be fired from the hill, near the Arsenal, the Court House and City Hall by Major S.G. Ladd's Artillery in three detachments,"* the May 11th Semi-Weekly News announced.

*DESERET NEWS, May 7, 1869: Flags will then be unfurled from the principal offices, banks, stores and private residences in the city. Bands will discourse music from the most suitable positions for the public gratification and at the meeting in the New Tabernacle, to commence one hour after firing the salute... During the meeting, the Memorial of the Utah Legislature of 1852-53 calling the attention of Congress to the advantages resulting from the "Great Highway" and urging its earliest practicable construction, will be read.*

With railroad links east and west, Utah's isolation was at an end. The territory gladly ceded its frontier status to become the crossroads of the West.

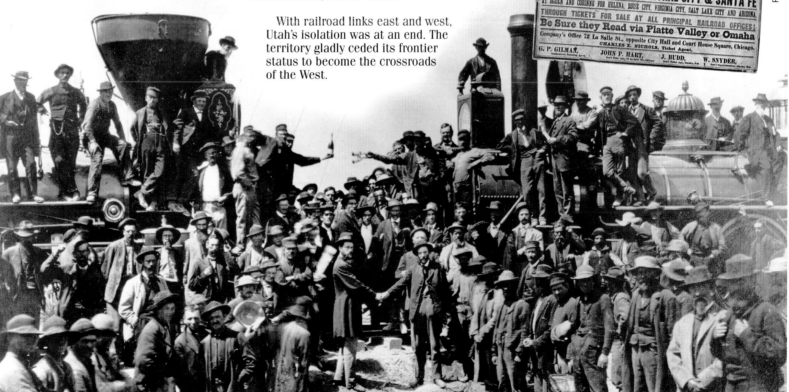

In a famous photograph by Andrew Russell, Grenville Dodge and Sam Montague shake hands before a crowd of workmen as the rails meet at Promontory Point.

# Indians
## Wars and treaties

**When Mormon settlers arrived in the Salt Lake Valley, they entered a territory that was visited by American Indians but not occupied by them. As settlers began to spread out in all directions, they did move into Indian homelands, and contact and conflicts increased. Brigham Young's well-known feed-not-fight policy was largely adhered to, but it did not prevent sporadic outbursts of violence.**

Chief Black Hawk

T he Deseret News reported such encounters with the language and biases of the times:

**DESERET NEWS,** *April 18, 1860: The mail carrier on the route between this and Brigham City reports, that on Thursday last, a small company of Indians who had visited Great Salt Lake City for the purpose of soliciting presents from the Government, as they were returning homeward quite dissatisfied at not obtaining what they came for, there being neither Superintendent nor Agent to be found in this part of the Territory, were very saucy as they passed through the settlements.*
*At Farmington they had some altercation with two men by the name of Barnard, on whom they made some demands. Near Kingston's Fort, three of them assaulted a man who was hunting stock on the range, and tried to run him over with their horses. One of the Indians was armed with bow and arrow, the others each had a war club; the one having a bow shot twelve arrows at the man, eight of which took effect, wounding him badly. The other two then came up with their war clubs to dispatch him; but one of them accidently dropped his club, which the wounded*

*man seized, and wielding it dexterously he soon drove the savage assailants from the field.*

Encounters with Indians were reported, but there was also a fascination with culture and customs. Typical is a report of the death of Peteetneet:

**DESERET NEWS,** *Jan. 1, 1862: The well-known Utah Chief, Peteetneet, as reported, died at or near Fort Crittenden, Cedar Valley, on or about the 23d ult. No horses were killed on the occasion, as is generally the case when an Indian of distinction dies, but a novel and brutal ceremony, by his express order, was instituted instead, and that was the killing of his wife, who was dispatched by beating out her brains with an axe, a squaw being the executioner. The Chief was buried after the manner of Indian sepulture in the mountains adjacent, and his murdered wife in the valley beneath.*

Concern for the condition of Indians was evident in news reports:

**DESERET NEWS,** *April 16, 1862: It is reported that in consequence of the cold, stormy weather, which has prevailed during the winter, many of the Indians, both north and south, are in a suffering condition, and some of them feel a little cross towards the representatives of*

*government because their wants have not been supplied, and in some instances, it is said they have killed cattle to satiate their hunger; but not in consequence of their entertaining any hostile intentions towards the whites…*

### Massacre on the Bear River

In July of 1860, the paper reported that Secretary Floyd had *"summoned Gen. Harney to Washington, with a view to the arranging for the campaign against the Shoshones and other Indians. It is to be planned on a large scale."* That campaign took place on Jan. 29, 1863, when Col. Patrick Edward Connor and his California Volunteers attacked a Shoshone village in what has come to be known as the Bear River Massacre. Reports reached the paper several days later:

**DESERET NEWS,** *February 4, 1863: Col. Connor and the Volunteers who went north last week to look after the Indians on Bear River have, in a very short space of time, done a larger amount of Indian killing than ever fell to the lot of any single expedition of which we have knowledge…*
*Two companies of the cavalry immediately crossed to the north side of the river, and had hardly got orders before the Indians showed fight — in the first fire, shooting one of the cavalry through the head. The Indians had selected for their position of defence, a deep ravine.*
*Not having a special reporter on the field, we are unable to give in graphic detail the fight, but have been informed that it was a hard contested battle that lasted between three and four hours…*
*Gradually the Volunteers got upon the redskins and drove them to the mouth of the ravine, where a portion of the cavalry met the retreating Indians and played dreadful havoc with them. In one pile forty-eight bodies were killed in*

The indian warrior, left, was a member of Chief Pocatello's tribe and died at the Bear River Massacre. Tomahawk was called a rabbit thrower.

Pioneer Memorial Museum

Utah State Historical Society

attempting to get into the river and after they reached it. We have no official data from which to give figures, but it is stated with the greatest confidence that from 250 to 300 Indians were killed and wounded. Only about 15 of the warriors were supposed to have escaped.

## The Black Hawk War

Attention then shifted to the south, where attacks and subsistence raids led by a charismatic chief named Black Hawk began to plague settlers. What later came to be known as the Black Hawk War lasted roughly from 1863 to 1868 and was the most destructive conflict between the pioneers and the Indians. It was unusual among Indian wars in the West in that it was fought by the settlers and not by militia. Although stealing cattle was the main goal of the Indians, lives were also lost. By the end, the final tally was about 70 settlers, and perhaps twice that many Indians.

But even so, reports were sporadic and rarely front-page news. Typical was this account, run under the headline "Indian Massacre:"

**DESERET NEWS,** *June 7, 1865: Through letters and verbal information we are enabled to present the following details of the recent tragic events in Sanpete and Thistle valleys: —*

*Thursday evening, May 25th, as br. Jens Larsen was gathering up the large flock of sheep in his charge, about 4 miles north of Fairview, Sanpete county, some Indians shot and killed him. He was an esteemed citizen, aged about 35 and left a wife and 2 children.*

*Friday morning, 26th, and about 12 miles north of Fairview, the same Indians, between daylight and sunrise, killed John Given, aged about 45, his* wife Eliza, aged about 40, his son John, aged about 19 and his daughters Mary, Annie and Martha, respectively aged about 9, 5 and 3.

*Balls, arrows and tomahawks or axes were used in the murdering, though none of the bodies were otherwise abused or scalped.*

In June of 1865, the Deseret News announced a treaty signed by Brigham Young and *"quite a large body of Indians"* assembled at the Indian Farm in Spanish Fork. The Indians agreed to move to Uintah Valley to a reservation. But the same account noted that *"Black-hawk and his band, who have been perpetrating the late atrocities in that neighborhood, are still in the mountains."*

Many of the announcements about Indian activity that appeared in the paper during these years almost took on the flavor of traffic reports. *"The Indians are reported to be troublesome in the neighborhood of Fort Reno, Powder river, on the route from Ft. Laramie to Montana,"* the paper reported on Aug. 23, 1866.

## Making peace

By 1869, however, most Indians, including Black Hawk, were more interested in peace:

**DESERET NEWS,** *May 25, 1869: Major Dymock B. Huntington, Indian Interpreter, informs us that, on the evening of Friday last, he had a visit from the notorious chief, "Black Hawk," who has been the prime mover in the Indian disturbances for the last few years in the southern portion of this Territory. "Black Hawk" said he was sent by the Pi-edes, who live west of Green River. They want peace and "Black Hawk" said he would* have them all, — men, women and children in Gunnison in one moon, so that the Indian Superintendent, Col. Head, and he, Dymock, might go and have a talk with them. He says they will not want to come to Gunnison, because they have nothing but horses they have stolen from the "Mormons" to ride on; they would rather meet a distance from the settlement. However, "Black Hawk" has kept his promise to keep the peace, given two years ago, it is very likely that he will bring them.

Black Hawk would continue his role as a peacemaker. In a letter dated Dec. 22, 1869, a Mrs. M. Patterson wrote:

**DESERET NEWS,** *Jan. 5, 1870: Dear Brother Cannon: — On the 16th instant, we had a big visit from Black Hawk, his brother, Mountain, and quite a number of his band. Black Hawk and Mountain talked to the people in the meeting house in the evening, bro. Shelton, from Beaver, being the interpreter. Black Hawk made great declarations of friendship and said he wanted a big peace. The day before his arrival, the Navajoes had made a raid on our horses, and a company of men were in pursuit. Black Hawk offered to go and bring the horses back, if we would furnish him and his men with fresh horses to ride, but it was not seen fit to accept his generous offer. He told us to catch the Navajoes, if we could, when they came to steal, and not kill them, but talk to them and show*

Ute chieftain Ouray is surrounded by his subchiefs, Warets, Shavano, Ankatsoh and Guero.

Utah State Historical Society

Pioneer Memorial Museum

**Veterans of Black Hawk War pose for reunion portrait.**

**Medallion was given to veterans of the Utah Indian War.**

**1860 Colt .44 cal. revolver**

LDS Museum

*that we do not desire to shed blood; send them back to their home and friends to tell what was said of them. This he said, would do far more good than killing them. — This is very good advice, but comes with rather bad grace from such a quarter. — Black Hawk's consumptive look and hollow cough indicate that he cannot last long.*

# The Civil War

## A remote outpost

**When Southern secessionists fired on Fort Sumter, South Carolina, on April 12, 1861, initiating America's Civil War, Utahns in their remote Western colonies followed the succession of events through the pages of the Deseret News.**

Several weeks after that event, on May 22, 1861, the newspaper proclaimed "A Battle Between North and South Imminent," based on Pony Express dispatches dated April 13. Such delayed reports were standard for the day.

Most pioneers had little direct involvement in the national conflict. Members of the Nauvoo Legion were assigned by the territorial governor to guard overland mail routes during the conflict, but they never saw action in the East. Many of the settlers believed the war to be fulfillment of a prophecy uttered by founding Prophet Joseph Smith. He had said in 1832 that the north and south would be pitted against each other and that the conflict would center on slavery and begin with rebellion in South Carolina.

As news of the escalating battle filtered into Utah, President Brigham Young said:

**DESERET NEWS,** *May 1, 1861: The whole government is gone; it is as weak as water … It will be the Christians against the Christians, and man against man, and those who will not take up the sword against their neighbors must flee to Zion.*

In the same issue, the newspaper recounted the burning of the Harper's Ferry Arsenal and riots in Baltimore. "Mobocracy Rampant," the headline announced.

*A St. Louis dispatch, on the evening of the 19th states that a terrible riot had taken place in Baltimore that day, on the occasion of the passage of northern troops through the city on their way to Washington… The railroad track was taken up and the troops, who attempted to march through the city, were first attacked by a mob with bricks and stones and then fired upon. The fire was returned. Two of the 7th Regiment of Massachusetts troops were reported killed and several wounded … The soldiers are reported to have killed ten citizens…*

By October, events were moving so fast that the Utah newsapaper, which was having troubles of its own because of a lack of paper for printing, had a hard time keeping current.

**DESERET NEWS,** *Oct. 23, 1861: "Many important events have transpired, that were exceedingly interesting on their first announcement, but in these troublous times, when important events follow each other in quick succession, the news of the day becomes stale on the morrow …*

The News then recapped the major events of the preceding month. Over the next few years, almost every edition of the paper had reports of the see-saw fortunes of the two armies fighting on the eastern battlefields. In April 1862, acting territorial governor Frank Fuller ordered a Nauvoo Legion unit to guard the overland mail route. Such assignments within the territory were the only Civil War-related tasks that fell to Utahns.

### Lincoln's assassination

In April 1865, in a black-bordered announcement, the newspaper advised its readers of the sorry climax to the war that had ended only days earlier — the assassination of President Abraham Lincoln.

**DESERET NEWS,** *April 19, 1865: WASHINGTON, 14th, Midnight — The President and wife, with other friends this evening visited Ford's Theatre for the purpose of witnessing the performance of Our American Cousins …*

*During the third act and while there was a temporary pause for one of the actors to enter, a sharp report of a pistol was heard, which merely attracted attention, but suggested nothing serious until a man rushed to the front of the President's box, waving a long dagger in his right hand, exclaiming: Sic semper tyrannis (death to tyrants.) He immediately leaped from the box, which was in the second tier, to the stage beneath, ran across to the opposite side of the stage, making his escape amid the bewilderment of the audience, from the rear of the theatre and mounting a horse, fled.*

*The screams of Mrs. Lincoln first disclosed the fact to the audience that the President had been shot, when all present rose to their feet, rushing towards the stage, many exclaiming, "hang him." The excitement was of the wildest possible description. Of course, there was an abrupt intermission of the theatre performance …*

**President Abraham Lincoln**

National Archives

Deseret News

THE DESERET

FROM THE ARMY OF THE POTOMAC.

*On hasty examination, it was found that the President had been shot through the head above and back of the temporal bone, and that some of the brain was oozing out. He was removed to a private house, opposite the theatre and the surgeon-General of the army and other surgeons were sent for to attend to his condition … A common single-barreled pistol was found on the carpet.∴ Abraham Lincoln died this morning (15) at 22 minutes after 7 o'clock.*

In Utah, the funeral was also observed:

**DESERET NEWS,** *April 26, 1865: Public buildings were closed and business suspended from 10 o'clock a.m. till 4 p.m.; and at an early hour people began wending their way to the Tabernacle. At 12 the building was filled to its utmost capacity … The Choir sang hymns suited to the occasion and the opening prayer by Elder Franklin D. Richards was followed by a feeling and appropriate adress by Elder Amasa Lyman and an eulogy by the Rev. Norman McLeod …*

A number of blacks who had come to Utah Territory as slaves were freed with announcement of the Emancipation Proclamation at the outset of the Civil War.

**Daniel Bankhead Freeman was the first freeborn Utah black.**

Utah State Historical Society

## Aug. 6, 1862

## MISCELLANEOUS NEWS

Martin Van Buren, the eighth president of the United States, died at his residence in Kenderhook, N.Y., on the morning of July 24, being 89 years of age … Mr. Van Buren was the first ex-chief magistrate of the undivided States, who has been "gathered to his fathers" on the memoriable Twenty-fourth of July… the anniversary of the entrance into these valleys of the pioneers, of a just people for whom, although they had a just cause, he could do nothing.

**(The reference is to Van Buren's response to an appeal from Joseph Smith for protection of the Latter-day Saints from mobs in Missouri and Illinois.)**

## Feb. 4, 1868

It is reported that the President, some two weeks since, placed a million dollars to the credit of the emancipation commissioners of the District of Columbia, to be paid pro rata to the owners of the slaves who have been set free by act of Congress. Three hundred dollars is the maximum allowance for each slave.

## July 27, 1868

(From Paris, Rich County, correspondent)
On Sunday last, N.C. Davis and Allen Davis of St. Charles, and Thomas Slight and J. Collings of Paris, with six women, were returning from Fish Haven, when about midway from the latter named place to St. Charles, their attention was suddenly attracted to a peculiar motion or wave in the water (of Bear Lake) about three miles distant … Mr. Slight says he distinctly saw the sides of a very large animal that he would suppose to be not less than ninety feet in length … It was going south and all agreed that it swam with a speed almost incredible to their senses. Mr. Davis says he never saw a locomotive travel faster, and thinks it made a mile a minute, easy. In a few minutes after the discovery of the first, a second one followed in its wake, but seemed to be much smaller, appearing to Mr. Slight about the size of a horse. A larger one followed this, and so on till four large ones, in all, and six small ones had run southward out of sight…

## April 23, 1869

## CONTEMPTIBLE.

— Packages of goods, frequently arrive from the East in this city, having, in addition to the address of the parties to whom they are sent, disgustingly obscene, and profane phrases inscribed upon the wrappers or cases in which they are enclosed, and this, too, in good calligraphy, proving that while the dirty scribes who are guilty of such meanness are among the vilest of the vile, they are not among the most ignorant and illiterate. Such conduct is beneath contempt; and they who are guilty of it are a disgrace to their mothers, and deserve a severe caning.

## April 23, 1869

## TIGHT ROPE PERFORMANCE.

— We understand that Professor De Houne will give another of his excellent performances on the tight rope, tomorrow afternoon, near Faust and Houtz' stables, during which he will cook a dinner in a common cook stove on the rope.

## June 12, 1869

We should have scarcely thought it necessary to mention that the fact of an advertisement appearing in our columns, does not necessarily carry with it our endorsement, had we not been told that some folks regard the advertisements as much the work of the editor as the leading article. We imagined it was everywhere understood, that when a merchant or any other person purchases a certain portion of the paper to specify his wants, or draw attention to his wares, that he has the right to do so in his own language, providing there be nothing contrary to morality and decency. That portion of the paper is his as long as he continues to pay for it.

## April 5, 1869

## MINUTES OF THE FIRST ANNUAL MEETING OF THE FEMALE RELIEF SOCIETY OF THE 17TH WARD, S.L. City

The Society, now fully organized, is composed of one Presidentess, two Counsellors, Secretary and Treasurer; sixteen Teachers or Visiting Committee, a Board of Appraisers, composed of four members; and one hundred and seventy members.

The financial condition of the Society is as follows:

Received in donations during the fiscal year, ending Feb. 17, 1869

| | |
|---|---|
| Cash | $62.40 |
| Provisions and merchandise | 935.62 1/2 |
| Cash from parties | 243.40 |
| Orders and merchandise | 26.90 |
| Total | $1233.32 1/2 |
| Amount Disbursed in behalf of the needy | $854.85 1/2 |
| Balance in treasury | |
| Cash | 182.85 |
| Store orders | 12.50 |
| Merchandise | 188.12 |
| Total | $1238.32 |

## Nov. 16, 1869

## A CURIOUS SURGICAL SUCCESS… TRANSFUSION OF BLOOD
(From the New York Post, October 28)

The "Medical Record" for Oct. 1st publishes an account by Dr. Joseph Buchser, of this city, of a successful operation, of a kind commonly dreaded and avoided by the most skillful surgeons:

The patient, a young German woman, lost much blood after an attack of typhus fever, became reduced in strength and was apparently dying. As a last hope, Dr. Buchser proposed to her husband the dangerous operation of a transmission of healthy blood from his vigorous body into her veins. The husband consented; and Dr. Guleke, who was called in consultation, assisted at the experiment… The patient, who could not possibly be anaesthetized, underwent the operation with ease… In three quarters of an hour the operation was accomplished. Pulse immediately after the operation had fallen to 116, respirations, 16; one hour later, pulse 108, respirations 18.

During the afternoon, patient felt very hungry and thirsty; took light food and drank a pint bottle of claret.

Of course, no unpracticed hands, and no mind unfamiliar with the history of transfusion, both in its few brilliant successes and in its terrible accidents, will venture to attempt such an operation as this. But a few such cases such as this would afford the hope that, in skillful hands, transfusion of blood may become a powerful agent for good, in an important class of cases.

## Nov. 23, 1869

## BRIEFS

Truth would be popular with us if it proposed only to correct the faults of others.

Discouragements are given us to bear and surmount, not to talk about and yield to. It is pluck and endurance that win.

True liberty allows each individual to do all the good he can for himself, without injuring his neighbor.

There are three times as many men engaged in selling liquor as in preaching the Gospel or teaching school.

A child six years old was recently run over in Boston. "Don't whip me, father, I'll never do so again," were his last words.

Laborers get seven cents a day and board in Switzerland.

# THE DESERET NEWS.

TRUTH AND LIBERTY.

March 14, 1860

## THE UNION ACADEMY

On the East Side of Union Square, G.S.L. City, will be ready for the admission of scholars on the 9th of April next.

This Academy will be under the general supervision of Professor Orson Pratt and will commence with Mssrs. Orson Pratt Jun., and James Cobb as Teachers to whose aid other teachers will be added whenever the number of scholars may render it requisite.

No tuition will be charged to those who study Algebra, Surveying or other higher branches of Mathematics, Astronomy, Chemistry, Mineralogy, Geology and Modern Languages, which, with whatever else may be taught, it is expected will be taught and learned in a thoroughly practical manner …

— Brigham Young Sen.

March 28, 1860

## TAKING THE LEAD

The people in the Thirteenth Ward are making the necessary arrangements for building, in the course of the summer, a commodious school house on the foundation that was commenced some time since — not after the original design, but upon a plan considered more economical and convenient and better suited to the purposes for which it may be required.

July 4, 1860

## A Favorable Report.

Bishop L. W. Hardy, who has lately been on a tour through Utah, Juab and San Pete counties, reports that the wheat crops in all the settlements he visited look remarkably well, never better, and the prospect of an abundant harvest in that region is truly cheering.

In San Pete, in consequence of the cold, dry weather during the spring, the wheat is somewhat backward, and will be late in ripening. It is said that there is, at least, ten thousand acres of wheat growing in that county, which, though late, bids fair to produce well.

Sept. 12, 1860

## Save your Paper Rags.

The inhabitants of Utah are requested to gather up and save their worn out wagon covers, and every description of cotton and linen rags for paper making, and deliver them, from time to time, to the Bishops of the several Wards, or the 'News' and 'Mountaineer' Offices or their agents, for which, when clean, they will be allowed five cents a pound. The rags can be sufficiently cleaned in pure water, without soap.

It is expected that, in a few months, all who wish can receive paper in exchange for rags.

— EDWARD HUNTER, Presiding Bishop

Oct. 2, 1861

## LAST IMMIGRANT COMPANY

On Friday evening, the 27th ult., Captain Sextus E. Johnston arrived in this city with his company of immigrating Saints, the last expected this fall, although there are one or two small freight trains yet expected to arrive. There were in the company between fifty and sixty wagons, but how many persons, no one, of whom inquiries have been made, could state definitely… It is estimated that between four and five thousand persons have come across the plains this season, intending to remain permanently in the Territory, and if they came here to live their religion and fully carry out their intentions, they will, of course, enjoy themselves better and be more satisfied with their condition and circumstances than while they have been living in Babylon … The opportunities for new comers to obtain the necessary things to make them comfortable during the following winter were never as good as they are this fall.

Oct. 23, 1861

## GOING SOUTH, BUT NOT SECEDING.

The development of the resources of Washington county and the entire Southern part of the Territory has long been considered of great importance to the people residing in these valleys, but the settlements formed there for that purpose have not flourished to the extent desired from various causes, not necessary now to state.

To accomplish the desired objects as soon as practicable, a company numbering over three hundred men with their families, have been either selected or have volunteered to go there this fall, as the winter, below the Rim of the Basin, is the best season of the year for building, fencing and opening farms for cultivation the ensuing year. Of this company, about two hundred are from Great Salt Lake City and county, some fifteen or twenty from Davis and Weber, a few from Tooele, about sixty from Utah, thirty from Sanpete and a few from Juab, Millard and Beaver counties.

With some of those going, we are not acquainted and cannot testify as to their fitness for the enterprise.

April 9, 1862

## Miscellaneous News Items.

The re-appearance of the Merrimac in Hampton Roads was much feared, although it was believed that the Monitor was a match for her. The *World* was of the opinion that if the Monitor could tow a small stone fleet into and blockade the Norfolk channel, there would be time to finish another iron-clad gunboat before the obstructions could be removed, if, indeed, her guns could not altogether prevent their removal.

April 16, 1862

## Parowan Cotton Factory.

The cotton mill at Parowan, owned by Ebenezer Hanks, Esq., which was so far completed as to be partially put in operation over a month since, is said to be doing tolerable good work, with a fair prospect that it will be a success, satisfactory both to the proprietor and the public. Only seventy-two spindles have yet been put in motion, but others will be ere long. The establishment is not very extensive but when put in complete working order may be expected to furnish a market for some considerable portion of the cotton that was grown in Washington county last season. As the cotton growing business in the southern part of the State is expected to be greatly increased, other and more extensive mills will of course be erected at no distant day.

Oct. 15, 1862

## CRICKET MATCH

On Thursday last, Oct. 9, a match was played between the Deseret Union and Springville Union Cricket Clubs, on the square in the 16th Ward.

The game commenced at 11 o'clock a.m. and finished at 5 p.m. The playing was very spirited and interesting throughout and elicited much applause from the spectators present. The Springville Union won by two runs. The following table exhibits the number of runs made by both clubs:

After the match, the Deseret Union entertained the

### SPRINGVILLE UNION.
*First Innings*

| | Runs |
| --- | --- |
| Richard Low, c. H. Luff | 5 |
| George Harrison, c. G. Luff | 6 |
| J.W. Cook, run out | 3 |
| A. Harrison, run out | 9 |
| James Stevenson, c. Bowring | 2 |
| H. Barlow, b. McEwan | 0 |
| Hugh M. Dougall, b. P. Margetts | 0 |
| Thomas Dallin, b. P. Margetts | 4 |
| Thomas Roylance, b. McEwan | 3 |
| J. Holley, not out | 10 |
| A. Warren, b. P. Margetts | 3 |

### DESERET UNION.

| | |
| --- | --- |
| Thomas Jessop, c. Cook | 14 |
| Henry Luff, b. Cook | 0 |
| William Cooper, b. Cook | 23 |
| George Luff, b. Cook | 7 |
| Henry McEwan, not out | 1 |
| Phillip Margetts, b. Cook | 5 |
| Henry Bowring, c. Roylance | 0 |
| George Knowlden, b. A. Harrison | 5 |
| Richard Treceder, b. Cook | 0 |
| Samuel Cooper, b. Cook | 2 |
| Charles Kidgell, b. Cook | 6 |
| Wilds | 4 |

players of the Springville Club at supper at Valley Home, which reflected great credit on "mine host" Hitesman as a caterer for the inner man. The evening was spent very agreeably.

Oct. 14, 1863

## THE THEATER

We were prevented from attending this place of entertainment on Saturday evening; but through persons who were present, we have learned, with great satisfaction, that the nut selling and nut cracking nuisance of the preceding Saturday evening was completely abated. We are obliged to the management for this timely squelching of the low, vulgar practice. We looked forward to the building of the theater in this city with kindly interest as an institution that was to edify, instruct and amuse. We should now dislike to get dissatisfied with it.

July 6, 1864

## THE FOURTH IN THE CITY

The dawning of the eighty-eighth anniversary of American Indendence was greeted with the usual honors. The artillery stationed at the head of East Temple Street boomed forth a national salute, the brass and martial bands mingled with the roar of cannon the sweet harmony of national airs, and in a short time, the city was astir and the holiday was eagerly greeted.

Early in the day a large sprinkling of the younger portion of the population were soon riding up and down the streets, and towards noon the sidewalks were lively with pedestrians moving to and fro, visiting and congratulating, while another portion "hanging about" apparently freed from all the responsibilities of life, were doing the loafing and consuming the ice creams.

The novelty of a Pyrotechnic display attracted a very large concourse of people towards the Arsenal as the evening fell and darkness began to be visible.

**ELIAS SMITH....EDITOR AND PUBLISHER**

**Aug. 3, 1864**

There is a gentleman in St. Louis who has two bushels and a half of children. His name is Peck, and he has ten boys and girls. Four pecks, one bushel.

There is a farmer in Putnam county, New York, who has a mile and a half of children. His name is Furlong and he has eight boys and four girls. Eight fulongs, one mile.

There is a lady in Boston who was husband to her husband before they were married and who has given him three husbands since marriage. Her name was Husbands, which was unchanged by marriage.

**Aug. 31, 1864**

## TAKE NOTICE

Left his home at Centreville, Davis county, Utah Territory, on the 4th of July, 1864, THOMAS LYON, about 12 years old. He had on light blue pants, blue denims shirt and a grey woolen cap.

Any persons giving information of his whereabouts to O.M. Duell, 15th Ward, G.S.L. City or to his Mother, on O.M. Duell's Farm, will confer a great favor.

Mary Lyon

**Sept. 14, 1864**

## BY TELEGRAPH

Washington War Dep't. Sept. 4

Sherman's official report of the capture of Atlanta is just received, dated 26 miles south of Atlanta yesterday morning. It has been detained by the breaking of the telegraph lines.

Our army withdrew from about Atlanta and on the 30th made a break for the East Point road and reached a good position from which to strike the Macon road. Howard was on the right, near Sonesboro. Schofield on the left, near Rough and Ready…

(Signed) Sherman

**Feb. 15, 1865**

## IRRIGATION

A mass meeting of the citizens of Great Salt Lake County, living on the East side of the Jordan river, was held on Saturday, Feb. 4th, 1865, in the Tabernacle in this city, to organize a company for the construction of an irrigation canal, according to the provisions of "An Act to incorporate Irrigation companies," passed Jan. 20th, 1865, and published in the NEWS of Feb. 1st, 1865. At that meeting, Twelve Trustees, a Secretary and a Treasurer were elected.

**Aug. 2, 1865**

## A SCHOOL TEACHER WANTED

A good, competent School Teacher can find constant employment in Tooele City School District, by applying within a reasonable time and furnishing good references. From 70 to 80 scholars in summer and from 100 to 125 attend through the winter months. A large and well appointed school room and fuel will be furnished.
A. Galloway
John Tate
George Craner, School trustees

**April 5, 1865**

THE SUEZ CANAL — Mr. Ferdinand de Lesseps gives public notice that his projected Ship-canal, uniting the Red Sea with the Mediterranean, was so far completed in 1864 that a daily boat has been run from Port Said to Suez since the 1st of last month — a large bark towed by a steamer, and conveying twenty to thirty passengers having passed from sea to sea within twenty-four hours. As yet, the depth of water would seem to be but four or five feet, with a width of thirty to forty; but it is confidently calculated that the canal will be prepared for effective transportation by April, when six steam-tugs are to be ready for service upon it.

This canal is ninety miles long, and is to have, when completed, a minimum depth of twenty feet, with a width of 330 feet at the surface. It was commenced in 1859 by a private company, on a subscribed capital of $40,0000,000.

**Feb. 20, 1869**

## THE BEST MANAGEMENT OF THE SILKWORMS FOR UTAH

The annual silkworm (Bombix Mori) which produces by far the best silk in Europe, is born in the spring, ordinarily about the middle of May. It feeds on the leaves of the mulberry tree and attains its full growth in about six weeks. During that period, it changes its skin four times and according to Mr. de Quatrefages, of the French Institute, increases its weight seventy-two thousand times…

I will do my best to simplify, in the full sense of that word, the process of raising these precious insects in Utah. To arrive at that end, the most natural mode ought to be adopted by our breeders. "Give the silk worm air, fresh and pure; let them be comfortably warm and dry and cleanly and with a sufficient space… The eggs are generally laid on paper or cloth and must be kept in a cool, dry place in the cellar, where, to prevent them from hatching, the thermometer never rises above fifty degrees…

After remaining in a warm atmosphere from five to eight days, the eggs will assume a whiteish color, a sure symptom of the formation of the worms inside. They will soon begin to show themselves, and the moment they make their appearance, they begin to look for food. Place some tender leaves from your mulberries on the paper and they will at once begin their occupation for life — eating. Etc.

**Feb. 20, 1869**

INFORMATION WANTED concerning John Montgomery, who left New York City, with the Saints of the Emerald Isle, Aug. 15, 1868. He traveled in that company until three days journey west of Benton, where all trace of him was lost. Any person knowing of his whereabouts will confer a favor by writing to his sister, Mary Montgomery, care of Wm. H. Miles, Esq., 117, John St., New York City.
(Frontier Index or Phoenix please copy)

**March 2, 1869**

## A FATAL ACCIDENT

Occurred on the night of Friday the 19th, which made a sad finale to a wedding. On that day a happy couple had come to Brigham City from the town located at the old crossing of Bear river, procured the services of a duly qualified gentleman and were soon yoked together in the harness of matrimony. On the return to Bear river, Charley Graves from Booth's hotel was engaged to drive the party, and on arriving, the joyous couple caused the whisky to circulate in any desired quantity. The driver drank too freely, drove off the road coming back and overturned the carriage, which fell on him, injuring him severely. This occurred on Friday night and he was not discovered until Saturday morning, the overturned carriage having lain upon him all night. He was brought to Brigham City, and Dr. O.C. Ormsby was immediately called in; but it was too late. He lingered on till Sunday and then died. I understand he was from New York State.

**June 8, 1869**

## THE UNIVERSITY OF DESERET

The first term of this institution closed on Wednesday; the second term commences on Monday next. The success which has attended the labors of Professor Park and his assistants during the past quarter is very gratifying to all the friends of education who are acquainted with the progress of the pupils… This institution supplies a want that has been long felt, and it is to be hoped that the efforts of the Chancellor and Board of Regents of the University to sustain it will meet with the cordial co-operation of the public. We have now the foundation laid for a first class college; if properly supported, it will undoubtedly become all that we can desire and be a renowned seat of learning…

**Nov. 23, 1869**

Singapore has a boa constrictor that has swallowed a young lady, who wore at the time a $15,000 dimands necklace. The young lady is of no value now, but the necklace is, so about thirty thousand natives are diligently searching for the snake.

# Statehood denied

In the early 1860s, when about a dozen Southern states were in various stages of removing themselves from the Union, Utah Territory made another attempt to get in. A new constitutional proposal was drafted and presented to the territory's residents for consideration.

**DESERET NEWS,** *March 19, 1862:*
*... upon canvassing the votes cast at the General Election, "for" and "against" the Constitution adopted by the Constitutional Convention on the 22d day of January, A.D. 1862, and submitted to the people for their rejection or ratification... I find that the said Constitution was unanimously adopted ...*
*(Signed) William Clayton*
*Secretary of the Convention*

John Bernhisel, Utah's elected territorial representative to Congress, was again directed to present the Utahns' petition. The newspaper reported periodically on the progress of the proposal as it negotiated the congressional process:

**DESERET NEWS,** *July 2, 1862:*
*FROM WASHINGTON*
*In the House of Representatives on the 9th (of May), Hon. J. M. Bernhisel, Delegate from Utah, presented the Constitution of the State of Deseret and the memorial accompanying it, asking for admission into the Union on an equal footing with the original states, which were received and referred to the Committee on Territories. On the 10th, the Vice President presented the same in the Senate ...*

By January, 1863, the petition still had not been acted upon. Brigham Young, who acted as "governor" of the State of Deseret within Utah Territory (which had its own governor), addressed the General Assembly:

**DESERET NEWS,** *Jan. 21, 1863:*
*[Our delegates to Washington] have labored assiduously for the admission of Deseret into the family of States. But Congress, during its last session, was heavily burdened with duties pertaining to the conduct of the war then and still is being prosecuted for the restoration of the Union and, so far as I have been advised, took no action upon our petition...*

*Beyond cavil it is the inherent and indefeasible right of American citizens to enjoy the untrammeled privilege of self-government, still we prefer, as hitherto, to conform with long-established usages, trusting that even those usages will soon concede to us the rights of self-government, so long withheld ... (We hope) that ere long, we also will be privileged with those constitutional franchises pertaining to a state government so justly our due and for which we have so long and so patiently waited and so loyally petitioned.*

Congress in fact was very nearly overwhelmed with Civil War issues. It did not act on the territory's petition. It did, however, take time for a debate on polygamy and in July 1862, passed the Morrill Anti-Bigamy Act. The bill outlawed bigamy in the territories still waiting for statehood. Violations called for a $500 fine and five years in prison. The bill also prohibited churches from owning more than $50,000 in real estate in any of the territories, a provision obviously targeted at Utah.

The Deseret News didn't give space to the Morrill bill. With the entire country focused on the war, there was little expectation that it would be enforced, and it wasn't. But the territory had had a taste of what was to come. The slavery questions that had bogged down statehood petitions in the 1850s were largely being resolved by the war. Polygamy — what the American Republican Party termed the second "relic of barbarism" — would be the stumbling block for Utah statehood for decades to come.

## The world of the 1860s
### A TIMELINE

**1860**— The port of Vladivostok, Russia, is founded on the coast of the Sea of Japan.

**1860**— The second Opium War ends with the signing of Sino-British and Sino-French conventions in Beijing.

**1860**— Abraham Lincoln elected president of the United States.

**1861**— Slave states join South Carolina in forming the Confederate States of America.

**1861**— Fort Sumter falls to Confederate troops.

**1861**— Alexander II frees 20 million serfs in Russia — a third of the population.

**1861**— Charles Dickens publishes first episode of "Great Expectations."

**1862**— Gen. Robert E. Lee assumes command of the Confederate armies of North Virginia.

**1862**— Victor Hugo's "Les Miserable" published in France.

**1862**— Abraham Lincoln proclaims the freedom of slaves in the Confederate states, effective Jan.1, 1863.

**1862**— Richard Gatling patents a gun that fires hundreds of rounds a minute through a cluster of rotating barrels.

**1862**— The Homestead Act offers every head of a family 160 acres of land free.

**1862**— Casualties in the Civil War are horrific: no fewer than 23,500 killed in one day at Antietam, Md.

**1863**— President Lincoln signs the Conscription Act.

**1863**— Confederate troops routed at Gettysburg, Pa., where 40,000 die.

**1863**— President Lincoln declares the last Thursday in November a national holiday of thanksgiving.

**1864**— A multilateral agreement on the Red Cross is signed at the Geneva Convention.

**1864**— Maximilian, Archduke of Austria, appointed emperor of Mexico.

**1864**— Abraham Lincoln elected to a second term as president.

**1865**— Charles Dodgson, writing as "Lewis Carrol," publishes "Alice's Adventures in Wonderland."

**1865**— Confederate General Robert E. Lee surrenders his troops, ending the Civil War.

**1866**— The Prussian army defeats Austria in the Seven Weeks war, changing the political map of Germany.

**1866**— A transatlantic telegraph cable successfully completed, linking the United States with Europe.

**1867**— By one vote, the Senate agrees to buy Alaska from Russia for $7.2 million, or 2 cents per acre.

**1867**— Karl Marx publishes the first volume of "Das Kapital."

**1868**— President Andrew Johnson escapes impeachment by one vote.

**1868**— The first patent granted for a typewriter.

**1868**— Spain's Queen Isabella is forced to seek refuge in France, leaving Spain in the hands of rebel generals.

**1869**— Count Leo Tolstoy publishes "War and Peace," one of the world's greatest novels.

**1869**— The Suez Canal opens.

**Paper currency, payable in merchandise, was issued by ZCMI.**

Charles Dickens

Karl Marx

Zions Cooperative Mercantile Institution
SALT LAKE CITY. October 6th 1870.
PROMISE to pay Leo Conkling or bearer
Five Dollars
Series A.
5
Oct. 16th 1868.
No. 2214

# Merchants
## in the kingdom

The occasional arrivals of wagons from the East or from California, carrying goods the pioneers could not grow, manufacture or trade among themselves, were times for celebration. Settlers hungry for the niceties of more firmly established civilization eagerly waited such announcements as:

**DESERET NEWS,** *Aug. 30, 1865: FORTY-SIX WAGONS JUST ARRIVED!!*
*We take pleasure in informing our friends and patrons that we have THIS DAY received our FOURTH TRAIN OF FORTY-SIX WAGONS, direct from the Missouri River, loaded with a SPLENDID ASSORTMENT OF GOODS of every description … WALKER BROTHERS*

Frontier commercial enterprises sprang up as fast as the population could support them. In the 1860s, the territory's varied businesses also became a reflection of the increasing push-and-pull between the Mormon settlers and a growing body of so-called "gentiles." Some of the most successful stores in blossoming Great Salt Lake City were founded by apostate Mormons such as the Walker Brothers — David, Joseph, Samuel and Matthew — or by non-Mormons like the Prussian-born Jewish clan of Frederick H., Samuel H., George S., Frederick S. and Herbert S. Auerbach. They competed with faithful Latter-day Saint concerns such as Kimball & Lawrence, Hooper & Eldredge, W. Jennings and W.S. Godbe (although Mr. Godbe eventually formed his own splinter group and became persona non grata with the Saints).

Brigham Young, still clinging to the desire for Mormon exclusivity and always anxious to keep his flock and their resources in the fold, began to urge his people to patronize merchants of their own faith. The newspaper editorialized his position:

**DESERET NEWS,** *Feb. 22, 1865: Perhaps in no country in the world have men engaged in ordinary mercantile trading been able to accumulate fortunes so rapidly, during the* past ten or twelve years, as in this Territory … When a new establishment is opened, the usual promises are made of "the cheapest goods," "the best value," etc. etc., which, if honestly interpreted, would read, "we only want to secure your custom, and when we have got it, and made a good start, we'll pile it on as heavy as anybody else."

*If our remarks give offence in any quarter, all we can say is, we advocate the claims of the public, and they are superior to private and personal interests.*

*We recommend the people to import as much as they can themselves, and bring along all the useful machinery possible and the means for manufacturing much of what we require among ourselves.*

By 1866, Young had issued a formal embargo on non-LDS purchases. A sudden decline in Deseret News commercial ads followed, but when they recommenced, the Walker Brothers still bought more ad space than just about anyone.

Church leaders had devised another plan to encourage support of LDS merchants. It was a cooperative marketing system that would involve a parent store — Zions Cooperative Mercantile Institution — with tentacles reaching out to smaller units in the Mormon communities. Brigham City had for several years been operating a prototype operation that was used as a model.

**DESERET NEWS,** *Feb. 20, 1869: ZION'S CO-OPERATIVE ASSOCIATION — IMPORTANT MEETING TODAY*
*At a meeting of the President and Board of Directors of Zion's Co-operative Institution, held at noon today, in the office of Eldridge and Clawson, an important decision was arrived at. The committee (assigned to select a building and study which goods should be offered) made their report, in which was embodied the propositions of various merchants, all of which, without exception, were exceedingly liberal. It gave the committee great pleasure to report, and the President and Board of Directors to hear, these propositions, as they were as fair as could be asked.*

*All who have the interest of this enterprise at heart will be gratified to learn that active steps have been taken to commence business with the Parent Co-operative Store immediately.*

Oxcarts and covered wagons stand outside first location of ZCMI in Jennings Eagle Emporium, at right, in April, 1869.

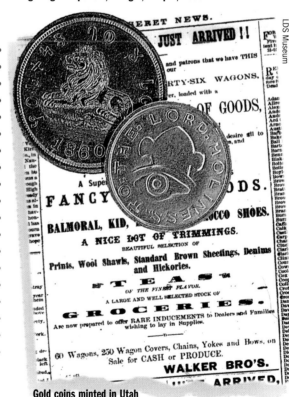
Gold coins minted in Utah included the Deseret Alphabet.

# Theater
## in the desert

"The people must have amusement as well as religion," pioneer leader Brigham Young declared, and that sentiment was impetus for the Salt Lake Theatre, the first of its kind west of the Mississippi River.

In 1861, approximately 12,000 pioneers were settled in Great Salt Lake City, a small group to finance and support a $100,000, 1,500-seat theater project. But rise it did, on the northeast corner of 100 South and State. Bricks were made of clay taken from the city's east benches and brought to a site where the Denver & Rio Grande Railway depot eventually was situated. Pine beams were dragged from Cottonwood Canyon. Iron was a scarce commodity in the young community, and pioneers scavenged enough from wrecks of government wagons on the Wyoming plains for the theater and other construction projects. When Johnston's Army pulled out of Camp Floyd, Hiram Clawson spent about $40,000 to purchase, at significantly cut-rate prices, building materials from the camp. Some of these items, too, went into the theater, giving rise to a local saying that Johnston's Army was sent to Utah to "benefit theatrics."

**DESERET NEWS,** *March 12, 1862, dedication: On Thursday evening, the members of the High Council, the bishops, the city, county and territorial officers, the workmen on the Theatre, the public hands, etc., with their families, were the invited, but finding the building insufficient for the whole, many had to reserve their tickets for the First Regular Night of the Season - Saturday.*

Workers were still putting the finishing touches on the theater, and Young *"wished the people to apprehend nothing, though a bench should roll over or a plank split a few inches — none should see in either circumstance the building falling upon them."*

President Daniel H. Wells of the First Presidency, an actor in his own right, offered a lengthy prayer (repeated word for word in the News) that blessed everything down to the dishes to be used in performances, as well as *"all the nails, screws, bolts, glue, putty, paint or other materials used for the construction and finishing of this building."* He prayed that the theater would "crumble to atoms" rather than be profaned by anything unworthy. It was rumored that his wife, Louisa, wondered facetiously if it would have been all right to have "left out the lath and plaster" in his long dedicatory blessing.

For a frontier establishment, the Salt Lake Theatre was a marvel of interior decoration. Three posts on each side of the stage held kerosene lamps to illuminate the performance area, and 382 oil lamps lighted the hall. Stoves around the perimeter kept the audience comfortable.

The theater offered an opportunity for pioneers to dress up and socialize. Those blessed with opera glasses used them alternately to watch the stage activity and to look around the audience to see who was there. Guns were checked at the door. When parents failed to respond to requests to leave babes-in-arms at home, they soon found themselves faced with a $10 surcharge. Country folk often turned up with produce, meat or dairy products to cover the price of a ticket.

Eventually, as one of the outstanding theaters in the country, the Salt Lake house drew the leading performers of the time — among them, P.T. Barnum, Billie Burke, Buffalo Bill Cody, Eddie Foy, Al Jolson, Edwin Booth, Lillian Russell, Oscar Wilde and the Barrymores. Ethel reportedly enthused that she would like to "play here until I am 100 years old." Initially, guest performers came by stagecoach, later by train. Sometimes they made it to the theater with minutes to spare before a performance.

Some local talent nurtured in the Salt Lake Theatre went on to bigger things, notably Maude Adams. The daughter of a performer, Annie Kiskadden, Maude spent much of her infancy in a basket behind the curtains. Young Maude began with bit parts in the Salt Lake Theatre and went on to international acclaim.

By the 1920s, the aging theater was seeing increasing competition from vaudeville, movies and the automobile, which took entertainment-seekers farther abroad. Despite a clamor to keep the historic building intact, church leaders sold the property in 1928 to Mountain States Telephone and Telegraph, and it was razed. The red pine ceiling beams refused to budge and delayed the demolition for several weeks, as if they clung to an historic era that would never return.

Culver

**Ethel Barrymore**

**P.T. Barnum**

**A velvet-covered box seat was often used by Brigham Young. The seats are from the regular auditorium.**

Pioneer Memorial Museum

Pioneer Memorial Museum

Pioneer Memorial Museum

**THEATRE.**

GREAT SALT LAKE CITY, U.T.

Manager, - - - - - H. B. CLAWSON.
Acting and Stage Manager, - JOHN T. CAINE.

ENGAGEMENT OF THE EMINENT ARTISTE,
**JULIA DEAN HAYNE,**
FOR A LIMITED NUMBER OF NIGHTS!

The Management take pleasure in announcing that they have engaged the

POTTER DRAMATIC TROUPE,
For the purpose of presenting to the patrons of the Theatre, the Eminent Artiste, JULIA DEAN HAYNE. She will be supported by the Popular Tragedian
**MR. GEORGE B. WALDRON,**
And the strength of the Stock Company, among whom are Messrs. J. S. POTTER, N. S. LESLIE, B. S. MORTIMER, C. GRAHAM, F. A. SHIELDS, and H. TAYLOR Miss BELLE DOUGLASS, Mrs. N. S. LESLIE, etc., etc.

**FRIDAY, AUGUST 11, 1865.**

Will be presented the popular and beautiful Play, in 5 Acts, entitled

# CAMILLE

"All Nature Hopes for Spring---Why Not 1?"

| Camille Gautier, | - | JULIA DEAN HAYNE. |
|---|---|---|
| Armand Duvall. | | Mr. GEO. B. WALDRON. |
| Monsieur Duvall. | | Mr. J. S. POTTER. |
| Monsieur De Varville. | | Mr. N. S. LESLIE. |
| Gaston. | | Mr. B. S. MORTIMER. |
| Gustave. | | Mr. C. GRAHAM. |
| Arthur. | | Mr. H. TAYLOR. |
| Messenger. | | Mr. F. A. SHIELDS. |
| Madame Prudence. | | Miss BELLE DOUGLASS. |
| Nanine. | | Mrs. N. S. LESLIE. |
| Nichette. | | Mrs. LESLIE. |

| Act 1st—Spring | The Supper. |
| Act 2d— | The Pledge. |
| Act 3 | The Sacrifice. |
| A | The Revenge. |
| Ac | The Return. |

NTH HOUR!!

FOR SPRING, AND WHY 1?!

**Maude Adams first appeared as a child in the theater, later becoming internationally famous. Above, a typical playbill and tickets.**

**D E S E R E T   N E W S**

# Mining
## gains a foothold
### 1870-1880

The Latter-day Saint pioneers who first settled Utah Territory wrested a living from its surface, but what lay beneath became, over time, one of the region's greatest assets. By the third decade of settlement, bounteous troves of valuable minerals had been found and mining began to shape the state's economic and political future.

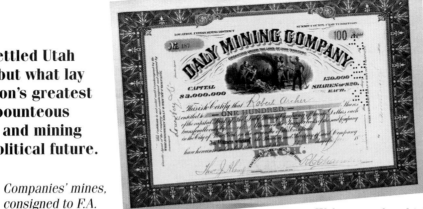

From the beginning of the 1840s hegira to the Great Basin, colonizer Brigham Young encouraged his followers to avoid the California gold rush, and he didn't particularly advise the distractions of prospecting for precious metals closer to home, either:

*DESERET NEWS, June 8, 1870: We are not anxious to obtain gold; if we can obtain it by raising potatoes and wheat, all right. 'Can't you make yourselves rich by speculating?' We do not wish to. 'Why don't you dig the gold from the earth?' Because it demoralizes any community or nation on the earth to give them gold and silver to their heart's content; it will ruin any nation. But give them iron and coal, good hard work, plenty to eat, good schools and good doctrine and it will make them a healthy, wealthy and happy people.*

There were some practical considerations, as President Young suggested. Coal and iron were greatly needed in the burgeoning Utah communities. With timber at a premium for building, the 1854 Territorial Legislature offered a cash prize for discovery of the first workable coal deposits. Apparently, no one collected. But by the early 1870s, the Deseret News was printing announcements such as:

*DESERET NEWS: June 26, 1870: THE FIRST COAL — Two car loads of coal from the Wasatch Coal Companies' mines, consigned to F.A. Mitchell, Esq., reached the city Thursday morning. This, we understand, is the first coal that has been brought direct to this city by the UCCR (Utah Central Railroad.)*

*DESERET NEWS, April 19, 1871: COAL — During the prevalence of stormy weather in March, the hauling of coal from the mines on the Weber to Echo City was almost entirely suspended. The result was that coal from those mines became very scarce in the city, so scarce in fact that it could not be purchased... Gentlemen of experience from Pennsylvania, who have examined the coal from that region, express the confident opinion that (Utah coal) will be found an excellent article for the manufacture of iron... Never did the coal from Weber stand so high in the estimation of the people as it does today.*

Acting on his desire for locally produced iron, Young dispatched families to the Cedar City area in 1850-51 to establish the Iron Mission. Ore from a mine southwest of Parowan was to be refined in a blast furnace near Cedar City. Production problems under pioneer conditions, however, stymied the project, and the mine and production works never became fully operational, although small amounts of iron were generated. The works were shut down in 1858.

After gold was discovered in California, prospectors roamed the west, including Utah, to find their fortunes. In 1870, the foundations of Utah's mining industry were dug into the mountains. Names such as Stockton, Ophir, Mercur, Park City, Tintic and Silver Reef became common in the newspaper. Great fortunes were indeed made, but more important to the state itself were the growing numbers of miners and laborers who found a home within its boundaries. Wealthy miners became influential in business and politics. Congress again denied statehood, while Episcopalians and Catholics dedicated their first churches. Women voted and were sent east to train as doctors. Brigham Young University was founded. Change was everywhere.

MINING MACHINERY.

THE EAGLE WORKS

Manufacturing Co.

P. W. GATES, President.

Office, 48 So. Canal Street,

CHICAGO, ILL.

MANUFACTURE

Mining Machinery

OF MOST APPROVED KINDS,

SUCH AS

Stamp Mills, Ore Crushers, Pans, Settlers, Mining and other Pumps, Portable and Stationary Engines and Boilers, Portable Circular Saw Mills and Shingle Mills, Flouring Mills, and Mill Machinery of all descriptions.

For further information, send for Circulars.

HIGHLY IMPORTANT

**An early assayer's table contained the chemicals and weights of the office. Stock certificate above was for a mine in Summit County.**

D E S E R E T   N E W S

Nitric acid was part of assayer's equipment.

"Outsiders" coming to Utah in increasing numbers didn't share Young's reservations about developing the area's precious metals. Aware of the rich deposits that were being exploited in surrounding states, they were not at all loathe to prospect and then dig.

Patrick E. Connor, who came to Utah at the head of a military unit that was the first to occupy Fort Douglas, made his most profound impact as a mining entrepreneur. The men in his regiment received generous leaves to go prospecting. Two things motivated Connor: getting rich and encouraging non-Mormons to flock to the mines. He hoped to dilute the influence of the church in politics and commerce by increasing the "gentile" population.

The mines did, in fact, prove a magnet for many groups of Europeans — Greeks, Welsh, Italians, Scandinavians, Slavs and others — who melded into the Utah population. Chinese who had helped build the railroad and were now out of jobs also drifted into the mining camps, often as service providers, adding another cultural dimension.

As the mines began to thrive, Young encouraged LDS men to benefit from employment in the works, but only to improve their homes and farms:

**DESERET NEWS,** *April 19, 1871:*
*We say to the Latter-day Saints, work for these capitalists and work honestly and faithfully and they will pay you faithfully. I am acquainted with a good many of them and as far as I know them, I do not know but every one is an honorable man. They are capitalists, they want to make money and they want to make it honestly and according to the principles of honest dealing. If they have means and are determined to risk it in opening mines, you work for them by the day. Haul their ores, build their furnaces and take your pay for it, and enter your lands, build houses, improve your farms, buy your stock and make yourselves better off.*

The standard mining pattern of fortune and failure relied on the luck of the draw. One Deseret News correspondent lamented:

**DESERET NEWS,** *July 13, 1870:*
*GALENA CITY, LITTLE COTTONWOOD — The Lavinia has a tunnel one hundred and sixty feet in length, with a breast of ore twelve feet deep; the prospects of this company are undoubtedly good, to say the least, but in juxtaposition to their prospects can be placed many a failure… Little Cottonwood cannot and will not pay back in dollars and cents the amount required to develop it. I look upon the investment of means in mining here to be the height of absurdity to say the least. Little Cottonwood has ore, Big Cottonwood has ore, Bingham Canon (sic) has ore, Rush Valley ditto; Tintic ditto; but what does it cost to obtain that ore; five hundred dollars to one received…*

Earlier, the same pessimistic outlook had been expressed about copper:

**DESERET NEWS,** *May 9, 1860:*
*COPPER — We have recently been presented with a specimen of virgin copper, found in Cedar county, some ten or twelve miles from Camp Floyd, which those well versed in mineralogy… pronounce equal to the best they have ever seen.*
*If it exists in that vicinity, as is alleged, in any considerable quantities, it would probably pay well for working, if any felt disposed to engage in such an enterprise, but in these days, gold is the principal thing sought after, and a man who would engage in copper mining in an inland country like this, might by some be considered in a state of insanity.*

As mining technology improved and production costs went down, such "insanity" became the key to huge fortunes for some and a good living for many others. In 1868 the Walker Brothers shipped the first loads of commercial copper by rail from the Bingham area to refineries in Baltimore.

Passage of laws to enhance and protect mining also encouraged the industry:

**DESERET NEWS:** *Jan. 17, 1872:*
(Gov. George Woods' message to the Territorial Legislature:) *Great changes have been wrought in Utah since the last session of the Legislative Assembly. The rapid and profitable development of her mines, unparalleled in richness and extent, has called hither a vast population and invited capital from every portion of the civilized world. In justice, therefore, to the owners of mines and for the peace and good name of the Territory, I earnestly recommend the passage of a plain, judicious and comprehensive mining law …*

Soon, such words as Silver Reef, Bingham Canyon, Highland Boy, Emma, Silver King, Ophir, Flagstaff, Ontario, Humbug, Black Dragon, Mammoth and Eureka were common coin among Utah residents. One of the most enduring and profitable commercial undertakings in the West had taken root in the territory and was blossoming.

**DESERET NEWS,** *Aug. 3, 1870:*

AMOUNT OF ORE MINED The shipment of ores from the following districts shows for the month of July (Pc. to the 27th ult.):

| | |
|---|---|
| Little Cottonwood | 314 tons |
| Bingham | 6 tons |
| Parley s Park | 40 tons |
| Rush Valley | 70 tons |
| Deep Creek | 10 tons |
| Tintic | 30 tons |
| Total | 470 tons |

Of this amount about eighty tons remain in the Territory at the smelting works of Woodhull Bros. About the same amount has been shipped per schooner *Pioneer* across Salt Lake to the railroad at Monument Point. Some ninety tons from Cottonwood are now being shipped to the new smelting works. From returns given by Meader, Woodhull and others, the average value of ores exported is $105.00 per ton or a total for the month of $19,350.00.

C.L. Stevenson, Mining Engineer

These hard-rock miners were drawn to Park City in search of gold.

# John Wesley Powell

**Between 1869 and 1872, John Wesley Powell, a one-armed soldier-turned-scientist, explored the last uncharted territory of the United States. Most famous for his trips down the Colorado River, he is also the man who discovered the Escalante, the last large river to be named in the U.S., and the Henry Mountains, the last chain to be added to maps.**

**Major Powell first navigated the Colorado in this craft.**

**H**is first trip down the Colorado was hazardous; in fact, for a time, reports had circulated that all in the expedition had been lost. It was a Deseret News scoop that set the record straight:

**DESERET NEWS,** *Sept. 7, 1869: By courtesy of Wm B. Dougall, Esq., of the Deseret Telegraph Line, we learn that the Powell expedition, concerning the supposed loss of which there was so much excitement a few weeks since, arrived safely at the mouth of the Rio Virgin, on the Colorado river, on the 30th ult. Major J.W. Powell himself had arrived at St. George in good health…*

The major and his brother stopped by the Deseret News on Sept. 14, on their way back home, and a report of that visit, again the first that the nation heard, was printed the following day: *"It was with feelings of pleasure that we met with the Major, in the enjoyment of excellent health, after having made his adventurous and hazardous descent of this remarkable river."*

After the success of this expedition, interest in Powell's work was greater than ever. And he was able to put together a return journey to survey and study surrounding areas. On May 10, 1872, a man named W.D. Johnson Jr. who was participating in this scientific venture, wrote a letter to the editor.

**DESERET NEWS,** *May 29, 1872: Thinking that a few items concerning our party would be interesting to your readers, I will try and entertain them a short time with the doings and intentions of Powell's Colorado River Exploring Expedition.*

Noting that the party had already been in the field for some time before he joined them, Johnson said his descriptions would be of the country

**Major John Wesley Powell talks with a Piute tribesman during an 1873 trip to northern Arizona.**

*Smithsonian Institution*

west and south of Kanab. He explained the process of triangulation used to measure heights and distances, noting *"we travel from one mountain or point to another to get angles and sketch the country, with pack animals, as it would be impossible to travel with a wagon."*

The party consisted of 12 men at that time, *"and all have different duties to perform, such as topographers, photographers, geologists and those who herd and tend to the horses and drive the pack train."*

His letter is filled with descriptions of this unusual country. He talks of traveling over a *"lava-covered country, which was barren and desert looking with only now and then a scrub cedar. Finding no water, we made what is called in this country a 'dry camp,' and we found it dry indeed."*

He talks of geology, *"which we found to be of the carboniferous formation, and composed mostly of lime stone, grey marble, of good quality, micacious shales and conglomerates."*

He notes the contrasts in weather, at one point commenting on the summer flowers, but on the first of May noting *"Mr. Jones and I spent our May walk in the snow from four to twenty feet deep."*

Throughout, Johnson is suitably impressed by the scenery. *"It is grand indeed, and it makes one feel the power and greatness of an all-wise God,"* he says of Mount Trumbull. And upon climbing a small mountain that gave them a view of the river some 5,000 feet below: *"The view is so grand and extensive that the eye cannot take it all in at once. While looking at some*

*wonderful and magnificent piece of scenery, another perhaps as grand or more so claims your attention. This one sight will repay anyone who may wish to see scenery rare and beautiful."* An inkling of the future of tourism?

At the end of the letter, written from Windsor Castle, in Arizona, he notes that work is almost done.

*"We have nearly finished the mapping of this country, with the exception of the river, which will be finished next summer. In ten or twelve days we will start for the Dirty Devil River, to get that country mapped, then from there to Paharia."*

The empty spots on the map were slowly filling in.

Deseret News files

**Gen. George A. Custer**

# Custer

**With memories of their own Indian troubles still fresh, Deseret News readers of 1876 no doubt were interested in news of the terrible rout suffered by Gen. George A. Custer on the Little Bighorn River (referred to in the news stories as the Little Horn).**

**C**uster, whose Army assignment was to round up the Sioux and Cheyenne Indians and settle them on reservations, had seriously underestimated his enemy at the Little Bighorn. He thought he faced about 1,000 warriors. In fact, some 2,000 warriors were camped on the Little Bighorn, including such noted braves as Crazy Horse, Gall and Sitting Bull. In a short running battle, Custer and his

estimated 210 soldiers all were killed. The controversial battle became grist for historians for years to come. Dispatches to the Deseret News contained exaggerations and errors but were a vivid description of the battle:

**DESERET NEWS,** *July 6, 1876:*
*EASTERN (Dispatch)*
*A FRIGHTFUL MASSACRE*
*GENERAL CUSTER AND THREE*
*HUNDRED SOLDIERS*
*SLAUGHTERED BY INDIANS*

*HELENA, Mont., — A special correspondent of the Herald writes from Stillwater, Montana, July 2: Muggins Taylor, a scout for Gen. Gibbons, got here last night direct from Little Horn River.*

*Gen. Custer found the Indian camp, consisting of about 2,000 lodges, on the Little Horn, and immediately attacked the camp. Custer took five companies and charged the thickest portion of the camp. Nothing is known of the operations of this detachment only as they trace it by the dead.*

*Major Reno commanded the other seven companies, and attacked the lower portion of the camp. The Indians poured in a murderous fire from all directions; besides, the greater portion fought on horseback.*

*Custer, his two brothers, nephew and brother-in-law were all killed, and not one of his detachment escaped. Two hundred and seven men were buried in one place, and the killed is estimated at 800, with only thirty-one wounded.*

*The Indians surrounded Reno's command, and held them one day in the hills, cut off from water until Gibbons' command came in sight, when they broke camp in the night and left.*

*The Seventh Cavalry fought like tigers, and were overcome by mere brute force.*

*The Indian loss cannot be estimated, as they bore off and cached most of their killed.*

*The remnant of the Seventh Cavalry and Gibbons' command are returning to the mouth of the Little Horn, where a steamboat lies. The Indians got all the arms of the killed soldiers.*

*There were seventeen commissioned officers killed. The whole of the Custer family died at the head of their column. The exact loss is not known, as both adjutants and sergeant major were killed.*

Springfield Carbine was carried by U.S. Cavalry.

*The Indian camp was from three to four miles long, and was twenty miles up the Little Horn from its mouth.*

*The Indians actually pulled the men off their horses in some instances.*

*I give this as Taylor told me, as he was over the field after the battle.*

*P.S. The above is confirmed by other letters, which say Custer met with fearful disaster.*

**ANOTHER ACCOUNT**

*A Times extra (Bozeman, Montana, July 3) says Mr. Taylor, bearer of dispatches from the Little Horn to Fort Ellis, arrived this evening, and reports the following: The battle was fought on the 25th, thirty or forty miles below the Little Horn. Custer attacked an Indian village of from 2,500 to 4,000 warriors on one side, and Col. Reno was to attack it on the other; three companies were placed on a hill as a reserve.*

*General Custer and fifteen officers and every man belonging to the five companies were killed.*

*Reno retreated under the protection of the reserve. The whole number killed was 315. General Gibbon joined Reno, and the Indians left. The battle ground looked like a slaughter pen, as it really was, being in a narrow ravine. The dead were very much mutilated. The situation now looks serious.*

**Sitting Bull**

U.S. Army Military History Institute

## Brigham Young Endows an Academy

Brigham Young supported education as he did everything else — with all his heart. So it was that he endowed a college to honor the Territory and its people. Still, when Brigham Young Academy was launched in Provo, it wasn't done with great fanfare.

He started with a Deed of Trust, drawn up in October 1875, of some of his property. It would be the financial foundation of the new school. The Deseret News took note of it:

**DESERET NEWS,** *Nov. 30, 1875: The Brigham Young Academy. — The revised deed of the above institution… has been received by the Trustees named therein as follows: A.O. Smoot, William Bringhurst, L.E. Harrington, W. H. Dusenberry, Martha J. Coray, Myron Tanner and Harvey H. Cluff… an organization was perfected by electing A.O. Smoot, Prest., W. H. Dusenberry, Secretary, and H. H. Cluff, Treasurer. A committee on by-laws and rules was also appointed, and yesterday this commitee reported a series of bylaws and rules, which were adopted…*

*We are informed that it is quite probably the Academy will be opened on Monday, December 6th, but will be able to state definitely by the middle of next week. We are also requested to state that all charges are payable in advance. We would therefore advise all parties interested to call upon the Treasurer, Mr. H. H. Cluff, and receive a permit for their attendance. — Utah County Times, Nov. 17*

The Academy did get started, but on Jan. 3, 1876, in a rather beat-up Lewis Building, with 70 showing up for the first experimental term. Two years later, the paper carried this notice:

**DESERET NEWS,** *April 10, 1878: A Model Academy… It is a model educational institution. From the standpoint of a Latter-day Saint it has no superior. Its system embraces education as a whole, cultivating the moral and religious as well as the intellectual nature. The academy is doing a large amount of good in the community. Its beneficial effects will reach far into the future. It has our hearty good wishes for its continued prosperity and success.*

That was a remarkably prophetic statement about the future Brigham Young University.

# Women voting:
## A new idea

**Outside of Utah Territory, stories circulated of the "oppressed, miserable, unenlightened and enslaved women" trapped in polygamous marriages sanctioned by the LDS Church. The truth was that the majority of the pioneer women who were plural wives were satisfied with their lot, progressive in their pursuits and enjoying a level of equality with males that went beyond that of their sisters in the States — they could vote. As poet, political activist and unswerving church leader Eliza R. Snow gloated:**

**DESERET NEWS,** *Jan. 19, 1870: Instead of being lorded over by tyrannical husbands, we, the ladies of Utah, are already in possession of a privilege which many intelligent and high aiming ladies in the States are earnestly seeking, i.e. the right to vote. Although as yet we have not been admitted to the common ballot box, to us the right of suffrage is extended in matters of far greater importance … they may reserve their sympathy for objects more appreciative.*

Snow referred to the traditional right of LDS women to vote on church matters, but her comments came just weeks before the franchise at the ballot box was also extended to them. Utah women, in fact, won the right for political suffrage twice — once essentially by default and the second time in a hard-fought battle preceding statehood in 1896. In the 1870s, the women's suffrage movement in the United States was building toward the crescendo that eventually led to the 19th Constitutional Amendment in 1920 granting universal suffrage to all Americans, regardless of gender. In Utah, suffrage was extended to women 50 years earlier, in February 1870:

**DESERET NEWS,** *Feb. 16, 1870: To the honorable Orson Pratt, Speaker of the House: SIR:*
*I have the honor to inform you that I have this day approved, signed and deposited in the secretary's office "An Act" conferring upon women the elective franchise. In view of the importance of the measure referred to, it may not be considered improper for me to remark that I have very grave and serious doubts of the wisdom and soundness of that political economy which makes the act a law of this Territory, and there are many reasons which, in my judgment, are opposed to the legislation; but whatever these doubts and reasons may have been, in view of the*

*unanimous passage of the act in both the House and the Council, and in deference to the judgment of many whose opinion I very much respect, I have, as before stated, approved of the bill … (Signed by S.A. Mann, acting territorial governor.)*

Although Mann reluctantly put his signature to the bill, he essentially bowed to pressure not from the Utah legislators, but from the outside political world. The assumption in the States was that if Utah women had the power to vote, they would free themselves from the "bondage" under which they suffered. Then-Deseret News editor George Q. Cannon saw it differently:

**DESERET NEWS,** *Feb. 16, 1870: The female suffrage question is now fairly before the nation; its advocates are as earnest in their labors as if the salvation of the world depended upon their success, and the triumph of the movement, we believe is only a question of time. The agitation of the question has reached the Rocky Mountains. In our neighboring territory, Wyoming, the cause has*

*Dress worn by Susan B. Anthony during her visit is on display at Pioneer Memorial Museum.*

Susan B. Anthony, third from right, and the Reverend Anna Howard Shaw, with her hand on chair, met with LDS women's leaders in 1895 to discuss suffrage.

**D E S E R E T   N E W S**

*triumphed; in Colorado the ladies are petitioning to have female suffrage legalized there. But… nothing short of an amendment to the Constitution of the United States to this effect will do … and this is now being eagerly sought … We believe in the right of suffrage being enjoyed by all who can exercise it intelligently…*

In the context of the times, the argument that women were more capable of voting than blacks was frequently raised in the debate over suffrage. Wyoming was, in fact, the first state to grant women voting rights, establishing its law in December 1869, only months before Utah Territory. But before that sparsely populated state held an election to afford women the opportunity, Utah women had already cast ballots for the first time in local and territorial elections. They were encouraged by their female leaders to make good use of the right. Snow, who headed the Female Relief Societies, told them:

**DESERET NEWS,** *June 28, 1871: In no other way can we fully testify our appreciation of the magnanimity of those noble-minded men who were instrumental in investing us with this high prerogative. Let us prove ourselves worthy of the trust reposed. The right of franchise opens to us a new field of duty, one in which, as yet, we have but little experience and we think that it would be wisdom to adopt such measures as would produce a concert of action, or at least, such as would prompt every sister to do her duty at the coming election … We suggest that all the Presidents, officers and leading members of the Female Relief Societies throughout the Territory take immediate action by appointing committees whose duty shall be to visit in person every legal voter, and if need be, awaken her to the importance of the occasion and … faithfully instruct with regard to the necessity of each woman critically examining the ticket she places in the ballot box, so as not to be imposed upon by unprincipled office-seekers.*

Political activity was not new for Utah women. At the same time the question of female suffrage was being debated in the

Territory, several proposals in the U.S. Congress were aimed at decimating the LDS Church and squelching polygamy. The proposals sparked widespread "Indignation Meetings" among the women in the territory. Protest meetings were held by Relief Society units throughout the area, and an estimated 25,000 signatures were added to resolutions decrying the proposed congressional edicts. LDS women were not eager to be freed from the "domination" under which they supposedly languished.

Because Utah women had already won what others throughout the country were zealously seeking, the leading voices in the suffrage movement chose to visit the territory in July 1871. Susan B. Anthony, whose name became inseparably attached to the movement, was first welcomed by the LDS suffrage leaders, but when she became critical of polygamy, the enthusiasm withered. The Deseret News took up the gauntlet in defense of the Mormon contingent. When an Eastern newspaper suggested that Anthony had "broken the Mormon line" the News quickly countered:

**DESERET NEWS,** *Aug. 2, 1871: (Our readers) will be curious to know when and where Miss Anthony uttered such wonderful prophecies which required so much daring to make public. She certainly had every opportunity that could be desired to say what she wanted; for Mrs. Stanton and herself had public meetings in the Tabernacle, which both sexes attended, and they had a private meeting to which none but women were admitted … How long will it require to satisfy preachers, politicians, editors, etc., that a break in the "Mormon Line" cannot be made?*

Anthony and her entourage found more welcome among non-Mormon suffrage activists in Salt Lake City. Eventually, however, they reconciled with the LDS group in support of the common cause. Many of the LDS women became actively involved in the national movement, traveling to cities in the East to add their voices to the plea for universal suffrage.

In 1887, aware that suffrage for Utah women had strengthened the church, not weakened it, Congress rescinded the voting right as part of the general effort to stamp out Mormonism. Not until Utahns began to put together a statehood document in the mid-1890s would the issue arise again.

# The United Order tested

**A**ttempts to initiate the United Order, a plan of communal living and common sharing of goods and services, were first made by The Church of Jesus Christ of Latter-day Saints in the 1830s. In the 1870s, now located and firmly established in Utah Territory, church leaders again felt the need to attempt the plan.

Some Utah communities, particularly Brigham City and Lehi, had implemented forms of the Order even earlier, but the movement got a new push after President Brigham Young visited St. George in 1874 and found economic conditions in a sorry state. He believed the mutual efforts and rewards of the United Order would solve the problems there and in other Utah Territory communities affected by new economic realities in the territory. During the April General Conference of the church that spring, Elder Orson Hyde presented the new plan:

**DESERET NEWS,** *May 6, 1874: We now want to organize the Latter-day Saints, every man, woman and child among them who has a desire to be organized, into this holy order. You may call it the Order of Enoch; you may call it co-partnership, or just what you please. It is the United Order of the Kingdom of God on the earth … As individuals, we do not want your farms, we do not want your houses and city lots, we do not want your horses and your cattle, we do not want your gold and your silver nor anything of the kind … We want the time of the people called Latter-day Saints, that we can organize this time systematically and make this people the richest people on the face of the earth … And what are we to have when we enter this order? What we need to eat, drink and wear and a strict obedience to the requirements of those whom the Lord sets to guide and direct … Organize the brethren and sisters, and let each and*

*every one have their duties to perform …*

Over the next few months, about 220 United Order plans were devised by the communities. They ranged from such simple things as cooperative manufacturing or farming schemes to full-fledged communal orders like the one established in Orderville in southern Utah. The Deseret News began to print reports from its correspondents in the communities:

**DESERET NEWS,** *Dec. 9, 1874: WILLARD, BOX ELDER CO.: Our people are identified with the co-operative movement in Brigham City, and our co-operative store, under the able management of John T. Thain, is in a thriving condition notwithstanding the scarcity of greenbacks.*

**DESERET NEWS,** *April 22, 1874: BEAVER: President Young and party arrived a few minutes before 4 o'clock on Saturday afternoon … At six o'clock in the evening, a meeting was held in the basement of the meeting house, when President G. A. Smith, Joseph A. Young, Milo Andrus and A.M. Cannon spoke upon the subject of the United Order, showing the benefits that would be derived in the people uniting together in all their labors… The intention is to elevate the poor and make them comfortable and happy as well as the rich … In the evening, the assembly met and organized by electing, for this Stake of Zion, John R. Murdock President…*

**DESERET NEWS,** *Nov. 25, 1874: ST. GEORGE: It is evident that the experience of the people of Southern Utah, in the practical workings of the United Order the past season, has laid the foundation of future success… The same general appearance of sterility and barrenness still characterizes the country, but there is… a reasonable assurance of a supply of the comforts of life in the future from resources still only partially developed.*

Some of the plans were never implemented, some flourished for a time and then were abandoned. Few lasted long.

Although the attempted resurrection of the United Order fell short, many of its principles of self-reliance and responsibility for the poor later were incorporated into the church welfare program.

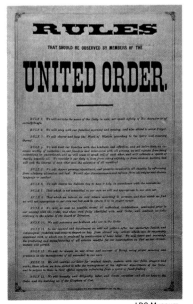

LDS Museum

# DESERET EVENING NEWS.

TRUTH AND LIBERTY.

SALT LAKE CITY, UTAH TERRITORY

Jan. 5, 1870

POLICE. — The festivities of Christmas have not so far been as fertile in regard to furnishing Alderman Clinton with cases to decided as one might naturally have expected at such a season. Still, a few patrons of Barleycorn, or something stronger, have been lodged in the elegant quarters furnished by the city authorities as an asylum for those who break the city ordinances. The last installments of this kind were Pat Morley and Mack Murphy, who had imbibed too freely of "bitters," and as a means of celebrating Christmas, engaged in a fight. Each one bore marks of the engagement when brought before the Doctor, who, on investigating the matter, decided that such pugilistic displays are contrary to the law and opposed to good order. Each gentleman (?) was therefore desired to contribute $10 to the city fund, or, in default, take apartments in the Rock House situated in the rear of the Hall.

Jan. 5, 1870

SABBATH SCHOOL PARTY. — A very pleasant company assembled last evening in the 20th Ward School House, on the occasion of a party given for the benefit of the Ward Sabbath School. Dancing commenced vigorously about seven o'clock, and "all went as merry as a marriage bell" until a late, that is, early hour this morning. The party was a complete success, and was favored with the presence of President Young, Elder Geo. Q. Cannon and other leading citizens.

Jan. 5, 1870

A Western man has invented an "ink pencil," which is said to be the best thing yet. It consists of a tube about the size of an ordinary pencil, containing ink. Near the point of the pencil is a little iron stopper, resting on a spiral spring inside. When the point of the pencil is placed on the paper, the stopper is forced up and the ink flows evenly, without blotting the paper. It needs no adjustment, and can be carried in the pocket.

Jan. 19, 1870

THAT MENAGERIE. — We are given to understand, by the gentleman with that unpronounceable Italian name, who cares for the "birds, beasts and fishes" at our home menagerie, that the enterprising proprietor thereof has engaged the services of an experienced, skillful, and daring trapper whose whole business will be to secure for the menagerie specimens of the wild beasts and birds of Utah. Our friends interested in zoology may soon expect many valuable additions to this growing institution of Salt Lake City.

Feb. 16, 1870

A NUISANCE. — Complaints have been frequently made of late concerning the practice of throwing household refuse, dead dogs, stable manure and similar matter into the water secs in the city. As a great many people depend for their supply of water upon that which comes down from City Creek, this infecting the water with putrid carcasses and impure matter is a public evil which should be stopped, and, we think, would never exist did those who are guilty of it reflect on the condition in which the water is thus sent through the city for use by the people. Bury the carcasses of animals under trees; keep manure in the proper heaps or pits and thus preserve a valuable fertilizer, and let the water course through the city in the same purity in which it comes from the mountains.

Feb. 23, 1870

## AN ORDINANCE
### TO ESTABLISH AN INSANE ASYLUM AND HOSPITAL

Be it ordained by the City Council of Salt Lake City that the buildings erected by the Corporation of the City in the Fifth Municipal Ward, known as the Sugar House Ward … be established as a place for the use and treatment of the sick; also the treatment and safe keeping of insane or idiotic persons …

June 6, 1870

EDITOR, DESERET NEWS: Dear Sir, will you please bid a pleasant good-bye for me to my many friends and relatives in Salt Lake City, whom I have not time to visit before my departure for the East. I have been in your city two months, and have never enjoyed myself better. I have not (although a Gentile) been attacked or molested by anybody, even to a bull purp (sic).

Respectfully,
C.S. Nichol

Feb. 23, 1870

The ear-ache may be almost immediately relieved, unless proceeding from tumors in the head, by the following treatment: Wash out the ear with soapsuds and a syringe, holding the ear down so the water will run out. When the inner surface of the ear is dry, drop into it three drops of a mixture composed of two parts sweet oil and one of chloroform; then tie up the head in a warm flannel.

Aug. 2, 1871

DIED, this morning, in the 9th Ward of this city, of teething and canker, Charles Abner, son of John and Ann Taylor, aged ten months and three days. Funeral will take place at the 9th Ward School House tomorrow at two o'clock p.m. Friends are invited to attend.

Feb. 21, 1874

That Lecture. — Mr. George M. Ottinger is a most decided favorite as a lecturer with all who have had the pleasure of hearing him. This was attested last night by the numerous audience which assembled to hear him on "How to Read a Picture," notwithstanding the cold, stormy character of the weather quite a large representation of ladies were present. As usual, the lecturer was easy and graceful in manner, prolific in ideas, and fluent in language… .

Mr. C.R. Savage is the next lecturer at the same place: He will elaborate, next Friday evening, on the "Solar Spectrum," when he expects to exhibit the electric light.

Feb. 24, 1874

Unavoidable. — Brother William C. Graham, our carrier for the lower part of the city, was unable to go his usual round last night, on account of a severe and sudden attack of illness. Subscribers who did not get their papers will please be kind enough to accept of this explanation and apology.

April 6, 1874

H. Dinwoodey has removed his FURNITURE from Main Street to his three-storey brick building, First South Street, half-a-block west of Co-op. clock, where he is prepared to do a wholesale as well as a retail business.

April 6, 1874

Too Attentive by Half. — A man in soldiers' clothes, and carrying more "spirit" than discretion, on Saturday, entered some houses on South Temple Street, and endeavored to make himself familiar and agreeable to the "women folks," but only managed to make himself disagreeable so, his room being considered infinitely preferable to his company. Some people have a way of making themselves more free than welcome.

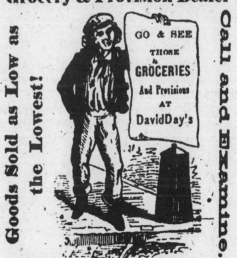

**April 16, 1874**

In the matter of long, dragging dresses, a reform is greatly needed. It spoils any dress to drag it upon the ground. That women, fine ladies, the most delicate half of the human race, should voluntarily consent to and obstinately persist in becoming street scavengers, and in sweeping up with their fashionable and costly dresses, all manner of filth, all manner of human and animal excretion, from the streets and sidewalks, is one of those extraordinary paradoxes, those inscrutable mysteries which constitute "woman an enigma."

**Oct. 4, 1875**

## DISCOURSE
## by
## ELDER JOHN TAYLOR
## DELIVERED IN THE
Old Tabernacle, Salt Lake City,
August 31, 1875.

### REPORTED BY DAVID W. EVANS

... Now then, with regard to this union of property, what is it? Why, it is something to draw the people nearer together, to prepare them for future developments. What is the Order? Well, we, here, have thought proper, at the suggestion of President Young, to act as stewards over our own property. In some places where there is not so much property as here it might be better to pursue another course; but as to that, no matter if our hearts are together, and we do what we do in all sincerity before God. What we are after is to give our hearts to God, to renew our covenants, and then be one in our temporal affairs; and this is to be under the direction of the living priesthood and not under any particular dead letter... . (Elder Taylor was discussing the United Order)

**June 30, 1876**

**For Fuller's Hill.** — At 11 o'clock on the Fourth the Odd Fellows, Red Men, Knights of Pythias, members of the G.A.R. and their respective friends, organized in due order of procession, will march from East Temple Street, on First South Street, to Fuller's Hill, along the route to which resort the street will be sprinkled, to keep down the dust. At the Hill the time will be spent in speech-making and other exercises ordinary to such occasions.

During the evening there will be a display of fireworks.

**July 1, 1876**

**Balloon Ascension** — On Monday evening, at 8 o'clock, there will be a balloon ascension in front of Dwyer's book store. The article is of goodly size,

and will be suitably illuminated.

**July 1, 1876**

Parties wishing to celebrate the glorious birthday of our nation in company with their families and friends, can obtain a sociable and pleasant day's enjoyment by purchasing tickets for the LADIES' CENTENNIAL EXCURSION to LAKESIDE and return on July 4th, 1876, leaving U.C.R.R. Depot at 8 a.m., returning at 7 p.m.

Speeches, dances, singing, bathing and old fashioned games will be the order of the day.

**July 1, 1876**

**A Novel Incident.** — In the First Ward a little bluebird has built its nest in a newspaper delivery box.

**July 1, 1876**

**The Centennial Fourth.** — On the glorious Fourth, the Centennial Fourth, the following places in addition to the celebration at Ogden, will be resorted to by the public of the city.

Glendale Gardens — Various games and amusements, etc.

Lindsey's Gardens — Various games and amusements, balloons, fire works, dancing.

Fuller's Hill — Benevolent Societies' reunion, various games and amusements, dancing, fireworks, etc.

Ladies' Centennial — Exhibition at Constitution Buildings.

Spring Lake Pleasure Grounds — Various games and amusements, boating, gymnastics, dancing, etc.

Theatre — Royal Illusionists, afternoon and evening.

**July 3, 1876**
**Return**

Mrs. Adkins, a poor woman, lost her purse, containing $6.80, on Saturday, on East Temple St. It was her whole stock of money. The finder will do a kind action in leaving it at this office for her.

**July 3, 1876**

**Centennial Silver Brick**. — We noticed to-day, in the express office of Wells, Fargo & Co., in this city, a large bar of silver bullion, from Homansville, East Tintic, Utah, the troy weight of which is 3,551 oz., being the product of Tintic mines, the values of the same being about three thousand dollars.

O.P. Rockwell

**June 10, 1878**

**An Old Citizen Departed.** — At six o'clock yesterday evening O.P. Rockwell, a pioneer citizen of this Territory, departed this life, at the office of the Colorado Stable, which he had been using for some time past, while selling stock. He was at the Theatre on Saturday night and went to the office above mentioned about midnight. Yesterday morning he vomited a large quantity of offensive matter. A few moments before his death he vomited again, was seized with a species of congestive chill and suddenly expired.

We understand that his family, who reside on the Rockwell ranch, in Rush Valley, were at once sent for. The remains were taken charge of by the city sexton.

We are informed that deceased was about 70 years of age, and, from the hardships through which he passed in his eventful life, must have had a very powerful constitution.

**June 10, 1878**

**From Manti.** — This morning we had the pleasure of meeting with our friend, Elder W.H. Folsom, who came up from Manti on Saturday evening.

Regarding the progress of the Temple we learn from him that the hands were somewhat reduced in number on account of the men having to leave to water their crops. They are now beginning to return again, and, when he left seventy men and several teams were at work.

The third terrace wall is nearly completed and the fourth is about half done. It is expected that the ground will be all prepared for the laying of the corner stones and for proceeding with the construction of the foundation by the time of holding the next Stake conference, about the middle of August.

A good feeling prevails among the people, a strong disposition being manifested by them to push the work on the temple to the extent of their ability.

**June 11, 1878**

**Horrible Depravity.** — A horrible case of depravity has been brought to light in this city. Dr. A.B. Spinney, of San Francisco, who has been in the habit of paying periodical visits to this city, was arrested and placed in jail last evening, on a charge of procuring an abortion for, and twice defiling the person of a young married woman. Some of the details are too filthy for publication.

It appears from the affidavits on file in the Justice's

court, that the woman visited Spinney twice in last December, and that he, according to her wish, procured an abortion for her, she being at that time two months pregnant. By his representations she was also induced to submit to the defilement by him of her person on two occasions. In addition, from this cause, she contracted a loathsome disease, for which she has been, since then, under treatment of one of our resident physicians.

The foregoing are the facts of the case, as alleged, and the affair is of the most repulsive and abominable description. If the allegations are true, Dr. A.B. Spinney is one of the most wicked and depraved characters living, and is deserving of the most severe punishment that the law admits of in such cases.

The woman who figures in this case is a resident of the Tenth Ward.

**June 12, 1878**

Roads. — ...The roads in Parley's and Silver Creek Canyons are in very bad traveling condition, rendering coal-hauling to this city, which is being carried on quite extensively, very tedious and difficult. The hauling of coal by teams should be encouraged and made as easy as practicable. Those whose duty it is to see that the roads are kept in repair should attend to that important matter.

**March 18, 1879**

## UTAH SCHOOL STATISTICS

The Territorial Superintendent of District Schools has compiled the reports of the County Superintendents for the year 1879 ... The following totals, taken from the (superintendent's) figures:

No. of schools in 1876, 310; in 1877, 327; in 1878, 346.

No. of children in counties, between the ages of 6 and 16 in 1876, 30,900; in 1877, 30,792; in 1878, 33,604.

No. of scholars enrolled in 1876, 19,886; in 1877, 19,779; in 1878, 21,710.

Percentage of names enrolled in 1876, 64; in 1877, 64; in 1878, 64.6.

No. of days school was taught in 1876, 143; in 1877, 146; in 1878, 137.

Amount of taxes appropriated to the use of schools in 1876, $18,229.23; in 1877, $323,202.59; in 1878, $382,112.90

**May 10, 1879**

## NOTHING SHORT
## OF UNMISTAKEABLE BENEFITS

Conferred upon tens of thousands of sufferers could originate and maintain the reputation in which AYERS's SARSAPARILLA enjoys. It is a compound of the best warrantable alternatives with the iodides of

Potassium and Iron, and is the most effectual of all remedies for scrofulous, mercurial or blood disorders. Uniformly successful and certain in its remedial effects, it produces rapid and complete cures of scrofula, sores, boils, humors, pimples, eruptions, skin diseases and all disorders arising from impurity of the blood. By its invigorating effects, it always relieves and often cures liver complaints, female weaknesses and irregularities and is a potent renewer of vitality. For purifying the blood it has no equal. It tones up the system, restores and preserves the health and imparts vigor and energy...

**June 14, 1879**

A GOOD IDEA —Mr. J. Williamson, who keeps the Seventh Ward meat market, has adopted a new and excellent plan for serving his customers, which cannot but meet the commendation of all. He has a large wire screen around his stand, by which the meat is protected from flies, and serves his customers through a slide wire door similar to that of a restaurant, through which the cook passes the food to the waiter in the dining hall. This idea is a very novel one and withal, very satisfactory.

**July 20, 1879**

## EXECUTION OF WALLACE WILKERSON

### Provo, May 16, 1879

The execution of Wallace Wilkerson took place precisely at 12 o'clock noon in the yard of the county jail in this place. Through the bullets striking him just above instead of through the heart, he did not breathe the last gasp for 27 minutes after being struck, being insensible, however, during the time.
**(No mention is made in a long story regarding the crime for which he was executed.)**

**April 6, 1876**

# TERRIBLE DISASTER

**Terrific Explosion of Forty Tons of Giant, Hercules, Blasting and other Powder.**

**Four Persons Instantly Killed and Others injured.**

**Great Damage to Property**

At 12 1/2 minutes to five o'clock yesterday afternoon the citizens of Salt Lake City, and probably the people of the surrounding country for many miles, were suddenly startled by a couple of reports of a most terrific and deafening character and so nearly simultaneous as to appear almost as one. These were followed by two others which were more distinctly apart. The writer, who was standing on the east side of City Creek, had a full view of Arsenal Hill, where the exploded powder magazines were situated. In connection with the reports, an immense mass of flame shot heavenward at each succeeding report, and rising above the fire, then shot a great shower of debris, which seemed to vanish with lightning rapidity, when the air was filled with missiles which whistled and tore through the atmosphere, scattering all around with a radius of over two miles, and a vast cloud of smoke which had arisen floated to the southeast. The concussion was so powerful that all around in a circuit of the extent already named houses tottered and shook, roofs, walls and ceilings were rent, windows innumerable were smashed, and hundreds of people were suddenly prostrated upon the ground.

## CONSTERNATION

seized upon the people, some rushed out of the houses, while others ran into them. Women and children screamed and many men turned pale. Crowds ran towards the vicinity of the explosion, while others sped away, and in fact people were running in every direction. Some shouted, "A volcano," others "An earthquake," while some comprehended the real cause. The scene was one that will never be likely to be forgotten by those who witnessed it...

### FATAL CASUALTIES

Considering the nature of the catastrophe, the immense shower of missiles from the size of small boulders to rocks weighing a couple of hundred pounds, pieces of iron, concrete,&c., it's marvellous that there were not a larger number of persons killed, there being, according to what has been ascertained, but four.

Arsenal Hill is now known as Capitol Hill, but in 1876 it was a storage site for 40 tons of powder, probably near the Daughters of the Utah Pioneers Building. Investigators were never sure what caused the powder to blow up, but they suspected two of the victims might have been shooting at birds and the paperwad from their shotgun ignited loose powder.

The explosion was felt as far north as Kaysville, and debris rained down on a two-mile radius from the site. Many buildings were damaged, including Brigham Young's flour mill a half mile away which was destroyed.

It was Wednesday, a day before the start of LDS General Conference, which would bring thousands of people to Temple Square just a few blocks away.

Two days later, the paper said it was the work of the "Prince of the Power of the Air" and had this comment:

**April 7, 1876**

It was an experience which compressed into a few moments the force of years of ordinary mental impressions and brought thousands of people face to face with the presence of imminent individual danger and apparent sudden death.

# The telephone comes to town

**The Deseret News called it a "TELEPHONIC MARVEL" but put the grand news at the very bottom of a page. A piece titled "Voices from Babylon" got much better placement than the one recounting the first telephones in Utah Territory:**

*DESERET NEWS, March 1, 1879:* Bell's Telephone was regarded as a wonder when its capabilities were first disclosed and demonstrated. But the improvements which have been made upon the instrument have vastly exalted its claims to the marvelous and greatly increased its usefulness. We have heard a great deal about the powers of the microphone, but until Friday last had never seen them exhibited.

Mr. L. E. Holden, the well-known mining magnate of this city, has a Telephone communicating with his elegant residence on South Temple Street, from his office over the Deseret National Bank. Mr. A. M. Musser, agent for the Bell telephone, having received some transmitters or microphonic attachments, has fitted a pair to Mr. Holden's Telephones. The effect is astonishing. Standing twelve feet from the instrument fastened to the wall of his office, Mr. Holden speaking in an ordinary tone could be as distinctly heard at his house six blocks distant as if he were conversing in the room. Whispers into the instrument at one place also were distinctly heard at the other, the ticking of a clock and, in the house on the corner of Fifth East Street the rumbling of wagons in Main Street could be heard when the window of the office was opened, as if they were just outside the dwelling house.

Provided enough subscribers can be obtained to insure the success of the enterprise, it is proposed to establish a Telephone system in this city, which will put its patrons in instantaneous communications with each other, connecting varied business and social interests at a nominal average cost of $3 per month. It is the intention to connect residences, offices, stores, hotels, livery stables, markets, lumber yards, wool and hide houses, doctors, lawyers, courts, drug stores, banks, assayers, smelters, gas works, factories, breweries, saloons, express offices, stage stations, Fort Douglas (etc. etc)… so that all may possess facilities for immediate, reliable and strictly private communication with each other.

When there is no Telephone connection, messages can be sent to the central office, conveniently located on Main Street, and promptly delivered by the messengers in waiting, who will do any desired errand. Communication will be thus established with all parts of the city and suburbs … Lady and her gentlemen friends at camp and in town may hold social conversations asking about train and mail arrivals, about passengers or theatres or order their supplies and in a hundred directions utilize this ever ready medium of speedy and certain communication without leaving their premises…

One is led to think of the Almighty power of the Creator when contemplating the developments of science. And the thought arises that if poor, finite man can bring forth such astonishing effects by a mere smattering of knowledge, why should any doubts be entertained of the omniscience and omnipotence of the Eternal God, to whom all the secrets of nature are as an open book…

Salt Lake City's system lagged behind the one established in Ogden earlier in the year. The first line there connected George A. Lowe's store to his warehouse. But the Ogden newspaper, the Junction, predicted it was only a matter of time until "wires run from one business house to another and from one residence to another, that telephone communication may be a settled fact in every household."

Mary Ferguson was Salt Lake's first "number please" lady. By 1890, the local system had 506 subscribers and 13 employees.

The city's wide streets, the pride of city designers, were a problem when it came to telephone wiring. Poles had to run down the center of the street and lines were "stacked" to accommodate telephone, electricity, telegraph and trolley cars. With the telephone lines at the top of the stack, linemen risked life and limb to keep things humming. However, Salt Lake's 60-foot Idaho cedar poles were soon recognized near and far as the "most beautiful in existence."

As the technology evolved, calls outside the area became possible, but long-distance was an adventure. Each party had to be at the central office of his service area. Often, a messenger from the company had a long horse ride to summon the person wanted for the call. The person who had made the call had to wait in his local office until the callee was rounded up. Such a call was a momentous occasion and not for frivolous messages.

Alexander Graham Bell's prediction that by the 20th century the "tiniest, farthest hamlet will be woven into the wire fabric" was coming true.

In 1914, Utah again became a "crossroads" as the last pole uniting telephone services coast to coast was put in place on the Utah/Nevada border.

Early switchboards had to be connected by hand.

The first telephone was an ungainly creation.

DESERET NEWS

# Midway
## on the temple

After the completion of the intercontinental railroad in 1869, a boom in rail building in Utah Territory was also a boon to building the Salt Lake Temple, which had been under way for more than 20 years.

I n April 1873, the Wasatch & Jordan Valley Line to the mouth of Little Cottonwood Canyon gave ready transportation for the granite blocks being mined in the canyon, expediting the work. The walls of the edifice were well above ground level now, a visual spur to church members to pay their tithes, in both time and money, to speed completion of the long-awaited temple.

*DESERET NEWS, June 27, 1876: WORK ON THE TEMPLE — The work on the Temple in this city is going forward nicely. Four more car loads of rock rolled into the block this morning and the stone cutters, in large force, are busily engaged... It is expected the walls will be taken up a considerable distance during the present season. The work is under the general and able supervision of the architect, Brother Truman O. Angell, who is necessarily kept most actively engaged ...*

*DESERET NEWS, June 30, 1876: THE NUMBER OF HANDS — One hundred and three hands, stone-cutters and laborers, are at work on the Temple Block, and in the vicinity of forty are in the quarry.*

While the Salt Lake Temple slowly rose, territory residents rejoiced that smaller temples were becoming available elsewhere:

*DESERET NEWS, April 11, 1877: (A Special Report from St. George regarding the April 6 dedication of the St. George Temple:) Elder Brigham Young Jr. spoke of the privilege which we at this conference enjoyed of meeting together in the first Temple which had been erected by the Latter-day Saints in these mountains. This privilege was one which had been looked forward to with earnest and prayerful aspiration by the people of God, who had been gathered ...*

Two years later, another announcement heralded the imminent construction of yet another temple:

*DESERET NEWS, April 29, 1879: THE MANTI TEMPLE — Monday, the 14th inst., being the day fixed upon for laying the cornerstone of the Temple in Manti, President John Taylor and eight others of the Twelve Apostles, with other of the authorities of the Church, left Salt Lake City on Friday, the 11th inst., and proceeded by train and team to Nephi, where they spent the night and held meeting with the Saints. On Saturday, the Apostles, Bishops and Elders distributed themselves so as to hold meetings in all the more populous towns of northern Sanpete. On Sunday and on Monday, all met at Manti. A large concourse of Saints assembled from the various Stakes of Zion composing this Temple District, the Nephi people bringing their brass band with them ...*

The Logan Temple, too, was under construction. Even though the LDS people of Utah Territory were in a struggle to gain recognition as a full-fledged state, they had already made the indelible trademark of their faith on the land.

Hand tools were used in building the Salt Lake Temple.

LDS Musuem

LDS Church Archives

LDS Musuem

Wedges driven into granite block show how the stone was cut for the temple, whose walls are about halfway up in 1870.

August 20, 1877

### DEATH OF PRESIDENT BRIGHAM YOUNG

AT ONE minute past four o'clock this afternoon, PRESIDENT BRIGHAM YOUNG departed this life, surrounded by his family and intimate friends. This announcement will thrill the whole Territory with grief. We feel the weight of this great loss to the world, and cannot at this moment express in the faintest degree, our deep sense of the void occasioned by his departure. He was a GREAT MAN in every sense of the term. And he has left a mark upon the age which the future will never efface, but which will grow brighter and broader as the man, his deeds and his sentiments become better known and appreciated...

He has, under God, rescued thousands from poverty and raised them to independence, opened the deserts of these mountains to colonization, preached the gospel of salvation to many nations, declared the counsel of heaven to the inhabitants of the earth, prepared the way in the Temples of God for the redemption of hosts of the dead, organized and consolidated the order of the everlasting Priesthood, and, having finished his work on earth, gone into the spirit world to join with Joseph, Hyrum, Willard, Jedediah, Heber, George A. and other great and glorious servants of the Lord, to continue the great work they all labored for on earth.

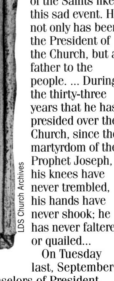

**Brigham Youg**

LDS Church Archives

August 30, 1877

### OBITUARY

THE tidings of the death of President Brigham Young, announced in last evening's DESERET NEWS, were telegraphed to all parts of the Union. The leading papers of the United States have each published an obituary notice, the cable has flashed the word to Europe, and all parts of the civilized world have been stirred to their depths by the sad news. The name of Brigham Young is familiar all over the globe. His greatness is universally acknowledged, but his goodness is known only to a few.

September 10, 1877

### EPISTLE OF THE TWELVE APOSTLES AND COUNSELORS TO THE CHURCH OF JESUS CHRIST OF LATTER-DAY SAINTS IN ALL THE WORLD

BELOVED SAINTS:

... Nothing that has occurred to us since we came to these valleys has touched the hearts of the Saints like this sad event. He not only has been the President of the Church, but a father to the people. ... During the thirty-three years that he has presided over the Church, since the martyrdom of the Prophet Joseph, his knees have never trembled, his hands have never shook; he has never faltered or quailed...

On Tuesday last, September 4th, the two counselors of President Young and ten of the Twelve Apostles, — two of the Twelve, Brothers Orson Pratt and Joseph F. Smith being absent in England, — held a meeting, and waited upon the Lord. With humble, contrite and saddened hearts we earnestly sought to learn His mind and will concerning us and His Church. The Lord blessed us with the spirit of union and condescended to reveal to us what steps we should take. Elder John Taylor, the senior apostle, and who has acted as the President of the Twelve, was unanimously sustained in that position. With the same unanimity also it was voted that the quorum of the Twelve Apostles is the presiding quorum and authority in the Church.

October 4, 1875

## VISIT of PRESIDENT GRANT

After the train left Ogden for this City, President Brigham Young, Honorables John Taylor, B. Young, Jr., and Jos. F. Smith, and all the other gentlemen and ladies of the special train party from Salt Lake City, were in turn presented to President Grant, who stood upon the platform of his car. The meeting between him and President Young was hearty and cordial. ...

The train arrived at the depot shortly before 2 o'clock. There were very few people within the enclosure, which had prudently been cleared by the police, to prevent confusion or accident. There was, however, a very large number of carriages in waiting, provided by the city, and, some by the private party already alluded to, for the occasion. The President was met here by a delegation of Federal office-holders and others, who escorted him to the Walker House, the route to which was lined with thousands of people. ...

During the afternoon, while an exceedingly large concourse of people were assembled, in front of the hotel, the President appeared upon the balcony, accompanied by Governor Emery, who introduced his Excellency, as the first President of the United States that had ever visited Utah. The Governor also said, in effect, that he was certain that he expressed the sentiment of the whole people, when, in their name and behalf, he bade him heartily welcome to the Territory.

**President Ulysses S. Grant**

This is the first time Utah has been honored with a visit from any Chief Magistrate of the nation, and we but speak the sentiments of Utah when we express the hope that his visit has been one of unmixed pleasure, and that he leaves with just impressions regarding this portion of the Republic, where live a people who are as loyal and true to constitutional principles, and who are, we believe we can say without boasting, as honest and industrious, as any community on the Continent, their works and the peace and good order that prevail among them testifying amply that such is the actual condition, peace and good will being their motto.

**Some folks still considered Salt Lake City a frontier town. But less than four decades beyond its earliest settlement, the city was a trend-setter. It was the fifth city in the world to have a central electric system, joining London, New York, San Francisco and Cleveland in flipping the switch.**

Early Salt Lake electric trolley car ran to Warm Springs.

**DESERET NEWS,** *April 1, 1881: A successful and satisfactory test was made of the Brush electric light on Main Street, at and in the vicinity of Walker Brothers' store last evening between 8 and 9 o'clock. A large multitude had gathered in anticipation of the exhibition, announced beforehand, and after waiting some time, were gratified by its appearance. The two post lamps, one at Walker Brothers' corner and the other in front of the store of Lipman and Davis, gradually began to lighten and continue to increase in brilliancy until the vicinity was flooded with a beautiful white light, which might resemble moonlight were the latter greatly intensified.*

*The whole length of the street was not ablaze with splendor as some had* been led to expect, but the gas in the store and in the street lamps near at hand were quite swallowed up, or presented a weak and very subdued appearance. Besides the two electric lamps spoken of, jets of the light were shining in the White House, Walker House, Post Office and other buildings in the circuit... Some persons complained of headache and said it was too much of a good thing altogether. Like many other things, it would doubtless have to become popular through use and habit ...

For the Salt Lake officials who sanctioned the experiment and for the Salt Lake City Light, Heat and Power Co., it was a triumph. Mayor William Jennings and the City Council were sold on the idea of municipal lighting after visiting a smelter south of the city, where they witnessed the illumination of two lamps which, they reported, "lit the building in brilliance second only to sunlight."

The first electric plant was in the center of the second block south of Temple Square, a 30-by-70-foot brick structure with four 60-horsepower boilers that drove a 150-horsepower buckey engine. The engine in turn drove three Brush generators to provide power to light 40 lamps each.

For years, service was sporadic and poor. Initially, power was on from dusk to 10 p.m. — until midnight on dance and theater nights. On Monday mornings, it went on for a few hours so housewives could get their washing done, and again on Tuesday so they could iron. By degrees, the system moved out of the downtown area and soon all the city's homes were served.

Ironically, the Deseret News was predicting that electric lighting was an impracticable flash-in-the-pan that would not soon be feasible:

**DESERET NEWS:** *Oct. 17, 1881: The tower system of*

Utah's first direct current, "electric light works" was a maze of pulleys.

# Electricity and trolley cars

## 1880-1890

Electricity and its technological promises enthralled Utahns. In the 1880s they weren't disappointed. They got their first street lights at the beginning of the decade and the telephone at the end. A new age was coming. Utah State Agricultural College started in Logan under the Land Grant Act and Weber Stake Academy, now a university, started in Ogden. The West was still wild, with outlaws such as Butch Cassidy and his Wild Bunch holding up banks and stealing payrolls. The United States, also riding a tide of immigrants, dedicated two of its greatest monuments: the Statue of Liberty stood up in New York and the Washington Monument arose in the nation's capitol. But throughout the years, tension mounted between the LDS Church and the federal government over plural marriage, and many citizens were imprisoned for their beliefs.

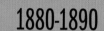

The first commercially-used, electric incandescent lamp from Thomas Edison.

UPI Photo

*electric lighting does not seem to succeed anywhere. Either the lights are unsatisfactory, or the towers get out of the perpendicular, or something else occurs to render them unsatisfactory... The Washington Star says: "So far as experience or observation here goes, Washington has seen little to commend in the matter of the electric light ..."*

As time and experience solved problems and proved the use of electricity to be feasible, however, the uses multiplied.

In Salt Lake City, a whole host of Missouri rat mules lost their jobs as the city's trolley system was electrified. It was the end of a colorful era marked by such announcements as this:

**DESERET NEWS,** *May 18, 1879: Street Car Accident: Car No. 9 of the 20th Ward line of horse cars met with an accident at the switch near the Ward store last evening. Becoming frightened at two ladies on the track ahead, one of the mules swerved around, got loose from the harness and, beside injuring himself, broke the tongue of the car. No one else was hurt, but a few minutes*

*excitement and "goodness gracious" were the spirits of the occasion.*

The mule-drawn cars were retired after serving the city since 1872. A gala celebration noted the coming of electric cars toward the end of the decade.

The first steetcar to run on Salt Lake City tracks.

Utah State Historical Society

**DESERET NEWS,** *Aug. 17, 1889: ELECTRIC INAUGURAL*
*It was a Great Success and Promises a Bright Future.*
*In accordance with previous arrangements, six of the new electric street cars moved down from the power house to the City Hall corner, to take on board, for a trip over the First South Street line, the guests who had received invitations from the company to participate in the formal opening of the electric service.*
*One of the cars was occupied by Held's*

*band, which discoursed fine music as the cars moved over the line. The remaining five cars were soon filled with guests, among whom were Presidents Wilford Woodruff, George Q. Cannon and Daniel H. Wells, Governor Thomas, Chief Justice Zane, Secretary Sells, members of the city council, officers of the city government and of the county, representatives of the railroads and of the press, and a large number of gentlemen of prominence. There were a number of ladies in the party.*
*The cars moved tandem from the point of starting to the D.& R.G. depot, where a stop of a few minutes was made, the band meanwhile discoursing music. The Utah & Nevada bathing train was a little late, which occasioned a delay of some minutes at the crossing of its track ...*

Over time, more than 100 miles of trolley track criss-crossed the city and a spider web of lines woven overhead kept the cars moving. For years, ladies properly be-gloved and be-hatted caught the trolley for Saturday shopping downtown and gents made it their coveyance to work. One LDS Church general authority, historians say, would send his wife out to hail the trolley and he would shortly emerge from his house, still dressing, to complete the job en route to his offices. The trolley system would serve Salt Lake until the 1940s, when its demise was announced, a victim of gasoline-fueled vehicles that now ruled the streets.

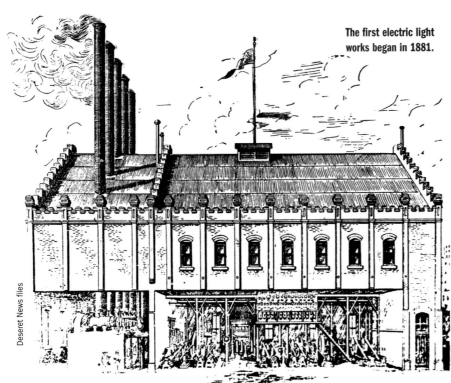
The first electric light works began in 1881.

Deseret News files

# A MADMAN'S FEARFUL CRIME! PRESIDENT GARFIELD SHOT THIS MORNING

**President James Garfield**

Deseret News files

**July 2, 1881**

(The following bulletins and dispatches have been coming in all day. We publish them as they come, notwithstanding they are in some cases slightly contradictory. Ed, D. E. N.)

WASHINGTON — Prest. (James A.) Garfield was shot twice at the Baltimore and Ohio R.R. Depot, Washington, this morning …

9:30 a.m. — Prest. Garfield was shot this morning at the Baltimore and Potomac Depot. Col. Corbin has just passed in the President's carriage with a physician on the way to the Baltimore and Potomac Depot.

10 a.m. — President Garfield is now lying in a private room in the officers' quarters of (the depot). Dr. Bliss, Surgeon General Barnes and Dr. Purvis (colored) are in attendance.

10 a.m. — It is reported that Prest. Garfield is dead, but the excitement is so intense that it is impossible to find out anything definite at present. The man who shot him has been arrested … The shooting was done by a slender man, about five feet seven inches in height. He refused to give his name, but it is said by persons who profess to know him that his name is Dooty.

(In fact, the assassin was Charles J. Guiteau, who bore the president a grudge because he had not appointed Guiteau consul to Paris.)

The prisoner was arrested immediately after the firing by officers in the depot… The shooting was done in the ladies' room of the depot, immediately after the President had entered, walking arm in arm with Secretary Blaine on their way to the limited express train, which was about to leave.

[Garfield was en route to a reunion of his class at Williams College.]

10:20 a.m. — The President is now being conveyed to the Executive Mansion under a strong escort of metropolitan police. Two companies of regulars from the Washington barracks have been ordered out to preserve quiet. Great excitement prevails.

The national calamity had its effects in Salt Lake City. Then-editor Charles W. Penrose wrote that:

Last night the arrangements were perfected for the grand celebration of the 105th anniversary of national independence in Liberty Park … It was supposed that nothing would bar the way to one of the largest and most glorious celebrations of the kind ever enjoyed in the Territory. But morning came and brought the startling and lamentable tidings of the attempted assassination of President Garfield. With the news came the conviction that the rejoicings of the season were at an end. The nation's Chief Magistrate lay at the point of death and whether he recovered or in the Providence of God should pass from this mortal sphere, it would ill become the people to be engaged in feasting and jollity while the head of the nation was lying prone, perhaps in the struggles of dissolution…

(LDS Church) President John Taylor endorsed the movement (to cancel the celebration) and feeling deeply moved by the sad event of the hour arose and made the following remarks: "In relation to the startling news that we have heard concerning the attempted assassination of President Garfield, whether it arises from private animosity or personal feelings of revenge, or whether it originates from a political clique, it is one of those things that all right feeling people will lament… We have our ideas of principle which amount to something like this: that God lifts up one man and puts down another according to His will… but while we have an understanding of this kind, we cannot but lament …"

Despite the cancellation of the July Fourth gala, the holiday was observed by a suspension of business. But the mood was somber:

**No Performance** — Owing to the lamentable news of the assassination of President Garfield, the Management of the (Salt Lake) Theatre decided this morning that the performances announced for this afternoon and evening should not take place. Money paid for the tickets will be refunded, or tickets will be good for the next performance…

Interest in the man who shot the president was intense:

**July 5, 1881:**

The statement that the prisoner was Guitteau (sic) was verified by the officer in charge, in the jail. The prisoner arrived and was placed in the cell about 10:30 o'clock, just one hour after the shooting occurred. He has a sandy complexion and is slight, weighing not more than 125 pounds. He wears a moustache and light chin whiskers and has sunken cheeks and eyes far apart from each other, giving him a sullen, or as an officer described it, a loony appearance. The officer in question stated that he has noticed the peculiarity of nearly all murderers, and that their eyes are set far apart, and Guitteau, he said, proves no exception to the rule…

During his later trial, Guiteau appeared insane, but the jury was not convinced. He was hanged in 1882. Initially, it appeared Garfield would survive the gunshot wounds, but one of the two bullets that penetrated his body eluded all his doctors' efforts to remove it. Alexander Graham Bell, inventor of the telephone, was called in to try to locate it with an electrical device, but was not successful. Infection set in and after lingering 80 days, Garfield died:

**Sept. 20, 1881:**

### Death

The President remained in a dying condition until 10:35, when he was pronounced dead. He died of some trouble of the heart, supposed to be neuralgia, but that, of course, is uncertain…

### New York Tribune

NEW YORK — The reaper Death gathers the bravest and the best. After a struggle that has kindled the admiration of the world for his heroic manhood, President Garfield has gone to the still heights where crime and pain come not. He looks down upon a mourning nation, which he hoped to help by a wise discharge of duty. Worthier men than Abraham Lincoln and James A. Garfield this country has never seen in high station, and each was taken early from us …

The News continued to follow the ceremony surrounding Garfield's funeral and his burial in Cleveland. It was the second assassination of an American president in less than two decades.

# The Wild West

## Legends are born

The Wild West was never as big, as wild, as romantic as later books and movies would portray it. But it was a violent place, governed largely by the law of the six-shooter. And even at the time, contemporary accounts of outlaws and gunslingers indicate a beginning fascination that would grow to legendary proportions.

**S**o it was when the Deseret News reported the "Particulars of the Killing of Billy The Kid," based on a telegraph report from New Mexico:

**DESERET NEWS,** *July 20, 1881: Billy had been stopping with Mexicans in that vicinity, disguised as one of them ever since his escape from the Lincoln county jail. Pat Garrett, sheriff of Lincoln county, has been on the track for some time, and on the day above mentioned, arrived at Fort Sumner, having been put on the track by some Mexicans. He had to threaten their lives in order to get them to divulge Kid's whereabouts. About 12 midnight, Sheriff Garrett entered the room of one Pat Maxwell, a live stock owner, residing at the Fort, and supposed to have knowledge of the fugitive's exact whereabouts. Garrett had not been in the room over 20 minutes, when the Kid entered in his stocking feet, knife in hand — ostensibly for the purpose of buying some meat. He immediately observed Garrett crouching at the head of the bed, and asking Maxwell what that was, drew his revolver. Maxwell made no answer, but proceeded to crawl toward the foot of the bed. Had he answered, giving Garrett's name, Billy would have killed him at once, as he is a dead shot. Billy moved slightly, and getting into the moonlight, then shining in at the rough window, Garrett recognized him, fired — the ball passed through the heart. He fell backward — his knife in one hand and revolver in the other…*

Billy the Kid posed for this photograph shortly before his death.

Some nine days later, an editorial note appeared in the paper:

**DESERET NEWS,** *July 29, 1881: The killing of "Billy the Kid," alias Wm. McCarthy, the New Mexico desperado, who has shot from eighteen to twenty-five men, will be applauded by all the good people of the region where he was a terror because of his skill with deadly weapons, and his utter recklessness and contempt for the law.*

Jesse James was also a notorious figure of the time. After one of his gang members was captured after a train robbery, readers got some insight into the workings of the James gang. A Mr. Land, in giving his confession, told of hooking up with the outlaw:

Jesse James led a gang that looted some $200,000 in robberies and killed at least 16 men.

UPI Photo

Culver Pictures and UPI

**DESERET NEWS,** *April 3, 1882: Immediately after shaking hands he and Mott walked away to the end of the platform and held a short conversation. Jesse then came up to me and said:*

*"Mr. Land, I understand you are going in with us to rob the train tonight."*

*"Yes, sir."*

*"Have you any arms?"*

*"Yes, a breech-loading rifle."*

*"Be sure and bring it with you. Meet us at the out back of Jack Cole's farm as soon after eight o'clock as convenient. Come alone. When you get within two or three hundred yards of the spot signal us by whistling twice. An answer will be once."*

*I then turned and went back home. My folks were all there except my brother… A little while after I got up, took down my rifle, and slipped out in my stocking feet, got away without raising any of the family. Upon arriving at the cut I gave the signal agreed upon. It was answered, and I stepped forward and was met by Jesse James. All the old gang were there, six of them, and Armstrong and Deerduff, who I knew before, and who had joined the regular gang a short time before. But I was the only one of the neighborhood boys who had got there…*

*Jesse James said: "Boys, we who are older hands at the business will stop the train, and go through the cars and get what there is there. You fellows run along outside and fire 15 or 20 shots apiece to scare the passengers."*

*Jesse stood upon a pile of rocks on the track, and swung a lantern and the train came to a stop within a few feet of the obstruction…*

The day after this account appeared, word came from Kansas City of the death of Jesse James:

**DESERET NEWS,** *April 4, 1882: The news of the killing of Jesse James created an immense sensation in this city, although the report was generally treated with incredulity, and even at this late hour many unbelievers can be found.*

Details were printed the next day, under the small headlines: "More of the Murder" and "Jesse James the Railroad Robber".

**DESERET NEWS,** *April 5, 1882: In a small frame shanty in the south part of the city, on a hill not far from the World's Hotel, Jesse James has lived with his wife since some time in November last. Robert and Charles Ford, two of his gang, have made their headquarters at his house… and the three have been making preparations for a raiding expedition, on which they were to start to-night. James and the two Ford boys being together in the front room about 9 o'clock this morning, the former took off his belt and laid his pistols on the bed, preparatory to washing himself when Robert Ford sprang up behind him and sent a bullet through his brain. The ball entered the back of his head at the base of the right brain, coming out over the eyes… .*

*Mrs. James was in the kitchen when the shooting was done. It was divided from the room in which the bloody tragedy occurred by a dining room. She heard the shot, and, dropping her household duties, ran into the front room. She saw her husband lying on his back, and his slayers each holding his revolver in his hand making for the fence in the rear of the house. Robert had reached it when she stepped to the door and called to him: "Robert you have done this; come back." Robert answered: "I swear to God, I did not." They then returned to where she stood. Mrs. James ran to the side of her husband and lifted up his head. Life was not extinct, and, when she asked if he was hurt, it seemed to her that he wanted to say something but could not. She tried to wash away the blood that was coursing over his face from the hole in the forehead, but it seemed to her the blood would come faster than she could wash it away and in her hands, Jesse James died.*

*Charlie Ford explained to Mrs. James that "a pistol had accidently gone off."*

*"Yes," said Mrs. James, "I guess it went off on purpose."*

Afew months earlier another of the West's legendary gunslinging events was reported in the paper:

**DESERET NEWS,** *Oct. 1881: A Tombstone dispatch says: Four cowboys, Ike and Billy Clanton and Francis and Tom McLowery, have been parading town for several days drinking heavily and making themselves obnoxious. The city marshal arrested Ike Clanton. Soon after his release the four met the marshal, his brothers Morgan and Wyathe Earp and J.H. Holliday. The marshal ordered them to give up their weapons, when a fight commenced. About 30 shots were fired rapidly. Both of the McLowery boys were killed and Billy Clanton mortally wounded, dying soon after. Ike was slightly wounded and arrested. Morgan Earp was severely wounded in the shoulder, Wyathe slightly, the others were unhurt.*

History would come to know this event as the shootout at the O.K. Corral. Just wait until Hollywood got hold of it…

Wyatt Earp was a careful gunshooter. Above, the real O.K. Corral in Tombstone, Ariz.

# A hostile Congress
## and plural marriage

**With the echoes of the Civil War fading away, American politicians in the 1870s and 1880s turned their attention to Utah, the LDS Church and plural marriage. That interest, combined with an influx of non-LDS settlers to Utah Territory, made polygamy a dominant political issue for a generation and the subject of thousands of news stories before the church discontinued its practice in 1890.**

**Wilford Woodruff**

Deseret News files

T
he plurality of wives was revealed to Joseph Smith and recorded in 1843, though it is evident from historical records that the principles involved had been known to him since 1831. It was openly announced by church leaders in Utah Territory in the 1850s and quickly became a focus for anti-Mormon sentiments. Politically, it was a major impediment to statehood.

Congress, which controlled the country's territories, passed a series of legislative edicts to outlaw polygamy. The Morrill Act of 1862 prohibited plural marriages, but it was largely ignored because of the war. A succession of increasingly stringent laws followed.

The Deseret News waged a fierce defense of what LDS leaders claimed to be a right under the U.S. Constitution's protection of religious liberty. Few editions of the newspaper failed to carry news or opinion about the debate. The News also had no qualms about printing derogatory articles in full from other newspapers, taking note particularly of the local competition, the Salt Lake Tribune. The occasional supportive articles from around the country also were reprinted; an example was this one:

**DESERET NEWS,** *April 22, 1882:*
*The Providence, (Rhode Island) Star, a journal which has said some severe things concerning the "Mormons," and cannot be accused of sympathy with our system, has the following:*

*The Mormon Conference at Salt Lake City, which closed on Sunday night, was a remarkable gathering. The reports that have been telegraphed to us of its doings, prepared as they are by men whose hatred of the Mormons is more bitter that than of the Irish for English landlords, has given us a very imperfect idea of the spirit which pervaded the gathering. Eleven thousand people, men and women, were assembled in the immense tabernacle on Sunday, and the*

*enthusiasm that was manifested, according to the dispatch of a special correspondent, was somewhat phenomenal. The entire proceedings were dignified and marked with a terrible earnestness.*

*The tone in which the Mormon Leaders addressed the people may be learned from the language used by President Taylor in his opening speech, which set the key for all who followed. "The antagonism we now experience here," said President Taylor, "has always existed, but we have always come out of our troubles strengthened. I say to you be calm, for the Lord God Omnipotent reigneth, and He will take care of us…"*

Every community was subject to harassment by deputy marshals. Typical is this report from the 1860s:

**DESERET NEWS,** *Oct. 23, 1866:*
*A RAID ON IRON COUNTY — This morning, about daylight, the quiet little burg of Enoch, situated about six miles north of here and attached to this ward, was visited by Deputy Marshals Thompson, of Beaver; Orton of Parowan; and assistants, who arrested, on the going charge [polygamy], John P. Jones and his eldest son, John L. The former is one of our veteran citizens, and one of the pioneers of southern Utah. He is now quite feeble and must be verging onto three score and ten years. His alleged plural wife was arrested at the same time, all of whom, together with four of the citizens of this city, who were subpoenaed by Deputy Orton, as witnesses in the above case are now en route for Beaver. We are informed by rumors that the next visit*

*is intended to be made on this city, as "game" is getting somewhat scarce in the north of this judicial district …*

In all, an estimated 1,000 men and some women were imprisoned. They found conditions deplorable in the State Penitentiary in Sugar House, and the ongoing raids kept families in turmoil as they tried to protect husbands and fathers, some of whom went into hiding to escape conviction.

In 1887 Congress passed the Edmunds-Tucker Bill. It disincorporated the church, dissolved the Perpetual Emigration Fund Co. that provided loans to church members to locate in Utah, abolished female suffrage and gave the attorney general of the United States the right to control the real and personal property of the church. Relationships between the Latter-day Saints and the U.S. government continued to deteriorate.

President Wilford Woodruff, fourth President of the

## THE MANIFESTO

Public Announcement in Relation to Plural Marriages, September 24, 1890, by Prest. Wilford Woodruff.

### OFFICIAL DECLARATION.

*To Whom it May Concern:*

Press dispatches having been sent for political purposes, from Salt Lake City, which have been widely published, to the effect that the Utah Commission, in their recent report to the Secretary of the Interior, allege that plural marriages are still being solemnized and that forty or more such marriages have been contracted in Utah since last June or during the past year; also that in public discourses the leaders of the Church have taught, encouraged and urged the continuance of the practice of polygamy.

I, therefore, as President of the Church of Jesus Christ of Latter-day Saints, do hereby, in the most solemn manner, declare that these charges are false. We are not teaching polygamy, or plural marriage, nor permitting any person to enter into its practice, and I deny that either forty or any other number of plural marriages have during that period been solemnized in our temples or in any other place in the Territory.

One case has been reported, in wh…

church, struggled with the situation. After much prayer and deliberation, he declared on Sept. 24, 1890, that the Lord had made it plain to him what he was to do, and that it was the right thing. The result was called the Manifesto, which was released to the nation's newspapers the next day:

**DESERET NEWS,** *Sept. 25, 1890:*
… Inasmuch as laws have been enacted forbidding plural marriages, which laws have been pronounced constitutional by the court of last resort, I hereby declare my intention to submit to those laws, and to use my influence with the members of the church over which I preside to have them do likewise… And I now publicly declare that my advice to the Latter-day Saints is to refrain from contracting any marriage forbidden by the law of the Land.
*WILFORD WOODRUFF,*
President of the Church of Jesus Christ of Latter-day Saints.

In the October general conference, the official declaration was read in full. The newspaper reported:

**DESERET NEWS,** *Oct. 6, 1890:* President Lorenzo Snow offered the following: "I move that, recognizing Wilford Woodruff as the President of the Church of Jesus Christ of Latter-day Saints and the only man on the earth at the present time who holds the keys of the sealing ordinances, we consider him fully

authorized by virtue of his position to issue the manifesto which has been read in our hearing and which is dated September 24, 1890, and that as the Church in General Conference assembled, we accept his declaration concerning plural marriages as authoritative and binding." The vote to sustain the foregoing motion was unanimous.

To reassure members of the church, President Woodruff closed the conference and bore testimony of the revelation that had come to him:

**DESERET NEWS,** *Oct. 18, 1890:* No matter what trials or tribulations we may be called to pass through, the hand of God will be with us and will sustain us… I say to Israel, the Lord will never permit me nor any other man who stands as the President of this Church, to lead you astray. It is not in the programme. It is not in the mind of God. If I were to attempt that, the Lord would remove me out of my place, and so He will any other man who attempts to lead the children of men astray from the oracles of God and from their duty. God bless you. Amen.

Into the 1900s, the church took increasingly stronger steps to dissociate itself from the practice and excommunicated those who followed it. With the discontinuance of plural marriage within the church, the way opened to a successful quest for statehood.

# DESERET EVENING NEWS.

July 6, 1881

Electricity has been successfully applied in Germany to land locomotion. Now comes its application to water travel. M.G. Trouve, of Paris, has constructed an electric apparatus which propels a boat on the Seine. The experiments with a small vessel containing six persons have been successful, and there appears no reason why the same principle will not apply to larger vessels. Out of all the discoveries and trials with electric current we have no doubt that a good steady light will yet be obtained, and a reliable, noiseless, smokeless, controllable motive power.

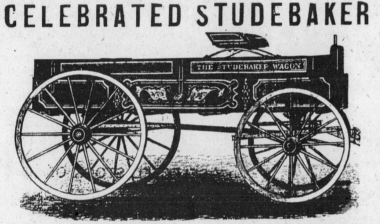

TRY THE
CELEBRATED STUDEBAKER

July 6, 1881

The Studebaker President.— Clem Studebaker Esq., President of the famous Studebaker Brothers Manufacturing Establishment, of South Bend, Indiana, whose arrival here we noticed the other day, will leave here the latter part of this week for his eastern home. He has just returned from a tour through the West, visiting the various agencies of his establishment, one of which in Sacramento is among the most extensive. He has called here on his way back to see how Studebaker interests are progressing in these parts, and expresses himself as highly pleased with the result of his observations.

July 27, 1881

Putting on the Roof.— We learn from the Logan Leader that the work on the Temple in that city has reached a very important stage, viz, the laying of tin on the roof. This was begun on Tuesday the 19th inst., and is being rushed with all speed. All the men who can work to advantage on the roof are placed there, the aim being to get the tin securely fastened down as soon as possible.

Oct. 26, 1881

## MYSTERIOUS MURDER
### JOEL HINCKLEY KILLED BY TWO MASKED MEN

The following special dispatch to the NEWS, from Mr. R.G. Lambert, sent from Logan was received today:

"Joel Hinckley, agent for the Utah & Northern Railroad, at Franklin, was shot by two masked men, last night, about 10 o'clock. The murderers escaped. No clue has been obtained. The town is out searching for the perpetrators of the crime. No cause for the deed is learned..."

Deceased was a fine young man, about twenty years old, son of Arza Hinckley, at Corn Creek, Utah.

April 1882

## BRIGHAM YOUNG ACADEMY
### REPORT OF PUBLIC EXAMINATION

Written exercises, Brigham Young Academy, Sixth Year, Third Term, ending March 31st, 1882. Number of Students registered.

| Department. | No. of Registers | Teachers |
|---|---|---|
| Primary B | 23 | Mrs. Zina Y. Williams |
| Primary A | 15 | " |
| Intermediate B | 45 | N.L. Nelson |
| Intermediate A | 109 | M.H. Hardy |
| Academic B | 69 | J.M. Tanner |
| Academic A | 79 | J.F. Talmage |
| Normal | 33 | By the Principal |
| Total attendance | 373 | |

May 31, 1882

The Bicycle Races. The place made most attractive to excursionists yesterday was Calder's Farm. Multitudes took advantage of the holiday to get out of the dusty streets and drive down through the green fields to rest and refresh themselves in the arbors and groves, and glide over the cool water of Spring Lake, while "Music arose with its voluptuous swell, etc." The most enticing feature of the entertainment was undoubtedly the bicycle contest for the gold and silver medals. The large semi-circular grand stand to the south of the arena, was crowded with spectators for over four hours, while hundreds ranged themselves around that end of the track on either side.

Shortly after 2 o'clock, eight uniformed riders of the Club, directed by captain D.L. Davis, mounted their glittering steeds and passed around the track, singly, in double file and four abreast...

May 31, 1882

Railroaders' B. B. Match.— Yesterday there was a friendly baseball match between the employees of the Utah Central and Denver & Rio Grande Railroad companies. It was a stoutly contested game, the U. C. boys scoring 25, while the D. R. G's. got 24.

July 17, 1882

## THE DESERET HOSPITAL
### DEDICATION SERVICES.

THIS morning, at 11 o'clock, a number of ladies and gentlemen interested in the establishment of a hospital for the care and treatment of the sick, under the auspices of the Church of Jesus Christ of Latter-day Saints, assembled at the building on Fifth East Street, between East Temple and First South, to attend the dedications and the opening of the institution.

Presidents John Taylor and Jos. F. Smith were present, also President W. Woodruff, Apostle F.D. Richards, Prest. of the Stake Angus M. Cannon and Counselor Jos. E. Taylor, Mayor W. Jenning, Elders L. John Nuttall, Joseph Horne and Chas. W. Penrose, the officers of the Institution, physicians, ladies of the Relief Society, etc...

### PREST. JOSEPH F. SMITH

This was a step quite necessary to be taken. It was in the interest of the afflicted and the poor. He would have been pleased if the institution could have been started in a better place. It was but a small beginning, yet it was better than none at all, and he expressed the hope that success would attend it, and the perfect union, harmony and good feeling would prevail among all who had the conduct of its affairs, so that the good spirit of the Lord might be with them...

The Rt. Rev. Daniel S. Tuttle, Episcopal bishop for Utah.

Aug. 26, 1886

## "SPEAK OF A MAN AS YOU FIND HIM"

A GENTLEMAN who has become identified with the history of Utah is about to leave the Territory to make his home in Missouri. His face is familiar to the people of Montana and Idaho as well as the denizens of the country near the shores of the saline Sea. Bishop Tuttle of the Episcopal Church, who was some time ago elected to the Bishopric of Missouri, will leave a favorable impression upon all who have become acquainted with him during his sojourn in the region of the Rocky Mountains. Kind, courteous and urbane, yet dignified and firm in his demeanor, he has made many friends among people of various shades of opinion.

Although very pronounced in his opposition to the "Mormon" faith, he has not acted as an enemy to the "Mormon" people. So far as we are aware he had not, like many of his cloth, used his ecclesiastical influence towards the oppression and spoliation of the Latter-day Saints, but has on many occasions borne testimony to their good qualities, in public and in private. We respect a consistent antagonist...

Bishop Tuttle is not only frank enough to express freely his dissent from the doctrine of the "Mormons" when among them, but brave enough to speak in defense of the unpopular people when in the midst of their enemies. There are few prominent men who dare do this…

We bid the gentleman farewell, with the best wishes for his welfare. We hope to hear that Bishop Tuttle and his partner in life are enjoying prosperity and contentment and the cordial feeling of a host of friends in his new field of labor in old Missouri.

---

April 23, 1889

## THE PROMISED LAND

The Time Has Arrived for Settlers
to Enter Oklahoma.

### ALL SORTS AND CONDITIONS OF MEN THERE.

The Fleetest of Horses Carry Them
to their New Homes.

### FIFTEEN THOUSAND PERSONS CAMPED AT GUTHRIE.

The Land Office is Besieged by Eager
and Determined Crowds.

By Telegraph to the NEWS.
**THEY MAY ENTER**

### A Motley Crowd Rushes Into Oklahoma.

St. Louis, April 22.—The Republic's Arkansa City special says:

Oklahoma is open. The trials, struggles and sacrifices of years are partially rewarded, but the events of today have made those of the days, weeks, and months to follow of much concern, and will prove how far the supply is below the demand, and necessitate further concessions to avert disorder, bloodshed, and other conditions but little short of anarchy. The history of the day will forever be a memorial in frontier annals, and will leave behind a heritage of litigation which will be fruitful to land sharks and claim attorneys, but destruction to the claims of poor and honest settlers.

---

May 6, 1880

### Base Ball

WASHINGTON, May 4 — The game today was a contest of the pitchers, in which both did great work. Clarkson saved them the game for the Bostons when in the ninth inning, with men on second and third, he succeeded in retiring the side without a run. Score: Washington, 2; Boston, 3. Batteries: Washington — Fearson and Mack, Boston — Clarkson and Bennett.

---

May 7, 1889

---

### "The Merchant of Venice."

The world produces only a few masters of the dramatic art. Among them Edwin Booth stands today without a superior, we think without an equal. In every movement, gesture, expression and intonation he is so natural and so fully interprets the design of the play wright whose ideas he embodies, that his acting is as near perfection as one could hope to see.

His Shylock at the Theatre last night was fully up to the mark of his former efforts… He did not look like Booth at all. In feature, expression and cast of countenance he was changed into the money-lending Hebrew thirsting for revenge against a taunting enemy…

Tonight Julius Caesar will be presented, when both the great actors will appear. (Barrett played Bassanio). It is to be hoped that those who attend will be in their seats by 8 o'clock, when the curtain rises, and that babies in arms will not be brought to spoil with family music some of the best passages of the play.

---

May 7, 1889

### Personal.

Mr. Hubert H. Bancroft is in town accompanied by Col. George W. Morrison. Mr. Bancroft's name is familiar to the people of Utah as the author of the great work, "The History of the Pacific State," now in process of publication. Col. Morrison is one of the History Company of San Francisco and a very pleasant and intelligent gentleman. They arrived here last evening and will remain a few days. We wish them a pleasant visit.

---

May 7, 1889

### A Storm of Frogs.

St. Paul, May 7. — A Pioneer Press special from Jamestown, Dak., says that during a storm last evening a large number of frogs were precipitated to the ground from a cloud. It is claimed a funnel-shaped cloud was seen in the west shortly before, and the theory is the frogs were caught up from some slough in a whirl-wind and carried in the air until it spent itself.

---

# Tit for tat with
# Oscar Wilde

**O**scar Wilde, English author and one of the leaders of the "art-for-arts'-sake" aesthetic movement of the late 19th century, visited Salt Lake City during an extended tour of the United States. He got a less-than-lukewarm reception from the Deseret News.

**DESERET NEWS,** April 11, 1882: The noted aesthete appeared in a cut-a-way black velvet coat, with vest and knee breeches of the same material. The coat was adorned at the neck and wrists with snowy ruffles. He is a tall, spare young man, the aesthetic or attenuated character of whose legs, combined with the peculiar cut of his coat caused him to resemble, in beauty of form, a grasshopper on end… His hair is long and flowing and his smooth face as destitute of manly adornment as his lecture is of hard common sense. The forehead recedes from where it joins the nose, the jaw is long and the mouth somewhat open and fluffy.

Wilde's views, the reviewer commented, "flit from his mouth like feathers." The visitor's arguments were either so self-evident as to be laughable or "as old as the hills… The lecture was without strength or argument, was delivered in the most flabby and meaningless manner imaginable, the whole forming an excellent burlesque on common sense."

Wilde reciprocated in kind. After a tour of the city, he later commented that the Tabernacle was "the shape of a soup kettle with decorations suitable for a jail." He wrote to his friend Mrs. Bernard Beere, in snide tones, that the "Opera House of Salt Lake (the Salt Lake Theater) is an enormous affair about the size of Covent Garden and holds with ease 14 (polygamous) families." He included an illustration showing several men, each flanked by several wives. In addition, he told a Denver reporter that his Salt Lake visit afforded him the opportunity to see the ugliest women he had ever seen.

And with that tit-for-tat exchange of insults, one of England's premier authors marked his visit to Mormonism's stronghold.

## The world of the 1880s
### A TIMELINE

**1880**— Tahiti is annexed by France.

**1880**—James A. Garfield elected president of the United States.

**1880**— The Cologne Cathedral is finished. It was begun in 1248.

**1881**— The Boers defeat the British at Majuba Hill, Britain recognizes an independent Transvaal Republic.

**1881**— The first U.S. Lawn Tennis Championship is played.

**1881**— Sioux Chief Sitting Bull gives himself up.

**1882**— The United States passes the Immigration Act, which prohibits Chinese immigration for 10 years.

**1882**— British troops bombard Alexandria, Egypt, and occupy Cairo.

**1882**— Tchaikovsky writes the "1812 Overture."

**1882**— The American Baseball Association is founded.

**1883**— Krakatoa volcano erupts in Java, killing 30,000 and blotting out the sun.

**1883**— Chicago is the site of the first skyscraper, 10 stories high.

**1884**— Grover Cleveland elected president of the U.S.

**1884**— Gold is discovered in the Transvaal, Johannesburg rises.

**1885**— King Leopold of Belgium takes the Congo as his own possession.

**1885**— Van Gogh paints "The Potato Eaters."

**1885**— Louis Pasteur creates the rabies vaccine.

**1885**— "Dr. Jekyll and Mr. Hyde" written by Robert Louis Stevenson.

**1885**— George Eastman creates a coated photographic paper.

**1885**— Golf comes to America after John Fox of Philadelphia learns it on trip to Scotland.

**1886**— British prime minister William Gladstone's government falls after 6 months.

**1886**— Charles Hall and P.L. T. Heroult of France produce aluminum by electrolysis.

**1886**— The eighth, and last, Impressionist exhibit held in Paris.

**1887**— Queen Victoria celebrates her Golden Jubilee.

**1887**— The first Sherlock Holmes book, "A Study in Scarlet," written by Sir Arthur Conan Doyle.

**1887**— Tchaikovsky composes the ballet, "Swan Lake."

**1888**— Heinrich Hertz discovers electromagnetic waves.

**1888**— Cecil Rhodes gains control of the Kimberly diamond mines in South Africa.

**1888**— Nikola Tesla builds an electric motor.

**1888**— Benjamin Harrison elected president.

**1889**— Washington, Montana, North and South Dakota all become states.

**1889**— The French Panama Canal Co. goes bankrupt.

**1889**— Von Mehring and Mikowski demonstrate that the pancreas releases insulin to prevent diabetes.

---

Feb. 21, 1885

## The Last of the Buffaloes

The year the Northern Pacific Railroad was completed there were some five thousand hunters along the line of the road engaged in killing buffalo and other animals for the hides. A Montana correspondent writes recently that the harvests of furs in the Northwest are about ended, for the buffaloes are near their final extinction. Hunters are daily returning from parts of the country where they formerly roamed in myriads, with the report that now no such game is to be found. Glendine shipped alone, within a short time, one hundred thousand robes, and great quantities were sent from the neighboring points. Notwithstanding the bison was the main dependence of the Indian for food, the animals did not numerically decrease until the white hunters began killing them, since which time their decline has been very rapid.

In 1868 the Transcontinental Railroad divided the buffaloes into two great bands, continuing their migrations and giving the hunters easy access to the feeding grounds. The men employed by the trade-men divided into gangs, each having a shooter and eight or ten skinners following him. The shooter would bring down from 80 to 100 buffaloes in a day, the hides being worth from 75 cents to $1 in the raw state. Only the best parts of the meat were preserved, the larger part being left to rot.

The herds in Texas, New Mexico and Arizona long since disappeared, and their feeding grounds are occupied by cattle and sheep. In the Northwest the bison went with the red men when the Government troops drove Sitting Bull from the grounds of his tribe. For some years the white skeletons along the railroad line were a special inducement for the tourist to undertake the journey across the prairies, but now collecting and selling these bones is a regular business. The buyers are to be seen at nearly every station, and large heaps of the bones ready for shipment. The bones which surveyors have put up for sighting points are taken with the rest, and within a few years this last monument to the former numbers of the American bison in the past will disappear.

---

Capstone of the Washington Monument is hoisted into place in 1885.

## The Washington Monument

When the great obelisk of the Washington Monument was finally completed, the entire country paid tribute to a man who was already an icon. Although George Washington resisted any such tribute to him while he was alive, the general outline of the monument was known and fund raising began as early as 1833. The project moved slowly, however, and not until 1876 did Congress vote funds to finish it.

When it was dedicated, the Deseret News, relying on telegraph reports, said "The day was very cold and raw, and spectators sat near the monument with their hats on and coat collars turned up." At the conclusion of the ceremonies, held in the hall of the House of Representatives, President Chester A. Arthur spoke:

**DESERET NEWS,** *Feb. 24, 1885: In the completion of this great work of patriotic endeavor there is abundant cause for national rejoicing; for, while this structure shall endure, it shall be to all mankind a steadfast token of the affectionate and reverend regards in which this people continue to hold the memory of Washington. Well may he ever keep the foremost place in the hearts of his countrymen. The faith that never faltered, the wisdom broader and deeper than any learning taught in schools, the courage that shrank from no peril and was dismayed by no defeat, the loyalty that kept all selfish purpose subordinate to the demands of patriotism and honor, the sagacity that displayed itself in camp and cabinet alike, and above all, that harmonious union of moral and intellectual qualities which has never found its parallel among men; these are the attributes of a character which intelligent thought in this century ascribes to the grandest figure of the last…*

In an accompanying editorial the newspaper echoed that thought:

*The last three days have been more or less devoted throughout the country to celebrating the natal day of one of the grandest characters of human history — George Washington… It is seldom that the qualities that go to make up a great warrior and a great statesman are found in one person. It is even rarer that a statesman who is great in times of peace shines with anything like the same splendor in times of war…*

*The base of Washington's greatness consisted of his unselfish devotion to the general weal, his public career giving no evidence that he was influenced by avarice or other sordid motives…*

UPI Photo

# The French give the world
# Two icons

**During the 1880s, two structures destined to take their places among the world's greatest attractions arose. The Deseret News gave plenty of space to the advent of both the Statue of Liberty in November 1886 and to the Eiffel Tower in Paris in May of 1889.**

**H**eadlined "THE GREAT DAY" the News story of the uncovering of Bartholdi's colossal Statue of Liberty in New York harbor glowed with superlatives:

**DESERET NEWS,** *Oct. 28, 1886: The French sculptor, Bartholdi, may well exclaim like Caesar, "Veni, Vidi, Vici!" And what a conquest is his! A conquest of a people, comparatively uneducated in high art and undeveloped in public spirit, a victory of the idealist over the utilitarian …*

*The mammoth figure stands, at last, upon its massive pedestal, symbolizing the incarnation of all that the nation has lived, and suffered, and fought for, in the awful sacrifices it has laid, in a single century, upon the altar of American Freedom. Towering above the blue waters, it rises a veritable goddess, a gigantic face, standing in eloquent silence like a guardian spirit before the gates of the city …*

President Grover Cleveland, who officially accepted the gift from the French, along with scores of American and French officials, participated in a grand parade. The newspaper duly listed all their names and declared the occasion *"all in all, an event not previously paralleled in the history of modern times."*

By contrast, the ceremonies that introduced the Eiffel Tower to Paris received only lukewarm reviews from the American reporter who covered the Paris Exposition.

**DESERET NEWS,** *May 7, 1889: PARIS, May 6 — At 2 o'clock this afternoon, surrounded by his ministers and many distinguished guests, President (Marie Francois) Carnot stood under the great dome of the Exposition building,* formally *to declare it open … The military display, which was inferior to many I have seen in Paris, was wisely curtailed to give the visitors an opportunity to see the charms of the most beautiful spot in Europe, whose natural loveliness is not over-matched by its historical association, in which romance and tragedy are so strangely commingled…*

The reporter said that the surprise of the day was that so many French diplomats were on the Exposition grounds, even though the government had officially disallowed them from assisting in the grand opening. Of the tower itself, his analysis was that:

A plaster cast of Liberty's head is sculpted at the Paris workshop in 1877. Copper sheets were then molded from the cast and riveted together.

AP/Bartholdi Museum

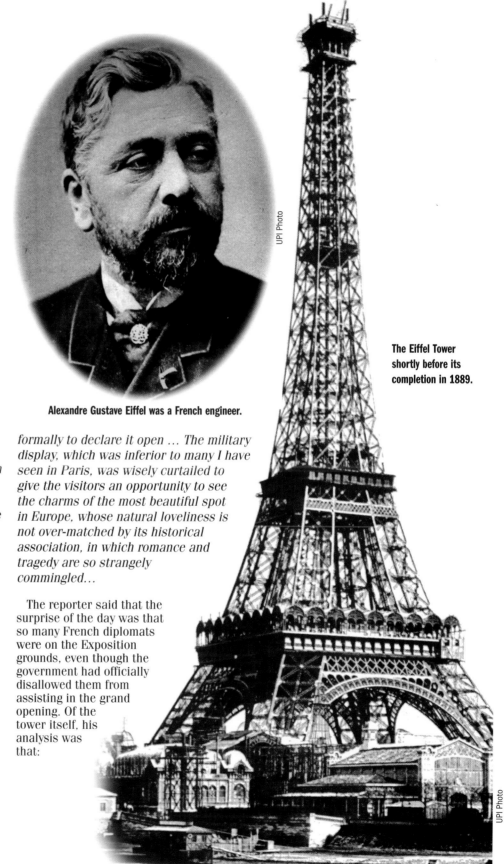

UPI Photo

Alexandre Gustave Eiffel was a French engineer.

**The Eiffel Tower shortly before its completion in 1889.**

UPI Photo

**DESERET NEWS:** *The Eiffel tower has been smiled at, as the great folly of the Exposition, but the giant manikin of iron threads professes a value apart from its ostentaciousness. One might mistake it at a distance for an elongated scaffold of an electric light, but on closer approach, it is seen to be a daring monumental achievement. From its highest balcony there is visible a beautiful panorama of seventy miles of hills, rivers, lakes, towns and hamlets which no painter can place on canvass (sic) and no poet transcribe in verse. The summit is at a total height of nearly 1000 feet, or nearly double that of the Washington Monument and higher than St. Peters in Rome. It will be utilized for scientific purposes, the public being permitted to ascend only about two thirds of the way in elevators which can provide transportation for 25,000 persons daily. Restaurants and saloons will enable pleasure parties to spend days in the air.*

With these introductions, Utahns kept pace with world interest in what remain more than a hundred years later two of the greatest tourist attractions on the globe.

After more than a century, the Statue of Liberty is an enduring symbol of American and French commitment to democracy.

Finely-detailed work of the Statue of Liberty up close. Below, it rises startlingly above the streets of Paris.

AP/Bartholdi Museum

UPI Photo

Surrender of Geronimo and his band.

# Geronimo

**DESERET NEWS,** *Sept. 6, 1886:* NOGALES, Arizona, 4. — Information has reached here that General Clark arrived at Calabasas last night with the intelligence from General Miles that while the latter was marching side by side with Captain Lawton, Geronimo came up saying the Indians were out of provisions and ammunition, that they were faint and hungry and would give up their arms and surrender unconditionally.

With that short notice the Deseret News reported the capture of the great Apache chief, who, with his band of 18 warriors, 14 women and six children, had eluded some 5,000 regular army troops. Geronimo's raids over 10 years caught the nation's imagination.

A month later, the paper went after those who, from 3,000 miles away, berated the officer for his decision to treat Geronimo, who had "made night hideous and daytime uncertain," as a prisoner of war. Miles made promises to Geronimo that others would not keep.

An aged Geronimo

**DESERET NEWS,** *Oct. 12, 1886:* It is always the way: Criticism is much easier than performance, and it is still easier to condemn than to carry out. Red tape and official solemnity are matters of education and opportunity, but actual exploits in the field are other and vastly different things.

The Indians are the wards of the nation… To treat them as savages in the field and as civil criminals when captured is something of an anomaly. To hang Captain Jack and banquet Sitting Bull… to make an exile of Geronimo shows that we are progressing very slowly in the matter of dealing humanely and justly with the native Americans because there is a painful lack of system and an almost absolute disregard of the ethics of national and native inheritance… General Crook, (who had pursued Geronimo) when once asked if he did not think the Indians were more sinned against than sinning, replied in his bluff way, 'Undoubtedly sir, undoubtedly.' These points are worthy of consideration.

# Statehood
## at last
### 1890-1900

**A**fter almost half a century, and seven official attempts to gain status as a state in the American Union, the day finally had arrived:

**DESERET NEWS,** *Jan. 4, 1896:*
*A PROCLAMATION*
*WASHINGTON — The President at 10 o'clock this morning signed the Proclamation admitting Utah to Statehood... Now, therefore, I, Grover Cleveland, President of the United States of America, in accordance with the act of Congress, and by authority thereof ... do hereby declare and proclaim ... That the creation of said State and its admission into the Union on an equal footing with the original States is now completed...*

The formal document, printed in full on the front page of the Deseret News, set off a frenzy of celebration, despite wintry weather:

**DESERET NEWS:** *At 9:15 this morning the usual early morning serenity of East Temple Street was decidedly disturbed owing to the fact that Superintendent Brown of the Western Union Telegraph Company was observed to rush frantically out of the office armed with an old reliable shotgun, the contents of which belched forth in two resounding reports. A small boy in the near vicinity dived for an adjacent doorway, his juvenile brain probably having grasped the idea that a holdup or bank robbery was in progression...*
*Towards noon decorations became apparent upon nearly every store in the city. Amongst the most ambitious ranks the bunting display of the ZCMI Shoe Factory ... Every man grasped the hand of every other man and the greeting of a few days ago, "A Happy New Year to you," was evolved into the very appropriate*
*salutation of "A happy New State to you..."* *At 11:30 the Battery of the N.G.U. took its position on Capitol hill and proceeded to fire a salute of twenty one guns accompanied by the ringing of bells, blowing of steam whistles and igniting of a half dozen bombs on the NEWS corner which the junior members of the establishment let off with the result that the concussion was felt for a long distance about...*

A parade was whipped up, with a platoon of police at the head and the Scandinavian Societies bringing up the rear. Sandwiched between were carriages with present and former territorial officials, surviving pioneers of 1847, a half dozen bands and anyone else who had an inclination to dress up and join the march. A special session of the Legislature was called for the following Monday. The call by the state's acting governor was *"on account of the Constitutional Convention failing to fix a time for its meeting,"* the News said.
Congratulatory telegrams flew back and forth between the national capital and the new state. A News editorial writer emoted:

**DESERET NEWS:** *At this grand and glorious consummation of her efforts, all Utah rejoices, and each patriotic heart within the commonwealth swells with emotions of gratitude to the Giver of all Good for the deliverance He has wrought in behalf of the people. Utah assumes the robes of State sovereignty with a courage to meet the increased responsibilities of the future and with a fixed purpose that in every act she will honor the sacred principles of liberty heralded to the world by the divinely inspired Constitution of the United States.*

The newspaper also printed a summary of the attempts, beginning in 1849, to gain recognition as a state.

Ironically, the seventh and successful petition to Congress was noted in the News in September 1893 as a simple footnote to other congressional business. House Resolution 352 was submitted by the territory's representative, Joseph L. Rawlins, who assiduously pressed the territory's arguments for statehood, earning himself the sobriquet "Father of the State."
Even though it was a foregone conclusion that statehood would soon close all the gaps in the union from coast to coast, Rawlins did not find the course easy. For several months after his petition had been presented to Congress, he fought against proposals to futher divide Utah:

**DESERET NEWS,** *Sept. 9, 1893: It (a particular proposal) would make of Kansas two states and would admit New Mexico and — cutting us through the middle, North Utah. South Utah and Arizona would be doomed to the cold territorial condition a little longer, an injustice most rank, as*

Utah shed its territorial status and finally became a state during the 1890s, long after many of its neighbors. It was a time of maturation: The Salt Lake Temple was finally completed after 40 years of volunteer labor, a constitution was written, political parties organized and elections began. Women regained the right to vote, and the first woman state senator in the nation was chosen. The Tabernacle Choir literally competed on a world stage for the first time. New interurban railroad lines, yesterday's light rail, began linking the cities. Two resorts opened: Lagoon on the Bamberger rail line and Saltair on the Great Salt Lake. But the decade ended on an ominous note. War engulfed Spain and the United States. Utahns, eager to show they were a full partner in the nation, provided more than its expected number of volunteers to fight it.

ZCMI sprouted banners and bunting to celebrate Utah's becoming the 45th state.

LDS Church Archives

*everybody will admit. Nevada singularly escapes mention in this startling program, but the design doubtless would be to bisect it also and divide it between North and South Utah.*

Fending off such threats to the integrity of what was left of Utah Territory, supporters of statehood triumphed, and on March 5, 1895, the News printed in its entirety the Enabling Act passed by Congress. Statehood still lay about a year away, as a Constitutional Convention was called to hammer out the proposed state's basic laws.

**DESERET NEWS,** *March 6, 1895: The Constitutional Convention today, after a superabundance of parliamentary sparring, occasioned principally by the attempted and finally successful enforcement of caucus calculations and rules, got squarely into the harness and elected a full set of permanent offices, with Hon. John Henry Smith at their head.*

For nearly two months the delegates fussed and fumed over details large and small. One of the first issues of contention regarded who would sit where in the meeting rooms of the Salt Lake City and County Building:

**DESERET NEWS,** *March 7, 1895: In the general readjustment which took place, it transpired that there were nineteen members who had passed the sixtieth annual milestone on life's journey and these aged gentlemen all got choice seats under the provisions of the resolution.*

Much headier issues lay ahead. Each aspect of the state's foundation document received fervid debate. Two issues, however, remained sticky to the end of the convention: women's suffrage and the location of the state agricultural college:

**DESERET NEWS,** *March 12, 1895: Whereas both political parties in the*

*Territories have declared in favor of woman suffrage; now therefore be it Resolved, that the rights of citizens of the State of Utah to vote and hold office shall not be denied or abridged on account of sex.*

The proposal was concise; the furor it set off went on for weeks, with delegations of women packing the meeting halls and delegates jabbing and lambasting to get their points across. Noted LDS delegate B.H. Roberts objected not so much as a matter of principle as for fear the question would hopelessly bog down the convention's work and stymy congressional acceptance. As the debate heated up, the News reported, committee chairman Kimball ordered the crowd to be quiet and rebuked the delegates for "unseemly conduct." Ultimately, the convention voted in favor of women's suffrage, making Utah the second state to grant the right, behind Wyoming. Utah had earlier granted women the right to vote, but Congress took it away in 1887.

The argument in the Education Committee to consolidate then-Utah State Agricultural College with the University of Utah failed to pass muster, leaving the land grant USAC on its Logan campus.

By mid-March, the News reported that the process of writing a constitution had been under way for 11 days, and was expected to continue 20 to 30 more, although a third of the $30,000 allocated for the convention was already spent. Not until May 8, 1895, did the newspaper announce "THE CLOSING HOURS: The Constitution signed by Ninety-Nine Delegates." The meetings closed with $8,000.50 still due delegates and no money available to meet the $1,500 printing costs. Congress was asked to cover the shortfall.

# Butch Cassidy

## Always good for a story

**Whether or not Robert Leroy Parker (Butch Cassidy) was as charismatic as modern movies have portrayed him, he certainly had a penchant for getting his name in the Deseret News, even to this day.**

George Parker, known as Butch Cassidy, and Harry Longbaugh, the Sundance Kid, were the targets of this "wanted" poster from the Pinkerton Agency.

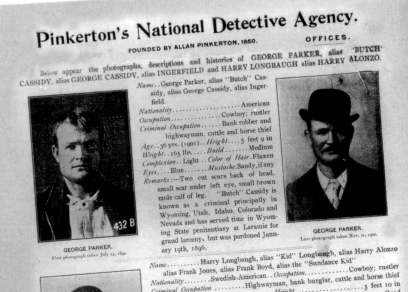

C̄assidy's escapades made him one of the most notable outlaws in the West. Family members depicted him as a good boy gone temporarily wrong. His victims, on the other hand, tended to picture him as one of the most brazen and successful criminals of the outlaw era. His Hole in the Wall Bunch, which took its name from the rugged San Rafael badlands where they fled to escape the law, gained notoriety for bank and train robberies.

One of the most egregious of the gang's holdups occurred April 21, 1897, in Castle Gate. Just after noon, E.L. Carpenter, paymaster for Pleasant Valley Coal Co., with two assistants, stepped off the Denver and Rio Grande train and headed for the company offices above a local store. They were carrying the coal company's payroll in heavy bags.

As soon as the train pulled out, Cassidy and a partner accosted Carpenter, told him to throw up his hands and relieved him and his aides of their bags. Although a score of people watched the robbery, only one, the company clerk, acted. He took a rifle in pursuit, but when it failed to fire, the thieves romped off with about $7,000 in gold. The following day, the Deseret News opined:

**DESERET NEWS,** *April 22, 1897: THE SAN RAFAEL BRIGANDS — Wednesday afternoon's episode at Castle Gate ought to give emphasis to the demand for the San Rafael mountains in east central Utah to be cleared of robber bands. There is no doubt that the two highwaymen who robbed Paymaster Carpenter, as related in Wednesday's NEWS, are of the* number of outlaws who find comparatively safe lodging in the San Rafael district …

… the two men are now almost certainly known to be Tom Gissell and "Butch" Cassidy — said to have figured in the Montpelier bank robbery — and not Gillis and Fowler as at first supposed …

The young man, Phelps (Carpenter's assistant) was struck on the head and compelled to drop a sack containing $1,000, which the thieves afterwards abandoned. Mr. Carpenter was forced to deliver a sack with $7,000 in gold, which was taken and T.W. Lewis, with a third sack that had $800 in silver, made a narrow escape into the store and the robbers rode away, in plain view for some distance. They appeared to be cool, and perhaps were more self-possessed than most of the spectators, but that they did not feel altogether masters of the situation is shown by their failure to pick up the thousand dollar sack …

The following day, the News reported on the progress of the search. But the newspaper mistakenly named Gillis and Fowler as the thieves. Afterward, it was ascertained that it was Butch and company who had done the deed:

**DESERET NEWS,** April 23, 1897: Wednesday evening Sheriff Storrs and Deputy Sheriff Henry joined the

Salt Lake officers who went to Castle Gate on the 8:50 R.G.W. train to investigate the robbery of Mr. Carpenter … Mr. Loveless of Huntington, who was in Provo yesterday, said (the robbers) were in Huntington last Sunday. He expressed a doubt about the officer being able to capture them, for the reason that the San Rafael country and its approaches is infested with a large body of desperadoes (sic), and he believes the posse will meet with some interceptions themselves on their way over from Green River. A larger posse would have gone from Green River but four horses were all that could be obtained at that point.

By 1901, with Pinkerton detectives hired by the railroad breathing down his neck, Cassidy tried to make a deal with Utah Judge Orlando W. Powers to get amnesty for all his crimes. In exchange, he would become a guard for the railroad. When government representatives failed to show up for a scheduled meeting, he was scared off. He may never have known that the men he was to meet had been delayed by a severe storm.

With his current partner in crime, Harry Alonzo Longbaugh (the Sundance Kid), Cassidy headed for South America. They spent some time in Argentina, where they owned land and were involved in several legitimate enterprises. Eventually, however, they returned to their thieving ways, robbing banks and trains. In 1909, word came that they had been killed in a shootout with Bolivian law officers.

Ironically, it wasn't the first time Cassidy's demise had been reported. In the spring of 1898, an erroneous report of his death was printed:

**DESERET NEWS,** May 14, 1898: CASSIDAY IS DEAD: Butch and His Partner Shot by the Officers. Butch Cassiday and his partner, Joe Walker, the noted and daring Robbers Roosters, were shot dead yesterday morning by a posse of officers. Last evening, the News received word of the shooting, which occurred at the head of Florence canyon, leading off from Green river. A week ago Billy McGuire and Bud Whitmore were held up by a gang in Box canyon and robbed of twenty-five cattle … Sheriff Allred immediately organized a posse … The posse came upon the gang … camped among the rocks near McPherson's summer camp at the head of Florence canyon … A hot fusillade from the posse soon brought Cassiday and Walker down … Upon proper proof and identification, the sheriff will pay the captors $500 each for Cassiday and Walker …

**DESERET NEWS,** June 13, 1898: NOT BUTCH CASSIDAY — Despite the positive identification of the man who was shot recently in company with Walker as Butch Cassiday, the fact is now pretty well established that it was not he … It now appears certain that the dead man is John Herring.

With the report from Bolivia in 1909, one of Utah's favorite mysteries was born. Some say Cassidy survived the gunfight. One of his sisters wrote a book in which she claimed he had, in fact, returned briefly to his old home in Circleville, visited with family members and then disappeared again. His burial place remains a family secret, the sister later told the Deseret News.

Old Folks Day at Lagoon in 1898, shortly after it opened.

## Lagoon: a great stop for the railroad

**DESERET NEWS,** July 6, 1898: This was Old Folks' Day.

Simple though they may be, the above words have a mighty significance, and brought to many good, old, honest-hearted souls, a joy inexpressible, a happiness almost boundless. Twenty-three years ago Old Folks' day was inaugurated and from that time until the present, those who have borne the burden and heat of the day have been remembered, if not twice a year, once at the very least. This year the Lagoon at Farmington was chosen for the outing, and Davis county did herself proud in entertaining the tottering souls as they were landed at that beautiful summer resort… .

The ride was made in just 50 minutes with not a jar or accident to mar the pleasure of the trip. Arriving at Lagoon, O what a sight was there!

Old Folks' Day that year was just a promise of what was to come at Lagoon, which had opened on Decoration Day in a new and improved version. Lake Park opened in 1886, but in recent years the resort suffered from a receding lake which left behind a sticky, blue mud that was unpleasant for bathers. In 1896 the resort was purchased by Simon Bamburger, who put his money and vision to work. He moved things 2 1/2 miles inland to the banks of a nice lagoon, added an arm of his railroad, and created a lovely setting.

Deseret News files/ James G. Campbell

Utah State Historical Society, Verne Jeffers Collection

# Temple dedication

For 40 years, through the stresses of settling a new country, fighting a battle for statehood, weathering the intrusion of federal troops and otherwise struggling to become established in the Great Basin, Latter-day Saints faithfully plodded on in the construction of a building more important to them than any other — the Salt Lake Temple.

N̄ ow it was done. General excitement characterized Deseret News articles in the week or so preceding the dedication services in April 1893, including a list of assigned times when Salt Lake Saints would attend sessions. Those from outlying areas were given other times during the dedication period, which extended to Sept. 5 to accommodate all who wished to attend:

**DESERET NEWS,** *April 4, 1893: The appointment of Salt Lake Stake, by wards, for admission to the Temple dedication services is given herewith. Should there be any not yet reported who are entitled to be admitted, they will probably be assigned to the morning session of April 19.*

The News also pleaded for help in accommodating the huge crowd of visitors expected for the occasion:

**DESERET NEWS,** *April 8, 1893: In a few days more and thenceforward for a period of several days the number of people requiring subsistence and shelter here will be considerably augmented, exactly how much cannot be told at present, but certainly 50 percent, with the chances in favor of a much greater increase than even that. Have the good people of Salt Lake stopped to think seriously over what this means … Be not backward in receiving within our doors those who require accommodation. This is the proper thing to do.*

A large special edition of the Deseret News prominently featured a rare expensive woodcut reproduction of the finished temple. The newspaper was then using illustrated advertising, but only rarely used art with news articles. The edition hailed the long-awaited dedication, expansively describing the temple and reporting on every possible attendant item related to the ceremonies.

**DESERET NEWS:** *The Loving Labor of Forty Eventful Years is Finished*

A historial descriptive sketch recalled the laying of the cornerstone on April 6, 1853, by President Brigham Young and his counselors. That date and the date of the first of the dedication rites on April 6, 1893, by President Wilford Woodruff were both memorialized, the article said, *"in a beautiful art window of one of its upper rooms, the two inscriptions flanking a large center-piece devoted to an accurate representation of the splendid structure, over whose spires and extending out beyond, appears the motto, 'Holiness to the Lord.'*

An outline of the historic Latter-day Saint devotion to temple building was given, including the temples earlier built and then abandoned in Kirtland, Ohio, and Nauvoo, Ill., as the Latter-day Saints were driven from place to place in the Midwest. The paper quoted then-Apostle Anthon W. Lund, who spoke during the dedication on the necessity to build temples:

*The essential mark of this people is the building of temples, wherein we may receive blessings which cannot be received outside of them.*

Other excerpts from the copious special edition included:

**DESERET NEWS:** *The work of surmounting the capstone with the figure representing the Angel Moroni was proceeded with after the ceremonies. This figure is of gigantic proportions, being twelve feet and a half inches in height. The idea conveyed by the statue is that of a herald, or messenger, in the act of blowing a trumpet, an embodiment of the fact of Moroni bringing the Gospel to the earth in this latter-day dispensation. It is made of 24 hammered copper and was constructed by W.H. Mullens & Co., of Salem, Ohio, after a model by Mr. C.E. Dallin of this city … Its effect is beautiful.*

*President Joseph F. Smith warned the people to be on their guard against*

**Workers on the temple's interior pause for a photograph during final rush to completion.**

*pickpockets and other bad characters who had probably been attracted to this city from other places by the Conference and dedication, "think it a good time to practice their trade among the crowds which would be drawn together on this special occasion."*

*The number of people who attended the ceremonies and who were on the grounds was probably about 40,000, besides many thousands more who crowded the adjoining streets and covered every building in the vicinity from which a view of the interior of the Temple Block could be obtained. The entire scene was imposing, presenting a spectacle that has not been duplicated on this continent in modern times …*

Even non-Mormons joined in observing the occasion. During the month preceding the dedication, the Walker Brothers store, whose proprietors had, ironically, left the church, ran an "IMPORTANT NOTICE":

**DESERET NEWS,** *March 31, 1893: To commemorate the important event of the dedication of the Temple, our Mr. Peifuss will erect a LARGE FACSIMILE OF THE TEMPLE in our handsome windows. This will be composed entirely of goods from our store. It will fill the whole window and you will talk about it for years … We invite every one to walk past the corner of Third and Main Street and see this handsome work.*

The dedication of a temple in Salt Lake City established the city finally and firmly as the center of what would grow to be a worldwide church. By the end of the 20th century, more than a hundred temples were built or planned over the earth, with many more coming, but the dedication of the Salt Lake edifice was a significant milestone, both for the city and the church.

**Ticket for admission to the dedication services was signed by Wilford Woodruff.**

LDS Church Museum

**Crowds gather for the placing of the capstones on the temple. (Line is from crack in glass negative.)**

Utah State Historical Society

# The world of the 1890s
## A TIMELINE

**1890**— The great German leader Bismarck dismissed by Kaiser Wilhelm II.

**1890**— 153 Sioux, half of them women or children, killed at Wounded Knee, S.D. by U.S. Cavalry.

**1890**— Idaho and Wyoming gain statehood.

**1890**— Vincent Van Gogh dies of suicide.

**1890** — Johns Hopkins Hospital in Baltimore uses rubber gloves in surgery.

**1890**— Publication of Emily Dickinson's poems, four years after her death.

**1891**— Paul Gauguin settles in Tahiti to paint.

**1891**— W.L. Judson invents the zipper.

**1892**— Tchaikovsky's "The Nutcracker" ballet first performed in St. Petersburg.

**1892**— Rudolf Diesel patents the first internal combustion engine.

**1893**— Queen Liliuokalani of Hawaii is deposed, and the islands become a republic in 1894.

**1893**— Antonin Dvorak premieres his Symphony No. 5, "From the New World."

**1893**— Karl Benz and Henry Ford build automobiles.

**1894**— Japan and China declare war, with Japan victorious in 1895.

**1894**— Jean Sibelius writes "Finlandia."

**1894**— Auguste Rodin sculpts his monumental "The Burghers of Calais."

**1895**— Wilhelm Roentgen discovers X-rays.

**1895**— Guglielmo Marconi develops radio telegraphy.

**1895**— King C. Gillette perfects the safety razor.

**1896**— Wiliam McKinley elected president of the U.S.

**1896**— First modern Olympics held at Athens.

**1896**— Nobel Prizes established.

**1896**— The first motion pictures are shown by the Lumiere Brothers, Auguste and Louis, and by Thomas Edison.

**1897**— The first American comic strip, "Katzenjammer Kids," begins.

**1897**— The malaria bacillus discovered by Ronald Ross.

**1898**— The U.S. warship Maine blows up in Havana harbor, leading to the Spanish American War.

**1898**— The married scientists Pierre and Marie Curie discover radium and polonium.

**1898**— Britain gains Hong Kong under a 99-year lease.

**1899**— France grants a pardon to Alfred Dreyfus, a Jewish officer accused of treason, whose trial has scandalized the country for five years.

**1899**— The Samoan Islands are divided between the U.S. and Germany.

**1899**— The educator John Dewey writes "School and Society."

# The Tabernacle Choir opens a new era

The choir had been evolving for several decades, from informal groups to the infant Tabernacle choir of the 1870s. (The first true Mormon Tabernacle Choir sang at the LDS general conference of October 1873.) It was now ready for an introduction on a larger scale. The great Chicago World's Fair in September 1893, marking 400 years since the discovery of America, provided the perfect showcase. In late August, Director Evan Stephens and 250 members of the then-350-member group were en route:

**DESERET NEWS,** *Aug. 29, 1893: At 3:10 o'clock this afternoon the largest, happiest and most select excursion party that ever left this Territory pulled out from the Union Pacific Depot. It consists of the Tabernacle choir accompanied by a host of hopeful and enthusiastic friends. Manager Whitney informed a NEWS Representative this afternoon that 408 tickets had been sold, with the prospective disposal of a considerable number more ... Attached to the train will be the splendid car Pickwick kindly and generously placed at the disposal of the First Presidency of the Church. The Pickwick is fresh from the shops and is regarded as one of the most comfortable cars of the kind ever manufactured. It is of walnut and mahogany finish of the rarest workmanship.*

A special News correspondent wired home daily descriptions of the journey east, lauding the performances of the choir at train stops along the way — Denver, Kansas City and St. Louis, where people gathered to hear the Salt Lake contingent.

**DESERET NEWS,** *Sept. 9, 1893: IT WAS UTAH'S DAY. And Right Royally Did She Observe It. Utah contributed her share towards entertaining the World Fair visitors and got her quota of advertising out of the great congress of nations by celebrating the anniversary of her enabling act in Festival Hall today ... curiosity to see the Mormon choir and to see the Mormon leaders drew 3000 or 4000 people together. To these an interesting two hours were given, and if they did not carry away with them enough facts about Utah to fill a volume, it was because they did not have their ears open. The choir was on hand with Radcliffe and Daynes at the great organ.*

The choir aroused a surprising amount of attention among fairgoers. Stephens finally asked his singers not to wear the badges identifying them as being members of the choir as people tended to stop them, and they were late for rehearsals. As the Salt Lake group took its turns in the Eisteddfod (a name given to traditional Welsh singing competitions) the reports by the News correspondent took on a definite biased tone. A choir from Scranton, Pa., had recruited some singers from Cardiff, Wales, to bolster its performances. The News writer — and some others — did not approve:

**DESERET NEWS,** *Sept. 8, 1893: Prevailing Favoritism for Everything Welsh. Yesterday's contralto contest was won by a girl from Wales, although the Utah party*

In 1893, members of the Mormon Tabernacle Choir prepare to leave for Chicago's World's Fair.

*think Bessie Dean Allison would have had an excellent chance had she entered. The absence of Welsh blood in her veins, however, might have operated against her.*

In the final sing-off, competition was so close between the Pennsylvania choir and the Tabernacle contingent that there was a general feeling that the first and second prizes would be combined and divided between them. Instead, the judges favored the Scranton singers.

**DESERET NEWS,** *Sept. 9, 1893: The big contest is over, the painfully awaited verdict is announced and tonight the Salt Lake choir starts for home with the second prize of one thousand dollars in their luggage and a laurel wreath worth many times more than that on their brow.*

Despite the temporary disappointment, the choir was welcomed home in the wee hours of Sept. 13. In an interview, Stephens expanded on the experience:

**DESERET NEWS:** *Sept. 13, 1893: On the whole, it was a glorious trip for all of us ... Everywhere I turned, the kindly, cheering smile of my singers greeted me ... Each choir, I have reason to believe, did the very best work they were capable of doing. I am certain mine did. Never have they tried harder or more effectually to excel ...*

# The first
# Woman
# senator

**The advent of statehood primed the political pump in the last elections of the 19th century. Many wanted to be the first to represent their peers in the new government bodies that were created when Utah was accepted into the Union.**

**T**he state election returns in the fall of 1896 were full of surprises. Three women were elected to the Utah Legislature, including a state senator, Martha Hughes Cannon, who was the first of her gender to hold such office not only in Utah but throughout the United States. Elected to the Utah House were Eurithe K. LaBarthe and Martha M. Campbell.

In a fascinating twist, Cannon, a physician and long-time supporter of women's suffrage, challenged and beat her husband, Angus, to win the Senate seat.

The Deseret News began weeks before the election to push voters, particularly women, to do their civic duty. The newspaper outlined an ideal Legislature and told voters:

*DESERET NEWS, Oct. 26, 1896: Utah needs a Legislature that will direct its labors for the good of the whole State, of all its*

Martha Hughes Cannon, shown here in later years, was the first woman in the country to serve as a state senator.

*Utah State Historical Society*

*industries and all classes of its people and that will do so upon the broad basis of well developed principles as they have been proved to be of force and applicability in the settlement and development of this region. It is for the voters of Utah to provide themselves with such a Legislature.*

The News did not get into the Cannon-Cannon debate, but other local papers were not so circumspect. The Tribune offered this advice to Angus: *"We do not see anything for Angus M. to do but to either go home and break a bouquet over Mrs. Cannon's head to show his superiority, or to go up to the Herald office and break a chair over the head of the man who wrote that disturber of public peace."* The reference was to a Herald article proclaiming Martha the superior candidate.

While taking no special notice of the success of female candidates, the Deseret News

did note that the majority of those who cast ballots in the 1896 election were women. In Salt Lake City, of 17,631 registered voters, 9,035 were women.

***DESERET NEWS,*** *Nov. 8, 1896: The women's vote was fully as large in proportion to that of the men, if in fact, it was not larger. Ladies were first at the polls … Women put the cross up by the rooster (the symbol of the victorious Democratic People's Party) and let it go at that.*

As a state senator, Cannon was successful in promoting many health and education issues. She sponsored legislation for education of mute, deaf and blind children; another bill creating the state Board of Health; and yet another requiring employers to be considerate of the health of their female workers (such as providing stools for them to sit on when not occupied with work.) In modern times, she was honored with her name on the new State Health Department building.

If the 1896 elections were tense, they were totally eclipsed by the 1899 go-round, when Utah's Legislature cast 164 ballots and couldn't muster the requisite 32 votes to sanction a candidate for the U.S. Senate. For two years, Joseph L. Rawlins was the sole Utahn in the body.

In addition, Congress refused in 1899 to seat duly-elected B.H. Roberts in the House because of his background as a polygamist. It was an era of intense political rivalry that paved the way for later eminent Utah congressmen who served long and well.

**LEGISLATIVE TICKET.**

**For State Senators—Sixth District.**
**[Vote for Five.]**

| | | |
|---|---|---|
| Angus M. Cannon | Independent Republican, Republican. | |
| John T. Caine | | 8054 |
| Martha H. Cannon | Democrat, People's Party. | |
| John S. Daveler | Democrat, People's... | 11686 |

# DESERET EVENING NEWS.

TRUTH AND LIBERTY.

April 15, 1890

## PAVING ORDINANCE PASSED.

The ordinance "levying the tax and for the assessment of property on both sides of State Street, from the south line of South Temple Street to the north line of Fourth South Street, for the purpose of paving said street," was taken up and passed...

The estimated cost of the improvement is $87,150, and the tax levied against the abutting property is $16.50 1/2 per front foot, and the assessor is instructed to levy the assessment. One-tenth of the total amount levied against each lot becomes delinquent within fifty days from the approval of the ordinances, and one-tenth each year thereafter until paid up.

The ordinance levying the tax and for the assessment of property on both sides of State Street, from South Temple to Fourth South, for the purpose of curbing and guttering said street, was then taken up and passed. The estimated cost of the improvement is $11,176, or $2.12 per front foot on the abutting property. The tax is to be paid in the same way as for paving.

Oct. 10, 1890

## THE PLANET MARS.

### Professor Pickering has Observed a Snow Storm on that Heavenly Body.

### ASTRONOMICAL OBSERVATIONS.

BOSTON, October 9 — Professor W. H. Pickering of Harvard College has for something like a year been devoting a great portion of his time to observations of the planet Mars...

"On the second occasion we found that THE WHITE SPACE in the southern hemisphere had increased during the twenty-four hours by an area nearly as large as the United States so, you see, if this white appearance is due to snow, there must have been a tremendous storm in Southern Mars on the 10th of April." Professor Pickering remarked in answer to a question about the northern hemisphere, that the southern half of the planet was far more interesting. It is that section where the dark places are located which are supposed to be water. The planet, in his opinion, being older than the earth, as well as smaller, has passed the stage in which the earth now is, and is approaching the condition of the moon, in other words is dying.

April 2, 1891

## A TYPEWRITER AT LAST

County Attorney Murphy, who has so frequently applied for authority to procure the services of a stenographer and type-writer at the expense of the county, was given permission to do so.

Feb. 17, 1893

## ARTICLES OF AGREEMENT

### Whereby the Islands Are to be Made a Part of the Republic

Washington, D.C. Feb. 10. — The preamble to the treaty declares that the government of the United States and the provisional government of Hawaii, in view of the natural dependence of those islands upon the United States, their geographical proximity, the intimate part taken by citizens of the United States in implanting Christian civilization... have determined to accomplish by treaty the object so important to their permanent welfare, and to this end confer full power upon their respective plenipotentiaries, who are agreed upon in the treaty.

In article I the government of Hawaii cedes, from the date of the exchange of ratification, to the United States absolutely all rights of sovereignty of whatsoever kind in and over the Hawaiian Islands and their dependencies, such islands henceforth to be an integral part of the territory of the United States...

March 12, 1893

### Attempt to Reach the Mysterious Region by Balloon.

STOCKHOLM, Feb. 28. (Special)—Chief Engineer S.S. Andree, the bold Swedish Aeronaut, has made up his mind to reach the North Pole by means of a balloon. If all arrangements can be finished in time the journey will be undertaken already this summer; in contrary case not before the summer of 1896.

April 1, 1893

## TRAGEDY AT EUREKA

### The Course of Striking Union Miners Bears Bloody Fruit.

Blood has been shed at Eureka. Hyrum S. Hyde, an employee at the Bullion-Beck mine, now lies at Eureka, suffering from a gunshot wound that is likely to prove fatal. His injury was inflicted in an affray with two striking union miners, Bat Sullivan and Albert Collins, who are themselves slightly wounded.

Last evening young Hyde was at the lower end of town, not far from the mine, when a quarrel ensued between him and Sullivan and Collins. Just how it began could not be ascertained from Eureka today, though it grew out of the feeling exhibited by the union miners against the non-union employees at the mine...

Sept. 6, 1893

## A SPENDTHRIFT SPIRIT

An example of the recklessness that has prevailed in the expenditure of funds taken from the city treasury during the present administration is set forth by the records of the council and street department, which show that two or three months ago the City Council ordered certain grading, by resolution, to be done at the intersection of First South and Thirteenth East streets, at a cost not to exceed $400. The matter was referred to Street Supervisor Hines, who was instructed to proceed with the work at once...

The work has been completed and at a cost of more than $3000. One councilman says that the amount will reach nearly if not quite $5000... There is no getting around the fact that Mr. Hines had spent at least $2600 of the city's money without authority.

Sept. 11, 1893

## A STRANGE VISITOR.

### A Mammoth Eagle Takes Up a Temporary Resting Place on the Temple.

Shortly after day-break this morning a large bird was observed perched on one of the west towers of the Temple, and there it remained until the bright rays of the sun shot over the peaks of the Wasatch and flooded the valley with light, when it flew to the eastern part of the building and circling about the central tower finally alighted on the crown of the statue of the angel Moroni. It was now discovered by the aid of a strong field glass belonging to Professor C.J. Thomas that the strange visitor was a magnificent eagle of the Golden Species...

A couple of Temple attaches ascended the tower as far as they were able to in order to get a plain, close-range view of his Imperial Eagleship, but the latter objected to such curiosity as being an uncalled interruption and accordingly ruffled his feathers, spread his wings and left his temporary resting place, flying over the city towards the southeast, presumably for his aerial home among the crags and peaks of the Wasatch.

March 12, 1895

## CARD FROM THE FIRST PRESIDENCY

Salt Lake City, Jan 25, 1895. Notice is hereby given that contributions to the monument to be erected in Salt Lake City in memory of Brigham Young and the pioneers will hereafter, and until further notice, be acknowledged through the columns of the DESERET NEWS...

We earnestly hope that the people will respond generously and promptly to this call so that if possible the monument may be completed, dedicated and unveiled to the public by the 6th day of next October

WILFORD WOODRUFF,
GEORGE Q. CANNON,
JOSEPH F. SMITH

March 28, 1895

## SPEAKS FOR THE RIGHT

Prof. C.A. Whiting, of the University of Utah, sends in the following:

EDITOR NEWS: As a citizen and educator thoroughly interested in the mental, moral, and physical development of the rising generation in Utah, I wish to enter a most vigorous protest against the present attempt to flood our Territory with cigarettes...

This is not the time or place to urge the evils arising from the tobacco habit, but I know of no competent authority who does not admit that disastrous results to boys arise from the use of tobacco.

Oct. 12, 1896

This week, the tomato canning department of the factory at West Bountiful will be shut down, as the cold weather closes the season for the tomato crop. Most of the (workers) are girls, since it does not require great physical exertion. A clever girl makes good wages at it too, during the season. For instance, in Saturday's run, when over 10,000 cans of tomatoes were put up, two of the young ladies made $1.77 1/2 each. This was the highest record of the day, working from 8 a.m. to 6 p.m.

Oct. 22, 1896

## MORE COLORED TROOPS COME

This afternoon witnessed the arrival in this city of the second squad of colored Federal troops. They were companies D, E and G of the Fort Bayard detachment of the Twenty-fourth infantry.

They came in on the Union Pacific between 2 and 8

o'clock and soon afterwards marched to Fort Douglas, where in the dispensation of army life they will be stationed for some time to come. Four other companies are scheduled to arrive here this evening. They too will immediately repair to the post and thus complete the regiment.

---

**Oct. 30, 1896**

Last Friday Mrs. Dickinson, a woman well known in the vicinity of Mount Angel, Oregon, after suffering from a severe illness, was supposed to have died … The announcement of the funeral had been made for last Sunday, to take place at the Catholic church at Mount Angels… After the home services, the undertaker, in placing the lid on the casket, had his attention attracted to the body. Whether by the effort to replace the lid or in some other manner, by a slight jar of the casket, at any rate, the spell was broken, for Mrs. Dickinson suddenly came to life, awakened from a trance, and the house of mourning was quickly transformed into a house of joy. The woman was speedily removed from the casket, within which she narrowly escaped being buried alive, and today is enjoying comparatively good health …

**April 21, 1897**

## COUNCIL MEETING

The sanitary inspector asked permission to employ a detective at $60 per month for one month to arrest parties guilty of violating the ordinances relating to the disposition of garbage. Referred to sanitary committee.

**April 30, 1898**

### Looking For a Nickname

Chicago baseball cranks are endeavoring to find a new nickname for their team in view of the fact that the club has decided to discard the title of Colts. Somebody has suggested Burnsides, in honor of the new manager, Tommy Burns, and it looks like a go. The idea of nicknaming ball teams is not a new one, as every team in the National league labors under some alleged pet name. Many of the teams are inappropriately named, however. To call the Brooklyns the Bridegrooms nowadays is enough to drive a rabid crank to a country retreat where he will never hear of baseball again.

### The New Coiffure.

The present season sees a new form of the ever popular pompadour coiffure. The hair is waved and mounted over a light cushion, or where the hair is very thin a set of false waves is put upon the head just over the forehead. With the new pompadour style of putting up the hair, partings have been done away with, for the waves are drawn straight back from the forehead. It is quite a simple fashion and any

ingenious woman after studying the illustration ought to be able to put up her own hair in this manner. The fluffier the waves the prettier the effect.

**May 19, 1898**

## LAST WORD SPOKEN

### Fervent "Amen" Uttered by England's Grand Old Man.

#### THE END CAME QUIETLY.

London, May 19.—The deepest manifestations of grief are seen throughout the country. Flags are half masted, the bells are tolling, shades are down and public galleries have the pictures of Mr. Gladstone draped with crepe.

The queen and the prince of Wales received an early intimation of the sad news and immediately sent touching expressions of condolence to the widow.

**(Report on the death of the statesman and prime minister William Gladstone.)**

**May 26, 1898**

FOR DINNER, 12 to 3, 15c, YOU GET soup, 2 meats, vegetables, tea or coffee, pie and pudding at Kimball Block Restaurant. 71 West First South.

---

LADIES CAN EARN $8 WEEKLY DOING needle work at home: no canvassing. Inclose self-addressed envelope for reply. Standard Novelty Co., 101 Beekman street, New York.

**May 28, 1898**

## VENGEANCE WAS SWIFT.

The quiet little city of Springville, Utah county, was the scene of the greatest excitement and sensation in its history today. The commotion was caused by the robbing of the Springville bank by two alleged members of the Butch Cassidy Robbers' Roost, Hole-in-the-Wall gang, and the subsequent capture of one them and the killing of the other. The men were both desperadoes of the most dangerous and daring

character, and at least one of them, I. Maxwell, had a price of $500 upon his head, placed there by Governor Wells recently, when the executive offered rewards for a dozen outlaws who have been preying upon the people of southeastern Utah for the past few years…

**May 31, 1898**

### Baby Carriages vs Bicycles.

Logan Journal: A well known young lady of the city, who has been extremely unfortunate of late in being mixed up in bicycle accidents, was going down Second street Thursday evening on her wheel, when she encountered two ladies who were trundling baby carriages in front of them, and consequently occupied nearly the entire width of the sidewalk. In trying to get around them the fair bicyclist was crowded into the ditch and the way she shot off her wheel into the water, reminded one of a boy diving after pennies in a pond. A nasty gash was inflicted upon her leg just below the knee, and she was badly shaken up. The two ladies who were the cause of the accident could not refrain from laughing at the unfortunate young lady's predicament, and as a consequence they received a most vigorous tongue-lashing from the injured damsel.

**June 21, 1898**

## LOST!

### $50 REWARD. $50

The foreman of our Baking Powder department, while overseeing the mixing of a batch of Saltair Baking Powder, lost a diamond stud, size 2 1-8 carats set in a combination for pin or stud. The diamond is a pure, white stone. It was presented to our foreman by his New York employers in recognition of his ability as a manufacturer of baking powder. We will pay the above sum in gold to any person returning same with the can of Saltair Baking Powder in which the diamond was found to our office room 46 O'Meara Building.
SALTAIR BAKING POWDER CO.,
Manufacturers of the celebrated Saltair Superior Baking Powder.
OFFICE, 46 O'MEARA BUILDING,
SALT LAKE CITY, UTAH.
Telephone 46-2 rings.
P.S.—Please call your friends attention to the above notice

**July 1, 1899**

### The Great Kraenzlein to Compete.

Far greater interest is being taken this year in the forthcoming competition for the all around individual championship of America than has been exhibited for some years past. There are two reasons for this, one being the greater activity that is being displayed this season in sports of all kinds, and secondly, because Kraenzlein, the great athlete from the University of Pennsylvania, will be a competitor. This young man is by all odds the finest athlete now in training.

**July 13, 1899**

## THE UNIVERSITY BUILDING PLANS

### The Four Buildings Which Will Form a Nucleus–Normal, Library, Museum and Physical Science.

The Great Kraenzlein

A meeting will be held next Wednesday night at which the plans now under consideration for the construction of the new University Buildings will be completed, after which work upon Utah's greatest educational institution will be at once commenced.

Since the appropriation was made for the building, plans for its construction have been receiving the careful thought and consideration due to the subject, and yesterday afternoon the board of regents of the University met to discuss and consider together the plans upon which the general features of the institution will be based, these plans including the laying out of the grounds, as well as the construction of the buildings.

The general outline agreed upon was that four buildings should form the beginning, or nucleus of the University structure, these to consist of the library, museum, normal and physical buildings. Each of these will be built of brick and native stone, with the roofs, and will be three stories high, the buildings to correspond in general design, while varying in essential details. The plan for each is far from ornate, but dignified and imposing.

**August 18, 1899**

… "Permit me to suggest that each board of trustees and each teacher in the county should secure and study the statutes relating to the control of contagious disease; since they become liable to prosecution for the admission of pupils or others from infected homes, to the schools or otherwise encouraging the spread of disease…

Will you kindly see that the school houses in all

infected localities are disinfected according to the following rules:

1. Brush off all ceilings, walls and furniture and sweep all floors.

2. Mop all floors and furniture with a solution of bichloride of mercury (one to one thousand). Chairs may well be immersed in a barrel of the solution. Polished wood work should be immediately wiped dry. (The bichloride of mercury can be bought in tablet at any drug store. Sixteen of the large tablets to an eight quart pail of water gives the required strength.)

3. Each room must next be disinfected with formaldehyde gas. (This requires an experienced man and special apparatus). Reasonable rates can be made with Druehl and Franken or Schramm Drug Co., or at similar rates a man will be sent out from the office of the county physician

Yours respectfully,
OSCAR VAN COTT,
County Superintendent,

# Saltair
## The glory of the lake

The lake that gave Salt Lake City its name was a source of endless fascination and recreation for early settlers. Only three days after arriving in the valley, church leaders went for a swim in the lake. Wilford Woodruff noted in his journal that "No person Could Possibly sink in it." The lake, he wrote, "ought to be added as the eighth wonder of the world."

Turn-of-the-century photo showed two lieutenants and their companions at the new Saltair.

The arrival of the railroad added a new dimension to lakeside recreation, as tracks of the Central Pacific and the Utah Western railroads ran close to the shore and cut the commute from a four-hour buggy ride to one hour by train. Resorts were built at Lake Side, Lake Point and at Garfield and Black Rock beaches.

But it was with a great deal of interest that readers picked up the paper in early January of 1893 to learn that a new bathing resort was in the works, to be built by the LDS Church. Noting that a new rail line would take bathers to Saltair "in Twenty Minutes and Back in Sixteen," the story went on to provide "A Detailed Description of its Magnificent and Costly Buildings" which had been designed by Richard Kletting:

**DESERET NEWS,** Jan. 14, 1893:
Utah in general and Salt Lake in particular have long offered innumerable attractions to tourists… . What her people do is usually done well, and in no one thing can this truth be more correctly or appropriately applied than to their erection of buildings which are not only often original and novel in architectural design but the administration of all whose pleasure it is to see them.

In this respect, Utah will soon have added another laurel to the many she has already won…

Noting that "Bathing in the surf in America's Dead Sea has already become world renowned," the article added that nothing like the resort that would open on "Decoration Day in May next" had ever been seen before:

The pavilion is a magnificent piece of architectural work, and with the approach and bath houses will cost $200,000 and will contain 2,000,000 feet of lumber…

While an entirely new and original style of arrangement and architecture seems to have been attempted so far as interior work goes the structure from without will have a decidedly mosque like appearance.

Every detail had been carefully thought out, even the disposition of sewage. General Manager Isaac A. Clayton noted: "We realized that we could not allow it to go into the lake, as that would ruin our bathing business. The water will be kept perfectly clear and pure, and every drop and pound of sewage and other refuse will be conveyed ashore by a private sewer system and conducted inland on our own property for a distance of two miles where it will be utilized for fertilizing purposes. So you see the public need not be alarmed on that score."

Construction proceeded apace.

**DESERET NEWS,** May 12, 1893:
Gradually order, wonder and beauty have been brought about over a 'chaotic, wilderness of water' a Saltair of late until today a most bewildering and magnificent scene presents itself at the Coney Island of the West.

Saltair opened as planned on Decoration Day, but the official grand opening ceremonies were not held until later.

**DESERET NEWS,** June 8, 1893: The formal opening of Saltair, the greatest bathing resort in the known world, occurred today under the most auspicious circumstances… . Music, dancing and speech-making were in progress this afternoon…

The next day, a glowing editorial again praised the resort.

**DESERET NEWS,** June 9, 1893: Of the vast host of people who yesterday

Mrs. Geneve Oliver, Deseret News files

visited the new health and pleasure resort on the shore of the Great Salt Lake, we venture to say nine out of every ten beheld a structure immeasurably larger and finer and more complete and perfect in all its appointments than their wildest imagination had pictured. The magnificent pavilion rising, Venice-like, out of the waves in stupendous and graceful beauty, deepened in its semi-Moorish architectural lines the suspicion that what one saw was not firm structural reality but rather a delightful oriental dream.

From the beginning, Saltair proved to be all that designers and builders hoped it would be, providing not only a place to swim, but also music, dancing, entertainment, bike racing, a giant roller coaster and more. The Flying Grigolatis; Lulu Beeson, the best dancer in the world; the Juggling Normans appeared. Orville and Wilbur Wright demonstrated their "heavier than air" machine by flying 80 feet above the ground. The Big Band era brought Artie Shaw, Glen Miller, Sammy Kay and Les Brown.

The church sold the resort to private

interests in 1925. By then its golden age had passed. But it managed to hang on, surviving fires and wind storms until 1959, when the declining resort was given to the state of Utah. Officials decided to close it. After years of abandon and neglect, what was left burned to the ground in 1970.

But those glory years were never to be forgotten, and periodic reminiscences would find their way into print:

**DESERET NEWS:** *It was the dances that I remember most. You'd take your girl out to Saltair and dance the first and last dances with her. The crowds were big and friendly then… . I remember one time when a 90-mile wind whipped across the lake and knocked the lights out at Saltair. The only light we had was the one on the front of the train, but the musicians didn't stop playing and we didn't stop dancing. — Pete Rock, Deseret News, May 20, 1961.*

*I remember when people on weekends would send youngsters out by train at 6 a.m. to reserve bowery space for the family later in the day. — Art Teece, Deseret News, Oct. 21, 1964.*

*The navy blue and black 'brilliantine' bathing suits, which we rented for*

twenty-five cents, had bloomers that came to our knees… . We wore bathing caps made of a rubber material that would almost float us if we got salt water under them. The mens' suits were modest knee length and their chests had to be covered. — Allie H. Packer, Deseret News, June 28, 1975.

*Those of us who lived the last years of Saltair still relish it the way New Englanders breathe in the smell of burning leaves in autumn. To us it means racing for the open-air car of the train that went out to Saltair, riding in the Giant Racer and screaming all the way, and dancing to Harry James and Louis Armstrong as the waves lapped at the pilings under the biggest outdoor dance floor in the world. And now, years after the grand Lady of the Lake burned to the ground, new folks or visitors smell that lake wind and say, "What is that strange sour smell?" We 'old timers' lick our lips, trying for a taste of salt, that stupid, pecky salt, and maybe trying, too, for a taste of our childhoods. — Terrell Dougan, Deseret News, July 14, 1975.*

*I remember celebrating my sixth birthday at Saltair in 1908. Of course, I had*

**Salt Lake, Garfield and Western Railroad trains unload their passengers at Saltair Resort.**

been there many times before. My family loved picnics and picnics had a special flavor at Saltair. Food tasted better because everyone was hungry after bathing in the lake. The lapping of the lake under the pavilion supplied a soothing kind of music. The golden sunset, with the sun a huge ball of fire dipping from sight on the distant lake shore, leaving a beckoning path of gold across the blue lake, was a picture never to be forgotten, even to a growing child. — Gertrude Lobrot, Deseret News, Sept. 3, 1982.

**Swimmers float in the salt in this photograph from the 1920s.**

**Its unusual Moorish-style architecture gave Saltair an imposing look. It was built upon pillars driven into the lake.**

# Remembering the
# Maine

**America's conflict with Spain over the possession of Cuba and the Philippine Islands, coming two years after Utah statehood, offered Utahns their first opportunity to serve the country of which they were now full-fledged citizens.**

Theodore Roosevelt led the "Rough Riders" in the Spanish-American War and returned a hero.

UPI Photo

Utah State Historical Society/National Archives

Utah artillery battery is in action near Chinese Church, the Philippines, in 1899.

**A**t the top levels, there was debate in Utah over how and how much the state should support the war. Utah's long fight to achieve statehood left some festering resentments and some of the state's die-hards remembered that in the 1850s, they were themselves the target of federal troops in the shape of Johnston's Army.

But as one of the sister states it was harder for Utah to resist the call to arms. In fact, Utah Sen. Frank J. Cannon was at the forefront of the movement in Washington to force war with Spain, even though many of Utah's leaders back home were urging restraint. The sinking of the battleship Maine in 1898 generated a groundswell of patriotism that was irresistible, even in the Beehive State. Utah enthusiastically joined the war effort:

**DESERET NEWS,** *May 27, 1898: The war spirit appears to be on the increase in Salt Lake. Men are so anxious to go to the front that they now as willingly accept enlistment in the regular service as with the Volunteers … Until a few days ago, a great preference was shown for volunteer enlistment, but when candidates for soldiers' honor presented themselves only to find the quota filled, they went away and began to think. The more war news that came and the more they thought, the more convinced they became that if they couldn't go with the volunteers, they would go with the regulars …*

In an accompanying editorial, the News encouraged men to sign up:

**DESERET NEWS:** *If the men of Utah who have shown an enthusiastic desire to serve their country will take the steps necessary to come to an understanding and to act in concert, it*

*will be an easy matter to make this the first of all the states to furnish its quota of the new call for volunteers. The number this state will be required to supply is 255, and it is conservative to say that twice that many of her citizens are anxious to enlist… It would be a credit to the youngest state in the Union to say that in a single day she enrolled her quota of recruits under the President's second call for volunteers …*

The departure of the main body of Utah's troops in May was the occasion for a spirited celebration:

**DESERET NEWS,** *May 20, 1898: GRAND PUBLIC DEMONSTRATION IN BEHALF OF THE BRAVE BOYS WHO, ANSWERING THEIR COUNTRY'S CALL, CHEERFULLY LEAVE.*

*Two more of Utah's Volunteer army organizations have said farewell to home and kindred and taken their departure for the field of duty … They left this city over the Rio Grande Western this afternoon for Ogden, where their train will be switched on to the Southern Pacific and whirled over desert and mountain to San Francisco, preparatory to embarking for*

*the Philippines to give succor and relief to brave Admiral Dewey and the gallant blue jackets who helped him to win the glorious battle of Manila Bay.*

*The scenes attendant upon the departure were such as to stir the hearts of the most phlegmatic and arouse to patriotic thought and action those who have heretofore looked upon war with undisturbed equanimity … It is conservatively estimated that not less than three fourths of the city's population was crowded into the business district to witness the state's noble Volunteers make their march to the trains …*

The News devoted considerable space to the war throughout the next year, particularly following the fate of the Utah warriors. They sailed on the Colon for the Philippines, pulling into Manila Bay July 17. On Aug. 13, Spain conceded defeat. But the civil conflict among the Filipinos kept the Utah soldiers busy for almost a year longer. Armed with some of the latest equipment available, provided initially for the Utah Guard shortly before the war broke out, they were a valued unit. For a time, they were the sole artillery support for a division headed by Gen. Arthur

MacArthur (father of Douglas). During their Philippines sojourn, the Utahns recorded 56 major encounters, 53 of them against the Filipino insurgents.

Letters home, many of them published by the newspaper, kept Utahns abreast of the conflict. In May 1899, Richard W. Young, head of the Utah troops, wrote: *"I have not slept without my trousers, shoes and stockings on more than once since the fracas started … Personally, I have been in 25 engagements, besides being under fire numerous other times when we were not replying. We have had 11 men die — eight killed and three of natural deaths, and have had 17 or 18 wounded. Our boys have taken our guns, all exposed, up to within even 60 yards of entrenched (enemy.)"* At the end of the conflict, Young stayed in the Philippines as the appointed chief justice of the newly organized Philippine Supreme Court.

In June 1899, as the war wound down, the Utah battalion prepared to return home. For weeks, the impending arrival was anticipated:

**DESERET NEWS,** *June 20, 1899: WASHINGTON, D.C. — Gen. Otis cables that the Utah regiments are now taking the transports to return home … The tidings were gladly received (at the state offices) as they were by those who crowded the sidewalk in front of the News office to read the bulletins on which the joyous information was portrayed. Secretary Hammond was asked as to what, in his opinion, should be done toward giving the boys a welcome on their arrival. He replied that he could not say at this time beyond that "their reception should be most royal."*

While the soldiers wended their way home, preparations were indeed made for a royal welcome. The state had special silver medals struck for its heroes. The Deseret News had a beautiful portfolio "in high art style" printed in San Francisco. It recounted the history of the war and featured the achievement of the Utah batteries, along with a complete roster of the volunteers from Utah, Idaho and Wyoming. Price: 30 cents. On the actual day, the city provided a gala welcome home:

**DESERET NEWS,** *Aug. 19, 1899: Fifteen months to the day after leaving Salt Lake to ship for war service in a land 10,000 miles over the seas, the Utah volunteers re-entered their homes. It was a perfect delirium of greeting, a frenzy of popular enthusiasm; the town turned itself topsy turvy with delight over its heroes and probably while life lasts, they will not forget the whole-souled nature of that welcome home… Main*

*Street sidewalks early became almost impassable; South Temple, leading to the Short Line depot, was a solid block of humanity for almost the entire distance, and around the depot itself, it looked as though half the population of the city was struggling to get into the yard.*

Earlier, the soldiers had been feted wildly in Ogden as the train passed through, the News reported:

*… the soldier boys steamed into town amid a shout of welcome that rose upon the sunny morn … One or two of the men could not resist the temptation of jumping out (of the train) and clasping their loved ones to their breasts. Sergeant Alford Ellis was among the first to reach terra firma with a couple of monkeys in his arms; he dropped his pets and the next instant he was kissing his father and brother with an abandon that put his "sparking days" to shame …*

Participation in a national crisis had cemented Utah's sisterhood with the Union and done much to erase barriers that had kept others aloof.

Welcome home parade for Utah troops featured a great arch at Second South and Main streets on August 19, 1899.

*Utah State Historical Society, C.R. Savage Photo*

The battleship Maine lies sunken in the waters of Havana, below. At left, pen and ink drawings illustrated the war for readers.

*UPI Photo*

U.S. troops march into Havana on Aug. 12, 1898, at end of the war.

*UPI Photo*

PICKET DUTY IN THE RAIN

CAPTURING A SPY

GLIMPSE

# The Park City
# Fire

Utah State Historical Society

**Firemen struggle to put out the remnants of the Park City fire that leveled the town in 1898.**

Utah State Historical Society

**A Miner's Union parade in Park City shows the town before the fire.**

**"DESTROYED! Park City Practically Wiped Out by a Raging Conflagration,"** the headline blared. The worst fire in Utah's history to that date left a scene of ruin and despair, with a loss conservatively estimated at over a million dollars.

The fire started on a Sunday morning during the lethargy following a payday night of revelry. Sheriff Thomas Walden immediately fired the three shots that signaled a fire, but things were already out of hand:

**DESERET NEWS,** *June 20, 1898: Park City, Utah's proud and prosperous mining camp, has practically been wiped out of existence, being visited yesterday by the most disastrous conflagration in the history of Utah. It may be that the city will be rebuilt and rise again from the ruins that now cover the canyon where it once stood, but it will be years before it can fully recover — if recovery is at all possible…*

*Not less than five hundred persons are homeless and destitute. They must have assistance at once, otherwise they will suffer greatly. The distressing plight in which so many are placed is the result of*

*a fire that had a very small beginning, but which cut a very wide swath as it went forth by leaps and bounds on its mission of destruction.*

*The fire originated in the Freeman or American House about 4 o'clock yesterday morning. The announcement of its discovery was made by an excited Chinaman. A general alarm was sounded from the Marasac mill. But before there could be any effective response, the hotel was completely enveloped and doomed to swift and certain destruction, as well as all contiguous buildings. There was no time for the removal of goods from stores, money from places of deposit, books and papers from shelves or safes, horses from barns — scarcely time to save human beings from being cremated alive. Everything was licked by the flames as they swept up and down the canyon, which resembled a great fiery furnace which illuminated the heavens in all directions.*

The Park City firefighters, whose four fire hoses had little effect on the blaze, appealed to the fire departments of Salt Lake, Coalville and Ogden. Special trains were commissioned to get additional fire department men and equipment to the burning town. Hundreds of volunteers did what they could while burned-out buildings collapsed behind them.

Some of them were still telling their stories years later. Fred Jennings reported being almost knocked over by a piano that tumbled from a saloon. His sense of humor still intact, he stopped fighting the fire long enough to play "There'll Be a Hot Time in the Old Town Tonight." Another story that was told and retold involved a Doctor LeCompte who lost his trousers when a spark set them on fire.

He tossed them into the flames and continued to work in a borrowed pair.

**DESERET NEWS,** *It is impossible to go into detailed description of the consuming conflagration. It spread so rapidly through the business district into the residence portion of the city as to make all efforts to extinguish it futile. There was only one thing to do and that was to resort to dynamite in blowing up houses in order to cut off the material upon which the flames were feeding. This was done to good effect, however.*

As the fire raged unimpeded, officials of the Marasac mill finally gave permission to breach the huge wooden flume that carried water to the mill from the mine situated on the hill above. Water rushed down the canyon to douse the flames. By noon, the fire was contained.

The News then listed a column of businesses that had suffered losses. Park City officials proudly asserted that they would rebuild without help from anyone, but other Utah communities rallied to provide aid. Salt Lake City donated $2,500, and Mount Pleasant chipped in $102.40. Many private citizens, churches and other organizations provided money or volunteer assistance.

Many newspapers around the country reported on the disaster, some giving it priority over the Spanish American War. The Deseret News left the war on the first page and dealt with the fire on the second. Some Park City residents looked at the rubble, threw up their hands and moved on, but others stayed to rebuild a new, more mature, less flamboyant Park City over the ashes of the disaster.

Move over, electric lights and telephone. A new love has captured the imagination of America's fickle public — the automobile. The dawning of a new century heralded the advent of a nation on wheels. Going farther, going faster and going fashionably was a national mania.

**T**he phenomenon actually began to take root as the 19th century slipped into history.

Deseret News women's writer Daisy Mae (Fashion's Fads and Foibles Airily Discussed daily) predicted:

**DESERET NEWS,** *July 15, 1899: There is no question in my mind that the Auto Girl is a worthy end-of-the-century institution, but she will never be so numerous as the Bicycle Girl and the Golf Girl. It costs money, and lots of it, to follow the new craze …*

Cost? Piffle! As an article concerning the great trek across the country noted:

**DESERET NEWS,** *July 18, 1899: As to the cost of the automobile as compared to that of a horse, Mr. A.S. Winslow of the National Motor Carriage company finds, the latter is the more expensive of the two. The automotor, he says, will cost for five years, including the first expense of $1,000 for the vehicle, $2,306.50, while the horse and carriage will cost during the same time $2,780. Still, the automotor is as yet too expensive to become popular for private use. It will probably become cheaper… With the cost reduced, what was at first an expensive plaything will undoubtedly become a general necessity.*

The gasoline engine was perfected to offset some of the obvious problems of electric and steam power:

**DESERET NEWS,** *Dec. 12, 1903: The necessity for a motor independent of the unreliable wind, the inaccessible water, the unavailable skill and the expensive and dangerous steam … was the mother of the invention of the gasoline engine… The evolution of the machine from an imperfect and complex aggregation of parts acting more or less out of harmony with each other, to its present simple and harmonious proportions and efficient and reliable action is truly wonderful…*

The novelty arrived in Utah as the new century took hold, and a spin in a horseless carriage gained bragging rights for local residents:

**DESERET NEWS,** *May 16, 1900: (LDS Church) President Lorenzo Snow enjoyed an exhilarating ride yesterday afternoon on Mr. Hyrum Silver's automobile, with Mr. Silver at the helm. Like many other prominent Salt Lakers who have enjoyed a whirl over the city with the Silver brothers the last ten days, President Snow pronounced the ride as being particularly fine and an indication of the possibilities of latter-day locomotion.*

Not everyone was agog at the new contraption:

**DESERET NEWS,** *Dec. 12, 1903: BUCKBOARD GONE WRONG A party of business men in the office of Henry Clews were discussing the automobile while the stocks went tumbling. The banker took part in the conversation to recall a recent incident at Newport. While one of the elderly natives was inspecting one of the newer forms of a motor, which stood at the curb, Mr. Clews asked: "Well, what would you call it?"*

*"That," replied the old man solemnly, "is the late lamented buckboard, died and gone to eternal punishment."*

*–Philadelphia Ledger*

One of Utah's first flivvers was homemade. Although the Deseret News did not take immediate note, a later article written by John Devey of Lehi, including photos, recounts the history:

**DESERET NEWS,** *April 23, 1921: Dear Editor:*
*I saw in the Deseret News a few days ago that*

Utah State Historical Society

**D E S E R E T  N E W S**

# Racing into a new
# Century

## 1900-1910

The 20th century hit the ground running, with many of the technological revolutions that would transform society just getting under way. Salt Lake City saw its first automobile early in the 1900s, and the first airplane wasn't far behind. X rays, wireless telegraphy, motion pictures – a whole spectrum of electronics was in place, waiting to be developed.  It was a time of great optimism as the horse and buggy era slowly came to an end and the North Pole was conquered.  In Utah, however, the decade was only five months old when searing headlines told of the nation's worst ever mining disaster at Scofield. Reforms and strikes began in the mining industry, and a great new open pit copper mine opened in the western part of the valley. It was a good start.

John Hutchings Museum of Natural History

**Mr. Moritz's automobile was able to hold a number of his friends in 1906. Above, early license plates were handmade of leather.**

A very early turn-of-the-century photo shows the first motorcar in the Ephraim area.

Utah State Historical Society

# Man flies!

Deseret News files

**Wilbur Wright**

the question arose as to when the first auto made its appearance in Salt Lake City. You say that it is certain that the Silver Brothers brought to Salt Lake City in 1900 a gas-powered buggy. Now the fact is that two of the brothers brought one each and used them in Salt Lake, but they were not gas-powered; they were steam-propelled. I know this because I made a special trip to Salt Lake to see them, thinking I might pick up something that would help me, as I was then making one of my own in the evenings, after working hours …

Mr. Silver then gave me my first ride in a horseless carriage, as they were then called.

Mr. Devey gave an accounting of the first autos, in his memory, to be driven in Utah, then continued his personal experience.

My horseless carriage was the first one made in Utah and I believe I am safe in saying, in the West. I commenced making this machine in 1899 and tried to get it ready so that I could drive it to conference in 1900. I was not able to complete it in time, but did so a little later… The roads in those days were not like they are now. The farmers then would dig irrigation ditches cross the wagon roads some two or three feet wide and two feet deep and if I had used small wheels, I might have gotten into a ditch and never got out again.

The machine was speeded up so I could make 20 miles an hour on good roads … Like most all early cars, I have been pulled home several times and more than once I pushed it home, as it only weighed about 750 pounds and was light enough so I could lift one wheel off the ground. I used this machine continually for eleven years and several prominent men had their first automobile ride in it.

With the advent of the auto came the advent of auto advertising. Almost simultaneously, the News began printing ads to lure would-be purchasers. The Utah Automobile Co. even specialized:

**DESERET NEWS:** Dec. 19, 1903: If you are a doctor, how can you get along without an automobile physician's car? It has a physician's cabinet and can do your work in one-fourth the time you can now with the horse and buggy and will add many times to your comfort.

## Utah Automobile Co.
INCORPORATED
57 MARKET STREET, SALT LAKE CITY, UTAH.

L. C. SNOW, President. W. L. PICKARD, JR., Treasurer.

THE UTAH AUTOMOBILE CO.

## The Winton & Oldsmobile
### LEAD THE WORLD

**1905 WINTONS**

WINTON & KING
Long live the King

**1905 OLDSMOBILES**

**WINTONS**
Are absolutely the FINEST LINE OF HIGH GRADE CARS BUILT IN AMERICA.

REMEMBER the Winton received the highest award at World's Fair at St. Louis.

**1905 OLDSMOBILES**

Early Deseret News ad sold autos for about $1,800.

**DESERET NEWS,** Dec. 18, 1903: A successful trial of a flying machine has been made near Kitty Hawk, N.C., by Wilbur and Orville Wright of Dayton, O. The machine flew for three miles in the face of a wind blowing at the registered velocity of 21 miles an hour and then gracefully descended to earth at the spot selected by the navigator. The machine has no balloon attachment but gets its force from propellers worked by a small engine.

Preparatory to its flight the machine was placed upon a platform near Kitty Hawk. This platform was built on a high sand hill, and when all was in readiness, the fastenings to the machine were released and it started down an incline. The navigator, Wilbur Wright, then started a small gasoline engine which worked the propellers. When the end of the incline was reached the machine gradually rose until it obtained an altitude of 60 feet. In the face of a strong wind blowing it maintained an even speed of eight miles an hour. The idea of the box kite has been adhered to in the basic formation of the flying machine.

Man flew, and the world would never be quite the same. It took the world a while to realize that, though. The whole notion of flying machines seemed fairly radical in those early days.

Only days before, the Deseret News reported the failure of the Langley Airship, built with help from the Smithsonian Institution. "The failure to fly was total and the wreck of the aeroplane was almost complete," the paper had reported on Dec. 9, 1903. Although the failure was attributed to "defects in the launching apparatus not a weakness in the machine itself," the crash put a damper on what seemed the most promising effort. No one at that time knew much about the Dayton bicycle builders who would actually succeed.

These were still the days when "aeronaut" meant balloonist, and in 1907, when the paper said "The present season promises to be a lively one for aeronauts and aeronautics," it meant the "gas balloon."

**DESERET NEWS,** May 4, 1907: The United States government — always a bit conservative in the matter of ballooning — seems to have waked up to the possibilities of air travel. It has gone so far as to establish a flying corps as a regular branch of the army. An order for three new balloons of the gas bag variety has been placed with Leo Stevens, the veteran ascensionist and balloon maker… .

At first thought it is rather disappointing that the government has made no advance in substituting some one of the numerous widely exploited airships of recent times for the old fashioned gas bag. The fact is, the government has become weary of the repeated failure that has followed every trial of a new principle and has also grown correspondingly wary.

Also making news that month was a return of the first balloonist to visit Utah:

**DESERET NEWS,** *May 18 1907: Sailing through the skies in a gas balloon was first practiced in Utah on July 4, 1883, and the man who rose out of Washington square above the gaze of 8,000 people, to land in Red Butte canyon, after a trip to the eastward at a height of 15,000 feet, is now back in Salt Lake for a return visit. Since leaving here 24 years ago, Prof. Van Tassell has grown from a young man to an old man, while the number of his ascensions has increased from 19 to many hundreds.*

Balloons had their day; but the new flying machines were here to stay and were increasingly in the news. But flying was not without its hazards. In 1908, Wilbur Wright's propeller broke during a test flight and struck one of the supports of the rudder, injuring him and killing a military passenger.

**DESERET NEWS,** *Sept. 18, 1908: Lying in the Fort Myer hospital with a fractured thigh and ribs, Orville Wright, the aeronaut, who fell with Lieut. Selfridge in yesterday's aeroplane accident, is making a manly fight for recovery. Through the night there was anxiety over the injured aviator's conditions, but as day broke and no indications of internal injuries developed… there was great relief expressed among those who were watching the progress of the patient… .*
*Many members of the Aero club and the Aeronautic society of this city [New York] look on the death of Lieut. Thomas E. Selfridge by the accident to the Wright aeroplane at Fort Myer as the severest setback that aeronautics has ever received, but E. La Rue Jones, editor of the Aeronautics, pointed out in an interview that in the history of aeroplanes there have been only four deaths compared with the great number in connection with the development of the balloon…*

So, experimental flights continued, in this country and abroad:

**DESERET NEWS,** *Aug. 2, 1909: Paris — At Port Aviation near Juvisy yesterday M. Peliot Gaudart in a Visin biplane rose to a height of 800 feet, beating the record established by Wilbur Wright and winning the Lazare Weiler prize… . The aeroplane remained aloft for nine and a half minutes, the descent being made with ease.*

A few days later, the Deseret News presented firsthand news of flight. It printed two pictures, one of Orville Wright going 15 miles an hour and another "bringing aeroplane out of shed."

**DESERET NEWS,** *Aug. 6, 1909: Attorney Joel Nibley has returned from a trip east, bringing with him some historic souvenirs in the form of kodak pictures taken by himself of the flight of Orville Wright recently at Ft. Meyer, Va.*

By 1910, airplanes were familiar enough to be used in advertising. Two ads appeared on Jan. 27, one from the

Mullett Clothing Company that included a tiny tot at the controls of the plane; the other from Butler Art Shoes, 11 floors high in the Boston Building, noting that "The airships are coming… . You can reach us via the elevator. Just take a flight and see how low we sell good shoes way up here…"

But soon Salt Lakers saw for themselves how these flying machines worked, in what was apparently the first flight in Utah.

**DESERET NEWS,** *Jan. 31, 1910: Before a crowd of 8,000 enthusiastic people, Louis Paulhan, the eminent French aviator, made a flight at the fair grounds lasting 10 minutes and 36 seconds, attaining a height of about 300 feet, describing all sorts of evolutions, showing perfect control of his machine, and then made a perfect descent while the shouts shattered the air strata which the man-bird had just left.*

**DESERET NEWS,** *Feb. 3, 1910: Louis Paulhan, by his successful flight in a heavier-than-air biplane, demonstrated at an altitude of more than 4,300 feet that man may, in time, be crowned king of the air. He did not attain a height of more than 300 feet from his starting place, though he tried many times during his flight here. Conditions were against him and he admitted after his*

landing that some sort of "freak" machine must be used at such altitudes before success will be achieved.

Before the next decade had ended, airplanes would find both commercial and military success. And the world would be forever changed.

**Pilot T.T. Maroney and David Cazier were photographed at Payson in 1916.**

**An early photograph in Utah captures the box-like construction of the first airplanes.**

D E S E R E T N

# A glittering
# palace
# of salt

**BICYCLE RACES TONIGHT!**
**Salt Palace Saucer Track, 8:15 P. M.**

WALKER VS. DOWNING, Match Sprint Race, ½, ¾, 1-mile heats.
ONE-MILE HANDICAP, PROFESSIONAL.
UNKNOWN DISTANCE LAP, PROFESSIONAL.
ONE-MILE MOTOR TRIAL AGAINST TIME, F. E. WHITTLER.
Record, 1:05 1-5.
THREE-MILE OPEN "WESTERN CHAMPIONSHIP," Amateur.
AUSTRALIAN PURSUIT, Amateur.
HELD'S MILITARY BAND.                    ADMISSION 25c.
Tickets on sale Stickney's CigarStore.
The Fastest Riders in the World.

Bicycle racing was a major sport as the century began. Illustrations above are from the Deseret News, and at right, "The Pride of Provo" poses for his photograph.

Utah State Historical Society

**DESERET NEWS,** *Aug. 22, 1899:*
*The Salt Palace is open. Amid a flourish of music and oratory the doors of the marvelous edifice were formally opened last night. There must have been 1,200 people in the building to witness the exercises, while there were perhaps twice that number on the grounds. The 900 incandescent lights on the exterior of the palace presented a gorgeous sight, the dome of the edifice looked as though it might be on fire. But the interior was even more a brilliant revelation than the outside. There were few who went to the palace last night who had formed anywhere near an adequate conception of its grandeur. The charm of the interior was in the beautiful blending of the colors in the dome, and the exquisite grace of the relief work, all as white as the driven snow. The walls and ceiling fairly scintillated under the many brilliant lights.*

Salt Lake City had a new palace, the likes of which had not been seen before. So if reporters got a bit carried away with their adjectives, they could be forgiven. The Salt Palace was, the paper noted, a "rare and radiant sight."

Gov. Heber M. Wells was lavish in his praise of the endeavor, located between State and Main Streets at Ninth South. Minnesota and Leadville have their Ice palaces, Sioux City had her Corn Palace, he noted, but it was for Salt Lake to build a Salt Palace. "The Governor thought the people of Salt Lake would show a due appreciation of the Palace, for it would prove to be a source of attraction for people all over the world. It would increase our population and advertise our resources and when we become a great throbbing midway metropolis we may look back and bless the day that Neiden built the Salt Palace."

The palace was designed by Richard K.A. Kletting, who could also list the State Capitol, Saltair and numerous downtown buildings on his resume. The palace was made of wood, encrusted and sprayed with powdered salt, and of "slabs of rock salt from Salina and incrustations from the shores of Great Salt Lake, compressed and cut into blocks."

Over the next 11 years it would live up to its promise as a place of exposition and entertainment.

A great wooden arena, one of the finest in the country, was part of the original Salt Palace complex.

Utah State Historical Society/Nicholas G. Morgan

The main hall, the primary reason of the palace after all, was filled with exhibits and displays featuring Utah industries: prized specimens of minerals and ores, manufactured products, field crops, fruits, educational and scientific endeavors.

On the Midway Plaisance was an exotic array, which included, according to a Deseret News ad, the DeKreko Brothers from the "renowned Streets of Cairo" with "the greatest Oriental aggregation in existance"; Hagenbach's Wonderful Trained Wild Animal Show; Wilson's Congress of Nations; Baby Estelle's Palace of Varieties; a Palace of Illusions; gondolas, merry-go-rounds, balloon ascensions, miniature railroads, a haunted swing and "many other attractions too numerous to mention."

Traveling shows also entertained the city.

**DESERET NEWS,** *June 1, 1900:*
*Commencing at 8 o'clock this evening, the Will Rising Comedy company will give three vaudeville performances in the pretty new theater. Every number on the program is new, breezy and original. Mme. Thelma, the modern Venus, will give beautiful new poses before the calcium, and she will also render selections on the violin in her inimitable style…*

*Captain Beach, the human fish, who has startled scientists of the continents, will give wonderful free exhibitions in the large aquarium on the Midway, eating, smoking and reading beneath the surface of the water…*

Nothing at the Salt Palace, however, was enjoyed more than the bicycle races. The large, wooden oval track, one of the world's first eight-lap board tracks, was designed by Truman O. Angell Jr. Some 4,000 spectators could sit around the top of the saucer, cheering on local favorites such as Hardy K. Downing, Carl Smith (known as "The Hard-riding Mormon") and Iver Larson, who set numerous records, including one for the half-mile: 23.9 seconds.

**DESERET NEWS,** *June 13, 1900:*
*What the Salt Palace would be without the bicycle races is not hard to imagine. This does not mean that there are not numerous other attractions well worth the price of admission, but that the race meets are distinctly the drawing card. The fact was well illustrated last evening when not less than 4,000 people assembled in the great arena to see the riders spin around the shining saucer like meteors…*

Halley's comet was seen in Salt Lake skies in 1910. Perhaps it is only coincidence that the meteoric ride of the Salt Palace also came to an end that year. On Aug. 10, 1910, a fire broke out in "The Third Degree," an electric concession on the midway, and the Salt Palace — every beam and salt cube — burned to the ground.

## CAMPING AROUND THE NORTH POLE

Sept. 16, 1919

Battle Harbor, Labrador, Sept. 15, by wireless via Cape Bay, N.F., Sept. 15 — "We hoisted the stars and stripes twice at the north pole," said Matthew Henson, Commander Robert E. Peary's colored lieutenant and the only civilized man, besides himself, according to Peary, who ever reached the pole.

Henson tonight gave to the Associated Press an account of one night and two days he and Commander Peary and four Eskimos camped at 90 degrees north latitude. Henson assisted in raising the American flag and he led the Eskimos in the cheers, an extra cheer for Old Glory in the Eskimo tongue being given…

"We arrived at the pole just before noon, April 6, the party consisting of the commander, myself, four Eskimos and 36 dogs, divided into two detachments equal in number and headed, respectively, by Commmander Peary and myself. We had left the last supporting party at 87 degrees, 53 minutes, where

UPI Photo

**Commander Robert E. Peary**

we separated from Capt. Bartlett, who was photographed by the commander…

"I kept a personal diary during this historic dash across the icefield. Our first task on reaching the pole was to build two igloos, as the weather was hazy and prevented taking accurate observations to confirm the distance traveled from Cape Columbia. Having completed the snowhouses, we had dinner, which included tea made on our alcohol stove, and then retired to rest, thus sleeping one night at the north pole…

## The Victorian era ends

**Her name alone described a historic era, a lifestyle philosophy, a type of architecture — Victoria, queen of England. Her death at age 82, after 64 years on the throne, was reported by newspapers around the world with respect and veneration:**

**DESERET NEWS,** Jan. 22, 1901:

QUEEN VICTORIA OF ENGLAND IS DEAD

London, 7:07 p.m. — The text of the Prince of Wales' dispatch to the lord mayor is as follows:

Osborne, 6:45 p.m. — My beloved mother has just passed away, surrounded by her children and grandchildren.

(Signed)     ALBERT EDWARD

The queen is said to have bade farewell in a feeble monosyllable to her family assembled at her bedside at mid-day. She first recognized the Prince of Wales, to whom she spoke a few words of great moment; then Emperor William and the others present filed past and heard a whispered good bye. All those in the bedroom were in tears…

With the members of the royal family gathered at the queen's bedside, the bishop of Winchester and the rector of Whippingham read prayers for those in extremis. Happily the queen was able to recognize those around her. They came to her bedside, but the physicians warned them against attempts to speak to her. Naturally, the family, while recognizing the claim for public information, insist that the details of the events around the death-bed shall be sacred for the present … The arrival of Lord Clarendon, the lord chamberlain, is considered ominous, because the arrangements for the succession to the throne will be in his hands.

**The death of Queen Victoria was the end of an amazing rule that began when she was 18 years of age. During her years on the throne, England's colonial interests throughout the world flourished. The wealth of India, Hong Kong, Australia, Canada and many other colonies flowed to the homeland, making England at that time the richest country on earth.**

**Internally, it was a time of great change for the nation. Victoria recognized the folly of ignoring the global shift to popular rule and she granted greater powers to Parliament, becoming England's first "figurehead" ruler.**

**The queen's private life also was a busy one. She married her cousin, Prince Albert of Saxe-Coburg-Gothe and they were the parents of nine children. His death in 1861 left her greatly bereaved and she essentially retired from the public view, if not from public responsibility.**

## The world of the 1900s
### A TIMELINE

**1900**— The Boxer uprisings in China bring an allied force of eight nations to rescue Europeans.

**1900**— Sigmund Freud publishes "The Interpretation of Dreams."

**1900**— Count Ferdinand Zeppelin builds the first airship.

**1901**— The first Nobel prizes are awarded from a fund endowed by Alfred Nobel.

**1901**— J.P. Morgan creates U.S. Steel Corp.

**1901**— Guglielmo Marconi transmits the first telegraphic messages across the ocean.

**1901**— George Eastman starts the Eastman Kodak Co.

**1902**— The Boer War in South Africa ends; 5,774 British and 4,000 Boers died.

**1902**— The Aswan Dam on the Nile is completed.

**1902**— Rudyard Kipling publishes his "Just So" stories.

**1903**— Marie Curie is the first woman to win a Nobel Prize.

**1903**— Jack London writes "The Call of the Wild."

**1903**— Henry Ford founds the Ford Motor Co.

**1903**— The first teddy bears, named after Pres. Theodore Roosevelt, designed by Richard Steiff.

**1903**— The first Tour de France bicycle race is held.

**1904**— Puccini premieres "Madame Butterfly."

**1904**— The Russo-Japanese War fought.

**1904**— Theodore Roosevelt wins presidential election.

**1904**— W.C. Gorgas conquers yellow fever in the Panama Canal Zone and work begins on the canal.

**1905**— Albert Einstein publishes the Special Theory of Relativity.

**1906**— U.S. troops are sent to Cuba and William Taft becomes its provisional governor.

**1907**— Oklahoma becomes the 46th state.

**1907**— The Boy Scouts movement founded by British general Robert Baden-Powell.

**1907**— "Mutt and Jeff," the first daily comic strip, begins the in the San Francisco Examiner.

**1908**— General Motors founded and the Ford Motor Co. makes its first Model "T."

**1908**— The Union of South Africa is founded.

**1908**— Jack Johnson is the first black to win the heavyweight championship of the world.

**1909**— Louis Bleriot flies across the English Channel in 37 minutes.

**1909**— President Taft says a naval base will be built at Pearl Harbor, Hawaii, to protect the U.S. from Japanese attacks.

# DESERET EVENING NEWS.

Jan. 1, 1900

## WAR ON THE NATIONAL LEAGUE

### Seven Hour Meeting of American Baseball Magnates.

The Chicago Times-Herald of this morning says: In a secret conference lasting for several hours, a majority of the American baseball league magnates decided to declare war on the National League and break the national agreement, which has been in force since February 24, 1896…

As a consequence unless the National League magnates can find measures to placate the belligerent western organization, Chicago and St. Louis in the West and Boston and Philadelphia in the East will be invaded next spring.

Feb. 13, 1900

## MILITARY FUNERAL FOR UTAH HEROES

With bowed heads and heavy hearts the people of Salt Lake today laid away in their own burying grounds, the hero dead, sent home by a grateful government, after yielding up their lives in war-visaged isles beyond the seas.

The day was not ideal, nor was it one that contributed to high spirits. On the contrary, lowering clouds, falling snow and dreary winds constituted the precursor of a feeling of deepest gloom. There have been many sad funerals in Salt Lake — funerals that have caused an almost universal sorrow, but few indeed that have occasioned the distinctive heart-aches that did the one of today.

April 23, 1900

## PADEREWSKI COMES, SEES, CONQUERS.

The Paderewski event on Saturday night will take its place near the head of the list of exquisite concerts which Salt Lake music lovers have listened to in the past twenty years. There was nothing about the entire affair that was not notable. The audience, while it fell short of anticipations, was in the highest sort representative of our musical taste and culture. Only fifty people paid the dollar rate and climbed to the top gallery. There were probably 150 in the second gallery, 200 in the first, and 250 to 300 in the downstairs portion, the receipts footing up about $1,300. The stalls were glaringly vacant, and while there were numerous full dress suits in evidence on the part of the gentlemen, "society" generally was not in attendance. Instead, there was over the house a hush, almost a devotional breathlessness, which told

unmistakably the character of the audience, and conveyed at the same time the highest kind of tribute to the distinguished artist. The applause on his first appearance was of a mildly enthusiastic character, rather decorous than pronounced, but before the night was over, the magnetism of the wonderful player rushed out over the footlights, overwhelmed the audience and caused a perfect whirlwind of enthusiasm…

No effect ever brought out of the piano could equal that produced by Paderewski in his sustained notes at the end of a phrase. The dying away of the chord was simply inspiring. It was listened to almost with awe…

May 16, 1900

## JUDGE TIMMONY'S COURT

Mike Boyle for once pleaded for clemency. "Let me go, judge, and I'll leave town?" "For how long?" "Oh, three months; no, I'll make it ten months." "Well, I'll suspend sentence, and you know what will happen to you if you don't go."

Eugene White, Eli Webb, Ralph Sevis, Ed. Viglinis and George Powell, boys, 16 years of age, were up for trespassing upon the property of the Oregon Short Line railroad company. Judge Timmony gave them a good lecture and told them they might go if they would promise to behave themselves in the future.

May 16, 1900

## Schools at the Lake.

The public school teachers of the city are endeavoring to arrange a date at SaltAir in the first week of June for the teachers and pupils of the schools. Excursion Agent Mann is helping the "school-marms" to bring arrangements to this end to a satisfactory conclusion. Every date in June, excepting in the first week, has been taken there being eighteen Sunday schools represented in the bookings.

## Opal Club to Lagoon.

The Opal Club, through Chas. E. Berry, has arranged with Excursion Agent Bean for a special day at Lagoon before the regular opening for the summer. A special train will be provided for members of the club, which will leave the depot at 7:30 in the evening. Arriving at the resort the club members and their guests will be given the freedom of the grounds and will regale themselves in a supper and also enjoy some dancing, for which the club furnishes its own orchestra.

May 16, 1900

## Baseball at Logan.

Logan, — The A.C. and B.Y. baseball teams met on the latter's campus yesterday and played as exciting a game as ever seen in this city. At the close of the ninth inning the score stood 12 to 12. Another inning was played, in which the B.Y.'s got rattled and let in 8 A.C. players. In the second half of the tenth, the A.C.'s put out one man on first, second man got to first, but the third knocked a fly to first, who doubled to second and the game was ended.

## SPORTING NOTES

The Z.C.M.I. and the Hansen Produce Rippers will play ball on Decoration day. Both teams are practicing assiduously for the contest.

June 11, 1900

## MEETS DEATH ON THE WIRES.

Alexander Stevenson, night inspector of the Utah Light & Power company, met his death Saturday night, as quickly as four thousand volts of electricity could do the work. The shocking affair transpired on Third South, between East Temple and State streets. Stevenson was making his regular nightly rounds inspecting the street lamps, accompanied by Daniel E. McBride, the lampman of the company. Stevenson perceived that the lamp in front of the First Methodist church was out, when he promptly ascended the pole to adjust the carbons which he supposed to be crossed. He had barely reached the top when a light flashed from the pole, the man uttered a muffled scream and his limp body sank down on the cross beam…

Oct. 6, 1900

## DALLIN WINS TWO MEDALS AT PARIS

A letter just received from C.E. Dallin, the Utah sculptor, says that he has been awarded a medal at the Paris exposition for his work "The Medicine Man…" Mr. John J. Daly especially said he felt confident the statue would be recognized by the judges. The honor conferred on Mr. Dallin is all the higher, that only five American sculptors have been similarly recognized, and that this is the second

medal he has been awarded at the Exposition…

"The equestrian statue of the "Medicine Man" was so well esteemed by the French artists that it was given a fine place in the salon of 1899, having no other statuary near it, and for background the green shrubbery — in fact, everything to show it to the best advantage. The critics of the "Petite Republique," the "Autorite" and the "Frankfurter Zeitung" heartily praised it, and it was a favorite with the visitors to the sculpture garden.

Dec. 5, 1903

## OLDFIELD GOES EAST.

Barney Oldfield, formerly a Salt Lake bicycle rider, now champion automobilist of the world, was in Salt Lake for a short time yesterday afternoon. He left last evening for the east. Before leaving Los Angeles, where he has been racing, he shipped his motor cars and for that reason was unable to give an exhibition of speed here.

Barney had a successful trip to the coast. He smashed records and made money. The world's record of 56 flat was reduced by him one second. But one day in practise he made the mile in 54 4/5 seconds.

Dec. 11, 1903

## AUTOMOBILIST ARRESTED

To Officer J.D. Brown belongs credit for making the first arrest for the infraction of the ordinance relative to fast driving over crossings. The arrest was made today just before noon, the victim being LeRoy C. Snow. Mr. Snow was not driving a fractious horse, but an automobile, and Officer Brown declares that he was going down East Temple street at the rate of fifteen miles an hour. The officer placed Mr. Snow under arrest and informed him of the charge to be booked against him. The latter asked the officer if he realized who he was arresting.

"It don't cut no ice with me who you are," said the minion of the law.

Mr. Snow explained that he was a teacher of French and German at the Latter-day Saints university.

"Well, that don't win you nothin'. If you are a professor, you should know better than to break the ordinance. Now don't put up no holler or I'll call the wagon …

"This looks good to me," said Brown as he climbed in beside his prisoner and rode with him to the police station. There Mr. Snow was booked for fast driving, but was released upon his own recognizance…

Dec. 12, 1903

## BEST SELLING BOOKS.

Record for October.

According to the records of all booksellers, the six books which have sold best in the order of demand during the month are:

1. The Little Shepherd of Kingdom Come. Fox $1.50
2. The Call of the Wild. London.............. 1.50
3. Rebecca. Wiggin... .................. 1.25
4. The One Woman. Dixon... ............... 1.50
5. The Adventures of Gerard. Doyle... .......... 1.50
6. The Sherrods. McCutcheon... ............. .. 1.50

We have the above and all the latest popular books of the day.

DESERET NEWS BOOK STORE
16 Main St.

Dec. 12, 1903

## LIFE OF MODERN FOOTBALL PLAYER.

How long does a football player usually last?

By the question it is not meant "how long does he live?", but how long is he effective as a football player? Reference is made to the able-bodied college pig skin chaser. There are exceptions, it is said, to all rules, but among those who pose as experts, it is generally conceded that the life of a football player is seldom more than four years. After that he begins to decline, sans nerve, sans power, sans everything else except the memory of former victories, applause, etc.

In the gentle(?) game of football it is not always the big, strong, husky man who is the most effective. The main qualification may be stated in one little word — Nerve.

Dec. 12, 1903

## AGAINST DANCING IN SCHOOLHOUSES

An action has been brought by I.T. Terry, a resident of Warren, Weber county, against Joseph Carver, Mattle Thomas and R.L. Short, trustees of county school district No. 2, to restrain and enjoin the defendants from permitting a public dance in the public schoolhouse at Warren, a temporary restraining order was issued yesterday afternoon by Judge Rolapp prohibiting the defendants from holding a dance at the schoolhouse last evening. The complaint alleges that the defendants as school trustees of the district have been permitting public dances in the school building, and that on such occasions the desks were taken up and piled in the corners, greatly to their damage and to the damage of the building.

Should the court grant the injunction it will work a hardship on the young people of several wards in the county where they have only the schoolhouse for pleasure purposes.

Dec. 12, 1903

## BRIGHAM YOUNG UNIVERSITY.

A second basketball team, denominated "The Scrubs," has been organized by way of attrition for the league team. Exhibit games will be held once a week till the opening of the league games in January. Enthusiasm for the novel sport is becoming general among the students, and there is talk of each class having its team with a view to local athletic honors.

## B.Y. COLLEGE

A grand kermiss or sociable has been arranged to be given by the amusement committee of the faculty...The Logan Knitting factory offers a beautiful silk shawl to the most popular young lady in school. Riter Brothers Drug company will give a handsome dressing case to the best lady waltzer, and one will also be given to the best gentleman waltzer.

Professor Hall spoke in chapel on Wednesday, and gave the students some very valuable instructions as to how they should study. He showed them the dangers of mind wandering and demonstrated the necessity of concentration practise, and of studying when in proper physical condition.

Dec. 12, 1903

## LATE LOCALS.

Word was received in the office of State Superintendent of Schools Nelson this morning from Superintendent Fry of Morgan that he is in need of a teacher for the rest of the year at Milton. The salary is $55 per month.

Dec. 12, 1903

## TYPOS AND THE TRIBUNE.

Truth today prints the following:

"The Tribune and its little brother, the Telegram, are at outs with the Typographical union, The union has a rule that matter set in type for one newspaper cannot after being used in that paper be handed over to another newspaper for use by it, unless both newspapers are owned by the same people. The Telegraph has been lifting matter bodily from the Tribune, which was used in that paper in the morning and running it in the evening Telegraph, thus saving the cost of setting up a second time...

Dec. 14, 1903

## RESIGNATION OF BENJ. CLUFF, JR.

### From Presidency of Brigham Young University — May be Succeeded by G. H. Brimhall.

Provo, Utah Co., Dec. 14. — A meeting of the Brigham Young university board of trustees will be held tomorrow evening to take action on the resignation of President B. Cluff, Jr., who has been the president of the institution for about 12 years. He has decided to devote his time to business pursuits, and expects to engage in the rubber business in Mexico as the superintendent of the Utah-Mexican Rubber company's business, when his connection with the university is ended...

It is believed that Dr. George H. Brimhall will fill the position made vacant by the resignation of Professor Cluff. Dr. Brimhall has been one of the faculty of the school for many years, and was the acting president while Professor Cluff was on his trip to Central and South America with the Brigham Young academy expedition.

Dec. 14, 1903

## WHAT RADIUM COULD DO.

"I have no doubt," said M. Curie, "that a kilogram of radium would be sufficient to destroy the population of Paris, granting that they came within its influence. They would feel nothing during their exposure to the radium nor realize that they were in any danger. And weeks would pass after their exposure before anything would happen. Then gradually the skin would begin to peel off, and their bodies would become one great sore. Then they would become blind. Then they would die from paralysis and congestion of the spinal cord."—Cleveland Moffet in McClure's.

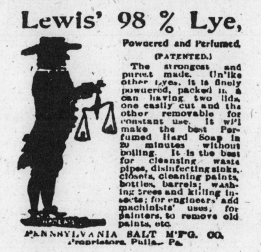

Dec. 14, 1903

## NARROW ESCAPE FROM LYNCHING.

### Soldier Who Assaulted Miss Edith Gill Last Night May Consider Himself a Lucky Man.

The solder who made a criminal assault upon Miss Edith Gill last night is now languishing behind the bars at the city jail. His name is Thomas R. Fuller, aged 28 years, and a member of the Twelfth battery.

That Fuller is not dangling at the end of a rope instead of being alive and under the protection of the city police authorities, is due entirely to the strategy of the officers at the post, and Sergt. Roberts and Officer Emil Johnson, to whom belongs the credit for making the arrest. A crowd of Fuller's own comrades were bent on lynching him when it became known that he was the man who committed the foul deed... But somehow the officers got wind of the scheme and at once placed the prisoner in the army ambulance under an armed guard in command of Lieut. Clark, accompanied by Sergt. Roberts and Officer Johnson...

Dec. 14, 1903

## ST. JOHN'S CHAPEL DEDICATED.

The new St. John's chapel of the Episcopal church on Eleventh South street, was dedicated yesterday afternoon, by Bishop Tuttle with impressive services. The attendance was gratifying, and the bishop preached an excellent sermon. The larger chapel has been much needed of late, as the number of Episcopalians in the southern part of the city is increasing.

May 26, 1906

## CHURCH BUYS HISTORIC PRESS.
### A MOST INTERESTING RELIC.

Newark, N.J., May 26 — Joseph F. Smith, president of the Church of Jesus Christ of Latter-day Saints of Salt Lake City, Utah, yesterday purchased the old Washington press upon which the first edition of the Book of Mormon was printed. The price paid to Col. Fred Clemons is said to be $500.

Inquiry at the office of the First Presidency today elicited the information that the above dispatch is correct, in so far as it pertains to the purchase of the press in question. The price paid for it, however, was $250, instead of the amount named in the Newark account of the transaction...

Feb. 23, 1907

Weekly Health Report — The weekly report of the city board of health for the week ending February

22nd shows 32 births reported during the week, 16 males and 16 females. Thirty-two deaths were reported during the week; 18 males and 8 females. Six were shipped here for burial. There were reported during the week 23 cases of contagious and infectious diseases consisting of 13 cases of diptheria; 1 of epidemic cerebro spinal meningitis; 3 cases of scarlet fever; 2 cases of measles; 1 case of mumps; 2 cases of meningitis and 2 cases of chickenpox. 6 cases of scarlet fever; 16 cases of diptheria and 3 cases of epidemic cerebro spinal meningitis remain in quarantine.

April 12, 1907

## OGDEN IN DARKNESS.

### Landslide in Canyon Damages the Big Power Plant Flume.

Ogden, April 12 — There was a serious landslide in the mouth of Ogden canyon this morning, which partially destroyed the pipe line of the Utah Light & Power company. An immense amount of earth slid slowly down the mountain side, cracking the pipe in many places. The water was stopped, and a large force of men was at once set to work to stop the slide from coming farther down, if possible. Should the slide pass the place where it is aimed to be stopped, it will do much more damage than has yet been wrought. There will be no street lights in Ogden tonight, but sufficient power has been secured from Provo and Bear River plants to partially light the business and residence districts. It is expected that it will take at least three days to repair the damage.

August 2, 1909

## JOSEPH C. PARCELL OF PROVO BENCH BADLY BEATEN

Provo Bench, Aug. 2 — Shortly after Saturday midnight, Joseph C. Parcell, Jr. while on his way home from Provo was waylaid by two young men of Lake View, named Neeley Souller and Abe Lunceford. He was knocked from his bicycle and badly cut up about the face, and would probably have been worse used had not passers by come to his rescue. His assailants then decamped and got away in a buggy which they had tied up nearby. A warrant has been sworn out against Parcell's assailants, and they will soon be arrested.

August 16, 1909

## ICE FAMINE IN SALT LAKE

The ice situation in Salt Lake City reached a critical stage yesterday when the last of the 3,000-ton reserve of artificial ice which is stored every year by the Utah Ice and Cold storage company was taken out for distribution. There is already considerable wailing around the city because of big cuts being made in the

daily supplies and this is likely to continue until the weather gets so cool that it will not be necessary. Briefly stated the situation is this. The daily needs of the city is from 200 to 240 tons, depending on the weather and the supply is only about 80 or 90 tons of artificial and about 50 tons of natural, making a total of 140 tons per day available. It is stated also that the supply of natural ice will be used up in the next two or three weeks, and the people will have to go through the most of September with only the limited supply of artificial ice…

The cause of the shortage is attributed to the excessive hot weather during the month of June, as well as the months of July and August thus-far, but the real trouble is said to be the fact that Salt Lake City has outgrown the plant of the Cold Storage company…

Sept. 22, 1909

## CITY CREEK WATER CARRIES TYPHOID

### J.W. Burnham Blames Land and Water Commissioner for Fever Outbreak.

According to J.W. Burnham, who lives at 39 North Capital street, the officials are on the wrong track in their attempt to fasten the origin of the present typhoid outbreak on the dairies…

"I have no hesitation," said Mr. Burnham this morning, "in placing all the responsibility of present conditions on the shoulders of the land and water commissioners. That the germs of typhoid have been carried into so many homes in Salt Lake City is due to the fact that hundreds of cattle and horses are allowed to graze all summer long, and for that matter all the year round. In some cases, in the various gulches along the City Creek, as well as in other canyons. I know what I am talking about, and I would like to lead a party of physicians and newspapermen and any others who would like to go over the hills and into the heads of these gulches. They would be surprised to see the conditions there. In the vicinity of a number of the springs which rise in these gulches and flow into the main creek, are the favorite bedding grounds of these cattle. They come there to drink, and the deposits in some places are worse than any barnyard you ever saw. As most of these cattle graze and bed there for four or five months of the year, you can imagine what the conditions are…

August 2, 1909

## WILL SOON ISSUE NEW LINCOLN PENNIES

Philadelphia, Aug. 2. — The Philadelphia mint will issue today the new Lincoln pennies, which the treasury department has caused to be designed and struck off in honor of the hundredth anniversary of the late president's birth…

The artist, Victor D. Brenner, is 27 years old and is a Russian who came to this country as a boy and sold matches in the street and studied art at night at

Cooper Union.

He saved up enough money to continue his studies in Paris and on his return opened a studio.

# Horrific news from
# Scofield

A mass burial for 150 of the Scofield mine victims was attended by 107 widows and 268 fatherless children.

**Shock waves of horror and grief fanned out from the Winter Quarters coal mine in Carbon County as the full impact of an underground explosion hit the small community on May 1. It was the most lethal mine accident ever in Utah and, at that time, in the United States.**

**O**f the 310 mine workers on duty, 200 died when coal dust exploded and sent deadly fumes circulating through two connected tunnels. Many were Finnish immigrants. The death record stood until Dec. 19, 1907, when an explosion in a Jacobs Creek, Pa., mine killed 239 workers.

The first Deseret News reports of a "Fearful Accident" lacked detail but conjectured that an "Army of Men has been killed":

**DESERET NEWS,** *May 1, 1900: SCOFIELD, Utah — At present the mining camp at Scofield is the scene of the greatest excitement on account of a terrific explosion at the Winter Quarters mine, which occurred about 10 o'clock this morning.*

*The cause is attributed to the blowing up of a number of kegs of blasting powder and the point at which the explosion took place is not as yet known. The scene before the mouths of the tunnels of the mines is a vivid one in the extreme.*

*Women and children waiting, moaning and crying out the names of their beloved ones and as every man is brought out from the mine on a stretcher, every one rushes forward, raises the covering from the face and shrieks awful to hear penetrate the dark and gloomy atmosphere as some one rushes forward only to faint at the foot of their husband's*

*or father's corpse.*

*Up to now it is positively known that the loss of life is a great one and up to now the corpses of twenty miners have been brought out and placed upon the ground awaiting arrival of strong-hearted men to carry them to their various homes.*

The second-day News headline, "The Disaster Grows," expanded on the scope of the explosion and the ensuing fire:

**DESERET NEWS,** *May 2, 1900:*

### TERRIBLE MUTILATION

**Bodies Now Being Removed are Burned Almost Beyond Recognition. Fins Refuse to Do Rescue Work. One Big Trench for a Grave. Plight of Widows. Coroner's Inquest. Bodies Buried in the Mine Tunnels.**

*At this time, 225 bodies have been recovered from the mines. Since last night, according to some accounts, the number is nearly 250, but the best posted men, those who have kept a close count on the bodies as they have come out, place the number at 225. Of the new bodies, 13 came from No. 4 at about 1 o'clock this morning. Nearly all are in a frightful condition. Few, if any, escaped the fire which wrapped them as in a sheet of flame.*

The numbers of the dead were overestimated in the News, and for some time they were not clear, even to mine officials.

Under a separate headline, the condolences of America's president were expressed:

### M'Kinley Extends His Sympathy.
**Expresses His Deep Sorrow to Governor Wells for the Wives and Children of the Victims.**

*WASHINGTON, May 2 — The President today sent the following telegram to the Governor of Utah: Governor Wells, Salt Lake City, Utah. I desire to express my intense sorrow upon learning of the terrible calamity which has occurred at Scofield, and my deep sympathy with the wives, children and friends of the unfortunate victims of the explosion.*

*WILLIAM M'KINLEY*

**DESERET NEWS,** *May 4, 1900: We found the dead in every conceivable attitude. One man had filled his pipe and sat down to light it. The damp [a deadly combination of gases] struck him and he died then and there with the filled pipe in his outstretched hand…*

*On a box where a dead Finlander was they picked up his watch. It had stopped when the explosion occurred and the hands marked 10:28 o'clock …*

*Death's winding sheet seems to envelop Scofield this morning. Every house, without exception, is a house of mourning and every household is preparing to receive its dead.*

Among the first party of rescuers was young Walter Clark. He was a mine employee but had been working outside when the explosion ripped through the underground mine. With others, he rushed to the mouth of the tunnel, fearful for the lives of his father and brother. The youth dashed recklessly into the tunnel, only to be "enveloped by the lurking damp." He was dead before others could reach him, bringing the Clark family toll to three. The total rose again when Walter's "beautiful 16-year-old sister, Lizzie," on being told of his death, dropped dead at her mother's feet of shock.

The mourning of widows and orphans filled the streets, the newspaper said. "A procession of them waiting and screaming follows the bodies as they come from the mine, and it seems impossible to quiet them… The whole state of Utah may be truthfully said to be clothed in the mantle of mourning over death's awful harvest among the coal miners at Winter Quarters."

In some households, every male member was dead. Robert Hunter died with three of his sons and four nephews. John Muir perished with his two sons and a son-in-law at his side. John James was found in the mine with his son clasped tightly in his arms. At least 20 of the dead were mere boys who worked with their fathers as couplers and trap boys.

The supply of caskets in the small town was soon exhausted, and more were ordered from Salt Lake City and Denver. On May 5, two huge funerals were held, one a Lutheran rite for the 61 Finns killed in the mine and a second for the LDS miners who shared their fate.

The cause of the Scofield blast never was determined, although there was speculation that the Finnish miners, anxious to make a good showing, had taken "Giant Powder" into the tunnel to rip out bigger chunks of coal. Utah's coal mines, in fact, had an enviable safety record at the time, but the Winter Quarters disaster led to the union movement and safety reforms of the new century.

# Cathedral
## in the desert

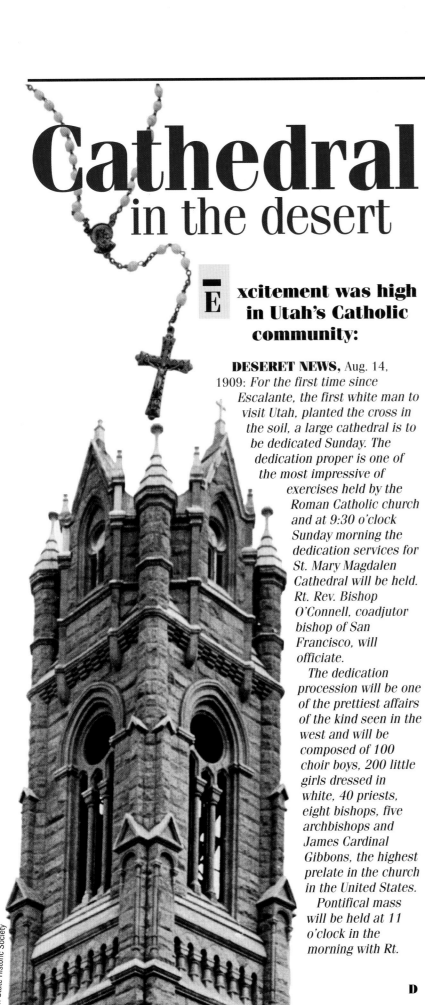

**E**xcitement was high in Utah's Catholic community:

**DESERET NEWS,** Aug. 14, 1909: *For the first time since Escalante, the first white man to visit Utah, planted the cross in the soil, a large cathedral is to be dedicated Sunday. The dedication proper is one of the most impressive of exercises held by the Roman Catholic church and at 9:30 o'clock Sunday morning the dedication services for St. Mary Magdalen Cathedral will be held. Rt. Rev. Bishop O'Connell, coadjutor bishop of San Francisco, will officiate.*

*The dedication procession will be one of the prettiest affairs of the kind seen in the west and will be composed of 100 choir boys, 200 little girls dressed in white, 40 priests, eight bishops, five archbishops and James Cardinal Gibbons, the highest prelate in the church in the United States.*

*Pontifical mass will be held at 11 o'clock in the morning with Rt.*

*Rev. Bishop Laurence [Lawrence] Scanlan in charge. The morning sermon will be preached by Archbishop J.J. Clennon of St. Louis.*

Construction on the Gothic-style cathedral began in 1899. The impressive dedication rites 10 years later were a triumph for Catholicism and the crowning moment for the faith's pioneering stalwarts who ventured into the mostly LDS bastion of Utah to establish their religion. For Father Scanlan, it was a personal culmination of enormous proportions.

As an Irish-trained emigrant to America, his lot as a priest fell among the frontier communities of California, Nevada and, ultimately, Utah Territory. "I took pastoral charge of the Church of St. Mary Magdalene, which was then the only church and Catholic institution in the Territory of Utah, one 14th day of August, 1873," he wrote in his personal history.

History has lost the date of the celebration of the first Mass in the territory, but it seems likely to have occurred in July 1859 when a priest, nameless in the records, officiated at the funeral service for a soldier at Camp Floyd.

Father Edward Kelly, a Catholic missionary, was the first officially assigned priest in Salt Lake City. In June 1866, he offered Mass for several Sundays in Independence Hall on west 300 South, a gathering place for Salt Lake's non-Mormon "gentiles." In the fall, he purchased an adobe structure on 200 East to be a chapel/rectory. Non-Mormons throughout the state supported him financially.

Father Kelly was reassigned when the Utah church fell under the auspices of the Vicar Apostolic of Denver, and a succession of short-term priests came and went until Utah fell under the direction of Archbishop Alemany of San Francisco. When Father Scanlan arrived in 1873, there were approximately 800 Catholics in his flock. His "parish" ranged from Ogden to the vociferous mining camp of Silver Reef near St. George. On one notable occasion, he celebrated a High Mass in the St. George Tabernacle, an indication of his amicable relationships with most Mormons.

Pressed by mine owners and workmen, he made an urgent plea for nuns to establish a hospital in Silver Reef. In 1879, three Holy Cross sisters were assigned. By 1883, the silver at Silver Reef had petered out, and the community's Catholic church burned to the ground.

Wooden scaffolds line the interior of the Cathedral of the Madeleine during construction. Photo taken Feb. 20, 1907.

By 1880, Father Scanlan's unstinting efforts were rewarded with the title of Vicar Forane, making him superior of all the priests working in Utah — at that time, six. In 1875, two sisters came to Salt Lake City to build and manage a school. In the same year, Holy Cross Hospital was founded, housed in a building on 500 East. Its service, particularly to miners, was one of Utah's notable medical success stories. The sisters soon offered a basic health-insurance program to miners for $1 per month. All Hallows College for young men followed in 1886.

On June 2, 1891, Father Scanlan was appointed bishop of the newly created Diocese of Salt Lake, and St. Mary's became a full-fledged cathedral. The marks of his wise stewardship were evident wherever Catholics gathered.

As the new century approached, he planned for a new cathedral at the corner of 100 South and 300 East. The property, however, was too small to accommodate his ambitious dreams, and he obtained the present cathedral site. With subsidies from the Pious Fund of the Californias, money gained through complex agreements made with Mexico when it ceded land to the United States,

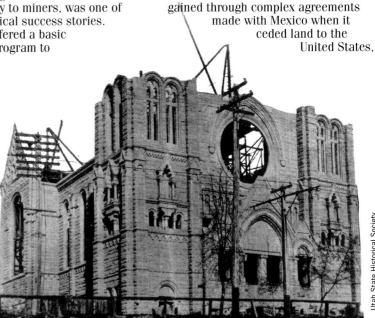

The cathedral's walls are about half way up in this photo taken around 1902.

and the support of the diocese, he began work on his imposing new church.

And now, in 1909, the grandeur and ritual of historic Catholicism were brought to Salt Lake City to note its completion.

Again in modern times, the cathedral, under the direction of Bishop William K. Weigand, was restored.

By then, it had become a rich community treasure. In a joint supplement with the Salt Lake Tribune, the Deseret News celebrated the restoration:

**DESERET NEWS,** *Feb. 20, 1993: [Quoting Bishop Weigand] The diocese has much to be grateful for and proud of as it completes this centennial project. True, we stand on the shoulders of incredible Catholic forebears. But the fact that we have just pulled off something far beyond our perceived ability tells me that the Catholic community of Utah remains a "gutsy" and vibrant people, not unlike those forebears in Utah.*

As part of the rededication, the remains of Most Rev. Lawrence Scanlan were removed from a crypt and reburied in a new altar tomb built from the cathedral's old high altar, a fitting gesture to one of the church's stalwarts of earlier days.

**Rev. Bishop Lawrence Scanlan**

# San Francisco
# Earthquake

April 18, 1906

## FOURTH EDITION – LATEST NEWS OF GREATEST EARTHQUAKE DISASTER IN AMERICAN HISTORY

## EARTHQUAKE, PANIC, DEATH, FIRE, DESTRUCTION

### DAY OF DOOM AND DISASTER

**Frightful Calamity Comes to San Francisco in the Early Morning Hours**

The greatest and most desolating of all earthquakes in the history of modern America occurred in San Francisco this morning. The first news of the dreadful calamity came to Salt Lake in the form of the following dispatch over the one remaining wire out of that calamity-stricken and unfortunate city:

Denver, April 18 — At 9:15 a.m. Postal Telegraph Company here received the following information from Los Angeles: It is reported that thousands of lives have been lost in an earthquake at San Francisco. Both the Postal and the Western Union telegraph buildings in that city are reported to have been destroyed. A disastrous fire is eating its way up the south side of Market street and at last accounts was within three blocks of the Palace hotel. Water mains were bursting and the fire department was absolutely helpless. Business is entirely suspended…

The city is now under martial law. It seems that the entire business section of San Francisco must be destroyed. Mayor Schmits has called for the assistance of the entire Oakland fire department and has ordered that all dynamite available be used to blow up buildings in order to stay the progress of the flames… The shock lasted three minutes, thousands of buildings were damaged and destroyed. The loss of life is reported to be great. There is no water and fire rages all over the city. All wires with the exception of this one are gone… Terror and excitement are indescribable. Most of the people, asleep, were suddenly aroused and rushed into the streets undressed. Buildings swayed and crashed, burying occupants. Panic in the hotels…

**The great San Francisco earthquake is still considered one of the worst disasters in U.S. history. Estimates place its magnitude at 8.0 on the Richter scale, and it was recorded as far away as Washington D.C. Up to 3,000 may have died and a quarter of a million lost their homes. Utahns were frantic for more news, and the paper met the challenge by publishing extra editions throughout the day and the following day.**

**Fires rage in San Francisco as stunned residents watch, surrounded by rubble of their destroyed homes.**

### SALT LAKERS ON THE COAST

The calamity of an earthquake on the coast comes home very sympathetically to Salt Lake, for the town is full of people to whom San Francisco is as next door neighbor, and to whom the catastrophe brings the most intimate concerns. The nearness of it all brought people in hundreds to the bulletin boards this morning, while the telephones in the newspaper offices and the Associated Press were constantly ringing… The entire editions of the Deseret News were sold as fast as the people on the streets could buy them and thousands more could be…and then the people began to crowd for the telegraph offices.

### SALT LAKE RELIEF

Unless present plans are changed in all probability the Commercial club will call a main meeting for tonight to discuss ways and means with the object in view of sending a relief train to San Francisco…

### ALL HOPE OF SAVING SAN FRANCISCO ABANDONED

April 19, 1906

A correspondent of the Oakland Tribune, writing from San Francisco at 10 o'clock a.m. says: "At this writing there seems to be practically no hope of saving any of the city. Those who were sanguine for the ultimate success of the firemen in controlling the flames have now given up hope, and are fleeing from the flames in despair. Many people are being buried alive, imprisoned in the downed buildings where the rescuers could not reach them… The flames seem entirely out of control. The workers have destroyed block after block of residences with dynamite in the

hope of stemming the flames, but after each effort the blaze would leap across a seemingly unpassable gulf."

**The story continued for days, as did the fires in the doomed city.**

April 21, 1906

### THOUSANDS OF REFUGEES HEADED TOWARDS UTAH.

Five hundred refugees from the San Francisco earthquake and the fires disaster arrived in Ogden today and a thousand more will reach there tomorrow. Probably a majority of these will come on to Salt Lake. Other trains from the coast will bring hundreds if not thousands more daily… The Ogden authorities say that they will shortly be deluged with fleeing people, and that they will be heavily taxed to care for them.

**Events were indeed desperate in San Francisco, now under martial law, patrolled by hundreds of troops.**

April 21, 1906

During the afternoon three thieves met their death by rifle bullets while at work in the ruins. The curious were driven back at the breasts of the horses that the cavalrymen rode and all the crowd were forced from the level district to the hilly section beyond to the north…

**Happening as it did in the early morning, it quickly galvanized the Deseret News newsroom. Extras updated the news throughout the day, and every issue was snatched up from the newsboys on the streets. The paper put out seven editions and sold more papers than ever before in its history for any one news story.**

# An
# assassination
## opens the century

Three hours before being shot, President William McKinley is flanked by Agriculture Secretary James L. Watson, left, and John G. Milburn, his host at the Pan-American Exposition.

**F**or the third time in less than a half century, the country was stunned by the painful news of a fatal assault on an American president:

**DESERET NEWS,** *Sept. 6, 1901:*
*PRESIDENT McKINLEY IS FATALLY SHOT*

*BUFFALO, Sept. 6 — President McKinley was shot twice in the stomach here this afternoon at the Temple of Music. His condition is serious. Two shots took effect in the stomach. He is now at the hospital in the Pan-American grounds. He was shot by a stranger...*

*The President was shot by a well dressed man with whom he was shaking hands... As the man approached the President, it is said, he had the revolver covered with a handkerchief and as he reached out his hand to shake the President's hand he fired. A bullet which had lodged against the breast bone has been extracted. The President is resting easy.*

With the rest of the nation, Salt Lake City was shocked and aghast:

*When the first bulletin was posted in the windows of the newspaper offices, men stopped and fairly gasped for breath. Almost in a trice large crowds were collected in front of the News, Herald and Tribune. Men, women and children stood and gazed with anxiety, pain and fierce indignation written on their faces.*

At first it appeared that McKinley might survive, but a week later the headline of the Deseret News confirmed the worst. Gangrene had taken the life of the president:

**DESERET NEWS,** *Sept. 14, 1901:*
*Milburn House, Buffalo, N.Y. — William McKinley, twenty-fifth president of the United States, died at 2:15 o'clock this*

*morning from the effects of an assassin's bullet. Theodore Roosevelt, twenty-sixth president of the United States, succeeds to the exalted office under the constitution and the laws of the country and with the administration of the oath of office today, he will begin to exercise the functions of President.*

*But for the moment, the transfer of the government is forgotten in the great sorrow which has fallen on the nation in the passing of President McKinley. Soldier, statesman, president, devoted husband and friend, he was beloved by all who knew him...*

*The President himself fully realized that his hour had come and his mind turned to his Maker. He whispered feebly, "Nearer, My God, to Thee," the words of a hymn always dear to his heart. Then in faint accents he murmured, "Good bye all, good bye. It is God's way. His will be done."*

Condolences came from around the world and the Deseret News, on the day of the death, added the sentiments of Salt Lakers:

**DESERET NEWS,** *Sept. 14, 1901: The die is cast. The end has come. President William McKinley is dead. The event is a calamity too great for words to express. We can only bow our heads in submission to the Divine will, while our eyes are filled with tears and our hearts ache with grief... A mighty soul has ceased to act among the sons of men. We doubt not that his allotted work was finished, and that what he was before appointed to do was accomplished. He has completed a noble career and has gone to his rest and his reward. His blameless life and loving devotion to an invalid wife have not only*

*gained the respect of friend and foe, but endeared him in the people's affections. He was loved as well as esteemed, and therefore his cruel death causes anguish unspeakable.*

In great detail the News followed the current of events, including the rush to fill the national void. A vast crowd awaited the arrival of Theodore Roosevelt in Buffalo, but he was whisked away to Milburn House, where he took the oath of office:

**DESERET NEWS,** *Sept. 14, 1901:*
*PREST. ROOSEVELT IS SWORN IN:*
*"I shall take the oath of office at once, in accordance with your request, and in this hour of deep and terrible national bereavement, I wish to state that it shall be my aim to continue absolutely unbroken the policy of President McKinley for the peace and prosperity and honor of our beloved country."*
*The President stepped farther into the bay window and Judge Hazel, taking up the constitutional oath of office which had been prepared on parchment, asked the*

*President to raise his right hand and repeat it after him. There was a hush like death in the room as the judge read a few words at a time and the President in a strong voice and without a tremor and with his raised hand as steady as if carved from marble, repeated it after him ... The hand dropped to his side, the chin for an instant rested on his breast and the silence remained unbroken for a couple of minutes, as though the new President of the United States was offering silent prayer. Judge Hazel broke it, saying, "Mr. President, please attach your signature," And the president, turning to a small table near by wrote, "Theodore Roosevelt" at the bottom of the document in a firm hand.*

Once more, an orderly succession to the American presidency had survived the outrage of murder.

The assassin, identified in the first news stories as Frank Nieman, actually was Leon F. Czolgosz, a Polish nationalist and anarchist. He later was electrocuted for the crime.

MRS. M'KINLEY AT THE BEDSIDE OF THE PRESIDENT.

# The Great War:
## seeds of conflict

**The nations of Europe had been pitted against each other in a deadly struggle for more than three years while the United States walked a tightrope of neutrality. From the trigger point — the assassination of Prince Franz Ferdinand and his wife in Sarajevo on June 28, 1914 — through three years of escalating battle, the Deseret News followed the fortunes of World War I.**

T hen in April of 1917, banner headlines informed Utahns that their country was going to war in Europe:

**DESERET NEWS,** *April 3, 1917:*
*PREST. WILSON URGES CONGRESS TO TAKE ACTION*
*WASHINGTON — President Wilson tonight urged Congress, assembled in joint session, to declare a state of war existing between the United States and Germany. In a dispassionate, but unmeasured, denunciation of the course of the imperial German government, which he characterized as a challenge to all mankind and a warfare against all nations, the president declared that neutrality no longer was feasible or desirable where the peace of the world was involved…*

Wilson's departure from neutrality was a response to increasing German attacks on civilian shipping, including the sinking of the Lusitania, a British steamship torpedoed off Ireland in April 1915. By 1916, the Germans had brought their U-boats uncomfortably near American shores. The News of Oct. 9, 1916, reported that the captain of a Nantucket lightship had seen three submarines off the coast near Newport, R. I. "GERMAN SUBMARINES PLAY HAVOC WITH BRITISH SHIPS IN AMERICAN WATERS," the headline roared. On April 2, 1917, only a day before Wilson asked Congress to declare war, the Aztec, an armed American merchant ship, was sunk off the coast of France.

In addition, American officials had learned of a German attempt to persuade Mexico to wage war against her northern neighbor, armed with German weapons and bolstered by German troops. The so-called Zimmermann Plot was disclosed to Congress and reported in the same issue of the News.

On April 6, the U.S. House signed the declaration of war earlier approved in the Senate. President Wilson signed the act at 1:11 o'clock, sending the country into a frenzy of preparation. On the same date in Salt Lake City, the annual April conference of the LDS Church began sessions. Church leaders who had supported neutrality in the war, given a new set of circumstances, urged church members to be loyal:

**DESERET NEWS,** *April 6, 1917: The eighty-seventh annual general conference of The Church of Jesus Christ of Latter-day Saints convened in the tabernacle this morning at 10 o'clock. President Joseph F. Smith presided and gave the opening address.*

*President Smith sounded the keynote of the conference, or rather the keynotes, for he voiced several sentiments each of equal importance with the others (including) the absolute necessity of loyalty and unity on the part of Latter-day Saints in the present crisis through which the United States is passing … He said if members of the Church shall be called to defend their country's honor, let them go with no hatred in their hearts, but with the desire to uplift and benefit mankind, if need be even by fighting or giving their lives.*

Utah Sen. Reed Smoot lost no time in introducing Senate bills "likely to make of Salt Lake a great military center," the same newsy April 6 edition reported:

## 1910-1920

The teen years of the new century started with great promise when an old dream came true. The waters of the Pacific Ocean mingled with the Atlantic in Panama, completing one of the great engineering wonders in history. But that same year technology and war turned out to be a bad marriage as they mixed with ancient enmities in the Balkans and Europe. In Sarajevo, Bosnia, an assassination triggered a bewildering set of alliances between countries and launched the Great War. World War I consumed Europe, eventually drawing Utahns to fight on far-off and dangerous battlefields. Great, doomed ships plied the waters — the Lusitania, the Titanic and even the S.S. Utah. To punctuate the misery, as the war neared its end a great, killing epidemic swept the world. Utahns were ready for happier times.

*Beat back the HUN with LIBERTY BONDS*

Utah State Historical Society

Deseret News files

The bills include establishment here of a government munitions factory, an aviation academy and a military supply depot. The munitions plant would be close to the raw materials, and in a protected place. The location of a supply depot here would necessarily mean a brigade post and training camp for all of the recruits of the intermountain country …

Smoot's proposals largely failed, but Utah mightily supported the war effort in many ways. Wounded soldiers were treated in a Fort Douglas hospital. Thousands of volunteers supported Red Cross work. Banks offered loans at 6 percent interest for folks to buy Liberty Bonds that paid 3 percent — and had takers. Families conserved precious commodities or did without. This was a war for home and family. Patriotic fervor was rampant. A few days after war was declared, Utah men were lining up to offer their time, service and lives for the cause:

**DESERET NEWS**, *April 9, 1917:*
*Recruiting for the navy and army is progressing at such a rate that unless the detachments now doing duty in the local districts*

receive additional help, the officers and men in charge will find themselves up against a serious proposition. Applicants for enlistment were so numerous this morning that seats had to be provided for them out in the hallway, while in the offices it was difficult to move around…

At the end of the war in November 1918, the News summarized that Utah had, overall, done better than the national average in providing manpower for the conflict.

For a year and a half, the News reported in detail not only the international and national aspects of the war, but as much as possible on the welfare of the state's own military personnel:

**DESERET NEWS**, *Oct. 26, 1918:*
*THREE BROTHERS IN FRANCE, ONE IS WOUNDED IN BATTLE*
*Lorenzo Young, son of Mr. and Mrs. B. M. Young of this city, was slightly wounded in going "over the top" in France and is now in a base hospital, according to a letter just received from his brother, Gaylen S. Young, who was with him just after the wounding. A third son of Mr. and Mrs. Young — Joseph S. Young — is also in France and recently has been placed in charge of one of the government warehouses there …*

There followed a letter from Gaylen from "Somewhere in France." Almost daily, reports came of the enlistees, the dead, wounded or captured as the early blushes of patriotism bogged down in the reality of an ugly war, the first in history to employ new weapons of mass destruction. Occasionally, in the confusion of the battlefield and mountains of information, mistakes were made:

**DESERET NEWS**, *Oct. 25, 1918:*
*Hyrum Shulsen of West Jordan, who was reported killed in action in France Aug. 4 and for whom military services were held, is alive and recovering in one of the base hospitals in France, according to*

word just received by relatives from the nurse who is attending him. Mr. Shulsen was shot through the throat and in the thigh. Intimation is given that he was left for dead on the battlefield, for one of his identification cards had been removed and he lay among the bodies of the dead. He was later found and sent to a hospital at the rear.

A year and a half after America entered the war, the Germans were beaten. The final awful battles in France routed the Central Powers, which were crumbling both from the beatings without and revolution within. A jubilant Deseret News, under a headline declaring "GLORY TO GOD ON HIGH AND ON EARTH, PEACE" filled pages with details of the armistice:

**DESERET NEWS**, *Nov. 11, 1918:*

**Poster for war bonds is full of patriotic appeal.**

"Good Bye, Dad, I'm Off To Fight For Old Glory. You Buy U.S. GOV'T BONDS"

**THIRD LIBERTY LOAN**

**An officer's tunic from World War I was a simple and sturdy affair. At right, Liberty bonds were sold to help finance the war.**

**DESERET EVENING NEWS.**
LAST EDITION
TRUTH AND LIBERTY.
SIXTY-SEVENTH YEAR
FRIDAY APRIL 6 1917 SALT LAKE CITY UTAH
24 PAGES

# UNITED STATES SEIZES GERMAN MERCHANTMEN

**Vessels Which Sought Refuge at Opening of War Taken in Charge**

MEANS SAFETY POLICY

**President Wilson Signs Resolution Of War and Issues Proclamation That State of War Exists With Germany**

**President Joseph F. Smith Opens Eighty-Seventh Annual Conference Urging Saints to Be Loyal to God and Nation**

Great Tonnage of German Ships Taken in Charge By American Authorities

TEUTON BOATS

WASHINGTON — With the granting of the armistice to the beaten German armies by Marshal Foch, the next step will be the arrangement for the meeting of the peace conference which will endeavor to reach a permanent settlement of the vast issues arising from the great world war... more than four and a half years of incredibly bloody strife have developed problems that may not be permanently adjusted for a generation...

The news set off a hullaballoo in Salt Lake City, a related story told:

**DESERET NEWS,** Salt Lake is celebrating with unprecedented enthusiasm the glorious news of the end of the world war. Cares and worries have been thrown away and men, women and children are joining in the most jubilant celebration ever held in the history of the city. It is a general holiday and only such work as is absolutely necessary is being done. The streets are thronged with joy-mad celebrants ...

A somber undertone, however, reminded Utahns of the cost. On another page of that day's newspaper was the copy of a letter written only a few weeks earlier, Oct. 20, from France. It was sent by Brig. Gen. Richard W. Young to Bryant S. Hinckley, general secretary of Deseret Gymnasium:

My dear friend, No doubt the cable has already conveyed to you the sad news of the death of your son, Stanford, which occurred at 6:30 last evening in the Base hospital near the city of Bordeaux... At noon yesterday I was advised that he was dying... I talked briefly with him and ascertained that there was no service that I could render... He lingered until evening. His funeral will occur tomorrow in the cemetery here. I shall... attend. You have my profound sympathy as have all who know and love him.

With great joy and great sorrow, Utah and the rest of the country noted the end of World War I. It was truly "a war of ones," begun for Americans at 1:11 p.m. on an April day in 1917 and ended on the 11th hour of the 11th day of the 11th month of 1918. Unfortunately, it would not be the last.

# The Russians revolt

**F**rom the beginning of the 20th century to its end, Russian affairs were on the front pages of the newspaper. The birth of communism in that country was duly recorded, but few readers at that time could anticipate what would follow. The century began with Czar Nicholas II in solitary power. He lost part of his authority in the revolution of 1905, which created a parliament. By 1917, facing violent strikes over shortages of bread and coal, he lost all authority when the Russian Duma, ignoring his calls to disband, set up a provisional government headed by Aleksandr Kerensky.

Then Vladimir Lenin, safe in Finland, made his move.

**DESERET NEWS,** Nov. 8, 1917:

KERENSKY'S REGIME FALLS.
London, Nov. 8. — Premier Kerensky has fled from the capital, the semi-official news agency declares. Orders, it states, have been issued for his arrest.
London, Nov. 8. — Premier Kerensky has been deposed. A Proclamation sent out through the wireless stations of the Russian government today and picked up here, states that the garrison and proletariat of Petrograd (St. Petersburg) have deposed the Kerensky government...

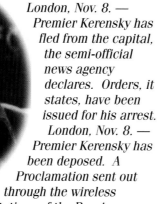

**Lenin**

## Proclamation Issued Sets Forth Aims.

The text of the proclamation of the military revolutionary committee in Russia reads:

We have deposed the government of Kerensky which rose against the revolution and the people. The change which resulted in the deposition of the provisional government was accomplished without bloodshed.

Announcing this to the army at the front [fighting World War I], the revolutionary committee calls upon the revolutionary soldiers to watch closely the conduct of the men in command. Officers who do not join the accomplished revolution immediately and openly must be arrested at once as enemies.

The Petrograd council of workmen's and soldiers' delegates consider this to be the program of the new authority:

First — The offer of an immediate democratic peace.

Second — The immediate handing over of large proprietorial lands to the peasants.

Third — The transmission of all authority to the council of soldiers and workmen's delegates.

Fourth — the honest convocation of a constitutional assembly.

The fate of the czar was resolved later.

**DESERET NEWS,** Nov. 17, 1917:
Efforts of the family of Nicholas Romanoff, the deposed emperor, to live in seclusion in Tobolak, Siberia, and the curiosity displayed by the natives toward the former royal family of Russia, was described by a correspondent... It was because of this curiosity on the part of the people that the former Emperor and his family were transferred to the Abolak monastery, 14 miles from Tobolak.

The Romanoffs occupied in Tobolak the house of the governor, which was guarded by soldiers day and night. In the daytime, the Romanoff children were often seen sunning themselves on the balcony and reading books, one in a little white hat and the other with uncovered head showing the short end after an attack of typhoid fever...

**DESERET NEWS,** July 20, 1918:
London, July 20. Former Emperor Nicholas of Russia has been shot, a Russian wireless statement today announces...

The former empress and the young Alexis Romanoff, the former heir apparent, have been sent to a place of security...

The message announces that a counter revolutionary conspiracy was discovered, with the object of wresting the ex-emperor from the authority of the soviet council. In view of this fact, the president of the Ural regional council decided to execute the former ruler and the decision was carried out only July 16.

The dispatch was, of course, not all true. The czar and his entire family were executed and buried in an unmarked grave. Many more would follow them.

**Czar Nicholas Romanov**

Beehive Collectors Gallery

# Joe Hill
## becomes a legend

**O**n Jan. 10, 1914, grocer John G. Morrison and his 17-year-old son, Arling, were killed during a robbery of their store on the corner of West Temple and 800 South.

A 35-year-old Swedish immigrant known variously as Joseph Hillstrom, Joel Hagglund and Joe Hill, was arrested for the murders. He came to Utah in 1913 to work in the Park City mines and was active in the Industrial Workers of the World movement. He was also known for his songs based on the experiences of the working man.

Evidence was mostly circumstantial: Hillstrom had been treated for an "ugly wound in the breast" at the home of a Murray physician about two hours after the robbery. He later wore a suit in which the name "Morrison" had been printed in the arms and pant legs with indelible ink.

Although Hillstrom maintained his innocence, the evidence was enough that a jury found him guilty of murder. He was sentenced to die before a firing squad.

Largely because of his IWW connections, the case drew worldwide attention.

**DESERET NEWS,** *Aug. 1, 1914: In a telegram from James Rohn, A.R. Douglass and Bob Scott purporting to represent 500 working men of Tacoma, Wash., Governor William Spry is notified that he will be held personally responsible for the well being of Joseph Hillstrom, alias Joe Hill…*

*The telegram was received this morning and is the last of a number of communications received by the governor during the last few days asking that the chief executive intervene in the Hillstrom case.*

Appeals and even two requests from President Woodrow Wilson managed to delay execution, but not to prevent it.

**DESERET NEWS,** *Nov. 18, 1915: Joseph Hillstrom will pay the death penalty tomorrow morning at the state prison for the murder of J.G. Morrison and his son, Governor Spry having declined to* reconsider the action of the board of pardons at the request of Prest. Woodrow Wilson. In a telegram sent to Prest. Wilson late this afternoon Gov. Spry takes the chief executive of the nation to task for his interference in the matter a second time.

And a reporter was sent to the prison to talk to the prisoner:

*At the state prison today, Hillstrom said this is his busy day, but he would grant a few moments time to a representative of The News. He smiled as he looked up from a letter he was writing, but could not hide his nervousness. The condemned man said he is not afraid to die as he has never done anything wrong in all his life. He was not voluble and what he said came as answers to questions. He said he has nothing to explain. It is, he said, "up to other people to explain."*

**DESERET NEWS,** *Nov. 19, 1915: Joseph Hillstrom was shot to death at the state prison at 7:42 o'clock this morning. When the signal was given to get "ready," Hillstrom shouted "Fire" but he waited several seconds before he paid the penalty for the murder of J.G. Morrison. The aim of the executioners was accurate and the condemned man whose crime and conviction had affected world-wide attention was pronounced dead just 1 minute and 14 seconds after the volley was fired.*

**DESERET NEWS,** *Nov. 19, 1915: Joseph Hillstrom when asked if he had a last will to make before he paid the penalty for the crime for which he was convicted, replied that he had nothing of which to dispose. He then wrote three short verses which was his will and which he asked to have delivered to Ed Rowan and his other I.W.W. friends. Hillstrom also wrote a last poem or song, composing his own music, and made several copies of it for different persons including one man who was on the death watch. This is of a sentimental nature and refers to the breaking up of families by war.*

USS Utah

Dec. 23, 1909

## Battleship Utah Rides the Stream

PHILADELPHIA — Declared to have no equal afloat as a first-class fighting machine, the battleship Utah, the greatest warship ever built in the United States, was launched at 11 a.m. today at the yard of the New York Ship building company of Camden, N. J. in the presence of several thousand people who crowded the docks and every vantage point in the vicinity of the yard.

As the big hull started to leave the thickly greased ways, Miss Mary Alice Spry of Salt Lake City, daughter of the governor of Utah, raised her arm and broke a gaily beribboned bottle of champagne against the cut-water of the great ship as she spoke the words that gave the vessel its name.

**The pride of landlocked Utahns proudly took its place in the U.S. fleet and served long and well. It figured prominently in the blockade of Vera Cruz during the Mexican revolution and saw its end in the infamous Japanese attack on Pearl Harbor. It remains sunken but visible in the harbor as a lasting memorial.**

Joseph Hillstrom, above in handcuffs after his arrest, drew international attention to his case.

# DESERET EVENING NEWS.

TRUTH AND LIBERTY.

Jan. 31, 1910

## WANTS ARIZONA STRIP

(Special to the News)

WASHINGTON — A bill for the annexation to Utah of that portion of Arizona lying north and west of the Colorado river, will be added as an amendment to the [Arizona] statehood bill by Senator Smoot. It is thought the rider will go through with the parent legislation.

Five thousands dollars has been asked by representative Howell in the Indian appropriation for the straightening of the Duchesne River at Theodore, Utah. The amount will be made good out of the sale of town lots and is to be expended under the supervision of the secretary of the interior.

Feb. 12, 1910

One of the most thrilling and entertaining exhibitions ever witnessed in the state perhaps, aside from Paulhan's flight at the fair grounds some time ago, was witnessed by thousands who stood anxiously as the huge crane operated by Jones company at the Hotel Utah, which is said to be the largest ever set up in the State of Utah, raised a Hupmobile 150 feet to mid air Thursday afternoon. Mr. A.E. White of the Motor company sat at the wheel and was reflecting into the probability of whether or not his life insurance policy would be paid as he hung suspended in space. As the crowd cheered, he raised his hat, smiled and tooted the horn.

April 22, 1910

## MARK TWAIN DIED PAINLESSLY

REDDING, CONN. — Samuel Langhorne Clemens (Mark Twain) died painlessly at 4:30 o'clock tonight of angina pectoris. He lapsed into coma at 3 o'clock this afternoon and never recovered consciousness. It was the end of a man outworn by grief and acute agony of body…

He recognized his daughter Clara (Mrs. Ossip Gabrilowistsch), spoke a rational word or two and feeling himself unequal to conversation, wrote out in pencil:

TWAIN'S LAST WORDS:

"Give me my glasses."

These were his last words. Laying them aside, he sank first into reverie and later into final unconsciousness…

May 18, 1910

## The Earth Now in the Tail of the Comet

Preparations have been made at all observatories, public and private, to note all unusual atmospheric, optical and electrical phenomena that may happen today. No man can say what is exactly going to happen, but on one point all astronomers are agreed, and that is the absolute harmlessness of the event. This morning at 3:30 the comet's tail stretched over one half of the visible heavens, beginning at the horizon below the square of Pegasus involving the lowest star, Gamma, which shone with but slightly diminished luster through it and ending in the milky way below Aquila…

Dec. 14, 1911

## PAPER TOWELS IN SCHOOLS

There is a controversy brewing among the members of the board of education as to the advisability of inaugurating sanitary paper towels in the public schools in place of the present linen towels, which are said to be breeders and dissemenators of disease.

At the request of many teachers the committee on teachers is seeking to have the paper towels adopted. The committee on public buildings is opposed to the idea on the grounds that the paper towel is not sanitary and that its use in other cities has proven a failure.

Aug. 14, 1912

## NO TELEPHONE IN CITY SCHOOLS

Service Would Cost $1,200 a Year, Which Board Thinks is Too High

Aug. 19, 1912

## Richards Returns From Olympic Games

Alma W. Richards, who represented Utah in the Olympic games in Sweden, winning first place in the running high jump, arrived in Salt Lake this afternoon. Richards is in the best of health and says that he enjoyed the trip immensely.

On Wednesday evening, he will be the guest of honor at a banquet given at the Roberts Hotel in Provo by the athletic committee of the Brigham Young University. Richards will be presented with a medal by the institution which he represented.

Coach E.L. Roberts of the BYU went to Thistle last night and met Richards there on the Denver & Rio Grande Western…

**Mark Twain**

(Richards broke the world high jump record in the Stockholm meet, fifth competition in the modern Olympics.)

Sept. 19, 1912

**PROGRESS OF STRIKE:** One thousand armed strikers are still holding possession of Utah Copper mountain; Deputy Sheriff Otto Witbeck rescues night watchman from Utah Copper pumping station; President Moyer (of Western Federation of Miners) announces that strikers have promised to stop shooting promiscuously… Garfield Smelter may soon be forced to close.

BINGHAM — After an extended conference of Gov. Spry, mine operators, state officials and others, this morning was decided that troops will not be ordered to Bingham until it has been shown that Sheriff Sharp and his men are not able to handle the situation…

Although hundreds of shots were fired at Bingham last night and the occasion was one of the wildest the camp has ever known, there were no casualties. All night long the armed foreigners who have entrenched themselves on the terraces of the Utah Copper mountain continued to shoot off fire arms.

Oct. 10, 1912

BINGHAM — One man was shot in the leg, another was knocked down and one arrest was made this morning as a result of men going to work this morning in the Utah Copper and Utah Consolidated properties. One steam shovel is now working steadily at the Utah Copper, over 100 men [imported strikebreakers] are at work…

Oct. 5, 1912:

## CHURCH WILL BUILD TEMPLE IN ALBERTA, CANADA

A proposition to build a temple in Canada was placed before the general priesthood meeting held in the assembly hall last evening and met with instantaneous and unanimous support. The temple will be built, according to the decision of the meeting, just as soon as possible and at a point within the province of Alberta, Canada, to be decided upon later and of such a character as to meet the needs of the people of the section in which it will be constructed…

Oct. 23, 1912

## Groundbreaking Ceremony

In a blustering breeze that gave the air an uncomfortable chill and under a sky which was overclouded and threatening, 1,500 people assembled at the University (of Utah) campus this morning to witness the laying of the cornerstone of the new administration building, to be the finest educational structure in the intermountain region…

In the underside of the stone a cavity had been chiseled for the sealed copper box containing various articles relating to the university and the new building and which rested upon the (base) stone… the granite block was lowered over it…

President Joseph T. Kingsbury stated the purpose of the gathering and called it an important event in the history of the state. He spoke of the value of higher education to the race and declared that without it, the world would move backward rather than forward…

Jan. 1, 1913

What shall we do for our annual Thanksgiving feasts when the turkeys are all gone? How shall we replace the toothsome white meat, the satisfying and succulent dark flesh and the drumstick and other bones that yield such satisfactory picking? With what else will the well-flavored cranberry go so well?

Idle questions? Not a bit of it! Soon the turkey, at the present rate of decrease, will be only a gastronomic memory… The census bureau in Washington has issued a bulletin showing that in 1910 there were only 3,663,708 turkeys on farms in the United States, while in 1900, there were 6,594,095. At that rate, the turkey will be practically extinct in 1920 …

Jan. 28, 1913

New York, Jan. 27. — James Thorpe, the Indian athlete and Olympic champion, today admitted that charges of professionalism brought against him were true and formally retired from amateur athletics…

The letter admitted that Thorpe had played baseball for a salary on a professional team three years ago while a student of the Carlisle Indian school, but said that on the same team there were several northern college men who were regarded as amateurs and Thorpe did not realize his participation was wrong. Thorpe added that he did not play for the money he earned but for the love of the game.

Thorpe's winnings of the Pentathlon and Decathlon

**Jim Thorpe**

events at the Olympic games in Stockholm and later his wonderful performances which won for him the all-around championship of the A.A.U. at Celtic Park last September have stamped him the most marvelous all-around athlete of modern times...

All the prizes and the honors which Thorpe has gained since 1909... must be transferred... to the men who finished second to the Indian in every event.

**Feb. 1, 1913**

## DISCUSSION OF EIGHT-HOUR LAW

The house committee on labor held another protracted session at the New Grand hotel yesterday for the consideration of H.B. 28 by Southwick of Utah county, which extends the eight-hour law to factories, coal mines and above ground workings....

George S. McCallister (president of the Manufacturers association of Utah) said that if the eight-hour law was made applicable to factories, then manufacturing in Utah must cease, for as it is the manufacturers are competing against higher freight rates and the 12-hour labor of the east.

Mrs. Elizabeth Cohen (of the Federated Women's Clubs) said that she did not care to ask that the eight-hour law be made to apply to women and girls. The women were well satisfied for the time at least with the nine-hour law passed by the last legislature . . .

**Feb. 1, 1913**

There are two plans for a Lincoln monument before Congress. One provides for the erection in Potomac park of a structure in the form of a Greek temple, sheltering a bronze statue of the immortal statesman. The other provides for a road from Washington to Gettysburg. Both plans have opponents, as well as supporters . . .

**Feb. 3, 1913**

## SIXTEENTH AMENDMENT

CHEYENNE, Wyo. — Not a dissenting vote was registered in either house of the Wyoming Legislature this forenoon on the joint resolution ratifying the income tax amendment to the federal Constitution. The resolution of ratification was introduced in Senate . . . and was taking the usual course until the legislators learned that only one state was needed to make the amendment effective. Thereupon, when the senate met this morning, Sen. Kendrick moved the resolution be taken up under a suspension of the rules and voted upon. This was done and immediately forwarded to the house, where it was expedited through . . . The resolution is now on its way to the governor for his signature . . . The income tax is now one of the provisions of the Constitution of the United States. Wyoming's ratification of the income tax amendment — the sixteenth change in the Constitution and the first since the reconstruction — completed a list of 36 states,

three-fourths of the Union, which have approved the provision.

**Nov. 24, 1913**

BERLIN — Emperor William's edict forbidding German army and navy officers to dance the tango and other steps while in uniform has been taken to heart here and the same rule has been introduced throughout the diplomatic circle.

A hurried change was made today in the program for the dance to be held after the Thanksgiving dinner of the American colony . . . .

**Nov. 24, 1913**

[By Walt Mason, who wrote a daily item, in verse, for the News]

MRS. PANKHURST: She has come across the sea/ To explain to you and me/Why the women of old England/Tried to pound their country flat./ Let us hope she won't incite/Native suffragists to fight,/ Won't stir up to bloody battle Rheta Dorr and Carrie Catt./ Mrs. Pankhurst is a duck/And I wish her bully luck/And I hope her suffrage coffers ne'er will seem an aching void./But I cannot help but think/That her errand's on the blink,/That a dame like Mrs. Pankhurst should be usefully employed . . .

**Dec. 14, 1913**

EXETER, England — Mrs. Emmeline Pankhurst, the militant suffragette leader, was lodged today in Exeter jail. The police who arrested her on board the Majestic on her arrival from New York outwitted the women sympathizers who had been watching to resist her arrest . . .

At her request, Mrs. Rheta Dorr, an American, was permitted to accompany her.

**Nov. 29, 1913**

## WARD ENTERTAINMENTS

EMERSON WARD — A farewell testimonial will be tendered Avard Fairbanks, the promising boy sculptor, Friday, Dec. 5 in the Emerson Ward Chapel. Mr. Fairbanks leaves shortly for Europe, where he will continue his studies . . .

**Dec. 13, 1913**

## LOST MONA LISA IS RECOVERED

FLORENCE, Italy — The authenticity of the Mona Lisa found yesterday in possession of Vincenzo Perugia, was confirmed by experts after further examination today.

The picture bears the seals of the Louvre and other galleries in which it has been hung, while the traces of repairs at the back of the canvas, known to have been made, are also visible.

The prisoner was again questioned by the police authorities this morning. He repeated his story of

having stolen the picture as an act of patriotic vengeance for Napoleon's depredations in Italy. He displayed the utmost indignation at his treatment by the police, declaring it unjust after the risks he had run and the abnegation he had demonstrated out of patriotic sentiment. . . .

News of the discovery of the Mona Lisa spread in the chamber of deputies in session at Rome, where extremist members were engaged in fisticuffs in an endeavor to prevent a vote on the election of a Nationalist deputy for Rome. The disorder ceased immediately. . . .

**July 30, 1914**

## FORTY STAGES HELD UP IN THE YELLOWSTONE

Mammoth Hot Springs, Yellowstone Park, July 29. — Two masked bandits held up about 40 stages near Shoshone Point this morning, robbing the 165 passengers of more than $3,000 in money. At the point of a rifle, one of the bandits forced the tourists to drop their money into a flour sack while his confederate kept the stage drivers under guard and prevented them from returning to Old Faithful geyser and spreading the alarm. So quickly did the bandits complete their work that the stages were less than an hour late in arriving at the Thumb lunch station. No shots were fired. . . .

As each stage coach drove up the approach to Shoshone point the driver was commanded to throw up his hands. The passengers were ordered out of the coaches and with the order of "Cash only, gents" the bandit with the rifle compelled them to drop their money in the sack . . .

**July 15, 1914:**

## WARNING TO CAFES WITH WOMEN ENTERTAINERS

The county attorney today sent word by personal representative to every cafe in town where women entertainers hold forth, advising the proprietors that girl singers must be kept upon the stage or platform and must not be permitted to parade around among the tables of guests; also that suggestive songs, actions or conduct will not be allowed. The clothing or costumes of performers must also be adequate and not immodest and the performers must conduct themselves in an orderly and decent manner . . .

The county attorney says that the Hotel Utah, whose entertainments are conducted in accordance with these suggestions and which is therefore in no need of the warning, is omitted from the list of those called upon.

**Aug. 13, 1914**

## TETZLAFF HANGS UP HALF-MILE RECORD FOR AUTO

Teddy Tetzlaff, the speed king, accomplished a world's record for a half mile yesterday afternoon on the salt beds at Salduro when he covered the distance in 12.6 seconds. In making the record, he attained a speed of 142.8 miles per hour. A mile course was marked off, but the heat waves wiggled so much that the timers were unable to catch the start that far away. At a half mile, the race could be easily timed and the Blitzen Benz was sent for the record.

**May 8, 1915:**

## 1364 WENT DOWN WITH S.S. LUSITANIA

### MANY AMERICANS LOST ON GREAT CUNARDER

LONDON — Fifteen hundred persons lost their lives, the British Admiralty estimates, when the Cunard Line steamship Lusitania was torpedoed yesterday afternoon off Old Head, Kinsale, on the Irish coast [by a German submarine.]

The known survivors number only 658, while there were 2,160 souls aboard the great liner when she was attacked . . .

The United States consul at that port can account for only 61 Americans saved out of 188 who were aboard . . .

The heavy loss of life among the . . . passengers is believed to have been due to the calmness and self possession they displayed in face of danger. Most of them were at luncheon when the steamer radioed her death blow and declined to rush for the boats and lifebelts. . . .

QUEENSTOWN, via LONDON — The various craft that yesterday afternoon went out from here to the scene of the Lusitania disaster returned to Queenstown last night and early this morning. All of them brought survivors in greater or lesser numbers. It is now estimated here that 600 will be the outside number of those saved. No trace has been found here of either Alfred G. Vanderbilt or Charles Froman. The latest rescue boats to arrive are bringing mostly bodies of the dead picked up from the water at the scene of the disaster . . .

WASHINGTON — Appalled by the tragic aspect

of the Lusitania disaster, as hourly developments disclosed its magnitude and far-reaching possibilities, with the probable loss of 157 American lives, President Wilson and his advisers are waiting for all the facts and for a crystalization of public opinion to aid in laying out the course the United States will pursue in this latest international complication, the gravest the president has faced since the outbreak of the European War . . .

LONDON — The Exchange Telegraph company has received today the following telegram from Copenhagen:

Berlin newspapers print the news of the sinking of the Lusitania in colossal type and hail the successful torpedoing of the ship as a new triumph for Germany's naval policy. The general impression is that England has got what she deserves.

*Oct. 12, 1916*

## CHURCH OFFICES NEAR COMPLETION

Construction work is nearing completion on the new Church office building being erected on east South Temple street between Main and State streets. It is expected that the opening, long delayed because of unfilled marble contracts, will take place about the first of the year, when one of the handsomest edifices in the city will be occupied by the officers of the general Church authorities. The whole structure, when completed, will be replete with the best of home products, from the golden travers marble in the entrance, from the Utah quarries, to the very granite blocks which finish the upper parapet . . .

*July 20, 1918*

The local headquarters of the Red Cross, at 70 East South Temple street, received another contribution this morning when Eugene Waring, 12 years of age, 1017 Second avenue, appeared before office hours and patiently waited until the doors of the Gardo House were opened. His contribution was 76 cents to aid in the great [World War I] cause, the proceeds of a magic lantern show which he had given at his home.

*Nov. 11, 1918 (Armistice Day)*

## LOVE PACT ENDS WITH DOUBLE TRAGEDY

Apparently the result of a mutual agreement, Bert Walker, a boiler-maker of Magna, yesterday morning shot and instantly killed Mrs. Glenda Titcomb Smith, 15-year-old war bride of Alma E. Smith, who is with the American expeditionary forces in France, and then fired a bullet into his own body, causing his death a few hours later. . . The tragedy, forming the climax of an unlicensed love affair between the two, occurred in a room at the Panama rooming house at Magna at 10 o'clock yesterday morning. A note left by the young woman indicated that the two had entered a death pact.

# THE LOPEZ MANHUNT

**On Nov. 12, 1913 Rafael Lopez "the devil-may-care dandy of the Latin community" went courting his lady, Inez Ocaro, of Bingham, and found her with Juan Valdez. He went home, loaded a powerful army rifle and two automatic pistols, then "cooly took his stand outside Ocaro's home" and waited for Valdez, whom he shot as he exited. With Valdez dead, Lopez took off running and for the next two weeks law officers chased him through Salt Lake and Utah counties. He killed three officers in the process, then circled back to Bingham and holed up in the Apex mine. Soon, two more men were dead.**

*Nov. 29, 1913*

BINGHAM — Rafael Lopez has added two more deputies to his list of victims. Deputy Sheriff Douglas Hulsey and an Austrian deputy named Tom Mandrich have been shot and one of them is either dead or mortally wounded; the groans of one of the men can be heard in the Andy tunnel of the Utah Apex mine.

Deputies Hulsey and Mandrich were shot by the Mexican fugitive from his hiding place in the blind Larson stope… Their intention was to build a fire of hay, sulphur and formaldehyde, and force Lopez from hiding.

*Dec. 1, 1913*

BINGHAM — Choking, blinding suffocating smoke and gases are pouring out of every tunnel entrance to the mountain in which are burrowed the workings of the Utah-Apex Mine. The entire hillside is covered with a poisonous vapor and all save the guards standing grimly at their posts have left the mountain side in an effort to escape from the smoke. If Rafael Lopez has not found a sealed refuge in the mine, he has either been strangled to death or will not live out the hour.

*Dec. 13, 1913*

BINGHAM — A new sensation was developed in the hunt of Rafael Lopez when it was reported last night to Sheriff Smith that Sam Rogers, a shift boss at the Utah-Apex mine, has been accosted by and conversed with Lopez in the Andy tunnel both on Thursday and yesterday… To Rogers, according to the latter's statement, Lopez declared "I'll die fighting," and although he realized that he is trapped, he would face it out until the end …

**Certain that Lopez could not have escaped the fumes they created, officials scoured the mine for two more weeks. No trace of Lopez was found. On Jan. 5, 1914, with law enforcement officials complaining about the cost of the manhunt and mine officials anxious to resume full operations, the search was called off. Lopez's whereabouts became one of Utah's unsolved mysteries.**

## You'll quit home baking if you try this delicious, big HOLSUM loaf

You've often wished you could stop bread baking. The terrific heat of the summer bake day—the danger of catching cold in winter—the demands it makes on your precious time—have made you long for the right kind of bread to take the place of yours.

You'll find the kind of bread you've longed for in the big ten-cent loaf of HOLSUM The large loaf means less waste, too! From the same dough, the big loaf is better quality than the small.

### For Quality and Economy Buy the Big Loaf

You'll find HOLSUM everything you can ask for in bread. It is close-grained, substantial, and with a wonderful flavor that

*"Takes You Back to Younger Days"*

## Made By Superior Baking Co.

# The world of the 1910s
## A TIMELINE

**1910**— Congress enacts the Mann Act, prohibiting transportation of women across state lines for immoral acts.

**1910**— Stravinsky's "The Firebird" ballet creates a sensation in Paris.

**1910**— Halley's comet visits.

**1911**— Raold Amundsen, a Norwegian, beats British Captain Robert Scott to the South Pole.

**1911**— Dr. Sun Yat-Sen becomes the provisional president of a new Chinese Republic.

**1911**— "Alexander's Ragtime Band" written by Irving Berlin.

**1911**— The Nobel Prize for chemistry is given to Marie Curie.

**1912**— New Mexico and Arizona become states.

**1912**— The Ottoman Empire's domination of the Balkans ends in bloody war with Serbia, Bosnia, Bulgaria and Greece.

**1913**— The Federal Reserve System established.

**1913**— Arthur Wynne invents the crossword puzzle for the New York World.

**1913**— Henry Ford produces automobiles on an assembly line and gears up for mass production of the Model T.

**1913**— Grand Central Terminal opens in New York City.

**1914**— "Pygmalion," a play by George Bernard Shaw, opens in London.

**1914**— Europe is at war, while the United States struggles to stay neutral.

**1915**— Albert Einstein releases his General Theory of Relativity.

**1915**— Edgar Lee Masters authors "A Spoon River Anthology."

**1915**— D.W. Griffith films "Birth of a Nation."

**1916**— The National Park Service is established in the Department of the Interior.

**1916**— The first Rose Bowl football game played: Washington State College defeats Brown University.

**1917**— Mata Hari is executed as a German spy by the Allies.

**1917**— The Trans-Siberian railroad, begun in 1891, completed.

**1917**— Finland proclaims itself a republic and breaks from Russia.

**1918**— The British government drops its plan for home rule for Ireland.

**1918**— Jerome Kern and Irving Berlin both have plays in New York.

**1918**— Knute Rockne becomes the head football coach at Notre Dame.

**1918**— Max Planck wins the Nobel Prize for physics after introducing the quantum theory.

**1919**— The League of Nations is formed to promote peace, but the U.S. Congress won't accept it.

**1919**— Ignace Paderewski becomes premier of Poland.

**1919**— The "Black Sox" baseball scandal stuns the nation.

**1919**— President Woodrow Wilson wins the Nobel Peace Prize.

**1919**— Dixieland Jazz wows the audiences in London.

# Refugees from Mexico

Mexico's longstanding civil upheavals of the early 20th century were watched closely by Utahns because of a half dozen Mormon colonies spotted throughout northern Mexico. The Deseret News sometimes gave more play to the action south of the border than to the bubbling troubles in Europe

Francisco Villa

AP Photo

In August 1912, when rebel general Pancho Villa rampaged through the area and threatened Americans, officials decided to abandon the colonies and bring the LDS settlers back to the United States. They left in haste:

**DESERET NEWS,**
Aug. 7, 1912:
[A letter to LDS Presiding Bishop (Charles W.) Nibley from Bishop O.P. Miller]
I visited the refugees late in the evening and found a condition that was most appalling. Quite a number of women and children were ill and several infant babes had been born en route and since the arrival at El Paso.
The government is furnishing some supplies and the people of El Paso have been very liberal with their means and have rendered very valuable assistance. One train came in last evening with quite a number of wounded soldiers, and it is reported here this morning that there is some firing across the line between some Americans and Mexicans…
The sight presented to my view is one of the most heart rending that I have ever witnessed — to see over 2,000 people, mostly women and children, driven from their homes without time to gather even their personal effects and most of them without a dollar to assist themselves with. We shall have to draw heavily upon the church for relief.

As the colonists continued to escape, some had brushes with the Mexican rebels:

**DESERET NEWS,** Aug. 17, 1912: EL PASO, Texas — For the first time since the western portion of Chihuahua was colonized by American followers of the "Mormon" religion more than 25 years ago, that state is entirely deserted by the colonists. From the American border at Hachita, New Mexico, to Colonia

FRANCISCO VILLA.

Chuichupa, 226 miles south, a territory that contains six "Mormon" towns, not a single colonist remains.
The last party of refugees, 42 men from Chuichupa, have arrived at Hachita after a 200-mile journey overland. They brought with them a band of 100 horses which were driven across the United States border in bond. Also, they brought an interesting story of their flight through the country that is now filled with federal soldiers who are driving the rebels out.
By the time the 42 evacuated Chuichupa the town had been captured by rebels who took possession of the homes of the colonists, looted their stores and made themselves at home. They did not attempt to prevent the colonists from leaving, for, as S.H. Vester said, "They knew we were going if we had to fight our way out."

When Villa's rebels crossed the border and killed 18 Americans in Columbus, N.M., U.S. leaders sent Gen. J. J. "Black Jack" Pershing to capture the Mexican strongman:

**DESERET NEWS,** April 10, 1916: General Pershing's Headquarters at Front, via Mexican telegraph to Juarez: Renewed reports have been received here by Gen. Pershing that Francisco Villa is dead and buried. These reports are under investigation. Meanwhile the hunt for the Villistas is proceeding with renewed vigor with the arrival at the front of Gen. Pershing.
Pershing never did catch up with the elusive Villa, who was, in fact, not dead. But the general had brought himself to the notice of America's top military officials and when war broke out in Europe, he made his lasting reputation as head of the American Expeditionary Forces.
The Mexican revolution lasted for several years longer, but interest in Utah declined with the advent of World War I and the loss of the Mormon colonies south of the border.

Feb. 15, 1913

## THE CORSETLESS GIRL.

The corset has been more or less under the ban for many generations. Sermons have been thunderous against it from the pulpit. Doctors have denounced it as not only unhygienic and injurious to the wearer, but a peril to the race. "Dress reformers" have endeavored to persuade their sisters to give up the contrivance and return to nature; but all in vain. The corset has persisted. Much thought has been given to perfecting its lines. Fortunes have been made by designers and manufacturers of styles that met the approval of the fair corset wearers.
The grandmothers frowned on the corset, but now they have reason to frown because the sweet girl graduates into society, the debutantes of Washington, have discarded their stays. The cry is now not "back to nature" but "back to the corset." The grandmothers, when they inveighed so earnestly against this mysterious garment, never suspected the advent of the turkey trot and the bunny hug and the various "dips" and "glides" that have made the waltz and two-step seem almost as tame to the younger set as the quadrille and the minuet seemed to the debutantes of five years ago. And there's the rub.
One fair young creature in Washington discovered that by discarding the corset she became without the slightest effort, the belle of the ball. The fateful secret soon became known to others. The corsetless girl instantly made her appearance in large numbers at every dance. Her elder sister, her cousins, her aunts, her mother and grandmothers are all imploring her to resume the corset. There is no question of hygiene, no question of personal discomfort or injury, no fears for the future of the race. The elder matrons maintain that the bunny hug and the turkey trot and the "dips" and "glides" make the corset imperative to the ballroom.
While the society leaders in Philadelphia and other cities are trying by every influence at their command to eliminate these very modern and very popular dances, it would seem as if discarding the corset would strengthen their hands. But then, all this must remain a mystery to mere man, and the solution of a very perplexing problems may well be left to the ladies themselves. — Philadelphia Press.

# Titanic

**Things like this were not supposed to happen in the gilded world of 1912. So it is not surprising that the first dispatches were optimistic.**

In 1912, German artist Willy Stoewer envisioned this scene of the Titanic sinking bow first.

**DESERET NEWS,** *April 15, 1912: Halifax, N.S. — The Canadian government marine agency here at 4:15 p.m. received a wireless dispatch that the Titanic is sinking... It is said the steamers towing the Titanic were endeavoring to get her into shoal water near Cape Race to beach her... While badly damaged, the Titanic is still afloat and is reported to be making her way toward Halifax under her own steam.*

It would not be long, however, before the truth of the matter became painfully clear. The Virginian arrived too late to render assistance. The Parisian rescued no passengers. Only the Carpathia had been able to pick up survivors: 868. The inconceivable had happened. The Titanic was lost.

The largest steamship ever built, the Titanic was 882 feet long and had 46,328 tons displacement. She was making her maiden voyage from London to New York, and her passenger list read like a who's who: Col. and Mrs. John Jacob Astor; Maj. Archibald Bett, military aide to President Taft; F.D. Millet, the artist; Mrs. and Mrs. Isador Strauss; J.G. Widener of Philadelphia; President Hays of the Grand Trunk railway... In all the liner carried 1,400 passengers and 800 crew.

At 2:20 on the morning of April 15, the glorious ship struck an iceberg just off the coast of Newfoundland and sank. Later dispatches filled in the tragic details:

**DESERET NEWS,** *April 16, 1912: The appalling magnitude of the wreck of the liner Titanic has been little mitigated by the fragmentary information which has filtered in today... The favorable details are insignificant compared with the fact that the Titanic is now at the bottom of the Atlantic and that the shattered wreck*

took with her about 1,350 victims to their death...

*Tearful crowds of relatives and friends of passengers on board the Titanic thronged the steamship offices in all the three offices, visiting hour after hour for news that more often than not meant bereavement and sorrow... Of the survivors on board the Carpathia by far the largest number are women and children. Many men of prominence on two continents are among the missing... The $100,000,000 steamship with cargo and jewels worth perhaps $10,000,000 more, is a total loss.*

**DESERET NEWS,** *April 17, 1912: The Cunarder Carpathia bearing 868 survivors of the sunken White Star liner Titanic was less than 600 miles from New York at noon today and the word was eagerly awaited that would shed light on the catastrophe.*

*Hope that the list of survivors of the sunken Titanic will be added to has practically been given up...*

**DESERET NEWS,** *April 18, 1912: President Taft today made public cablegrams received from the king and queen of England and the king of Belgium, conveying their sympathies to the American people in the sorrows which have followed the Titanic disaster. The president's response to both messages was made public.*

And finally...

**DESERET NEWS,** *April 19, 1912: Seven hundred and forty-five persons, mostly women, sick in heart and body, wrote in the annals of maritime history today the loss of the biggest steamship ever built by man. They were the survivors of the White Star liner Titanic which sank, bow foremost, with 1,595 souls aboard, her captain at the bridge, her colors flying and her band playing "Nearer, My God, to Thee" in 2,000 fathoms of water on the banks of Newfoundland under the starlit skies at 2:20 a.m. Monday.*

*With one voice they told of the splendid heroism of those who remained behind to*

find a watery grave that they might live.

*Capt. Smith died, they said, as a gallant sailor should, after having first placed all the women who would go aboard the lifeboats. There were many who stayed behind to die in their husbands' arms.*

*From their narrow lives stand out in relief the following facts:*

*The Titanic was making 21 knots an hour when she struck the iceberg.*

*No one at first thought she would sink. She remained afloat more than two hours.*

*The iceberg ripped open the hull below the water line.*

*Instant panic was averted by Capt. Smith's terse appeal to his crew: "Be British, my men."*

*A small number of steerage passengers tried to rush for the lifeboats and were held back by the crew and other passengers.*

*The Titanic turned her nose for the bottom when the last lifeboat was less than a hundred yards away, reared her stern high in the air and trembled for a moment before seeking the bottom.*

*There were two explosions when the inrushing waters reached her boilers.*

*When she sank there was silence; a moment later the cries and supplications of 1,500 dying men rose in chorus indescribable over the spot where she went down.*

For days afterward, the grim reports continued to come in: more bodies recovered, more reports of the death struggles of the victims, more names revealed. Mixed in were a few tales of heroism: how Fifth Officer Harold Lowe rescued 23 people from death; how John Bruce Ismay, president of the International Marine company, had to be forced into the last lifeboat; how Mrs. Isador Strauss refused to leave her husband, remaining with him to the last.

Congress immediately began holding hearings to try to make sense of it all. Survivors testified, experts analyzed, the ship's designer questioned.

No ship is unsinkable, they concluded. But out of it all came one glaring mistake: There simply were not enough lifeboats aboard the Titanic to carry all the passengers to safety.

At least no ship would ever set sail in that condition again.

# Panama Canal:
## a 'stupendous achievement'

**DESERET NEWS,** *Aug. 13, 1914: The first steamship to pass through the Panama canal — the Cristobal — made the trip from the Atlantic to the Pacific in 11 1/2 hours.*

*The return trip, however, was made in 8 1/2 hours, which probably marks the average time that will be consumed by merchant men when all of the machinery of the canal is in smooth operation. The Cristobal made the experimental voyage Aug. 3 and 4 and at the time was drawing 25 feet of water.*

*Last Sunday Gov. Geothals in recognition of their services allowed a number of the old employees to traverse the canal from one ocean to the other on the steamer Advance and it is reported that everything is in perfect order for the formal opening of the canal next Saturday.*

The idea of a canal to join the Pacific and Atlantic oceans was dreamed of as early as 1517, when Vasco Nunez de Balboa, the first European to reach the Pacific, talked about the possibilities.

Early attempts considered by Great Britain and the United States would have put the canal in Nicaragua. In 1878, the French began digging across the isthmus of Panama, but the company went broke before much was done.

In 1903, following a revolution in which Panama declared independence from Colombia, the United States signed a treaty that gave it use and control of a canal zone. In 1904, the Americans took over the French property and went to work.

Construction of the canal was an engineering marvel, costing the United States $310 million. Along the way, great strides were made in medicine as well, in learning methods to reduce yellow fever and malaria.

Ten years later, the canal was finished.

**DESERET NEWS,** *Aug. 15, 1914: The United States warship Ancon today made the passage through the Panama canal, and transit through the waterway is now officially open to the traffic of the world.*

*The Ancon left her berth at Cristobal at 7 o'clock this morning and made her way to the end of the deep water channel from the Atlantic to the Gatun locks. She went through these locks, which have a lift of 85 feet, in seventy minutes. She continued through the waterway from deep water on the Atlantic to deep water on the Pacific side without incident.*

The 50-mile canal goes from Limon Bay on the Atlantic Side to the Bay of Panama on the Pacific side. Passage through the canal shortened a voyage between New York and San Francisco from 13,000 miles to less than 5,200 miles. That had important commercial and military implications in a world shadowed by the war in Europe.

**DESERET NEWS,** *Aug. 15, 1914: Vessels drawing not more than thirty feet of water may now make the passage. It would be possible to put the big American dreadnoughts through at any time.*

*Any of the foreign warships now in the Atlantic and Pacific waters could now make the trip, but the naval plans of the European powers which have vessels off both coasts of the United States are not known here.*

*No embarrassment will face the United States should one of the vessels of the belligerents seek passage. Strict rules are laid down in the treaty for the perpetual neutralization of the canal and every detail will be under the direction of Governor Goethals and his staff.*

The impact of the canal was immediate:

**DESERET NEWS,** *Aug. 17, 1914: The sum of $25,000 was taken in yesterday in tolls by the Panama canal...*

*Three steamers already today are going through the waterway and four more probably will start before nightfall. The total receipts in canal tolls up to the present time amount to $100,000.*

But the long-term potential was even greater:

**DESERET NEWS,** *Aug. 17, 1914: So closely the various steps in the progress of work on the Panama canal have been followed in the United States that the dispatches on Saturday bringing news that the formal opening of the waterway "free and open to all vessels of commerce and of war of all nations on terms of entire equality" failed to make the impression that should have marked the event. "Its stupendous undertaking has been finely accomplished and a perpetual memorial to the genius and enterprise of our people has been created," wrote Secretary of War Garrison in a congratulatory letter to Col. Goethals, the genius who brought the titanic effort to a successful culmination... .*

*On October 16, 1913, President Wilson touched an electric button in Washington that set off the charge of powder which blew out the Gamboa dike and the waters of the Altantic met and mingled with the waters of the Pacific. And on Saturday the canal was thrown open to the world's shipping. Indeed, it was an event which should thrill the American people with pride in the accomplishment of the task that had baffled the brightest engineers of the other nations of the world.*

President Woodrow Wilson officially opened the canal by blowing out a dike. Below, steam shovels were the real diggers on the canal. Here they complete the bottom of the Culebra Cut in 1913.

AP Photo

# A windfall capitol

**Eighteen years after Utah became a state, its government still had no permanent home. The Legislature met in several locations, including the Council House, Social Hall and the Salt Lake City-County Building. State offices were scattered around Salt Lake City.**

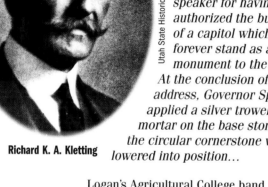

Richard K. A. Kletting

**N**ot lack of desire, but a lack of money delayed plans for building on the 20 acres that had been donated by Salt Lake City for the purpose. The Legislature eventually appropriated money for an additional 20 acres to give the capitol an imposing perch at the top of State Street with an unimpeded view of Salt Lake Valley.

But the building itself came into being after the death of E.H. Harriman, one of Utah's railroad entrepreneurs. Early in the history of railroading, Harriman took 60,000 miles of decrepit Union Pacific Railroad lines, a Utah corporation that was described as a "streak of rust," and built them into a huge success that left him worth an estimated $100 million at his death in 1909. Utah's share in his inheritance tax, about $750,000, became the germ seed for the State Capitol.

On April 4, 1914, when the cornerstone was laid, the Deseret News printed a replica of the tax check, drawn on Guaranty Trust Company of New York by Harriman's widow, giving the windfall due credit for this big occasion. The following Monday (the News then had no Sunday paper), the gala ceremonies were reported:

**DESERET NEWS,** *April 6, 1914: In the presence of several thousand persons from all parts of the state, William Spry, governor of Utah, laid the cornerstone of the state capitol at 5 o'clock Saturday afternoon... Glowing tribute to the thrift and industry of the people of Utah was paid by the speaker for having authorized the building of a capitol which will forever stand as a monument to the state. At the conclusion of the address, Governor Spry applied a silver trowel to the mortar on the base stone and the circular cornerstone was lowered into position...*

Logan's Agricultural College band played the Star Spangled Banner and the vast crowd, "in breathless silence," watched the huge stone being lowered into place, then burst into applause that lasted for several minutes.

One of the debates among designers as the work went forward was whether to use Utah marble or Georgia marble to face the interior. The commission heading the project was determined to use Utah products when possible, but Georgia marble was cheaper and could be obtained in larger slabs. In the end, Georgia marble was used on the main floor and Utah marble in the legislative chambers and Supreme Court.

When the building was ready for occupancy, about 10,000 Utahns gathered again for more hoopla, more speeches, more music:

**DESERET NEWS,** *Oct. 10, 1916: More than 10,000 people, representing practically every county in the state, formally accepted the new capitol*

*yesterday. The motion to accept the building was made by W. J. Robinson, following the conclusion of the address by Gov. Wm. Spry, and the multitude answered with a rising voice, filling the great building with the sound of a tremendous cheer.*

*The formal dedicatory exercises began in the afternoon, but the crowds of visitors began to arrive early in the morning, arriving in a steady throng. Most of them visited every nook and cranny of the edifice. It was estimated that between 35,000 and 40,000 visited the building during the day.*

Gov. Spry waxed eloquent, turning the capitol over to the people "For it is your capitol, my friends; it always has been; it always will be." The Tabernacle Choir, unfortunately, was "not able to attend the ceremonies." In their place, poetry written by Herbert S. Auerbach, one of the city's pioneer merchants, was read. President Joseph F. Smith recounted efforts to relocate the capitol building, but "this was the place picked out by the pioneers and they knew what they were doing." He predicted the building would stand "until God shall shake the earth and the mountains fall to the ground."

The capitol was designed by Richard K.A. Kletting, who also drew the plans for several other important Utah buildings. Its ultimate cost was more than $2.7 million — a shocking amount for its time. Even so, statues that were to decorate the niches according to the original plan were never put in place for lack of funds.

Utah's Corinthian-style capitol, which closely resembles the national capitol in Washington, D.C., has been proclaimed to be among the most beautiful of the 50 statehouses in the Union.

The new State Capitol Building takes shape in May, 1914 photo.

A Red Cross motor corps is shown on duty during the 1918-1919 influenza epidemic.

# A worldwide killer

**Two killers were on the loose at the end of the decade — World War I and the Spanish influenza pandemic. Worldwide, the virus killed some 20 million people, about 500,000 of them in the United States.**

In comparison, the loss of American soldiers in the war reached 116,516, with another 234,428 wounded. Many of the military casualties were attributed to the virus, not to combat. Of the 299 Utah soldiers listed as fatalities, 93 died of disease and 12 of non-combat accidents.

Utah's 1918 and 1919 death statistics also reflected the extent of the scourge among civilians. About one in every three deaths in the two-year period were related to influenza and pneumonia, often a secondary complication of the disease.

**DESERET NEWS,** *Oct. 10, 1918: In all places where Spanish influenza has been reported schools are closed and all announcements and arrangements for public gatherings have been cancelled, pursuant to the order issued Wednesday by the state board of health… Salt Lake City, Ogden and Murray and many other smaller towns are closed tight … All collegiate study has been suspended at the University of Utah for the period of the influenza epidemic on the order of President John A. Widtsoe… Thirty university men were yesterday removed to the Fort Douglas isolation hospital.*

The newspaper listed rules to combat the disease, the foremost being to avoid crowds. "Your nose, not your mouth, was made to breathe through — get the habit," and clean hands were a must. Opening windows at night was considered beneficial, as was avoiding tight clothing. "Seek to make nature your ally, not your prisoner." A special hospital was speedily set up to care for the stricken, the same issue of the newspaper said:

*The Red Cross people are making every effort to open the Judge Mercy emergency hospital by Friday, to be ready to receive influenza patients. Mrs. Matilda Thompson, a prominent Red Cross worker and formerly superintendent of the Judge Mercy hospital, will again act in this capacity…*

*An urgent call is now made to all who can contribute clean old rags, such as tattered table linen, sheets, etc., to bring them immediately to local headquarters, so they may be used as compressors at the new hospital… An order was received today for 5,000 masks to protect doctors, nurses and patients. They protect the patient from spreading the disease and the attendants from contracting the same.*

Some hardy souls hoped to cheat the bug, the Oct. 10 newspaper suggested:

*Football practice will likely not be hindered by the blanket order compelling schools, theatres, churches and all public gatherings to suspend wherever a case of Spanish influenza is reported. Although no definite ruling has been handed down by the state board of health, which issued the order of closing, it is expected that because of its healthful nature, the grid game will go on unhindered.*

The following day, their bubble was burst:

**DESERET NEWS,** *Oct. 11, 1918: Spanish influenza wins. Tommy Fitzpatrick had hoped that the ban placed on public gatherings and school sessions by the state board of health because of the alleged prevalence of Spanish "flu" would not affect football practice. When the little Irish mentor hied himself to Cummings field yesterday afternoon for practice, however, he found only a few grid candidates scattered here and there. Most of the boys had lost no time in hitting the trail for home sweet home.*

As fatalities mounted, almost daily obituaries told the fearsome tally of the dead. The Oct. 25, 1918, News noted, on just one page, the flu-related deaths of two Provo residents, Herman Vacher and Edward Farrer, a well-known local businessman. In Payson, Mrs. Lula Wilson Dunstand and Lynn Keel Manvill were both dead. The bodies of two stockmen from Uintah County were found in a cabin a short distance from Price after townspeople noticed their stock wandering unattended. Their deaths were attributed to influenza.

Ingenious ways were devised to help families whose finances were adversely affected:

**DESERET NEWS,** *Oct. 28, 1918: If a plan suggested by Robert H. Siddoway, state fish and game commissioner, is accepted by city health officials, families suffering from the Spanish influenza may receive free ducks as gifts of hunters who come home with a surplus of the birds…*

By early winter, the disease seemed to be on the wane. The Nov. 12 issue of the News reported that flu cases were departing and the emergency hospital was being closed.

Despite all warnings against gatherings (even the October LDS Church General Conference was canceled) Utahns couldn't restrain themselves when news of the armistice in Europe was declared, ending World War I. Huge crowds gathered in Utah communities to celebrate the end to the war, and in doing so lost a major battle to the disease:

**DESERET NEWS,** *Nov. 15, 1918: Exactly 126 new cases of Spanish influenza were included in the final official report of the city board of health as a result of yesterday's canvass, and indirectly a result of the unrestricted celebration of last Monday night. Only one death occurred yesterday …*

With a sigh, private and government groups that had planned gala "peace parties" cancelled them. Theater owners, deprived of their audiences, tried to ignore the rules, but were brought back into line by the state health commissioner.

Through the winter of 1918-19, the disease continued its ravages. Through the decades since, periodic world influenza epidemics have been noted, but the development of medications to treat secondary infections such as pneumonia have greatly reduced the death toll. Never since 1918-19 has an infectious killer done such deadly work.

**SECOND SECTION** Local News and Sports **DESE**

FOUNDED 1850

## Many Towns Are Closed By Order Of Health Board

Theatres, Churches and All Public Gatherings Under Ban For Present--Spanish Influenza Spreading Rapidly.

**RULES TO COMBAT "FLU"**

# Prohibition:
## An experiment turns sour

**The Volstead Act, which became the 18th Amendment to the Constitution, prohibited the manufacture and sale of intoxicating beverages.**

The culmination of a long campaign for temperance, the act passed in 1919 and was ratified by enough states that Prohibition, as it came to be called, went into effect in January of 1920.

Herbert Hoover called it a "noble experiment."

LDS President Joseph F. Smith left no question in anyone's mind on where he stood on the issue back when the debate began:

**DESERET NEWS,** June 3, 1911: *"Any man who will darken the door of a saloon to drink intoxicants is a criminal in the sight of God, and an enemy to society... I hope to goodness every man and every woman will do his and her duty on the 27th day of June and vote that we can say throughout the state of Utah that it is white and not black, that you vote 'dry' and not 'wet.' "*

However noble the ideal, however, the practice was something else. Instead of turning the country into a nation of sober, hard-working citizens, it created a nation of law-breakers. Rum-runners. Bootleggers. Moonshiners. Bathtub gin-makers. A whole new category of criminals sprang into action. Federal agents did what they could, but they couldn't do much. Even Utah had its problems.

**DESERET NEWS,** April 17, 1923: *The most scientific "moonshine factory" with which federal prohibition officers have been required to cope, and which was operating full blast in an exclusive residence of the city, distributing its product termed to be "100 per cent proof" over a wide territory was raided Monday afternoon and its operations brought to a close.*

*Mrs. M.A. Anderson, said to be the caretaker of what was described by federal prohibition agents as a luxuriously appointed mansion at the rear of 240 east South Temple street, was the only one arrested at the time of the raid.*

*April 6, 1926: Four thousand gallons of liquor were seized and 42 alleged violators of the prohibition law were arrested by federal officers during March... Along with this, the federal officers assisted local officers in capturing 13 other suspected violators.*

*May 19, 1927: A whisky still of 75 gallons capacity, running full blast, the fumes being carried out through a large hole in the ceiling and roof by means of a large electric fan, was discovered Thursday morning on the third floor of a three-story dwelling at 314 First avenue.*

*Aug. 27, 1927: John E. Holt of Salt Lake Saturday was fined $250 in the federal court for possession of material which, if assembled, would have been suitable for use as a liquor still.*

In 1924, federal officials were optimistic. "Prohibition Success Growing Declares Daugherty," proclaimed a banner headline on Feb. 24. "Respect for Law Increasing, Attorney General Tells President; Penalties Heavier."

But by 1926, they were still not on top of things. An executive order issued on May 21 by President Coolidge added 10,000 more men to the "federal dry agent army" and gave the treasury the power to "enlist at a nominal salary, state, county and municipal officers as special federal dry agents."

Part of the problem was that organized crime found a gold mine in the trade of illegal booze. Chicago, in particular,

### 1920-1930

We call them the Roaring Twenties. The war was over, inhibitions were falling and the stock market was rising. Jazzy speak-easies flourished. Barnstorming pilots roamed the country, bringing aviation to rural Utah. First letters, then passengers began flying out of Salt Lake's Woodward field. Utahns also had a new set of heroes: Babe Ruth, Lou Gehrig, Charlie Chaplin, Mary Pickford. The greatest of them all was a skinny young pilot who flew the Atlantic by himself and landed into history. The Deseret News launched a radio station, a Utahn came to the Supreme Court and a Piute fought what was generously called the last Indian war. For most, it was a great time, right up until October 1929, when Wall Street, as the headline in Variety noted, laid an egg.

Carbon County lawmen discovered this elaborate and illegal still around 1929. Bill Lines is at left and Sheriff Marion Bliss at right.

Edna Bliss Mahleres

**Woman Pays $100 For Having Liquor**

Youth Fined For Taking Moonshine To Fair.

Alice White of 62 south West street, admitted she was successful in concealing two bottles of whisky from... she failed...

became the battleground for rival bootlegging gangs run by the likes of Al Capone, Dion O'Banion and George Moran.

**DESERET NEWS,** *Jan. 24, 1924: The Windy City, it seems, isn't dry after all.*

*Discovery that the closing of 5,000 saloons and coffee shops hadn't ended the anti-Volstead violations resulted from the shooting of Davy Miller, West Side gangster and prize fight referee, who was dropped in the crowded lobby of a LaSalle theater Sunday night.*

*The first evidence of a flourishing rum ring came when police running down a clue in the shooting found a liquor price list on a wall…*

*Other detectives stumbled upon a booze cache from which was distributed to transients, through hotel bellhops, hundreds of gallons of whisky gin daily.*

As trade picked up, gang violence escalated in the infamous St. Valentine's Day Massacre:

**DESERET NEWS,** *Feb. 14, 1929: Seven members of the North Side gang of George "Bugs" Moran were lined up against a wall and summarily executed today by a band of men who invaded the north side headquarters of the gang posing as police officers. After forcing the men to raise their hands, the gangsters shot them down…*

*Today's slayings, in the form of a massacre, was something new in Chicago gang warfare. Heretofore, the gangsters took their victims for a "ride," luring them into automobiles and then killing them, or else swept past in automobiles and raked their victims with gunfire.*

In February 1933, Congress passed the 21st Amendment, which would repeal the 18th and it went out to the states for a vote. A headline on Nov. 8, 1933, told it all: "Utah Goes Wet; Amendment Repealed." Utah became the 36th state to vote for repeal, the last one needed. The "noble experiment" had ended in failure.

# Getting off the ground

**W**hen military contracts were canceled after World War I, it was a setback to the fledgling air industry. Other directions were clearly needed — and soon found.

**DESERET NEWS,** *May 12, 1920: The government air mail service will celebrate its second birthday anniversary Saturday, the operations of the past year having been marked with "phenomenal success," according to post office department. Statistics for the entire year show an average performance of 37 per cent, including flights under most adverse conditions.*

The announcement soon followed that Salt Lake was to be added to the route.

**DESERET NEWS,** *May 15, 1920: First class mail service between Salt Lake and New York in 21 hours will be established by September according to a reported interview with Otto Prager, second assistant post master general at San Francisco…*

*Salt Lake will be required to establish a flying field and hangar and the government will spend fully $26,000 in improvements.*

By then planes were popular in Salt Lake, no doubt about that. Even the Deseret News had one.

**DESERET NEWS,** *May 21, 1921: SOME GLIMPSES OF SALT LAKE AS THE CITY LOOKS TO THE BIRD MEN. Here are some of the views obtained by a Deseret News staff photographer in a flight over the city. Obtaining pictures from such low altitudes was made possible by the daring work of Rex Smith, Deseret News staff aviator, who maneuvered the "ship" in dangerously close proximity to the roofs of some of the city's taller buildngs.*

Other air news making headlines during

Swallow biplanes carried air mail for Varney Air Lines, a predecessor to United Air Lines. Leon Cuddeback, shown here, was Varney's first pilot.

the decade was an around-the-world flight undertaken by "the cream of the United States Air Service," which left from Santa Monica, Calif. on Mar. 17, 1924. But later came more life-changing news:

**DESERET NEWS,** *May 22, 1926: Opening of passenger service between Salt Lake and Los Angeles by the Western Air Express, Inc., Sunday marks the dawn of commercial aerial passenger traffic in America…*

*It will be the first time in the history of aviation in this country that daily aerial passenger service has been offered by a commercial air line on a fixed schedule, according to Mr. Woolley. He declared the new service will cut 19 hours from the traveling time between Los Angeles and eastern points and that Salt Lake will become an important junction for both air and rail travel…*

*Passenger service will be available every day unless weather conditions are such that it would be dangerous. There are two seats that may be occupied.*

It was an idea whose time had come. By Sept. 16, 1927, the paper reported that "395,000 Ride On Air Liners Over U.S. in 6 Months; Operators Fly 12,000,000 Miles."

But not all air news during the decade was positive. News of crashes began

showing up with increased frequency. One was particularly devastating; all the victims — three men, a woman and two children — were Utahns:

**DESERET NEWS,** *Sept. 4, 1928: POCATELLO — Six passengers and a pilot were killed at noon here today when their plane, landing from Great Falls, Montana, crashed from a height of only 30 feet… . Attendants at the field cannot explain the smash beyond the fact that a sudden gust of wind must have caught the plane.*

Sad news did not deter flying, however. By 1928, Salt Lake Airport News became a regular part of the paper:

**DESERET NEWS,** *Sept. 22, 1928: Lieut. Russell Maughan, Utah's famous transcontinental dawn-to-dusk flier, arrived in Salt Lake Saturday from Los Angeles, where he attended the national air races.*

*Again breaking all records, the Boeing Air Transport company sent two ships from Salt Lake to Chicago, Saturday, carrying 2,815 pounds of mail, 20 pounds of express and K.T. Davies as passenger.*

*Flying a Ryan plane, Tommy Thompson and W.R. McKnight, merchant, left Friday to attend the opening of the new airport at Debeque, Colo.*

# The movies make Hollywood

**Utahns had a new pastime: the movies. D.W. Griffith's landmark "The Birth of A Nation" opened in 1915 and the idea of telling stories through pictures was an immediate hit.**

**M**ovie theaters, complete with organs to provide background music for the then-silent films, sprang up everywhere. Hollywood "stars," who in early films had remained nameless, now attracted huge followings. And readers of the Deseret News found a weekly "News of the Photoplayers" feature. Trends, gossip and eccentricities found their way onto the pages:

Charlie Chaplin in "The Little Tramp."

Hearthrob Rudolph Valentino works his charms on Agnes Ayres.

Deseret News files

**DESERET NEWS,** *May 1, 1920: The "back to old clothes" movement has hit the Hollywood, California, motion picture colony where it is expected to meet with particular success. Marshall Nellan startled his organization when he arrived at the studio clad in a pair of old overalls and a jumper which had seen considerable service around the garage. Marjorie Daw, as soon as she saw Nellan in his attire, rushed home and came back to the studio attired in an old middy-blouse and walking skirt.*

*May 15, 1920: An announcement of release that will attract attention in the motion picture world is made by the president of Selznick enterprises, who states that between now and this time next year 537 subjects will be produced and distributed by the various Selznick organizations. This gigantic program according to Mr. Selznick, has never been equalled.*

*July 30, 1921: Ever interested in why Buster Keaton's face is so long? Up to now the secret has been cloistered in the solemn comedian's heart. To all questioners he has turned the weary eye, and requested that he be allowed a few thoughts unto himself.*

*But the hidden truth is out … His studio has a past… Think of the ghosts that gambol by night in the gloom of the cluttered sets — led by the shuffling specter with arms that flap and feet that flop in ghoulish glee…*

*The fun-maker with his awesome mien simply can't smile in that environment. By the spirit of the 10,000 laughs he is elevated above the plane of careless mirth.*

Not everyone was in favor of this new industry. A writer for the Yale Review was quoted in the paper, decrying the "morals of the movies":

**DESERET NEWS,** *May 1, 1920: When a picture is made to illustrate a very unsavory subject about which people, as a rule, do not freely speak, and that picture is advertised at a great rate at the street side… I revolt at the spectacle… I must conclude that their interest in the subject is not educational at all. They are like the faker with a medical museum…*

Others worried about the Hollywood lifestyle.

**DESERET NEWS,** *Jan. 25, 1924: Why are movie people such failures as husbands and wives? The oft-asked question is repeated as Hollywood contemplates the wreck of the marriage venture of George Melford, director, and his wife…*

*Perhaps the psychologists are correct in their diagnosis. The people of the screen, they explain, are human sieves through which are sifted constantly the characters they play. Eventually the make believe character weakens the real one.*

But most people recognized that the movies and their stars were here to stay.

Hollywood powerhouses Douglas Fairbanks, Mary Pickford, Charlie Chaplin and D. W. Griffith on the set of one of Chaplin's early movies.

**DESERET NEWS,** *May 22, 1927: Because motion pictures have now become one of the necessities of life, Cecil DeMille maintains that they merit the intelligent consideration of every far-seeing business man as an integral part of our societal and industrial framework.*

**DESERET NEWS,** *April 3, 1926: Who are the biggest movie stars? The public, which makes the stars and breaks them, is the best judge. The "biggest stars" then are the players with the highest "box office value."*

A list followed, ranking stars by studio. Paramount: Gloria Swanson, Pola Negri; Metro: Lilian Gish, Norma Shearer; First National: Colleen Moore, Norma Talmadge; United Artists: Charlie Chaplin, Douglas Fairbanks, Mary Pickford, Rudolph Valentino; Warner Brothers: Monte Blue, Irene Rich; Fox: Tom Mix, George O'Brien; Universal: Reginald Denny, Hoot Gibson.

And Utah was beginning its association with the industry in several ways:

**DESERET NEWS,** *May 8, 1920: The Mary Pickford club of Heber City, Utah, with Mina La Rue Wilson as president, has been adjudged the winner of the Mary*

*Pickford picture contest recently conducted through the photoplay department of The Deseret News. Miss Pickford herself acted as the final judge.*

*The club will receive at an early date the large autographed art photograph of Miss Pickford, which she offered as the first prize.*

**DESERET NEWS,** *Sept. 9, 1927: The great walls of Zion Canyon will form the scenic background for the motion picture production of "Ramona," Helen Hunt Jackson's enduring novel of early Spanish and Indian life in southern California.*

On Oct. 6, 1927, "The Jazz Singer," the first of the "talkies," premiered in Hollywood. The industry would never be the same, although it would take awhile for the rest of the country to catch up.

**DESERET NEWS:** *May 17, 1929: Starting Saturday at the Star theatre will come all talkie pictures. The popular family playhouse on east First South has been completely rebuilt to make perfect acoustics. Special plaster has been placed on the walls and the lobby has been redecorated. The initial picture will feature Gary Cooper and Nancy Carroll in "The Shopworn Angel."*

Dec. 28, 1922

## Egyptian Relics See Daylight First Time for More than 3000 Years

LUXOR, Egypt. —(AP) Some of the priceless treasures found in the tomb of King Tutankhamen saw daylight for the first time in more than 3,000 years yesterday, when Howard Carter and Arthur Mace, excavators of the Metropolitan Museum of Art in New York, superintended their removal to the tomb of King Seti II, a half mile away.

One of the objects thus transferred was a magnificent inlaid box upon which was depicted King Tutankhamen and his queen at a lion hunt. The box contained the queen's robes and jewelry, including a large black amber necklace.

An alabaster vase, containing a substance believed to be balm for the dead similar to that mentioned in the Bible also was removed to the Seti tomb, where all the treasure will be subjected to a further preserving process.

Feb. 21, 1930

## Curse of King Tut Gets Another Victim in London

LONDON —(AP) His mind harried by thoughts of the Pharaoh's curse and the recent death of his son, 78-year-old Lord Westbury today fell to death from his bathroom window on the seventh floor of St. James's court…

Lord Westbury for months has worried over the strange circumstances of the death of his son, Richard Bethell, 46, who was secretary of Howard Carter, whose investigations in Egypt disclosed the treasures of ancient Tut-Ankh-Amen… His was the tenth death among people concerned with the exploration of Tut-Ank-Amen's sepulchre…

**The curse has long since been judged a folk fantasy, but the discovery of King Tut's tomb on Nov. 26, 1922, stunned the world. It set off a huge interest in Egyptian art, inspiring, among other things, the motif for several Egyptian Theaters.**

# The Deseret News

Sept. 16, 1920

## Orphans Entertained At Local Playhouse

Sixty-five children from St. Ann's Orphanage and 75 from the Orphan's Home and Day Nursery were entertained at the Strand theatre yesterday by Manager Allen Curtis of the theatre and Charles Doychert, who owns the rights in this territory to the picture, "The Confession." Watermelons and balloons were provided for the small guests as well as bags of candy.

May 12, 1922

## The Children's Home.

The dedication of the Children's Home by President Heber J. Grant last evening marks an event which merits more than passing note. The Primary Association has long stood for charity of the noblest kind — the proper training of children. In its new activity it will supply a need long felt and one which this community and the whole Church will greatly appreciate. The first aim of the Home is to furnish a place with the best environment for convalescent children; the second is to maintain a neighborhood house for children whose mothers have to work. Thus by charity a need for charity is overcome. Mothers whose duties to children prevent them from earning a living may now be given a chance.

The spirit of helpfulness and service which will permeate the Home will extend itself to all the Primary Associations, and kiddies the Church over can now plan to help their unfortunate companions.

(This was the predecessor of Primary Children's Hospital.)

Sept. 6, 1922

## JUSTICE SUTHERLAND

That title has a good ring to the ears of the people of Utah, who will quite universally rejoice in the honor that has come to this state through the appointment of George Sutherland to the Supreme Court; an appointment, it is announced, in which the United States Senate took only ten minutes to affirm.

**George Sutherland**

Were Dr. Karl G. Maeser still living, no man in Utah would take greater pleasure in the appointment of Mr. Sutherland to the Supreme Bench than this master educator. George Sutherland was for years a student of Dr. Maeser, and the young man's brilliant career in the Brigham Young Academy at Provo, his early home, was one that Dr. Maeser often referred to with delight. The Brigham Young Academy was a Church school; Mr. Sutherland knew its advantages, which he enjoyed for a number of years although not a member of the Church which the school represented.

Utah pays its heartfelt respects to the man whose high appointment brings distinguished honor to the state.

Dec. 16, 1922

## Harnessing The Colorado

With the signing of what is destined to become a historic pact for settlement of interstate water rights, interest in the development of the Colorado River is centered in the attitudes which will be taken by the several state legislatures in ratifying that compact into law.

... representatives of seven states and the federal government agreed last month to provisions of a document designed to settle any future controversies which might have arisen as between states over the utilization of the waters...

Briefly, the compact provides for a division of the Colorado River into two basins separated at Lees Ferry, about one mile below the Pahreah river in Arizona. The upper basin embraces such portions of the states of Wyoming, Colorado, Utah and New Mexico as naturally drain into the main channel of the river... Nevada, California and Arizona (are) in the lower basin.

Dec. 23, 1922

A group of ruins of ancient cliff dwellings never before seen by men, was discovered in Zion National Park at the close of the season just past.

Walter Ruesch, acting superintendent of Zion National Park, says "These dwellings are in what is known as Parunuweap Canyon, seven miles beyond the farthest point of which an automobile can penetrate and accessible only on horseback or afoot... (they) are even more interesting than those that have been known and studied heretofore. This is due to the fact that the roof is still intact and the buildings are almost perfect, as the hand of vandalism has not destroyed their beauty nor taken from them anything of interest."

March 10, 1923

## Enjoyable Concert.

Before 200 or more music lovers in the First Congregational church last evening, Alva Woodward, basso, appeared in concert with Miss Becky Almond as pianist and assisting artist. The program rendered was an excellent one, the most pleasing feature being Massenet's "Vision Fair." This number was given with such success that the musicians were recalled many times by their appreciative audience.

Sept. 23, 1923

## SEACOAST CITY WASHED AWAY

### 150,000 DEAD

### Summary of Japan Disaster

The situation in Japan resulting from one of the greatest disasters in history as disclosed by advice from all sources up to this morning is as follows:

Estimated that at least 100,000 persons are dead, one report even gave this figure for Tokyo's dead alone.

Shocks believed to be the settling shocks of the original temblor were recorded on American seismographs.

Tidal waves of great intensity followed the first shocks.

Communication with Japan continued virtually paralyzed... most of available information emanating from Iwaki radio station 166 miles north of Tokyo.

Martial law declared in Tokyo and Yokohama and no one allowed to enter the former unless he carries his own food supplies...

Numerous volcanoes are reported in eruption...

June 13, 1925

## Wendover Road Opens
### Forty-Mile Highway Over Mud Flats Proclaimed Victory for Engineering Science.

SALDURO, June 13. — (Special) — The 40-mile gap that has barred traffic through Utah over the direct route to the Pacific harbors since the west was settled was closed Saturday.

Following fitting ceremonies, Secretary of Agriculture William M. Jardine, assisted by Governor George H. Dern of Utah and J.G. Scrugham of Nevada, shoveled a salt barrier from the path beneath a great salt arch when the highway was declared open for all the world to use and the assembly passed through.

The Secretary and the two governors wore long white dusters with enormous straw hats, each of which shaded the salt for several yards under the shovelers.

The Wendover cut-off crosses the filled-in bottom of what was ancient Lake Bonneville.

June 17, 1925

PRICE, June 17. — (Special) — Marshal James M. Burns of Castlegate died at 10 p.m., Tuesday of wounds received Monday night when he was shot down by Robert Marshall, negro miner, who lay in wait for him and opened fire without warning.

Marshall has apparently made good his escape, for since he exchanged shots with Deputy Sheriff Mack Olsen Tuesday morning he has not been seen.

June 18, 1925

## 1000 CITIZENS TAKE PART IN PRICE HANGING

PRICE, June 17. — (Special) — Robert Marshall, slayer of Deputy Sheriff James M. Burns, of Castlegate, was lynched at 10:20 a.m. Thursday by a mob of more than 1,000 persons at the A.W. Horsley ranch, after a sensational overpowering of arresting officers in front of the courthouses here.

Marshall was cut down once by deputy sheriffs, but when it was seen he was alive the mob a second time overpowered the forces of the law and strung him up again.

A tip from a negro at Castlegate at 9 a.m. led a posse to the cabin where the fugitive had been living...

He was taken out to the auto where (Chief Clerk Joe) Parmeley searched him, finding the pistol of Burns, the man he slayed, in his pocket.

**(The lynching was later blamed on the Ku Klux Klan.)**

April 6, 1926

## Jazz Will Die In Ten Years, Says Composer

DENVER, April 6. — (Special) — American jazz today was given a mortality rating of not to exceed 10 years.

At the expiration of this period, the equivalent of a musical incarnation will take place and modern jazz of syncopated fame will give way to a new order of rhythm.

This is the essence of a statement by Henry Eichheim, noted composer of Oriental music and for 21 years, first violinist of the famous Boston symphony orchestra.

Jazz will disappear, but the vibrancy of its stimulating rhythms will remain.

Aug. 23, 1927

## B.Y.U. President Back After Year Trip Around World

PROVO, Aug. 23 — Having traveled more than 47,000 miles during his year's absence from Provo, Dr. Franklin Stewart Harris, president of the Young university returned Saturday. It lacked four days of being a year since Dr. Harris left on his world tour. While away he visited Hawaii, northern and southern China, Korea, Manchuria, Japan, Philippine Islands, India, Egypt, Palestine, Syria, Turkey, Greece, Italy, Switzerland, France, Belgium, Holland, Denmark, Sweden, Norway, and the British Isles.

"While on my tour around the globe I was impressed with the great goodness and sincerity of mankind," said Dr. Harris in commenting on his trip. "The most fundamental quality of mankind everywhere is the tendency to worship. Men differ in their religious views but whether Mohammedan, Buddhist or Christian, they are sincere."

Aug. 30, 1927

## FLOWER EXHIBIT ATTRACTS 5,000

Bigger and better than ever, the summer show of the Salt Lake Flower Garden club completely occupied the mezzanine floor of the Hotel Utah on its opening at noon Tuesday.

Nearly 500 exhibits were seen on the spacious tables all around the balcony, with practically every variety of out-door summer flower seen in full bloom, giving the entire place not only an atmosphere of vari-colored beauty, but an aroma which pleased the sense of smell even as one entered the outer doors of the hotel.

Sept. 11, 1928

## Salt Lake Garners First Pennant

BOISE, Idaho, Sept. 11. — (AP) — The Salt Lake Bees crowned themselves champions of the Utah-Idaho league Monday by defeating the Boise Senators 10 to 2 in a game that had little of championship character except the name.

It was Salt Lake's first championship in upward to 30 years in organized baseball... .

Sept. 11, 1928

## Brings Salt Lake First Pennant

Pursuing the succulent statistics with uncertain aim, you learn that Salt Lake City won her first baseball championship in organized baseball on September 10, 1928. Salt Lake City teams played in the Pacific National Union Association, Pacific Coast and Utah-Idaho leagues for upward of 30 years without the semblance of a pennant. Now comes Bobby Coltrin, "Bustlin' Bobby" and chases the buxom Bees of 1928 in ahead as Utah-Idaho league champions. The fans doff their hats today to Coltrin. He put us on the map this year for certain!

Sept. 11, 1928

## Salt Lake Airport News

Watkins Davies, 77 year old optometrist from Stockton, Calif., flew back to Oakland on Boeing Air Transport company's westbound plane Monday. He arrived in Salt Lake Saturday after flying from Oakland to Salt Lake in five hours and 14 minutes, flying time. He intended going on through to Cheyenne, Wyo., but due to heavy mail loads east, there was no room for a passenger.

J.M. Sleger, owner of several moving picture theatres in Montana left Monday morning with the regular planes going to Butte.

Sept. 11, 1928

## MEAD LEAVES TO VIEW NORTH UTAH

Dr. Elwood Mead, United States commissioner of reclamation, and a party of federal and state officials and a number of Salt Lake business men, left at 8 a.m. Tuesday in automobiles to view several proposed dam sites in northern Utah. The group went to the Hyrum and Porcupine damsites in Little Bear river canyon in the morning and planned to travel through Cache valley up to the Idaho line and return to Huntsville valley in the afternoon, looking over the Magpie damsite in the south fork of Ogden canyon.

An early photograph of Maude Adams.

Pioneer Memorial Museum

Sept. 18, 1928

## MAUDE ADAMS ASKED TO PLAY AT FAREWELL

The Salt Lake Theatre is to go down on Oct. 16, so it is proposed that a farewell show be given there within the next month. An attempt will be made to let the playhouse go as it was in the heyday of its career. Though nothing definite has yet been decided, it is hoped that Maude Adams, most noted of all stage people from Utah, can be persuaded to step out of her retirement onto the stage of the old temple of the drama where in the past she acted so charmingly...

It is a number of years since Miss Adams retired to her home in New York state, since which time she has resisted every call to return to the stage. She was born in Salt Lake and made her debut on the local boards as a baby... .

The Mountain States Telephone & Telegraph company, present owners, have deferred dismantling the theatre until Oct. 15, so that a farewell show may be given.

Sept. 19, 1928

## TURKEYS SAVE UTAH ORCHARD FROM HOPPERS

BRIGHAM CITY, Utah, Sept. 19. — (AP) — An army of turkeys, rushed to the battlefront in motortrucks, has exterminated a devastating horde of grasshoppers on an 80-acre peach orchard near here.

Advancing from the west, the hoppers were systematically eating up the peaches on the trees in the orchard of Dr. A.D. Cooley. Liberated from the trucks, the turkeys marched up one row and down another, devouring the insects as they went.

Within a few days they had routed the enemy and were taken to another orchard nearby and later to a grain field, where they continued their campaign.

Sept. 21, 1928

## 'Scarface Capone' Wounds Self In Pistol Accident

CHICAGO, Sept. 21. — (INS) — Alphonse Capone, the big booze and beer man of Chicago, was able to cavort around his hotel suite here today, fully recovered from an extremely embarrassing situation for Capone.

Capone was shot in the leg and groin. The worst part of it was that Capone shot himself. In all his long days as ruling czar of Chicago badlands, his scuffles with police and gangsters who have vowed to kill him, Capone never had been even grazed by a bullet until last Sunday.

While playing golf... Capone became tired carrying

his heavy and trusty .45 automatic in his belt. So, while climbing bunkers and replacing divots, "Scarface" shifted the weapon to the hip pocket of his plus-fours. He forgot all about the weapon until he sat down in his automobile and the gun exploded.

Oct. 21, 1929

## President Hoover Pays Tribute Of Nation to Edison

BY GEORGE R. HOLMES.
(Special Leased Wire Service to The Deseret News)

DEARBORN, Mich., Oct. 21 — President Hoover came to Detroit today for a visit with Henry Ford and to join with the auto magnate and other national figures in honoring Thomas A. Edison on the fiftieth anniversary of his perfection of the incandescent light bulb.

A cold October drizzle was falling when the presidential special drew into the station, some miles from Detroit proper. The president and Mrs. Hoover were met by Mr. and Mrs. Henry Ford and Mr. Edison at the station. The Fords and the city of Detroit share the duties of being host to the distinguished gathering of notables here to honor the aged inventor.

Oct. 19, 1929

# DOROTHY DIX

Most men and women marry to get companionship. The thing that lures them into the bondage of matrimony is neither romance nor the sex appeal. What they fall for is the prospect of getting some one to whom they can talk endlessly. Somebody who will laugh at their jokes and encore their stories. Somebody who will listen with bated breath while they tell all the details of their daily lives and what they said to the boss and the boss said to them or how they got a bargain that was marked down from $5 to $4.98. Somebody to whom they can tell all their hopes and plans and ambitions, who will extol their triumphs and blame somebody else for their failures.

That is the sort of companionship that every man and woman who enters into the holy estate expects to find in it, but few ever realize their fond hopes. After the honeymoon has waned, a deadly pall of silence settles down over the great majority of homes and husbands and wives have nothing to say to each other beyond a perfunctory discussion of bills and the children and the routine business of existence.

It is a rare thing to see a married couple who take any genuine pleasures to each other's society and who can pass an enjoyable evening chatting with each other…

Oct. 22, 1929

Taylor Nuttall, 17, 371 Third avenue, high school student, will not be permitted to operate an automobile within the corporate limits of the city for a period of 60 days, and must also pay a fine of $20. If he drives a car within that time, or does not pay the fine, he must serve 60 days in the city bastille.

This was the edict of "hizzoner" in police court Tuesday in the case of young Nuttall charged with speeding 50 miles an hour on east South Temple street Monday. It was charged he was driving the chassis of a car, and that young women were "hanging on as best they could." Nuttall pleaded guilty to the charge.

Oct. 29, 1929

## With the Amateur Athletes

by Jimmy Hodgson

The departure of the Utes from Fort Collins this year was a much different procedure than two years ago. This time the goal of a championship pennant was still brightly in view, two years ago all hopes had been put asunder by the contest. A good time was had by all and Ike [Armstrong] in particular wore a great big grin when the win was in the bag.

Les Goates surely started something when he called the big Ute fullback, "Powerhouse Pom." [Dean Olsen] The name has been taken up all over the conference and will no doubt stick to the great young gridder as long as he is in the college sport.

Big Marwin Jonas was given a double serving of everything on the trip and proved his need of the double portion by doing two men's work in the game. Marve is a big fellow and needs a little more nourishment than the average man. Trainer Einer Nielson saw that the needs of "old Tarzan" were not neglected.

Trainer Nielson becomes the unanimous favorite of the entire squad on the football trips. You see, Nielson orders all the dinners.

## The last Indian battle

The last of America's Indian "wars" was fought in the spring of 1923 in the bleak desert canyons of San Juan County. The so-called Posey War was decidedly unbalanced in favor of settlers and amounted mostly to a rout of vastly outnumbered Native Americans.

For a long time, feelings between ranchers and local Indians festered as the newcomers took up land and usurped animals and plants the Indians had depended upon for survival. The 1923 conflict began when Posey, a Paiute Indian married to a Ute, engineered a jail break for two young Utes who were being held in Blanding as suspects in the robbing of a sheep camp, killing a calf and burning a bridge. The events quickly became a national media event and front-page news in Salt Lake City:

**DESERET NEWS,** *March 20, 1923:*
*(Special to the News) MONTICELLO — Posses from nearby towns have reached Blanding and the combined forces have driven the attacking Indians off, who are now headed for San Juan River, according to a courier who arrived here this afternoon. Neutral Indians are being held under guard in Blanding until the excitement is over.*

*Old Posey captured a posse in an auto, but only shot holes in tires, radiator and windshield, allowing posse members to escape unmolested after disarming them.*

*The Allen Canyon band of renegade Indians are again on the war path. Blanding is isolated, the redmen having cut telephone wires, and the last word from the Indian-beleaguered village was brought here at 4 a.m. today by a courier asking for the formation of an armed body of men to aid the inhabitants of the town. The Indians, according to the courier, engaged in a pitched battle with ranchers Monday in an attempt to rescue from custody Dutch's Boy and Bishop's Boy, Indian youths being held for the robbing of a sheep camp recently …*

The following day, the newspaper reported that three settlers were missing and feared

held hostage, rumors that ultimately proved false. A Ute, one of the young men sprung from jail, was killed and another two wounded. On the settlers' side, the News reported that a horse had been shot from under John Rogers and a bullet went through his trouser leg.

On March 24, a deputy U.S. marshal was en route to San Juan to deputize more men for the search for Posey and his band. The marshal prepared for all-out combat:

**DESERET NEWS,** *March 24, 1923: Marshal (Ray) Ward also requested his deputy to bring his high power battery commander field glasses used during the world war when the marshal commanded the Ogden battery of the 145th Field artillery, and also to secure six pair of field glasses from the national guard for use by the possemen. Fort Douglas (was asked) to furnish additional ammunition for the army rifles in use and accordingly the adjutant of the post had prepared several bandoliers which will be taken to the scene of action…*

*Desperately wounded in the leg, Old Posey, leader of Utah's latest and probably last Indian uprising, was today hiding in the rocks with Bishop's oldest boy as the sole remnant of his little band that last Monday defied the "pale face" law and fled with two prisoners …*

*A general roundup of the redmen was in effect today… Forty members of the tribe are in the stockade at Blanding and the five captured in battle are en route there strongly guarded to prevent their escape.*

The News accounts, complete with the unpolitic pejoratives of that time, referred to a hastily constructed "bullpen" where Indians were held until Posey and his renegades had been rounded up. Posey died of his wounds, although Indians maintained his captors fed him poisoned flour. Possibly the last victim of a confrontation between settlers and the indigenous natives, he became a symbol of the losing battle fought by Indians as outsiders took over the West.

**Posey**

Utah State Historical Society

## First Zion, then, surprise! Bryce are national parks

Automobiles and roads to accommodate them accounted for the rise of a new American pastime at the beginning of the 20th century — national park hopping. Utah, with some of the most spectacular and unique vistas in the country, became the destination for more and more scenery-seekers as its wonders were recognized and set apart as parks.

In the 1920s, two of the state's national monuments were upgraded to park status. On Nov. 19, 1919, President Woodrow Wilson signed legislation making Zion the Beehive State's first national park. For the previous 10 years it had been Mukuntuweap National Monument. That was too much of a mouthful for most people, it was decided, and the area was dedicated in September of the following year as Zion:

*DESERET NEWS,*
*Sept. 16, 1920: The dedication of Zion National Park Sept. 15 was a success exceeding the most ardent expectations, according to General Passenger Agent D.S. Spencer of the Oregon Short Line, who returned [to Salt Lake City] today.*

*Mr. Spencer says 800 people attended the dedication held at the Wylie Camp in Zion Canyon Wednesday. He says nothing like it was ever before witnessed in that part of the state...*

*The festivities started the evening before. They were made attractive by a bonfire of huge proportions. General manager and Mrs. W. W. Wylie had provisions ready for the crowds, and while all could not be housed, much was done for their comfort. The state furnished cots and mattresses in sufficiency, but through some oversight, there were no blankets. However, enough were secured for the women visitors, while the men utilized their overcoats ...*

*On the opening day at 6 a.m. the*

**Bryce Canyon National Park**

*Deseret News files*

*combined bands played "The Star Spangled Banner."*

*There was not a breath of air stirring ... The quietness of the gorge seemed supernatural, when there came the grand outburst of the national anthem. The effect, as the sound waves reverberated from cliff to cliff and from gorge to gorge, from one side of the great canyon to the other, were inspiringly sublime and the entire assemblage was deeply affected.*

*Speakers enthused about the park's wonders and the foresight of national*

officials in setting it aside as one of the country's treasures. S.T. Mather, superintendent of national parks, said the purpose of such parks was to provide recreation centers for the American people. He pledged himself to the effort to identify and protect such natural wonders throughout the country.

Utah's second national park sneaked up on most people unawares, almost exactly eight years later:

*DESERET NEWS,* Sept. 18, 1928:

### Surprise Sprung In Creating Park

*Presenting Utah's second national park to the folks at home, members of the party that made the wonderful tour around the scenic loop through southern Utah, including the north rim of the Grand*

*canyon, returned Tuesday morning.*

*The Union Pacific lodge at Bright Angel Point was formally opened, the Kaibab trail from the rim to the river was dedicated, the mile-long tunnel out of Zion canyon to Mt. Carmel was inspected and later "holed through." Everything went off as scheduled, except the one item of the new national park — that was not on the program, but came as a fitting surprise and climax.*

*No doubt Stephen T. Mather, director of national parks, and others, had an idea that it might happen, but it was kept on the quiet until all the government and legal formalities were out of the way, ready for the actual ceremony.*

*And so, Bryce Canyon, formerly a national monument under the direction of the forest service in the department of agriculture, is now a national park under the direction of the park service in the department of the interior ...*

With this terse announcement, Bryce became second on the growing list of Utah parks. Over the years, Arches, Canyonlands and Capitol Reef followed, giving sparsely populated Utah a disproportionate number of national attractions. Only Alaska with seven and California with six outnumber the Beehive State on the national parks rolls.

## The world of the 1920s

### A TIMELINE

**1920**— Pancho Villa, Mexican guerrilla leader, surrenders.

**1921**— Sacco and Vanzetti found guilty of murder after a sensational trial.

**1921**— President Harding signs a peace decree to end the war with Germany and Austria.

**1922**— The Reader's Digest comes out in its first edition.

**1923**— The great Finnish runner, Paavo Nurmi, posts a 4-minute mile.

**1923**— The first electric razor is patented by Col. Jacob Schick.

**1923**— Ford produces its 10 millionth car.

**1924**— J. Edgar Hoover becomes head of Bureau of Investigation, renamed the Federal Bureau of Investigation, in 1935.

**1924**— George Gershwin's "Rhapsody in Blue," combining jazz and symphony elements, performed for the first time.

**1924**— Adolf Hitler writes "Mein Kampf."

**1925**— Chrysler Motor Co. founded by Walter P. Chrysler.

**1925**— John Scopes, a biology teacher, is found guilty of teaching evolution in a state school.

**1925**— The first "motel" opens in San Luis Obispo, Calif.

**1926**— Gertrude Ederle swims the English Channel, the first woman ever to do so, and does it in record time.

**1926**— A.A. Milne publishes "Winnie-the-Pooh."

**1926**— Harry Houdini, the great escape artist, dies.

**1927**— The first Ryder Cup professional golf tournament is won by a U.S. team..

**1927**— The movie industry produces its first "talkie"— "The Jazz Singer" starring Al Jolson.

**1928**— A new star is born when Mickey Mouse makes his debut in "Steamboat Willie."

**1928**— Prof. Alexander Fleming discovers the wonder drug penicillin.

**1928**— Emperor Hirohito is crowned in Japan.

**1929**— Gang warfare in Chicago reaches an apex with the St. Valentine's Day Massacre.

**1929**— The first Academy Awards are held.

# Disaster at Castle Gate

Avery, Kenneth. Acord, R.V. Ambrossi, Joe. Anderson, J. R. Anderson D.R. Alexander, Prince. The alphabetical listing of the victims seemed to go on forever. Gittins, Brinley. Gionini, Steve. McDonald, Otto. Men and boys from nearly every home in Castle Gate. Perkins, Ed. Tyler, Matt. One hundred and seventy-two in all. The worst fears of any mining town had come true.

- 
- 
- 
- 
- 
- 
- 
- 
- 
- 
- 
- 
- 
- 
- 
- 

**DESERET NEWS,** *March 8, 1924: Three successive explosions wrecked the portal of Mine No. 2 Utah Fuel company at 8:30 a.m., strewing the canyon with timbers, leaving a 50 foot hole at the mouth of the tunnel and entombing 175 miners, mostly married men.*

*The first blast was followed by two others and as a result the portal was almost impassable…*

*Up to 1 p.m. rescue parties were unable to enter further than 200 feet. Even there two were overcome and it was necessary to return with them almost immediately to the surface. One recovered almost immediately but the other, Thomas Hilton, is in the emergency hospital.*

For awhile hope lingered that some of the miners might escape by making their way to the far end of the tunnel to an exit opening on Willow creek on the lower level. But it was not to be. Devastation was complete.

**DESERET NEWS,** *March 10, 1924: Youths, born and raised in Castlegate, sons of coal miners all, together with their fathers perished in the explosion that caught 175 in mine No. 2 on Saturday. Records of the company reveal that in seven instances, fathers and sons perished. In two instances, the deadly explosions followed by the accumulation of death dealing gases claimed as their victims, a father and two sons…*

*Bob Dodd and Ben Thomas, two of the victims, were killed less than an hour after they had entered the mine for the first time as regular employees.*

**DESERET NEWS,** *March 10, 1924: Andrew Gilbert, 73 years old, hero of the Winterquarter's disaster of May 1, 1900, when 200 men lost their lives in the worst mining catastrophe in the history of Utah, paid with his life Saturday as a result of his devotion to the mining industry.*

*To his companions of Castlegate he was plain Andy, despite his advanced age, but to the Utah Fuel company he was known as one of the best coal miners that ever picked up a shovel.*

**DESERET NEWS,** *March 10, 1924: Bereavement over losses in the Castlegate disaster strikes at the heart of families all over the state. As the names of men caught in a living grave in the mine workings become known, inquiries are made from all sections.*

*Losses strike at families not only in the more populous sections but appear to come in some instances from remote corners where a head of a family or son had left the farm or ranch for employment in the Carbon county coal fields.*

There were no survivors. But it still took time to recover the bodies.

**DESERET NEWS,** *March 11, 1924: Ninety-four bodies had been recovered late Tuesday… The progress of the rescue crews was slowed by cave-ins and twisted pipes…Virtually no fires have been encountered.*

The last of the bodies would not be located and removed until March 15. In the meantime, the identification process continued. Rescue work was winding down, but the grieving had just begun.

**DESERET NEWS,** *March 11, 1924: Castle Gate's community house and recreational center, the largest building in this small mining camp, holds for the last time all that is mortal of the men who have in the years past entered into the festivities for which it was erected…*

*Bodies recovered at mine No. 2 are removed in conveyances to the morgue and there are fixed for burial. As soon as the bodies have been placed in coffins they are removed to the auditorium of*

*the "hall" there to rest until final arrangements are completed for the burial of the victims.*

*Women, widowed by the three cruel blasts… children of these same women, many of them in arms and others in the full bloom of life, wended their way Tuesday to the recreational "hall" there to gaze upon the faces of their loved ones.*

There was the search for reasons why.

**DESERET NEWS,** *March 11, 1924: Original cause of the Castlegate explosion may never be known, O.F. McShane, chairman of the state industrial commission, declared on his return from Castlegate Monday.*

*The explosions which followed, however, were believed by many to have been of coal dust stirred up and ignited by the original blast.*

*"Force of the charges is shown on every hand," Mr. McShane declared. "The entrance reminds one of the clean bore of a gigantic cannon."*

John Psaroudakis, left, and Joseph Sargetakis outside Castle Gate Mine No. II. Sargetakis lost his life in the explosion soon afterward. Below, flowers bedeck the coffins during a mass burial service for some of the Greeks killed in the explosion.

Utah State Historical Society, Helen Papanikolas

Utah State Historical Society, Helen Papanikolas

# Lucky Lindy
## comes to town

**In two days in May 1927, the exploits of one young man shrunk the ocean breaches between the world's continents from days to hours. Capt. Charles Augustus Lindbergh, alone in the Spirit of St. Louis, flew non-stop from New York to Paris and captured the imagination of all the world.**

T he news media covered all aspects of the historic aviation coup, as excerpts from the Deseret News show:

**DESERET NEWS,** *May 20, 1927: WASHINGTON — Naval hydrographic experts calculated late today that if Charles A. Lindbergh maintained the pace he set in the early stages of his trans-Atlantic flight and meets with no mishap he will reach Paris about 3:30 p.m. tomorrow…*

*Captain Charles Lindbergh in his monoplane "The Spirit of St. Louis," had flown more than 600 miles on his flight to Paris at 2:30 o'clock eastern daylight time, this afternoon, and was right to the minute on his time schedule that was taking him over the great circle to the French capital. The "Flying Fool" was booming along at one hundred miles an hour and as the small villages in Nova Scotia sighted him in flight it was apparent that his motor was functioning smoothly and that he was keeping to his charted course…*

*… Lindbergh's trans-Atlantic flight is linked closely, in interest at least, with Woodward field, Salt Lake. About three years ago, Lindbergh passed through the pursuit course for army flyers at Kelly Field as a pupil of Lieut. Russell L. Maughan, Utah's "dawn to dusk" aviator … Lieut. Maughan said that*

*Lindbergh in one plane crashed with another in the air at a point over the head of the instructor. Both pilots left the wrecks to find their unguided way to earth, landed gently under parachutes and began to discuss the adventure as one that sometimes mars a practice flight…*

Utahns following Lindbergh's flight heaved a collective sigh of relief as he landed in Paris, more than two hours before the anticipated time:

**DESERET NEWS,** *May 21, 1927: LE BOURGET FLYING FIELD, France — Captain Charles Lindbergh, American aviator, landed here safely tonight completing his non-stop flight from New York to Paris. Lindbergh came over the LeBourget flying high slightly to the east of the field. He circled twice slowly, then settled down 200 yards west of the main building. He made a wonderful landing … The crowd of 250,000 gave a great roar and rushed forward. Dozens of persons were swept off their feet in the wild excitement to reach the wonderful American.*

The plaudits of the world were heaped upon the young pilot, including a congratulatory telegram from President Calvin Coolidge and presentation of the Legion Cross by French President Doumergue. But for Utahns, the best was yet to come. A personal visit by the famed aviator three months later set Salt Lake City on end:

**DESERET NEWS,** Sept. 3, 1927:
### ENTIRE CITY GOES WILD IN CHEERING AS PLANE COMES
#### Great Hero of the Air Greeted by 200,000 as He Circles Valley

*Falling with a driving engine, Col. Charles Lindbergh passed westward over the 35,000 people gathered at Woodward field, at terrific speed. Those who thought the conqueror of the Atlantic was headed for the Pacific Ocean, however, were soon set at rights.*

*The wheels of the Spirit of St. Louis touched the ground at Woodward field at 2 o'clock to the second.*

*Passing over the field, Lindy banked his plane and drove the stout monoplane upward at almost a vertical angle while he circled the field twice in three minutes and came to a landing so gently that the dust was hardly stirred. The throngs at Woodward field were taken by surprise, as were the thousands in the city with eyes fastened on the Wasatch skyline, when the monoplane, appearing the size of a seagull, was sighted overhead at an altitude of 15,000 feet …*

The News editorialist compared Lindbergh to Brigham Young in his ability to dream a dream, formulate a plan and carry it out.

UPI Photo

**Looking very young, Charles Lindbergh stands beside the Spirit of St. Louis before beginning his 33-hour solo flight to Paris.**

# Golden days for
# baseball

**Babe Ruth**

Deseret News Files

**Earl Combs**

**Lou Gehrig**

Some said then — and some say now — that the '27 Yankees were the best there ever was. With their famous "Murderers Row" — Babe Ruth, Lou Gehrig, Tony Lazzeri, Bob Meusel, Earl Combs — they powered their way through the season and into the record books.

**DESERET NEWS,** *Aug. 23, 1927: As the major league baseball teams slipped into gear for service again yesterday on the same old base paths, the New York Yankees were within hailing distance of a total of 100 victories. There is no reason in baseball why they should not attain the century mark unless the team suffers a total collapse.*

*As many games as the Yankees win above the 100 mark will help to rate them with the great baseball teams of all time.*

*Sept. 23, 1927: In the American league, the Yankees collectively and individually, continued their assault upon various world's records. Ruth hit his 56th homer and needs only four more to break his record. Gehrig drove in two runs, setting a new world's record of 172 runs for this specialty and breaking the old mark of 170 made by Ruth. Earl Combs set another record by hitting three consecutive triples. By beating Detroit 8 to 7, on Ruth's homer in the ninth, the Yanks tied the American league record of 105 victories in one season.*

*Sept. 23, 1927: Babe Ruth equaled his 1921 record of 59 home runs in a season by hitting his second circuit drive of the day in the fifth inning of the Yankees' game with the Senators today. He hit No. 58 in the first inning.*

Number 60 would come on Sept. 30; not for 34 years would anyone approach that number again. The Yankees won 110 regular-season games.

The World Series that year pitted the Yanks against the Pittsburgh Pirates, and even Salt Lakers were caught up in the furor:

**DESERET NEWS,** *Oct. 4, 1927: The Yanks will win!! No? All right, the Pirates will win! No again?*

*Well, then, come see for yourselves on OLD MAGNETO in front of the Deseret News beginning Wednesday with the first game.*

*OLD MAGNETO shows the whole works, even to the calm or nervous disposition of the player at bat. And when the player hits the ball, you see exactly where the ball goes, who is brought into the play and what each player does.*

*Above, is a picture of the OLD BOY himself taken at a time many Salt Lakers will not forget. Direct wires keep him posted on every move at the game and he reflects it like a mirror.*

Sports fans and historians alike would look back on the decade of the '20s as the "golden years" of baseball. It didn't start out that way, however. The "Black Sox" scandal, where Chicago White Sox players were accused of throwing the 1919 World Series, rocked the sports world. They were acquitted in a trial that began on June 27, 1921, and ran through Aug. 2 (by that time most evidence had long disappeared). But that didn't impress the new baseball commissioner, Judge Kenesaw Mountain Landis, who banned the players from the sport for life.

**DESERET NEWS,** *Aug. 3, 1921: None of the American league players who were acquitted last night of an alleged criminal conspiracy to throw the 1919 world series has any immediate prospect of being restored to organized baseball, according to a statement issued by Judge K.M. Landis… "Just keep it in mind that regardless of the verdict of juries, baseball is entirely competent to protect itself against the tricks both inside and outside the game."*

To say that Babe Ruth single-handedly saved the game may be overstating things a bit. But there's no question that he came along — with big bat and power numbers — at just the right time.

His performance and his personality brought baseball back.

And when the Yankees opened a new stadium, it was reasonable to call it "the house that Ruth built."

**DESERET NEWS,** *April 18, 1923: If Ruth had not been transferred to New York suitably wrapped and packed as any costly bit of bric-a-brac should be wrapped and packed there might never have been this mammoth structure rising out of the Harlem marshland…*

*This new structure is not a stadium in any sense. It is one half of a colossal amphitheatre.*

Ruth and his Yankees were not alone in these glory days. Other names of the '20s are still spoken with awe today: the Senators' Walter Johnson, the Cardinals' Grover Cleveland Alexander, Philadelphia's Lefty Grove and Jimmy Foxx, the Detroit Tigers' Ty Cobb.

And there was Rogers Hornsby of the St. Louis Cardinals. His batting average led the league for six consecutive seasons, and topped .400 for three. On Sept. 30, 1924, when the Deseret News printed an inauspicious little list of the "Leading Major League Hitters," Hornsby was on top with an impressive .424. Who knew that the world of baseball would never see such a number again?

# Radio

**"Hello! Hello! Hello! This is KZN. KZN, the Deseret News, Salt Lake City, calling. KZN calling. Greetings! The Deseret News sends its greeting to all of you far and wide."**

The voice of Harry "Flash" Wilson, broadcasting from the roof of the Deseret News Building in downtown Salt Lake City, was heard for 1,000 miles in every direction, the newspaper reported.

**DESERET NEWS,** *May 5, 1922: A flash of electrical fireworks, followed by a dull hum of generating energy and "mysterious messages" took flight… High above the drone of Salt Lake street traffic, the News radio operator, H. Carter Wilson, set his wonderful scientific radio apparatus in operation… The words formed by his lips were hurled hundreds of miles out in space, to be flashed in on the radio receiving sets with the same audibility as where they were spoken… Conceive, if you can, anything to parallel the significance of the installation of the powerful machine. News traveling with the speed of light along an ether wave for the satisfaction of the numerous radio fans of the intermountain country, and not only news, but programs of music and entertainment, such as people travel hundreds of miles to enjoy…*

Only a few days earlier, the system had gone through a trial run. Tearing through downtown Salt Lake City, Nate Fullmer raced from the News building on South Temple to his friend William Elder's business on Third South to see if the radio signal actually was working.

"She's coming over, Nate! She's coming over!" Elder assured Fullmer as he arrived, breathless.

Well before the inaugural broadcast, the News had been advertising "receiving sets" so Salt Lakers would be prepared when the magic was turned on. Small crystal sets, complete with ear phones and "cat's whiskers" enabled enthusiasts to tune in.

KZN's first official speaker was LDS President Heber J. Grant. The message was consistent with his position — a testimony of the divinity of Jesus Christ and the verity of the church founded by Joseph Smith. The church quickly made use of mass communications to reach a rapidly growing congregation throughout the world. President Grant also committed the first "blooper" on the new medium. "Turn off the heat!" he said in mid-broadcast, forgetting to remember that everything he said was now being aired for the benefit of all those listening. Screening out such unintentional background noise was one of the great challenges of early radio.

For months, the novelty of radio made top headlines:

**DESERET NEWS,**
*May 11, 1922:*

### THE DESERET NEWS RADIO CONCERT PROGRAM TONIGHT

*The Deseret News radio concert program for tonight from 8 to 9 o'clock: Solos, "Struck" and "Ain't We Got Fun" and "Mammy" …*

A photo of Mammy, a hefty black entertainer, accompanied the program. At first, only half-hour programs reached the eager listeners glued to their cat's whiskers. Over time, the program duration was expanded. In late 1922, famed orator William Jennings Bryan, three times an unsuccessful candidate for U.S. president, was a local speaker. In 1929, the Tabernacle Choir began its tradition as the longest continuously broadcasting group in radio history. KZN left the Deseret News rooftop and evolved into KSL.

# Wall street crashes

**Ā** merica's stock market crash of late November 1929 came across as a mild thud in Salt Lake City. For days after the biggest financial failure in American history, the Deseret News treated the event as a minor story and predicted a quick resurgence of the market. A story out of Port Arthur, Texas, glaringly headlined "Lovers Ambushed and Killed" took precedence over the stock market news, as these headlines showed:

**DESERET NEWS,** *Oct. 29, 1929: Wall Street Crash Fails to Bring Financial Troubles to Bankers; Financial System Weathers Crisis with no Show of Ill Effects for the First Time in History; Care in Lending Helps; Prices go up Rapidly; Mart Closes Strong.*

The report on what was really happening on Wall Street was tucked away in a very small box:

*All records were smashed on the New York Stock Exchange and the New York Curb Exchange during one of the most frenzied sessions of selling in history. Tickers were thrown far behind the market and final quotations were not available for publication today.*

The only front-page concession the News made to the story out of New York three days later was a montage of pictures showing the disarray of the crowd on Wall Street and the faces of Charles W. Mitchell and J. Pierpont Morgan, two of the country's premier bankers. Banking leaders had called three conferences during the near-panic in an effort to halt the "mad sales of stocks," the News said.

J.C. Royle, special Deseret News correspondent in New York, followed up with a positive article the day after the crash:

**DESERET NEWS,** *Oct. 30, 1929: NEW YORK — The next 12 months may see expansion in some lines unparalleled in the world, sponsored by those who never 'sell America short,' no matter what the stock market may do. Federal reserve officials and*

*bankers in general anticipate an era of easy money and low-priced money as a result of the throwing overboard of huge blocks of stocks by the public in the last fortnight.*

The newspaper's business pages continued to paint a rosy picture even as banks affected by the shock waves out of New York collapsed on every hand:

**DESERET NEWS,** *Oct. 31, 1929: NEW YORK — Stock prices advanced from 1 to 17 1/2 points today on the heels of a 1 to 36 point gain yesterday and when the final gong rang, it was evident that the market had regained its poise and stability… A buoyant rally marked the opening…*

The next day, another headline suggested the "Sound Economic Condition of U.S. Proven in Panic":

**DESERET NEWS,** *Nov. 1, 1929: NEW YORK — Stability of the basic business structure of the United States was amply indicated this week by the steady course of commerce, industry and trade during the upheaval in stocks… Business went on as usual with only minor diminution of volume.*

*When business can take blows like those administered in the last ten days and come back with its chin up, it warns financiers never to "sell America short."*

The next few months would prove the optimists seriously wrong. A quick recovery was not in the offing. With only two months of the old decade left, America was poised to slide into the seemingly bottomless pit of the Great Depression. Along with compatriots across the country, Utahns felt the sting.

# The Great Depression

## A state in shock

In the early 1930s, as the nation slipped into the Great Depression, Utah found itself with some particular problems. The state's high birthrate and heavy dependence on mining and agriculture helped make it more vulnerable to the economic crunch than many other states.

**A**s the financial noose tightened, the state's statistics became more grim: In 1933, the average per capita income was $300 per year; 35.8 percent of Utahns were unemployed, the fourth highest rate in the country; the wage level for those who did have jobs shrank 45 percent and their work week 20 percent. Thirty-two percent of the state's population got part or all of its food, clothing and other necessities from government programs; business failures increased by 20 percent and more than a fourth of the state's banks

The 1936 photograph by Dorothea Lange of a 32-year-old woman in a California migrant-worker camp symbolized the era.

had closed their doors.

- The statistics translated into people: Farmers offering prayers of thanks if they could sell their produce at a break-even point; would-be workers wandering the streets or leaving their families to travel in search of jobs; clusters of makeshift tents springing up in empty city lots to shelter the homeless; men, women and children lined up for a bowl of soup at a charity kitchen; youngsters who should have been in school looking for odd jobs to help support their families.
- Utah, not that far from its pioneer roots, had always encouraged in-migration.
- Ironically, the state now holed up within its boundaries and fended off newcomers who might compete for jobs and charity:

**DESERET NEWS,** Nov. 26, 1930:
*S.L. ACTS TO PROTECT JOBLESS AGAINST TRANSIENTS*
*A determined effort to keep Salt Lake free of "floaters" at this time of unemployment is being made by the police department.*
*Acting under orders of Chief Joseph E. Burbidge, more than 500 men, who came to Salt Lake looking for work from other sections of the country, have been picked up during the past three days by members of the police department and sent on their way. Officers working in the west part of the city rounded up more than 75 Tuesday evening, built a large fire around which the men kept warm during the night, and Wednesday morning sent them on their way.*
*Every vigilance will be used, said Chief Burbidge... to see that the residents of Salt Lake who are now so wonderfully co-operating in meeting this unemployment situation are not imposed on by men from places where nothing is being done to relieve the situation.*

Hungry, desperate people became restive. Several marches on the State Capitol alerted Utah lawmakers to the depth of the discontent. In one such confrontation, a spokesman for unemployed workers accused legislators of paying more attention to booze, carps and suckers than to the plight of the jobless. Legislators, however, had pressing problems on another front — by 1932, the state was $2 million short of meeting its budget. In more than one instance, the push and pull of the various groups led to violence:

**DESERET NEWS,** Feb. 23, 1933:
*Tear gas was used to clear the sheriff's office of a mob that broke through the doors in the city and county building Thursday afternoon.*

An Oklahoma farmer and his sons battle the wind in a memorable image of the Dust Bowl in 1936. Arthur Rothstein took the picture for the Farm Security Administration.

**DESERET NEWS**

## 1930-1940

The 1930s began and ended with Utah in a deep slump, stunned by the Great Depression that started with failures on Wall Street and Main Street. The Depression scarred a generation for the rest of their lives. Every third person in Utah was out of a job, and those who had one saw their wages fall. Hoboes rode the rails looking for someplace to work, marking homes where housewives would feed them from their own meager stores. An alphabet soup of federal programs emerged, bringing murals to post offices and writers to record history. Conservation Corps members dug watershed projects still visible from the valleys. It was an age of criminals: In America they became folk heroes, but in Germany, a once-imprisoned corporal rose to power and Utahns watched with growing dread.

### UTAH AND THE Depression

**From 1929 to 1933**

Per capita income fell from
...... **$527 to $300**
Farm income fell from ...
**$69 million to $30 million**
Manufacturing dropped from ...
**$23 million to $10 million**

**Unemployment was 36 Percent vs. national rate of 25 percent**

Source: Utah, The Right Place

*Rioting started on the west steps of the building where Chief Civil Deputy Heber G. Taylor was offering six Salt Lake homes and one farm for sale following mortgage foreclosure. Deputy sheriffs attempted to protect the sale with a fire hose, but upwards of 200 got through the water barrier and seized the hose.*

*To save the papers, the deputy and others from the office fought through the crowd to the sheriff's office on the ground floor of the building. After the doors were slammed, the rioters broke the windows and forced the locks and brought the running hose*

**Photograph of unemployed man was taken in 1936.**

*inside the building, flooding the ground floor.*

*Two tear gas bombs exploded in the sheriff's office quickly cleared the rooms…*

Fifteen people were arrested, found guilty, fined and sentenced to brief jail terms.

**DESERET NEWS,** *Aug. 21, 1935: Four deputy sheriffs and an undetermined number of civilians were injured today in rioting at the Salt Lake county Emergency Relief Administration headquarters, 2236 Highland Drive…*

*Eight men were arrested and placed in the county jail on charges of inciting a riot. R.C. Jackson and Larry Carrigan, deputy sheriffs, were severely hurt, the former being trampled on by five men during the fighting and the latter suffering numerous cuts and bruises…*

*The rioting was the result of continued protest on the part of agitators against the budget cut in the FERA appropriations for September… Mimeographed handbills announcing this morning's demonstration had been passed around Salt Lake for the past three days…*

For many Utahns, the failure of the American economy created a moral dilemma. Their religious beliefs were founded in self-sufficiency and hard work. Initially, the LDS Church advised against accepting government "hand-outs," but as the depression hunkered down for the long haul, necessity overruled pride. Resistance to aid became less adamant. The church also responded with its own "security program," forerunner to the current highly acclaimed Welfare Program:

**DESERET NEWS,** *April 6, 1936: AN IMPORTANT MESSAGE … if those now on work relief should continue thereon, the cost of maintaining the balance of those actually needing relief and without means of self-help would, at Church relief rate, cost approximately $842,000 per year.*

*This makes clear the size of the problem… The curtailment of Federal aid, which is now forecast, makes it imperative that the Church shall, so far as it is able, meet this emergency.*

The 1936 edict asked that church members able to do so pay fast offerings and tithing to help the needy and that wards unite to assist one another, rather than serving only their own members. Soon the News was running stories about such activities as a wood-cutting project in the Liberty Stake. Unemployed men chopped wood at the stake's "work center" and prepared to distribute it to families in need. The object was not to provide outright charity, but to give opportunities for work whenever possible. Over time, the program was recognized as a unique approach to welfare.

**DESERET NEWS,** *Dec. 18, 1937: Many things have been said and written about the Church Security Program. Perhaps no activity of the Church has been so widely discussed nationally and even internationally as has this effort to provide economic independence and security for the membership of the Church principally by promotion of a spirit of co-operation…*

But even the church programs could not fully address the depth of the depression in Utah. Federal charity outstripped the fledgling LDS welfare project 10 to 1 in contributions to the poor. For every dollar the state sent to Washington in taxes, $7 came back through such programs as school lunch, adult education, summer recreation, road construction, civic improvements, sewer construction and other projects were noted:

**DESERET NEWS,** *May 11, 1931: About $775,000 in federal funds will be spent this year in the Salt Lake district by the airway division of the department of commerce, W.E. Kline, airways engineer in charge of this, announces.*

*Of the total, $425,000 will be expended on maintenance and $150,000 for new improvements, Mr. Kline stated.*

The 1930s were a troublesome decade for many Utahns, one that left a lasting impression on the minds of a generation. Not until World War II would the state's economy and the nation's fully rebound, ending the Great Depression.

# A long recovery

**Dragging America out of the abyss of the Great Depression became the biggest national priority of the '30s. Recovery began with the election of Franklin Delano Roosevelt, a president whose stated objectives seemed to presage a turnaround:**

**DESERET NEWS,** *March 4, 1933: WASHINGTON (INS) — Franklin D. Roosevelt assumed the arduous duties of the presidency today with a ringing appeal to the nation to rally to meet the national emergency and a promise of quick action by the new administration in both executive and legislative branches…*

*"This great nation will endure as it has endured, will revive and prosper…"*

The road to that revival and prosperity was lined with a plethora of federally financed programs, many of which benefited Utahns. The need was painfully apparent when 1,500 Utah Democrats lined up to compete for the 300 jobs available in Utah as the "spoils" of the 1932 Demo election sweep. The State Legislature struggled to close a $2 million gap in the state budget and contemplated issuing "scrip" to help thousands of unemployed Utahns find jobs.

The president's massive reforms sounded a lot like socialism to many wary Utahns, despite their crying need for relief. The Deseret News announced the advent of Social Security in a two-inch story at the bottom of the first page:

## SECURITY MEASURE SIGNED BY PRESIDENT

**DESERET NEWS,** *Aug. 14, 1935: WASHINGTON (AP) — President Roosevelt sent the nation into a momentous governmental venture today by signing the social security bill.*

**Franklin Delano Roosevelt**

**D E S E R E T   N E W S**

*The president signed the bill in the presence of congressional leaders who sponsored it. Also with him was Secretary Perkins, who will have a part in the gigantic attempt to provide unemployment insurance and old age pensions…*

*He described the law as representing a "cornerstone" in a structure which is being built, but is by no means complete."*

The News paid more attention to another government program that was not as long-lasting, but had a great impact on Utah:

**DESERET NEWS,** *April 5, 1933: WASHINGTON (AP) — The first 25,000 men who will form part of the conservation corps will be sent to military camps for conditioning, beginning tomorrow … President Roosevelt by executive order today made available $10 million to finance the beginning of work. The first contingent will be selected from among men most in need of help and whose circumstances are fully and accurately known… Pay will be at the rate of $30 a month, payable twice a month.*

In Utah, men longing to have $25 a month sent to their families, with $5 left over for spending money, lined up for CCC jobs:

**DESERET NEWS,** *May 4, 1933: "I wish we could take them all," said Gus P. Backman Thursday, as, with a corps of*

*20 young women aids, he took applications from upwards of 4,000 youths of Salt Lake county who wish to go to work in Utah forests for Uncle Sam.*

*From the applicants who registered at the City and County building Thursday, 140 young men will be selected and sent to Fort Douglas for preliminary conditioning for a season of strenuous work on projects in the state…*

Two months later, 1,400 men from throughout the state were sent to camps in American Fork Canyon, Soapstone, Nebo, Pine Valley and Desert range, where there was work to be done. The state soon had 20 camps, primarily in national forests. The CCC workers built erosion control projects, dams, terraced hillsides and diversion dams to prevent flooding. Forest campgrounds were improved and ranger stations built. A road from Escalante to Boulder was constructed, so local residents no longer had to make the trip on muleback. The corps' experimental terracing above Bountiful became a standard for flood and erosion control in mountain terrain everywhere.

During the life of the CCC, 116 camps operated in Utah at various times. The federal infusion of funding amounted to $52 million. Many men trained on CCC projects in jobs that could be carried to the private sector.

A second federal program that profoundly affected Utah was the Works Project Administration. Through the recovery years, the News printed such headlines as: "Washington Okehs Million Dollar WPA County Road Project"; "WPA Gives $80,000 Fund for Arsenal Improvements"; "Three New Utah WPA Jobs Okehed."

WPA looked out for the interests of arts and sciences. In Utah, artists were paid to produce hundreds of works to decorate public buildings. Salt Lake's Art Barn was a WPA-sponsored project. And in 1935, the humble seeds of the Utah Symphony were planted when five indigent musicians who were receiving public dole were recruited by the Federal Music Project, a WPA offshoot, to form the Utah Sinfonietta.

As the economy gradually improved, the federal programs withered or evolved into other forms. The concerted effort of local, state and federal governments, combined with native stubbornness and ingenuity, ultimately saw Utah through the worst financial setback of its history.

May 7, 1937

## SABOTAGE HINTED AS CAUSE OF HINDENBURG DISASTER

BULLETIN — New York, May 7, — Capt. Ernst died here late this afternoon.

**by the Associated Press**

LAKEHURST, N. J., May 7 — The flaming destruction of the once-seemingly impregnable dirigible Hindenburg brought swift action today by the American and German governments to determine the cause of the disaster.

Thirty-three persons were known dead or missing.

Of the 97 passengers and members of the crew aboard when the greatest of all airships exploded, burst into flames and crashed to earth last night — just as it was lowering to the mooring mast, and only 200 feet above the ground — 68 persons survived; the known dead or missing were 13 passengers, six of the crew and ten others, mostly crew members. The one dead on the ground brought the total to 30.

The ruins of the luxurious liner of the skies lay crumpled on the landing field at the naval air station — a junk heap of black metal, a mass of ghastly, grisly framework.

**Cause Mystery**

On the lips of everyone was the question — what caused the crash, what was the matter! Twenty times had the Hindenburg crossed the North Atlantic safely.

**Craft Largest, Most Luxurious Of All Airships**

LAKEHURST, N.J., May 7 — (AP) — Here is what the Hindenburg was like before her crash:

The ship: Largest and most luxurious airship ever built, 803 feet long — cruising range of 8,500 miles — capacity of 50 passengers and 60 crew and 24,606 pounds of freight — four 1,000 horsepower Diesel engines giving it a maximum speed of 84 miles an hour.

# Killers and gangsters

**The Great Depression and Prohibition were ready-made incubators in the 1930s for scofflaws and criminals. The combination of financial desperation and a national thirst for illicit liquor provided a rich seedbed for those who were willing and eager to flout the rules. And while liquor was often the starting point, many of the criminals of the 1930s ranged far beyond to steal, intimidate, kidnap and kill.**

**S**ome of the most notorious names in American criminal history became household words in the 1930s.

Dozens of hoods tied into rival gangs and their crimes were methodical, blatant and broad in scope. Such characters as John Dillinger, Baby Face Nelson, Bugsy Segal, Pretty Boy Floyd, Machine Gun Kelly, Alphonse (Al) Capone and Ma Barker with her nefarious offspring competed for headlines, cutting a wide swath of illegal booze, thievery, prostitution, racketeering and murder.

They were desperate times that called for heroic remedies. Enter J. Edgar Hoover, the quintessential American crime-fighter, creator of the Federal Bureau of Investigation as it now exists and a deadly enemy to the 1930s gangsters. Later there were charges that Hoover became obsessed with ferreting out "crime" and overstepped his bounds. But for several years, his G-men were the nemesis of crooks who had operated virtually unchecked in some American locales. Backed by more restrictive laws regulating kidnapping, extortion, bank robbery and other crimes, they wreaked

havoc on hoodlums. The score card:

July 22, 1934, John Dillinger killed resisting arrest in Chicago; Oct. 22, 1934, Pretty Boy Floyd killed on an Ohio farm resisting arrest; Nov. 27, 1934, Baby Face Nelson, fatally wounded in a gunfight in Illinois; Jan. 8, 1935, Russell Gibson of the Barker-Karpis Gang, killed in Chicago; Jan. 15, 1935, Ma and Fred Barker, killed in Florida; May 1, 1936, Alvin "Old Creepy" Karpis, arrested by Hoover himself in a New Orleans raid and deported to Canada.

Of all the 1930s gangsters, probably none excited the American imagination more than Clyde Champion Barrow and his "moll," Bonnie Parker Clyde Barrow. Clyde was considered one of the most sadistic of the hoods who pillaged the country, killing for the sheer joy of it. His haphazard gunplay made him unpopular even among the brotherhood of criminals. The sudden demise of the two was front page drama:

**DESERET NEWS,** *May 23, 1934: BLACK LAKE, La. — Clyde Barrow and his gunwoman companion, Bonnie Parker, were beaten to the trigger pull by Texas officers today.*

*Their crime career ended in a blaze of riot gun fire when, disregarding a command to halt and unable to get their weapons into play, the desperado and his cigar-smoking girl crumpled up in the front seat of a car traveling at about 85 miles an hour. The car careened into an embankment and was wrecked.*

*In the wreckage, the officers, who had set the trap for the Southwest's public enemy number one and the Parker woman, found both bodies riddled with bullets. Bonnie's was*

*almost doubled over the machine gun she had held in her lap. Barrow's broken body was twisted behind the steering wheel, a revolver gripped in one hand... Barrow was regarded as one of the nation's most dangerous killers, shooting at the bat of an eye and fleeing in fast automobiles...*

**J Edgar Hoover**

Unfortunately, the good guys didn't always survive unharmed. Samuel P. Cowley, born in Franklin, Idaho, reared in Logan, Utah, four-year LDS missionary in Hawaii, holder of a law degree and finally, FBI agent, was one who fell. He directed and executed the plan that finally netted John Dillinger and in November 1934 was hot on the heels of Dillinger's partner, Baby Face Nelson (born Lester M. Gillis.)

Alerted that Nelson had been seen in a suburb of Chicago, Cowley and his partner, Herman E. Hollis, undertook a pursuit. On the 27th, the lawbreaker and the law met with disastrous results:

**DESERET NEWS,** *Nov. 28, 1934: CHICAGO (INS) — George ("Baby Face") Nelson was found shot to death today in Niles, Ill., a Chicago suburb, the gruesome discovery bearing mute evidence that he died in retribution for killing two government agents last night... Nelson, it was evident from the*

**Bonnie and Clyde**

**Al Capone**

**John Dillinger**

manner of his death, had been fatally wounded in the terrific gun fight with Samuel P. Cowley and Herman E. Hollis, federal agents, whom he killed on the northwest highway near Barrington, Ill...

A solemn pledge by the United States government to avenge the slaying of Inspector Samuel P. Cowley was given to the federal agent's father, Mathias F. Cowley (in Salt Lake) today.

Advised of the killing of another federal agent and the fatal wounding of Inspector Cowley, J. Edgar Hoover, chief of the bureau of investigation of the Department of Justice, wired Mr. Cowley at his residence... "Inspector Cowley is a most courageous officer and devoted public servant."

Cowley's effectiveness and courage as an agent and his ultimate sacrifice in the course of his duty were lauded throughout the nation. Finally, the efforts of such men brought an end to the gangster era. Crime didn't cease but became less brazen, less flamboyantly glamorized, less public. It tended to go underground, where its perpetrators were faceless and nameless to the ordinary American, unlike the daredevil crooks of the 1930s.

FBI Inspector Samuel P. Cowley tracked down Dillinger, but was killed by "Baby Face" Nelson.

# The Lindbergh outrage

**In a day of big crimes, the one that most incensed Americans involved a small baby. The 20-month-old son of popular aviator Charles Lindbergh and his wife, Anne Morrow Lindbergh, was snatched by a kidnapper from his second-story bedroom, and the news rocked the country:**

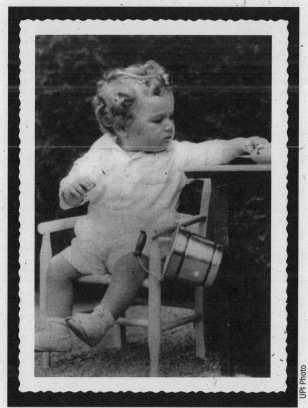

Charles Augustus Lindbergh Jr.

**DESERET NEWS,** *March 2, 1932: NEWARK, N. J. — A communication believed to be from the kidnaper of the Lindbergh baby and intended for his father, Col. Charles A. Lindbergh, today was found by a letter-carrier in the mailbox ...*

*"Baby safe," it read. "Instructions later. Act accordingly..."*

*Charles Augustus Lindbergh Jr. was stolen from his nursery crib as he slept last night between 7:30 and 10 p.m. and his parents said authorities were convinced the job was accomplished by a professional kidnaping gang.*

The Lindberghs paid $50,000 in ransom, but the baby was found dead in a shallow grave near their home six weeks later. It would be more than two years before a suspect was arrested:.

**DESERET NEWS,** *Sept. 20, 1934: NEW YORK (INS) — The Lindbergh kidnaping case, one of the most baffling crimes of the ages, broke wide open today with the arrest of a man charged by police with receiving the $50,000 paid by Col. Charles A. Lindbergh in the fruitless attempt to ransom his abducted infant son. In a formal statement issued late this afternoon, Police Commissioner John F. O'Ryan announced that Bernard (sic)Richard Hauptmann, 35, of the Bronx, had been taken into custody as the man who received the money tossed over the wall of a Bronx cemetery... It was widely reported that Hauptman's apprehension resulted from the alertness of a Bronx filling station attendant who received one of the $10 gold certificates paid as ransom when he sold the prisoner five gallons of gasoline ...*

Hauptmann, an illegal alien from Germany, steadfastly denied any guilt, and the trial went through several appeals. Ultimately, he was convicted on circumstantial evidence:

**DESERET NEWS,** *April 4, 1936: TRENTON, N. J. — "This man is dead." With those words, spoken by a physician in the crowded prison death house at 8:47.30 last night, was told the end of New Jersey's case against the Lindbergh baby killer — the end of Bruno Richard Hauptmann. He died as most people thought he would — unspeaking, unshaken, cold, unsmiling.*

Bruno Richard Hauptmann

## The world of the 1930s
### A TIMELINE

**1930**— Constantinople becomes Istanbul.
**1930**— Robert Frost publishes his "Collected Poems," which will win a Pulitzer Prize.
**1930**— "American Gothic" painted by Grant Wood.
**1930**— Clyde Tombaugh discovers the planet Pluto.
**1930**— Bobby Jones wins all four world golf titles in a "Grand Slam."
**1931**— Boris Karloff is a smash hit in "Frankenstein."
**1931**— Thomas Alva Edison, one of the greatest inventors ever, dies.
**1931**— Empire State Building completed in New York.
**1932**— Franklin D. Roosevelt elected president in a landslide.
**1932**— Aldous Huxley publishes "Brave New World."
**1932**— "The Grand Canyon Suite" composed by Ferde Grofe.
**1932**— First Winter Olympics in the United States held at Lake Placid, N.Y.
**1933**— Frances Perkins becomes the first woman to serve in a cabinet, appointed Secretary of Labor.
**1933**— Germany engages in an orgy of book burning, builds its first concentration camps.
**1933**— "King Kong" becomes a film classic.
**1933**— The School of American Ballet founded by George Balanchine and Lincoln Kirstein.
**1934**— S.S. Queen Mary luxury liner launched.
**1935**— "Porgy and Bess," George Gershwin's American opera, opens.
**1935**— John L. Lewis founds the CIO (Congress of Industrial Organizations).
**1935**— Persia becomes Iran.
**1936**— The Spanish Civil War begins.
**1936**— "How to Win Friends and Influence People" published by Dale Carnegie.
**1936**— Boulder Dam completed.
**1937**— Nylon, an artificial silk, is patented by Wallace Carothers.
**1937**— Japanese troops occupy and begin massacres of Nanjing in China.
**1937**— "Snow White and the Seven Dwarfs" produced by Walt Disney.
**1937**— The Golden Gate Bridge opens for traffic in San Francisco.
**1938**— Thornton Wilder's "Our Town" wins the Pulitzer Prize for drama and Marjorie Kinnan Rawlings' "The Yearling" wins for fiction.
**1938**— Lajos Biro invents the ballpoint pen in Hungary.
**1939**— John Steinbeck's "The Grapes of Wrath" wins the Pulitzer Prize.
**1939**— "God Bless America," written by Irving Berlin, becomes an American classic.

# The Deseret News

## Feb. 20, 1930

### Ice Cream Is Stolen, Boys Held

Judge Oscar W. McConkie of the Third district court, was nearly "cheated" out of his refreshments at a party Wednesday night at the home of Mrs. William Facer, 524 First avenue.

When the hostess prepared to serve refreshments she discovered that ice cream left on a back porch was gone. Police were called.

About two minutes later, a police car pulled up at the curb and Patrolmen C. J. Larson and Alva Johnson carried the missing freezer to the door.

The officers explained they chased four boys in a flivver toward the foothills and found a loaded revolver and a freezer of ice cream in the car.

## May 19, 1931

### Utah Fails To Grasp Dam Benefit, Report

Utah does not fully sense the tremendous opportunity for trade offered by activities at Hoover dam, according to the opinion expressed by R. A. Hart, chamber of commerce industrial secretary, upon his return Tuesday from the dam site… .

Mr. Hart made the trip to the Hoover dam site to survey the activities there and determine in what ways Salt Lake and Utah might best profit from the spending of the $165,000,000 for the big project.

He declares that he was first impressed by both the vastness and diversity of the activity in progress. The Union Pacific system has just completed its connection with Boulder City, including adequate terminal facilities; a 2,000,000 gallon water tank has been erected at the government city, and a mess hall capable of seating 1,000 men… .

Mr. Hart Tuesday issued a warning for all jobless persons to stay away from Hoover dam unless work has been assured them there.

## May 4, 1931

### Ground broken for Zoological Park

Ground was broken Monday for the new zoological gardens on the tract southeast of the city, given recently by Mr. and Mrs. James A. Hogle. Preliminary building is expected to be begun Tuesday. Some of those at the ground breaking ceremony were… John M. Wallace, E. G. Shell, Dr. George A. Allen, president of the Zoological society; Ed L. Vetter, Miss Jane Cannon, taking out first shovelful of dirt; Dr. W. A. Pettit and the Rev. Henry A. Post.

## May 25, 1931

### Picnic Arranged At New Zoo Park

At the spot made memorable by the pioneers of 1847 where Emigration canyon opens up to a view of the valley, Salt Lake citizens will be given a graphic picture of what the new zoological garden will look like on Tuesday at noon, when a picnic luncheon of zoo directors, members, friends and state and city officials will be held under auspices of the Salt Lake Zoological society.

Dr. George A. Allen Monday said that the idea originated with Dr. Charles G. Plummer, an officer of the society and city zoological park board, and was to enable all those interested in the development and planning of the city to express their opinion regarding the zoo project to locate the animals now in crowded quarters at Liberty park, in large, natural surroundings… .

Big stakes will be displayed all over the 32-acre tract, which is known as Hogle Gardens in honor of the donors, indicating the location of each house, cage and enclosure on the architects' drawings, which will be explained by Julian M. Bamberger, vice president.

## April 2, 1932

### Maude Adams, Otis Skinner Win Applause In Shakespeare Drama

Recalled time after time by an audience obviously insisting on a curtain speech, Salt Lake's own Maude Adams, most beloved of American actresses, made her first appearance here in 14 years Friday night at Kingsbury Hall with Otis Skinner in Shakespeare's comedy, "the Merchant of Venice."

But despite the clamorous applause, which after one scene brought her and Mr. Skinner to the footlights for 13 curtain-calls, Miss Adams, true to the tradition which has almost become legendary with her, refused to present herself in any way to the public except as a character.

**Johnny Weismuller**

## April 2, 1932

### Jungle Thriller Now At Capitol theatre

"Tarzan, the Ape Man," the current attraction at the Capitol theatre, establishes a new record for screen thrills. This Edgar Rice Burroughs romance becomes strikingly realistic drama under the able interpretation given it by the excellent cast. Johnny Weismuller, the swimming champion plays the title role and Maureen O'Sullivan, Nell Hamilton and C. Aubrey Smith play strong featured roles.

## April 6, 1932

### Phar Lap "The Red Terror"
#### (Phar Lap means lightning in Javanese)

MENLO PARK, Calif. April 6 — (INS) — Declaring himself mystified at the death of Phar Lap, Australia's great thoroughbred, Dr. William Nielsen, veterinarian, told International News Service today he planned to ask for a pathological examination of the famous animal's stomach.

"I hesitate to say Phar Lap was poisoned, but I also hesitate to say it was a natural death due to colic, as appears on the surface," Nielsen declared.

"But in all my 13 years experience as a veterinarian I've never seen a horse die so quickly. He was apparently only slightly indisposed in the morning. That afternoon he was dead."

At the peak of a racing career that stirred the admiration of the world, Phar Lap died at 3 o'clock yesterday afternoon in his stall at the stables of the Ed Perry ranch here. … David J. Davis, broken hearted owner of Phar Lap, was inclined to accept the general consensus that death was due to colic caused by a foxtail, or a bit of alfalfa, or barley, sodden with dew, picked up while Phar Lap was exercising in an adjoining field.

## Feb. 4, 1933

### Senate Indorses Dern For Cabinet
#### Motion Passes Unanimously After Mild Protest

Under a resolution adopted by the senate Friday afternoon former Governor George H. Dern is indorsed for the secretary of interior portfolio in the cabinet of President-elect Franklin D. Roosevelt.

The former governor now has united support of both houses of the Utah legislature.

## Feb. 23, 1933

### Utahn in Cabinet Faces Heavy Task

WASHINGTON, Feb. 23 — (AP) — In the face of troublous conditions in several parts of the world the big problem confronting the incoming secretary of war will be to provide adequate national defense at minimum expense.

George H. Dern, former governor of Utah, is the man upon whom that duty will fall.

What the army wants is to maintain its present status. Any cut in its trained man power, officers contend, would weaken the main props of this country's national defense. .

Demands of the budget for curtailed expenditures gave General Douglas MacArthur, chief of staff, an opportunity to warn the House appropriations sub-committee that any further reduction of the land forces would "destroy the military framework of our system of national defense."

## July 12, 1933

WASHINGTON, July 12 — (INS) — A virtual ultimatum to public utility services throughout the country to reduce rates 10 per cent has been ordered by Assistant Secretary of War Woodring.

Acting in the interest of governmental economy but with a view to bringing relief to household budgets throughout the nation, Woodring has dispatched orders to all corps area commanders to serve notice upon the public utility services that war department contracts for such services will not be renewed for the fiscal year 1934 unless a 10 per cent reduction rates is granted.

Dec. 5, 1933

## UTAH CASTS 36TH VOTE FOR REPEAL

Twenty-one affirmative votes by members of the Utah State Constitutional convention at the capitol today, put an end to prohibition, both within the state and within the nation.

Shortly after the recess for lunch, members reconvened at 3:45 and started the form or procedure leading up to the ratification of the Twenty-first amendment.

Earlier in the day, two other states, Pennsylvania and Ohio, had completed the same formalities, leaving the way open for Utah's final action on repeal.

By its action Utah became the thirty-sixth state to ratify the Twenty-first amendment and thereby put repeal immediately into effect throughout the entire country.

Nov. 10, 1934

## Roosevelt Places Utah Financier In Charge of System

WASHINGTON, Nov. 10 — (AP) — Marriner S. Eccles, Ogden, Utah, banker whose financial views are classed as liberal, was appointed today as governor of the Federal Reserve board.

The 44-year-old financier succeeds Eugene R. Black, who resigned three months ago to return to his old post of governor of the Atlanta Federal Reserve bank.

Eccles entered public office for the first time last January when he was named assistant secretary of the treasury. He had a leading part in formulating the administration's housing legislation...

"A group of the leading financial institutions of Utah and Idaho, with resources in excess of $50,000,000, in whose organization and development

**Jascha Heifetz**

Mr. Eccles had taken a leading part, and of which he was the head, came through the banking crisis in such splendid condition as to reflect great credit upon his ability as a bank executive," the announcement added.

The Federal Reserve Bank system is intended to furnish an elastic policy to afford means of rediscounting commercial paper and to establish a more effective supervision at banking and credit in the United States.

Dec. 26, 1934

## OGDEN EMPLOYES SURPRISE PEERY

OGDEN, Dec. 26 — City employes in departments directed by Mayor Harman W. Peery, surprised him Monday with a Christmas present consisting of a silver and gold mounted Colonel Bill Cody Bridle, martingale and spurs, with hand-tooled leather fittings of an oak-leaf design. The bridle bit extends between two silver and gold six-shooters.

Dec. 27, 1934

## World Famed Violinist To Give S.L. Concert Jan. 14

Ranking as an outstanding musical event of the season, the appearance in Salt Lake City on the night of Monday, Jan. 14, of Jascha Heifetz, world renowned violinist, will draw to Salt Lake music lovers from all over the state.

The Heifetz concert is being brought to Salt Lake under the auspices of the Auerbach company, which has agreed to underwrite the guarantee for the undertaking and give the proceeds to charity.

Under the present arrangement, after all expenses have been deducted, the receipts will be equally divided by the Auerbach company between the L.D.S. Relief society, the Community Chest, and the Junior League relief fund.

August 16, 1935

## Bodies Near Pt. Barrow
### Engine Misfires When Noted Flier Attempts To Take Off at Point 15 Miles From Destination

JUNEAU, ALASKA, Aug. 16 — (AP) — A large Pan-American Airways airplane under directions received from Col. Charles A. Lindbergh and officials at New York, left here today for Fairbanks to fly the bodies of Will Rogers and Wiley Post back to Juneau.

BARROW, ALASKA, Aug. 16 — (AP) — An airplane crash at the "top of the world" today had taken the lives of two world-famed figures — the loved humorist Will Rogers and the aerial world girdler Wiley Post.

Their crushed bodies were taken from the wreckage of Post's new monoplane at the mouth of a small river 15 miles southwest of here. Post's wrist watch had stopped at 8:15 p.m. (P.S.T.) last night.

Native runners brought word of the accident to Barrow late last night and Staff Sgt. Stanley R. Morgan, signal corps operator, stationed at this, America's most northerly white settlement, hired a fast launch and went to the scene.

## Sergeant Who Found Bodies Of Fliers Native of Utah, Brother Lives in S.L.

Sergt. Stanley R. Morgan, the army radio operator at Point Barrow, Alaska, who recovered the bodies of Will Rogers, noted film humorist, and Wiley Post, famed aviator, from their wrecked airplane and reported the tragedy, is a Utahn.

Sergt. Morgan was born at Payson in 1904.

Dec. 10, 1936

## EDWARD SURRENDERS THRONE THAT HE MAY WED AMERICAN

(By The Associated Press)
LONDON, Dec. 10 — King Edward of England abdicated his ancient, mighty throne today.

He will marry Wallis Warfield Simpson, as man, not monarch.

Albert Frederick Arthur George, the tall 40-year-old Duke of York, will rule over the 495,000,000 subjects of the greatest empire on the earth.

He will reign as George VI...

Rather than give up the twice divorced American woman who waited today within the rain splashed walls of a villa on the Cote D'Azur, in France, balked by state and church in his desire for morganatic marriage, Edward VIII signed this morning the decree of abdication...

April 1, 1937

## Stalin Demands 'Merciless' Extermination

MOSCOW, April 1 — (AP) — Joseph Stalin called upon Russia today for "merciless" extermination of all Bolshevist enemies in what was interpreted as a virtual death sentence for hundreds under arrest as counter-revolutionaries.

The demand of the Soviet leader, regarded as an ultimatum to the Communist party, was made in the Kremlin March 5 before the closing session of a plenum of the central committee of the party and was published today.

"I think it is clear," the secretary of the central committee declared, "that the present wreckers and

diversionists — no matter whether they have masked themselves under the flag of Trotzkyism or Bukharinism — have lost their influence in the worker's movement and have become simply an unprincipled and idealless band of professional wreckers, diversionists, spies and murderers.

"It is quite clear these gentlemen should be destroyed, exterminated mercilessly as enemies of the working class and enemies of our country.

"This is clear and does not demand further interpretation."

May 4, 1937

## 'Gone With the Wind' Wins Prize

NEW YORK, May 4 — (AP) — Margaret Mitchell wrote 1,037 pages for "Gone With The Wind" but she could find only four words with which to greet the news that her book had won the annual Pulitzer prize.

"I'm astounded," was the first reaction of the Atlanta author. She groped for words. Then — "I'm overwhelmed."

**Amelia Earhart**

July 6, 1937

## 'Cannot Hold Out Much Longer,' Is Word;
### Earlier 'Flares' Believed From Amelia Caused By Meteors

SAN FRANCISCO, July 6 — (AP) — Coast guard headquarters here today announced it was informed an Oakland radio amateur reported picking up a message purportedly from Amelia Earhart, missing aviatrix, at 6:35 a.m. (Pacific Standard Time.)

The amateur's name was withheld while a coast guard officer hurried to Oakland to investigate the report.

No other station apparently picked up the report,

but coast guard officials said they were informed the Oakland amateur heard a message, which he quoted:

"281 miles north Howland. Cannot hold out much longer. Drifting northeast. Motor sinking in water."

July 6, 1937

HONOLULU, (AP) — Hopes for the rescue of Amelia Earhart skyrocketed early today, then suddenly fizzled out when the coast guard cutter Itasca reported it had apparently mistaken a meteor for flares from the round-the-world flier's plane.

Despite the severe disappointment the search continued today, its center probably shifting southward 500 miles from a point 280 miles north of Howland Island to the Phoenix Islands.

Dec. 29, 1937

## New Building Planned For Child Hospital

Plans For Up-To-Date Home Announced By First Presidency

Decision to erect a new building for the Primary Children's Hospital was announced today by the First Presidency.

Pres. Heber J. Grant announced that the Presiding Bishopric had been instructed to make immediate plans for a new, up-to-date, fireproof building to be erected on the site of the present hospital, 14 West North Temple Street.

The new building, he explained, has long been needed by the hospital, to provide adequately for its needs.

Dec. 1, 1938

## TWENTY-ONE KILLED IN S.L. SCHOOL BUS TRAIN STRIKES CAR; 21 INJURED

### Speeding Freight Strews Dead 2 Blocks

#### By Theron Liddle

Twenty-one identified dead — two unidentified dead — four feared dying — eight others critically injured — nine others less severely injured.

That was the toll of Utah's and the nation's worst traffic accident in history when a speeding D. & R. G. W. freight train plowed into a crowded Jordan District High School bus 15 miles south of Salt Lake City early today.

#### Strikes Bus In Center

The giant, four-piston D. & R. G. W. freight locomotive, heading a train of 50 cars, struck the bus squarely in the middle and scattered bodies of the dead and injured and the wreckage half a mile up the track.

Of the estimated 45 children on the bus, only two were able to walk when ambulances and first aid crews arrived at the site of the tragedy. Mangled bodies were strewn on both sides of the right-of-way.

Of the injured, 12 were reported seriously hurt, while nine suffered minor injuries. No one on the bus escaped unscathed.

The bus, nearing the destination of its scheduled run, was filled to capacity.

According to eyewitnesses and train crew members, the bus, driven by Ferald H. Silcox of Riverton, who was killed instantly, stopped for the crossing and then pulled onto the tracks. Fog and a light snow made visibility poor.

Engineer E. L. Rehmer halted the train within its length and members of the train crew immediately sent calls for all available ambulances, doctors and nurses.

Jan. 12, 1939

## Work Starts On Utah Field House

Working on the north rim of the University of Utah Stadium this drag line and caterpillar are cutting off the north slope of the bowl to allow a $175,000 field house to become a part of the 'U' Athletic plant. The work is the first on the field house, long a need at the school and will provide for the southeast end of the field house. A tunnel will be built from the field house into the Stadium from the north, making it possible for football and track and field teams to use the modern dressing rooms of the new structure. The new plant will be ready by next fall.

[A photo accompanied the story.]

March 8, 1939

## $1,350,000 Proposed For Deer Creek Project

An appropriation, of $1,350,000 to continue work on the Provo River Deer Creek project by the Bureau of Reclamation was recommended to the House today by its appropriation committee, according to an Associated Press dispatch from Washington, D.C.

The appropriation cut $150,000 from budget estimates, was included in recommendations for the allotment of $50,622,600 for construction, operation and maintenance of western reclamation projects during the next fiscal year.

The total allotment recommended was $100,000 in excess of budget estimates and included $23,000,000 for the Grand Coulee dam in Washington and $10,000,000 for the California Central Valley project, the two biggest water developments in the West.

March 11, 1939

MARIAN ANDERSON, Negro contralto, sings for Salt Lake Civic Music Association members at Kingsbury Hall, Tuesday night at 8:30 o'clock and what a program.

Numbers by Purcell, Bizet, five gems from the lieder of Schubert including "Der Doppelganger" and "Erlkonig," the dramatic "Casta Diva" aria from Bellini's "Norma," a song of her accompanist and a group of seldom-heard Negro spirituals form the list of selections... .

When Miss Anderson returned to America four years ago, the New York Times reported: "Let it be said at the outset: Marion Anderson has returned to her native land one of the greatest singers of our time..."

March 14, 1939

## Faux Pas In Nice Society Pointed Out By Emily Post

### Dating

Q: Is it tactful for a man to ask a girl for a date by saying, "are you going to be busy Saturday night?"

A: No (This is a "trap" invitation. If she answers "no" she has to accept whatever he invited her to do.)

Q. Would it be better for a man to say, "Will you go to the dance with me Saturday evening?"

A: The definite invitation to a dance is best, though the request for a date is quite all right. (For wrong way to ask, see answer to preceding question.)

April 22, 1939

## S. L. Executives Turn Out Early For Daily Exercises

If local business men walk with more spring in their step and are less grouchy with their employees, it's probably because they are doing the "hands on hips; one, two, three, bend" and other calisthenics in the early morning class at the Deseret Gymnasium.

At 7:30 a.m., three days a week, more than a score assemble at the gym, where, under the direction of H. C. Mortensen, they line up for exercises, and follow this with a plunge in the gym pool.

June 12, 1939

## OGDEN AIRBASE BILL ADVANCES

WASHINGTON, June 12 — (AP) — Immediate expenditure of $8,000,000 for an air depot at Ogden, Utah, and $4,000,000 for an airbase at Fairbanks, Alaska, was recommended to the House today by its appropriations committee.

The committee provided for the projects in a $222,198,047 supplemental military appropriations bill, introduced following extensive hearings.

### July Work Start Urged

Plans for the two bases, vital links in the War Department's expanded national defense program, were discussed at length at the hearings by army officials, who expressed hope work would be underway shortly after July 1.

Gen. H. H. Arnold, chief of the army air corps, said establishment of the depot at Ogden for the repair and storage of planes and the handling of ammunition for coast airbases and the construction of an inland base in Alaska were essential to national defense.

Nov. 1, 1939

## Edwin C. Hill Eulogizes Utah Television Inventor

In a day when warlords and politicans are conspicuous, we are apt to overlook more important men who will get a higher rating when the returns are all in. Less than 1,000 men have contributed to the basic discoveries and processes which have made the modern world, and a nation's score in bringing such men out in front is to a great degree the measure of its real attainment.

This observation is touched off by the news that television will soon begin to filter into little roadside homes and that, again, it is a young American hayloft inventor who brings through the miracle. He is Philo T. Farnsworth, 33-year-old, who first discovered and applied the unique principle of electronic television. His story makes one realize that in our age centuries of normal change are telescoped into a decade or two.

Jan. 30, 1939

## SILVER QUEEN'S TREASURES SELL FOR MERE TRIFLE

PASADENA, Cal., Jan. 10 — (INS) — Mrs. Susan Emery-Holmes Delitch, "Utah Silver queen," and 74 year old society leader was in seclusion today, following an auction sale in which treasures she had valued at $7,000,000 were disposed of for $100,000.

Eighteen jeweled goblets once owned by Czar Nicholas II of Russia were sold for $65 each. A triple framed ikon, once the property of the Grand Duke Boris, brought $499.

The sterling silver tea and coffee service the American people presented to Admiral George Dewey was sold for $1100.

The Amelia bed on which Brigham Young had slept brought $1,000.

Names of purchasers were not disclosed.

# Escape into fantasy

**Joan Crawford**

**M**ay Mann, Deseret News' very own Hollywood correspondent, certainly got around. One week she was talking to Shirley Temple, another she was taking Mae West up on her invitation to "come up and see me sometime." The "Brigham City girl" strolled down Hollywood Boulevard, hobnobbed with the glamorous stars, and shared it all with her readers:

**DESERET NEWS,** *Aug. 1, 1936: Little misses between four and ten years would do well to take a lesson from Miss Shirley Temple, watch her capricious little ways and beguiling smile and profit thereby. … The child is a real actress, as you soon discovered watching her before the camera out on the Fox lot in Beverly Hills. They say smile and Shirley turns one on and then off just like we'd turn on a water faucet.*

*"What is that nice tall gentleman doing, the one in Salt Lake City who came out to see me last year?" she inquired and as I reflected, puzzled, she added: "The one with the mustache — a cute little one — he wrote a story about me."*

*"That must be Ted Cannon of The Deseret News," I replied as the description seemed to fit him better than anyone else I could think of for the moment. "That's the one!" she said. "I liked him, he knew some funny pencil tricks," and those mischievous brown eyes turned on me as if to say: "It's too bad you don't know some, too."*

Pencils or no, the little actress seemed to like May Mann. A few days later, the Deseret News printed her letter:

**DESERET NEWS,** *Aug. 10, 1936: "Hello May Mann: Did you get back to Utah yet, or are you still in Hollywood? I'm on my vacation with Mother and Daddy. We got our dog, Corky, back again. Corky was lost for a week, but some people took him in and brought him back to me. That was nice of them, wasn't it? You were nice, too, to print the stories about me. Didn't we have a good time when you visited me? Say hello to any people you see who know me. Love, Shirley Temple.*

And then there was Mae West:

**DESERET NEWS,** *Aug. 17, 1936: "Sit down, now lie right back and you'll get the full effect," and Mae West, one of four foremost ladies on the screen, sat on a white satin boudoir chair and urged me to sample that famous bed in her bedroom, noted for its mirrored ceiling, white bear skin rugs and white satin furnishings.*

*The place, Mae West's apartment, and I was actually in it, one of very few women ever privileged to do so. And Mae West was sitting there talking to me in the most friendly manner and obviously quite amused at my exclamations of awe when I stepped in to call.*

**Mae West**

As the dreary days of the Depression dragged on, Utahns were no different from the rest of the world — finding escape from real life in the glamor of the silver screen. No news was too trivial: wig-makers reveal that Shirley Temple's head is 1 1/2 inches larger than Mae West's. Carole Lombard and Spencer Tracy will be teamed for the first time in "Exclusive." The "talkies" are now 10 years old, and don't those old silents seem silly?

Even more exciting was the news that Robert Taylor, "America's No. 1 matinee idol at the present time" would talk on the telephone to one lucky Salt Lake girl in a contest sponsored by the Deseret News. The winner, Kallie Foutz of 120 C Street, who "bombarded the star with questions and heard the answers with considerable satisfaction."

**DESERET NEWS,** *Aug. 11, 1936: He had a few words to say on his coming picture opposite Joan Crawford, "The Gorgeous Hussy" and speaking of the future, expressed a wish to play in a heavy dramatic role. His hobbies are swimming, boating and horseback riding. He has* stopped off in Salt Lake on several occasions and likes it here.

*Miss Foutz was accompanied by a goodly group of fans, all of whom thrilled to the conversation over an extension phone. "Ohs" and "Ahs" were plentiful.*

Despite the glitz and glamor, the end of the decade brought an indication that not all of Hollywood's work was transitory.

**DESERET NEWS,** *Aug. 16, 1939: Filmdom, ever hunting things new, finds two of them…*

*A production, titled "The Wizard of Oz," which gets far away from the everyday formula of movie making...*

*L. Frank Baum's classic of childhood was unveiled to the public last night at Grauman's Chinese Theater, bringing… an almost unheard of outburst of raves from usually blase critics…*

**DESERET NEWS,** *Dec. 13, 1939: "Gone with the Wind" is now ready for all those who always intended to read the book, but never got around to it, as well as for the vast number of faithful readers who wondered how Hollywood would treat it… . No film which caused so much speculation about treatment and casting, before production, and which runs for three hours and 57 minutes, in its final form, belongs in the everyday classification…*

Movies, of course, were not all that could take Deseret News readers' minds away from the grim realities of life. Comics had come into their own in the '20s; and by the '30s were not only a part of the daily paper, but also had an 8-page section on Saturdays. The Lone Ranger, Li'l Abner, Nancy, Tarzan, the Nebbs, The Captain and the Kids, Hawkshaw the Detective, Ella Cinders, Buck Rogers and the 25th Century and more provided a welcome escape into a fantasy world where no one had to wonder where the next paycheck would come from.

No one was bigger at the box office than Shirley Temple, shown here with a 22-inch prototype doll based on her costume in "Stand Up and Cheer."

2 Famous Theatres
CAPITOL
NOW!
Shirley TEMPLE in "BRIGHT EYES"
A FOX Picture with JAMES DUNN
Starts SATURDAY
EDDIE Cantor in "KID MILLIONS"
Released thru UNITED ARTISTS

# The rise of evil

Just released from prison on a conspiracy charge in 1925, Adolf Hitler visits a local Nazi Party group in Bavaria.

**DESERET NEWS,** *Jan. 30, 1933:*
*Adolf Hitler, picturesque leader of the German Fascists, was made chancellor of Germany today, succeeding General Kurt Von Schlechler who resigned last week.*

*But in granting him the ambition of his political lifetime President Von Hindenburg surrounded him with a cabinet of Conservatives... .*

*The new chancellor, who is only 43, took the appointment in his stride.*

*"Well, we shall see," was all he said to the correspondents as he returned to the hotel from the president's office, "now let's eat."*

Germany had been in turmoil since the end of World War I. Embittered and burdened by terms of the Treaty of Versailles, further devastated by the worldwide Great Depression, workers especially were susceptible to the promises made by the charismatic Hitler: jobs, an end to reparation payments, new business, the re-arming of the country. Hitler's National Socialist German Workers' party, known as the Nazis, made steady gains in the Reichstag (the lower house in the Weimar Republic) in the early '30s, to the point where Hitler manipulated himself into power.

And the world would indeed see what that meant.

**DESERET NEWS,** *Feb. 24, 1933:*
*Charge that the door to President Paul von Hindenburg has been closed to the public since Adolf Hitler became chancellor was before the German electorate today... .*

*The threat of Hitlerites that they will retain the helm of government by force, if necessary, if the Reichstag and Prussian diet elections go against them has given rise to many expressions of doubt concerning the influence of the president.*

*Feb. 27, 1933: A disastrous fire of incendiary origin tonight gutted the Reichstag building, one of the most imposing governmental structures anywhere in the world.*

*While no coherent account regarding the origin of the blaze could be obtained owing to the intense confusion which prevailed after the fire broke out, there were rumors that political terrorists might have been responsible.*

*Mar. 6, 1933: The electoral endorsement of the Hitler government's "Nationalistic revolution" with its policy of suppressing Communists and Socialists leaves no doubt that the next few months will be devoted to wiping out the last vestiges of both democracy and communism.*

While the world waited to see how things would play out in Germany, other disturbing news was making headlines around the globe:

**DESERET NEWS,** *Feb. 22, 1933:*
*Japan today hinted to the world that she expects the present campaign in Jehol to end in conflict with the United States and the League of Nations on the decks of battleships in the great arena of the Pacific ocean. Japanese naval leaders openly predicted this today, as the actual outcome of the Manchurian dispute. Japan's withdrawal from the League of Nations, they declared, will place responsibility for settlement on the navy... .*

*Oct. 2, 1935: Italian Troops Invade Ethiopia. Duce Ready To Declare Africa War.*

*Benito Mussolini, premier of Italy and Fascist leader, today pledged his nation to meet force with force and to bear economic sanctions "with discipline."*

*"War," he said, "would be met with war."*

*Oct. 9, 1936: Nazi Germany, despite its demand for return of the Reich's pre-war colonies, will not ask Japan to return Germany's former island possessions in the Pacific ocean which Japan has been secretly fortifying in the face of frequent warnings by the United States and a specific ban by the League of Nations.*

*Oct. 26, 1936: Rome Hints Fascist-Nazi-Nippon Pact Against Communism*

From the beginning, Hitler dreamed of Anchluss: unification of the two German-speaking nations, Austria and Germany. By 1938, growing support in Austria led him to action.

**DESERET NEWS,** *Mar. 12, 1938: About 1,000 German infantrymen, landed from planes, began marching into Vienna at 5:06 p.m. (11:06 a.m. E.S.T.) today as Hitler returned in triumph to his native Austria. ...*

*The German Fuehrer was hailed as a savior when he entered Linz, capital of upper Austria at 4:12 p.m. (10:13 a.m. E.S.T.).*

*"Long live the liberator of Austria, Adolf Hitler!" yelled crowds in the main square.*

## Deutsche! Wehrt Euch! Kauft nicht bei Juden!

Benito Mussolini, Italy's Fascist dictator, strides away from a war memorial day celebration May 9, 1940. The sign warns Germans not to do business with Jews.

Hitler then turned his eye toward Czechoslovakia, where 3 million Germans lived in an area known as the Sudetenland. He gambled on the fact that neither France nor England, despite treaties with the Czechs, wanted war, and his gamble paid off.

**DESERET NEWS,** *Sept. 30, 1938: Prime Minister Chamberlain and Reichsfuehrer Hitler today added a new Anglo-German declaration of peace to the four-power Munich accord that gave Germany part of Czechoslovakia and averted a European war.*

*After the British and German chiefs had signed with Premier Mussolini of Italy and Premier Daladier of France the pact for Czechoslovakia's dismemberment, they made a joint declaration of the will of their "two peoples never to go to war with one another again."*

*German troops were at the border to begin the gradual occupation of the Sudetenland at midnight…*

*Chamberlain expressed belief that Munich would open the way "to appeasement in Europe." On this note of peace, he flew back to London.*

Looking back, many historians pick this as the point when a tough military stand by France and England could well have been enough to defeat Hitler, thus avoiding the drawn-out conflict that would spill into the next decade. At the time, however, when world leaders were still taking Hitler at his word, they sincerely believed peace was a viable option.

It would not be long before they realized how wrong they were. And not just on the military front. Early in 1939 came news of disturbing trends inside Germany.

**DESERET NEWS,** *Jan. 12, 1939: Germany, angrily blaming Jews for mysterious shots fired at Nazi buildings in The Netherlands, warned today that Jews in Germany would be made to suffer if the incidents continued…*

**Neville Chamberlain**

*Nazi newspapers let loose a scathing blast against international Jewry, warning of the dire fate awaiting their German co-religionists if another attempt is made on the life of Germans.*

By August of 1939, Hitler was once again looking toward eastern Europe. Next up would be Poland. And even in the U.S., the implications were clear.

**DESERET NEWS,** *Aug. 22, 1939: "I look for a German military assault on Poland within a a short time."*

*So spoke U.S. Sen. William H. King, ranking member of the senate foreign relations committee and student of international affairs, upon his arrival in Salt Lake today from a hectic session of Congress.*

*The senior Utah senator looks for the assault as part of "military conspiracy" among Hitler, Mussolini and Japan.*

*He declined to predict what America would do if a general European war ensues, but expressed a "sincere hope that we'll be able to stay out of it."*

Through the end of August, headlines reflected the world's turmoil: Aug. 23: "Chamberlain Says Britain Will Fight," Aug. 24: "Hitler Ultimatum to Poland Expected Hourly," Aug. 29: "War Or Peace Decision Up To Hitler; London Stands Beside Poland."

And then on Sept. 1 the news came in gigantic type across a Deseret News Extra: "WAR! NAZI PLANES RAIN BOMBS ON POLAND."

Utahns felt the impact.

**DESERET NEWS,** *Sept. 1, 1939: The*

*Deseret News files*

*following statement regarding the situation of missionaries in Europe was issued today by the First Presidency.*

*"The last missionaries left Germany last Saturday; they are all now in Denmark. By present plans a very few of them will remain for work in Germany if proper arrangements can be made; others will be sent to some of the neutral European countries for the present at least."*

*Sept. 1, 1939: Will the Polish conflict develop into a general European war? Is Germany justified in attacking Poland?*

*A reluctant "Yes" to the first and a resounding "No" to the second were given by a cross-section of Salt Lake's man-on-the-street in a survey made today by the Deseret News.*

*A.L. Henderson, Main Street art light tender, said: "A general European war is bound to come from the present situation in Poland. It won't take much to turn the squabbling and bickering of all the European nations into an armed battle."*

*Miss Betty Jean Saville, pretty candy clerk, believed: "Hitler has put his foot in it so far now he can't back out."*

*Echo Johnson, blond airline stewardess, answered the conflict question with a question of her own: "How can the European nations possibly avoid becoming involved?"*

*Harry R. Jones, tours salesman on Main Street, said "Hitler has lied too much. England and France don't believe him any more. They'll fight him before they listen to his promises again."*

And on the editorial page that day, a sense of what was to come:

**Spotlight Of War Focuses On Rumania And Balkans**
Newest developments in war-embroiled Europe are shown on this map as Russia shifts political attention from Finland to the Balkans. The Reds are demanding that Bessarabia secede from Rumania and warn Turkey of "dangers" in Anglo-French alliance. Meanwhile the Soviets continue their war on Finland.

*Sept. 1, 1939: Without formal declaration of war on the part of any country, hostilities which may lead to the downfall of nations and even to the destruction of civilization itself are under way… At this critical hour in the world's history, men and nations should bow in humility and in soberness and beseech the Supreme Power which guides the destinies of the universe, that this conflict may be avoided; that this blotch upon the face of civilization may be averted; that all men may return to their sober senses and realize the hopelessness and futility of any such action as now is contemplated.*

But for now the rest of the world could only watch.

- Informational map from 1939 shows shifting allegiances. Russia and Germany are allies; Russia is bogged down in its war with Finland but threatens the Balkans.

- At left a medal struck by the Germans to celebrate the return of the Saar region.

# Sports:
## A needed break

**The '30s were a time of hellos and goodbyes in the baseball world:**

Jesse Owens, U.S. hero of the 1936 Olympics in Berlin.

Deseret News files

**DESERET NEWS,** *July 5, 1933: Without seeming to be too flip with their millions, the baseball people estimate with no trace of a boastful nature that something approximating $5,000,000 worth of talent, at the current market values, will be put on display Thursday in the American and National league all-star contest at Comisky park.*

The idea of an all-star game, a promotion in connection with the Chicago World's Fair, had been greeted with skepticism at first. But it proved so successful that it became a classic part of summer. Players participating in that first game included Babe Ruth, Lou Gehrig, Chuck Klein, Lefty Grove, Frankie Frisch and Pie Traynor.

Other firsts during the decade included the first night game: May 24, 1934; and the first inductions into the Baseball Hall of Fame. Names were announced early in 1936, although the Hall itself didn't open until 1939.

But for all the comings, there were some goings. Babe Ruth played his final game on May 30, 1935. And in 1939, the baseball world said goodbye to the Iron Horse:

**DESERET NEWS,** *July 5, 1939: Baseball reached the most dramatic moment of its lifetime yesterday afternoon at the Yankee Stadium when Lou Gehrig, victim of a hideous wasting disease which medical science cannot cure, limped up to a microphone at home plate to speak of the light and the heavy things that lay in his heart…*

This, then, was the man who stepped up to the microphone to say, from his heart, "I think I'm the luckiest man on the face of the earth."

Baseball was big in those days, but it wasn't the only game in town. In fact, on Feb. 15, 1933, when Associated Press sports writers chose the dominating athlete of the past decade, it wasn't a baseball player who got the honor, but rather golfer Bobby Jones, edging out Babe Ruth by a margin of 207 to 202. Boxer Jack Dempsey came in third, followed by Big Bill Tilden, Helen Willis Moody, Paavo Nurmi and Red Grange.

Closer to home, Utahns watched with the rest of the world as Ab Jenkins began setting record after record at the Bonneville Salt Flats.

**DESERET NEWS,** *Aug. 8, 1933: AB JENKINS SETS 60 SPEEDWAY RECORDS AT SALDURO*
*Aug. 5, 1935: JENKINS PREPARED TO BREAK COBB'S RECORDS*
*Aug. 12, 1939: Ab Jenkins Sets Seventeen Records; Utah Driver Satisfied And Calls It Quits For 1939.*

In 1936, Deseret News readers got involved:

**Ab Jenkins**

**DESERET NEWS,** *Aug. 7, 1936: Here is how the new moniker "Mormon Meteor" will look on the rudder of Ab Jenkins $40,000 racing automobile, except that it appears more attractive here because Miss Ruth Jenkins, daughter of the famous driver, graces the picture. The name "Mormon Meteor" was chosen by means of a contest sponsored by The Deseret News Sports Department, collaborating with Mr. Jenkins.*

In 1933, Alf Engen was making headlines by winning the world's pro ski title for the third straight year. In 1935, Joe Louis and Max Baer were top names on the boxing circuit. The 1936 Summer Olympics in Berlin turned Jesse Owens' name into a household word — and also created controversy over whether or not black members of the U.S. track team had been deliberately snubbed by Adolf Hitler. By 1939, Bobby Riggs was the dominant name on the tennis circuit. But the title of "No. 1 Capitalist In ProSportsdom" for the decade went to Sonja Henie.

Throughout the '30s, Deseret News readers were treated to the style and opinions of national sports columnist Grantland Rice, while Les Goates kept readers apprised of local happenings. In 1934, Goates provided this assessment:

**DESERET NEWS,** *May 26, 1934: No native Utahn, versed in the traditions of the commonwealth, will deny that the Utah vs. Aggie football game leads in public appeal. For color, action, drama and suspense this event invariably takes top place on the list.*

*From the viewpoint of general interest throughout the state the high school basketball tournament carries far more comment than any other sporting topic in Utah.*

*Utah is fast coming to the fore in golf… . Sandlot baseball continues to hold its place as the favorite sport of many thousands of Utahns. The semi-pros haven't* as yet made a real challenge for the amateur patronage.

Deseret News files

And speaking of coming attractions, the sports world closed out the decade with a subtle hint of what was ahead:

**DESERET NEWS,** *Nov. 1, 1939: 'Twasn't always thus on the gold rush gridiron.*

*With turnstiles clicking a mercenary symphony, the National Professional Football League, one of sportsdom's poor relations, moves into another bonanza season. Campaign after campaign the attendance numbers have continued to wax fatter. In 1938, for instance, the figure topped 1,100,000. …*

*The play-for-pay major league is truly a phenomenon when you consider that after a much pooh-pooh'd birth it rose to its present prosperous condition right in the teeth of the depression, as it were.*

**New York Yankees Add Another World's Title And More Series Records**

THE WORLD'S CHAMPIONSHIP NEW YORK YANKEES still have no competition. They won their fourth straight world's title yesterday beating the Cincinnati Reds 7 to 4. They became the first team in history to win that many consecutive championships. Moreover they took their 28th series victory in 31 games, another record. The New York players shown above are BACK ROW, L-R: Bill Dickey, Red Ruffing, Joe Di Meggio, Oral Hildebrand, Steven Sundra, Paul Schreiber, Johnny Murphy, Lefty Gomez, Atley Donald, Tom Henrich, Art Jorgens, Marius Russo. MIDDLE ROW, L-R: Bump Hadley, Monte Pearson, Marius Russo, Lou Gehrig, George Selkirk, Bill Knickerbocker, Doc Painter, trainer. FRONT ROW, L-R: Buddy Rosar, Charlie Keller, Spud Chandler, John Fletcher, Manager Joe McCarthy, Earle Combs, John Schulte, Red Rolfe, Babe Dahlgren, Frank Crosetti. In front, Mascot Tim Sullivan. Absent, Joe Gordon. (AP Wire Photo)

The 1940s opened with war already raging in Europe and a deep sense of foreboding. Americans watched war clouds gather on the horizon as Hitler's voracious appetite swallowed his European neighbors and Japan's growing military ambitions spread chaos across Asia. Many Americans hoped to remain neutral but still gave indirect support to an embattled Great Britain as it struggled against Germany. Utahns watched, waited and made their feelings known:

# A world engulfed in
# war
## 1940-1950

The 1940s will forever be known as the war years. The decade started with Britain fighting for its life and Nazis walking the streets of ancient capitals. When the betrayal at Pearl Harbor brought the United States into the war, it truly became a global conflict. An estimated 50 million people died, the majority of them civilians, and whole countries were laid waste. Cruelty on a scale never before seen left scars that would not heal for generations, and the task of rebuilding would take years. In its insulated geographic location, Utah became a military stronghold and finally shook off the Great Depression. But the war gave birth to a new, nuclear age and a Cold War.

Pearl Habor

*DESERET NEWS, Nov. 17, 1941:* The Utah Chapter of the Committee to Defend America today joined with similar groups over the entire nation in protesting "massacres … by the totalitarian powers." The protest was contained in a resolution affirmed to by more than 2,000 Utahns who attended a meeting of Defend America yesterday evening in the Assembly Hall.

By the fall of 1941, the News was reporting German incursions into Libya and Moscow. Negotiations were under way with Japan in hopes of averting war in the Pacific. On Dec. 2, 1941, the News headline read: "Roosevelt Demands Japanese Explain Movement of Troops." Three days later: "Japan Voices Hope for U.S. Peace." An editorial cartoon showed Prime Minister Tojo with several conflicting masks, trying to decide which one to wear.

One of modern history's most treacherous acts, the unannounced Japanese attack on Pearl Harbor, Dec. 7, 1941, left no doubt:

Deseret News files

*DESERET NEWS, Dec. 8, 1941:*

### U.S. DECLARES WAR ON JAPAN
*WASHINGTON (AP) — President Roosevelt asked Congress today to declare war against Japan. He made the solemn, historic request after disclosing to the nation that yesterday's sudden Japanese attack on Hawaii had cost the United States two warships and 3,000 dead and wounded.*

*"I ask," the chief executive declared, "that the Congress declare that since the unprovoked and dastardly attack by Japan*

*on Sunday, Dec. 7, a state of war has existed between the United States and the Japanese Empire." The president said that yesterday was "a date which will live in infamy."*

In fact, the damage was much greater. Several columns of news supported the president's position. The news also carried a small box on the front page:

#### All Members of Church in Hawaii Safe
*Missionaries and members of the two Church missions in Hawaii are safe and well, according to cablegrams from Honolulu, received this morning by the First Presidency.*

The United States was committed to war in the Pacific. Three days later, Congress again acted, declaring war on Germany and Italy:

*DESERET NEWS, Dec. 11, 1941: WASHINGTON (AP) — Congress voted war against Nazi Germany and Italy today in a swift response to President Roosevelt's appeal for a "rapid and united" effort for the cause of victory "over the forces of savagery and of barbarism."*

Beehive Collectors Gallery

# U.S., Britain Declare War Against Japan
Japs Claim Sea Supremacy

Big and bold headlines were mandatory for the day following Japan's sneak attack on Pearl Harbor. Above, the battleship Arizona is engulfed in flames as it sinks. At right, many would receive the bronze star for valor.

Beehive Collectors Gallery

All vehicles carried a federal use tax stamp on windshields. Below, a GI with a full field pack would be carrying trench shovels, rations, clothing and ammunition along with his M-1 rifle.

FEDERAL USE TAX
ON MOTOR VEHICLES

$5.00

THIS STAMP
EXPIRES
JUNE 30, 1943
KEEP THIS STAMP
POSTED ON VEHICLE

STAMP TRANSFERABLE
WITH VEHICLE

12001835

John Clark

AP Photo

As fast as a roll call could be tallied, the Senate unanimously, and the House without a single "no" vote, accepted the challenge of Adolf Hitler and Benito Mussolini, Axis partners of Japan with whom the nation went to war Monday.

Over the next few years, the world split into two war machines — the Allies, which eventually had the support of 50 nations, and the Axis with nine. The most costly war in history in terms of death and destruction settled in for a long stay. With the war a fact, Utahns rushed to support the cause:

**DESERET NEWS,** *Dec. 12, 1941: Defense bonds topped news of defense activities in Utah today. The U.S. Grazing Service with national headquarters in the Walker Bank building, reported that 69 of its employees had purchased $7,000 in bonds and had pledged to purchase $500 each month…*

*The Utah Central Credit Union today petitioned the U.S. Treasury Department for a charter to sell defense savings bonds at all of its offices in the state…*

*Also taking part of the defense spotlight was the announcement by the Utah Pharmaceutical Association that more than 200 drug stores in the state will act as first aid stations in the event of any disaster…*

*The City Commission today took under advisement emergency requests of Fire Chief LaVere M. Hanson for purchase of three air raid sirens and for the hiring of 25 additional firemen or alternative training of volunteer civilian firemen to comply with requests of the State Defense Council…*

*Patriotism isn't limited to men. Recruiting officers in Salt Lake reported today with the information that scores of women have applied for military duty. … "They are willing to take any job which will help Uncle Sam's fighting forces," Sgt. S.D. Gratz of the U.S. Marine Corps recruiting office said.*

John Clark

A Utah inspection sticker from 1942 reminded users to keep their speed under 40 and contribute to victory.

As needs became more acute, women did, in fact, join the military ranks in unprecedented numbers. And as the war absorbed more and more Utah men, women left their kitchens and entered the work force:

**DESERET NEWS,** *March 10, 1942: Women are being trained to take over the work of nearly 100 men in the U.S. Grazing Service, it was stated today by Director R. H. Rutledge, with the announcement of two transfers of women to replace men called into military service …*

Utah Oil Refining Company Stations and its dealers sponsored an ad asking that customers *"Think about the woman or man at the gasoline pump … Wartime demands have taken the experienced manpower from most industries. We realize, frankly, that in many instances you are not getting the service you expect and which we would like you to receive. There's simply no substitute for experience and the folks now at the stations are doing the best job they can under very trying circumstances…"*

The same edition pointed up the continuing need for enlistees in the various services:

*The butcher, the baker and the candlestick maker can no longer walk past the recruiting poster of "Uncle Sam Needs You" with a free and easy conscience.*

*The Navy today announced it will enlist qualified men with trades and technical experience between the ages of 17 and 50 who can pass the required physical examination …*

Like their counterparts across the country, Utahns coped with rationing, carefully managing their "stamps" to pay for such short-supply items as gasoline, tires, sugar, meat and children's shoes. They scoured their homes and environs for scrap metal and bought war bonds. They tried to carry on normal activities with their lives disrupted. The News reported on "wartime romances," with marriages

arranged during a soldier's leave. Some families welcomed war brides who came to the state to join the husbands they married in foreign countries. Beehive Staters turned off lights in response to air raid wardens' requests; they zipped their lips to prevent inadvertently helping the enemy with loose talk. And they slowed down to conserve cars and tires:

**DESERET NEWS,** *Aug. 25, 1942: Stringent measures to crack down on truck drivers and passenger motorists exceeding their 40-mile war time speed limit were authorized today by the State Highway Traffic Advisory Committee to the War Department, acting in conjunction with the ODT, the State Tire Rationing Board and the State Highway Patrol.*

Thousands of young men and a fair number of young women enlisted or responded to draft calls, willing to put their lives on the line for world peace:

**DESERET NEWS,** *Aug. 20, 1942: Mothers, with proud eyes shining wet, had priority even over sisters and sweethearts for a last hug today as "God speed" rang along the lines and 63 Mormon boys were mustered aboard a train at the Union Depot. They had been sworn into the U.S. Marine Corps to form the second platoon of the Mormon Battalion during impressive ceremonies last night at Memory Park.*

*The boys left here dressed in their civilian clothes and marching without regard to size, place and without benefit of a drum. Soon they will look different. They don't just "issue" uniforms to the Marines. These boys will be measured first. The Marines have some grim business appointments in their date books, but they will keep the dates in clothes that fit.*

Before long, many of those brave and

issing, One Wounded In

TECH. SGT. JOHN M. OLD-
ROYD has been reported missing in action.

four brothers, Cpl. Hyrum R
. aylor and Pfc.

The newspaper was full of stories about Utah's young men who were missing, killed or wounded, or had been promoted or moved. Military news was, of course, a high priority for the editors.

They Set The Pace For America's War Effort

Officers at Kearns, Utah, the nation's fastest built and staffed replacement training center, inspect the serried ranks composed of men who have been soldiers but a short time.

Messerschmidt BF109

Japanese soldiers shout "Banzai!" as they gain control in the Philippines, forcing U.S. troops to withdraw to Bataan. Above, Kearns became an Army training center

UPI Photo

confident young men were added to the lists of those dead, wounded or missing. Daily, the News carried stories of the state's military.

Awards, promotions and heroic stories counterbalanced news of casualties. On March 4, 1944, a half page was devoted to an "Honor Roll of Utah World War II Casualties." The list included the names of 25 newly reported dead, along with scores of others whose deaths already had been noted. The "lists" took on shape, substance and reality with poignant stories:

**DESERET NEWS,** *March 8, 1944: Second Lt. Garth B. Larsen, son of Mr. and Mrs. Niels P. Larsen, 2219 E. 3020 South St., is missing in action, his parents learned in a letter from his twin brother, Second Lt. Gordon P. Larsen, stationed in England.*

*The brothers were stationed within 40 miles of each other and the authorities telephoned Gordon when Garth did not return from a raid over Gotha, Germany, Feb. 24…*

Despite the horrifying carnage, the war left some lasting, positive effects in Utah. For the first time since the Great Depression, there was a major shift in the state's economy. Military-related industry became the leading source of income. As the war in Europe ended, the News noted more than a dozen new or improved industries:

**DESERET NEWS,** *May 8, 1945: Never before in such a short space of time has an industrial development been known comparable to that resulting from the all-out war effort of a freedom-loving people during the great world holocaust which now, with the vanquishment of Germany, gives promise of coming to a welcome end…*

*That same dry valley where "an ear of corn would not ripen" has become the nucleus of probably the heaviest concentration of government sponsored industry of any area in the western United States. Within a radius of less than 50 miles has sprung up, almost as if they were the result of Aladdin's magic lamp, more than a dozen huge war industries which have brought millions of dollars and thousands of new people into the state…*

*"Keep 'em Flying" is the motto in deed as well as word at Hill Field. Recently the 11,000th aircraft engine was overhauled in the engine repair department, maintenance division, at this $25 million plant …*

*The first soldiers to set foot in the little border town of Wendover in August, 1941 little dreamed that within a few short months a mighty air field would rise there from which trained gunners and bombardiers would be flying the skies in combat…*

*One of the first of Utah's war installations to start sending supplies to the armed forces on the battle fronts of the world was the Utah Army Service Forces Depot at Ogden. Three months before the bombing of Pearl Harbor, on Sept. 15, 1941, that depot was activated and within a few hours after the first bomb landed on the Pacific outpost on that memorable Sunday, the first supplies began moving from the depot to the battle front.*

*The greatest war-born industry in all the West and the largest single war project financed by the Defense Plant Corporation, the $200 million steel plant at Geneva, Utah, came into being with the speed of a streamlined racer. In the short space of only 21 months, 1.5 million cubic yards of earth were moved, 600,000 cubic yards of concrete were poured, 85,000 tons of structural steel were erected, 83 acres of steel sheeting to enclose the building was put up and tens of millions of bricks were laid, all to build the most modern steel plant in America.*

*One of the largest Utah war installations in point of area is the $30 million, 27,000-acre Tooele Ordnance Depot, which handles every type of combat equipment except chemical. In connection with this huge installation, there has grown up a village that is second largest in Tooele County.*

*The Deseret Chemical Warfare Depot 17 miles south of Tooele was set up to take over from the ordnance department the entire incendiary bomb program and the handling of gas warfare materials.*

*"What's the Navy doing in Utah?" is the puzzled question of many a person hearing first of NSD, Clearfield, one of the two largest inland naval supply depots in the world. Yet, this huge $32 million Naval Supply Depot, approximately 750 miles from the nearest ocean, is an integral part of America's unparalleled two-ocean navy and comprises almost one-tenth of the navy's total supply storage space.*

*From wheat field and wastelands to Utah's third largest city; from arid flats to an intelligently planned civilization, all in a record short period of time: that is the story of the development of the AAF Overseas Replacement Depot at Kearns, Utah. This army camp, from the selection of the site on April 2, 1942 and the official opening on July 20 of that year, has grown to a 6,000-acre, $50 million community of 1,000 buildings. It has within its boundaries the largest rifle range in the West, second largest in the nation.*

Also on the list of Utah's war-related plants was the Eitel-McCullough Co., which manufactured essential radio and radar tubes, and the Utah Ordnance Plant operated by Remington Arms. The latter, one of the largest of Utah's war installations, also was one of the shortest-lived. From January 1942 to December 1943, the bustling plant employed as many

MEAT RATIONING RETURN PLANNED IF NECESSARY

Nation Must Aid Starving, Truman Says

John Clark

Gasoline ration stamp A was highly coveted, but still restricted driving. Below, women were recruited to work in defense plants and other vocations to fill the gaps left by men serving in the military.

SOLDIERS *without guns*

Deseret News files

as 12,000 workers at a time, turning out millions of machine gun bullets, including incendiary tracing bullets, one of the war's technological advances.

Utah also had some less tasteful assignments during the war. Several prisoner of war camps were located within its borders.

In addition, war hysteria led to the creation of a number of Japanese relocation centers in the country, one of them at Topaz, in the desert wastes near Delta. Highly secret preparatory meetings in early 1942 did not make it into the News columns, and there was little mention in the paper of the camp from its opening Sept. 11, 1942 to its demise in October 1945. The camp accommodated 8,000 internees in fairly primitive conditions. In 1943, the News made a rare observation about Topaz:

**DESERET NEWS,** *Dec. 18, 1943:*
*Thousands of tons of produce on the farms and in truck gardens and in the factories of the Intermountain area have been harvested and processed with the assistance of hundreds of Americans of Japanese ancestry who formerly resided in the War Relocation Authority in Topaz, Utah, according to Charles F. Ernst, project director. Nearly 2,100 persons from the center, or more than one half of the eligible workers, have left the center on indefinite or seasonal leave to assist in the war effort by relieving the manpower shortage in communities from Nevada to the Atlantic seaboard, Mr. Ernst pointed out.*

*These men and women are either citizens or aliens who have been determined as loyal to the United States and who have given their services in the best way possible for them by entering industries wherever possible.*

When given the opportunity, 105 of the Topaz interns joined the American military,

giving faithful service despite what many felt was an injustice. After its closure, the camp was dismantled.

By spring 1944, the handwriting was on the wall in Europe. The June 6, 1944, landings on five Normandy beaches (including Utah Beach) initiated a relentless but bloody push:

**DESERET NEWS,** *June 6, 1944:*

### ALLIES PENETRATE NAZI SHORE DEFENSES IN INVASION OF FRANCE

*SUPREME HEADQUARTERS, ALLIED EXPEDITIONARY FORCE (AP)–*
*The Allies landed in the Normandy section of northwest France early today and by evening had smashed their way inland on a broad front, making good a gigantic air and sea invasion against unexpectedly slight German opposition.*

*Prime Minister Churchill said part of the record-shattering number of parachute and glider troops were fighting in Caen, nine miles inland, and had seized a number of important bridges in the invasion area…*

With the Allies definitely on the offensive, Americans celebrated. However, the News reported, the invasion found Salt Lake calm:

*In decided contrast to many American cities, Salt Lake today received the news of the long-awaited European invasion quietly and many persons were unaware of the great news for some time after arising. No sirens, whistles or bells were sounded during the night and the first word many Utahns received was when Deseret News boys screamed "EXTRA" through the streets…*

Utahns learned some new geography: Cherbourg, Caen, then Paris itself, the Meuse River and the infamous Ardennes Forest, nicknamed the Bulge. With the Russian armies pushing toward Berlin from the east, Hitler abandoned his armies to their fate, holed up in an underground bunker and committed suicide. The end of the despised "Fuhrer" was a matter of conjecture.

**DESERET NEWS,** *May 1, 1945:*

### ADOLF HITLER DEAD

*LONDON (INS) — Adolf Hitler died "at post of battle," according to German radio broadcast.*

*Whether Adolf Hitler actually died at his command post in Berlin today, as the German radio said, the world may not know with assurance for some time — perhaps never. He may have been dead for days or weeks; he may be still living and this announcement only a ruse to help his escape plans. However, the Hamburg radio announcement could mean that this is the official end of Adolf Hitler, as far as what authority remains in Germany is concerned …*

Finally, the Deseret News joined sister newspapers throughout the world in joyfully announcing the end of World War II in Europe:

**DESERET NEWS,** *May 8, 1945:*
*LONDON (AP) — The guns fell silent on the Western Front tonight and President Truman and Prime Minister Churchill proclaimed the victory to the world.*

*All hostilities were ordered ended by 4:01 p.m. Eastern War Time. The cease-fire orders had gone out earlier from*

supreme headquarters. The U.S. Third Army, it was disclosed, had been ordered to hold its fire at 2 a.m. yesterday, six hours after Germany's representatives had acknowledged their defeat to Gen. Eisenhower…

The war in Europe was over. But in the Pacific, a formidable foe awaited, even though in June of 1942, the Battle of Midway shifted the course of the war, giving the Allies the upper hand:

**DESERET NEWS,** *June 8, 1942:*

### Battered Japanese Fleet Makes Escape from Battle of Midway

*PEARL HARBOR, (AP) — A once mighty Japanese naval force, reported to constitute the bulk of the Imperial Fleet, today limped westward in desperate retreat from Midway Island, its proud units pounded by an American defense turned into a shattering offense.*

*"The enemy appears to be withdrawing," said Admiral Chester W. Nimitz, commander in chief of the Pacific Fleet…*

*But even should the Japanese make good their escape, it will be only at the cost of at least three warships sunk, 11 or more others damaged and the virtually complete destruction of their protecting air arm…*

Despite the battering, and with American troops almost at the doors of her island empire, Japan fought on, determined not to surrender. Heavy casualties were expected if the Allies invaded Japan. But a fearsome new weapon was in the wings, one that would make global war unthinkable.

**As the war drew to a close, German soldiers seem happy to surrender and raise their arms to be searched.**

# The Deseret News

March 16, 1940

## Unusual Building Project of Welfare Program Described

Salt Lakers will soon witness a most unusual building feat — a structure taller than the Walker Bank Building rising to full height in 15 days.

That is the length of time estimated by construction engineers for erection of the grain elevator for the Church Welfare Program on which work is now underway at the Welfare Center, Seventh South and Seventh West Streets.

This almost unheard of speed in construction is of necessity and not by choice. Because of the tremendous weight of the wheat to be stored in the large bins, the greatest strength in concrete available is needed...

March 16, 1940

## Zanuck Signs Dean Jagger For 'Brigham Young' Role

**By Louella O. Parsons**

HOLLYWOOD, March 16 — (INS) — May I present Dean Jagger whose name you are going to hear many times within the next few months? He has been signed to play "Brigham Young" and so quietly was the signing done that no one even knew Jagger was under consideration...

Well, "Brigham Young" which Henry Hathaway directs next month, ought to provide the path to stardom if Jagger has what it takes.

May 7, 1940

## 'Grapes of Wrath' Wins Pulitzer Novel Award

NEW YORK, N.Y. (INS) — John Steinbeck's novel "The Grapes of Wrath," a story of refugees from the Dust Bowl, was awarded the Pulitzer Prize today as the most distinguished American novel of 1939.

William Saroyan's play, "The Time of Your Life," won the drama prize.

"Abraham Lincoln, the War Years," by Carl Sandburg, was accorded the prize for the most distinguished work in American history ...

May 7, 1940:

## Tonsils Vs. Singing

**By Logan Clendening, M.D.**

Does the removal of the tonsils affect the voice?

Singers used to be cautioned against having their tonsils out. It was said that their removal would influence the register of the voice so that the whole range would be lowered.

According to modern beliefs, removal of the tonsils enlarges the throat cavity, both in breadth and height, which tends to result in a fuller and more resonant voice. If the operation is advisable, the singer can be assured that no unfavorable change will take place. In fact, the removal of the tonsils does not affect the singing or the speaking voice either one way or the other in most instances.

Only if a heavy scar remains is the voice changed for the worse.

Dean Jagger as Brigham Young.

Deseret News files

Sept. 16, 1940

## President Calls For Registration For Draft Oct. 16

WASHINGTON — The text of President Roosevelt's proclamation upon all men from 21 through 35 to register Wednesday Oct. 16 for compulsory military service follows:

... In a free society the obligations and privileges of military training and service should be shared generally in accordance with a fair and just system of selective compulsory military training and service. Therefore ... 1.The first registration under the selective training and service act of 1940 shall take place on Wednesday, the sixteenth day of October, 1940, between the hours of 7 a.m. and 9 p.m.

2. Every male person (other than persons exempted by Section 5A of the aforesaid act) who is a citizen of the United States or an alien residing in the United States and who, on the registration date fixed herein, has attained the twenty-first anniversary of the day of his birth and has not attained the thirty-sixth anniversary of the day of his birth is required to present himself for and submit to registration...

Oct. 24, 1940

## 40-Hour Week is Law

WASHINGTON — The 40-hour work week became the legal standard for the nation's interstate industry today and from now on employes covered by the wage-hour law will be entitled to time and a half pay for more than 40 hours work.

The 40-hour standard prescribed by the act became effective at midnight, replacing the 42-hour work week inaugurated a year ago...

The 40-cents-an-hour minimum wage, one of the major goals of the wage-hour law, will not be required in all industry until 1945, but by the use of industry committees, the agency has already established minimum rates running up to 40 cents in many industries. The minimum rate now is 30 cents.

Sept. 27, 1941

## Guns Or Housing Is U.S. Choice

Must Americans choose between guns and housing?

This is a vitally important question in view of the fact that tens of thousands of families who have needed new homes for years now have the money for the down payment required for new home ownership and the further fact of a shortage of about two and one half million dwellings.

To be specific, the army needs powder for its new guns. Construction of its powder plants is being rushed. They will be built of wood and take a billion feet of lumber, along with large quantities of cement, plumbing, heating, and electrical equipment and other building materials. And they will require a large body of building labor....

Sept. 29, 1941

## Turkey Men Will Boost Production

Leaders of America's largest turkey cooperative assembled in annual convention at the Newhouse Hotel today, prepared to launch a campaign to increase gobbler production for defense by 10 per cent in keeping with a request from Agricultural secretary Claude R. Wickard.

Great strides in the science of producing the erstwhile "holiday birds" has taken them out of the luxury class and made them a staple important in defense, it was pointed out...

Sept. 29, 1941

## Bergen Finds Competition When He Visits Hospital

As Charlie McCarthy says, when Edgar Bergen tells the story of Robinson Crusoe you won't recognize it. But when McCarthy, Bergen, and the children of Primary Children's Hospital collaborate it's something neither Mr. DeFoe nor Mr. Bergen would contemplate.

The immaculate Charlie and the no less impeccable Bergen gave an impromptu performance at the children's hospital this morning that almost proved their undoing...

Both Bergen and Charlie were in fine fettle and the quips of the little upstart kept the children in gales of laughter, particularly when he interrupted Bergen when a horn honked outside and the telephone rang in the next room. "If that's Sarah," Charlie shouted, "I'll talk"...

Nov. 25, 1941

## 'U' May Get Full Medical Unit

Chance that the University of Utah might obtain a complete four-year medical course of study was seen today by Dr. Fred C. Zapffe, secretary of the Association of American Medical Colleges, and Dr. Maurice Rees, executive board member of the association, who have been investigating the situation at the Utah institution.

"Conditions are ideal here in Salt Lake for the university to have a complete medical school," Dr. Zapffe declared. "Since the last two years of medical study are clinical," he stated, " the university medical plant would not have to be enlarged, for local hospitals could absorb the seniors in practice and internship work."

Charlie McCarthy

Deseret News files

Dr. Zapffe further explained that getting the additional two years of schooling depends on the local and university reaction, rather than on his association's sanction....

## Jan. 10, 1942

### Louis Batters Baer to Bits in First Round

NEW YORK (AP) — Any tendency to start recalling nostalgically the young Joe Louis who "killed" his man with a punch can be spiked right now; for the mature Joe Louis who knocked out Buddy Baer in the first round at Madison Square Garden last night is as great a fighter as the world has seen.

At 205 3/4 pounds — which is the heaviest he ever has weighed — the Negro champion looked as fast as ever in his career and it is doubtful he ever threw a harder punch than any one of the three that dropped the 250-pound Baer to the canvas as though he had been shot.

Baer, shaking his battered head cheerfully, said: I know now what they meant when they said the man who beats Joe will have Father Time in his corner. Maybe my next child will be a son and I can raise him up for the job."

## May 23, 1944

### Dogs Ordered Quarantined

Delivering an intended death blow to the spread of rabies in Salt Lake County, the State Board of Health today declared a county-wide canine quarantine.

Meeting at a luncheon session this afternoon at the University Club, 130 E. South Temple St., board members adopted severe measures directed against the spread of the disease that has broken out in the county during the past few weeks...

"During the period of quarantine all peace officers are impowered to kill or capture all dogs not held in restraint on private premises.

"All peace officers and representatives of boards of health are authorized to examine and enter upon any private premises for the enforcement of this quarantine"...

Dr. McKay pointed out that no person had been known to recover from a fully developed case of rabies. The Pasteur treatment, he said is effective in preventing the development of the disease....

## June 18, 1945

### General Met By Thousands

WASHINGTON (AP) — Gen. Dwight D. Eisenhower, returning triumphantly to his homeland from victory in Europe, declared today his

soldiers "passionately" believed "the problems of peace can and must be met."

Climaxing a spectacular homecoming that saw him ride over the Capital's historic triumphal parade route — Pennsylvania Avenue — past wildly cheering men and women, General Eisenhower told a joint session of Congress and the Supreme Court:

"The genius and power of America have, with her allies, eliminated one menace to our country's freedom— even her very existence. Yet still another remains to be crushed in the Pacific before peace will be restored…

Hundreds of thousands of wildly shouting men, women, and children, veterans of this war and the last, wounded veterans, the old and the young, raised their voices in a mighty tumult as the general of the army rode through their midst.

It was one of the greatest ovations the nation's capital ever rendered...

## June 26, 1945

Charlie McCarthy, the world's best-known dummy, is missing. Edgar Bergen's companion was absent from the baggage compartment when the ventriloquist arrived by plane late yesterday from a USO hospital tour...

It was the original Charlie, too — the one with the personality — and not one of the several imitations Bergen has had made.

## Nov. 23, 1945

# RATIONING TO END

WASHINGTON — (AP) — All meat rationing ends tomorrow. At the same time, all foods become point-free.

Secretary of Agriculture Anderson made these announcements...foods freed from the ration program include butter, margarine, lard and shortening. The meat rationing termination also applies to canned fish.

Sugar is now the only food left on the ration list... .

Anderson estimated that lifting of rationing will make meat available for civilians in December at an annual rate of 165 pounds per capita compared with an annual rate of 110 pounds during early spring and summer....

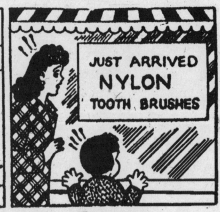

Nancy was a tremendously popular comic star. The strip reflected current issues, including the war-time shortage of women's nylon hose.

## Be Sure to Save Ration Book

WASHINGTON (AP) — OPA today cautioned the public to be sure and save ration book number four for buying sugar.

A spokesman for the agency said, however, that with the termination of meats and fats rationing tomorrow, all other stamps in book four will be valueless. So, he added, are the red tokens that were given as change for meats-fats coupons.

## Feb. 8, 1946

### Listing of All Job Openings For Vets Asked.

Utah businesses and industry leaders must "do everything in their power to see that veterans are placed on jobs equal to their service-attained or original skills and abilities," John M. Wallace, president, Walker Bank and Trust Co., said today.

Speaking in his capacity as chairman of the business and employment opportunities committee of the Salt Lake Veteran's Advisory Council, Mr. Wallace urged employers to list all jobs with the U.S. Employment Services, 55 West Third South St....

## Feb. 15, 1946

### New Mineral Discovered In Cave Near Utah Mine

A hitherto unknown mineral composed of phosphate of iron has been discovered by Dr. Bronson Stringham of the University of Utah geology department in a cave near the Tintic Standard Mine, according to analysis received from the University of Minnesota this week.

Dr. Stringham has named the new mineral tinticite after the region in which it was found… The new mineral could be used for fertilizer, if a large enough deposit were found, but the amount Dr. Stringham discovered is not large enough to be put to any practical use.

## Feb. 15, 1946

### 8-Year Old Boy Takes Bus Ride

PROVO — An eight-year-old boy is held by juvenile authorities in Provo this morning, bringing to an end a free joy ride on a Burlington Trailways bus, which he began yesterday afternoon.

When questioned, the lad told local officers he sneaked on a bus in Salt Lake, rode as far as Provo where he got off and went to a show.

After the show he boarded a Price-bound bus, thinking it was traveling back to Salt Lake. However, before the bus started, the driver discovered the boy had no ticket and turned him over to local authorities.

## Feb. 16, 1946

### Airline Space Now Available For Civilians

The trip by air that Joe Doaks, the lowly civilian, has had to postpone so service men could be transported, is his for the asking today as all wartime restrictions on air travel were lifted, according to Sam B. Kellogg, district traffic manager, United Air Lines.

According to Mr. Kellogg, the lifting of restrictions will release approximately 500 seats daily on the coast-to-coast route of United Air Lines. Since Dec. 3, 1944, the company has been holding 70 percent of all eastbound transcontinental space for returning servicemen…

## Feb. 16, 1946

### Poor Grocer! Can He Help It If Butter is Scarce?

Salt Lake retail grocers who have placidly been taking the abuse heaped upon them by irate "butter-less" customers today reared up in righteous wrath to say "Don't blame us!"

"Butter in Salt Lake is just about as hard to get

Gen. Dwight D. Eisenhower

today as a fresh drink of water was for the Ancient Mariner," a grocer said. "And housewives seem to feel the fault lies with the retailer."

As one retailer put it: "We've been blamed for all the wartime grocery inconveniences the public has had to stand. You'd think we were directly responsible for rationing and shortages."

One woman called a local chain store today and rasped into the poor manager's ear: "I've been trading at your store for many years. Why can't I get butter?"

"Well, madam," the manager replied, "There isn't any. When we get some, you can have one-quarter of a pound like the rest of the customers."

## June 5, 1947

### Bradley Sets GI School Bill at 12 Billions

Gen. Omar N. Bradley, veteran's administrator, said today it may cost the government $12,000,000,000 to educate the ex-GI's.

The cost for the 20 months since the war ended is nearly $3,500,000,000, he said and of 2,300,000 students now in colleges 1,200,000 are veterans getting their education at the government expense...

## June 5, 1947

### COBB LEAVES FOR SALT BEDS

John Cobb, London fur broker and speedster, will leave England on the Queen Elizabeth, July 25, en route to Salt Lake to complete plans to race on Bonneville Speedway during the last two weeks of August, Gus P. Backman, director of the Centennial, said today....

Mr. Cobb will attempt to best the world's land speed record of 369 miles by reaching a peak of 400.

## June 5, 1947

### U.S. Launches Investigation Into Russ Coup

President Truman today denounced the Communist coup in Hungary as an outrage and asserted that the United States does not intend to stand idly by in that situation...

Until last week, Hungary's non-Communist government was the sole break in an otherwise solid lineup of Moscow-controlled nations extending from the Baltic to the Adriatic Seas...

## July 25, 1947

### Princess Alice Okehs Julie As Pal At Zoo

Everyone can uncross his fingers now.

Princess Alice — who as Salt Lake's lone pachyderm ruled supreme over the municipality's zoo world for lo these many years — has decided to share the local animal kingdom with trick-doing, carnival elephant, Julie.

A few days ago, when zoo officials skeptically brought Julie to Hogle's Zoological Gardens, the waters were anything but smooth. Oldster Alice went into a two-hour sulk, while the gentle, friendly Julie made all the overtures...

## Oct. 14, 1947

### Meatless Day Effect Is Nullified

Salt Lake City's weekly meat consumption apparently has not dropped despite a temporary decline registered in meat sales both on today's and last week's meatless Tuesday...

One manager reasoned that Salt Lakers are going without meat on Tuesday — as per federal request — but they are eating more meat on the other six days of the week.

Meanwhile, today the evidence was that a majority of Salt Lakers complied with the meatless Tuesday request of President Truman. Many shoppers remarked to store clerks that they were not purchasing meat today because of the food conservation program.

## May 7, 1948

### Wanted–A Name For Baby Tiglon

The most talked-about baby in Salt Lake City today was the little "tiglon" born yesterday to Daisy, a tigress presented to the Hogle Zoological Gardens... by the Deseret News. This baby is unusual, because his father is a lion.

Since the parents of the zoo's latest addition are unable to name their offspring, The Deseret News is sponsoring a contest to name the little tiglon. A $25 prize will be given to the winner of the contest. Send your name

Shasta the liger, offspring of a lion and tiger, was just a few days old.

suggestions to Swen Teresed, in care of The Deseret News. All entries must be mailed by midnight Thursday, May 13....

The tiny cub, one of the rarest hybrids in animal history, is the second of its kind known to have been born in captivity and the first to be born in the United States, according to Joseph I. Sloan, supervisor of Salt Lake City parks...

**(The "tiglon" was determined to be a liger, and was named Shasta.)**

## June 11, 1948

### NANCY BECOMES STAR THE HARD WAY

Like the story of a bush-leaguer in baseball coming up the hard way to become the nation's top player is the career of Nancy, the lively little girl who plays the star role in the comic strip, NANCY, which appears daily and Sunday in THE DESERET NEWS.

NANCY started out as a "bit" player in the comic FRITZI RITZ. Ernie Bushmiller, the artist, drew her in just "to give Fritzi something to worry about."....

In a survey by B. H. Grant Research, Inc., an independent readership rating service, the comic strip NANCY placed first in the nation.

## April 3, 1949

### Shriners To Begin Hospital Building

DENVER (AP) — Denver El Jebel Temple officials said Saturday a gift of $50,000 from an elderly Colorado widow will permit Shriners to start construction Monday on a new 60-bed hospital for crippled children in Salt Lake City.

The donor is Mrs. Frances S. Simpson of Matheson. She became interested in the shriner program after she lost an infant son who had been crippled from birth....

The new Shriner Hospital will receive crippled children from Colorado, Wyoming, Utah, Idaho, and Arizona...

## April 4, 1949

### Lee Approves Decontrol Of Ogden Rent

Removal of rent controls in Ogden was authorized Monday by Gov. J. Bracken Lee in response to a request by the Ogden City Commission.

It was expected the decontrol order would go into effect immediately, the governor's office declared...

In Salt Lake City Mayor Earl J. Glade announced the city commission would "explore" the rent situation before making any recommendations...

## Aug. 16, 1949

### Bombers Rout Chickens; Owner Sues U.S.

Havoc in a chicken run from the thunder of 12 big Army bombers is described in a suit filed against the U.S. government in the federal court Tuesday.

Mike Boskovich, the plaintiff, said that on Aug. 1, 1946, he was the owner of 3500 hens and young pullets in a wire mesh enclosure at Midvale.

Twelve heavy bombers flew over the chicken run in formation at less than 500 feet above the chickens, he alleges.

The plaintiff asserts that many of the chickens were killed or maimed as they flew into the wire with great force. Many more were smothered as they piled up in the corners...

## Aug. 16, 1949

### Famed Author of GWTW Dies Of Injury

ATLANTA — (AP) — Margaret Mitchell, the author of "Gone With the Wind," died Tuesday. She was struck down by a speeding automobile on Peachtree Street last Thursday night...

The quiet author of the famous Civil War novel was hit by a car as she and her husband, John H. Marsh, an advertising executive, crossed the street while walking to a movie near her home.

Police charged the driver of the car, Hugh D. Gravitt, 28, with suspicion of manslaughter... police records show he had had 23 traffic violations previously against him...

## Apr. 3, 1949

### Tabernacle Choir Will Record on Columbia Discs

By Conrad B. Harrison

WITH ITS COLUMBIA recording sessions now set for June 2 and 3 and its great easter program in the offing, the Tabernacle Choir, under its famous conductor, J. Spencer Cornwall, is sharing the music spotlight with no one these days ...

Ivor Sharp, general manager of KSL, announced the dates for recording two "Twentieth Anniversary" choir albums Saturday

Performances will be placed on Columbia Masterworks labels and the works will be under supervision of Goddard Lieberson.

Each album will contain four 12-inch records to be issued first in conventional shellac and vinylite and later on the new Columbia long-playing microgrooves, Mr. Sharp said.

Nov. 3, 1948

## Polltakers Busy Trying to Explain Upset

NEW YORK (AP) — It was precisely as President Truman predicted:

The faces of the poll takers were red today, the morning after election.

The President said the polls, which proved statistically he was beaten before the ballots were cast, were wrong. "Sleeping polls," he called them.

And wrong they were.

Not since 1936 when the Literary Digest poll picked Alf Landon over Franklin D. Roosevelt (final official result: Roosevelt won 46 states to Landon's two) have the polls taken such a whipping.

Dr. George Gallup, director of the American Institution of Opinion, who had predicted a Tom Dewey victory in the presidential race, was one of the few pollsters up for early comment. He said, "This is the kind of a close election that happens once in a generation and is a nightmare for poll-takers. Everyone is asking, 'what happened?' Why did all the polls underestimate Truman's strength? The answer to this question will likely be found in an analysis of the voting…"

**Thomas Dewey**

---

**In a major political upset, Harry S Truman squeaked into office with less than 50 percent of the popular vote. The Chicago Tribune actually released its early editions proclaiming a Dewey victory. Returns from some later-voting states such as California tipped the scales in Truman's favor.**

## The world of the 1940s
### A TIMELINE

**1940**— The "Luftwaffe" razes one-third of the city of London in the biggest air raid of the war.

**1940**— Vought-Sikorsky Corporation holds first successful helicopter flight in the U.S.

**1941**— U.S. Savings Bonds and Stamps go on sale.

**1942**— Disney's "Bambi" comes out.

**1942**— Magnetic recording tape is invented.

**1942**— Coconut Grove nightclub (Boston) fire kills 487, most of asphyxiation when trapped by exit doors that opened inward instead of outward.

**1942**— Bell Aircraft tests the first U.S. jetplane.

**1943**— Penicillin is used successfully to treat chronic diseases.

**1943**— Zoot suits become popular in the U.S.

**1944** — Franklin Delano Roosevelt is elected for fourth term.

**1944**— Tennessee Williams writes "The Glass Menagerie."

**1945**— World's first general-purpose computing device starts operation.

**1945**— Charles de Gaulle is elected president of France.

**1945**— Frank Lloyd Wright designs the Guggenheim Museum, New York.

**1945** — Vietnam formed as an independent republic with Ho Chi Minh as president.

**1946**— A U.S. scientist claims that smoking could be a cause of lung cancer.

**1946**— First session of United Nations held.

**1946**— Benjamin Spock writes "Baby and Child Care."

**1946**— Xerography process invented.

**1946**— Atomic bomb is tested at Bikini Atoll.

**1946**— Joe Louis gets the world heavyweight boxing title for the 23rd time.

**1947**— Chuck Yeager is the first man to travel faster than sound.

**1947**— The transistor is developed.

**1947**— Princess Elizabeth marries Philip Mountbatten, Duke of Edinburgh.

**1947**— The Dead Sea Scrolls are discovered in Wadi Qumran.

**1948**— Gandhi is assassinated.

**1949**— RCA invents a system for broadcasting color television.

**1949**— Long-playing, 33 1/3 rpm vinyl records are produced.

**1949**— Arthur Miller writes Pulitzer Prize drama "Death of a Salesman."

**1949**— USSR tests its first atomic bomb.

**1949**— South Africa establishes its apartheid program.

U.S. Navy

**USS Missouri, 1944**

*Boeing B29 Superfortress.*

# A fearful peace at last

With the war in Europe over, only Japan stood between the Allies and their "final triumph." The stubborn resistance of Japanese leaders, even though American troops were making an inexorable and bloody march through its island fortresses, called for drastic measures.

**A** fter careful deliberation, President Harry S Truman authorized the use of a powerful new weapon. A B-29 named Enola Gay, whose crew trained at Utah's Wendover Air Base, delivered the bomb that would finally force defeat upon the Japanese:

**DESERET NEWS,** *Aug. 6, 1945: WASHINGTON (AP) — An atomic bomb, hailed as the most terrible destructive force in history and as the greatest achievement of organized science, has been loosed upon Japan.*

*President Truman disclosed in a White House statement at 11 a.m. today that the first use of the bomb — containing more power than 20,000 tons of TNT and producing more than 2,000 times the blast of the most powerful bomb ever dropped before — was made 16 hours earlier on Hiroshima, Japanese army base. The atomic bomb is the answer, President Truman said, to Japan's refusal to surrender…*

*SAN FRANCISCO (AP) — The Japanese Imperial High Command admitted today that the new atomic bomb dropped on Hiroshima wreaked extensive destruction and revealed that damage may have been so terrific that it could not believe only a single bomb was used …*

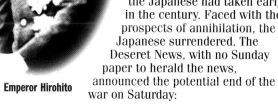

AP Photo

**Emperor Hirohito**

Still no surrender was forthcoming, and on Aug. 9, the world stood in horrified awe as the second demonstration of atomic power unfolded in Nagasaki:

Deseret News files

**DESERET NEWS,** *Aug. 9, 1945: GUAM (AP) — The world's most destructive force, the atomic bomb, was used for the second time against Japan today, striking the important Kyushu Island city of Nagasaki with observed "good results"…*

*The Japanese had had time to study the devestation wrought at Hiroshima, where they reported "practically every living thing " was destroyed.*

While the Americans unleashed a new power that would change the world forever, the Russians were closing in from the west, reclaiming Chinese territory the Japanese had taken early in the century. Faced with the prospects of annihilation, the Japanese surrendered. The Deseret News, with no Sunday paper to herald the news, announced the potential end of the war on Saturday:

**DESERET NEWS,** *Sept. 1, 1945: YOKOHAMA (AP) — The world's bloodiest war will come to an official end tomorrow when emissaries of Japan step aboard the battleship Missouri for a surrender ceremony starting about 9 a.m…*

*At that hour General MacArthur and other high Allied officials will surround the agents of Emperor Hirohito who have been designated to scratch their names to a document yielding up an empire built on conquest… At the height of the ceremony, President Truman in the White House in Washington — where Japanese warlords expected this war would end — will begin speaking to the world by radio…*

Salt Lakers of all faiths gathered to express gratitude:

**DESERET NEWS,** *Sept. 3, 1945: Thousands of Salt Lakers of all religious denominations are expected to fill the Salt Lake Tabernacle to capacity tomorrow night in a huge mass meeting of thanksgiving for peace, which came officially yesterday with the proclamation of V-J Day…*

In the coming weeks and years, the world would count the cost of World War II — almost 10.5 million Allied military dead; 5.7 million of the enemy killed; millions of wounded, some of whom would heal, others not; heavy civilian losses; approximately 6 million Jews and others considered "unworthy" by the Third Reich displaced, tortured and killed. Chaos in the world's economies promised a long recovery period. A new "Cold War" began that endured long after the fighting ceased.

Weighed against that were major advances in science and technology that would eventually lead into the Space Age, although at a terrible price. And out of the ashes would arise powerful new allies from the ranks of the vanquished.

The Second World War changed the world forever.

The Japanese mainland was hit by two atomic bombs, as the Deseret News reported below. The final surrender documents were signed Sept. 2 aboard the battleship Missouri under direction of General Douglas MacArthur.

ATOMIC BOMB SENDS SMOKE SOARING OVER NAGASAKI—Smoke columns ascended more than 20,000 feet over the Japanese city of Nagasaki within three minutes after the atomic bomb explosion on Aug. 9.

## Nagasaki Hit by Worse Blast Than Hiroshima

German leaders on trial at Nuremberg include, center row, Hermann Goering, Joachim von Ribbentrop, Gen. Wilhelm Keitel and Alfred Rosenberg.

# War's aftermath

The devastation wreaked on the world by four years of war from 1941 to 1945 took many years longer to remedy. Reconstruction began immediately. Nations rebuilt shattered cities, saw to the needs of their people, shored up their alliances and tried to revitalize their tattered economies.

**T**he first item of business on the minds of some was justice and vengeance. An international tribunal met in November 1945 to try the men most closely associated with Adolf Hitler — those who carried out his orders of death and destruction:

**DESERET NEWS,** *Nov. 20, 1945: NUREMBERG, Germany (AP) — A strangely assorted score of gloomy Nazis sat dejectedly today before an international military tribunal and heard themselves formally accused of Nazi war crimes, the murder of 10,000,000 Europeans, plunder, horror and torture.*

*Throughout the opening session of the historic trial for their lives, Hitlerian followers such as corpulent Hermann Goering, vague Rudolf Hess and defiant Field Marshal Wilhelm Keitel listened through earphones while spokesmen of the nations which crushed their*

heirarchy recited crimes the world had never before witnessed.

The first trials lasted almost a year. Nineteen of the first 20 tried were convicted. Twelve received death sentences, and 10 were hanged on Oct. 16, 1946. Goering committed suicide before he could be hanged. Martin Bormann was missing and tried in absentia. From 1946 to 1949, 12 more trials took place in Nuremberg, involving 185 defendants. The unprecedented trials documented extensively the events of World War II and rejected the argument that "following orders" excuses individuals from culpability in excessive war cruelty.

Allied nations that survived the most horrible conflict in human history vowed, if possible, to prevent a recurrence. They banded together in peacetime organizations. Fifty nations formed the nucleus of the United Nations:

**DESERET NEWS,** *June 26, 1945: SAN FRANCISCO (AP) — Delegates of 50 nations united by war today signed the charter upon which they pin their hopes to remain united in peace.*

*Dr. Wellington Koo of China brushed his name down on the page of history, and the first of the United Nations to be invaded by the Axis became the first to affix a signature. Thus began an eight-hour ceremony in which 153 delegates moved in alphabetical order — after China, Russia, Britain and France had signed — to the great blue table, surrounded by the flags of all the United Nations, centering the Kleig-lighted auditorium of San Francisco's Veteran's Building.*

The United States was last to sign,

partly from courtesy as the host country, but also to accommodate President Harry S Truman, who could be there more conveniently in the afternoon.

Unwilling to rely solely on debate and diplomacy to protect world interests, the United States also entered into an agreement with its closest allies to promote military preparedness — the North Atlantic Treaty Organization:

**DESERET NEWS,** *April 4, 1949: WASHINGTON (AP) — President Truman, rejecting Russia's charge that the Atlantic Treaty is "aggressive" Monday hailed the historic pact as "a shield against aggression and the fear of aggression ..." Truman asserted the people of the West are determined that "the sickening blow of unprovoked aggression" shall not "fall upon the world again ..." In effect, he blamed Russia's policies in the United Nations for making such a regional security system necessary. He said the United States and other countries had hoped to establish an international U. N. police force, but their efforts "have been blocked by one of the major powers..."*

The reference was to Russia's heavy-handed use of its veto power in the international body. The creation of NATO also acknowledged new world friendships. Allies in World War II, the U.S. and USSR now were acknowledged adversaries in the Cold War that followed.

The United States, the richest and least physically affected of the Allies, pledged to help rebuild the countries devastated in

President Harry S Truman

the war. The Marshall Plan, named for U.S. Secretary of State George C. Marshall, poured millions of dollars into the reconstruction effort:

**DESERET NEWS,** *June 5, 1947: CAMBRIDGE, Mass. (AP) — Secretary of State Marshall called upon the countries of Europe today to work out together a great new program of reconstruction.*

*He promised American economic assistance and support "so far as it may be practical," and at the time he pledged the United States to oppose "any government which maneuvers to block the recovery of other countries."*

Based on an extensive survey, the U.S. looked for ways to "provide a cure rather than a mere palliative." A year before the war ended, Congress acted to provide support for American veterans:

**DESERET NEWS,** *June 22, 1944: WASHINGTON (AP) — President Roosevelt today signed the "GI bill of rights," setting up a vast government aid program for veterans of this war. With congressional leaders and heads of veterans' organizations looking on, the chief executive put his signature to the measure authorizing federal loans, hospitalization, job insurance, schooling and other ex-service benefits estimated to cost between $3 billion and $6.5 billion.*

In Utah, the bill had significant effects — the establishment of the Veterans Administration Hospital, a boom in college and university enrollment that put pressure on the higher education system and a slew of new government offices that would still be working at the end of the 20th century to administer veteran benefits.

# 100
## years in the valley

Forget about those earlier problems the U.S. government had had with those pesky Mormons in Utah. By 1947, all was forgiven. And President Harry S Truman sent his congratulations on the pioneer centennial:

**DESERET NEWS,** *July 24, 1947: Utah stands in proud place among her sister commonwealths. Her rich agriculture, her business and industry, her pioneering in the social services, her zeal for education, and not the least, her men of wisdom and valiant women have given her a prestige unexcelled by any other state.*

Utahns had a lot to celebrate, and they were determined to do it right. Months of preparation culminated in activities and festivities like nothing that had gone before:

**DESERET NEWS,** *July 14, 1947: Nauvoo, Ill. — A party of 143 men, three women and two children will break camp here tomorrow morning and begin an eight-day trek to Salt Lake City.*

*The trek, sponsored by the Sons of Utah*

An automobile is decked out as a covered wagon led by a team of oxen to commemorate the 100th anniversary of the arrival of Mormon pioneers in 1947. A convoy of the vehicles retraced the pioneer route.

The Post Office issued a commemorative, 3-cent stamp.

*Pioneers,… is composed of the exact number of men, women and children who reached the valley July 22, 1847… Unlike the early pioneers whose uncomfortable journey in covered wagons and on horseback took months, the modern pioneers will travel by automobile, but the tops of the cars will be covered with prairie schooner rigging.*

*July 19, 1947: Advance ticket sales to "Promised Valley," musical drama opening Monday evening in the University of Utah stadium bowl, are setting an intermountain states record, Gus. P. Backman, Centennial director, said today.*

*July 21, 1947: Sold out! Yes, the Centennial Edition of the Deseret News issued last Saturday was a complete sell-out.*

*There may be a few more available copies of this prized edition and they will be handled by regular street salesmen in*

*downtown Salt Lake.*

*July 23, 1947: The curtain on 100 years of Utah's unique history was dramatically raised today in downtown Salt Lake when the Centennial Parade passed in review for nearly 100,000 applauding spectators.*

*July 24, 1947: As an enduring symbol of religious freedom, industry, faith and courage exemplified in Utah's exploration and settlement by pioneers from 1776 to July 24, 1847, the great "This is the Place" monument was unveiled and dedicated this morning as the highlight of many weeks of Centennial celebration.*

Practically every community in the state planned a celebration. For weeks the paper filled up with pioneer stories. Seven Utah pioneers, all over 80, were flown back to Nauvoo. A 3-cent centennial stamp came from the U.S. Postal Service. And for months, the suspense had been building as to who would win a very special contest:

**DESERET NEWS,** *July 28, 1947: Everybody had 'em but today the Sons of Utah Pioneers "whisker derby" was just a memory to most contestants. Serge J. Olsen, Logan, was named grand champion in the state-wide contest, for his two-toned chin spinach.*

# Radio
## taps into imagination

The Utah Symphony plays its first concert at the University of Utah's Kingsbury Hall on May 8, 1940, with Hans Heniot conducting.

**DESERET NEWS,** *Sept. 27, 1941: As far as youngsters are concerned, Bob Burns, the "Arkansas Traveler" is the greatest artist in the country. For Bob is tops at making "windies." He's heard every Tuesday at 6 p.m. over KSL...*

- *When the theme notes of "Evalina" introduce Lum and Abner to their air audiences on Monday, Sept. 29, as their new time on the Pacific Coast Red Network on NBC, the Pine Ridge sages will begin a new chapter in their radio history — the beginning of a new transcontinental series. They are heard over KUTA at 8:30 p.m...*
- *With summer vacations a thing of the past many of the famous NBC radio stars will return to the air in the next two weeks. Fibber McGee and Molly and Bob Hope, favorites on KDYL each Tuesday night, are back on the job... Jack Benny leads Sunday's stars on October 5, 1941, when he and the Benny company make their fall debut... Basil Rathbone as Sherlock Holmes and Nigel Bruce as Dr. Watson will also return on October 5, 1941...*

It was the golden age of radio. In the early 1940s, the Deseret News listed the programs for six radio stations: KUTA, KSL, KVNU, KOVO, KDYL and KLO. Audiences found a full line-up of comedy, sports, news and music (including broadcasts of the Mormon Tabernacle Choir) .

But Utah was increasingly concerned with the technology side as well.

**DESERET NEWS,** *Nov. 30, 1943: Earl J. Glade, mayor-elect of Salt Lake City, told the Senate Interstate Commerce Committee today that the radio industry was making steady progress in its efforts to "elevate broadcasting standards."*

And by the second half of the decade came a preview of the future:

**DESERET NEWS,** *Feb. 7, 1946: Television, that wonder of radio science they've been talking about for exactly 14 years, is almost ready to make its debut in Salt Lake City.*

*That is, almost. It will be a year if the radio-wise estimate of O.B. Hanson, vice president and chief engineer of the National Broadcasting Co., New York City, comes true.*

In the meantime, there was still Bing Crosby and Fred Allen on the Philco Radio Hour... The Guiding Light... Arthur Godfrey ("he's your man!") ... Harold (The Great Gildersleeve) Peary... the Lux Radio Theater... Lassie... The Shadow, a Real Thriller... and so much more to be found on the radio dial.

# Creating an orchestra

**T**he first Salt Lake Symphony Orchestra gave a concert on May 17, 1892, in the Salt Lake Theater. In 1902, George D. Pyper, director of the theater, persuaded his board of directors to come up with $1,500 to subsidize an orchestra. Again in 1923, a S.L. Symphony was organized and concerts given at "the old Hippodrome, the Wilkes, the Salt Lake Theater and the Orpheum."

So, the announcement in April 1940 that Utah would have a new orchestra, part of the government's WPA program, was greeted with enthusiasm.

**DESERET NEWS,** *April 13, 1940: Right at this moment, the most important development in recent years of music activity appears to be the formation this week of the Utah State Symphony Orchestra Association as a department of the Utah State Institute of Fine Arts.*

*May 8, 1940: Music lovers of Salt Lake City and Utah today were eagerly awaiting the placing of a large milestone along the road of Utah musical history tonight, when the newly organized Utah State Symphony Orchestra makes its first public appearance.*

*May 9, 1940: In a short talk delivered from the stage during last night's performance, Dr. Bennion, first vice president of the Utah State Symphony Orchestra Association said:*

*"Tonight we are making history! The appearance of our own symphony orchestra gives us a metropolitan atmosphere which we have not had before — I feel nearer to New York tonight than I have in a long, long time."*

And in 1947 came another momentous announcement:

**DESERET NEWS,** *June 18, 1947: "There need be no relationship between the size of a city and its cultural taste," Maurice Abravanel, newly appointed conductor of the Utah Symphony, said today. "There is no reason for a city to be artistically provincial, simply because it does not have as many opportunities as the so-called 'sophisticated' cities," he said...*

*Enthusiastic about America's development during the past 11 years, he declared, "Through the grace of God and Mr. Hitler, America now has the greatest musicians in the world."*

*He will begin rehearsals Oct. 20 with the Utah orchestra.*

Born in Greece, the 44-year-old Abravanel came to America in 1936 to escape oppression and war. Enthusiastic, optimistic, he was beginning an association with the Utah Symphony that would last 33 years and build a world-class orchestra.

# A championship era

**March Madness not quite being then what it is now in basketball, Utah's victory did not even merit a front-page story. But it did get nice play on the sports pages:**

The University of Utah basketball team won the NCAA championship in 1944 after losing out in the first round of the National Invitational Tournament (NIT).

AS UTES WON NATIONAL CAGE TITLE: Herb Wilkinson of Utah, (TOP) retrieves a rebound in the national championship finale last night against Dartmouth in Madison Square Garden. Extreme left is Bob Lewis and far right is Dick Smuin. LOWER: Utah's players carry Wilkinson off court a few seconds after he shot winning goal, giving the Redskins the title.

**DESERET NEWS,** *Mar. 29, 1944:* Utah and St. John's, of Brooklyn, the two most surprising teams of the post-season championship college basketball tournaments, will clash at Madison Square Garden Thursday night in a recognized championship game for the benefit of the Red Cross.

Utah, a seven-point underdog, upset mighty Dartmouth, 42 to 40, to win the NCAA title in an exciting extra period game before 17,990 at the Garden last night. St. John's, a similar underdog, toppled favored Depaul, 47-39, on Sunday to win the National Invitation tourney.

It was pure chance that Utah was even playing in the NCAA tournament. The team received invitations both to it and to the NIT but accepted the NIT bid and then lost to Kentucky in the first round.

In the meantime, four members of the Arkansas team were injured and a coach killed in an automobile accident and that team withdrew from the NCAA meet. Utah was a last-minute replacement. Led by all-American Arnold Ferrin, they did the impossible.

**DESERET NEWS,** *Mar. 29, 1944:* That the Redskins, mostly 17-year-olds, with a couple of youngsters of 18 and two 4-Fs, could beat the great Dartmouth quintet, Eastern champions and heretofore unbeaten by any collegiate aggregation, is almost beyond belief, especially in view of the fact that the Hanover, N.H., aggregation is star-studded with college-graduate, navy trainees from all over the Atlantic seaboard. In age and experience, the Utes had no business in the same league with Dartmouth, but still they won the national championship.

Collegiate basketball was not the only place the impact of the war was being felt in these early years of the '40s. The entire sports world was affected.

**DESERET NEWS,** *Aug. 4, 1942:* Joe Louis, world's heavyweight boxing champion, tightens the bit on his horse preparatory to a ride at the Cavalry Replacement Training Center at Fort Riley, Kansas, where he is undergoing basic training.

*Aug. 5, 1942:* Hank Greenberg, formerly of the Detroit Tigers, became a second lieutenant in the army air force upon graduation from the Officers Candidate School today.

Allen Tolmich, former Wayne University hurdler, and Gruek Fenske, the miler, also were commissioned as lieutenants after completing their 12-week courses.

Early in the decade, the sports community found reasons to celebrate. At the end of the 1941 baseball season, the final major league batting champ was Ted Williams, batting .406. File that under numbers that would never be seen again.

And this one, too:

**DESERET NEWS,** *July 18, 1941:* The baseball season lost some of its zest last night when Joe DiMaggio's phenomenal hitting streak came to an end, but the pennant aspirations of the New York Yankees may be better off.

Throughout the country millions of fans have been anxiously following the feat of the lean, poker-faced outfielder in rolling up an all-time major league record for hitting safely in 56 consecutive contests.

These records might never be broken again, but something even more important would be broken in '40s baseball: the color barrier.

**DESERET NEWS,** *April 9, 1947:* Jackie Robinson, the most controversial ball player in the country, said today he believes he can make good as a major leaguer if given the chance. The Negro star, whose .349 batting average with Montreal last year was good enough to lead the International League, doesn't know where he will play this year.

*April 11, 1947:* Jackie Robinson's first appearance in the white flannels of the Brooklyn Dodgers was greeted with a roar of approval by a crowd of about 10,000 early birds at Ebbets field today, two hours before the scheduled exhibition between the Dodgers and the New York Yankees.

*April 16, 1947:* Brooklyn's Negro first-baseman, and first of his race to reach the majors since 1884, failed to get a hit in three official trips to the plate, but his sacrifice-error play in the seventh inning set up the subsequent tying and winning runs.

Robinson would end up as the Rookie of the Year. And at the end of the decade a couple of other unusual athletes were making their way into the record books:

**DESERET NEWS,** *June 12, 1947:* Mrs. Babe Didrickson Zaharias of Denver, became the first American ever to win the British Women's Amateur Golf title today… Mrs. Zaharias, winner of 15 straight tournaments in the United States before she came here for the "only major title I have left to win," consistently outdrove her opponents.

**DESERET NEWS,** *June 13, 1948:* Citation won the triple crown of America's racing today, wrapping up the Belmont Stakes easily… "He's the greatest horse I've ever seen, let alone ridden," [Eddie] Arcaro said.

Jackie Robinson

Deseret News files

**D E S E R E T     N E W S**

# The Society Pages:
## Hemlines and visitors

Christian Dior set women's fashions on its ear with his "New Look" creations in 1947. Here, modern models wear a cocktail dress, left, and a two-tiered evening gown.

**DESERET NEWS,** *Mar. 3, 1940:* "Youth, a World Problem" was foremost in the discussion today when the Salt Lake District of the Utah Federation of Women's Clubs conducted an institute on public welfare at the Newhouse Hotel.

"Youth demands nothing but opportunity to serve and become a normal member of the society that gave him birth," said Miss Thompson, local director of the National Youth Administration.

Building on foundations laid in the 1920s and '30s, Salt Lake clubwomen were going strong in the '40s. Social issues, social events and a society section of the newspaper had all become standard fare.

**DESERET NEWS,** *Mar. 16, 1940:* Gov. and Mrs. Henry H. Blood will act as chief hosts at the forty-first anniversary dinner of the Utah State Institute of Fine Arts Monday evening at 6:30 in the Newhouse Hotel, it was announced today by Mrs. Seymour Wells, chairman of the reception committee.

Guests at the affair, which marks the opening of a statewide campaign for Institute members and the encouragement of the arts in Utah, will be greeted by prominent cultural leaders and representatives of organizations who will compose receiving lines.

In the spring of 1942, the society pages were filled with events commemorating the 100th anniversary of the Relief Society, "the world's oldest continuously existing women's organization."

During the war, many of the events benefited and recognized those performing war service.

**DESERET NEWS,** *Mar. 10, 1944:* Mother Hubbard had nothing on the American Mothers Sentinel League, for they, too, are finding their cupboards bare.

This organization, which has been sponsoring a free Snack Bar for servicemen, open on Saturday night til 2 a.m., has been serving up roasts of meat, and baked cakes and gallons of hot beverages, all home-cooked and all at personal expense to members to some 400 servicemen each week. But the food, and the funds, are running low.

A benefit concert scheduled March 20 in the Rose Crystal Room of the Newhouse Hotel at 8:30 p.m. has been agreed upon.

**DESERET NEWS,** *Mar. 25, 1944:* Honoring the members who are serving in the various branches of the Red Cross and other wartime agencies, the Ladies Literary Club will meet Friday at 2 p.m.

But social events were not all that filled the society section. In the '40s, Salt Lake retained enough "small town" atmosphere that comings and goings were an important part of the news.

**DESERET NEWS,** *April 8, 1940:* Mr. and Mrs. Sheldon B. Christenson and sons Niel and Richard, 1525 Mill Creek Way, will leave Wednesday to make their home in Los Angeles.

**DESERET NEWS,** *Mar. 18, 1942:* Her many friends in Utah will be interested to learn that Mrs. Reed Smoot, widow of the late Sen. Reed Smoot, a member of the Council of the Twelve, has arrived in Salt Lake for an indefinite stay.

Mrs. Smoot, who has been visiting in Washington, D.C., with her daughter and son-in-law, Mr. and Mrs. J.W. Marriott, arrived in Salt Lake this morning and is staying at the Hotel Utah.

**DESERET NEWS,** *Aug. 20, 1942:* A popular summer vacation visitor in Salt Lake is Mrs. Melvin Cannon and her young daughter, Bonnie Gay, who are here for a two-week stay. Mrs. Cannon is the wife of Dr. Melvin Cannon, a member of the staff at the Mellon Institute of Industrial Research at Pittsburgh, Pa. Dr. and Mrs. Cannon and their small daughter are guests of Dr. Cannon's father, Tracy Y. Cannon, at 1176 South Eighth West Street. They are also visiting with Mrs. Cannon's mother, Mrs. Annie S. Holland. The Cannons will motor back to Pittsburgh about Aug. 30.

Fashion was also an important part of the mix. In 1940: "Slimmer, Straighter Skirts Head This Way From Parisian Designers; Waistline is Lengthened, Smoothing Curves." In 1942: "Utility Watchword Of Styles Because Of War Conditions; Gone Are Ribbons, Other Extra Feminine Things." In 1947: "Well-Dressed Girl of 1948 Won't Show Knees." In 1948: "Take Your Gloves In Hand; Proper Care Means Longer Wear."

Women were also becoming more important as consumers. In 1940, they could buy an Easy Washer, "including autobit transmission, famous Easy Turbulator washing action, 1940s Streamline Wringers" for only $74.95. And a 1940 Magic Chef gas range for only $89.50. Of course, even then, not all shopping had to be practical:

**DESERET NEWS,** *Mar. 14, 1940:* When milady shops for dresses of black and white, she likely will be attracted to a dish of ice cream featuring the same colors, George W. Hennerich of Washington, D.C., managing director of the Ice Cream Merchandising Institute, contended today...

"When everyone is playing up black and white, for instance, why shouldn't a choice blackberry vanilla ice cream banana split also catch the fancy?" he asked.

**Even before the fires of World War II were fully doused, the chill of a Cold War emerged and lasted through several decades. A growing and mutual distrust between the United States and the Soviet Union and their respective camps was apparent during the peace talks at the end of the war. It blossomed in the events that followed.**

# Spies, bluster and fallout shelters

I n March of 1946, British Prime Minister Winston Churchill warned a conference of allies that "an iron curtain has descended across the Continent of Europe" and the phrase became the symbol of the ideologic barrier between communism and democracy.

The mistrust turned to war in Korea, one of the few Cold War stand-offs to turn into a shooting war. When the U.S. actively joined the war, there was serious concern that it would escalate into a world conflict:

**DESERET NEWS,** *April 5, 1951:*
*WAR JITTERS GRIP CAPITAL*
*The Nation's capital had World War III jitters Thursday after an official warning that America stands in "face of*

*terrible danger" and perhaps a world conflict. The fear was that Russia was about to throw her armed forces into the Korean war and that the fighting then might spread to Europe...*

Lurking in the background of every confrontation — even every potential confrontation — was the specter of atomic war. Americans saw what atomic power could do in Hiroshima and Nagasaki. Paranoia at the international level trickled down into the lives of common citizens. The uneasy feeling that all-out war was constantly imminent colored normal everyday lives:

**DESERET NEWS,** *Sept. 6, 1955:*
*Thinking of adding a new patio or outdoor dining room to your home?*
*An air raid shelter may be more appropriate, believe members of the Salt Lake City Board of Health. And a shelter to protect against "radioactive fallout from nuclear weapons" (atom bombs and such) can be built for about the same amount as a patio would cost, the health authorities say.*
*Responsibility of the individual for his own survival of an atomic attack is emphasized in a statement released by the seven-man health board.*

Such doomsday thinking was fed by "what-if" scenarios like this:

Deseret News files

**Sen. Joseph McCarthy**

*July 12, 1957:*
*HILL AFB 'BLASTED' IN UTAH RAID*
*A simulated atom bomb with the explosive force of 50,000 tons of TNT was dropped on Utah's Hill Air Force Base at 12:27 p.m. Friday to kick off the state's major Civil Defense program.*
*The simulated blast theoretically destroyed everything within a 15-mile radius, cutting off traffic on much-traveled U.S. Highway 91, according to Civil Defense officials...*
*Gov. George D. Clyde declared a simulated state of emergency through the state, and a simulated freeze on the sale of all food supplies and gasoline was ordered throughout Utah to prevent hoarding...*

Take out the oft-repeated "simulated" and

'Poor Old Rip Ivan Winklov—Just Back From 20 Years In Siberia For Having Said Stalin Was A Tyrant'

Time magazine chose Russian premiere Nikita Khrushchev for its man of the year for 1957 after his triumphs in the Cold War and in space. He also began debunking Stalin myths, right.

## 1950-1960

A magazine dubbed them "The Fabulous Fifties." At mid-century the country was ready to enjoy the good life, even as the Cold War raged in Korea and spies were thought to be everywhere. It was the decade when Disneyland opened, when the Interstate Highway System got under way, when Everest was conquered and the four-minute-mile barrier fell. Man-made satellites orbited the Earth. Utahns enjoyed a boom in uranium mining, thought about building fallout shelters, and innocently watched the skies light up when nuclear tests went off in Nevada. It seemed like a good time for the country, but beneath the surface an ominous tension was building. Federal troops escorted a young girl to school in Little Rock, Ark., and a Baptist preacher led a boycott of buses in Montgomery, Ala.

it was enough to send shivers down anyone's spine. Public statements by high-ranking officials such as Clyde ("We're looking straight down the barrel of a nuclear gun") kept the fears alive. The general unrest was blamed for new attitudes, especially among young Americans. If nuclear annihilation was inevitable, why bother with life? Some took the position that Americans were "Better Red Than Dead."

The death of Joseph Stalin, architect of Russia's communistic government, and the rise of Nikita Khrushchev did little to assuage American fears:

**DESERET NEWS,** *Nov. 19, 1956: MOSCOW (UP) — The Western envoys walked out on Communist Party Secretary General Nikita S. Khrushchev again Sunday night when he gave them another tongue-lashing and hinted that God would be on the side of the Communists — "if we believed in the existence of God."*

*"We will bury you," Khrushchev told the western diplomats at a reception at the Polish Embassy to mark the signing of a Soviet-Polish agreement giving Poland the right to pursue an independent course of communism.*

*"If you do not like us," the Vodka-drinking Khrushchev told the American, British and other envoys, "do not accept our invitations and do not invite us to you."*

On one memorable occasion, the Russian leader pounded on the podium during a United Nations session with his shoe to accentuate a point. Later, he blamed the incident on a problem with his watch. With a frantic race among nations to join the nuclear arms club, the ingredients existed for conflict on a grand scale. For obvious reasons, American officials jealously guarded the secrets of this new weapon, and when Russia became privy to those secrets through espionage, there was a severe reaction:

**DESERET NEWS,** *April 5, 1951: NEW YORK (UP) — The man and woman who stole America's A-bomb secret for Soviet Russia and "altered the course of history" were sentenced to death in the electric chair.*

*The supreme penalty was inflicted upon Julius Rosenberg, 32, and his wife, Ethel, 35. They are to be executed, the judge specified, during the week beginning May 21. However, the execution date is certain to be postponed by appeals.*

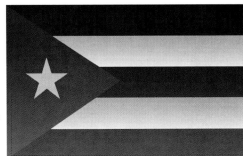

A CBS film released in 1957 shows Fidel Castro cheering with some of his troops. Castro's success in turning the Cuban Revolution to his benefit relied heavily on aid from the Soviet Union.

*If the Rosenbergs die, they will be the first persons ever executed for espionage after trial in the United States civil courts. The tough federal judge (Irving Kaufman) told the couple, parents of two small children, that their crime in delivering the essentials of America's A-bomb secret to Soviet Russia was "worse than murder."*

Despite pleas for clemency from such notables as Albert Einstein and Pope Pius XII, the Rosenbergs were executed in Sing Sing prison in Ossining, N.Y. Ethel's brother, David Greenglass, who had worked as a machinist at Los Alamos, N.M., during the development of the bomb and who aided the Rosenbergs in passing information to Russia, spent 15 years in prison.

All this provided fertile soil for a man like Sen. Joseph R. McCarthy. Suddenly, it seemed there were communists everywhere and McCarthy, as head of the House Un-American Activities Subcommittee, was able, apparently, to find one under every bush. Hundreds of Americans were accused of communist leanings, often based on precious little evidence. High-ranking military personnel, educators, journalists, clergymen, government bureaucrats — even movie stars — were fair game for what became a modern-day witch-hunt. It was an era of blacklisting and loyalty oaths.

In the mid-1950s, Congress recognized that McCarthy was out of bounds and acted to curb him:

**DESERET NEWS,** *Dec. 2, 1954: WASHINGTON — The Senate gave overwhelming approval to one censure resolution against Sen. Joseph R. McCarthy*

*Wednesday night. The first blow fell heavily when the Senate voted, 67 to 20, to adopt the first of two censure counts returned by a special committee. It censured McCarthy for "repeatedly abusing" a 1951-52 subcommittee.*

The McCarthy censure hearings were of particular interest to Utahns. One of the state's senators, Arthur V. Watkins, conducted the proceedings.

The Cold War took another uncomfortable turn in early 1959 when Fidel Castro took over control of Cuba, only 90 miles off America's eastern shores:

**DESERET NEWS,** *Jan. 1, 1959: HAVANA (UPI) — President Fulgencio Batista fled the country Thursday. He was succeeded by a three-man military junta which indicated it would make a peace offer to rebel leader Castro...*

*Diplomatic sources said they understood this would include a direct appeal to Castro's rebels to end the two-year-old revolution which has spread throughout the eastern half of Cuba and cost thousands of lives and millions of dollars...*

On Jan. 16, Deseret News columnist Roscoe Drummond called the Cuban revolution a good thing and predicted that "the new Castro Government is intent upon bringing about the needed and widely desired reforms." Castro quickly disillusioned Drummond and others who hoped for an off-shore ally by aligning himself with the Russian communists.

The Cold War had moved in next door, and Americans squirmed.

UPI Photo

# Deseret News
## Salt Lake Telegram

**Feb. 2, 1950**

What Janice Valois Putnam thinks of the weak response to the March of Dimes is nobody's business.

She's disgusted. Janice, a pretty 17-year-old, contracted polio last year. This year, to show her gratitude, she's offered her services to the drive.

But Janice is disgusted. She went to a meeting of some 250 local businessmen in one of the downtown hotels. She asked to place some coin boxes around. Then she waited from 12:30 to 4 p.m. when the meeting was over to collect the money.

Do you know what she found? Two nickels.

**Feb. 3, 1950**

## Actor to be given deed to all Utah

Utah will be given away, but it won't go back to the Indians.

Gov. J. Bracken Lee is scheduled to hand a "deed" to the state to Movie Star Vincent Price who arrives in Salt Lake City Saturday morning on behalf of Utah's polio campaign.

Even though it is cold in Salt Lake, the star is looking forward to his visit to Utah.

"Ever since I was martyred when I played Joseph Smith in 'Brigham Young' I've been interested in your city," he said. "So below zero or not I'll arrive there with my beard and leave without it."

**Feb. 6, 1950**

## Wayne Set For Films Until '55

**By LOUELLA PARSONS**

SITTING DOWN in Florida, sunning myself at this beautiful hotel, I'm handed a communique about still another big war picture for John Wayne, "Operation Pacific," at Warners. Boy — does he work!

John is booked solid for movies until 1955 ...

**Feb. 6, 1950**

Beginning today, "Tom and Jerry" start in

**John Wayne**

the Deseret News exclusively in this area. Their escapades, appealing to young and old alike, have come in for considerable Academy Award attention, and now they're going to cavort in the News.

**Feb. 9, 1950**

## Man O' War Acclaimed Best Horse

**By JAMES F. FOWLER**

MIAMI, Fla. (AP) — Whenever horse lovers meet sooner or later the talk turns to the greatest of them all, the immortal Man O'War. They talk of his 20 victories in 21 starts; of his five record breaking races and of the only time he was beaten, by a horse named Upset...

Samuel D. Riddle, now 88 years old, and still racing horses, smiled as he was told Man O'War had been picked the horse of the half century.

"They're right," he beamed, "they picked the right horse."

**Aug. 16, 1950**

## Teacher Pinch Seen For Areas in Utah

Utah school districts are having difficulty lining up kindergarten, first, and second grade teachers, N. Blaine Winters, state director of teacher personnel said Wednesday.

He said that although the teacher supply is fairly good for the higher grades and high schools, there is a shortage of high school home economics teachers.

**Sept. 17, 1951**

## Utah Counts 49 New Polio Cases

Polio continued a swift upward trend in Utah last week with 49 new cases reported, more than three-fifths of which struck in Salt Lake City and County.

The total number of cases climbed to 331, higher for the month than in the state's disastrous epidemic of 1943. Twenty-six deaths from polio have been recorded for the year, already higher than the 24 during the 1943 epidemic.

**Sept. 21, 1951**

## No Romance, Colleen Avers

**By MAXINE MARTZ**

Colleen Kay Hutchins, in her role as "Miss America," set Salt Lake reporters straight on any romance in her life.

"There just isn't anyone," the stately blue-eyed blonde declared at a press conference Thursday evening at the Newhouse Hotel.

She said that's what she told eastern reporters, but sometimes they "made things up."

**(She posed with her brother, Mel Hutchins, who rated All-American honors at BYU in basketball.)**

**Sept. 23, 1951**

## Ground Broken For New Los Angeles LDS Temple

**By HENRY A. SMITH**

LOS ANGELES — Groundbreaking for the Los Angeles Temple of the Church of Jesus Christ of Latter-day Saints took place Saturday noon under the direction of the First Presidency.

The ceremonies conducted at the temple site, at Santa Monica Boulevard and Selvy Avenue, Westwood, signaled the start of construction on the imposing edifice, which has been projected for more than a decade. It is a continuation of development of the property acquired by the Church in 1937, which was begun with the erection of the Beverly Hills chapel.

President David O. McKay was in charge of the groundbreaking and dedicatory exercises. ...

**Agriculture Secretary Ezra Taft Benson**

**Nov. 24, 1952**

## Elder Benson Named Agriculture Secretary

**From AP, UP and INS Wire Services**

NEW YORK — President-elect

Eisenhower Monday announced the appointment of Elder Ezra Taft Benson of the Council of the Twelve of the Church of Jesus Christ of Latter-day Saints to be secretary of agriculture in his cabinet.

Elder Benson of Salt Lake City is a former official of the National Council of Farmer Co-operatives.

The 53-year-old churchman was a supporter of Sen. Robert A. Taft's campaign for the Republican presidential nomination.

**June 2, 1953**

## Britain Crowns Elizabeth Queen

WESTMINSTER ABBEY, LONDON (INS) — Elizabeth II — touchingly young and lovely — was crowned Queen of Britain Tuesday under the fascinated gaze of 4-year-old Prince Charles, who himself may ascend the throne some day in this same abbey and with the same ancient rituals.

The queen — resplendent and regal in golden garments — must have appeared strange and awesome even to her own son at the moment the Archbishop of Canterbury placed the great crown of St. Edward on her shining head.

**Prince's Face Grave**

The young prince stood erect in the royal box, his hands clasped before him and his chubby face grave, as the crowning ceremony ended at 12:34 p.m. (4:34 a.m. MST) and a triumphant "God save the Queen!" roared from the throats of assembled noblemen and women from every corner of his mother's realm.

**Nov. 11, 1953**

## Idaho Boy, 11, Lives — Thanks to S.L. Medic

Thanks to the skill of a Salt Lake surgeon and his assistants, an 11-year-old boy, whose heart stopped beating for 28 minutes during an operation, was on his way home to Idaho Falls, Ida., Wednesday.

Robert Hudson's heart stopped beating while he was undergoing an operation at the LDS Hospital on Oct. 20 to correct a heart defect he had had since birth. The heart then went into a disordered type of movement called ventricular fibrillation.

The surgeon performing the operation pumped the heart with his hand to keep blood flowing to the brain, and during the 28 minutes, 21 shocks of electricity were sent to the fibrillation.

Feb. 17, 1954

## Ice Cream Popularity Shows Rise in Winter

Plain vanilla still is the odds-on favorite ice cream flavor in Utah despite competition from a growing number of yummy mixtures.

But whatever the flavor, Utahns now are consuming 20 per cent more ice cream in the wintertime than before the war. In fact, they are eating only one-third less ice cream in January than in July....

It is estimated that Utahns will consume more than 12 tons of cherries during February, mostly in the form of cherry vanilla ice cream.

Feb. 18, 1954

## Rock-Throwing Korea G.I.s Riot In Eagerness To Ogle Marilyn

WITH MARILYN MONROE IN KOREA (UP) — Stone-flinging American soldiers rioted Thursday in their eagerness to see actress Marilyn Monroe and one infantryman was trampled by a pushing mob.

**Marilyn Monroe**

Six thousand soldiers of the U. S. 45th Division staged the wildest demonstration yet seen in Miss Monroe's three-day "Something for the Boys" tour of Korea.

Dec. 15, 1954

Douglas R. Stringfellow's startling confession that his war record with the OSS was a hoax was, almost without question, the top local news story of the year during 1954.

Most Utahns vividly remember the night of Oct. 16

when the Republican congressman confessed that his story of serving on a secret mission with the OSS during World War II was a hoax.

Dec. 25, 1954

## Wars Absent From World Scene Today

**United Press**

This Christmas Day finds the world at peace and the fear of a third world war becoming less acute.

There may be a skirmish between the Nationalists and the Communists off the coast of China. But for the first time in many years there is no real war.

The unity of the free, God-fearing nations against the menace of atheistic Communism has never been so firm. Issues which divided the free nations and embittered their relations have been settled.

March 7, 1955

## Shock Waves Shake Homes In Salt Lake

ATOP MT. CHARLESTON, NEV. (UP) — The most powerful atomic weapon of the 1955 test series was exploded in the Nevada desert Monday with a roaring flash that shook houses some 370 miles away in Salt Lake City and lit the skies over an 1,800-miles diameter in 10 Western states.

The nuclear device, which could have been the prototype of a warhead for an intercontinental guided missile, was triggered on schedule in the predawn darkness of the Nevada proving ground...

Residents in Salt Lake City, 370 airline miles distant, complained the shock wave rattled their houses.

With its customary reticence the Atomic Energy Commission refused to disclose the exact yield of the device.

March 7, 1955

## U.S. Asks Reckoning by April 15

If you bought and sold penny uranium stocks during the "splurge" of 1954 you must reckon with Uncle Sam on or before April 15, the Bureau of Internal Revenue said Monday.

You must list your gains (or losses) on your income tax return.

There is a special form, schedule D, to be filled out and returned along with schedule 1040.

April 5, 1955

## Churchill Steps Down

LONDON (UP) — Sir Winston Churchill, the grand old man of the empire, officially resigned as prime minister of Great Britain Tuesday.

Tears glistened in his eyes as he presented his resignation to the Queen.

Sir Anthony Eden will be his successor.

Churchill, who battled and defeated every enemy save the relentless passage of time, presented his resignation to Queen Elizabeth II at Buckingham Palace.

April 22, 1955

## Utah Starts Polio 'Shots' As Salk Vaccine Arrives

Enough anti-polio vaccine to immunize 47,000 children arrived in Salt Lake City by air Friday morning and immediately was started on its way to all parts of the state.

The cargo of vaccine touched down on the Salt Lake Airport runway at 1 a.m. Friday after a flight from Parke-Davis & Co. in Detroit. It was brought in by United Air Lines.

Immediately after its arrival, bottles of the life-saving liquid were placed in the highway patrol cars and rushed to Sanpete and Summit counties for distribution Friday. Vaccine for the Tooele area was picked up by Dr. Tura Aldous, Tooele health doctor...

Shots will be started next Wednesday in Salt Lake City Schools.

**Liberace**

*Deseret News files*

July 12, 1955

## Liberace Dated August 9 in S.L.

Liberace, the smiling, wavy-haired pianist of television and the movies, is scheduled to present a concert in Salt Lake City Aug. 9.

The event is scheduled at the Fairgrounds Grandstand under aegis of Eugene Jelesnik, Salt Lake violinist...

He was one of the most successful artists to appear in a Las Vegas night spot. For a two-week schedule, he drew $40,000 per week.

His Nevada appearances were held coincidentally with the atomic bomb blast tests...

Oct. 1, 1955

## Young Movie Star Killed In Sports Car Smashup

HOLLYWOOD (UP) — Speed-loving James Dean, Hollywood's latest bobby sox idol, was killed Friday night in the head-on collision of his $7,000 German sports car and another automobile.

Dean, 24, was driving from Hollywood to a road race in northern California at the time of his death on a darkening highway 28 miles east of Paso Robles. A car driven by Donald Turnispeed of Tulare, Calif., a 23-year-old student, turned left in front of Dean's light aluminum Porsche Spyder and the two automobiles crashed head-on.

Dean died instantly ... Dean had only last week finished work on "Giant," one of the top pictures of the year. His co-stars, Elizabeth Taylor and Rock Hudson, and director George Stevens heard the news as they watched the day's "rushes" in a projection room at Warner studios.

**James Dean**

*Deseret News files*

Oct. 7, 1955

## Utahns Among 66 Air Victims

MEDICINE BOW PEAK, WYO. — Rescue teams Friday brought the first bodies down from the summit of this mountain peak where a giant United Air Lines DC4 crashed Thursday, killing 66 persons.

A human chain of rescue workers passed other broken bodies along the rock-strewn slopes below the fire-scarred cliff where the Salt Lake City-bound air coach crashed Thursday morning.

The 63 passengers and three crew members aboard the plane, including 21 Utahns, perished when the westbound air coach crashed head-on into a sheer rock peak less than 50 feet from the crest.

It was the nation's worst civilian air crash in history.

... The Utah victims included five members of the Salt Lake Tabernacle Choir returning home from the recent trip to Europe.

**Oct. 7, 1955**

It's possible that bows and arrows will become popular in modern warfare.

They will for sure if Jimmy Holmberg, 10, has his way. Jimmy, the son of Mr. and Mrs. Durmont Holmberg, 3234 Redwood Rd., thinks he has found a new way to bring archery back into the Army.

"Why throw hand grenades when you can shoot them with a bow and arrow?" asks Jimmy. And to prove his point, he has his own model for demonstration.

**April 19, 1956**

## Grace, Prince Married In Church Rites

MONACO (UP) — Beautiful Grace Kelly and a nervous Prince Rainier III became man and wife in the eyes of the church as well as the law Thursday. The bashful prince had to have help in placing the wedding band on Grace's finger…

Naval armed forces of the United States, France, Italy and Great Britain stood rigidly at attention along the route which Grace and her father rode to the cathedral.

**April 27, 1956**

## Negroes Extend Boycott Of Buses

MONTGOMERY, ALA. (UP) — An estimated 5,000 cheering Negroes voted unanimously Thursday night to continue their boycott of Montgomery's buses in the face of the city's threat to bring court action against the bus operators for removing the color bar.

A shouting throng which packed the Bay St. Baptist

Church roared its approval of a resolution calling for continuance of the boycott, now in its 21st week, until desegregation is officially okayed.

**Oct. 30, 1957**

HOLLYWOOD (INS) — Elvis Presley's ample sideburns bristled today in defense of his rock 'n' roll cult against a blast from Frank Sinatra.

Sinatra, in a Paris magazine article, said rock 'n' rollers were "cretinous goons" — in the class of idiots, according to Webster.

Presley called a news conference to express righteous wrath over Sinatra's description of rock 'n' roll as "the most brutal, ugly, degenerate, vicious form of expression, it has been my misfortune to hear."

Presley declared:

"It's the greatest music ever, and it will continue to be so. I like it, and I'm sure many other persons feel the same way. I also admit it's the only thing I can do."

*Deseret News files*

**Elvis Presley**

**Aug. 27, 1958**

## Solons Vote Power to Shut School

LITTLE ROCK, ARK. (UPI) — The Arkansas Legislature Wednesday overwhelmingly approved bills to close any school faced with forcible integration and rushed to put them into law Thursday.

The votes empowering Gov. Orval Faubus to defy federal laws integrating Negroes in Arkansas schools were unanimous in the state Senate — 33 to 0….

Then the two chambers recessed briefly and prepared to exchange their bills later in the day and push through final passage Monday about the same time the U.S. Supreme Court meets to hear arguments on the delay in opening Little Rock's Central High School.

**Dec. 24, 1958**

## Freedom Given 72 Inmates For Christmas

Seventy-two prisoners in the Salt Lake City Jail will be given freedom on Christmas Day in the annual yuletide "kickout" granted by City Judge Arthur J. Mays.

Wednesday in police court, Salt Lake lawyer Roscoe Irvine, former city prosecutor, presented a motion to the court that the remainder of the jail sentences against 72 prisoners be suspended so that

they can spend Christmas out of jail.

Judge Mays granted the motion for amnesty.

**Feb. 6, 1959**

## Public To Have 'Say' Soon On Belt Route

A public hearing on the much discussed belt route circling Salt Lake County has been tentatively set for Feb. 27 by officials of the Utah State Road Commission…

Elmo R. Morgan, state director of highways … said that considerable criticism of the proposed route had prompted the commission to seek alternate routes from the San Francisco engineering firm that plotted the proposed location of the highway.

The belt route will circle the county and provide an emergency bypass to the new federal interstate system of highways that are now beginning construction.

**April 10, 1959**

## Astronauts Face Atlas 'Test Ride'

WASHINGTON (UPI) — Some or all of the seven Americans chosen as the first U.S. Astronauts will get a ride in the nose of an Atlas intercontinental ballistic missile over the South Atlantic as part of their

UPI Photo

America's first astronauts: Donald K. Slayton, Alan B. Shepard Jr., Walter M. Schirra Jr., Virgil I. Grissom, John H. Glenn Jr., Leroy G. Cooper Jr. and Malcolm S. Carpenter.

training…

To assure that every precaution is taken before the future spacemen even board an Atlas, animals first will be sent on the missile ride. Monkeys, dogs, pigs and possibly bears will be used in the tests.

The seven "Mercury Astronauts," chosen above all others for the honor and the glory and the danger of being the first to carry their country's colors into space, were presented publicly Thursday for NASA.

The men — one Marine, three Navy and three Air Force test pilots — were described as the Americans best qualified for Project Mercury, as the manned satellite program is called.

## The world of the 1950s
### A TIMELINE

**1950**— First human kidney transplant is performed in Chicago.

**1950**— The U.N. building in New York is completed.

**1950**— World population is approximately 2.3 billion; the U.S. population is 150,697,999.

**1951**— 22nd Amendment passes, limiting president to two terms.

**1951**— Peace treaty with Japan is signed.

**1951**— Color television introduced in the U.S.

**1952**— Albert Schweitzer wins the Nobel Peace Prize.

**1952**— Agatha Christie's "The Mousetrap," opens in London.

**1952**— The "Revised Standard Version" of the Bible is published for Protestants after 15 years' work by 32 scholars.

**1952**— The U.S. explodes the first hydrogen bomb at Eniwetok Atoll in the Pacific.

**1953**— Queen Elizabeth II crowned.

**1953**— USSR explodes a hydrogen bomb.

**1954**— Roger Bannister breaks the 4-minute mile, doing it in 3 minutes 59.4 seconds.

**1954**— IBM markets an electronic calculating machine for businesses.

**1954**— The Boeing 707, the U.S.'s first passenger jet, makes its maiden voyage.

**1954**— Ernest Hemingway wins the Nobel Prize for literature.

**1954**— Dr. Jonas Salk starts inoculating Pittsburgh schoolchildren against polio.

**1955**— Protests in Montgomery, Ala., against segregated city bus lines.

**1956**— Prince of Monaco marries Grace Kelly from Philadelphia.

**1956**— Martin Luther King leads the fight against segregation.

**1956**— Boxer Rocky Marciano retires undefeated, after 49 fights.

**1957**— Teamsters Union is expelled from the AFL-CIO.

**1957**— Dr. Seuss writes "The Cat in the Hat."

**1957**— Leonard Bernstein's musical "West Side Story" opens in New York.

**1957**— Major John Glenn Jr. sets a speed record from California to New York in a jet.

**1958**— The complete works of Tolstoy are published in the USSR (90 volumes).

**1958**— Van Cliburn, from the U.S., wins the Tchaikovsky piano competition in Moscow.

**1958**— National Aeronautics and Space Administration is established.

**1959**— Fidel Castro becomes premier of Cuba.

**1959**— Hawaii becomes the 50th state.

**1959**— Synthetic diamonds are produced.

**1959**— 1.25 million people have been killed in U.S. auto accidents (more than have died in all U.S. wars combined).

# Atomic energy:
## Boom amidst the fallout

**The Atomic Age was definitely a mixed blessing for Utah. It brought a new industry, but it also brought radioactive fallout.**

I n the '50s, nuclear power seemed about to come into its own, with the promise of hundreds of peaceful uses aside from its civilization-crunching capabilities. And the raw material of atomic power — uranium ore — could be found in Utah.

The mineral had been mined in Utah earlier to provide raw material for the research of Pierre and Marie Curie but had dribbled out as that need ended. But uranium came back in the '50s. The Atomic Energy Commission offered a $10,000 bonus to prospectors who found new pockets of high-grade uranium-laced pitchblende ore, along with other incentives such as production support and high prices.

Charles A. Steen was one of many who went in search of a uranium bonanza. A 1953 News article told the story:

**DESERET NEWS,** *Dec. 10 1953: "He dreamed because he was a geologist-prospector on the*

*trail of uranium, and he had a wife and four kids holed up in a shack with not enough to eat. The actual discovery of the mine came dramatically. Steen's (mining) claims were on ground that the AEC had already looked over and rejected because it felt the uranium ore was too low grade to mine in the wilderness. Steen figured a richer vein lay 200 feet below ...*

*He hired a drilling rig with money scraped up by his mother and (R.M.) Barrett. The rig broke in the first hole. Steen tossed a few unlikely looking core samples in the jeep and headed to town to see if he could scrape up money to recover the drill tools. On the way, he found a friend testing samples with a Geiger counter. The ticking was so feeble that Steen bet that even his samples would make a better showing.*

*The test of his samples made the counter tick crazily, Steen said. Charlie Steen had found a million dollar uranium deposit.*

Southern Utah boomed. Salt Lakers invested in a frenzy of penny uranium stocks. Mines and mills sprang up to fill new nuclear orders for atomic submarines and power plants as well as bombs. Fortunes were made — and lost — in a rags-to-riches-to-rags cycle. Moab earned the sobriquet "Uranium Capital of the World." By 1955, around 800 mines on the Colorado Plateau were producing uranium. There was an ominous use for it.

**DESERET NEWS,** *Jan. 11, 1951: WASHINGTON (UP) — The Atomic Energy Commission announced Thursday it will stage test atomic explosions in the country at the bombing and gunnery range near Las Vegas, Nev.*

*When the first atomic test blasts are to be set off was not divulged.*

*When they are, they will be the first atomic explosions in the United States since the first A-bomb test at Alamogordo, N. M., on July 18, 1945.*

Officialdom continued to assure Utahns and Nevadans that all would be well:

**DESERET NEWS,** *Jan 19, 1955: LAS VEGAS, Nev. (UP) — Utah and Nevada residents have nothing to fear from next month's nuclear tests at the Nevada Proving Grounds.*

*This was the assurance Wednesday of a group of Atomic Energy Commission scientists. The scientists began a tour Wednesday of Utah and Nevada cities, stretching from Las Vegas to Salt Lake City, to brief residents on the spring series tests to be held at Yucca and Frenchman's Flats.*

*Although fallout from nuclear explosions has been a constant problem to the AEC, none of it has ever reached a fraction of the amount needed to produce any physical change in the human body, the scientists said. However, as a precautionary measure, residents of St. George were urged to stay indoors for several hours after one test last year because one of the clouds from the test site passed overhead.*

By 1955, some people were convinced that the dirty air that followed each test blast was not healthful. The first suits against the AEC began to hit the courts:

**DESERET NEWS,** *March 1, 1955: Five suits involving claims of $176,964 have been filed against the government by Iron County sheepmen. The plaintiffs, in complaints filed in Federal District Court in Salt Lake City, allege that they suffered losses as a result of the*

*1952 and 1953 atomic blasts on the Nevada Proving grounds.*

*Their herds were ranging within 60 to 80 miles of the probable point of detonation, the complaints maintain.*

*May 2, 1955: WASHINGTON (UP) — The Atomic Energy Commission has advised Congress three suits have been filed against the government claiming "personal injury caused by radioactive fallout" from the atomic tests in Nevada...*

*It said the commission's medical experts deny the damage claims...*

*All three were filed before the current series of tests.*

Gradually, even the government began to concede that atomic fallout might not be as benign as it had claimed:

**A test in 1957 lights up the Nevada desert.**

**DESERET NEWS,** *Oct. 26, 1957: A study of possible radioactive fallout danger in Utah will be made by the U. S. Public Health Service.*

*Lynn M. Thatcher, director of the Bureau of Sanitation, State Department of Health, said Thursday that officials have agreed to undertake the investigation in Utah...*

*He explained that federal health workers are presently making a complete evaluation of results of fallout in the state during the past year.*

*"It's a new science and there are not many experts in the field," Mr. Thatcher said. It will be a chance to get some of these experts into Utah."*

Over the next few decades, the full story emerged. Government agencies admitted to concealing evidence about the health effects of fallout. Legislation provided compensation for those hurt by fallout. As a new century dawned, arguments still continued about how and with whom to share the money.

Utah State Historical Society

UPI Photo

UPI Photo

One of the largest mushroom clouds ever seen from Las Vegas rises 40,000 feet over the Nevada Test Site, 65 miles away, on June 24, 1957. The bomb was dropped from a helium balloon. Above, a geiger counter to measure radiation.

# Korea:
## At war again

**A**merica's determination to stop the spread of communism found the nation again at war in the 1950s, this time in the troubled Asian country of Korea. Fighting under the umbrella of the United Nations, the United States provided 90 percent of the troops committed to the conflict.

**Purple Heart**

**DESERET NEWS EXTRA**

**U. S. PLANES, WARSHIPS ORDERED TO AID KOREA**

House Opens Debate on Tax Measure

Truman Takes Stand Against Red Invaders

ISSUES COMMAND

Bombers Enter Into Korean W

---

**DESERET NEWS,** *June 30, 1950: WASHINGTON (AP) — President Truman Friday authorized the use of American ground troops in Korea. The President announced he has authorized: The United States Air Force to fly specific military missions into Northern Korea whenever necessary; a naval blockade of the entire Korean coast; Gen. Douglas MacArthur "to use certain supporting ground units" in the efforts to turn back the Communist invaders of Southern Korea.*

Utahns again rose to the occasion:

**DESERET NEWS,** *Aug. 19, 1950: Saturday morning, Utah sent its first military units into federal services. In Salt Lake City, in Logan, in Cedar City and in a dozen smaller communities, men answered early muster calls, in uniform again after five years.*

*No one knew how soon those uniforms would go into storage again.*

**DESERET NEWS,** *Jan. 16, 1951: Utah's first two Air Force Reserve Units were alerted for active duty Monday. The units are the 497th General and Technical Supply Squadrons, based at Hill Air Force Base. Some 240 local men and their families will be affected, Air Force officials said.*

*Alert orders received Monday indicated the two units will go into active duty Feb. 15. They will go to Kelly AFB, San Antonio, Texas … The Air Force has authorized both unit commanders to recruit additional personnel who already have military skills.*

Many World War II veterans found themselves on the lines again. Utah's Army National Guard also provided

---

manpower, with 2,070 officers and men — almost 62 percent of the Utah Guard's complement — sent to Korea.

And more Utahns were added to the lists of those who have given the ultimate sacrifice in behalf of their country:

**DESERET NEWS,** *Jan. 15, 1951: Another Utah man has been killed and three Mountain West men are missing in action in Korea, the Department of Defense reported Monday. Two more have been wounded:*

*Killed in Action:*

*PFC. Burt Ervin, USMC, father of Miss Joyce M. Ervin, 17 Wilson Ave., Murray.*

*He was killed in action in Korea on Dec. 8, his daughter was informed. Private Ervin made his home in Murray for the past several years. He was employed by the Denver and Rio Grande Western Railroad. Temporary burial will be in the locality where death occurred, according to an official telegram …*

Of the 7,564 Utahns who served in Korea, 436 paid the ultimate sacrifice. The state also contributed its share of heroes, often at a terrible cost:

**DESERET NEWS,**
*Jan. 11, 1951: The wife of a Salt Lake City lieutenant reported missing in action in Korea returned Wednesday evening from Washington, D.C. "completely overwhelmed" by ceremonies in which she received the Congressional Medal of Honor on behalf of her husband.*

*Mrs. Lavon Henry, 1045 Harvard Ave., was the recipient of the second top medal to be presented in the Korean war. She still clings to the hope that her husband, Lt. Frederick H. Henry, is alive…*

*Lt. Henry was reported missing after staying behind alone to cover the retreat of his men from advancing Communist troops.*

Many Utahns were

**Truman Braces Self For Ouster Defense**

Constitution, Laws Cited by President

GOP Leaders Talk About Impeachment

---

affected by the war in a particular way through their membership in the LDS Church:

**DESERET NEWS,** *Jan. 16, 1951: Clearance from draft boards must be obtained before the First Presidency of The Church of Jesus Christ of Latter-day Saints will issue any calls to men between the ages of 19 to 25 to fill missions.*

*Young men of draft age who have received calls to fill missions, but who have not reported to the missionary home, now must obtain clearance from draft boards, President (David. O.) McKay said.*

Another more notable hero fell from favor during the course of the Korean conflict:

**DESERET NEWS,** *April 11, 1951: WASHINGTON (UP) — President Truman Wednesday dismissed General of the Army Douglas MacArthur from all Far East commands on charges of failing to support United States and United Nations plans to defeat Communism.*

*Mr. Truman cited against MacArthur the law and the Constitution. He named Lt. Gen. Matthew B. Ridgway to succeed MacArthur at once.*

*The Truman administration braced itself against an expected blast from Tokyo and political explosions here at home. Most Republicans in Congress immediately called the action a blunder. Democrats were prepared to back the president.*

---

UPI photo

**Soldiers of the 40th Division, which included many National Guardsmen, keep a watchful eye from their snowy bunker where they man a forward machine gun post.**

# The good life of the '50s

War had not been eliminated; injustice had not been overcome; mass destruction posed a dramatic threat. But for all that, most people who lived through the 1950s looked back on them with fondness. For many, the decade came to epitomize the good life.

A booming economy, varied consumer goods and services, new fields of entertainment, optimistic plans for the future, warm and fuzzy holidays — that's what the '50s were all about.

**DESERET NEWS**, *July 15, 1955: Probably everyone who has driven out in the suburbs and marveled at the way costly, spacious new homes are sprawling over the foothills, or at the way every second car on the highway seems to be this year's model, has asked himself the same question:*

*"Where on earth is all the money coming from?"*

*Well, part of that answer lies in the fact that for the first time in the nation's history, personal income is at a rate of more than 300 billion dollars a year. Civilian employment in May was at an all-time high of 62,703,000 jobs. Industrial production is also at a peak.*

While some economists worried about a growing debt level as buying on the installment plan became popular, many consumers reveled in the selection and choice they had.

**DESERET NEWS**, *Feb. 10, 1950: Featuring longer body length and increased room, the new 1950 Cadillacs were scheduled to go on display Saturday in the showrooms of the Fred A. Carleson Company, 535 South*

Main. Company officials said the new line features the widest changes in the General Motors line.

**DESERET NEWS**, *Feb. 11, 1950: Introduction of a new automatic dishwasher in stores in Provo, Logan, Ogden and Salt Lake City… will be made next week by Sears Roebuck and Company… . The new machine features a washing operation, two clear water rinses and an electrical drying operation.*

In 1951, Safeway shoppers could buy beef roast for 69 cents a pound; golden ripe bananas, 13 cents a pound; delicious preserves, 49 cents for a 31-oz. jar; Heinz cream of tomato soup, 10 cans for $1; sugar, $10.10 for 100 pounds; and Quaker Oats for 36 cents.

At Sears Roebuck and Co., shoppers could buy a 7.7 cu. ft. Coldspot refrigerator for $179.95 ($27.50 down, $10.50 a month); a 20-inch TV for $279.98; a Kenmore vacuum cleaner for $44.88; and a Kenmore gas range for $88.88 ($13.50 down and $5 a month) .

In 1953, shoppers might be tempted by Jack & Jill Cat Food, "so economical, so handy"; Blue Bonnet margarine, offering "Flavor! Nutrition! Economy!"; or a "new, finer, nonfat dry milk" from Sego that provided milk at about "9 cents a quart."

In 1954, a popular product was Wonder's Brown 'N Serve Rolls, "guaranteed foolproof!" And by then, another favorite was going strong:

**DESERET NEWS**, *Dec. 20, 1954: The Clover Club Company started in a small automobile showroom with four sacks of potatoes, hard work by the couple and financial sacrifice. (Mrs. Sanders sold her prized piano to help finance the project.)*

*Today the company is housed in a huge factory in Kaysville, and a $100,000 addition nearing completion. The new*

addition, to be used to store potatoes for conditioning, will hold 40 carloads of spuds.

Another American tradition began. By 1958, Harmans Cafe had "4 take-home locations" where you could buy a bucket of Kentucky Fried Chicken for $3.50 and "Give Mom a break!"

What were Salt Lakers doing with their spare time now that they had all these convenience foods and labor-saving devices?

Movies were still popular. In April, 1954, Walt Disney's "Living Desert," in its ninth week at the Tower Theater, set a new "continuous run record in a single theater for pictures in Salt Lake." "The Robe" had played in Salt Lake for seven weeks, but at two theaters. Also passed were records of films such as "The Jolson Story" and "From Here to Eternity."

By the end of the decade, Salt Lakers had a popular new way to watch movies: the drive-in. In 1958, places such as the Autorium, Woodland, Motor-Vu, Park-Vu and Oakhills Drive-In were showing "Tank Battalion," "Proud Rebel," "Desire Under the Elms" and "Ten North Frederick."

On the other hand, why go to the movies, when you could bring entertainment into your very home? This was the decade of ever-increasing television.

**DESERET NEWS**, *Feb. 12, 1950: KSL-TV will begin afternoon programming two days a week (Tuesdays and Thursdays) beginning Feb. 14, it was announced today by Lennox Murdoch, in charge of KSL-TV operations.*

*In addition to the new afternoon schedule, KSL-TV will go on the air one-half hour earlier at 7 p.m. Monday through Thursday. A combination of highly colorful children's programs including "Uncle Roscoe and His Story Sketch Book" will occupy this early time.*

*Sept. 21, 1951: KSL has begun preliminary construction on a mountain-*

Fess Parker, 'Davy Crockett'

Deseret News files

With its heavy chrome and swooping tail fins, the 1959 Cadillac Coupe was symbolic of the excess of the 1950s.

Deseret News files

**CHUCK ROAST**

**Beef Roast** U. S. Graded Shoulder Cut    lb. **69c**

**Pork Liver** Rich in vitamins and so tasty served with sliced bacon    lb. **35c**

| | | | | |
|---|---|---|---|---|
| **Pork Roast** Boston Butts | lb. 55c | **Bacon** Morrel's Pride | lb. pkg. 59c |
| **Boiling Beef** U. S. Graded Tender Plates | lb. 39c | **Fryers** A Grade, Pan Ready, Fresh or Frozen | lb. 69c |
| **Pork Chops** Loin Ends | lb. 63c | **Whiting** Tasty Freshwater Fish | 1½ lb. 39c |

**Hams** Armour's Shankless and Skinless Butt Shank   lb. **59c**   Center Slice Piece   Lb. **98c**

top television site that will provide television service to two-thirds of the homes of Utah, it was announced Friday by Ivor Sharp, executive vice president... "This will give KSL the highest television transmitter in the world — approximately 9,000 feet above sea level," he said. "From this height, an excellent signal will be beamed directly into Ogden, Logan, Provo and many other towns."

When it came to informing readers about what was happening on television, the Deseret News had the redoubtable Howard Pearson:

**DESERET NEWS,** *Dec. 16, 1954: A new hero probably came into being for American youngsters Wednesday night. His name is Davy Crockett. He came to life through the dramatic genius of Walt Disney, whose Disneyland has been surpassing championship fights and other highly rated programs on television.*

*July 12, 1955: Lawrence Welk and his Champagne Music (Ch. 2) bowed in over the weekend and we've heard a lot of praise for the free-flowing rhythm, the fine entertainment quality.*

**Walt Disney opens Disneyland.**

*April 23, 1956: The shakeup season has hit television. Three long noted personalities are bowing off their programs either by choice or request. They are Arthur Godfrey, Jack Paar and Robert Q. Lewis.*

*Oct. 4, 1957: Erle Stanley Gardner, the noted mystery writer who took his first plunge into television with his Perry Mason series (Ch. 5) last Saturday, starts his second show tonight. The new series is based on his Court of Last Resort.*

If television gave the country a new

common denominator, uniting us culturally, another development of the '50s would unite us physically. In his State of the Union address on Jan. 4, 1956, President Eisenhower renewed his appeal for "a big highway building program," which he said, "is even more urgent this year."

**DESERET NEWS,** *June 28, 1956: By 1970, Utah will be criss-crossed by splendid four and six lane divided highways. This is the prime conclusion to be drawn from a study of what the new 13-year road building programs just passed by Congress means to the state. The state now has some 700 miles of interstate highways and the bill provides for a rebuilding of an amount equal to this mileage.*

So, Utah, you have a brand new highway system. Where are you headed? How about to Disneyland. Linda Liddle was one of the first Utahns to visit this new park:

**DESERET NEWS,** *July 19, 1955: Daddy says I am one of the very first children from Salt Lake City ever to see Disneyland, and that I ought to tell the other children all about it.*
*If I were writing this for California children, I guess I would be supposed to use words like colossal and stupendous, whatever they mean. But for Salt Lake children I'm not going to use words like that, because, for one reason, Daddy and I think it would be exaggerating a bit...*

That first year, admission to the park was $1 for adults and 50 cents for children. "Individual rides will be 25 and 35 cents with a 50 cent tab being charged for the rocketship to the moon."
When it came to magic, Disneyland had it. But so did holidays. And nothing was quite like the Christmases of the '50s, with all those wonderful toys.
In 1951, a full-page ad from Montgomery Ward offered a furnished metal doll house for $3.97, a sparkling Disney train for $3.77, a set of wood tinkertoys for 87 cents, and a Snoopy Sniffer dog for $1.97.

**Disneyland, 1955**

In 1954, Grand Central was selling Lincoln Logs for $1.88, Royal Racer sleds for $2.98 (40-inch) and $3.95 (45-inch). An ad from ZCMI offered 32 gift ideas for $1. Among them: men's hankies, sofa pillows, Cannon towels, Viewmaster reels (3 for $1), bow ties, tray bibs and girls' purses.
In 1958, bikes costs $16.99 at Penney's, where you could also get a tricycle for $10, molded rubber basketballs for $1.99 and a special-purchase walking doll for $1.
Letters to Santa printed by the paper revealed the hopes and dreams of the children:

**DESERET NEWS,** *Dec. 19, 1958: Dear Santa: I am 7 years old would you please bring me a tiney tears doll I would like to have something else if you would like to bring it to me...*
*Dear Santa: There are 4 of us and we can each have one thing. Casey wants a chemistry set. Delta Lyn wants a game, Vernie wants a electrict train and our baby Loralyn wants a rubber dollie. We are real good and will be even better if you'll bring us something else as a surprise...*
*Dear Santa: I want a doll with clothes for her and a toy mouse and some clothes for me and everything you want to bring me. And some nutty putty.*

The papers of the '50s were filled with wishes for peace, accounts of Christmas entertainment, heart-warming tales of good deeds, winners of lighting contests, Christmas I Remember Best stories and more. Christmas then, as now, was universal and timeless.

Disney's "Mickey Mouse Club" was so successful that the company held periodic talent searches such as this one to find new Mouseketeers. Above, Lawrence Welk's musical show was so popular it still appears in reruns.

# Coping with rock 'n' roll

Elvis Presley was going to be on the Ed Sullivan show, and it rated a brief paragraph in the TV listings and a tiny picture. When TV editor Howard Pearson watched the show, he was more caught up in watching both his TV sets at the same time than in Elvis. First, there was both a ballgame and a tennis match:

**DESERET NEWS,** *Sept. 10, 1956: That wasn't as confusing as when 8 p.m. came and we wanted to see both the Ed Sullivan show, minus Sullivan, and the four gubernatorial candidates… Things started out all right.*

*That wonderful Charles Laughton introduced Sullivan's show and Del Leeson, KTVI's efficient announcer, introduced the candidates. By the time Elvis Presley had sung a number, I was a little confused whether J. Bracken Presley was talking about education in Utah or Elvis Lee was going to get through "Go, Man, Go" without a breakdown. And a person just had to keep both sets tuned on and watch both of them. There was always the hope that on the Sullivan show Presley might bend backwards so far he could not straighten up…*

Cultural historians would look back on the Sullivan show appearance as one of the huge milestones in the rock 'n' roll era. Didn't we know what a big deal it was?

Not then. It is safe to say that Elvis was not a favorite among the over-30 generation, who feared for the morals of that day's teenagers. The phenomenon was enough to merit a harsh editorial:

**DESERET NEWS,** *Sept. 28, 1956: Whose fault is it that day-after-day Elvis Presley continues to break more records than Rudy Vallee, Bing Crosby, Frank Sinatra and Johnny Ray ever did individually or collectively?*

*Is Presley's popularity a stinging indictment of the tastes of American teenagers? We think so. His popularity is not based primarily on his songs; it is based on his sensual, his vulgar,*

Elvis Presley, who became the "King of Rock 'n' Roll, rehearses in 1956 for his appearance on The Ed Sullivan Show.

UPI Photo

*obscene and revolting gyrations and physical mannerisms that make every conscientious parent cringe.*

Even though psychiatrists tried to analyze it — "they say he represents a revolt against parental authority and a symbol for many female fans" — and film producers tried to explain it — "So far as teen-agers are concerned, Elvis is what I call a safety valve," David Weisbart said. "By that I mean they can scream, holler, articulate and let go of their emotions when they see him perform" — no one could deny his power.

**DESERET NEWS,** *Nov. 14, 1956: Elvis Presley is rocking up the merchandising world with as much impact as he rocks 'n' rolls the bobbysox set. The 21-year-old ex-truck driver has endorsed 51 products which his business agent predicts will gross more than $20 million this year — a boom that would dwarf the Davy Crockett craze.*

And Salt Lakers were not immune.

*Nov. 10, 1956: Ol' Elvis Presley ain't nothin' but a houn' dog.*

*He was in Salt Lake City at the Union Pacific station from 10:05 to 1:50 p.m. Friday night on a stopover enroute to Las Vegas, and he didn't let anybody know.*

*All that charm and personality just a wastin' at the station.*

*Two Salt Lakers showed up, however. Miss Lorraine Maszarenas, 465 Penny Ave., got a call from her sister in Green River Friday afternoon. "Get down to the station tonight," she screamed, "Elvis is on the train!"*

*Miss Maszarenas and a girl friend hustled on down expecting a milling crowd, but the side-burned idol was surrounded mostly by train passengers. Miss Maszarenas had this comment to make Saturday: "Ooooh! Is he good looking!"*

**Buddy Holly**

Deseret News files

Elvis, of course, was not the only name in lights.

*Mar. 20, 1957: A United Press survey of record sales disclosed that Elvis, after a 12-month run on top, now is the second hottest popular record artist in the nation. Harry Belafonte has moved to the number one position, thanks to the latest calypso fad.*

Particularly after Elvis was drafted into the army in October of 1957, his popularity began to wane. (His comeback was later.) Nor was he the only musician in town. Salt Lakers lined up for everyone from Liberace to the Lennon Sisters during the '50s, when musical tastes of the country took a decided and diverse twist away from the Big Band Era. And sometimes it was hard then to really tell what it all would mean later.

**DESERET NEWS,** *Feb. 4, 1959: MOORHEAD, Minn. (UPI) A troupe of rock 'n' roll performers went on with the show before 2,000 subdued teenagers Tuesday night despite the deaths of three of their stars in a plane crash.*

*The 13 troupe members who had arrived here by bus for a one night stand at first canceled their date in Moorhead. However, they later decided to honor their commitment in the tradition of showmanship.*

*The stars of the group — among the biggest names in rock 'n roll — and their pilot were killed Tuesday when their chartered plane crashed in an Iowa farm field near Clear Lake shortly after takeoff.*

*The singers killed were Ritchie Valens, 17, a recording star billed as the "next Elvis Presley"; J.P. (The Big Bopper) Richardson, 26, and Buddy Holly, 21. The dead pilot was Roger Peterson, 21, Clear Lake.*

Didn't we know that was "the day the music died?"

# Beyond the sky and below the sea

**Humankind has always found new challenges to overcome, new mountains to climb. And the 1950s were no different:**

Mt. Everest

Thor Heyerdahl

Thor Heyerdahl's Ra I embarks.

**DESERET NEWS,** *June 2, 1953: (UP) — The British Union Jack waved Tuesday where man never had set foot before — atop 29,002-foot Mount Everest.*

*E.P. Hillary, a New Zealand beekeeper, and Tensing Brutia, a rugged Sherpa guide, reached the summit of the previously unconquered world's highest mountain last Friday and planted the British flag.*

*They sent down a signal that "all is well," that man finally had won his greatest physical victory over nature and the elements.*

*Col. H.J.C. Hunt, leader of the British expedition, immediately dispatched a runner to Katmandu, nearest town of Everest's dangerous slopes, with the glad news that the mission had been accomplished before Queen Elizabeth II's coronation. It took the runner three days to get here.*

So perhaps it's not too surprising that early reports didn't quite get all the names right. But there was no question that the world had found a new hero, who received a hero's welcome wherever he went:

**DESERET NEWS,** *Mar. 2, 1954: Lord Edmund P. Hillary, who along with Tenzing Norgay climbed to the roof of the world last May 29, made a brief stop at the Salt Lake Airport Tuesday morning.*

*The world-famous New Zealand mountaineer stopped at the airport for 25 minutes and enjoyed the "warm" sun with his wife on the*

*terminal ramp.*

*Asked how it felt to scale Mount Everest in the Himalayas and actually be on top of the world, Lord Hillary said simply, "We were pretty tired when we got there, but it felt jolly good."*

*The tall, rugged climbing expert, who along with Norgay only spent 15 minutes on Mount Everest, said the ascent was worth it.*

Heights were being conquered. And adventurous seamen were tackling the depths as well:

**DESERET NEWS,** *Aug. 25, 1958: (UPI) — The submarine Nautilus came home to a hero's welcome Monday with a new record under its belt and the Navy's controversial Rear Adm. Hyman Rickover aboard to share a nation's acclaim…*

*Cmdr. William Anderson, the daring skipper who took the nuclear sub on history's first voyage from Pacific to Atlantic under the North Pole, set a new Atlantic speed record for submarines on the voyage here from Europe. The Nautilus made it in six days, 11 hours and 55 minutes.*

One Utahn was aboard the Nautilus, Earl R. Diamond. With some help from the Deseret News, which arranged to get her a seat on an east-bound plane, his wife was able to get to New York to "dance tonight at a big party being given in New York City in honor of the Nautilus crew."

The atomic-powered Nautilus was about as modern as it got in those days. But Salt Lakers were fascinated by primitive seacraft as well.

Norwegian explorer Thor Heyerdahl sailed across the Pacific on a bamboo raft in 1947. In May 1951, the Deseret News carried a 14-part account of that journey — along with news that a full-length feature movie, "a photographic record of the trip," would be shown at the Studio Theater beginning June 1.

And throughout the decade, Salt Lakers, like the rest of the world, were fascinated by outer space — both real and imagined.

**DESERET NEWS,** *Dec. 16, 1954: (UP) — Pres. Eisenhower threw cold water Wednesday on the theory that "flying saucers" come from outer space.*

*He said an Air Force official, whom he trusted, told him some time ago that so-called "saucers" do not originate out of this world.*

*The President, who made the statement in reply to a news conference question, did not say whether he thinks "saucers" are real or where they might come from.*

*Oct. 5, 1957: (INS) — A new moon circles Saturday in the earth's heavens, placed there by Soviet scientists to open the Space Age… The satellite weighs 184 pounds and is 23 inches in diameter, according to the Russians. This is about the same size but nine times heavier than the full-size satellites planned by the U.S.*

*Oct. 5, 1957: A Bountiful radio "ham" believes he may be among the first to have heard signals from the Russian "moon" satellite.*

*Edward Ancell… said he turned to*

*the frequency at 1:23 a.m. Saturday and heard the signal for about three minutes.*

The Russians were first with their Sputnik, and for a time, it appeared the United States would not catch up:

**DESERET NEWS,** *Aug. 8, 1958: The United States made an unsuccessful reach for the moon Sunday morning with an 88-foot rocket. The effort was snuffed out 77 seconds and 10 miles from the launching pad. An explosion in the engine of the first stage destroyed the 52-ton rocket, scattering pieces into the Atlantic.*

But our time would come.

Sir Edmund P. Hillary

# Lifeblood
## of the desert

Often poised high above the river, workers tediously pieced together the dam that created Lake Powell.

*U.S. Bureau of Reclamation*

**F**rom the very first, Utahns realized the importance of water in this dry, arid climate. As large as it was, the Great Salt Lake was not much help because of the expense of removing salt and minerals. But a number of rivers ran through the state, and it was hard to see all that water going downstream without being used. Reservoirs, dam-building and reclamation were the new marching orders.

Congress hammered out plans for the Colorado; the Upper Colorado compact came in 1948, and in 1956 came the Colorado River Storage Project bill.

**DESERET NEWS,** *April 11, 1956: The Upper Colorado River Storage Project bill was signed into law Wednesday by President Eisenhower at Augusta, Ga., giving final authorization to a water system dreamed of for more than half a century...*

*Final authorization of the bill marks "an historic milestone in the annals of the Upper Basin states and of the nation," said Interior Secretary Douglas McKay... "Future generations will owe a debt of gratitude to the President and Congress for their conservation foresight in enacting this legislation."*

Indeed, it had been a long, hard haul to get to that point. Original plans called for dams to be built in Glen Canyon, Flaming Gorge and in Echo Park. The last one stirred a great deal of opposition.

Man's ingenuity and skill at Glen Canyon tamed the mighty Colorado and provided Utahns needed water for homes, agriculture, industry and recreation.

*Deseret News files*

**DESERET NEWS,** *Dec. 9, 1954: Representatives from the Upper Basin States will meet in Salt Lake City Friday to map plans for a national campaign geared to secure Congressional authorization of the Upper Colorado River Storage Project, including the controversial Echo Park Dam...*

*The state committees, which have the backing of the river commission, were set up to formulate a national publicity campaign "to sell" the proposed billion-dollar project.*

*George D. Clyde, director of the Utah Water and Power Board and also a member of the river commission, said the state committees will report Friday on money obtained so far for the national publicity campaign. Initial goal is $40,000, Mr. Clyde said.*

In the end, the grassroots efforts of the Aqualantes (water vigilantes) as they came to be known, succeeded. They lost the fight for Echo Park, but the other dams would provide Utah's water. With the bill signed, construction began that same year on Flaming Gorge and Glen Canyon.

**DESERET NEWS,** *May 6, 1961: The question: Is it desirable and feasible — and if so, how — to keep the water backing up behind Glen Canyon Dam from invading the Rainbow Bridge*

*National Monument?...*

*There is another argument, aside from dollars and cents, for letting the water back up to the Bridge. In the 51 years since Rainbow Bridge was discovered, an average of only 308 persons a year have seen it. With the tremendous recreational boating Lake Powell will bring, and with the opportunity of taking boats through the awesome gorges of Aztec and Bridge Creek canyons almost to the Bridge itself, tens of thousands of persons can be expected to see it each year.*

That view prevailed. Lake Powell began to fill. On Aug. 7, 1964, Lake Powell reached a milestone when it held 5.97 million acre feet of water — enough to test the electrical generators. But Flaming Gorge was finished first. Its dedication was cause for a great celebration.

First Lady Lady Bird Johnson joined local royalty, including Miss Navajo (Sarah Johnson) to dedicate Glen Canyon.

*Deseret News files*

**DESERET NEWS,** *Aug. 17, 1964: The First Lady of the United States, Mrs. Lyndon B. Johnson, Monday became the first lady in history to dedicate one of the West's huge reclamation dams.*

*Standing on a specially constructed platform atop a 502-foot pile of concrete, Mrs. Johnson Monday dedicated the $65 million Flaming Gorge complex...*

*In her dedicatory speech, Mrs. Johnson referred to the "spirit of the West" and the tendency of the pioneers to dream big and then set out to make those dreams come true.*

*She said John Wesley Powell, famed Colorado River explorer, envisioned a string of dams which would cause this arid land to flower.*

Two years later, Lady Bird was back:

**DESERET NEWS,** *Sept. 22, 1966: Mrs. Lyndon B. Johnson Thursday dedicated the Glen Canyon Dam — the seventh highest in the world — and said that it shows "our country is entering a new era of wise water conservation.*

*"Glen Canyon is not just a Colorado River dam," she declared in her prepared remarks. "It belongs to the nation. Many hopes were born because of Glen Canyon. Many hopes will be fulfilled because of it. Water is a vital commodity in the Southwest."...*

There would be battles ahead, Utah's Dixie Reclamation Project, and the long, drawn-out Central Utah Water Project among them. But for now, this "incredibly beautiful and creative work," as Lady Bird termed it, brought a lot of satisfaction.

*Deseret News files*

# Vietnam
## divides a nation
### 1960-1970

**A** t first almost everyone was supportive. The idealism of President Kennedy's pledge to "pay any price, bear any burden," in the cause of liberty still echoed in the land.

**DESERET NEWS,** *Aug. 4, 1964: The U.S. has no choice but to react swiftly and firmly to the attack made the other day by Communist North Vietnamese gunboats on the American destroyer Maddox.*

*This unprovoked attack in international waters was an act of war... Of course, Viet Nam is well worth saving. Unlike Laos, it has shown willingness to fight for its own freedom. Moreover, if South Viet Nam falls, the positions of neighboring Cambodia and Thailand might be rendered untenable.*

Communism was threatening; it was time to act.

**DESERET NEWS,** *Aug. 5, 1964: (UPI) — Senate leaders Wednesday cleared the way for approval Thursday of President Johnson's resolution voicing U.S. determination to take any steps necessary to keep peace in Southeast Asia.*

This would come to be known as the Gulf of Tonkin Resolution. Even then, the country sensed it had turned a corner. A UPI story gave an almost hour-by-hour account of Johnson's "Decision Day":

**DESERET NEWS,** *Aug. 5, 1967: (UPI) — President Johnson's day Tuesday began with easy conversation at breakfast about domestic policies and ended in tension near midnight when he told the nation that air attacks had been ordered on Communist North Vietnam.*

Southeast Asia had been a thorn in the West's side ever since the French tried to carve out Indochina back in the 1950s. The U.S. got involved as advisors when communist factions took over the north, and the country split into North and South Vietnam. Had Johnson's decision been different, history would have been different. As it was, a new word became part of our everyday vocabulary: escalation.

**DESERET NEWS,** *Mar. 8, 1965: (UPI) — Combat-ready U.S. Marines landed by plane and ship in South Viet Nam Monday and took up defense positions around the vital Da Nang air base only 80 miles from Communist North Viet Nam.*

*It was the first Marine landing in a combat zone since the Korean War.*

*Oct. 7, 1965: (UPI) — U.S. military strength in Viet Nam soared to a new high of 140,000 men Thursday when final elements of the 1st Infantry Division poured ashore. U.S. and Vietnamese planes meanwhile continued to pound Communist targets in both North and South Viet Nam.*

*Sept. 19, 1966: With the disclosure this week that American troops in Viet Nam now total 308,000 men and that they are being increased as rapidly as they can be accommodated, an unflinching look should be taken at the possibility of reducing U.S. forces in Europe. [An editorial].*

*Jan. 19, 1967: (UPI) — U.S. fighting men*

**Abbie Hoffman**

AP Photo

History views the 1960s as one of the most divisive decades the country has ever survived, yet it ended in a great triumph. Three assassinations staggered the country: John F. Kennedy, the popular and articulate president who raised the nation's hopes; Robert Kennedy, shot while campaigning for the presidency in hopes of ending an unpopular war; and Martin Luther King, civil rights crusader and Nobel Prize winner. The Vietnam War opened a generational wound that took decades to heal and left campuses in turmoil. Riots left cities in ashes. But great dams arose in the West, and at decade's end men left their footprints on the moon.

Beehive Collectors Gallery

**U.S. Marines, pinned down near the old citadel of Hue, Korea' ancient capital, keep low to avoid sniper fire during the infamous Tet offensive.**

UPI Photo

*UPI Photo*

**The helicopter came into its own in Vietnam.**

suffered their heaviest casualties of the war last week while American troop strength in Vietnam was being escalated to the 400,000 mark, military spokesmen said Thursday.

Jan. 26, 1967: (UPI) — The United States has suffered 49,024 casualties in the Vietnam war, an American military spokesman said Thursday. He said this included 8,542 killed, 39,997 wounded and 485 captured or missing.

The casualties exceeded the total number of American casualties in the Revolutionary, 1812, Mexican and Spanish-American wars. They totaled 38,931.

Utahns, who had hardly heard of Vietnam a few years before, were as involved as anyone, not exempt from the excitement or the pain:

**DESERET NEWS,** Sept. 13, 1964: The "they shoot first" war in Viet Nam comes home to Kearns every few days when a couple there gets a letter from a son who's a machine gunner on a U.S. Army helicopter.

Robert Pester… has flown more than 25 combat missions as a helicopter machine gunner looking down for orange bursts of flame.

Sept. 16, 1966: "Someone has to do the dirty work," were the words a Riverton youth in Viet Nam wrote his mother this week after he received the Army Commendation medal with "V" for "heroic actions against the Viet Cong." **[He was Pfc. Steven Jarvis.]**

Jan. 23, 1968: Three Utah servicemen serving in Vietnam have been killed in action recently, the Defense Department announced Tuesday.

They were identified as Army S. Sgt. Vaughn M. Angell, 31, Salt Lake City; Marine Pfc. Curtis Burke Bugger, Kearns; and Sp.4 Fred Jon Pinsonault, Roy.

Mar. 2, 1968: "There are more LDS servicemen fighting the war in Vietnam than our own members and people in general realize."

So said Navy Lt. (Chaplain) Preston N. Kearsley of Victor, Idaho, as he paused in Salt Lake City on a leave of absence… helping to serve 5,000 LDS servicemen as well as those of other faiths.

Mar. 6, 1968: Three more Utahns have been killed in action in Vietnam…

In what would become known as the Tet Offensive, North Vietnam launched a major campaign against the south on Jan. 30, 1968. The communists were eventually pushed back. But this long, drawn-out action, coming into U.S. homes each night on television, became an even stronger rallying point for increasing numbers of Americans who were opposed to the war.

**DESERET NEWS,** Jan. 19, 1968: (UPI) — Negro songstress Eartha Kitt, eyes flashing with anger, stunned guests at a White House luncheon Thursday by declaring that American youth are rebelling because of the Vietnam war. Her impassioned remarks left Mrs. Lyndon B. Johnson in tears.

Jan. 22, 1968: (AP) — Hollywood and Broadway performers appeared at a benefit Sunday night to raise funds for Democratic senators and congressmen opposed to the Johnson administration policy in Vietnam.

Mar. 26, 1968: For the first time since the United States became heavily engaged in the war in Vietnam, the American people's confidence in this country's ability to handle the situation there by military means has sharply declined. By 52 to 31 percent, the people are opposed to sending another 100,000 troops to Vietnam.

Nowhere was the opposition to the war more keenly demonstrated than on college campuses and at political conventions.

**DESERET NEWS,** July 2, 1968: BERKELEY, Calif. (AP) — The curfew clamped for three nights on this city to curb street demonstrations was lifted today by the city… More than 100 arrests have been made by 700 massed police… windows have been smashed and fires set since the demonstrations began Friday.

Aug. 29, 1968: CHICAGO (AP) — Some 3,000 antiwar demonstrators and Chicago police battled beneath the windows of the Conrad Hilton Hotel, the Democratic National Convention headquarters Wednesday night…

Police used clubs in subduing the demonstrators, most of them white youths, some of them bearded and sandaled, and some clean-cut. Police arrested 140 youths.

Utahns also joined in the protests.

Oct. 16, 1969: The Vietnam War, a thorn in America's side for a decade, pricked thousands to a show of conscience in Utah Wednesday, including those who want a stepped-up campaign.

A local response to a student-organized National Moratorium Day, the state's reaction was also student dominated with activity on at least five college campuses and with about 3,000 students making up the main task force for Salt Lake City's downtown march and rally…

Interspersed with students and other young people were a sprinkling of housewives pushing baby carriages, college professors, clergymen, nuns.

These were unsettled times in America. Growing disillusion with the war, increasing

*UPI Photo*

A weeping Vietnamese woman comforts her wounded husband during fighting at Ray Ninh, northwest of Saigon. Such photos fueled American protest.

agony over its divisiveness, rebellion against authority, new social mores — all these were adding more terms to our daily lexicon: counterculture, sit-in, hippie, psychedelic drugs, Woodstock.

**DESERET NEWS,** Jan. 17, 1968: "Send us your hippies, your peaceniks and your dissenters." That's the word a Marine on Con Thien sent back from Vietnam with Jack Peterson, Utah State University student newspaper editor, who went to Vietnam. "We don't shave or bathe up here — and we hold sit-ins in the bunkers during the daily artillery attacks from the north — they'd love it here."

By decade's end, weary war dragged on. And with it came a gloomy pessimism even in Deseret News editorials:

**DESERET NEWS,** Dec. 31, 1969: Too many Americans have lost confidence in the ability of their country to overcome pressing social and economic problems. Too many of us, exhausted by the longest war this country has ever fought — the one in Vietnam — have reached the point of fearing that honorable peace is beyond our grasp. Too many of us, seeing crime and riots all about, walk in fear and distrust of each other.

By decade's end, "Vietnam" had become another word for futility, and "the Sixties" became synonymous with a deeply troubled society.

**Jimi Hendrix**

*Deseret News files*

# Deseret News
## Salt Lake Telegram

Jan. 20, 1961

## Secy. Benson, Ivy Priest Lock Offices Last Time

WASHINGTON — Secretary of Agriculture Ezra Taft Benson and U.S. Treasurer Ivy Baker Priest performed a ritual Friday that marked a major milestone in their lives…

Mr. Benson has made it plain that his future will be doing the work he loves best of all, serving the Church of Jesus Christ of Latter-Day Saints as a member of the Council of the Twelve.

Mrs. Priest, who is from Bountiful, has disclosed no definite plans. She has been reliably reported, however, to be in line for a high position with a New York bank…

April 17, 1961

## Rebels Invade Cuba In Air-Sea Attacks

A strong force of rebel troops invaded Cuba Monday in an attempt to overthrow Premier Fidel Castro.

By parachute and landing craft, the assault force swarmed ashore only 90 miles from Havana and established a beach-head. Castro emotionally proclaimed a state of national emergency. He took personal command of defense operations.

The invaders struck in the swampy area around Bahia de Cochinos, the Bay of Pigs, shortly after midnight….

One broadcast indicated the casualties were heavy. Castro himself underscored the gravity of the events in statements read over the country's biggest radio station after a 12-hour silence.

April 20, 1961

## Castro Claims Victory, Speeds Up Executions

*Firing Squads Shoot Third Yank In 2 Days*

**By United Press International**

Fidel Castro proclaimed triumphantly Thursday the destruction of a Cuban invasion force and capture of its equipment including American-made Sherman

Fidel Castro

tanks. He followed this with a new wave of executions to tighten his grip on the country.

Havana radio announced that seven persons including an American — the third in two days — were executed by firing squads at dawn in Havana Thursday. It named the American as Diaz Bencom and said he led a plot to kill Castro. His home was not given.

A communique read over Havana radio early Thursday said Castro's regular army and militiamen overran the invaders' last position at Giron Beach on the Bay of Pigs at 5:30 p.m. Wednesday. But he admitted his men suffered "tragic losses" along with the invaders.

Aug.12, 1961

## East Germans Flee In Record Numbers

BERLIN (UPI) — A total of 2,017 East German refugees — an eight-year record — crossed the border into West Berlin Saturday fleeing the threat of sweeping new Communist measures to close the escape route to the West….

Saturday's flood of refugees swept past strict border controls at highway control points and subway and elevated train stations. Communist police held back hundreds of refugees but were unable to halt the rush….

The refugees were alarmed by the blank-check powers to halt escapes granted to the East German government by its parliament Friday, and by the possibility that the Berlin crisis might erupt into war.

Aug. 18, 1961

## Block Wall Seals Off Key Route

BERLIN (UPI) — The Communist regime of East Germany signed up young men for army service, formed factory defense guards and strengthened border barriers Friday in obvious preparation for long-term enforcement of its blockade between East and West Berlin….

The Communists sealed off the dividing line between East and West Berlin still tighter with a huge concrete and barbed wire barricade at Potsdamer Square and by cementing doors to East sector houses fronting on West Berlin streets.

May 8, 1962

## The Deseret News Wins A Pulitzer

NEW YORK CITY — The Deseret News and one of its staff writers have won a Pulitzer Prize, the most coveted award in newspaper journalism, it was announced here Monday.

The award for local reporting under deadline pressure went to Robert D. (Bob) Mullins, manager of the Deseret News Carbon County Bureau in Price.

With the distinction goes a $1,000 prize ,.. Mullins was cited for his "resourceful coverage of a murder and kidnaping at Dead Horse Point, Utah."

Mullins worked on the sensational case last summer for eight days, from the slaying of a Connecticut woman, the wounding of a companion and the kidnaping of her daughter, until the accused slayer killed himself. During the coverage, Mullins traveled more than 1,800 miles in some of the roughest terrain in Utah, and worked up to 30 hours at a stretch without sleep. He never missed a deadline.

Aug. 4, 1962

## Utahn's Spouse Has Role In Current Movie

Robert Redford, husband of a Provo girl, has one of the leading roles in "War Hunt," currently at the Lyric and Highland as second feature to "the Miracle Worker."

Mr. Redford is the husband of the former Lola Van Wagenen of Provo….

The Redfords visited with Mr. and Mrs. Van Wagenen for several days last week, and during that time they attended a special showing of the movie.

Afterwards, they left for Hollywood, where Mr. Redford is slated for a starring role in a Dr. Kildare episode being produced in color.

Aug. 4, 1962

## Kennedy Approves Decoration For Aide Who Blocked Drug

HYANNIS PORT, MASS. (UPI) — President Kennedy Saturday authorized the government's highest civilian decoration for Dr. Frances O. Kelsey, the medical officer who blocked the general sale of the

fetus-deforming drug thalidomide….

Press Secretary Pierre Salinger said Dr. Kelsey would be cited for her "high ability and steadfast confidence in her professional decision" to prevent the marketing of the drug, a sedative which has been blamed for birth deformities.

Aug. 5, 1962

## Marilyn Monroe Dies Of Drug Overdose

HOLLYWOOD (UPI) — Marilyn Monroe was dead Monday at 36, victim of an overdose of drugs which ended a tempestuous, glamorous rocket ride to fame and personal tragedy.

The figure on which she rose to stardom was found stretched across the bed of her modest Brentwood home, her lifeless hand grasping a telephone.

Her body was discovered by her psychiatrist, Dr. Ralph Greenson, who used a fireplace poker to smash through the bedroom window shortly after 3 a.m. Sunday morning.

Aug. 30, 1962

## U.S. To Provide Funds For Park City Project

Robert Redford

WASHINGTON (Special) — Rep. David S. King (D-Utah) was advised Thursday by the White House that the Area Redevelopment Administration will make a $1.3 million industrial loan Saturday to the United Park City Mines Co. of Park City.

Rep. King said the loan will enable United Park City to convert 10,000 acres of mining properties in the area into a large tourist and recreation complex.

The development will create 144 direct jobs, Rep. King said. It also will save the more than 200 jobs in the company's current operations.

Included in the recreation plan is development of ski lifts, lodges, picnicking and camping sites, a major resort hotel, a fine arts center, motels, golf course, airstrip and mountain home sites.

The mining company also hopes to develop an abandoned mine as a tourist attraction. Park City Mines first asked for $2.5 million, but was turned down by ARA.

Jan. 26, 1964
## Curator Dies Of Viper Bite

Jerry de Bary, 37, curator of Hogle Zoo, died at 6:30 a.m. Monday in a Salt Lake hospital from the effects of a deadly puff adder's bite late Saturday night.

Death came despite several injections of antivenom serum flown from San Diego, Calif., and around-the-clock efforts of several physicians.

Sept. 13, 1964
## President Signs Utah Park Bill

WASHINGTON, Sept. 12 — President Johnson signed Saturday a bill creating the Canyonlands National Park in southeastern Utah.

About 90 percent of the 257,640 acres within the boundaries spelled out in the new law are already federally owned. The remainder, owned by the state, will be exchanged for federal land elsewhere of comparable value.

The new law will preserve a rugged and colorful area near the confluence of the Colorado and Green rivers.

June 4, 1965
## Long Hair Has Got To Go

NEW YORK (AP) — A note for the cringing parents and graying school principals: it looks like the phenomenon known as the Beatle haircut may be on its way out. An Associated Press survey showed Friday that long, stringy hair is going the way of all fads and, in this case, is winding up on barber shop or home bathroom floors.

Nov. 12, 1965
## Landing Ends In Flames

**Deseret News Staff Writers**

A sleek United Air Lines jetliner made a "hard" landing at Salt Lake Airport Thursday at 5:54 p.m., then burst into flames and left 40 passengers dead in the charred ruins.

Another 50 persons, including all six crew members, escaped the inferno, but several were injured, some seriously.

The Boeing 727, distinguished by its high tail and three rear-mounted jet engines, was making the last intermediate stop on a flight from New York to San Francisco.

Cause of the crash was unknown, but comments of passengers and physical evidence indicated the craft

**Face of Gail C. Kehmeirer, pilot of crashed 727, registers horror.**

hit hard about 300 feet short of the runway....

Particularly tragic was the report by firemen and police that had there been no fire, all aboard would likely have escaped death or serious injury.

[The final death toll was 41].

Dec. 13, 1966
## 'Bid Adieu To The Shilling'

LONDON (UPI) — Britain sounded the death knell today for its 12-century-old currency system. It will keep the pound, lose its shillings and gain new pence when it switches over to decimal coinage in February 1971.

The old currency system was founded during the reign of Holy Roman Emperor Charlemagne (742-814)....

The pound, worth $2.80, will remain the major unit of currency for international and domestic reasons. But the 20 shillings that make up a pound will go, taking with them such coins as the shilling (14 cents), the florin (two shillings or 28 cents), the half crown (two shillings and sixpence or 35 cents), plus the 10 shilling note ($1.40). The 12 pennies that make up a shilling will also go.

Dec. 13, 1966
## 1966 — It Was Intriguing

**By HACK MILLER**

From all directions 1966 was one of the most intriguing years in sports...

Maybe the Utah rise to fourth place in national NCAA basketball was the year's best story. Maybe BYU's win in the NIT would claim the same for intercollegiate basketball.

Certainly the floodlights were on the Utah and BYU teams during these tournaments — and the buildup period until mid-March. Consider the story on Utah's bid for the winter Olympics — our delegation to Rome. We took a sound licking but we learned a lesson or two for the next time around. Virgil Carter and his BYU football records came into the front, too...

Dec. 14, 1966
## BYU Extends Ban On Coeds' Slacks

PROVO — Brigham Young University extended its ban on slacks for co-eds to the hobby shop and recreation area of the Student Union Tuesday, causing something of a stir among students....

A university spokesman said Wednesday, "Formerly, girls were permitted to wear slacks in the hobby shop

and bowling games area, but you can't reach them without going through the building or crossing the campus, so we just cut them out altogether. This is nothing new," he added. "The standards of dress on the BYU campus follow Church recommendations. This is in contrast to other campuses. People who come on campus immediately know students are better dressed than elsewhere."

Jan. 23, 1968
## North Korea Hijacks U.S. Navy Ship

WASHINGTON (UPI) — A North Korean air and naval force seized a U.S. intelligence ship on the high seas Tuesday and forced it to put into a Communist port. The White House said it was a "very serious situation." The president was awakened shortly after 2 a.m. EST to be told that four Communist patrol boats, with MIG fighters flying support overhead, had forced the USS Pueblo into the North Korean port of Wonsan.

The Pentagon announcement of the seizure did not mention any American casualties, but sources said some crew members were injured in the incident.

The lightly armed American vessel with 83 men aboard apparently surrendered without firing a shot. It marked the first time in more than 100 years that an American vessel had been captured at sea.

Jan. 27, 1968
## Museum To House 'Utah'

A lavish Museum of Natural History with more than 170 colorful exhibits will open at the University of Utah in 1969.

The museum, the first of its kind in the state, will be housed in the massive old library building on the U. Campus. Remodeling of the structure is expected to start soon.

Its educational exhibits will bring all the wonders of Utah's natural history under one roof. The geology, geography, biology, resources and anthropology of the state will not only be shown, but vividly explained as well.

March 15, 1968
## KCC, Unions Reach Tentative Accord

**BY GORDON ELIOT WHITE**

WASHINGTON — The Kennecott Copper Corp. and its unions reached a tentative contract agreement today covering its four-state Western Mining Division and an electrolytic refinery in the East....

The agreement was announced jointly by Kennecott officials and members of the Steelworker-led union coalition that has been bargaining here since Mar. 4....

The agreement, if finally approved, will bring at least partial end to the longest copper strike in U.S. history.

The previous record for Kennecott was a 173-day walkout in 1960.

March 15, 1968
## Total Strike Loss Estimated at $100 Million Plus

**BY CLARENCE S. BARKER**
Deseret News Staff Writer

Loss to the state in wages, taxes, sales, increased welfare etc. from the eight-month-old copper strike probably tops $100 million, Gov. Calvin L. Rampton said today.

Most of this, $91,385,000, represents lost wages and purchases of supplies and materials by Kennecott.

The governor estimated the tax loss at $7 to $10 million at all levels — state, local government, and schools.

**Sheep killed by nerve gas were buried where they fell.**

March 22, 1968
## Nerve Gas Test Linked To Death Of Sheep

SKULL VALLEY, Tooele County — The Army admitted today that it conducted tests of lethal nerve gas at super-secret Dugway Proving Grounds March 13 — the day before thousands of sheep began dying in nearby Skull Valley.

However, the Army did not concede that this caused the deaths of 5,000 to 6,000 sheep.

A delegation of senior military and civilian scientists was dispatched from Washington this morning to investigate the sheep deaths...

Baffled by the wholesale sheep destruction, animal medicine specialists ruled out the disease and placed the blame on a "mysterious poison." The poison affected the animals' central nervous system.

Aug. 16, 1968

## Inmate 'Stuck' In Trash Truck

UTAH STATE PRISON – Trying to escape from Utah State Prison in a garbage truck is not the best way, inmate Gary Lynn Reed, 24, can attest.

Reed, serving five years to life for robbery, suffered two puncture wounds in the lower abdomen after guards dutifully probed a load of trash Thursday afternoon.

Sept. 5, 1968

## Osmonds Home For Short Rest

Utah's high flying Osmond Brothers have arrived home for a short visit in Huntsville, but they'll soon be on their way again for more fair and television appearances that won't give them a breather until March.

In a week, they will head to New Jersey and 10 days of shows with Andy Williams, on whose television programs they have appeared. In October, they will perform at Sparks, Nev., on a bill to be headlined by Sergio Franchi, a singer who has turned actor for movies.

Sept. 21, 1968

## Dedicates Up-To-Minute Facilities

Utah's leaders gathered under one roof Friday — the bright copper roof of the new Deseret News Building — to dedicate one of America's most modern newspaper plants.

"This is one of the best facilities in the country," said Elder Mark E. Petersen, president of the Deseret News Publishing Co....

The special open house included a luncheon in the paneled board room on the first floor of the new Deseret News building, a tour of the plant and a film "Today's News Today," showing the production of today's Deseret News.

Nov. 6, 1968

## 2-1 Vote Kills Liquor Option

Liquor Initiative Petition No. A — perhaps the most hotly debated matter on Tuesday's ballot in Utah — went down to defeat with opponents polling a whopping 65 per cent of the vote.

With all districts reported, the tally stood at 144,239 votes for the bill and 270,132 votes against it.

A jubilant Richard A. Van Winkle, who headed the committee which battled the initiative, said the near two-to-one triumph was due "to the efforts of thousands of enthusiastic volunteers."

So complete was the liquor bill's downfall that it carried in only three counties — Carbon, Daggett and Grand.

[The petition would have allowed liquor to be sold by the drink.]

Dec. 28, 1968

## Gas Blamed In Sheep Case

WASHINGTON — An investigator for the American Association for the Advancement of Science said here Friday that chemical tests had proven "beyond doubt" that Skull Valley sheep killed last March died of nerve gas agent released from Dugway Proving Ground.

The Army has accepted legal responsibility for the sheep deaths and paid nearly $400,000 in indemnities to ranchers and Indians in the affected area, but it has continued to deny that its nerve gas actually caused the sheep to die.

Dec. 28, 1968

## Split Threatens Beatles

### BY MARILYN BECK

HOLLYWOOD (Bell) — All is not golden with the Beatles these days. John Lennon has put on several glittering performances — away from the stage — that are about to split the group wide open. John is so occupied with other things these days that his concert appearances have been disasters and recording sessions aren't much better.

Besides dissatisfaction with John's actions in general, the other Beatles are fed up with the way gal friend Yoko Ono has been directing his life. It was her idea, say they, that her and John pose for that nude album cover, and he went along in spite of protests from George, Ringo and Paul.

Costumed Beatles tout successful 'Sgt. Pepper's Lonely Hearts Club Band.'

Oct. 10, 1969

## Girl Scouts Lose On Poster

NEW YORK (UPI) — A federal court judge has turned down a petition by the Girl Scouts of America to halt the sale of a pop-art poster of a smiling, pregnant Girl Scout with the motto "Be Prepared."

The Girl Scouts filed a $1 million damage suit and sought an injunction to prevent Personality Posters Manufacturing Co., Inc. of New York from distributing the poster. The suit called the poster a malicious defamation of the Girl Scouts.

Judge Morris E. Lasker turned down the application for the injunction and said he doubted anyone could defame the Girl Scouts.

The Beatles – 1964

Deseret News files

## The Beatles

DESERET NEWS, *Aug. 19, 1964: Beatles, we love you, Yeah! Yeah! Yeah! This refrain sounded across the broad expanse of the U.S. Wednesday. In cities all over the country, it was the same. The mop-topped quartet from Britain took San Francisco by storm in person, but they were taking many other cities, including Salt Lake, through a movie.*

On their first American tour in 1964, the famed Beatles appeared on the "Ed Sullivan Show," then began a city-hopping tour of the country. Salt Lakers had to settle for the premiere of "A Hard Day's Night." Several hundred lined up beginning at 6 a.m. to see the first feature-length movie featuring the group. Lyric Theater manager Mike Pillaris called for police help but didn't really need it. The crowd was loud but not unruly. Musical icons of the '60s, the Beatles became the symbol for change, revolution, radical lifestyle flip-flops, drugs — the experimentation that engrossed a generation of Americans.

## The world of the 1960s
### A TIMELINE

**1960** – A record 10 Oscars are won by "Ben Hur."

**1960** – U.S. admits to aerial surveillance of USSR after Francis Gary Powers' U-2 plane is shot down.

**1960** – The U.S. nuclear submarine "Triton" completes first circumnavigation of the Earth under water.

**1961** – Peace Corps is founded.

**1961** – Yuri Gagarin from the USSR orbits the earth, and Alan Shepard makes the first U.S. space flight.

**1961** – A communications satellite is put in orbit by AT&T, with signals rebroadcast to stations in the U.S., England and France.

**1962** – Charles M. Schulz publishes "Happiness Is a Warm Puppy".

**1963** – Kremlin to White House hotline goes into operation.

**1963** – Valentina Tereshkova from Russia becomes the first female astronaut.

**1963** – First heart machine used by Dr. Michael De Bakey during heart surgery.

**1964** – The Beatles' first day in America.

**1964** – Nelson Mandela sentenced to a life term for treason.

**1964** – Martin Luther King Jr. wins the Nobel Peace Prize.

**1964** – Pope Paul VI makes a pilgrimage to the Holy Land.

**1965** – Medicare bill becomes law.

**1965** – Electrical blackout affects 30 million people in northeastern U.S. and parts of Canada; birth rate increases nine months later.

**1966** – Rubella vaccine is developed.

**1966** – Indira Gandhi becomes prime minister of India.

**1966** – The new Metropolitan Opera House opens in New York.

**1966** – Miniskirts become fashionable.

**1967** – China explodes its first hydrogen bomb.

**1967** – The world's first heart transplant is performed in South Africa by Dr. Christiaan N. Barnard.

**1967** – Mickey Mantle, with the New York Yankees, hits his 500th home run.

**1967** – Lost Creek Dam, Utah, completed.

**1968** – Jacqueline Kennedy marries Aristotle Onassis.

**1968** – Peggy Fleming, figure skater, wins the only U.S. gold medal at the Winter Olympics.

**1969** – Duke Ellington celebrates 70th birthday and receives Medal of Freedom from President Nixon.

**1969** – Food additive cyclamate is removed, and monosodium glutamate limited, after findings of cancer links.

**1969** – Mariner space probes send back pictures of Mars.

**1969** – Pants become acceptable everyday wear for women.

Malcolm X

# Malcolm X

DESERET NEWS, *May 13, 1964: NEW YORK (UPI) – National civil rights leaders were shocked almost to disbelief Friday by the advice of militant Negro leader Malcolm X that Negroes should form "rifle clubs."*

*Most said they agreed that the break-away leader of the Black Muslim movement could endanger civil rights progress and domestic peace with his urging that Negroes begin to "fight back in self defense."*

*"I can't believe he's serious," said James Farmer, national director of the Congress of Racial Equality (CORE.) He said that to unleash such violence could be "ultimately suicide."*

*Malcolm Thursday opened formally his announced campaign to organize a politically oriented black nationalist movement.*

**Civil Rights Leaders Aghast**
## Negro Rifle Clubs Proposed

By DAVID M. ALPERN

NEW YORK (UPI)—National civil rights leaders were shocked almost to disbelief Fri-

*"There will be more violence than ever this year," he said at a news conference in a hotel here. "White people will be shocked when they discover that the passive little Negro they had known turns out to be a roaring lion."*

All over America, blacks who had the same desires at heart found themselves in different camps. The pacifist sentiments of such men as Martin Luther King Jr. found a counterpart in the leadership of men like Malcolm X. Such internal wrangling diffused the civil rights efforts to a degree.

# Woodstock

DESERET NEWS, *Aug. 18, 1969: WHITE LAKE, N.Y. (AP) – The great rock festival ended today in the same spirit of peace and sharing that enables 400,000 young people to gather for three days of music, marijuana and mod living without a major incident.*

*"There has been no violence whatsoever, which is remarkable for a crowd of this size," said Dr. William Abruzzi, the festival's chief medical officer. "These people really are beautiful."*

*As the great exodus of tired, thirsty, hungry youths began Sunday, security officials reported three deaths and close to 5,000 persons treated for injuries, illness or adverse drug reactions during the three-day span…*

With this brief story on the bottom of an inside page, the conservative Deseret News slid over Woodstock, the largest gathering in honor of lifestyle ever. Performers such as Jimi Hendrix kept hundreds of thousands of yippies, hippies, flower children and assorted beautiful people spellbound. (Hendrix segued into a rock version of "The Star Spangled Banner" to salvage a somewhat lackluster performance, some said. He died in 1970, at 27, of a drug overdose.)

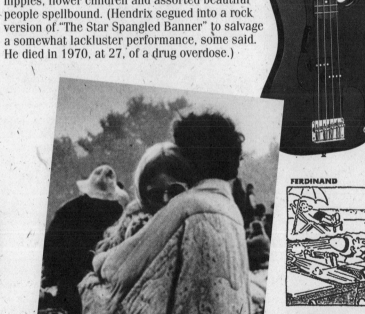

Gathering of several hundred thousand at Woodstock symbolized a generation in revolt.

# Arnold Palmer

DESERET NEWS, *Jan. 21, 1961: ROCHESTER, N.Y. (UPI) – Arnold Palmer, proud new wearer of the $10,000 diamond-studded Hickok belt, said Tuesday he will try for golf's "grand slam" – victories in the Masters, PGA, U.S. and British opens – this year.*

*The 31-year-old Latrobe, Pa., pro voiced his intention of becoming the first man ever to win all four of those titles during the same year after being honored here Monday night by the Rochester Press and Radio Club as the "Professional Athlete of the Year" for 1960.*

*Winner of the U.S. Open and the Masters last year, Palmer said his biggest disappointment in 1960 was his failure to win the British Open. "I had a feeling I was going to win it," he said, "and when I didn't, I was tremendously disappointed."*

Arnold Palmer

Palmer didn't have long to wait to salve this particular wound. On July 17, 1961, the Deseret News reported that he had joined golfdom's immortals by winning the British Open by one stroke. At that point, the only major golf event he had not yet conquered was the PGA championship, which was being played that year at the Olympia Fields Country Club of Chicago, and he was en route there after leaving England. For decades, News readers followed the ups and downs of Palmer's career, joining thousands of "Arnie's Army" followers without leaving their easy chairs.

FERDINAND

HI AND LOIS

# Gunshots in
# Camelot

**In the confusion of the 1960s with its Cold War standoffs, America's countercultural revolution and strident demands for civil equality, President John F. Kennedy's proposals for a "New Frontier" echoed well in the ears of millions of Americans.**

Young (43 when elected,) handsome, charismatic, politically savvy and surrounded by a "fairy tale" family, Kennedy intrigued the nation. In his inaugural address, he invited Americans to share the burden of liberty: "Ask not what your country can do for you — ask what you can do for your country."

Kennedy's Washington Camelot, however, was no bed of roses. His tenure in the White House was marked by several international threats. Not long into his presidency, the world came very close to war again when he challenged the Soviet Union's right to keep missiles in Cuba and then refused to back down:

*DESERET NEWS, Oct. 28, 1962: UNITED NATIONS — Acting Secretary General U Thant, accompanied by a high-powered team of U.N. officials, will leave for Havana Tuesday morning for a round of talks with Cuban Premier Fidel Castro. This decision, taken late Sunday, is the most significant step in attempts by Thant to obtain a powerful solution to the Cuban crisis.*

*The United States kept its guard up in the Caribbean Monday while President Kennedy sought speedy fulfillment of Russia's promise to pull her missiles out of Cuba ...*

Castro raged, calling Soviet Premier Khrushchev derogatory names and accusing him of cowardice, but the interests of world peace had prevailed. Kennedy also worked with other world leaders to engineer a treaty outlawing most forms of atomic testing. The United States was experiencing unprecedented prosperity, cheering its first manned space flights and preparing to send astronauts to the moon. It appeared certain that Kennedy would continue a presidency marked with laudable achievement at home and abroad.

But in a single instant, an assassin's bullet brought his presidency to an end. The Deseret News chronicled Kennedy's murder in a rare EXTRA edition:

**DESERET NEWS,** *Nov. 22, 1963:*
*KENNEDY ASSASSINATED*
*By Merriman Smith*
*DALLAS (UPI) — President Kennedy was assassinated Friday in a burst of gunfire in downtown Dallas. Texas Gov. John Connally was shot down with him.*

*The President, cradled in his wife's arms, had been rushed in his blood-spattered limousine to Parkland Hospital and taken to an emergency room. An urgent call went out for neurosurgeons and blood.*

*The President, 46 years old, was shot once in the head. Connally was hit in the head and wrist.*

*Police found a foreign-make rifle. Sheriff's officers were questioning a young man picked up at the scene.*

*The President was conscious as he arrived at the hospital. Father Huber from Holy Trinity Roman Catholic Church was called and administered the last rites of the church. Vice President Lyndon B. Johnson, who now becomes President of the United States, was in a car behind the Kennedys and Connallys. He was immediately surrounded by secret service men until he could take the oath of office as President.*

Stunned Americans glued themselves to television and radio stations as the tragic events of Dallas unfolded — the arrest of Lee Harvey Oswald, an admitted Marxist believed to have been the assassin; his shooting at the hands of Dallas nightclub owner Jack Ruby (Rubinstein) witnessed by

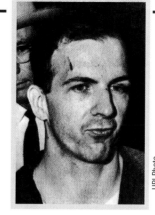

**Lee Harvey Oswald**

a worldwide television audience; the swearing-in of Johnson aboard an airborne plane; the pageantry of Kennedy's funeral; the ongoing debate swirling around the assassination; and the report of the investigative Warren Commission — all were shared with Utahns through the News pages.

The nation and the world nursed its collective wounds, but for the Kennedy clan, another personal tragedy was in the offing:

**DESERET NEWS,** *June 5, 1968:*
*ROBERT KENNEDY SHOT*
*LOS ANGELES (UPI) — Sen. Robert F. Kennedy was critically wounded early today by a swarthy gunman as he was leaving a jubilant primary election celebration. After undergoing nearly four hours of surgery doctors said his condition was "extremely critical."*

*Kennedy was shot in the head and neck. His aides quickly subdued the alleged gunman. At midmorning the suspect was identified as Sirhan Bishara Sirhan, 24, of nearby Pasadena...*

*Dr. Henry Cuneo said that even if Kennedy lives, he might suffer extensive brain damage... Cuneo said that several major arteries were severed and Kennedy's brain suffered extensive loss of blood and oxygen as well as several blood clots.*

Eight years the junior of his brother John F., Robert Kennedy had aspirations of his own. He served as U.S. attorney general from 1961 to 1964, most of the time in President Kennedy's Cabinet, and as U.S. senator from New York for three more years. He challenged President Johnson's war policies and was stumping for the Democratic nomination for president, feeling confident, when he was shot down in Los Angeles.

The brutal deaths of the Kennedys and the end of their dreams was a sour legacy for the country. It mourned not only their loss but the loss of its own innocence.

**Moments after this photo was taken during a Dallas cavalcade, President Kennedy was dead.**

**Robert Kennedy**

# The new battle over
# civil rights

**The rallying cry of the 1960s was civil rights. From one end of the decade to the other, Congress passed a succession of laws that sought to bring all people into the American mainstream, but particularly blacks. A hundred years after being freed from slavery, blacks were determined to finally gain the equal benefits of citizenship they were entitled to.**

Medgar Evers

ILLINOIS SUBURB
## Riot Rocks City A Second Night

CHICAGO (UPI)—Riot-trained police Tuesday patrolled the tense streets of south suburban Dixmoor, where dogs and tear gas Monday night quelled the town's second consecutive night of Negro riots.

The rattle of gunfire greeted police as they scattered on angry mob of 200 Negroes milling around a liquor store set afire by five "Molotov cocktails." At least 40 persons—27 of them white—were arrested but no one was reported injured.

Cook County Sheriff Richard B. Ogilvie said the two nights of rioting, rock-throwing and sporadic gun fire in the racially mixed suburb "appeared to be more than spontaneous combustion." He said there were "outside agitators" in the crowds of Negroes.

But Gene Callahan, executive director of the Chicago Conference on Religion and Race, said Monday night's flare-up would not have erupted into a riot if police from suburban Midlothian had not set dogs on the crowd without authorization.

GOT LOOSE

An unconfirmed report said one of the dogs accidently got loose from his handler and charged into the crowd.

The trouble Monday night a liquor store broke

Teams like this police dog and officer moved in on rioters in Illinois suburb to disperse mobs. Police used tear gas. More than 40 were arre...

Sixties race riots disturbed peace of dozens of American cities.

he struggle involved sit-ins, marches, voter registration drives, freedom buses and outright riots. Blood was shed. Long-suppressed discontent over racism boiled over in more than 50 American cities during the decade, leaving a trail of destruction and growing resentment:

**DESERET NEWS,** *June 7, 1963: LEXINGTON, N.C. (UPI) — Seven Negroes and two whites were jailed Friday in connection with a race riot in which one man was killed and another wounded...*

*Aug. 17, 1964: CHICAGO (UPI) — More than 1,000 rioting Negroes hurled chunks of concrete at white motorists, jeered police and looted store windows Sunday night and early Monday until they were driven back by massed police forces using tear gas. At least two persons were shot, close to 60 were injured, two building fires were set and 25 to 30 people were arrested in the fighting which broke out in south suburban Dixmoor over a bottle of gin.*

*Aug. 14, 1965: LOS ANGELES (UPI) — The nation's worst Negro uprising in two decades was crushed Saturday by 2,000 rifle-carrying National Guardsmen and armed police, but sporadic violence and nearly uncontrolled looting went on throughout the area.*

*At least 17 persons were killed, a thousand arrested and "astronomical" damage in the millions was caused in the three days of rioting.*

The rioting in the Los Angeles suburb of Watts hit close to home. Wary Utah officials predicted it couldn't happen here, but they were taking steps, nevertheless, to short-circuit race-incited events:

**DESERET NEWS,** *Aug. 16, 1965: Though most people did not believe that rioting could occur in Salt Lake City, law enforcement agencies quietly were taking steps to make sure they were equipped to handle any eventuality. Most of the measures, such as special riot training for officers, purchase of more than 200 extra-long night sticks, doubling of tear gas weapons and better communications with various police groups, were started after a (minor) riot in Liberty Park on May 30 ...*

Watts, Chicago, Detroit, Harlem, Selma, Washington, Baltimore, Little Rock and dozens of other cities became embroiled in the new "civil war" that rocked America.

However, many blacks chose to follow less violent paths to equality. The names of several young heroes and heroines who quietly but steadfastly refused to be barred from "white" schools were added to American history texts.

Linda Brown was one of them. When a white school in Topeka, Kan., refused her father's request to admit her, he filed a lawsuit. Ultimately the case of Brown vs. Board of Education reached the Supreme Court, which ruled in the Browns' favor. School segregation on the basis of race became illegal. Ten years after the decision, the News recapped the case:

**DESERET NEWS,** *May 17, 1964: On a spring day in 1951, a Negro clergyman in Topeka, Kan., went to*

*school with his daughter. Linda Brown attended Monroe Elementary, an all-Negro school, 20 blocks from her home. She rode the school bus most of the way. But on that day, the Rev., Oliver Brown did not take his daughter to Monroe. Holding Linda's hand, he led her to an all-white school,*
*Sumner*
*Elementary.*
*It was four*
*blocks*

*away. They walked.*
*In the building, the Rev. Mr. Brown attempted to enroll Linda. This brief sequence soon was to go into American legal and social history as part of the monumental decision by the U.S. Supreme Court that segregation in the schools is*
*unconstitutional.*

Some of the black leaders who chose

Some police units used dogs as allies in confrontations with blacks. Conflict ultimately raised questions of police brutality.

the nonviolent path to equality, promoting peaceful marches and changes in laws, fell prey to the very violence they wanted to avoid:

**DESERET NEWS,** *June 12, 1963: JACKSON, Miss. (UPI) — Mississippi's most outspoken civil rights leader, Medgar Evers, was shot to death from ambush early Wednesday ... Scores of Negroes poured into a Negro business district Wednesday afternoon in a renewal of the anti-segregation protest marches that Evers had directed until his death.*

*April 6, 1968: MEMPHIS, Tenn. (AP) — The assassination of Dr. Martin Luther King Jr. triggered Negro violence across the nation and caused President Johnson to cancel his planned trip to Hawaii.*

*The 39-year-old Dr. King died in a Memphis hospital Thursday night less than an hour after he was shot in the neck as he stood on the balcony of his motel here. Police searched for a white gunman. President Johnson called on the nation today — all men and all races — to "stand their ground to deny violence its victory" in the wake of the slaying of Dr. King.*

The central figure of America's civil rights movement was dead at the hands of James Earl Ray. King's advocacy of nonviolent protest could not save him from the violence that marked the mid-1960s. A Baptist minister, he was an eloquent speaker who used his skills to sway both blacks and whites to peacefully pursue equity. His "I have a dream" speech stirred all who heard it, and his birthday eventually became a national holiday.

Soon, social analysts went to work. It was not difficult to identify discrimination in education, employment, housing, government services, voting and other accepted American "rights" as the multiple roots that nurtured racial unrest. The effort to resolve these inequities began with establishment of the U.S. Civil Rights Commission and came to fruition on July 3, 1964, when the Civil Rights Act of 1964 passed the U.S. Congress:

**DESERET NEWS,** *July 3, 1964: WASHINGTON (UPI) — The civil rights bill, born in the violence of the Negro protest movement against discrimination, completed its congressional journey Thursday and was rushed to the White House for President Johnson's signature. The vote was 289 to 126.*

*The House, operating within strict procedural rules that limited debate on the measure to one hour, voted final approval of the bill one year and two weeks after the late President John F. Kennedy sent it to Congress... The House originally passed the bill on Feb. 10 and sent it to the Senate, where it became bogged down in the longest filibuster in the nation's history. Finally, on June 19, the Senate acted on an amended version and sent it back to the House for approval...*

*"This act is a challenge to all of us to go to work in our states and communities, in our homes and in our hearts, to eliminate the last vestiges of injustice in America," Johnson said.*

Utah, with a highly homogenous white population, (then less than 3 percent minority representation) stood a little aloof from the civil rights debate. The issue seldom surfaced and when it did, the notion of resolving inequities didn't appear to be a concern:

**DESERET NEWS,** *June 11, 1963: Salt Lake City has no power either to enact or enforce an ordinance with respect to civil rights, city attorney Homer Holmgren said Tuesday. Mr. Holmgren noted that Utah does not have civil rights legislation and therefore, in his opinion, the city cannot legislate with respect to civil rights...*

*The issue arose two weeks ago when a Negro, 65, told the City Commission that he and five other Negroes had been denied service in a cafe on 200 South. Mayor J. Bracken Lee directed Mr. Holmgren to draw up a resolution urging business people to*

*respect the rights of all persons...*

A state commission empaneled as advisory to the federal commission found that blacks, Indians and Mexican-Americans in Utah were, in fact, discriminated against. In its August 1966 report, the panel said that Negroes "paid more money on less favorable terms than whites for housing they purchased in predominantly white neighborhoods ... real estate brokers and salesmen refrained from selling or renting to Negroes outside their traditional residential neighborhoods; virtually no apartments were available for rent to Negroes and they paid higher rents than whites for comparable accommodations."

Indigenous Utah Indians, now consigned to reservations, also suffered discrimination, the commission found, largely due to being "inordinately shy, unprepared for any sort of real assimilation into urban society, unskilled for urban employment... The real or fancied inability of the Indian to 'hold his liquor' is a constantly repeated justification for the inequalities practiced..." In fact, America's Indians had not enjoyed citizenship, except in particular circumstances, until 1924.

Passage of the Utah Civil Rights Act in 1965 established equal treatment of all, regardless of "race, color, sex, religion, ancestry or national origin." The act decreed equal accommodation of all people by businesses that were subject to state regulation and banned discrimination in housing.

Federal and state legislation was a beginning, but it did not immediately correct civil inequities or nullify long-standing hatreds. Utah had its brush with irrational racial bigotry in 1980 when two young black men were shot while jogging near Liberty Park. Joseph Paul Franklin, a known white supremacist, was accused of the killings:

A sea of 200,000 people brought their demands for equal rights to the nation's capital in 1963, where they heard Dr. Martin Luther King's famed "I have a dream" speech.

**DESERET NEWS,** *Oct. 6, 1980: A nationwide hunt is under way for Joseph Paul Franklin, wanted in connection with the shooting deaths of two black joggers [Ted Fields and David Martin] and sought for questioning in four other sniper attacks on blacks, including Urban League President Vernon Jordan Jr...*

The long Franklin saga found he had committed racially motivated murders in several states. He ultimately was tried in Salt Lake City and sentenced to a life term in a federal prison in Illinois.

Throughout the '60s the ugly monster of blatant prejudice and its more subtle cousins of discrimination and unfairness were brought into the light of public scrutiny. But a full resolution of such inequities lay decades away.

Dr Martin Luther King Jr.

# From
# Fullmer through
# Maris to Namath

Deseret News files

The power behind Mickey Mantle's swing shows in 1964 photo, above. Roger Maris, right, set a 61-homer season record that stood for decades.

Deseret News files

**H**omegrown boys were doing just fine in the sports world of the 1960s:

**DESERET NEWS,** *Dec. 15, 1961: Gene Fullmer might go down as the year's most "awarded" athlete.*
*Gene has been named the winner of the Los Angeles Times "Fighter of the Year" award and will be on hand Dec. 29 for this honor.*
*He has been named for the same honor in Phoenix where he will appear for another honor.*
*This is in addition to the Edward Neil Award as Fighter of the Year on the New York Boxing Writers vote, Jan. 14.*

Gene Fullmer amazed the boxing world when he defeated Sugar Ray Robinson for the world middleweight championship in 1957, and his career had been going strong ever since. But he wasn't the only one.

**DESERET NEWS,** *Nov. 10, 1964: (UPI) — Merlin Olsen feels that the vaunted Los Angeles Rams "fearsome foursome" defensive forward wall has even more potential than it has shown this season.*
*And those four stalwarts — Olsen, Roosevelt Grier, Lamar Lundy and David Jones — have been the scourge of the NFL's Western Conference this season.*
*The articulate defensive tackle from Utah State told the Southern California Football Writers Monday, after receiving a golden helmet award as pro player of the week, that he and his teammates would be even better after a few more years of playing together.*

*Nov. 2, 1966: (UPI) — Billy Casper, who's been winning money at a record pace this*

*year, added another gem to his collection when he was selected PGA 1966 Player of the Year.*

*Playing against the likes of Arnold Palmer and Jack Nicklaus, Utah's Casper was again honored in 1968 as the professional golfer of the year "by the nation's golf scriveners who traipse across the fairways on the heels of the play-for-pay swatters."*

Of course, Utahns weren't the only ones making headlines throughout the decade. In baseball, the Yankees' Mickey Mantle and Roger Maris were stirring up a lot of interest:

**DESERET NEWS,** *Aug. 17, 1961: (UPI) — If Roger Maris or Mickey Mantle achieves the magic 61 number in 1961, that feat of breaking Babe Ruth's home run record will be hailed in America, at least, as the greatest sports accomplishment of the century.*
*Maris Thursday was only 13 homers short of the goal after hitting his 47th and 48th round trippers Wednesday, and Mantle is right behind him with 45 blasts.*

*Oct. 2, 1961: UPI) — Roger Maris claims "the ordeal is over," but actually the controversy merely started Monday over whether he or Babe Ruth should be recognized as baseball's official all-time home run king.*
*Emotionally exhausted and looking as if someone had put him through a wringer, the 27-year-old Maris accepted congratulations in a semi-daze Sunday after becoming the first major leaguer ever to surpass Ruth by hitting 61 homers in a single season...*
*Commissioner Ford Frick has ruled that two separate records will go into the books.*
*One will be Maris' mark of 61 homers for a 162-game season and the other Ruth's record of 60 in 154 games.*

The most famous asterisk in all of sports had

UPI Photo

**Joe Namath**

made its appearance.
The only punctuation that was being used on the football side of sports, however, was the exclamation point — put behind a new championship tradition:

**DESERET NEWS,** *Jan. 10, 1967: (UPI) — All the trappings of a world championship were falling in place today for the Super Bowl game between the Green Bay Packers and the Kansas City Chiefs.*
*The latest addition was a world championship trophy, an actual-size sterling silver football 20 inches in height, which National Football League Commissioner Pete Rozelle will present to the winning team in its dressing room after Sunday's game at Memorial Coliseum.*

*Jan. 16, 1967: (UPI) — Coach Vince Lombardi won't come right out and say so, but indications today were that he felt the Kansas City Chiefs were out of their league in more ways than one when they tangled with his mighty Green Bay Packers.*

Green Bay won the first Super Bowl 35-10. They won the second one 33-14, over the Oakland Raiders. But the lowly AFL would have its turn. In 1969: New York Jets 17, Baltimore Colts, 7. And Deseret News sports editor Hack Miller applauded:

**DESERET NEWS,** *Jan. 13, 1969: During the week one might have suggested that one Joe Namath keep his big mouth shut. He was talking too big for a little old AFL quarterback...*
*But this Monday there will be little said about Namath's tirades against the Baltimore Colts and one Earl Morrall, the Colt quarterback who was named the best man in the NFL.*
*Namath called his shots — and called them so completely that this day there are more who respect him than revile him. Big mouth or not!*

UPI Photo

**Vince Lombardi**

# A world of ballet and Beatles

The Beach Boys

**DESERET NEWS,** Aug. 13, 1964: The three top records of this week are: "Hard Day's Night," by — guess who? — the Beatles; "Something New" by, ho hum, the Beatles and "All Summer Long" by the Beach Boys.

This department has no quarrel with this listing except to point out that Utahns are also part and parcel of this adoration for music of this level...

That 20 times as many Utahns attended the first concert of the Beach Boys a month ago than attended the concert in the same hall of the Utah Summer Symphony Pops is some kind of indice to the preferred cultural level that is not quite as complimentary to our musical tastes as one would hope.

This is a long way of course of getting to the point that those who prefer music of a higher order ought to rise en masse and attend the final concert of the Utah Summer Symphony Pops next Thursday.

As much as Deseret News music critic Harold Lundstrom might hope otherwise, Beatlemania was raging, Beach Boy fever was going strong, the Rolling Stones were gathering no moss. These were the '60s, after all.

But fine arts were flourishing around the country, as well. Major orchestras were led by the likes of Arthur Fiedler, Georg Solti, Eugene Ormandy. America's ballet companies were considered on a par with Russia's Bolshoi.

Culture took a decided upturn on the homefront, as well.

**DESERET NEWS,** July 2, 1962: William Shakespeare will live again for two weeks beginning Monday at 8:30 p.m. when trumpets blare the opening of the first annual Shakespearean festival sponsored by the College of Southern Utah.

July 17, 1964: Utah's Tabernacle Choir and Philadelphia Orchestra fans and patrons have reason to be out turning cartwheels as part of their "Days of '47" celebrations!

The two international-famed musical organizations — perhaps "institutions" is the better noun — will, officially or otherwise, kick off the 1964-65 concert season when they combine forces for a joint concert Friday, Sept. 4, in the Tabernacle.

The big Choir news in the summer of 1964, however, was that the revered singing group was heading East.

**DESERET NEWS,** July 24, 1964: The Salt Lake Mormon Tabernacle Choir celebrated Pioneer Day at the [New York] World's Fair Friday following a successful command performance in the White House Thursday afternoon.

President Lyndon B. Johnson praised the choir at a concert specially held for him in the East Room of the executive mansion.

He called it a "deeply moving experience for me," and said it is "fortunate that under the American system the voices of all can be heard in this building."

That summer (the same summer, by the way, that Utahn Robert Peterson came home for the first time since getting the role of Sir Lancelot in Broadway's "Camelot,") news came that a "million dollar music theater" would be constructed in North Salt Lake for production of Broadway-cast musicals.

By the mid-'60s, the Utah Symphony was also breaking new ground — off on its first international tour.

**DESERET NEWS,** Sept. 16, 1966: ATHENS — Deservedly basking in the fantastic demonstration accorded violinist David Oistrakh by the shouting audience was our own Utah Symphony Orchestra and Maurice Abravanel who accorded him strong collaboration. Together they played with spirit and insight that proved to be a happy blend of exhilaration and sentiment.

Sept. 20, 1966: BELGRADE — The Utah Symphony and native son pianist Grant Johannesen made their Yugoslavian debuts here Monday night to the cries of "Bravissimo" and "Bis" (encore) from a demonstrative Balkan audience.

Sept. 23, 1966: VIENNA — The Utah Symphony orchestra under the direction of Maurice Abravanel, Tuesday night was called back six times for bows by the usually restrained Viennese audience.

The tour was a triumph. And news that came in 1968 didn't surprise Utahns at all:

**DESERET NEWS,** Aug. 27, 1968: The Utah Symphony Orchestra is one of the 12 best in the nation. Good management and popular support have helped make it that.

This is the report of Fortune Magazine to be published tomorrow.

Ballet was also going strong in Utah. What had started as the Utah Civic Ballet, under the skillful leadership of Willam Christensen, was trying to broaden its appeal.

**DESERET NEWS,** Aug. 16, 1969:

Utah Civic Ballet soloists Barbara Hamblin and Ken Mitchell, shown in 1967, helped bring prominence to Utah dance programs.

At first glance the problem seems formidable. How can a sparsely-settled land of deserts, mountains and cowboys hope to offer the same cultural benefits as the East?

Now, midway through its first year under a new name, Ballet West thinks it has found the answer — and with it the key to its survival as a major art form.

The idea of Ballet West is that it can draw upon the combined resources of the full west — and particularly those states forming the Federation of Rocky Mountain States. That was the reason for the name change from the Utah Civic Ballet to Ballet West last December.

The arts were on the move.

# Beyond the earth

**DESERET NEWS,** *May 5, 1961: (UPI) — Reports from the Mercury Control Center — and from the astronaut — told in tight phrases the story of the epochal flight: "Ignition." "Liftoff." "There it goes." "Looking good." "Trajectory okay." "Pilot in good voice communication." "Four Gs." "Now out of sight." "Astronaut okay." "Taking over manual control of all attitudes... Control okay." From Shephard: "What a beautiful view." "Voice communications still good." "Retro rocket package jettisoned." "Astronaut is working like a test pilot, reporting facts and procedures." "Going into re-entry attitude." "Parachute out." "Spotted by recovery forces." "The space craft has landed in the sea." "Astronaut is aboard helicopter." "Spacecraft is on (carrier) deck."*

There it was. The first American in space. And the country was jubilant. Who cared if the Russians had been first, with Cosmonaut Yuri Gagarin. Only 23 days later, 37-year-old Alan Shephard went 115 miles up and back. "Man, what a ride!" he said. Besides, all reports were careful to point out, Shephard actually controlled the vehicle.

It was a heady step for the U.S. space program, but it was only the first toward President Kennedy's stated goal of sending a man to the moon and back before the end of the decade. Much more was to come.

**DESERET NEWS,** *July 21, 1961: (UPI) — Virgil I. (Gus) Grissom became America's second spaceman Friday but had to swim the last 65 to 70 feet of his 303-mile trip to get away from his sinking spacecraft.*

**DESERET NEWS,** *Feb. 20, 1962: (UPI) — John H. Glenn flew triumphantly three times around the world in space Tuesday and was plucked safely from the sea at the end of his historic trail-breaking mission America.*

*The 40-year-old astronaut jumped into the sky atop a flame-spouting Atlas rocket at 9:47 a.m. MST. At 1:43 p.m. MST, 4 hours and 56 minutes later, he splashed down in the Atlantic only about six miles from the destroyer Noa.*

Utahns were as excited as the rest of the country.

*Feb. 20, 1962: On all three orbits John H. Glenn passed over the American continent far south of Salt Lake City.*

*The first pass took him over northern Mexico and the second near the U.S.-Mexican border. On the third trip Glenn's space vehicle came as far north as Phoenix, Ariz.*

*Feb. 21, 1962: The day after John H. Glenn Jr. rocketed around the earth, leading Utahns hailed his feat as "just the beginning" of America's march into space...*

*Dr. Henry Eyring, dean of the Graduate School at the University of Utah and a noted scientist in his own right, said the orbit reflected "technical excellence in every direction. We're not matched by anybody"...*

*Dr. Carl J. Christensen, director of the Engineering Experiment Station at the U. of U., said, "I have a feeling this is the beginning of a long series of this sort of thing. Where the end is is anybody's guess."*

Astronauts were our new heroes. And we were fascinated by every detail of their training:

**DESERET NEWS,** *Aug. 12, 1964: (UPI) — Fourteen fledgling astronauts journeyed to remote areas of the Nevada desert Wednesday for a practical test of their classroom lessons on survival...*

*The men will be required to fashion Arab-style clothing and shelters from parachutes, improvise digging tools, learn a signal system and solve a navigational problem at night. Their only food will be whatever desert animals, such as lizards, snakes and rabbits.*

*They were introduced to the strange food they can expect Tuesday when an instructor passed around some canned butterfly. One astronaut observed, "It'll never beat steak."*

By the mid-point in the decade, orbits had become routine and were replaced by new space adventures.

**DESERET NEWS,** *March 23, 1965: (UPI) — Astronauts Virgil I. Grissom and John W. Young whirled three times around the earth Tuesday and splashed down on schedule in the Atlantic after performing "truly historic" spacecraft maneuvers in orbit.*

*The Gemini 3 "space twins" soared into space at 7:24 a.m. MST.*

*June 3, 1965: (UPI) — Astronaut Edward White left the Gemini 4 cabin high over the Pacific Thursday and took a walk in space which so enthralled him that he had to be*

Astronauts James McDivitt and Edward White take simulated ride in Gemini spacecraft. World watched, awestruck, as American space program went into orbit.

NASA Photo

UPI Photo

NASA Photo

coaxed back in by fellow astronaut James McDivitt.

White was a particular favorite with Utah readers because he had visited the state en route to a cross-country assignment in 1963. He took part in some of the Days of '47 festivities, including leading the children's parade, and visited with LDS Church President David O. McKay.

**DESERET NEWS,** *June 3, 1965: He chatted with the white-haired Church leader about the space program and listened intently as President McKay recited a 100-year-old Church poem which told of the grandeur and eternity of space and God's creations. Afterwards, he asked if he could have a copy of the poem.*

And Utahns mourned deeply with the rest of the country when horrifying news came on Jan. 27, 1967, that three astronauts died in a fire that swept through their space capsule as it sat atop the launching pad during a test. Dead were Virgil (Gus) Grissom, Edward White and Roger Chaffee.

**DESERET NEWS,** *Jan. 28, 1967: Capt. Edward H. White, the Texas astronaut who was one of three killed Friday at Cape Kennedy, stood in the Salt Lake Tabernacle nearly four years ago and said:*

*"Stepping into space is the greatest adventure we've ever had, and the fruits of it will be beyond imagination."*

*Capt. White said he recognized the dangers of the space program. "Risks are just part of the job," he said.*

*Jan. 30, 1967: Edward H. White, one of three astronauts who burned to death on the launch pad at Cape Kennedy Friday, saw his mission as part of "the flame that will rekindle a fabulous new era of discoveries — a renaissance — which could possibly reveal to us some of the mysteries and secrets of those other worlds."*

*Col. White's testament of belief was contained in a letter written to Mrs.*

Kenneth B. Done, 2818 East 2960 South, in November, 1965, shortly after his "walk in space." Mrs. Done had written him asking his views on man's relationship to God, in preparation for a lesson... to be taught in a Relief Society theology class...

*"As to evidence of God's presence during our journey in space and during the short period that 'I walked in space,' I did not feel any nearer to Him there than here but I do know that His sure hand guided us all the way during that four-day mission!"*

While the nation mourned, it also worried that the tragedy would be a major set-back to the space program, but NASA was soon back on track with the Apollo flights. Finally, came the flight that took men around the moon.

**DESERET NEWS,** *Dec. 27, 1968: (UPI, AP) — America's amazing Apollo 8 astronauts blazed perfectly to a bull's-eye in a Pacific Ocean splashdown from a yuletide journey around the moon today and reported it was now "made of American cheese."*

*Dec. 27, 1968: If the Aircraft Carrier Yorktown were located on Temple Square, the three astronauts in their spacecraft would have landed less than 3 1/2 miles away or at the turnoff to the old Salt Lake Airport on U.S. 40, 2300 West North Temple St.*

*Dec. 28, 1968: Two of the most dramatic moments in Apollo 8's flight to the moon — the critical firing of rockets to drop into lunar orbit and to get out of orbit and head home — were also tense times for Dr. James C. Fletcher, president of the University of Utah.*

*"When those motors worked I felt just great," he recalled.*

NASA Photo

Dr. Fletcher's interest in the vital Apollo 8 engine was intensely personal —he helped plan, design and build the motor and helped solve some of the problems it later developed during tests.

*Dec. 30, 1968: (UPI) — Apollo 8 moonflight commander Frank Borman reported from lunar orbit that the moon surface 69 miles below him was "a vast, lonely, forbidding... expanse of nothing."*

Then, at last, the great moment arrived. A riveted world watched on July 20, 1969, as Neil Armstrong and Buzz Aldrin set foot on the moon. Deseret News science writer Hal Knight, was sent to Florida to cover the event:

**DESERET NEWS,** *July 21, 1969: CAPE CANAVERAL — It was a heart-stopping, emotional experience to follow Apollo 11's dramatic landing on the moon and see man step out to explore the desolate lunar surface.*

*The feat ushered in a new era in human history. For better or worse, mankind has irrevocably turned its face toward the stars.*

*Words fail to describe adequately the feeling raised by this enormous event. The sense of awe and wonder was overwhelming as the scenes unfolded.*

What did it all mean? Historic perspective would come later. But even then, some sense of the accomplishment prevailed.

**DESERET NEWS,** *July 21, 1969: Man's landing on the moon has opened a window on a heretofore mysterious and forbidden planet that has been an object of human awe, wonder and dream for centuries.*

*"Every accomplishment that lessens*

man's fear of the unknown is important to mankind psychologically," Dr. Jack Tedrow, Salt Lake psychiatrist said today in answer to a Deseret News inquiry.

**DESERET NEWS,** *July 21, 1969: (AP) — Eyes glistening, Archie Moore, 53, soaked it all in, motionless, not even a glance to the side.*

*Then the former light-heavyweight boxing champion of the world smiled a gentle smile.*

*"I know a boy who walked on the moon many years ago," he said.*

*"No, I ran on the moon. I ran and ran and ran.*

*"These brave men," he continued weighing his thoughts, "have given us the event to unlock the imagination of the young. Daydreams, you know, can be real."*

AP Photo

**Edwin E. "Buzz" Aldrin is photographed as he backs out of lunar module, headed for moon surface. The photographer was Neil Armstrong, first to alight.**

Beehive Collector Gallery

# Nixon's
## fallen presidency
### 1970-1980

The Vietnam War finally came to an end in the 1970s, concluding an unhappy chapter that began in the 1960s. The nation found another enemy, inflation, partly born from that war and the determination to have both guns and butter. President Richard Nixon, whose early success was in fighting communism, sent first his emissaries, then himself, to China in a brilliant coup that altered the relationship between the world's most powerful country and its most populous. But genius abroad would not save him from disaster at home when the Watergate hearings led to his downfall. After all that, the country celebrated its 200th birthday, its institutions secure and its power growing.

Beehive Collecors Gallery

**President Nixon. Now more than ever.**

As the full depth of Watergate emerged, President Nixon tried to hold on, buoyed by lingering support indicated by "Now More than Ever" button.

Deseret News files

**The rise and fall of President Richard M. Nixon in the 1970s was indicative of a new American mood. After the raucous 1960s, citizens were ready for quieter times and highly intolerant of shady business in high places.**

**N**ixon's short-cutted tenure as president began with a squeaker election. It was a vindication for Nixon, who had been defeated twice in a row in runs for office in the previous few years:

*DESERET NEWS, Nov. 7, 1968: WASHINGTON (AP) — Richard M. Nixon, his narrow presidential triumph cemented by late election returns, chose the privacy of a Florida retreat today to start forming the new Republican administration he hopes will "bring the American people together."*

Over the next four years, President Nixon scored important coups in foreign policy. He dazzled the country by visiting China in February 1972, thawing an icy standoff between the two countries who had fought each other in Korea. In May of the same year, he went to Russia, where he forged new trade agreements and a pact to limit the proliferation of nuclear arms. Under his leadership, U.S. involvement in the unpopular Vietnamese War decreased. Apparently, these successes in foreign affairs offset his failure at home to control wage and price inflation. In 1972, he and his globe-trotting national security adviser, Henry Kissinger, won popular acclaim:

*DESERET NEWS, Dec. 24, 1972: NEW YORK (AP) — Time magazine announced Saturday that President Nixon and Henry A. Kissinger, his national security adviser, had been chose as its "Men of the Year." "Describing the pair as an "odd couple, an improbable partnership," the magazine said they were selected for the annual*

"Man of the Year" because "They have been changing the shape of the world, accomplishing the most profound rearrangement of the earth's political powers since the beginning of the Cold War."

Despite the accolades, events were already under way that would ultimately cause Nixon to resign, the only president in American history to do so. A seemingly simple break-in at the Watergate Hotel in Washington blossomed into a full-scale political nightmare.

*DESERET NEWS, June 19, 1972: WASHINGTON (AP) — Disclosure that a salaried Nixon campaign security expert was one of five men arrested during a break-in at the Democratic National Committee headquarters has prompted Democratic accusations of "political espionage" and Republican denials of involvement.*

*Democratic National Chairman Lawrence F. O'Brien said Sunday the affair raised "the ugliest questions about the integrity of the political process that I have encountered in a quarter-century of political activity..."*

The scandal surrounding Nixon and his associates grew into a massive spider web of accusations covering a range of wrong-doing. The Watergate burglars were tried and convicted, but that did not end the affair.

Meanwhile, another blow hit the administration. Nixon's vice president, who was accused of accepting illegal kickbacks while governor of Maryland, resigned:

*DESERET NEWS, Oct. 10, 1972: WASHINGTON (AP) — Vice President Spiro T. Agnew resigned Wednesday, his historic decision announced by a weeping staff secretary.*

Agnew then pleaded no contest in federal court in Baltimore to a single count of federal income tax evasion.

The vice president, his face drawn, entered the plea before U.S. District Court Judge Walter E. Hoffman. Hoffman told the vice president he considered the no contest plea the equivalent of an admission of guilt. He sentenced Agnew to the maximum $10,000 fine and placed him on probation without supervision for three years.

Beleaguered and amidst growing evidence that he had been less than honest, Nixon vowed to "stand and fight." He tried to maintain a "business as usual" approach. In his January 1974 State of the Union address, he challenged Congress to focus its attention on solving inflation and the energy crisis then plaguing the country:

*DESERET NEWS, Jan. 31, 1974: In a hard-hitting 45-minute speech to a joint session of Congress and a broadcast audience of millions of Americans Wednesday night,*

AP Photo

**Nixon's resignation made Gerald Ford, left, the first un-elected vice president ever to become president.**

**D E S E R E T   N E W S**

Nixon dramatically asserted his intention to remain in the presidency despite inroads of the scandal on his administration. "I want you to know that I have no intention whatever of walking away from the job that the people elected me to do."

But the president's popular support was suffering serious erosion. Finally, after the Supreme Court said he could no longer keep critical tape recordings private, he released them:

**DESERET NEWS,** *Aug. 5, 1974: WASHINGTON (AP) — President Nixon on Monday released transcripts of three 1972 conversations which he said "may further damage my case," admitting he kept the evidence from his lawyers and omitted it from his public statements on Watergate.*

*Acknowledging that his impeachment by the House is "virtually a foregone conclusion," he said tapes of all 64 conversations he is giving U.S. District Judge John J. Sirica also will be turned over to the Senate for use in his impeachment trial...*

*"Portions of the tapes... are at variance with my previous statements," Nixon said in a written statement... "this was a serious act of omission for which I take full responsibility and which I deeply regret."*

The Deseret News criticized him editorially:

*Aug. 6, 1974: President Nixon's belated confession that he misled the American people about his knowledge of the Watergate cover-up is devastating to his efforts to remain in office. Since Mr. Nixon didn't take his own lawyer into his confidence until he virtually had to, how can the public be sure it has been told all the pertinent facts even now?*

Only days later, the inevitable end came:

*Aug. 9, 1974: WASHINGTON (AP) — Richard M. Nixon took tearful leave of the White House and his devastated presidency today, telling the men and women who served him that only a man in the deepest valley can know "how magnificent it is to be on the highest mountain." Then he flew to California, one last journey aboard Air Force One, departing a scant two hours before the formal passage of presidential power to Gerald R. Ford.*

In his last address to his staff before leaving office, Nixon said, "Always give your best; never get discouraged; never be petty. Always remember, others may hate you. Those who hate you don't win unless you hate them. And then you destroy yourself."

In his later years Nixon became something of an elder statesman, giving advice on foreign affairs. He died April 22, 1994.

*Waghorn*

Robb Barr and Leslie Cannon caught disco fever in Salt Lake City, but the dance craze was global.

*Deseret News files*

# Disco fever

**DESERET NEWS,** *April 27, 1979: The sounds are hot. The steps are lively. In Italy, they call it "Travoltisimo." Here, it's disco fever — one of the hottest rages to hit the country since the Big Band craze of the 40s.*

*It's become a national mania that has changed the way people dress, the way they play and the way they spend their time and money. Psychologists have analyzed it, marketeers are making big business of it and everyone down to your Aunt Beulah has tried it.*

*Before (John) Travolta — the great shining knight in a white three-piece suit —rode into the picture to resurrect disco, the fad was pretty much limited to clubs along the East Coast. Now the Disco Belt is expanding to encompass a worldwide phenomenon.*

# The priesthood announcement

News that had been long anticipated and yearned for by many members of The Church of Jesus Christ of Latter-day Saints arrived on a June morning.

The full text of an historic statement, over the signatures of then-President Spencer W. Kimball and his counselors, N. Eldon Tanner and Marion G. Romney, was printed on the front page of the News:

**DESERET NEWS,** *June 9, 1978: As we have witnessed the expansion of the work of the Lord over the earth, we have been grateful that people of many nations have responded to the message of the restored gospel, and have joined the church in ever-increasing numbers. This, in turn, has inspired us with a desire to extend to every worthy member of the church all of the privileges and blessings which the gospel affords.*

*Aware of the promises made by the prophets and presidents of the church who have preceded us that at some time, in God's eternal plan, all of our brethren who are worthy may receive the priesthood, and witnessing the faithfulness of those from whom the priesthood has been withheld, we have pleaded long and earnestly in behalf of these, our faithful brethren, spending many hours in the upper room of the Temple supplicating the Lord for divine guidance.*

*He has heard our prayers and by revelation has confirmed that the long-promised day has come when every faithful, worthy man in the church may receive the holy priesthood,*

*Deseret News files*

President Spencer W. Kimball

*with power to exercise its divine authority, and enjoy with his loved ones every blessing that flows therefrom, including the blessings of the temple. Accordingly, all worthy male members of the church may be ordained to the priesthood without regard for race or color...*

The news galvanized the church, and for several days, favorable comments on the action came from around the world. For black church members who had patiently awaited the opportunity to be fully involved, the announcement brought particular joy:

**DESERET NEWS,** *June 10, 1978: Tears of joy and happy surprise welled in the eyes of many black members of (the church) when they learned of a revelation opening the church priesthood to all worthy male members, including blacks.*

*Monroe Fleming, who has been a church member for 27 years, said he is very happy about the revelation, something he had long hoped for and "something the general public was hoping for..."*

*"We have all waited for this, but I didn't think it would come in my lifetime," said Lucille Bankhead, 73, a lifelong member of the church.*

The policy led to rapid expansion of the church in parts of the world dominated by black populations, including Africa. In 1998, President Gordon B. Hinckley became the first head of the church to visit the nations of Africa, where he was greeted with enthusiasm and love.

# DESERET NEWS

## SALT LAKE CITY, UTAH

Mountain West's First Newspaper    .    122 Years Of Service

March 30, 1971
## A Dramatic Plea For Calley's Life

FT. BENNING, GA. (AP) — Lt. William Calley's aged defense attorney, his voice choking with emotion, pleaded with the jury today "that this man should not be given the death penalty."

Calley, 27, sat at the counsel table nearby, his head down, as attorney George Latimer of Salt Lake City appealed to the jury that convicted him of premeditated murder at My Lai not to impose the death sentence.

Later sobbing Calley told the six jurors who can give him death that at My Lai "I had to value the lives of my troops, and I feel that's the only crime I ever committed."

**[Calley was convicted of killing 22 Vietnamese civilians. His life sentence was reduced to 10-years. He served 4 1/2 months in military prison.]**

Sept. 6, 1971
## S.L. Wins PCL Crown

TACOMA — Not since 1959, has Salt Lake City had a Pacific Coast League championship. But Sunday, the Salt Lake Angels ended a 12-year drought by defeating Tacoma, 6-4.

Salt Lake won the PCL championship by beating the Tacoma Cubs three games in a five-game series. The Angels had won the Southern division title and the Cubs won the Northern Division.

Angels' Greg Gossen, who was obtained by Salt Lake in a trade with the same Tacoma team earlier in the season, started things off with a three-run homer in the first inning. Ray Oyler added insurance with a two-run blast in the sixth inning.

Sept. 11, 1971
## Nikita S. Khrushchev Dies

MOWCOW (AP) — Nikita S. Khrushchev, who ruled the Kremlin for 11 years and pushed his country into the space age, died today in the obscurity to which his rivals had banished him.

The successor to Joseph Stalin had suffered from heart trouble for several years, and he evidently succumbed to a heart attack. He was 77.

April 3, 1972
## Search For Skyjacker Shifts Southeast ...

Lt. William Calley

UPI Photo

PROVO — Search for a hijacker who parachuted from a United Air Lines 727 jetliner with $500,000 ransom Friday night shifted from the Provo area to about 60 miles southeast this morning after the FBI announced it had a lead on a suspect...

The hijacker, a cool, bespectacled man armed with a pistol and grenade, plunged into the cold night at about 11:25 p.m. with the half million dollars and a bugged parachute.

**[Provoan Richard F. McCoy was later convicted of the spectacular crime.]**

May 2, 1972
## Columnist, Times Win Pulitzers

NEW YORK (AP) — The New York Times has won the 1972 Pulitzer Prize for meritorious public service for its publication of the Pentagon papers, the 47-volume study of how the United States became involved in the Vietnam war.

The national reporting award went to syndicated columnist Jack Anderson for his disclosure of administration policy-making during the India-Pakistan war, as the trustees of Columbia University announced the annual prizes Monday...

In the awards for letters, the trustees gave the fiction prize to "Angle of Repose," by Wallace E. Stegner, a professor of English and director of the writing program at Stanford University.

May 6, 1972
## Passengers Safe After Cuba Trip

MIAMI, Fla. — A Western Airlines 737 jetliner hijacked on a flight out of Salt Lake City Friday night arrived back in Miami at 10:57 a.m. MDT today after being commandeered to Havana, Cuba...

A pistol-wielding hijacker, threatening death to President Nixon, forced the jetliner with approximately 60 persons aboard to fly to Cuba, after stops at Los Angeles, Dallas and Tampa.

May 16, 1972
## George Wallace Rallies

SILVER SPRING, Md. (UPI) — George C. Wallace is paralyzed from the waist down as a result of spinal injury from a bullet wound at the hands of a would-be assassin, doctors reported today. They said he was making a remarkable recovery but that the paralysis could be permanent.

Even as the 52-year-old Alabama governor fought back from the attempted assassination Monday afternoon at a big shopping center in Laurel, Md., while campaigning for today's Maryland Democratic presidential primary, a top aide predicted Wallace would resume his campaign.

June 16, 1972
## Irving, Wife Get Prison

NEW YORK (UPI) — Author Clifford Irving was sentenced to two and a half years in prison and fined $10,000 in federal court today for his part in the bogus Howard Hughes autobiography.

Irving's wife, Edith, who admitted she forged the name "Howard Hughes" to withdraw Swiss bank checks intended for the billionaire recluse, was sentenced to serve two months of a two-year term and also fined $10,000.

Sept. 5, 1972
## Arab Gunmen Kill Israelis, Hold Hostages In Munich

MUNICH (UPI) — An Arab vengeance squad shot its way into the Israeli quarters of Olympic Village today, shot and killed an Israeli coach and were reported to have killed a second Israeli official. They took at least eight Israeli athletes hostage and threatened to execute them unless their demands were met.

The Olympic committee suspended the games temporarily for the first time in modern history and there were open fears that the violence and political turmoil the incident brought could mean the end of the Olympic Games as they are now held...

The Arab guerrillas demanded the release of 200 Arab prisoners held by the Israelis, demanded planes to carry their hostages to an unspecified country and said they would shoot the Israelis if their demands were not met. They set several deadlines but postponed action.

Jan. 23, 1973
## Nation Mourns Johnson

AUSTIN, TEX. (UPI) — The people who knew Lyndon B. Johnson best — his family, friends and neighbors from the Texas hill country — filed by his body in the marbled great hall of the LBJ Library today to honor and mourn the 36th U.S. president.

Johnson, whose pursuit of the Vietnam War divided a nation to which he had pledged a "Great Society," died Monday of a heart attack. He was 64.

The tall Texan who described the white House as the "Lonely Acres" was a man who loved and needed people. And they came to him today to pay their final respects.

Oct. 6, 1973
## Utah's Answer To Bob Hope Tours Again

"Utah Sunshine" will light up U.S. military bases in Taiwan, the Philippines, Thailand, Guam and Hawaii for six weeks this October and November.

"Utah Sunshine" is the official title of USO Show No. GA-190, which will tour the Pacific for 42 days, beginning Oct. 13...

Conducted and directed by Eugene Jelesnik, Salt Lake violinist-composer, television personality and conductor of the Salt Lake Philharmonic Orchestra, the troupe consists of four pretty and talented singers, who combine acrobatics, dancing and guitar and piano playing with vocal accomplishments.

**[The singers were Linda Almstedt, Susan Erickson, Chris Showalter and Connie Sommercorn.]**

Oct. 15, 1973
## ZCMI Facade Comes Down, To Go Back Up Next Year

Part of the historic facade on the old ZCMI building started coming down today to be refurbished and restored and then reassembled as part of the new store front next year.

Stephen T. Baird, Salt Lake architect, is in charge of this phase of the dismantling project, and was at the Main Street site today directing operations of the crane which lowered the cornice of the north bay down in one piece.

Baird explained that the store was built in three bays.

The original store is the center bay, built in 1876. Two years later the south bay was built. These two sections have the original cast iron fronts, but when the north section was built in 1903, ornamental sheet metal was used instead of cast iron.

"It's beautiful work in itself," he said, "made from sheet metal to look like cast iron."

### Oct. 5, 1974
## 'Family' series king

With three Nielsen ratings for the new season already reported, the No. 1 series again appears to be All In The Family.

The show placed second in the first Nielsen and then first in the second and third. And, despite the problems with Carroll O'Connor, who plays Archie Bunker, the series seems to be heading for its fifth straight as the king of television.

### Aug. 1, 1975
## Police find no trace of missing Hoffa

BLOOMFIELD HILLS, Mich. (AP) — Police searched today for former Teamsters union President Jimmy Hoffa, who hasn't been seen since Wednesday when his car was abandoned in a parking lot.

Police said early today that they have no clues as to the whereabouts of the 62-year-old Hoffa, whose career has been dotted with incidents of violence.

Hoffa has been trying to regain leadership of the 2.1 million-member union, largest in the nation.

Authorities planned to question a reputed high-ranking organized crime figure in Detroit today in connection with the Hoffa disappearance, police said.

### Aug. 11, 1975
## Ford, buddy split tab

VAIL, Colo. (UPI) — James Brown, of Tremonton, Utah, is going to split the daily rental of a luxurious condominium with an old buddy so the two can save a few dollars. The old buddy is President Gerald Ford.

White House press secretary Ron Nessen Sunday said Ford and his wife, Betty, will stay in the home of Dallas oilman Richard T. Bass, which normally rents for $175 a day during the off season at this ski resort.

The normal rent on Ford's own condominium here is $110 a day and Bass will stay there. Instead of paying the $65 difference between the rent on Bass' home and his own, Nessen said Ford is taking in boarders — Brown and his wife, Gloria.

When the venerable ZCMI, touted as America's first department store, got a facelift, the end result was a facade reminiscent of the original.

Deseret News files

### Aug. 15, 1975
## Once loved Wilbur

Stripper **Fanne Foxe** says she divorced her husband a year ago because she was in love with **Rep. Wilbur Mills**. But she says the American public "hasn't relaxed enough to allow a congressman to marry a stripper." So Miss Foxe, whose real name is Annabel Battistella, said she has moved to Connecticut, and at the age of 39 has begun a new career as a writer, movie actress and night club entertainer. She said in an interview Thursday she'll see the Arkansas Democrat again but "it won't be the same."

### Feb. 10, 1976
## Farewell to the linotype

The Deseret News retired its last linotype machine Monday, an occasion marked with few tears but many nostalgic sighs.

The linotype was donated by the Newspaper Agency Corp. to the University of Utah journalism department, where it will be housed along with other printing relics.

### Feb. 10, 1976
## But it's too big for the door

While Deseret News employes were indulging in a bit of nostalgia on the retirement of their last linotype, University of Utah faculty members were faced with grim reality.

It seems nobody bothered to measure the size of the Mergenthaler Comet, and when the machine arrived on campus, the journalism faculty discovered the linotype would not go through the door.

Said one faculty member, "Maybe we ought to sneak back to the NAC dock tonight, dump the linotype and run."

### July 20, 1976
## An incredible trip and a fantastic view

PASADENA, Calif. (UPI) — America's Viking 1 space robot landed gently on Mars today and radioed back the first pictures taken from the planet's surface — "incredible" photos showing a sandy, rocky Martian desert with a gently rolling horizon.

The three-legged spacecraft rode a cushion of rocket exhaust to a gentle touchdown at 6:12 a.m. MDT in a lowland considered one of the best places for its

instruments to conduct the first search for life on the red planet...

The first picture from the surface of Mars showed a hard, sandy terrain. "There are rocks and surface," said Dr. Thomas Mutch, Jet Propulsion Laboratory. "This certainly doesn't have the feel of a lunar surface. It's very dictinctive." The camera slowly scanned the surface, disclosing small rocks and medium-sized boulders lying on the desert-like floor in the late afternoon sun. The lander's footpad came into view so clearly that the rivets could be counted.

### Dec 17, 1976:
## Utahns remember MIAs

While many Utahns will enjoy reunions with family members during the Christmas holiday, some will find it a time for remembering those of their circle who are still listed as Missing in Action from the Vietnam era.

Several such persons attended the dedication of an undecorated Christmas tree at Fort Douglas Thursday afternoon...

Mrs. Barbara Endicott was among those who attended. Since 1972, she and others of her family have attempted to learn the fate of her brother, a captain in the U.S. Air Force, who is numbered among the 728.

Bruce Walker, then a lieutenant, was flying an OV-10 reconaissance craft over Vietnam on April 7, 1972. He was shot down in the demilitarized zone. For 11 days, military personnel had contact with him as he evaded capture and hoped for rescue...

"We know he was alive. We know where he was and that he was captured. Now all we want to know is what happened to him," Mrs. Endicott said.

Spain's Canary Islands airfield of Tenerife was scene of worst aviation disaster. Ironically, neither of two planes involved had left the ground.

AP Photo

### March 28, 1977
## Two 747s collide, killing 562 in aviation's worst disaster

SANTA CRUZ DE TENERIFE, Spain (UPI) — Provincial governor Antonion Oyarzabal said today that the worst aviation disaster in history occurred Sunday when a Pan American 747 turned into the path of a Dutch KLM 747 roaring down the runway at 186 miles per hour for takeoff.

Oyarzabal said 562 persons were killed in the collision and the subsequent explosions so fiery that the asphalt runway melted. He said 72 of the 634 persons aboard the two jumbo jets survived the accident but that some of them were in critical condition. Among the crash victims were four women from Ogden, Utah.

The U.S. embassy put the death toll at 599 and the Spanish Aviation Ministry put it at 559. Oyarzabal said official figures showed that the KLM plane carried 244 persons, mostly Dutch tourists... All those on the KLM jet were killed.

The Pan Am plane carried 390 persons, mostly American tourists from Los Angeles. A total of 318 of them were killed and 72 survived.

**[The final death toll was 582.]**

### June 9, 1978
## L.V. jury declares Hughes will forgery

Howard Hughes

LAS VEGAS, Nev. (UPI) — Refusing to believe tales of desert rescues and secret couriers, a District Court jury declared Thursday the will left with The Church of Jesus Christ of Latter-day Saints was not written by Howard Hughes.

The panels' decision wrecked the hopes of Melvin Dummar that three pages of yellow paper would make him an heir to the Hughes fortune.

Although the trial ran more than seven months, the jurors deliberated only 11 hours before deciding the scrawled document was a forgery.

### Sept. 6, 1978
## Fest focuses on film history

A lot of history and lore of the movie industry will be represented in films to be shown during Utah-US Film Festival, which opened at Trolley Corners today.

Names of some of Hollywood's outstanding pioneer personalities appear as stars, directors or producers of pictures to be shown during the Festival, which continues through Sept. 12.

For instance, the late John Ford is represented in eight of his own productions to be shown during the Festival and a John Ford Medallion Dinner is scheduled. Ford also will be remembered through two special retrospectives, "Directed by John Ford," and "On Working With John Ford," scheduled at 4 and 5:30 p.m. Sept. 11. Admission to these will be free.

**[The festival later evolved into the Sundance Film Festival.]**

**Nov. 20, 1978**

## Guyana toll rises; 400 die of poison

GEORGETOWN, Guyana (UPI) — A Guyana government official said Monday the band of American religious fanatics who massacred a California congressman and four members of his party had begun a wave of mass suicide and murder that left 400 persons dead and 600 missing.

Guyana Minister of Information Shirley Field-Ridley, who at first reported the mass suicide, said Guyanese troops Monday captured the headquarters of the Peoples Temple in the jungle city of Jonestown and found that some of the victims apparently were murdered...

She said a man who fled from the religious community headed by a Californian, the Rev. Jim Jones, reached a police station in the jungled interior of Guyana Sunday and reported that leaders of the sect were preparing for a mass suicide by poisoning.

Jones, 46, variously called himself the "prophet of God" and "father" and preached a flamboyant mixture of old-time faith healing, racial integration and socialism.

**Feb. 26, 1979**

## 90 pct. eclipse darkens N. Utah

A dull twilight settled on northern Utah for a few minutes Monday morning as hundreds of excited watchers had a clear view of an eclipse which blanked out more than 90 percent of the sun.

The eclipse was total in a narrow band running through the Pacific Northwest.

**March 28, 1979**

## N-cooler fails, Eastern plant leaks radiation

HARRISBURG, Pa. (UPI) — A cooling system leak, probably the most serious nuclear reactor accident to date, Wednesday released radiation and triggered an automatic shutdown of Three Mile Island nuclear power plant, forcing evacuation of the facility.

Blaine Fabian, spokesman for Metropolitan Edison Co., part owner of the plant located near Harrisburg, said some radioactive steam escaped and was vented into the atmosphere....

In Washington a Nuclear Regulatory Commission spokesman said details were sketchy but the accident appeared to have been a very serious one, knocking out the main reactor cooling system and forcing the use of the emergency backup cooling.

**Rev. Jim Jones**

San Francisco Examiner

**April 6, 1979**

## Abravanel will take his final bow

Conductor Maurice Abravanel will retire as music director of the Utah Symphony at the end of this season after leading the orchestra for 32 years, Symphony Board President Wendell J. Ashton announced Friday. Retirement is his doctor's recommendation.

The 76-year-old conductor did not appear for a regularly scheduled concert with piano soloist Andrew Watts two weeks ago after conducting a similar concert the preceding evening in Ogden. The reason given was fatigue, and the Salt Lake concert was led by the orchestra's associate conductor, Ardean Watts...

In November 1976, Abravanel underwent open-heart surgery. Before that time, according to Utah Symphony officials, he had never missed a concert or rehearsal since his engagement as music director in 1947.

**April 11, 1979**

## Friberg painting returns

HOLLADAY — Arnold Friberg's painting of England's Prince Charles arrived back in Utah Monday, delivered safely to the artist's studio by two top Canadian government officials.

Victor Irving, director, Department of Public Services, Administration of Justice (equivalent to the U.S. attorney general) and R.L. James, inspector of legal offices, North West Territories, hand-delivered the massive treasure after its unveiling in the presence of the prince last week in Yellowknife.

Friberg was commissioned to paint the portrait of the heir to the throne standing beside his favorite mount, "Centennial," for the opening of the Prince of Wales Heritage Centre museum just completed in Yellowknife on the shores of Great Slave Lake. When finished, the painting will hang permanently in the museum.

**Feb. 26, 1979**

## Khomeini supporters seize Iran, round up scores of Americans

TEHRAN, Iran (UPI) — Revolutionary forces of Ayatollah Ruhollah Khomeini completed their takeover of Iran Monday —

spelling an end to the monarchy. Khomeini followers rampaged through the streets and rounded up scores of Americans.

Khomeini's forces sealed their victory by capturing the shah's Niavaran palace and nearby headquarters of the elite imperial guard.

Khomeini immediately installed his hand-picked prime minister Mehdi Bazargan to run the country in the place of Shahpour Bahktiar, the shah's appointee who abandoned the post when he lost military support Sunday.

**May 17, 1979**

## Skylab fall due July 2

WASHINGTON (AP) — The space agency, in a revised estimate, said Thursday that July 2 is when the 85-ton Skylab space station most likely will fall apart and plunge to Earth. About 400 pieces are expected to survive the fall and hit the globe.

The National Aeronautics and Space Administration said there was a 90 percent chance the pieces would hit Earth between June 26 and July 9, with July 2 the most probable day.

**May 31, 1979**

## Girls rest in separate cribs

"I love those girls. I wish they were home, safe," Dr. Stephen Minton said Wednesday afternoon as he disclosed not only the medical drama but the tense emotional setting of surgery that separated Siamese twins Lisa and Elisa Hansen.

In another part of University Hospital, the objects of his affection lay in separate cribs for the first time since they were born, joined at the head, on Oct. 18, 1977.

Quietly jubilant, emotionally spent and repeatedly cautious about the prognosis for the twins, Minton and other hospital personnel explained to representatives of the news media that the twins still are in extremely critical condition. Weeks, months, even years of evaluation will determine the true degree of success in the history-making surgery performed Tuesday and Wednesday.

**Ayatollah Khomeini**

UPI Photo

**Nov. 2, 1979**

## His career is just ducky

"I started out to be in medicine. I went to school to get into pre-medicine. But I became the voice of Donald Duck and ended up as one of the greatest quacks in the world."

This was the observation, during a telephone interview, of Clarence Nash, who has supplied the voice of Donald Duck for 45 years...

Donald actually started on the Merrymakers radio show in 1930. "I recited 'Mary Had a Little Lamb.' Walt heard it and said he wanted the man who could do the duck voice. He didn't contact me. However, later, I left my calling card at the studio and, as fate would have it, I did the Duck voice for a receptionist who turned on Disney's intercom system, where Walt heard the voice, and I was hired." Donald is the only cartoon character where the voice came first. He was on radio and the animators created the duck character after hearing Nash do him.

**Nov. 5, 1979**

## Iranian students hold U.S., British embassies

TEHRAN, Iran (UPI) — Iranian students, following up their seizure of the American Embassy and two U.S. consulates, stormed the British Embassy Monday and seized 27 British citizens as hostages.

The students, numbering less than 30, took control of the British Embassy, without any resistance from the Revolutionary guardsmen, who patrolled the outer walls. The guardsmen then entered the compound while the takeover was on.

At the nearby U.S. Embassy, student invaders called reporters to display "incriminating evidence" against about 60 embassy staff members held by them as hostages since Sunday morning.

**Jan. 19, 1979**

## Polygamist John Singer killed in arrest try

Polygamist John Singer, who refused to allow his children to attend public school despite court orders, was shot to death Thursday afternoon during an arrest attempt by state and local law enforcement officials.

Ten law officials under the direction of the Summit County sheriff converged on Singer about 12:30 p.m. as he stepped off his farm property in Marion, Summit County and walkerd toward his mailbox.

Singer, 47, was wanted on a contempt citation stemming from his refusal to enter his seven children into the public school system. He also was wanted on charges of aggravated assault when an abortive arrest attempt last October when lawmen posed as newspaper reporters. Singer drew a gun during that incident.

Singer's wife, Vicki, their children and three other children were taken to the Salt Lake County Detention Center. The latter children lived with Singer since July, when he married their mother, Shirley Black, in a ceremony he performed himself on the farm. Mrs. Black was still legally married at the time to Dean Black of Kamas.

# Home from
# Vietnam

**T** he most unpopular war in American history — and the longest — continued to creep along in Vietnam with no signs of a resolution as the 1970s began. At home, frustrations over the war erupted into violence on the nation's college campuses:

**DESERET NEWS,** *May 5, 1970: KENT, Ohio — Four Kent State University students were dead today and three others remained hospitalized as investigators began piecing together events that turned a silent antiwar demonstration into a maze of violence and bloodshed Monday...*

*The university, ordered evacuated after the shooting, was virtually deserted this morning and under heavy police and military guard...*

At the University of Utah, an unquiet week followed the Kent State violence. Beginning with a peaceful rally tinged with hope, the Utah demonstration advanced to a more combative confrontation between students and police and ended with suspected arson:

**DESERET NEWS,** *May 6, 1970: Protesters at the University of Utah campus today hoisted a flag resembling the U.S. emblem, but with a peace symbol instead of stars in the blue*

**Death and dismay dogged Kent State University after a student demonstration turned violent. Campus unrest across the country underscored opposition to Vietnam War.**

*corner. About 300 persons gathered near this flag west of the Union during the morning, some carrying picket signs calling for a general student strike...*

*May 8, 1970: Student protest hardened into a confrontation sit-in at the University of Utah Thursday, with campus police arresting 85, including 16 non-students and four high school students.*

*May 12, 1970: Fire officials said today they felt "quite sure" arson was involved in the burning of an abandoned building on the University of Utah campus Monday afternoon, less than 100 yards from a peaceful student rally.*

While antiwar sentiment flared on American campuses, U.S. soldiers continued to wage a war they were not permitted to win. And the death toll mounted:

**DESERET NEWS,** *Nov. 3, 1970: First*

UPI Photo

DESERET NEWS — SALT LAKE CITY, UTAH — WEDNESDAY, JANUARY 24, 1973 — Longest U.S. War Ends Saturday

*Lt. Stuart B. Lamkin, who was killed in Vietnam March 10, has been honored posthumously with the Bronze Star with "V"*

*device for heroism and the Purple Heart. The medals were presented to the soldier's parents, Mr. and Mrs. Kay Sebrands, 1306 McClelland St.*

*A 1969 business administration graduate from the University of Utah, where he was commissioned a second lieutenant, Lamkin left for Vietnam last Feb. 23. His father, Maj. Stuart B. Lamkin, was killed during World War II in Sicily.*

In all, Utah lost 358 of its military to Vietnam casualties. Finally, after 12 years, the U.S. left Vietnam.

**DESERET NEWS,** *March 29, 1973: SAIGON (UPI) — The United States' direct military role in the Vietnam War came to an official end at 5:53 p.m. today 12 years, two months and 29 days after it began — the longest war in American history.*

*At that moment the last of a fleet of gleaming military transport planes left*

*Saigon's Tan Son airport with the final group of the 2,501 departing GIs...*

*They had waited until Hanoi's jails were emptied of the last 67 American prisoners of war known to be in North Vietnamese hands and the men were flown safely out. As the POWs boarded the planes in Hanoi, U.S. Navy Lt. John C. Ensch, 35, of Springfield, Ill., summed up their feelings: "It's real! It's real! By God, we're leaving!"*

Questions about soldiers missing or held prisoner prolonged the misery. For some, there was a happy ending.

**DESERET NEWS,** *Nov. 22, 1973: Thanksgiving Day at the Jay C. Hess home was the fulfillment of a six-year dream.*

*Last Thanksgiving and five others before that, Lt. Col. Jay Hess observed the uniquely American occasion with simple services in a North Vietnamese prison camp.*

*Today the retired Air Force veteran was thousands of miles from Vietnam and the prison camp as he spent the day with his wife, five children and other relatives...*

Such happy endings eluded other Utah families. Years after the country had moved on to other things, their loved ones came home only for burial:

**DESERET NEWS,** *March 25, 1989: Cmdr. Gene Albert Smith was eulogized as a man of honor, dedication, great intellect and discipline Friday. He was praised for his dedication to family and for the example he set both as a father and a husband.*

*Smith died June 27, 1966, his aircraft shot from the skies over North Vietnam ...*

The fates of the majority of the MIAs remained unresolved.

# Inflation
## comes home

**At the beginning of the decade, the economic news was not all that good:**

**DESERET NEWS,** *Feb. 2, 1970: In purchasing power, today's dollar is worth approximately 27 cents compared to the 1913 dollar. If we hold to the present five per cent rate of inflation the dollar 25 years from now will be worth a 1913 dime.*

*In the past 20 years the Consumer Price Index has gone up 52 percent, despite the fact that business profits have declined from 4.3 percent of sales to 3.3 per cent. It is true that the average weekly earnings of a factory worker have increased far faster — 135 percent to be exact. But even this most fortunate sector of the American economy has seen its real purchasing power rise only 35 percent after federal withholding taxes.*

The economy was bad, and it would get worse. Suddenly in the '70s, shopping wasn't fun anymore. Almost daily price increases plagued purse and pocketbook; life was haunted by a new specter: inflation. And everyone wondered where it would end:

**DESERET NEWS,** *Nov. 19, 1970: If you had been earning $10,000 in 1949, you'd need $17,049 to get along with today — and a whopping $5,526 of*

Gasoline was only 41.9 cents per gallon — if you could get it. Inflation gnawed at Utahns' pocketbooks, spawned shortages and generally wreaked economic havoc.

the increase would have been lost through inflation.

The Chamber of Commerce's study estimated that if inflation continues at just the same rate during the next 28 years that it has in the last 28, then this would happen:

— $7,200 in wages now would have to be $16,800.

— $3,000 cars today would cost $7,000.

— $25,000 homes would cost $58,000.

— A $4,000 college tuition would be $9,400.

— A $125 suit of clothes would cost $290.

Nor was inflation the only shadow across the land:

**DESERET NEWS,** *June 24, 1972: (NFS) — Most of the crises publicized by the government and the media are viewed by the public largely as abstracts. The gold crisis, the dollar crisis, the balance of payments crisis and the Middle East crisis all exist, of course. Yet rarely do they directly affect the average American's daily life.*

*But now there is a crisis looming that*

is guaranteed to touch the lives of millions of Americans and its effect may well be felt within the next few months.

*If the summer of 1972 turns out to be a hot one, city dwellers all around the country will routinely turn on lights and switch on air conditioners — only to find that the power they take so completely for granted no longer exists in quantities sufficient to meet their daily needs.*

*For the United States — once thought to be blessed with a virtually endless supply of nearly every energy source known to man — is slowly but inexorably running out of power.*

*Oct. 17, 1973: (UPI) — Eleven Arab oil-producing nations announced Wednesday they would reduce oil production by five percent every month until Israel withdraws from occupied Arab territories and the rights of Palestinians are restored.*

The good life was an image of the past. Americans had to tighten up, make sacrifices, try to get by.

**DESERET NEWS,** *Nov. 20, 1973:*

*(UPI) — The Senate voted President Nixon the sweeping powers he requested to deal with the energy crisis, and the administration was reported considering a plan to ban Sunday gasoline sales.*

*Nov. 26, 1973: (AP) — President Nixon says he is cutting 15 percent from deliveries of gasoline and home heating oil to stave off severe fuel-shortage damage to the nation's economy.*

*The moves will mean homes six degrees cooler than normal this winter and not enough gasoline to go around.*

**DESERET NEWS,** *April 1, 1974: Five cents isn't worth a plug nickel these days. You can't get a newspaper, send a postcard, you can't even find a pickle for a nickel any more.*

The government tried price controls. It imposed a 55 mph speed limit. Energy-saving and cost-cutting became national pastimes. New administrations tried new measures. But the headlines were grim:

*Oct. 8, 1974: Ford unveils anti-inflation plan: higher taxes, public jobs, oil curbs*

*Dec. 9, 1974: No doubt at all — a recession*

*July 2, 1976: Jobless rate goes to 7.5 pct.*

*July 14, 1976: Use of energy outpaces rise in population*

*April 28, 1977: Carter's switching course on inflation*

*May 19, 1979: Inflation tops income rise*

And life had changed for Utahns as well as the rest of the country:

**DESERET NEWS,** *July 23, 1979: Hardly ever a night out on the town, no more pleasure drives, even hamburger has become a luxury, cooler temperatures in the winter — hotter in the summer – getting by with the old car, the old sofa, the old winter coat.*

*Sound familiar? If so, then you're like many Utahns who are facing a bare-bones lifestyle brought on by the pressures of inflation, the energy crunch, the uncertain economy.*

# A magnificent
# Birthday party

**T**wo hundred years had passed since the Declaration of Independence was signed and America embarked on its great experiment in democracy. By and large, it weathered the centuries well, surviving war and scandal and economic upheaval. The country was in the mood to party — and to reflect on where we were and where we were going.

**DESERET NEWS,** *July 1, 1976: (UPI) — President Ford began a busy round of Bicentennial activities today with a salute to the nation's past and present and a prediction that "the best of the American adventure" will be in the future.*

*July 1, 1976: (UPI) — Old-fashioned Yankee Doodle Dandy Fourth of July celebrations may be out of style, but to many Americans the hoopla marking their country's 200th birthday is pretty wonderful.*

*"I'm proud to be a part of this country," said Charles Scales, who shines shoes in Boise, Idaho.*

*July 1, 1976: What do Americans wish for their country on its 200th birthday? The Deseret News asked passersby in Downtown Salt Lake City Wednesday afternoon and got responses ranging from "peace" to "no more Bicentennials."*

All kinds of festivities were planned. In the nation's capital, the original Declaration of Independence was on display for a 76-hour salute. The Mormon Tabernacle Choir, in town for the dedication of the Visitor's Center at the Washington Temple, sang to a crowd of 14,000 at the Capitol Center.

Salt Lakers celebrated with music, a marching band and fireworks, as "wall-to-wall" people gathered at Derks Field for the annual Deseret News Cavalcade.

But nothing captured the imagination and passion of the country more than the gathering of the tall ships in the New York Harbor.

**DESERET NEWS,** *July 2, 1976: (CSM) — There has never been anything like it before, and there probably will never be again... It has been described as a dramatic salute to a historic past, honoring the role of "wooden ships and iron men" in the discovery, settlement and development of the United States.*

*Bows smothered in foam, the giant square-riggers symbolizing an age when America was growing up and out, have charged across the Atlantic with sails pulling like great Percheron draft horses.*

*July 3, 1976: (UPI, AP) — On the water, sailors from dozens of foreign nations saluted America with champagne toasts, ceremonial cannon firings and the blaring of whistles and Scottish bagpipes.*

*"What an absolutely glorious chaos," shouted James Myatt, skipper of the Great Britain II. "it's absolutely wonderful. Hooray for the lovely, lost colonials."*

All in all, it was a party to remember.

**DESERET NEWS,** *July 6, 1976: (AP) — It turned out to be a big, warm surprise party. We surprised ourselves.*

*There was just a disposition, a hunger to feel good. Not just well, but good. We felt good.*

*At long last, the grim cliches of more than a decade — "The American malaise," "the sick society" — were scarcely heard in the land, praise God...*

*In all the land, there seemed to be a kind of truce in fights and causes. Even the critical young*

Tall-masted ships in New York Harbor were tribute to "wooden ships, iron men" that made America.

Christian Science Monitor

*seemed less critical. Nobody profaned the cathedral. And did you see all those young people jumping with joy at the Boston Pops concert led by that lovable American square, Arthur Fiedler? Imagine, if you can, American adolescents waving flags and dancing happily to "The Stars and Strips Forever."*

The party was over, but its legacy would linger for a long time.

**DESERET NEWS,** *July 5, 1976: Long after the echoes of the three-day Independence Day revelry have diffused and the burst of fireworks become only a twinkle in the mind's eye of a little boy who remembers, the Bicentennial observance will continue to have an impact on Utahns...* "The activities of this year have reached into the lives of many Utahns," said Richard P. Sorensen, executive director of the Utah American Revolution Bicentennial Commission.

"Bicentennial projects not only will improve the quality of life in Utah communities, but have involved people working together. We hope that the spirit roused by the observance will continue to inspire people to work toward community unity," he said.

Those projects were many and varied: Gov. Calvin Rampton's "A Million Trees for a Million People" tree-planting project; the Bicentennial concert hall-art center in downtown Salt Lake; renovation of the Capitol Theater, restoration of Willard's pioneer cemetery; new playground equipment in Hyde Park; restoration of the Union Pacific Railroad Station in Ogden; and many more.

1776 1976
THE LIBERTY
PURSUIT OF
AND THE
HAPPINESS

Bicentennial medal

# Stars
## snag title;
# Jazz
## come to stay

Deseret News files

It was a heady time for Utah basketball fans. Their own Stars had netted an ABA title and the celebration was on. After Stars went out, Jazz came in.

**They Did It!**
## Stars Are ABA Champs

Chances Slim
On Averting
Steel Strike

- Utah's love affair with sporty z's began in 1970, when the American Basketball Association's Los Angeles Stars moved to Utah. The centerpiece of the team was No. 31, Zelmo Beaty. Big Z, they called him, and Utah fans loved him:

**DESERET NEWS,** *April 16, 1971: Around the American Basketball Association, Zelmo Beaty casts a giant shadow.*

*It is not because of his height (6-9, 235-pounds) or the fact that he was runner-up this season in the league's Most Valuable Player balloting. No, it is because, in the words of Utah Stars' coach Bill Sharman, "He's a 100 percent gentleman at all times."*

They called him "The Franchise," "the glue man," the player that held the team together and powered it to greatness. And greatness was what the Utah Stars found that very first year with Big Z.

**DESERET NEWS,** *May 19, 1971:*

### Utah Nabs ABA Title

*The greatest sports story that the state of Utah has known unfolded in the Salt Palace arena and the Utah Stars' dressing room Tuesday night.*

*The actions of Stars' forward Willie Wise, who approached superstar status during the playoffs, were typical of the rest of the team in the locker room.*

*"Do you want to see what I think and feel?" questioned Wise as he walked into the shower with his uniform on. "This is how I feel. I want to wear this uniform forever."*

*Veteran center Zelmo Beaty has been at the professional basketball game for eight years and never known what it is to win a title."*

*"But right now I feel like I'm on top of the world. It took eight years of playing for me to do something like this. I've played with some great guys before but not like these guys."*

Unfortunately, that euphoria was a one-time thing. On court, the Stars provided exciting red, white and blue basketball, if no more championships. But off-court, the team was a struggling franchise in a small market. The whole ABA had a hard time competing with the more powerful, more glamorous NBA. The two would eventually merge, but not in time to help the Stars, caught in the economic turmoil of the '70s.

When Big Z left for the Lakers in the summer of 1975 because of a contract dispute, many saw that as the beginning of

an end that soon came:

**DESERET NEWS,** *Dec. 3, 1975: After a quick fire-sale of four players to the Spirits of St. Louis — Ron Boone, Randy Denton, Moses Malone and Steve Green — Bill Daniels' Utah Stars' American Basketball Association club was dissolved officially Tuesday at a league meeting in Chicago... .*

*The Utah Stars is the third ABA team to fold this season along with San Diego and Baltimore.*

One final indignity would come later:

*Oct. 1, 1977: The defunct Utah Stars professional basketball team will have its name lifted from 1st South Street, the city commission decided today.*

*After the basketball team won its league championship in 1971, the commission changed the name of 1st South between Main and West Temple streets to Stars Avenue in honor of the champions.*

The Stars were gone, but more z's were to come.

**DESERET NEWS,** *May 17, 1979: A strong possibility exists that the New Orleans Jazz basketball team will relocate in Salt Lake City, Salt Palace Board members were told this week.*

*About 3,000 $25 good-faith checks, indicating people will purchase season tickets if the team does come to Utah, have been received by the Salt Lake Area Chamber of Commerce.*

*May 22, 1979: BATON ROUGE, La. (UPI) — A former aide to Gov. Edwin Edwards admits it probably*

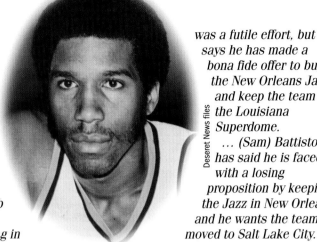

**Adrian Dantley**

UTAH JAZZ

*was a futile effort, but says he has made a bona fide offer to buy the New Orleans Jazz and keep the team in the Louisiana Superdome.*

*... (Sam) Battistone has said he is faced with a losing proposition by keeping the Jazz in New Orleans and he wants the team moved to Salt Lake City.*

*July 3, 1979: Moving day is never a joy and it is even less fun when there are 19 desks and only seven small offices.*

*Monday the Utah Jazz began moving into offices formerly inhabited by the extinct Stars and it became apparent early there was not enough room...*

With the likes of "Pistol Pete" Maravich, Adrian Dantley and Ben Poquette to lead the way, the Jazz, hoping that speed would compensate for height, set up shop.

**DESERET NEWS,** *Oct. 22, 1979: It has been a long time between tipoffs, but professional basketball — brown ball style — officially returns to the Salt Palace Monday night when the Utah Jazz hosts the Milwaukee Bucks...*

*General manager Frank Layden has been trading so furiously the players are hesitant to send out their laundry. Because of the newness of the players, (Tom) Nissalke, after the 101-85 belting at Portland Friday evening, warned of some rough sledding in the early going, predicting the Jazz, the youngest and maybe the smallest team in the NBA, would not begin to jell until midseason.*

**Future Jazz Star Karl Malone**

Better times were ahead.

# Fighting over women's rights

**DESERET NEWS,** *Aug. 17, 1970:*
*"Women may be looking to a recently published report to help open hitherto-locked doors for them, to help them fulfill their personal capabilities, and assume a more realistic share of the nation's leadership."*
*So said Miss Virginia R. Allan, chairman of President Nixon's Task Force on Women's Rights and Responsibilities…*
*Mrs. Barbara (Ted) Burnett, chairman of Gov. Calvin L. Rampton's Advisory Committee on Women's Programs, explains that Utah needs revisions in its laws and attitudes concerning women.*
*She reports, "Counselors on the junior and senior high school levels frequently guide young women into the 'feminine' occupations without regard to interests, aptitudes and qualifications."*

*Mar. 18, 1972: In a sense, only one senator and 11 representatives represent 53 percent of the registered voters in the United States — women.*
*Almost four of every ten workers in the United States are women. On the average,* they are paid $3 for every $5 paid a man.

Women's role in society had been in a state of flux for decades. In the '20s, all women got the right to vote. In the '40s, they moved into the work force to replace soldiers — and many stayed there. But the June Cleavers of the '50s were popular as well.
The so-called "Women's Lib" movement arose out of the activism of the '60s and was gaining more and more momentum as the country moved into the '70s.
In 1972, Congress passed the Equal Rights Amendment to the Constitution, which set off a nationwide debate. Some saw a Constitutional Amendment as too extreme; others saw it as not nearly enough.

**DESERET NEWS,** *Jan. 23, 1973: The Equal Rights Amendment, the number one topic of off-floor discussion since the 1973 Utah Legislature convened, will be officially debated Wednesday afternoon in the House of Representatives.*

*May 23, 1973: The Equal Rights Amendment, shot down by the Utah House of Representatives in January, is far from dead, says a local member of the National Organization for Women.*

It would go on like that for 10 years. By the end of the allotted 10-year period, 35 states ratified the amendment (three short of the necessary number). Utah did not vote for ratification.
That wasn't the only issue creating national debate. The Roe vs. Wade decision would be controversial for years:

**DESERET NEWS,** *Jan. 22, 1973: (AP) — States may not forbid women to have abortions during the first six months of pregnancy, the Supreme Court ruled 7 to 2 Monday.*
*Only in about the last three months, when the unborn child is developed enough to live outside the mother, may the state interfere with this "right of privacy," said Justice Harry A. Blackmun.*

**DESERET NEWS,** *Jan. 23, 1973: (UPI) — A Supreme Court decision that allows abortions on demand in early stages of pregnancy is being applauded by women's rights advocates but criticized* by Roman Catholic churchmen as a "tragedy" and "catastrophe" for the nation.

In 1977, designated International Women's Year, Utah women held mass meetings throughout the state. The 10,000 turnout in Salt Lake surprised even IWY organizers.

**DESERET NEWS,** *June 24, 1977: What appeared to be the largest women's meeting in the country today heard the keynote speaker deplore "anything that would adversely affect the femininity of women or impair the quality of her home and family life."*
*Keynoter Belle Spafford told the men and women gathered for the Utah State International Women's Year (IWY) conference in the Salt Palace that liberation is a "choice and wonderful blessing." However, she added, it can sometimes lead the overzealous to faulty attitudes and extreme actions.*

By decade's end, signs of change were seen:

**DESERET NEWS,** *Sept. 24, 1979: (UPI) — More than 10 million women will seek jobs in the next decade, leaving only 25 percent of America's wives staying home full time with their children by 1990, a new book from the Urban Institute predicted Monday…*
*"For better or worse, many more women will be joining and remaining in the labor force and planners — private and public — must anticipate the consequences," said editor Ralph Smith, an economist with the Labor Department.*

But the debate would continue.

# The '70s look

*Diane Keaton as "Annie Hall"*

**T**he Nehru look was dead. The mini skirt was supposed to be on the way out. Fashion designers came up with a new look. There was only one problem:

**DESERET NEWS,** *Oct. 18, 1970: (AP) — The midcalf skirt — the midi — is a flop so far this fall. Mrs. America just isn't buying it… An important Dallas retailer said, "The midi is failing to dominate the market… we are not happy with the ways sales have gone."*

Welcome to the crazy world of fashion in the '70s when polyester was queen and nothing too extreme. Mini, midi and a whole lot more:

**DESERET NEWS,** *Jan. 7, 1980: What made fashion history in the Seventies:*
*1970 — … Hot pants sizzle — briefly.*
*1971 — Chubby-looking fur jackets are all the rage…*
*1972— … Halston is making big money with Ultrasuede.*
*1973—… Diane Von Furstenberg does the wrap dress.*
*1975 — The big, droopy, sloppy look comes on the scene. Sweatshirts and T-shirts begin stealing the show… And the daring, baring string bikini shocks the world.*
*1976: — … Calvin Klein makes headlines with those skin-tight jeans…*
*1977-78: Droopy, baggy clothes and long lengths are "in." So is challis. So is gauze…*
*1978-79: Annie Hall droopy look gives way to fit and chic and nostalgic retro clothes that hark back to the Thirties, Forties and Fifties.*

# The death penalty returns

UPI Photo

**William A. Andrews**

Deseret News

**Pierre Dale Selby**

Deseret News

**Gary Mark Gilmore**

S.L. County Sheriff's Office

**Theodore Robert Bundy**

**Multiple murderers marched across the pages of the Deseret News in the 1970s. Theodore Robert Bundy, Gary Mark Gilmore, Pierre Dale Selby and William A. Andrews made mesmerizing, but spine-chilling, reading. The magnitude of their crimes outraged the public.**

**S**uave, handsome, articulate, a law student, Bundy was the most heinous serial killer of young women in the history of the United States. A trail of bodies from his native Washington State to Florida — with stops in Utah and Colorado — was imputed to him. Near execution, he admitted to more than two dozen.

The law caught up with him in Utah, where he was charged not for murder but for a bungled kidnapping that almost surely would have ended in death.

**DESERET NEWS,** *Nov. 18, 1976: UTAH STATE PRISON — Convicted kidnapper Theodore R. Bundy will spend at least the next 30 days in maximum security… Bundy, 29, is serving 1 to 15 years for aggravated kidnapping of a 17-year-old Murray girl Nov. 8, 1974, at Fashion Place Mall. Colorado authorities have also charged him with the murder of a Michigan nurse near Aspen, Colo.*

Utah authorities had strong suspicions that Bundy killed at least three Utah teenagers but couldn't prove it. They gave him to Colorado, which seemed to have a stronger case. Bundy escaped from Colorado facilities — twice. He made the FBI most-wanted list and for a time the trail grew cold. Then:

**DESERET NEWS,** *Feb. 17, 1978: PENSACOLA, Fla. (AP) — Theodore Robert Bundy, a cunning fugitive accused of one murder and suspected in 25 others, has been tracked to a jail cell by FBI agents who used fingerprints to penetrate his latest guise — that of a college track star.*

*Bundy was questioned today by investigators in the Jan. 15 bludgeon murders of two Chi Omega sorority sisters at Florida State University in Tallahassee.*

After years of appeals he was sentenced to die, not for the sorority sisters murders, of which he also had been convicted, but for the death of a 12-year-old Lake City, Fla., girl.

**DESERET NEWS,** *Jan. 24, 1989: STARKE, Fla. — The only living witness lives no more. Theodore Robert Bundy, 42, a charming young man who also happened to be America's most notorious serial killer, was executed in the Florida electric chair early Tuesday morning. Bundy was pronounced dead at 7:16 a.m. EST after some 2,000 volts of electricity surged through his body.*

The path to Bundy's execution was paved by another killer, Gary Mark Gilmore.

**DESERET NEWS,** *July 21, 1976: PROVO — The night clerk of a Provo motel was shot and killed Tuesday night in what appeared to be the second robbery-murder in two nights in the Provo-Orem area.*

*A Spanish Fork man arrested at 1:30 a.m. today in Pleasant Grove was charged with first-degree murder in connection with the deaths…*

*Gary Mark Gilmore, 35, Spanish Fork, was arraigned before Provo City Judge E.*

Patrick McGuire today…

Convicted, Gilmore attracted worldwide attention by demanding to be executed. He also carried on a jail-house romance with a young woman while he waited. His drawings and tender love poems were printed for all the world to share. His execution became a media circus:

**DESERET NEWS,** *Jan. 17, 1977: UTAH STATE PRISON — A last-minute court decision cleared the way today for the execution of Gary Mark Gilmore, 36, and moments later the condemned killer was shot to death here by a firing squad.*

*Gilmore, who killed two young men in two robberies in Utah County last July, became the first man to suffer the death penalty in the U.S. in nearly 10 years. His execution was fought literally down to the last minute by opponents of capital punishment…*

Unlike Gilmore, whose justice was relatively swift, the two men convicted in the Hi Fi murders used every legal tactic available to delay their executions.

**DESERET NEWS,** *April 24, 1974: OGDEN — Two airmen were arrested Tuesday night at a Hill Air Force Base barracks in connection with the brutal killings of three persons during the Monday robbery of an Ogden music store.*

*Taken into custody without resistance about 10 p.m. were Dale S. Pierre, 21, Brooklyn, N.Y., and William A. Andrews, 19, Dallas, Tex. Both men are helicopter*

*mechanics and have been at Hill AFB between six and eight months.*

*The two-hour robbery took place some time after 6 p.m. Monday at the Hi Fi Shop, 2323 Washington Blvd., where five persons were tortured by bandits and then shot in the head.*

For years, the gruesome details of the Hi Fi murders resurfaced as they fought their sentences. During his imprisonment, Pierre changed his last name to Selby. He was the first to exhaust his appeals:

**DESERET NEWS,** *Aug. 28, 1987: UTAH STATE PRISON — Calmly, Pierre Dale Selby blinked his eyes and licked his lips. He took deep breaths, his eyes fixed on the bright lights above his head. He wiggled his toes and muttered a quiet prayer. A fly buzzed around his body. Then, toxic chemicals dripped relentlessly into his bloodstream… Selby, 34, a native of West Indies, was pronounced dead at 1:12 a.m.*

Eventually, Andrews too lost the battle:

**DESERET NEWS,** *July 30, 1992: His last, blinding grin startled reporters. Strapped to a gurney, IV tubes running into both arms and moments from death, William Andrews lifted his head and flashed his toothy grin. When he saw his sister, niece and friends watching him through a window from a nearby room, his face broke into a radiant smile. He blew them a kiss and mouthed the words, "I love you."*

# A big mess at the
# Teton Dam

- Just as the first harbinger of
- trouble at the Teton Dam in Idaho
- was only a trickle, the first notice
- in the Deseret News of the dam's
- failure was just a small bulletin at
- the top of the front page:

**DESERET NEWS,** *June 5, 1976:*
*REXBURG — Residents of this city, St. Anthony and Sugar City were frantically being evacuated this afternoon as a wall of water from the crumbling Teton Dam rushed down towards the cities...*

*The dam is on the Teton River about seven miles upstream from its junction with the Snake River... the dam was recently completed and not quite finished off.*

Taken by surprise after its Saturday deadline and with no Sunday newspaper, the News scrambled to provide a full report the following Monday with extensive coverage of the Idaho disaster:

**DESERET NEWS,** *June 7, 1976:*
**IDAHOANS SAY LOSS MAY TOTAL $559 MILLION**
*New dangers faced residents returning to their devastated homes and businesses in Rexburg and Sugar City today — pesticide-poisoned waters, rattlesnakes and disease from cattle carcasses.*

*At least six persons were reported dead, 80 were treated for injuries and numerous others were listed as missing in the wake of the catastrophic flood which raced through the Upper Snake River Valley when the controversial earth-fill Teton Dam burst Saturday...*

News reporter Dexter C. Ellis flew over the scene in a plane and reported:

*Seen from 10 or 15 miles away, the flooded area looked like a shimmering desert mirage into which roads and lush green fields disappeared. Then the light plane arrived overhead and the newsmen aboard gasped.*

*This was, without question, a major disaster, something that happens in the Midwest, never in the sheltered Mountain States. Rippling, chocolate brown water poured in an ugly torrent from a wedge-shaped gap in the Teton Dam. It spread in waves over the communities of Sugar City and Rexburg.*

*The destruction appeared to be total in Sugar City,* the smaller of the two towns (population 617) with only the tops of business firms and homes protruding from the water. Houses were splintered and twisted off foundations, heavy school buses tossed about like toys and scores of autos abandoned to the flood waters...

Another Newsman, Dale Van Atta, just happened to be in Idaho Falls attending a wedding. Borrowing a camera, he hitched a ride to Rexburg and soon was wading through 2-foot-deep water on the town's Main Street. After describing a warm, lazy day in the small town, he chronicled the destruction wreaked by the flood:

**DESERET NEWS:** *... a wave of water from the bursting Teton Dam swept through the Upper Snake River Valley, leveling all objects in its path as easily as one's hand clears a Monopoly board of hotels and motels...*

*"I was expecting a lot of blue water," Kay Lloyd noted, and remembered vividly the swift, seething mass of muddy water that overcame the town in less than twenty minutes. When it roared through the downtown section of Rexburg, [Idaho bank manager Henry] Weick and his wife, Dawn, sped up the steps to the bank roof. On the hillside, spectators watched houses bob by like cordwood, dozens of huge pieces of lumber and telephone poles go crashing through barns and silos and several saw a Greyhound bus snag on a building before running ahead...*

The response from charitable organizations was immediate.

For weeks, thousands of people formed volunteer clean up crews from northern Utah and throughout Idaho. Many traveled hours by bus, spent a full day at work and then drove back home. As soon as the immediate danger was past, distraught Idahoans began clamoring for an investigation.

While blame for the disaster shifted among all of the concerned agencies, Deseret News editorial writers were more direct. They placed responsibility squarely at the feet of the U.S. Bureau of Reclamation for poor planning and shoddy workmanship on the Idaho dam. A flurry of reviews went forward on similar dams throughout the West. Teton had proved that the worst could happen.

## The world of the 1970s
### A TIMELINE

**1970**– A typhoon hits the eastern part of Pakistan, killing 150,000.

**1970**– An unmanned Soviet spacecraft, Venera 7, lands on Venus.

**1971**– 18-year-olds can vote after ratification of 26th Amendment.

**1971**– Federal and state aid to parochial schools is found unconstitutional by the Supreme Court.

**1971**– "Fiddler on the Roof" becomes the longest running Broadway musical.

**1972**– Britain imposes direct rule on Northern Ireland.

**1972**– 2.5-million-year-old human skull found in northern Kenya.

**1972**– Mark Spitz captures record seven gold medals at Summer Olympics but Games are marred by killing of 11 Israeli athletes.

**1973**– Pioneer 10, U.S. probe, transmits television from within 81,000 miles of Jupiter.

**1974**– Dr. Henry Heimlich develops a procedure to prevent people from choking to death.

**1974**– Aleksandr Solzhenitsyn is stripped of Soviet citizenship and exiled.

**1975**– 6,000 life-size clay warrior statues are discovered in northern China.

**1975**– Beverly Sills debuts at the Metropolitan Opera.

**1975**– Junko Tabei, Japan, is the first woman to climb Mt. Everest.

**1975**– First-class stamps go from 10 cents to 13 cents.

**1976**– North and South Vietnam are reunited as one country.

**1976**– The Episcopal Church approves ordination of women.

**1976**– National Academy of Science reports spray can gases can damage the ozone.

**1976**– Mysterious illness kills 29 people at an American Legion convention.

**1976**– Henry "Hank" Aaron retires, holding a career record 755 home runs.

**1976**– Enterprise, U.S. space shuttle, makes its first flight atop a 747.

**1977**– "Star Wars" by George Lucas opens in theaters.

**1977**– Supersonic passenger jet starts operation between New York, Paris and London.

**1978**– Pope John Paul II becomes first non-Italian pope in over 400 years.

**1978**– A Gutenberg Bible is sold for the highest price ever for a printed book, $2 million.

**1978**– First test-tube baby is born in England.

**1979**– Margaret Thatcher becomes the first woman British prime minister.

**1979**– Mother Teresa receives the Nobel Peace Prize.

# Cold war battles

## 1980-1990

When the 1980s began, the world was fiercely divided between the Soviet bloc and the Western world. By the end of the decade, great cracks appeared in the communist bloc. A debate raged over how to protect the country from a missile attack, one solution being to mount mobile missiles on railroad tracks in valleys throughout Utah. That didn't fly, but technology did. This was the era when people started using personal computers at work and recording TV programs at home. So they weren't surprised by artificial hearts and cold fusion, technologies with great potential but weak legs. Nature had its own surprises: Mountain runoff created the State Street River in Salt Lake City and a new lake at Thistle. And far-off Mt. St. Helen kept its promise and blew off its top.

**A**fter the frenetic '60s and '70s, many Americans welcomed a new wave of conservatism under President Ronald Reagan. The actor-turned-politician faced worsening U.S.-Soviet relations abroad and inflation/unemployment problems at home, but Americans as a people were more united than they had been for two decades.

Nevertheless, Reagan had enemies:

**DESERET NEWS,** *March 30, 1981: WASHINGTON — President Reagan was shot in the chest by a gunman Monday outside a Washington hotel. He was reported conscious and in stable condition at George Washington University Hospital. The gunman, firing at close range, also wounded White House press secretary James Brady in the head before being wrestled to the ground.*

John W. Hinckley was tried for the attack but found not guilty by reason of insanity, unleashing a debate on the complications of such decisions.

By the end of Reagan's two terms in office, personal economics had improved, but the federal deficit was at an all-time high. America had outspent the Russians as the price for a noticeable thaw in the Cold War.

After the Russian invasion of Afghanistan, Reagan shored up American and allied military resources. Eventually, he and Soviet Premier Mikhail Gorbachev signed the historic Nuclear Test Ban treaty in 1987. He stepped into internal conflicts in Central America to try to fend off communism.

**DESERET NEWS,** *Oct. 24, 1983: WASHINGTON (AP) — President Reagan said Tuesday he ordered the invasion of Grenada because a large number of Americans were in great danger from a new government run by a "brutal group of*

**Oliver North**

*leftist thugs." The United States had "no choice but to act strongly and decisively," he said.*

*Oct. 24, 1983: BEIRUT, Lebanon — (AP) U.S. Marines reinforced security barriers, bulldozed smoldering rubble and awaited replacements Monday after a suicide terrorist bombing that killed 183 comrades, left an undetermined number dead under tons of concrete and wounded at least 75.*

*Oct. 8, 1985: Palestinian hijackers who seized a luxury Italian cruise ship carrying 413 people claimed Tuesday to have killed two Americans, according to Western diplomatic sources in Syria. The hijackers threatened more deaths unless 50 Palestinian prisoners in Israel are freed. The 23,629-ton Italian liner Achille Lauro was hijacked off Egypt Monday.*

Such incidents kept tensions high during the Reagan years, but none did the damage, politically, that the so-called Iran-Contra affair did. A covert decision to bypass congressional approval and illegally sell arms to Iran, ostensibly to gain freedom for Americans held hostage (three ultimately were released) started the affair. Channeling money from the sales to the Contra rebel army in Nicaragua — a move also banned by Congress — compounded the irregularity.

Oliver North, until then an obscure member of Reagan's National Security Council, accepted responsibility for the Iran-Contra deals, and congressional hearings began in July 1987:

**DESERET NEWS,** *July 14, 1987: WASHINGTON (UPI) — Lt. Col. Oliver North, in the final hours of a grueling six-day appearance before the congressional Iran-Contra committees, was criticized Tuesday for playing a leading role in a "chilling and frightening plot" that was a "prescription for anarchy in a democratic society."*

Americans, confused by the moral issues involved, tended to line up in two columns: Those who thought North was a patriot and a hero who did some questionable things for good reasons and those who thought North was an egotist who felt himself above the law.

**DESERET NEWS,** *Sept. 13, 1987: Utahns like Lt. Col Oliver North. They don't want him prosecuted for his involvement in giving Contras money from the Iranian arms sales, even though they believe he acted illegally. They say North is a hero and patriot who didn't act out of hope for personal gain.*

Reagan denied authorizing the Iran and Contra deals. North was convicted by the congressional committee on three counts, but an appeals court overturned one of the convictions. In September 1991, the case against North was dismissed.

**President Reagan**

# Mount St. Helens blows

**The first reports seemed almost like science fiction. Mainland Americans were not accustomed to volcanoes going off in their back yards.**

**DESERET NEWS,** Mar. 27, 1980: Mount St. Helens, a volcano about 40 miles northeast of Vancouver, Wash., may be getting ready to erupt. Quakes have shaken it recently, causing avalanches. If recent disturbances have come from activity near the surface, a once-in-a-century eruption is imminent. Most of the area's 60 residents have left their homes.

Mar. 28, 1980: An "eruptive plume" of volcanic gas and ash spewed four miles high, and mudslides oozed down the snowy slopes of Mount St. Helens Friday in the first eruption of the volcano in more than 120 years...

"The mountain is heating up," said Don Swanson, an official of the U.S. Geological Survey, who flew over the volcano early Friday. "One could surmise the snow would be melting and this is what is causing the mudslides. We could conceivably have activity for a considerable period of time."

Those first reports didn't seem too bad. People had been evacuated; the eruption didn't seem life-threatening. They also got us thinking about our own back yard:

**DESERET NEWS,** April 1, 1980: Only yesterday, geologically speaking, volcanoes erupted in Utah.

And they could erupt again, but it's not very likely, experts say.

"You always get surprised," said Dr. Myron G. Best, a professor of geology at Brigham Young University and one of the few experts on volcanoes in Utah.

But geologists' educated guess is that there's little chance what is happening this week at Mount St. Helens in the Cascade Mountain Range of Washington will ever happen in Utah.

Into April, the volcano watch was on. On the 2nd, a new cloud of smoke and ash belched from the crater. On the 3rd, a change in seismic readings indicated that lava might be moving up. On the 4th, ominous tremors rumbled. On the 5th, "desk-sized ice cubes" were spit out. Then things quieted down; rumblings and tremors stopped. Could it be that the show was over? Not likely:

**DESERET NEWS,** May 19, 1980: (AP, UPI) — Abrasive volcanic ash coughed up by Mount St. Helens drifted over three states Monday following a volcanic eruption that killed nine people, left 21 missing, and forced thousands to flee a mile-wide wall of steaming mud.

The ash... fell half an inch deep on the ground up to 500 miles away following Sunday's convulsion that turned day into night in much of eastern Washington, Idaho and western Montana.

A plume of steam and ash was still billowing 14,000 feet high from a crater a half-mile wide Monday, but there were no sightings of the fuming rivers of mud and rock which roared down the flanks of the peak earlier. There were no sightings of lava flows during the eruption.

May 22, 1980: (AP) — President Carter flew within three miles of the volcanic summit of Mount St. Helens in southwest Washington Thursday and declared, "Someone described it as the moonscape, but the moon looks like a golf course compared to what's up there."

Flying into a mountainside snowstorm at 1,500 feet in a small Marine Corps helicopter, Carter told reporters he saw great piles of mud "that used to be mountains," deep craters and steamy melting ice that he called icebergs.

"It's a horrible-looking sight," the president said. "I don't know if there's anything else like it in the world."

As surreal as the landscape seemed, it was causing real problems: travelers stranded by ash-clogged highways and airports; torrents of hot mud crashing into rivers which in turn threatened to flood tiny towns; a cloud of billowing volcanic ash spreading as far east as Kentucky and Tennessee; a death toll that rose to 57 altogether.

Another major eruption came on July 22.

Shoppers in Spokane, miles from the spewing volcano, donned gas masks to protect their lungs from fine ash.

And then the mighty mountain went back to sleep, leaving the country to deal with the aftermath. What do you do with tons of ash? Bottle it and sell it to tourists, of course. A much harder question: How do you show respect for a life that was lost?

**DESERET NEWS,** Sept. 15, 1980: (AP, UPI) — To the auctioneer, it was just another estate, but for about 100 bidders it was a memento of Mount St. Helens legend Harry Truman.

The crusty, 84-year-old Truman apparently died along once-placid Spirit Lake in southwest Washington when his lodge was destroyed by debris from the volcano's devastating May 18 blast.

He ignored repeated warnings to leave the area, scoffing at the idea that the mountain he had lived on for 50 years might turn against him.

His body has not been found, but all Truman's possessions were sold Saturday... The first item was sold to Vicki Sassaman, of Skamania County, who paid $12.50 for Truman's metal hardhat.

"I don't really care if it's worth something," she said. "I just wanted it as a keepsake for Harry. I have a lot of respect for him because he did what he wanted."

Billowing clouds of ash spread across several states as Mt. St. Helens lost its lid. The eruption made a monster of the picture-perfect mountain shown below.

# MX
## That bird won't fly

In the 1980s, any Utahn who hadn't heard the term "MX" just wasn't paying attention. A grandiose, multibillion-dollar plan by America's military to spread a massive network of rail-connected missile bunkers across desert lands in Utah and Nevada generated a war of words that lasted several years.

**DESERET NEWS,** *Oct. 2, OMAHA (UPI) — The Air Force chief of staff said Sunday it is "likely" the MX missile system will be located in the Southwest, rather than in the Nebraska Panhandle and adjoining areas of the High Plains…*

*States most commonly mentioned by defense officials for the MX, the World Herald said, are Arizona, Nevada and Utah.*

The debate began. Military brass hurried to tout the benefits of their magnificent new weapon to an audience aware that war with Russia was always a heartbeat away:

**DESERET NEWS,** *April 21, 1980: A description of MX — missile experimental — the new intercontinental ballistic missile proposed to be based in the Utah-Nevada Great Basin, reads like the opening of a Superman serial.*

*It's big, it's accurate, it's able to carry 10 nuclear warheads to pre-programmed targets in a single launch…*

Ponderous MX missile, designed to deliver 10 warheads at one blow, never found a home in the Utah/Nevada desert, due to opposition, changing world affairs.

*Deseret News files*

But Utahns asked how the state could balance the promise of a revitalized economy against vast environmental impacts and the likelihood that their state would become a prime target in a nuclear war. The report from a Delta hearing summed up the confusion:

**DESERET NEWS,** *Jan. 16, 1981: Some are for it. Some are against it. Some are confused by it and all of them wonder about it. But all in the Delta area would be touched by the MX Project if the Air Force decided to base the gigantic project in their backyard.*

Many Utahns had no difficulty at all coming to a conclusion. Some, like State Sen. Frances Farley, called the proposal the "biggest land grab in the history of the country." Ultimately, the most significant opposition to the MX plan came from a powerful source. In early May 1981, the LDS Church issued a statement:

**DESERET NEWS,** *May 5, 1981: The First Presidency of The Church of Jesus Christ of Latter-day Saints issued a statement Tuesday deploring the nuclear arms race and expressing "grave concern" over concentration of the MX missile system in Utah and Nevada.*

*Such concentration may invite a first-strike attack with near-annihilation in western valleys and deadly fallout spreading over much of the nation, the statement said. The construction project would have adverse sociological, ecological and water impacts in the area, the statement signed by the three members of the First Presidency continued.*

The church's statement galvanized the opposition. In addition, the world changed. The Soviet Union began to crumble from within, and a new administration headed by President Bush was determined to cut military spending. MX, on the scale proposed in the 1980s, faded into the Western sunset.

# Wilberg
## Fire in the hole

Among Utahns, the words "mine" and "accident" used in the same sentence are certain to generate fear and anxiety. It happened again in December 1984 when a fire trapped 27 miners inside the Wilberg Mine in Emery County:

**DESERET NEWS,** *Dec. 20, 1984: ORANGEVILLE, Emery County — A stubborn fire kept 27 coal miners trapped thousands of feet inside a Utah Power & Light Co. mine seven miles north of Orangeville Thursday as federal mining inspectors sent a rescue team into the mine after them.*

*But the team was forced back out, probably by the heat… Officials were forced to turn their efforts to other rescue options.*

*The blaze broke out on a conveyor belt about 5,000 feet into the mine at 9:30 p.m. Wednesday. The workers were mining about 3,000 feet beyond that…*

Frantic rescuers started drilling two airshafts to a safety chamber where they hoped the miners might have fled. Those who tried to enter the mine were repelled by thick smoke and carbon monoxide when the fire surged out of control. Photographs showed thick plumes of smoke pouring out of the hillside. Families watched and waited, while hope dwindled and then died:

**DESERET NEWS,** *Dec. 23, 1984: HUNTINGTON, Emery County — They rode an emotional roller coaster for more than 70 hours, their hopes rising and falling with each report from the rescue teams.*

Smoke billowing from deep inside the Wilberg Mine was mute evidence of the fires that kept rescuers at bay for months. The disaster claimed 27 miners.

*LDS Church*

For the families who learned the fate of their loved ones at the Wilberg Mine, there was the trauma of shock after the long wait, followed by grief and then tears.

For months, the stubborn fire and fumes permeated the mine and robbed survivors even of a body to bury. Repeated attempts to reach the bodies were frustrated. Almost a year passed before the last of the dead miners was brought to the surface:

**DESERET NEWS,** *Dec. 16, 1985: ORANGEVILLE, Emery County — Emery Mining Corp. crews Monday found the last two bodies of 27 miners who perished in a fire last December at the Wilberg Mine, company spokesman Bob Henrie said.*

*The discovery of the remains about 9:30 a.m. came just three days before the one-year anniversary of the Dec. 19 disaster.*

Among those dead was Nanette M. Wheeler, 33, Castledale, the first female miner to die in a Utah mine accident.

Immediate questions arose over the Wilberg Mine's safety record. The mine was closed during hearings, which went forward amid protests from family and media members who were barred from the proceedings. Repercussions continued for months, but for many of the survivors, comfort began to come with dedication of a monument to the memories of those who died:

**DESERET NEWS,** *Sept 30, 1985: CASTLE DALE — A monument to 27 dead miners was dedicated Sunday afternoon in a short but solemn service. The monument, in front of the Emery County Courthouse, is dedicated to the memory of the 26 men and one woman who lost their lives almost a year ago in the Wilberg Mine fire.*

# Hearts and fusion for Utah

**The University of Utah caught the world's attention in science during the 1980s. The first permanent artificial heart was implanted, sparking a media sensation around the globe. Then an announcement that cold fusion had been achieved brought first cheers, then consternation. The announcement was apparently ahead of the science.**

University of Utah

**Barney Clark**

For more than two years before the actual artificial heart implant, there were hints that human experimentation was near:

**DESERET NEWS,** *Aug. 13, 1980: Almost certainly within the coming year, a human somewhere in the world — very possibly in the University of Utah Medical Center — will get a new lease on life through an artificial heart, Dr. Willem J. Kolff believes.*

The university collaborated for years on development of a heart model but spent two years overcoming barriers — permission from the U.S. Food and Drug Administration, approval by the university's own human experimentation board and then a search for the perfect patient to meet strict FDA guidelines. The announcement finally came:

**DESERET NEWS,** *Dec. 1, 1982: A piece of history will be added to medical annals Thursday if the University of Utah Medical Center proceeds with its announced intention to implant an artificial heart in a human. A hundred years from now, the name of the 61-year-old prospective recipient may be well-known to surgeons of a new era to whom the history of Utah's efforts will be a milestone in the development of artificial organs...*

The then-unnamed recipient, Dr. Barney Clark, a former Utahn and then a Seattle dentist, was deteriorating so rapidly that the surgery was expedited. Dozens of reporters from all parts of the United States and several foreign countries tensed themselves for the long wait.

**DESERET NEWS,** *Dec. 2, 1982: At 5 a.m. Thursday the announcement came. The Jarvik 7, Utah's artificial heart, was pumping in the chest of Barney B. Clark, a 61-year-old dentist from the Seattle suburb of Des Moines*
*At that point, the mechanical device had sustained his life for 50 minutes. As the morning ticked away, the news remained the same. The long-awaited human test of the artificial heart appeared headed for success...*

It was an achievement of major proportions. But troubles lay ahead. Pulmonary bleeding, seizures and a failure of one of the artificial heart valves followed each other in short intervals. Finally, after 112 days, the end came for Dr. Clark:

**DESERET NEWS,** *March 24, 1983: Dr. Barney Clark died a quiet, dignified death at 10:02 p.m. Wednesday, leaving a medical legacy on which the future of artificial heart use will be built...*
*A medical team, after considering the ups and downs of Clark's continuing battle to stay alive in the face of obvious deterioration and the collapse of one body system after another, made the decision to turn off the heart...*

Work on artificial hearts has continued in Utah and throughout the world. The expectations for the Jarvik 7 [after inventor Robert Jarvik] proved premature, but as one researcher said, the Utah events in 1982 were to the future of heart care what the first flights of Orville and Wilbur Wright were to aviation.

The cold fusion saga began on the same world-intensive scale with a university announcement:

**DESERET NEWS,** *March 23, 1989: University of Utah officials were to announce Thursday a breakthrough in fusion energy that reports say could provide virtually unlimited, clean and inexpensive energy...*
*"Yes, we did it" (B. Stanley) Pons told the Associated Press.*
*Scientists, who since 1952 have spent millions of dollars to achieve controlled hydrogen fusion, have generally believed that it could take place only under the millions of degrees of heat and density that exist on the sun.*

*March 24, 1989: Only time will tell if a break-through in nuclear fusion energy by a University of Utah chemist and his British colleague will find its place in history alongside Newton's apple and Bell's telephone.*
*But some scientists already are calling the "school-level" chemistry of Martin Fleischmann and B. Stanley Pons the greatest scientific accomplishment of the 20th Century...*
*During a press conference Thursday, the scientists confirmed that they have successfully created a sustained nuclear fusion reaction for 100 hours at room temperature...*

The announcement set the scientific world on its ear and brought hundreds of interested experts to Utah. Then first notes of caution surfaced:

**DESERET NEWS,** *April 2, 1989: New scientific ideas are always met with skepticism, but the University of Utah's claims of cold nuclear fusion are doubly doubted...*
*There is a growing number of physicists who say even if the experiment does work and the great amounts of heat Pons and Fleischmann have seen are repeated, they believe it isn't nuclear fusion taking place, but some strange form of chemistry.*

The university got financial support from the state and set up a research institute. Eventually, with the tempest surrounding cold fusion growing and contention high, Pons and Fleischmann left for France, and the Cold Fusion Institute closed its doors.

University of Utah

**Cold fusion test tube**

University of Utah

**Dr. William C. DeVries was the only surgeon authorized to implant the heart.**

Deseret News files

**B. Stanley Pons had a private aside for co-researcher Martin Fleischmann during a cold fusion discussion in autumn of 1989. Their announcement proved premature.**

# When streets became
# rivers

Men and machines tried to stop a mountain slide in Spanish Fork Canyon, but it was a losing battle. The tiny town of Thistle took the brunt of flooding.

 **F**irst came the rains.

**DESERET NEWS,** *Sept. 27, 1982: Gov. Scott M. Matheson signed an executive order Monday declaring a state of emergency so state agencies can assist Salt Lake County in flood cleanup work after Sunday's devastating storm.*

*The deluge flooded homes and streets, backed up sewers, caused mud and rock slides and set new day, month and water year precipitation records.*

The novelty of a river running down normally dry State Street brought out sightseers, many armed with cameras.

Then it snowed — heavy snows all winter long. Even so, the situation didn't seem that out of the ordinary. Then the ground began to move.

**DESERET NEWS,** *April 16, 1983: THISTLE JUNCTION — Three Utah construction companies are working around the clock to stop a moving mountain.*

*The mountain, above Spanish Fork Canyon, is sliding on a strata of slick clay at the rate of a foot an hour — pushing aside a river, a highway and a railroad bed.*

*April 17, 1983: THISTLE JUNCTION — Emergency officials have given up trying to keep the road or the railroad open through Spanish Fork Canyon and will now concentrate on keeping residents of Thistle and nearby areas from being flooded.*

*April 18, 1983: THISTLE — Elva Jackson Webb, 75, was brave, even a bit cheerful when people were around*

Sunday helping her evacuate her home of 42 years, yet the tears were close when she thought she was alone.

*She was one of the 22 families forced to carry out their belongings and leave their homes in Thistle because of rising water.*

Thistle was no more. In its place was a lake backed up behind the slide. And grim news awaited the rest of the state:

**DESERET NEWS,** *April 20, 1983: White-knuckle time is here for flood control officials.*

*They are making final preparations along canyon streams expected to flood this spring as snowmelt runs off the mountains. The runoff is expected to push City and Emigration creeks to flood level within 10 days, with runoff peaking in early May.*

*May 24, 1983: Officials say a landslide in Sanpete County's 12-Mile Canyon that forced closure of the canyon road is bigger in size, if not economic impact, than the slide in Spanish Fork Canyon that swallowed the town of Thistle.*

*May 26, 1983: Crews intentionally turned a Salt Lake street into a river Thursday morning, while Mother Nature did the same thing herself elsewhere and caused mudslides, loosed avalanches and contaminated water supplies.*

*City workers started pumping water down sandbagged 1300 South west of the Sixth West viaduct so underground conduits could carry more of the heavy runoff coming from melting snow in the canyons.*

Even so, Salt Lakers headed into Memorial Day weekend with plans for a normal holiday. But temperatures in the 80s and 90s quickly melted the canyon snowpack and turned roads into rivers.

**DESERET NEWS,** *May 29, 1983: Swift increases in City Creek's streamflow Saturday afternoon flooded downtown Salt Lake City, turning North Temple into a river blocking Main and State streets and threatening landmarks like Temple Square, the Salt Palace and the LDS Church Office building.*

*The all-time record flows in City Creek also flooded parts of the city's west side...*

*Residents and crews frantically sandbagged near Memory Grove, creating a four-foot high dam that diverted the creek into the road, and lined Canyon Road with sandbags to protect homes... City crews and volunteers later used sandbags to build a three-foot wall to divert the water down North Temple, blocking Main and State streets. Water was flowing so fast along State Street that it knocked over crews trying to build sandbag walls.*

Volunteers rallied in great numbers to try to keep the water under control. In all, an estimated 3,000 people came to fill sandbags in Salt Lake City alone. Numerous businesses donated food and drinks. State Street was turned into a river, and downtown Salt Lake turned into a mecca for tourists, who came to view this aberration of nature. Despite the trauma, a bit of festivity crept in.

The State Street River flowed until June 13, when streams of cars replaced the water, and life returned to normal.

# DESERET NEWS

Jan. 29, 1980

## Goodnight, Durante — wherever you are

SANTA MONICA, Calif. (UPI) — Jimmy Durante, "schnozzola" to his fans and friends for more than half a century, died of pneumonia Tuesday at St. John's Hospital, where he had been under treatment since Jan. 7. He was 86.

His death was announced by a family friend, Joe Bleeden, and confirmed by the hospital, which said the comedian, whose career spanned the era of honky-tonk speak-easies to modern television, died at 4:27 a.m. PST...

Bald, wizened and energetic, Durante excelled in every medium of entertainment — nightclubs, burlesque, vaudeville, the Broadway theater, radio, motion pictures and TV.

He earned a fortune and gave most of it away to good causes.

April 12, 1980

## Fayette links past, present of Church

FAYETTE, N.Y.– Taking a giant step forward into the futuristic world of communications, the Sesquicentennial conference of the Church also took a step back into the nostalgic past.

For the first time in its history, the Church held general conference in two different locations nearly a continent apart at the same time, linked together by satellite. In addition to the sessions originating in Salt Lake City, portions of the Sunday April 6 sessions were telecast live from Fayette, the birthplace of the Church, where so many important events in early Church history took place.

... Through modern technology, the telecast switched back and forth from Salt Lake City to Fayette with virtually no difficulty.
[From the Church News.]

Dec. 9, 1980

## Gunman slays ex-Beatle

NEW YORK (UPI) — John Lennon, the former mop-haired Beatle whose music set the beat for a revolutionary youth generation in the 1960s, was shot to death outside his Manhattan home by a man who earlier obtained his autograph on the rock star's new record album, police said Tuesday.

The assailant was identified as Mark David Chapman, 25, who was only 7 when the Beatles first burst upon the world stage in 1963 with "I Wanna Hold Your Hand."

Police said Chapman killed Lennon Monday night with a snub-nosed .38-caliber Charter Arms revolver he bought in Honolulu just six weeks ago. He was charged with second degree murder...

Police said Lennon's wife, Yoko Ono, looked on in horror as Chapman assumed a combat stance and pumped five bullets into the rock star's chest and arms.

Jan. 20, 1981

## At last! Hostages leave Iran

Iran freed the 52 American hostages Tuesday on the 444th day of captivity in exchange for return of its $8 billion in frozen assets, giving Jimmy Carter a dramatic victory in the closing minutes of his presidency.

The liberated captives flew from the Moslem nation just after nightfall aboard two Algerian 727 aircraft.

Word of the release came at 11:35 a.m. EST by telephone to London from Tehran airport officials at the end of a day of non-stop negotiations in four capitals involving bankers and government officials in the largest financial transaction in history...

Their freedom came just minutes before the engineer of the triumph, Jimmy Carter, surrendered his presidency to Ronald Reagan despite finally prevailing over the dilemma that contributed to his crushing election defeat Nov. 4 — ironically the anniversary of the seizure of the hostages in Tehran.

July 7, 1981

## Reagan selects woman for Supreme Court seat

WASHINGTON (AP) — President Reagan Tuesday chose Arizona Judge Sandra D. O'Connor to become the first woman justice in the history of the Supreme Court, calling her "truly a person for all seasons," and fulfilling a promise he made on the way to the White House.

Reagan said he did not name a woman successor to retiring Justice Potter Stewart "merely to do so," but because Mrs. O'Connor has the qualities needed on the high court.

"She is truly a person for all seasons, possessing those unique qualities of temperament, fairness, intellectual capacity and devotion to the public good which had characterized the 101 brethren who have preceded her," the president said in his nationally broadcast and televised announcement.

**Lady Diana Spencer and Prince Charles**

July 29, 1981

## Prince weds a radiant Lady Diana

LONDON (UPI) — Prince Charles married a dazzling, radiant Lady Diana Spencer Wednesday in a ceremony of such magnificence that the presiding archbishop called it "the stuff of which fairy tales are made."

Cheered by at least 900,000 flag-waving people, and watched and heard worldwide by an estimated 1 billion more, the 32-year-old heir to the throne made an irrepressibly smiling Diana, 20, Princess of Wales and the nation's future queen.

"Here is the stuff of which fairy tales are made — the prince and princess on their wedding day," said Archbishop of Canterbury Robert Runcie in his sermon to the St. Paul's Cathedral congregation of 2,500 people, including crowned heads and statesmen from around the world...

London erupted with color as it did with fireworks the night before. Neighborhood celebrations, most of them timed for after the ceremony, blanketed the country like the wedding-eve spider's web of 101 beacon fires.

Sept. 30, 1982

## 3 die from Tylenol laced with cyanide

ARLINGTON HEIGHTS, Ill. (AP) — The deaths of two brothers and a 12-year-old girl in the past two days were caused by Tylenol pain remedy capsules that had been contaminated with cyanide, officials said Thursday.

Dr. Edmund R. Donoghue, deputy assistant chief medical examiner of Cook County, said officials were examining two 50-capsule containers of Extra-Strength Tylenol in which "we have definitely confirmed the presence of cyanide."

Police in the two suburbs where the victims lived had been alerted and were attempting to learn the source of both bottles, Donoghue said, adding that the Federal Drug Administration's regional office in Chicago had been notified.

Feb. 4, 1982

## Utah Supreme Court welcomes 1st woman justice

Being the first woman on the Utah Supreme Court isn't going to be easy, said Justice Christine Durham, 36, as she was sworn in Wednesday afternoon and donned her black judicial robes.

"It has both good and bad sides," she told newsmen after taking the oath of office.

"It's good in the sense that you have the support of a lot of people you don't even know — other women. It's bad in that if you fail, you also are failing for others," she said.

However, failure was far from everybody's mind as Justice Durham was sworn in by Chief Justice Gordon R. Hall...

Feb. 9, 1982

## 66,000 seat BYU stadium approved

**Deseret News special**

PROVO — Final approval for a full-scale expansion project to increase Brigham Young University's football stadium to 66,000 seats was announced Tuesday by BYU President Jeffrey R. Holland.

Layton Construction Co. of Salt Lake City is beginning work immediately under a $12.4 million contract that calls for completion of the project in time for the start of the football season in September...

Glen C. Tuckett, BYU director of athletics, said excellent locations are still available on a donation basis in the loge, box and general seating areas of the stadium.

**John Lennon**

May 25, 1983

## The S.L. debut of 'Jedi' attracts truly dedicated

Why would anyone wait in line all day to see the first public showing of "Return of the Jedi," a movie that will probably play in Salt Lake City for at least a year?

— *"Just to tell everybody I've seen the movie."*

Scott Howard

— *"Because there are so many unanswered questions from 'Empire.'"*

Brooke Collard

— *"For fun."*

Joe Cartwright

— *"Because otherwise some yo-yo will go in and see it and spoil it for me."*

Brook West

— *"Because it's an event."*

Tonya Bell

**Star Wars robots R2D2 and C3PO**

"Star Wars" fans started lining up outside the Centre Theater at 10 a.m. Tuesday to be among the first in the country to see the third and final episode in the first-produced of three planned Star Wars trilogies.

Deseret News files

May 26, 1983

## AIDS threat to public is minimal

WASHINGTON (UPI) — Casual contact will not spread acquired immune deficiency syndrome, the mysterious disorder that has killed more than 550 people, a top government health official says.

"On the contrary, our findings indicate that AIDS is spread almost entirely through sexual contact, through the sharing of needles by drug abusers and, less commonly, through blood and-or blood products," the official said.

Edward Brandt, assistant health and human services secretary, told a news conference early this week promising leads were emerging in the search for the cause of the ailment, which afflicts mainly homosexuals, drug abusers, hemophiliacs and Haitian immigrants to the United States.

**[By the end of 1999, AIDS has killed 15 million people worldwide since its identification.]**

Sept. 16. 1984

## A beauty from Utah wins studded crown ...

ATLANTIC CITY, N.J. (UPI) — Miss Utah, Sharlene Wells, a strawberry blond jogger who grew up in South America, was crowned Miss America 1985 Saturday night to cap the most controversial year in the pageant's history.

The 20-year-old BYU junior, who wants to be a television anchorwoman, smiled broadly as tears rolled down her cheeks after master of ceremonies Gary Collins called out her name to climax the pageant's two-hour television extravaganza.

Wells paused while Suzette Charles, Miss America 1984 since a flap over a set of nude pictures dethroned Vanessa Williams, placed the rhinestone-studded crown on her head. Then she slowly took the traditional stroll down the Convention Hall runway as a capacity crowd of 21,000 stood and cheered wildly and millions more watched at home.

April 28, 1985

## Utahn Don Lind will realize a 19-year dream on Challenger

CAPE CANAVERAL, Fla.– When the Challenger roars into the Florida sky on Monday, as now scheduled, Dr. Don Lind of Midvale will realize the aim of 19 years of space training…

He was scheduled to fly to the moon on Apollo 18, 15 years ago, when that mission was scrubbed by congressional budget cutbacks. The huge Saturn V rocket booster that was to have driven Lind into space now lies on display here…

Lind was also tapped to fly on an earlier space shuttle mission that was scrubbed.

June 16, 1985

## Anchorage wins '92 Olympic bid; a stunned S.L. comes in 2nd

INDIANAPOLIS — Before the winner was announced, one member of the Anchorage, Alaska, contingent mentioned having a cardboard torch he was planning to pass to Salt Lake City as a goodwill gesture should the Olympic bid go to Utah.

But no torch was passed in Indianapolis Saturday afternoon. Instead, the cardboard cutout will stay in Anchorage, as the U.S. Olympic Committee executive board threw away the script and picked Anchorage to be its 1992 standard-bearer. Salt Lake City was second in the voting.

Anchorage will move to the international bidding war to see who will be host of the 1992 Winter Olympics...

Although no tears were shed by Salt Lake organizers when the announcement was made, there was an awful lot of head-scratching. Local Olympic boosters had thought their primary competition would come from

Lake Placid, N.Y., or Reno-Lake Tahoe, Nev. No one took Anchorage seriously.

June 30, 1985

## Americans return to freedom, appear 'in excellent condition'

WIESBADEN, West German (AP) — Thirty-nine weary Americans freed after a harrowing hijacking and more than two weeks' captivity in Beirut were welcomed to freedom Monday with embraces and cheers from relatives and countrymen and a hearty American breakfast.

"We are here, we are in good shape, they did a good job," said former hostage Steve Willett, 36, of Choupic, La.

A flag-waving crowd of about 100 people greeted the freed hostages with a shout of "Welcome back," as they got off buses that transported them to the U.S. Air Force Hospital at Wiesbaden, where they were offered free medical and psychiatric checkups.

Sept. 7, 1985

## It's no wonder stereo had a hissing sound

After a customer complained his woofer had turned out to be a hisser, the technicians at an electronics store in Cherry Hill, N.J., looked through the stereo speaker for bugs.

They found a snake.

The speaker returned by the irate customer had become the home of a 6-foot boa constrictor.

The boa was removed from the 4-foot-tall speaker and put in a cardboard box.

Workers at the store said they believed the beast slithered into the speaker through a 4-inch hole in the back.

Sept. 7, 1985

## Michael Jackson's no oddball

**Michael Jackson**

Michael Jackson's manager scoffs at reports of outlandish quirks ascribed to the reclusive singer and says, "We see ourselves as a couple of regular guys."

"He's utterly devoted and very disciplined," Frank Dileo said in an

interview in the Sept. 14 issue of People magazine. "It sounds boring and stupid, like I'm hiding something, but I'm not."

He denied that Jackson proposed marriage to actress Elizabeth Taylor or that he maintains a shrine to her at his 22-room Encino, Calif., mansion.

Dec. 20, 1985

## USU's 'Right Stuff' has made his mark on shuttle journeys

LOGAN, — Friends call him "Right Stuff."

"I just work hard," Scott Thomas said when asked about his nickname.

And that hard work for the junior studying physics at Utah State University has meant that Thomas has flown more experiments on space shuttle flights than any other person in the world.

That record and his work with astronauts who, according to Tom Wolfe's book on the history of space flight, have the right stuff, led to his nickname.

Dec. 20, 1985

## They'll be singing Mickey M-a-o-u-s in French Disneyland

PARIS — Mickey Mouse eating a croissant?

The once fantastical idea will become a reality within five years following the signing Wednesday of a tentative agreement between Walt Disney Productions and the French government to build the first European Disneyland 20 miles east of here in Marne-la-Vallee.

France won out over stiff competition from Spain and the victory left the French brimming with pride — despite some fear that Mickey could harm its culture.

April 29, 1986

## Nuclear reactor accident a 'disaster,' Soviets say

MOSCOW (UPI) — The Soviet Union said Tuesday the nuclear accident at its giant power plant north of Kiev was a "disaster." One unconfirmed report from the area said the death toll may have reached 2,000.

A statement issued in Moscow said only that two people were killed in the Chernobyl nuclear power plant accident. It said people living around the plant and in some nearby population centers were evacuated.

The statement distributed by the official news agency Tass, said the "radiation situation" at the plant had been stabilized and medical aid given to those affected.

# THE DESERET NEWS

## May 16, 1988
### 1,200 Soviets complete first leg of pullout

KABUL, Afghanistan (UPI) — A convoy of 300 armored personnel carriers, tanks and trucks began the Soviet Union's withdrawal from Afghanistan with a harrowing, eight-hour ride through rebel-infested mountains that ended safely in Kabul.

The withdrawal began Sunday at about 7:30 a.m., when 1,200 Soviet troops abandoned the Afghan army garrison in the strategic eastern town of Jalalabad and boarded the vehicles for the more than 60-mile ride west to Kabul, officials said. The convoy reached the capital by late afternoon, encountering no resistance from U.S.-armed Moslem rebels.

## May 16, 1988
### When Leno put mirror up to modern America, Utah audience roared

"Utah. A pretty, great state," chided Jay Leno. He had arrived in Salt Lake City a few hours earlier and he had seen those Chamber of Commerce billboards encouraging Utahns to like themselves.

"A pretty great state? I bet it took a million dollars to come up with that one. It's hard to believe the Japanese are ahead of us.

"A pretty great state? That's like a man saying to his wife, 'You know, honey, you're mildly attractive.'"

And that was just in the first two minutes of his Friday night concert. By the time he wound up almost two hours later, he had held up a mirror not only to Utah but also to most of modern American civilization...

**Jay Leno**

## May 24, 1988
### Eagles return triumphant to cheering crowd

Winger Martin Simard rode with "Tina" Turner in a bunk on the team bus from Flint to Detroit Monday morning.

The Golden Eagles, being on a first-name basis with the Turner Cup now that they've won it twice in a row, have nicknamed it "Tina," for obvious reasons, and Tina and the Eagles had their day in Salt Lake City Monday.

Hundreds of fans, television cameras and reporters greeted the Eagles at the airport at about 10:15 a.m. as they returned from their second straight championship tour, and a hastily planned parade in downtown Salt Lake City at noontime caught shoppers and the lunch bunch by surprise.

## June 10, 1988
### Bishop dies with last apology on his lips

*"Jesus, thou Son of God, have mercy on my soul."* — *Arthur Gary Bishop, in a final statement to witnesses at his Friday execution.*

Five times in five years, Arthur Gary Bishop killed without remorse. Five times he satisfied his perverted hunger, using a hammer, a pistol, even his bare hands to take human life.

Early Friday, the fear was etched on Bishop's own face as seven leather straps bound his arms and legs to a tan-colored gurney.

"Give my apologies to the families of the victims," he muttered one last time, lifting his head to look around. He closed his eyes and breathed deeply. His left leg twitched nervously...

Bishop, 36, a former honor student, Eagle Scout and missionary, admitted responsibility for the Oct. 16, 1979, murder of 4-year-old Alonzo Daniels; the Nov. 8, 1980, murder of 11-year-old Kim Petersen; the Oct. 20, 1981, murder of Danny Davis; the June 22, 1983, murder of Troy Ward; and the July 14, 1983, murder of Graeme Cunningham.

All five had been sexually abused and then murdered.

## March 25, 1989
### Tanker runs aground on reef, spilling Alaska crude

VALDEZ, Alaska (UPI) — The tanker Exxon Valdez, maneuvering through ice-clogged waters with 1.3 million barrels of oil, ran aground on a charted reef Friday and spilled 200,000 barrels, closing the nearby port of Valdez and creating an oil slick five miles long, the Coast Guard said.

The oil terminal is a major American oil port and source of one-fourth of domestic crude that travels down a pipeline from Prudhoe Bay.

The 987-foot tanker, bound for Long Beach, Calif., went aground on the charted reef 22 miles south of the port of Valdez, traveling through an area where it should not have been, said Chief Mark Peterson of the Coast Guard Marine Safety Office in Valdez...

Oil leaked rapidly for 12 hours, and a slick stretched five miles south of the tanker toward the center of Prince William Sound — an important fishing area — before the leak slowed to a trickle by afternoon, said Petty Officer John Gonzales.

## The world of the 1980s
### A TIMELINE

**1980**– Alfred Hitchcock, 80, died.
**1981**– AIDS identified for the first time.
**1981**– IBM releases a version of a personal computer (not the first) and starts an acceptance of computers for personal use.
**1982**– Pope visits Britain, first time in 450 years.
**1982**– Princess Grace of Monaco dies in a car crash.
**1983**– Terrorists in Beirut kill 216 U.S. Marines by bombing their headquarters.
**1983**– Sally Ride becomes the first U.S. woman in space.
**1983**– An Australian crew wins the America's Cup, ending 132 years of American victories.
**1983**– Martin Luther King's birthday becomes a national holiday.
**1984**– Fatal gas leak at a fertilizer plant in Bhopal, India, kills 2,100.
**1984**– Martina Navratilova wins her fifth Wimbledon singles title.
**1984**– A gunman kills 20 people at a McDonald's in California.
**1985**– 7.8 earthquake hits near Mexico City.
**1985**– The Rainbow Warrior, a Greenpeace ship, is blown up.
**1985**– The Italian cruise ship, Achille Lauro, is hijacked by Palestinians; American Leon Klinghoffer is killed.
**1986**– Nuclear accident at Chernobyl in the Ukraine, believed to be the worst in the history of nuclear power.
**1987**– A West German teenager lands his small plane next to the Kremlin wall in Moscow.
**1987**– Soviet Union and America sign first treaty to reduce nuclear arms.
**1987**– Ivan Boesky is given a three-year jail sentence for insider trading.
**1988**– Benazir Bhutto is the first woman to head a Moslem nation (Pakistan).
**1988**– One in every 61 babies born in New York this year has AIDS.
**1988**– The Shroud of Turin is investigated, said to be an ancient fake.
**1989**– A 6.9 earthquake strikes the San Francisco Bay area causing 270 deaths, 3,000 injuries and $1 billion to $3 billion in damages.
**1989**– Tiananmen Square (China) demonstration leaves 2,000 dead.

**Alfred Hitchcock**

AP Photo/Jeff Widener

# Tiananmen Square

**A lone Chinese man facing four tanks became a symbol of the futility of protest against repressive communist government. The man was pulled away by onlookers.**

In April 1989 the death of Hu Yaobang, a former Chinese communist leader who was popular with dissident students, triggered a number of demonstrations. For several weeks, an escalating stand-off between students, their non-student supporters and the government grew toward a deadly clash in Tiananmen Square:

**DESERET NEWS,** *June 3, 1989: BEIJING (AP) — Chinese riot police fired tear gas Saturday on crowds near Tiananmen Square in a renewed attack against pro-democracy students occupying the central square. Witnesses also reported at least 30 people were beaten by police outside the Beijing Hotel.*

*June 4, 1989: BEIJING (UPI) — Troops backed by tanks and armored cars fought savage battles with thousands of civilians Saturday and Sunday as a crackdown on the pro-democracy movement exploded into a city-wide insurrection, leaving more than 200 people dead and 600 injured, witnesses and hospital officials said.* **[Students later claimed 2,000 were killed.]**

*A gray, smoke-filled dawn broke Sunday over the blood-covered streets of the city of 10 million while the military continued pouring soldiers, trucks and armored vehicles mounted with machine guns into the center of Beijing.*

*About 5 a.m. Sunday, after hours of mayhem, a massive force of soldiers, tanks and riot police wrested control of Tiananmen Square from thousands of students who had occupied the political heart of the capital since May 13 to press demands for greater freedom.*

Meanwhile, Chinese students and Chinese-Americans living in Utah joined others across the United States protesting the Chinese government's actions:

**DESERET NEWS,** *June 5, 1989: About 500 Chinese students and Chinese-Americans rallied on the steps of the State Capitol Sunday afternoon in a show of solidarity with Chinese students and supporters killed in a crackdown by the government in Beijing. The Utah demonstrators wore black armbands with white flowers as a sign of mourning for the people killed during pro-democracy demonstrations at Beijing's Tiananmen Square. Many held banners and signs deploring the violence.*

Although the 1989 student revolt was successfully squelched, China was slowly moving toward a more open government and a return to free market policies.

April 6, 1988

## Readers vote Calvin & Hobbes most popular strip

Deseret News readers (3,774 of them) went to the polls (OK, really mailboxes) early this presidential election year and voted overwhelmingly for Calvin and Hobbes as their favorite daily comic strip.

Calvin won almost 2-1 (4,810-2,554) over runner-up and defending champion Family Circus. (First place votes got three points, second got two, third one.)

Rounding out the top 10 favorites Ziggy was third, Far Side fourth, Hi & Lois fifth, Rex Morgan sixth, Mother Goose & Grimm seventh, Bloom County eighth, Goblin ninth and Spider-Man 10th.

Although the survey was not conducted in a scientifically valid way, the large amount of mail indicates that readers take the comics seriously… If nothing else, the overall voting results revealed that EVERY comic strip has at least a few people who love it or hate it.

**[Creators of Calvin and Hobbes, Bloom County and the Far Side all retired at their peak, Goblin was canceled and the rest were still running by 2000.]**

ZIGGY — BY TOM WILSON

BLOOM COUNTY — BY BERKE BREATHED

# The Space Shuttle
## Routine and disaster

**W**e put those delectable moon landings behind us and were moving on in new space directions. Utah hoped to play a major part in the space program, coming up with elaborate designs for a spaceport near Wendover. But that was not to be:

**DESERET NEWS,** *Jan. 6, 1972: President Nixon's decision Wednesday for a "modified" space shuttle program apparently has shot down Utah's chances to be named as the nation's spaceport.*

*In an announcement at San Clemente, Calif., the President said the U.S. would embark on a $5.5 billion, six-year program which would make the space shuttle operational by about 1978.*

*Unlike original plans, the project now calls for an unmanned booster rocket to be used instead of a piloted booster which could be landed like an airplane… "I'm afraid this about eliminated us from consideration, at least for now," said Raymond L. Hixson, executive secretary, Utah Spaceport Committee.*

The first space shuttle flew into space in 1981. And Utah was involved, after all.

**DESERET NEWS,** *Mar. 5, 1981: The liftoff target date for the Columbia — America's space shuttle — is April 7 and the work is on schedule. The shuttle will be sent aloft with solid fuel motors designed and manufactured at the Wasatch Division of Thiokol Corp., Brigham City.*

*April 14, 1981: EDWARDS AIR FORCE BASE, Calif. — Astronauts John W. Young and Robert L. Crippen flew America's first space shuttle flawlessly through the fire of re-entry Tuesday to the first airport landing from orbit, opening a new era of space travel.*

*The shuttle Columbia, gliding without power, touched down on a long dry lake bed runway at 11:21 p.m. MST.*

*"What a way to come to California," Crippen said.*

America was back in space, and the country was ecstatic:

*May 30, 1981: The American people have rallied behind the space shuttle's first mission with widespread public support, speakers on Friday night's Civic Dialogue television program said.*

*"It did trigger many of the deep feelings of the people in the country. We were searching for something to get behind at this point in our history," said Joe Kilminster of Thiokol, who worked on the space shuttle Columbia mission.*

Columbia glided through space again in November, and a new fleet of shuttles developed: Challenger, Discovery, Atlantis. In September 1983, Thiokol landed a $220 million shuttle contract for work on space shuttle motors. But much of the state's focus turned toward research:

**DESERET NEWS,** *Dec. 16, 1983: An experiment that might reveal more about how the human body fights disease is slated to go aboard the next flight of the space shuttle Challenger.*

*The project, already shipped to Florida, was designed and built by four University of Utah mechanical engineering students, and it will determine whether high-quality crystals can be grown in weightless space.*

Space shuttle flights had become almost routine. And then — on the 25th shuttle flight, the 10th for the Challenger — the unthinkable happened:

**DESERET NEWS,** *Jan 28, 1986: (AP) — Space Shuttle Challenger exploded into a gigantic fireball 75 seconds after liftoff Tuesday, apparently killing all seven crew members, including schoolteacher Christa McAuliffe.*

*Fragments of the $1.2 billion spacecraft, one of four in NASA's shuttle fleet, fell into the Atlantic Ocean 18 miles southeast of the Kennedy Center launch pad.*

No American astronaut had been killed in space before, and the nation mourned as investigations tried to determine the cause so work could press on.

Blame was eventually placed on faulty O-ring seals in the Thiokol motors. More than 2 1/2 years' of research, re-design and testing were needed before America could return to space. Discovery lifted off at last on Sept. 29, 1988 and returned safely to earth four days later. We were back in space, but things would never be quite the same again.

The disintegrating Challenger painted crazy smoke trails on the Florida sky as it fell back to earth.

The crew of the ill-fated Challenger were: seated from left, Michael Smith, Francis Scobee and Ronald McNair; back, from left, Ellison Onizuka, Christa McAuliffe, Greg Jarvis and Judy Resnick.

# VCRs, PCs
## what next?

**B**ig things were happening in home electronics as the '80s arrived. Video cassette recorders, introduced in 1978, were quickly gaining popularity. Consumers loved the freedom these machines offered, even as industry officials worried about their impact:

*DESERET NEWS, July 26, 1982: The popularity of video recorders has added another dimension to home taping. By 1980 more than a million videocassette recorders were in use in the U.S.; and industry watchers predict that by 1987, 25 percent of all homes — about 25 million — will own video recording systems.*

But VCRs weren't the only thing changing television:

*June 2, 1980: (AP) — It began with a report on President Carter's visit with wounded civil rights leader Vernon Jordan in Fort Wayne, Ind., and "it won't ever stop."*

*As several hundred well-wishers gathered Sunday afternoon outside the Cable News Network's $20 million broadcast center, the nation's first 24-hour-a-day, all-news television network beamed its signal to cable systems across the country.*

*Sept. 30, 1982: (UPI) — In an era in which everybody is a critic of television, it takes courage to defend mediocrity, but Norman Horowitz says that's all that holds us together as a nation.*

*Furthermore, as TV fragments its*

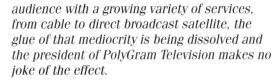

*audience with a growing variety of services, from cable to direct broadcast satellite, the glue of that mediocrity is being dissolved and the president of PolyGram Television makes no joke of the effect.*

On another electronics front, the introduction of personal computers was making waves:

*DESERET NEWS, Mar. 12, 1984: Sure, they're wonderful — revolutionizing the world as we know it. Sure, they are fast and efficient and can do everything but feed the cat. But what can a home computer really do for me?*

*That's the question a lot of people are asking these days. Amid all the sales pitches and hype that promise the moon and deliver a computer, you want to know exactly what this conglomeration of wires and chips and keyboards and discs can do for you.*

*And the answer is: pretty much anything you want.*

*But there's the rub. You have to know what you want. Computers are not magic machines, after all, but only tools. All that will come out is what you put in.*

In those days, consumer surveys revealed that game-playing, word-processing and record-keeping topped the list of personal computer uses. We hadn't met the Internet yet.

# The **forgery** bombings

**The explosions of two bombs in Salt Lake City in October 1985 blew open one of the most bizarre forgery and murder cases in American history:**

*DESERET NEWS, Oct. 16, 1985: As investigators probed Wednesday for clues in Tuesday's two bomb slayings — murders they believe may have been carried out by a professional killer with ties to organized crime — police were kept hopping by reports of suspicious packages, including one to the first victim...*

*Investigators are also probing the business dealings of the financially troubled CFS Financial Corp., one possible link between the deaths of Steven F. Christensen, 31, and Kathy Webb Sheets, 50.*

*A third explosion followed fast on the heels of the initial two, this one in a car parked near the downtown area. Suspicion suddenly pointed in a new direction:*

*Oct. 17, 1985: Authorities said Thursday they will seek criminal charges against Mark W. Hofmann in connection with this week's fatal bomb explosions as speculation surfaced that the bombings are tied somehow to a forgery operation involving historic Mormon*

Caught in the coils of a forgery trade that was beginning to unravel, Mark W. Hofmann resorted to murder. The road led him to Utah State Prison for the remainder of his life. Below: one of his forgeries.

*documents.*

*Hofmann was critically injured Wednesday when a bomb — the third in two days — exploded in downtown Salt Lake City. Revenge, perhaps fueled by business deals gone sour and possibly connections with a forgery operation are motives police are investigating ...*

Over the next 18 months, investigators uncovered a convoluted maze of deals, most of them involving forgeries of historic documents that Hofmann had claimed to be related to the LDS Church. Hofmann, whose dealings in documents began years earlier, apparently had come upon hard financial times and turned to forgery to fill his pockets.

Reams of newspaper copy piled up in Hofmann's file as the story unfolded. He was brought to trial on assorted charges from murder to making bombs. In January 1987, a plea bargain allowed him to plead guilty to some of the less serious charges, avoid a jury trial and bypass any chance of receiving a death penalty:

*DESERET NEWS, Jan. 23, 1987: "Due to the indiscriminate nature of the killings and the type of devices employed ... I want you to serve the rest of your natural life in the Utah State Prison."*

*With these words, 3rd District Judge Kenneth Rigtrup Friday sentenced Mark W. Hofmann to one prison term of 15 years to life and three other prison terms of 1-to-15 years for his role in the bombing deaths of two people and the forgeries and frauds that led to those murders...*

An outcry against the plea bargain had no effect. Hofmann was given into the custody of prison officials and prepared to spend the remainder of his life behind bars.

# A blue and white
# championship

**W**hen the 1984 Cougars beat Pittsburgh 20-14 in their opening game, everyone thought they had a pretty good team. Just how good would appear as the season unfolded:

BYU 47, Baylor 13
BYU 38, Tulsa 15
BYU 18, Hawaii 13
BYU 52, Colorado St. 9
BYU 41, Wyoming 38
BYU 30, Air Force 25
BYU 48, New Mexico 0
BYU 42, Texas-El Paso 9
BYU 34, San Diego St. 3
BYU 24, Utah 14
BYU 38, Utah State 13

Then came the Holiday Bowl:

**DESERET NEWS,** *Dec. 22, 1984: In a season filled with miracle comebacks, in a bowl game where such has become almost expected, the Brigham Young Cougars went to the well one more time to pull out another breathless victory.*

*With 1:23 left in Friday night's Holiday Bowl in San Diego's Jack Murphy Stadium, Robbie Bosco threw a 13-yard touchdown pass to give BYU a 24-17 victory over the University of Michigan.*

Only one honor was left: the National Championship. But would it come? The rest of the country, it seemed, had not quite caught the vision:

**DESERET NEWS,** *Dec. 18, 1984: The Cougars went 12-0 and, 11 weeks into the season, were voted No. 1. They were the talk of the country. The national press and TV networks descended on Provo almost daily. A book was commissioned to tell The BYU Story. And then the uproar. The year college football became a democracy. Bryant Gumbel grumbled. Barry Switzer campaigned. BYU's ranking was under attack.*

*Jan. 3, 1985: (Washington Post) — With all their hearts, with all their souls and with all their might, the people at the core of the Orange Bowl — the coaches, the organizers*

*and the network executives — tried to peddle their game between Oklahoma and Washington as the one, true, legitimate battle for the national championship.*

*B.Y.Who?*

*Barry Switzer, the Oklahoma coach who so obviously lusted for the No. 1 ranking, was always available to denigrate the quality of Brigham Young's conference and schedule, while boosting his own...*

*Switzer and Washington coach Don James then proclaimed the Huskies No. 1 after Washington's 28-17 Orange Bowl win.*

*It's swell that Switzer and James agree that a team that wasn't good enough to win its own conference is good enough to win the national championship.*

*Swell, but wrong.*

*BYU is No. 1. And Wednesday, the major polls reflected that. They couldn't have done otherwise.*

*At 13-0, BYU is the only unbeaten major college team.*

The AP, UPI and CNN/USA Today polls all agreed: BYU was No. 1. It was all over but the cheering!

Robbie Bosco

*Deseret News*

---

# Political
# Olympics

## In the 1980s sports and politics clashed:

**DESERET NEWS,** *Feb. 20, 1980: AP) — The United States will not participate in the Moscow Olympics since there is no sign the deadline imposed by President Carter for a Soviet troop withdrawal from Afghanistan will be met, State Department spokesman Hodding Carter said Wednesday.*

*The U.S. Olympic Committee, which will have to decide whether or not a team is sent, declined immediate comment on Carter's statement, but has said in the past that it would go along with whatever the government wants to do.*

The announcement was followed by more bad news for Moscow:

*Feb. 21, 1980: No U.S. at Games; no Levi's, either*

*Mar. 21, 1980: Coke withdraws as Olympic drink*

Western allies also boycotted the games. Deseret News photographer Tom Smart, on assignment with Associated Press, was not alone in thinking the games were a big disappointment:

**DESERET NEWS,** *Aug. 9, 1980: "But, the Games, well, the Olympic spirit was*

*gone. The competition was a joke... I remember walking around Montreal and seeing the athletes laughing, joking, just having a good time. There was a lot of camaraderie... In Moscow there was none of this."*

Four years later, the Soviet Union had its turn:

**Mary Lou Retton**

*AP Photo*

*May 8, 1984: (AP) — The Soviet Union said Tuesday it won't take part in the 1984 Summer Olympics in Los Angeles, citing the United States' "cavalier attitude" toward the Olympic charter and asserting the Americans don't intend to ensure the security and rights of athletes.*

But this time, while the athletes may have missed the competitors, America didn't care. From the time the Olympic torch was carried cross-country on the way to the games (it passed through Utah June 26-29) until the closing ceremonies, Olympic spirit reigned.

And when the games were over we had new heroes: track star Carl Lewis, diver Greg Louganis, marathoner Joan Benoit, and, of course, that perky, little gymnast:

**DESERET NEWS,** *Nov. 24, 1985: (AP) — Olympic superstar Mary Lou Retton won one gold medal in gymnastics, while Valerie Brisco-Hooks won three in track and field. But Retton is opening shopping centers and eating Wheaties for pay, while Brisco-Hooks hasn't even snipped a ribbon at a service station. Retton gets $8,000 every time she shows up at a shopping center to sign autographs.*

**The Russian bear just didn't come across as cuddly when the 1980s Olympics ran into opposition. American athletes and others boycotted the Moscow games as a protest against USSR invasion of Afghanistan.**

# A roller-coaster ride up

## 1990-1999

Just as the 1930s will be known as the Depression years, the 1990s will be known as the boom years. The Cold War ended in a whimper when the Soviet Union collapsed and a decade of prosperity set in. Inflation was negligible, the stock market soared to amazing levels and jobs were plentiful. As predicted, regional conflicts consumed our attention in the Gulf War and proved that ethnic hatreds and genocide were very much with us in Somalia, Bosnia, and Kosovo. At home, Utah prospered and finally won the right to host the Olympics, but paid a heavy price as a bribery scandal tarnished the victory. The nation's biggest construction job was under way on its Interstate roads, trolleys once again ran on light rails, and a tornado paid a visit.

Christian Science Monitor

**New York Stock Exchange**

### The decade started on a good economic note for Utah:

**DESERET NEWS,** *Dec. 26, 1990: (AP) — Utah retailers may have a merrier Christmas than merchants elsewhere in the nation, whose sales have flagged amid predictions of recession.*

*A spot check of shopping malls on Christmas Eve indicated holiday sales are up from last year...*

As KeyCorp economist Jeff K. Thredgold said in his year-end economic report for the state: "Utah economic performance during 1990 has ranked with the best of the 50 states. Solid Utah economic growth has been characterized by strong job creation, low unemployment, rising income levels, increased home construction and home sales activity, and continued state budget surpluses.

"The recessionary tendencies of much of the nation have, as yet, had only minimal impact upon the Utah economy," Thredgold said.

The song would get stronger as the decade went on:

**DESERET NEWS,** *Sept. 18, 1991: Despite a "sluggish national economic performance," Utah's business conditions remain healthy and the prognosis for the fourth quarter is favorable, says First Security Bank economist Kelly K. Matthews.*

*Jan. 6, 1994: The seven good economic years Utah has had since 1987 should continue in 1994 and could possibly last into 2002, the year Salt Lake City is attempting to host the Winter Olympic Games.*

*That assessment of the Utah economy comes from Thayne Robson, director of the University of Utah Bureau of Economic and Business Research.*

AP Photo

**A trader makes his bid. The market rose 8,000 points in the decade.**

Eventually, the rest of the nation caught up. And prosperity felt good.

**DESERET NEWS,** *Nov. 21, 1995: (AP) — If you think the Dow Jones industrial average reached the 5,000 mark Monday only because a bunch of Wall Street insiders are pouring money into the stock market, you're wrong.*

*Chances are, you, your family, friends or neighbors are doing it, too.*

*Aug. 2, 1997: (AP) — The industrial economy expanded again last month for its strongest performance in nearly three years, but the growth came with signs of rekindled inflation.*

*May 5, 1999: Despite some minor blips, the Dow keeps climbing and climbing. After celebrating the breaking of the 10,000 barrier in March, it only took 24 trading days to move from 10,000 to* above 11,000.

*July 2, 1999: America's cheerful spending spree is zooming right along, and the shopping center was a dominant force in retail sales last year.*

*Shopping centers in America broke the $1 trillion sales mark in 1998 with a 5 percent increase over 1997 sales, according to the International Council of Shopping Centers.*

Looking back, many analysts saw a '50s glow in the financial scene of the '90s. Happy days *were* here again.

May 3, 1999
**11,014.69**

8000

Nov. 21, 1995
**5023.55**

Feb. 23, 1995
**4003.33**

4000

April 17, 1991
**3004.46**

**Stock trading was fast and furious — and productive for many. The Dow made a super jump, cracking 11,000 for the first time on May 3. America's economy was rosy.**

2000

AP Photo

1000

1990          1995          2000

# Victory
## in the Cold War

East German soldiers repelled Berliners at the Brandenburg gate shortly after travel restrictions were lifted. Anxious crowds awaited official word to breach the 30-year barrier.

AP Photo

**M**apmakers had their hands full as the Cold War became history and a new world emerged.

Germany, split into East and West for four decades, reunited. The Soviet Union, a collection of 15 republics for 74 years, fell apart. The communist world came unglued all over eastern Europe and old alliances dissolved. A new openess in commerce erased border constraints that had lasted through decades.

One of the most powerful signs that the USSR had lost its influence with other east European communist countries was the dissolution of the Warsaw Pact. It dated back to May 1955 and was formed by eight communist nations as a response to the NATO agreement linking the U.S. with its European allies. The communist agreement grew mushy with the withdrawal of Albania, and disintegrated as one after another country adopted democratic reforms:

**DESERET NEWS,** *Feb. 25, 1991: BUDAPEST, Hungary (AP) — Foreign and defense ministers of the once-mighty Warsaw Pact signed a historic agreement Monday formalizing the end of the alliance's defunct military functions by March 31, Hungarian state radio said…*
*Czechoslovakian Defense Minister Lubos Dobrovsky, before entering the one-day meeting, told reporters, "a new era is beginning."…*
*Revolutions throughout eastern Europe in late 1989 overturned communist rule there and essentially ended any chance those nations would act in concert with the Soviets.*

Like dominoes falling, each nudged by the one before, communist countries made historic changes. Divided Germany faced increasing pressure from citizens on both sides of the Berlin Wall. Finally, in November 1989, East German authorities succumbed and the wall, one of the most visible emblems of ideologic separation, fell. Eric Hyer, an assistant professor of political science at Brigham Young University, was in both East and West Berlin for a week in late October, just before the fall of the wall. He wrote for the News:

**DESERET NEWS,** *Nov. 22, 1989: We*

AP Photo

**Mikhail Gorbachev loosened the grip of communism, only to have his Soviet Union fall apart. Below, with fall of Berlin wall, a joyous celebration broke out.**

UPI/Reuter

*are witnessing a revolution in the postwar geopolitical order in Europe.*
*The communist regime in East Germany was imposed by Stalin following World War II. His successor in the Kremlin, Khrushchev, consolidated Soviet control by erecting the Berlin Wall in 1961 and from the mid-1960s to the 1980s, Brezhnev propped up the repressive regime by threatening to use military force if necessary. Gorbachev has now made it clear that he is intent on economic and political reform and is unwilling to use Soviet troops to maintain this anachronistic Stalinist regime any longer.*

Hyer was already home when the wall actually fell, setting off a celebration that reverberated throughout the world:

**DESERET NEWS,** *Nov. 10, 1989: East Germany said Friday it was permanently lifting travel restrictions on its citizens and West Germany's foreign minister said workers would begin knocking new holes in the Berlin Wall, which for 28 years trapped*

East Germans in their rigidly controlled country.

One nation again after almost four decades, Germany faced significant challenges in melding currencies, tax burdens, philosophies and politics, but it now could begin the healing process.
Leaders in the Soviet Union had plenty of problems at home to divert their attention. The defection of the Baltic republics of Estonia, Latvia and Lithuania was evidence that the union was crumbling from within:

**DESERET NEWS,** *Dec. 9, 1991: The new alliance of the Soviet Union's three Slavic republics could lead to bloodshed, is unlikely to solve the nation's economic problems and probably spells curtains for Mikhail Gorbachev, specialists in Soviet affairs say.*

The collapse of the long-feared Soviet Union was imminent. One by one the member states demanded self-determination, opposing the heavy-handed central control under which they operated. The end came on Christmas Day 1991.

**DESERET NEWS,** *Dec. 25, 1991: MOSCOW (AP) — Mikhail S. Gorbachev, the eighth and final leader of the Soviet Union, announced Wednesday night that he is resigning as president of the now-dissolved communist empire…*
*Speaking in front of a Soviet flag, Gorbachev blamed the failed August coup against his government for bringing the "general crisis to its limit." He said, "The worst thing about this crisis is the collapse of statehood."*

The Soviet Union's claimed historic imperative to "bury" its democratic foes died with the USSR.

**DESERET NEWS,** *Dec. 12, 1991: The old Soviet system of a planned economy failed and was abandoned before there was anything resembling a market economy to take its place…*

Outbreaks of civil strife, war in Bosnia and Kosovo and other legacies of the fall of communism in Europe make it apparent that the end results will be for future history books to report.

# War
## in the desert

**F-16**

T he United Nations demanded that Iraq withdraw and called for a trade embargo against the invaders. President George Bush engineered a coalition of 39 countries, including the United States and Canada, who sent armed forces to the gulf region as a show of force. They set a Jan. 15, 1991, deadline for Iraq to leave Kuwait. When Hussein defied them, the Gulf War broke out.

At night on Jan. 17 (Baghdad time, Jan. 16 in the U.S.) Baghdad came under a fierce bombardment:

**DESERET NEWS,** *Jan. 17, 1991: "It was tremendous. Baghdad was lit up like a Christmas tree," said a U.S. wing commander back from bombing the Iraqi capital. "There were lots of bombs going off. It was an awesome display," said another pilot who took part in the first raids of the gulf war to drive Iraq out of Kuwait.*

*Tomahawk cruise missiles launched toward Baghdad from American warships. U.S. and Saudi F-15E fighter-bombers, British and Saudi Tornadoes, French Jaguars and Kuwaiti Hawks were among hundreds of planes that flew from bases in Saudi Arabia in a United Nations-sanctioned assault.*

Americans had front row seats for the war, thanks to modern technology. Television repeated its film footage of the attacks over and over. School children became familiar with the terms Desert Storm (the code name for the assault) Scud (the Iraqis' favored missile) and Patriot (the American anti-missile missile.) On the second day of the war, the U.S. experienced its first losses:

**DESERET NEWS,** *Jan. 18, 1991: A 33-year-old Navy pilot, father of two young children, is the first American combat casualty of the Persian Gulf War. Also identified were two other Navy pilots missing since Thursday…*

*The Pentagon identified Lt. Cmdr. Michael S. Speicher of Jacksonville, Fla., as missing in action after his single-seat F-A-18 Hornet fighter-bomber was shot down by an Iraqi surface-to-air missile over Iraq. Speicher was listed as missing because his body was not recovered. Defense Secretary Dick*

*Cheney had said earlier that the pilot was killed.*

Many Utahns had a personal stake in Desert Storm. For months, units from Hill Air Force Base and the Utah National Guard left for the gulf to participate in Desert Shield, a massive build-up of Allied forces:

**DESERET NEWS,** *Sept. 3, 1990: Three hundred yards of tarmac and a world in crisis separated the planeload of servicemen and women from their loved ones Sunday morning, and the only way to reach them was via the Persian Gulf… Routine it is… Even though Desert Shield is only three weeks old, Sunday's deployment was the third large contingent of Air Force support personnel to leave (Hill Air Force Base) for (the Gulf.)*

*Oct. 2, 1990: Thirty-seven Utah Air National Guard members flew out of Salt Lake City Tuesday morning for a month-long tour in Saudi Arabia. The deployment, in support of Operation Desert Shield, is the second trip to the Middle East for*

**Saddam Hussein**

*some of the Guard members, who fly and provide ground support for KC-135 aerial refueling tankers.*
*The wife of one guard member said through tears it was easier to see her husband go the second time. She and her children joined several dozen of the soldiers' family members who watched the plane roll down the runway just before dawn Tuesday.*

When the war broke out, security measures tightened at Hill and in surrounding cities. Everyone kept a close eye on developments in the gulf:

**DESERET NEWS,** *Jan. 18, 1991: HILL AIR FORCE BASE — A sense of somber relief pervaded this sprawling air base Thursday afternoon. There was relief that in the first stages of the Persian Gulf War, things must be going well for Hill's men*

**In February 1991, soldiers of the U.S. Army 82nd Airborne unit rode past the burned-out remains of an Iraqi tank. Desert Storm was winding down.**

and women deployed to the Middle East, because American casualties were low in the air war. And there was relief that a tense period of waiting for action had ended at last.

As the air war ebbed and the ground war began, it was clear Desert Storm would not last long. By late February, many Iraqi leaders were conceding defeat:

**DESERET NEWS,** *Feb. 27, 1991: KUWAIT CITY — With Iraq's shattered occupation army in chaotic flight, Baghdad announced it was willing to drop all claims to Kuwait if the allied assault would only stop. But deep inside rain-darkened Iraq, U.S. forces and Saddam Hussein's best troops were locked in a fierce tank battle.*

*Baghdad radio, in an offer swiftly rejected by the White House, announced that in exchange for a cease-fire, Iraq would accept a U.N. resolution that declared its annexation of Kuwait null and void. It also would accept a resolution that lays the groundwork for Iraqi reparations and the prosecution of Iraqis for human rights violations.*

Within days, terms of a cease-fire were worked out. But Deseret News editorial writers, along with thousands like them, issued a word of caution:

**DESERET NEWS,** *Feb. 27, 1991: Now that allied forces seem assured of sweeping victory in the Persian Gulf, the resulting elation must not obscure a painful fact of international life:*

*Victory in war does not automatically translate into victory in the ensuing peace...*

Such opinions were prophetic. "Peace" with Iraq consisted of an ongoing stand-off on such issues as policing that country's re-stocking of arms, including potentially deadly nuclear and chemical weapons. The United States continued to attack military targets from the air. A new century is not likely to see swift resolution of the problems that led to Desert Storm.

# The Clinton affair

**President Clinton**

**Monica Lewinsky**

Impeachment, a word feared by presidents, was on every American's mind as the 1990s neared their end. President Bill Clinton's two terms were pockmarked by investigations into questionable business dealings and charges of extra-marital dallying. Then Monica Lewinsky, a White House intern, told a friend she had an affair with the president. The friend taped the conversation and told Clinton's enemies. Clinton's denials, followed by his retractions and apologies, primed the impeachment hearings.

Opinion, from readers and editors, printed in the News reflected two schools of thought: 1. That a president's personal life has no bearing on his ability to run the country and 2. That a man who can't keep his own life in order has no business trying to run a country, as this letter to the editor said:

**DESERET NEWS,** *Dec. 20, 1998: Yes, Clinton is human; yes, he had an affair (like 40 percent of all married men and slightly fewer married women). No, that does not mean that he should be ridiculed and publicly humiliated as though he were a serious criminal. I do not believe that Clinton has committed an impeachable offense, and he should be allowed to finish his term with a little bit of dignity left.—* Bethany Hewes

*Dec. 16, 1998: We concur with President Clinton about how unsettling the impeachment procedure is, how unpleasant a trial in the Senate would be if he was impeached and that the process is an ordeal for the American people.*

*Where we obviously part company is in laying blame for causing the American people such agony and disruption...*

*Our commander in chief can identify the culprit by simply looking into a mirror. William Jefferson Clinton is the one who is responsible for the current turmoil and he alone must shoulder the blame and be held accountable. [Editorial]*

Charged with lying under oath and obstructing justice, the president faced the House of Representatives, which acted in late December:

**DESERET NEWS,** *Dec. 19, 1998:* **House impeaches President Clinton for perjury, obstruction of justice** *WASHINGTON — The House of Representatives impeached President Clinton Saturday for obstructing justice and lying under oath about his sexual affair with Monica Lewinsky, voting largely along party lines to send his case to the Senate. It was only the second presidential impeachment trial in American history. (Andrew Johnson barely escaped impeachment conviction in 1868.)*

*The House approved two of four articles of impeachment lodged against Clinton, formally recommending that he be tried in the Senate...*

The Senate did not concur with the House recommendation.

**DESERET NEWS,** *Feb. 12, 1999:* **Clinton acquitted by Senate** *WASHINGTON — The Senate failed Friday to convict President Clinton and remove him from office, nearing the end of a rancorous 13 months during which his disclosure of an affair with an intern turned into the second presidential impeachment trial in history. The Senate voted 55-45 to reject an impeachment article alleging perjury in his testimony before a grand jury.*

A shaken Clinton immediately began fence-mending:

**DESERET NEWS,** *Feb. 12, 1999: WASHINGTON (AP) — Offering and asking forgiveness, President Clinton said today his impeachment acquittal should begin "a time of reconciliation and renewal for America."*

Another crisis was weathered, but the fallout would color American politics for years to come.

# From Waco to Oklahoma City

**I**t began as one of those bizarre little events that should have been nothing more than a footnote to history. But it set off a chain of happenings with deep repercussions for all of society.

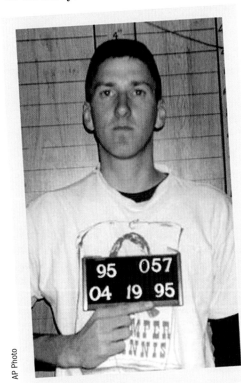

Lined up for a jail photo, Timothy McVeigh was just starting out on a legal process that would end in his conviction in Oklahoma bombing case.

**DESERET NEWS,** Mar. 1, 1993: (UPI) — Negotiators Monday tried to talk a man who claims to be Christ into surrendering with his followers at a heavily armed compound where five people have died and 15 have been injured in two bloody gunfights.

Four agents of the Bureau of Alcohol, Tobacco and Firearms died Sunday at Waco hospitals after the initial gunfight early Sunday. About nine hours later, a cult member was killed in a second gunfight, the ATF said.

David Koresh, the leader of the sect called the Branch Davidians, said a small child was killed in the compound Sunday, but the ATF has been unable to confirm that.

The cult, which had split off from 7th-Day Adventists back in 1934, had a history of dissidence and violence, but nothing like this. The standoff in Waco dragged on for weeks:

**DESERET NEWS,** Mar. 3, 1993: (AP) — An armed cult leader has told federal authorities he will end a bloody siege when he receives "further instruction from God," the FBI said Wednesday.

Mar. 27, 1993: (AP) — The high-pitched tone of an off-the-hook phone screeched from loudspeakers Friday. It was another selection from federal agents in an escalating war of nerves designed to end the month-long standoff with armed cultists.

And then the end came — in a way that no one had expected:

**DESERET NEWS,** April 19, 1993: (AP) — The compound where cult leader David Koresh and 95 followers holed up for 51 days burned to the ground Monday after FBI agents in an armored vehicle smashed the buildings and pumped in tear gas. The Justice Department said cult members set the fire.

April 21, 1993: (SHNS) — Federal authorities have found about 40 bodies so far in the charred remains of the Branch Davidian compound, including three that appear to have been shot, the Justice Department said

Smoke poured from the Branch Davidian compound where more thn 40 died. The Waco standoff generated sticky questions about how to deal with anti-government cults.

Wednesday. The bodies in and around the compound include the remains of 10 women and children…

The Waco standoff was over, but it would not be forgotten. Among those watching the event was apparently one Timothy McVeigh, who planned and carried out his own form of revenge two years later — although it took awhile for that connection to become apparent.

**DESERET NEWS,** April 19, 1995: OKLAHOMA CITY (AP) — An explosion believed caused by a bomb shattered a downtown federal office building Wednesday, blowing out a huge chunk of the nine-story structure and killing at least eight.

The explosion at the Alfred Murrah Building, which occurred shortly after 9 a.m. could be felt 30 miles away. Black smoke streamed across the skyline, and glass, bricks and other debris were spread over a wide area…

An initial investigation indicated the explosion was caused by a large bomb, perhaps 1,000 to 1,200 pounds, located outside the building, perhaps in a car.

The death toll quickly rose: to 19, to 110, to finally stand at 168. Because a day-care center had been housed in the building, many of the casualties were children. An identification number on the charred scrap of the vehicle that delivered the bomb led federal officials to McVeigh and a co-conspirator, Terry Nichols. In a lucky fluke, they found McVeigh was stopped in Perry, Okla., on a traffic violation 90 minutes after the blast and arrested because he carried a gun. McVeigh, 27, was outspoken about his anti-government sentiments and his

criticism of the Waco standoff.

He was tried, convicted and sentenced to death in 1997 for the Oklahoma City bombing. Friends and relatives of the victims were still trying to find ways to deal with their losses:

**DESERET NEWS,** June 3, 1997: One by one, the families lined up at the slippery elm that had outlived the Oklahoma city bombing. They came to nourish it with water representing tears they had shed for the dead.

Some poured all they had, symbolizing the grief they had resolved. Others sprinkled only a few drops; some tears will never be forgotten. Slowly, the ground beneath the tree became muddy.

Oct. 26, 1998: (AP) — John Taylor says the tears don't come as easily.

He joined thousands of people who watched groundbreaking ceremonies for a memorial to honor the 168 people killed in the Oklahoma City bombing — among them, Taylor's 41-year-old daughter, Teresa Lauderdale.

The people of Oklahoma City were finding ways to move on. But terrorism had struck deep in the heartland, and the country had lost another sizeable chunk of its idealism.

First reports about Oklahoma City's bombed Murrah Building grossly under-estimated the damage and deaths.

# Bringing back
# the past

At East Canyon a team of mules rocketed down a steep slope. The wagon flew apart on the way down and several passengers suffered minor injuries.

**N**ostalgia had a heyday in Utah in the late 1990s. The 100th milestone of statehood in 1996 was followed the next year by the 150th anniversary of the arrival of the first Utah pioneers in Salt Lake Valley.  Top hats and sunbonnets — or reasonable facsimiles thereof — became the mode of the day from "Pickleville to Panguitch," as one News headline writer wrote.

Fillmore, which enjoyed a brief term as Utah's capital in the state's early years, kicked off several days of events in early January:

**DESERET NEWS,** *Jan. 3, 1996:*
- *Millard County lit the fuse on Utah's yearlong statehood centennial celebration Tuesday, jumping the gun by two days on the official Jan. 4 anniversary.*
- *Fillmore's gala began with an afternoon parade of state and local dignitaries and ended with an impressive fireworks display...*
- *Gov. Mike Leavitt said, "This is a moment we've all been waiting for." The centennial, he said, is a "time for thanksgiving for the wonders of the state, a time to reflect on the past and a time to plan for the future."*

For the actual Statehood Day festivities, attention shifted to Salt Lake City, which had long since become the state's capital:

*Jan. 4, 1996: With songs, dancing and a fusillade of gunfire that set downtown Salt Lake City's concrete canyon echoing, Utahns heralded the state's first hundred years.*

*... at 9:13, the "real" statehood telegram arrived, and [state history director Max] Evans duplicated the two shots fired by Marion B. Brown, Western Union manager on Jan. 4, 1896. His shots let waiting Utahns know that with President Grover Cleveland's signing of the official proclamation, they had shucked territorial status and were bona fide residents of the United States...*

In 1997, already in a look-back mode, Utahns dug back to the events that started it all. Disregarding the out-of-sequence historicity of the celebrations, they marked the coming of the first Mormon pioneers to Salt Lake Valley in late July 1847.

**CHURCH NEWS,** *April 26, 1997:*
*From the banks of the Mississippi to the banks of the Missouri, President Gordon B. Hinckley on the same day dedicated a park in Nauvoo, Ill., and a visitors center at Winter Quarters (near Omaha,) Neb., both designed to tell the epic story of the*

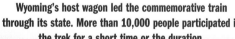

*Mormon migration to the West.*

*... he dedicated the Nauvoo Pioneer Memorial Park (where the pioneer exodus for the West began) on the afternoon of April 18... That evening, President*
Hinckley dedicated the new Mormon Trail Center at Historic Winter Quarters, more than 300 miles from Nauvoo, in the Omaha suburb of Florence.

The next day, he and other church and government leaders gave a send-off to a wagon train that re-enacted the historic march over the Mormon Trail, a grueling 1,100 miles of prairie and mountain that was the pathway to Salt Lake Valley for tens of thousands of 19th Century pioneers.

**DESERET NEWS,** *Aug. 30, 1997: Approximately 300 people from 130 different news organizations joined the wagon train sometime during the three-month trek. Among others were television crews from Russia, the Czech Republic, Romania, Italy, France, Belgium, Poland, Hungary, Austria, Ecuador, Philippines, Japan and three networks in Germany...*

The kind of stories they shared with readers and viewers included:

*May 21, 1997: With more than 300 miles of the trip behind them, the 1997 Sesquicenntenial Mormon Trail Wagon Train encountered Nebraska's sand hills Tuesday. Although the modern train is actually following developed roads most of the way, it paused for a demonstration of what it was like for their predecessors...*

*There was a moment of stark reality as several representative wagons traversed the sand hills. The second wagon, Wyoming's official vehicle, was coming down a hill and began to teeter on the uneven terrain. After righting itself a couple of times, it made another tilt and landed on its right side, probably creating a modern version of what happened to more than one early wagon crossing the dunes.*

*July 22, 1997: Predictions that Monday would be the most hazardous segment of the 1,100-mile re-creation of the Mormom Pioneer Trail came true minutes after the wagon train left its encampment here.  (East Canyon Reservoir.)*

*Fewer than a dozen wagons had filed off the steep incline leading off the plateau before a run-away wagon tore through the brush, bounced hard and flew apart... Six passengers received what appeared to be minor injuries.*

On July 22, exactly 150 years after scouts of the vanguard pioneer train entered Salt Lake Valley in 1847, the wagon train filed out of Emigration Canyon.

More than 10,000 people took part in the three-month re-enactment, mostly traveling a portion of the trail (about 200 made the full trek from Omaha to Salt Lake City.) Hundreds of thousands more greeted them along the way, and many times that number experienced it via the media. It was a milestone to remember.

Wyoming's host wagon led the commemorative train through its state. More than 10,000 people participated in the trek for a short time or the duration.

# Champions

O̅n the eve of the Jazz's first foray into the NBA Finals, Frank Layden remembered the early years:

**DESERET NEWS,** *June 11, 1997: In Layden's first two years of coaching the team — from 1981 to 1983 — the Jazz won 65 regular season games. Under Sloan this past regular season, they won 64.*

*But if Layden started low, he didn't stay there long. In 1984, after only his second full season as coach, he was named NBA Coach of the Year for guiding the Jazz to their first playoff berth and a 45-37 record, which doesn't seem like much in today's currency, but in 1984 it represented the first-ever above-.500 record for the Jazz and a 15-win jump from the year before.*

*The Jazz have not had a losing season since.*

*Five seasons later, after getting the team off to an 11-6 start in 1988, Layden, as team vice president, stepped down as coach, promoted himself to team president, and gave the car keys to Jerry Sloan, his assistant, with the gas tank on full. The Jazz haven't slowed down since.*

*Along the way, they picked up the dynamic duo of Karl Malone and John Stockton. In 1993, they hosted the NBA All-Star game, to show off their new home, the Delta Center. Although Michael Jordan complained ("Why not keep it in a warm place? Let us play golf for a couple of days, let us relax"), the*

Deseret News

Karl Malone and John Stockton took on Dennis Rodman and the Bulls in two NBA Finals. The Jazz fought valiantly, but ultimately lost each time.

*game was deemed a success, and Malone and Stockton were named co-MVPs.*

*The Jazz continued to improve, making it to the playoffs, and sometimes deep into the playoffs, each year. By 1997, they had added Jeff Hornacek to the roster and arrived at the Finals, facing Jordan's formidable Chicago Bulls.*

**DESERET NEWS,** *June 11, 1997: What Wednesday night's Game 5 at the Delta Center (7 p.m.) offers is a clash between one team riding a wave of confidence, and another team struggling with the sudden realization that it isn't invincible. If nothing else, the Bulls are acknowledging that the Jazz just may be their toughest Finals foe.*

*"In terms of talent that we've faced, by far this is the best talent from the standpoint of maturity and the players they have that make up that team," said Michael Jordan. "In that sense it has to be the biggest challenge that we have faced thus far."*

*The Jazz fought. But it was not to be:*

*June 14, 1997: Someday, someone's going to read a line in an NBA record book showing that the Chicago Bulls beat the Utah Jazz in six games and assume this wasn't a particularly close series.*

*But you know better. Three of the Bulls' wins were by a combined eight points, and that includes Friday night's series-clinching win, 90-86, ending the Jazz's fairy-tale season.*

*To few people's surprise, the same two teams were back for the 1998 Finals. And once again it was with the same results:*

**DESERET NEWS,** *June*

*15, 1998: Greg Foster stopped speaking and swallowed, the tears almost spilling out. When a reporter in the back asked if he could speak louder, Foster said softly, "C'mon man," and stared at the locker room floor.*

*"It's sad, it's disheartening, but we'll go out with our heads up," he said.*

*Draw the shades. Turn out the lights. Put on the Blues Brothers dark glasses. Hit the off button. Those shirts with "Utah Jazz: NBA Champs, 1998" can go in the box beneath the stairs. Better yet, send them to the Salvation Army…*

*The end of the season came Sunday night in predictable fashion. Michael Jordan had spoken earlier in the NBA Finals of sticking the knife in and twisting. So he did, cutting the heart from the Jazz. He stole the ball in a late possession. He made the basket on the last crucial shot. Could it have really ended any other way?*

That was, in fact, the end of Jordan's career. When the 1998-99 season opened (or didn't open because of an acrimonious labor dispute), it was without "His Airness."

Due to the NBA lockout, the last season of the decade was cut to 50 games, and was overshadowed by all the squabbling. So, although the Jazz bowed out early once again, the season had already lost some of its magic because of the dispute. Business took precedence over sport.

And basketball was not the only game having labor troubles in the '90s. A lengthy players' strike in 1994 cost baseball a World Series and a great deal of fan support. Industry watchers weren't sure if the game would ever recover, but along came a couple of heroes to help make amends:

**DESERET NEWS,** *Sept. 8, 1995: Darn it, baseball. We had given up on your so-called American pastime — and gosh, did you deserve it — until Wednesday*

Deseret News

Michael Jordan

night when Cal Ripkin Jr.'s 2,131 consecutive games played record was matched by 2,131 goosebumps along the arms and legs of a certain TV sports writer.

*Sept. 9, 1998: (Reuters)* — Mark McGwire hit his 62nd homer of the season Tuesday night in his 145th game, something the legendary Ruth couldn't do in 154 games or Roger Maris in 162 games.

And if that weren't enough, McGwire is being credited with saving the game, unifying the country, taking the nation's mind off sex scandals and even helping the global economy, because the stock market soared on that very day.

McGwire's home run set off an 11-minute celebration that halted the game against the Chicago Cubs and included McGwire hugging the grown children of the late Roger Maris… And he bear-hugged Chicago right fielder Sammy Sosa, who… had been shadowing McGwire for the last two months and has 58 homers himself.

Baseball was making friends and headlines on the homefront as well during the '90s.

**DESERET NEWS,** *Sept. 5, 1991:* The 1987 team that put the Salt Lake Trappers in the Baseball Hall of Fame with a professional-record 29 straight victories was the franchise's most-celebrated group.

But the 1991 team that won the Pioneer League championship Tuesday night in Derks Field, 2-1 over the Great Falls Dodgers, might have been better than the Streakers.

In the early '90s, Derks Field, once home to the Salt Lake Bees and more recently the Salt Lake Gulls and now the Trappers, was showing its age. A new stadium was needed; the only question was where.

**DESERET NEWS,** *Jan. 26, 1993:* Derks Field emerged the winner Tuesday in Salt Lake City's hunt for

a place to build a new baseball stadium.

Mayor Deedee Corradini announced the choice less than a week after the City Council recommended Derks as one of two possible sites. Her decision means professional baseball will remain at 1300 South and West Temple, where it has been for most of this century.

*April 10, 1994:* For the record, let history note that Franklin Quest Field officially opened Saturday morning in cold, drizzly Salt Lake City…

If you build it, they will come, the mayor told Salt Lake City a little more than a year ago. On Monday night, the Salt Lake Buzz will come to play in their new home.

AAA baseball was back in Salt Lake City. The decade also saw the departure of the popular Golden Eagles Hockey team and the arrival of the

**Mark McGwire**

*Associated Press*

International Hockey League's Grizzlies, which set up home in the new E Center in West Valley. The city also flirted with professional soccer, first the Sting and then the Freezz.

But professional sports weren't all that was making news. College sports, particularly football, basketball and gymnastics, also enjoyed tremendous popularity. In a decade filled with achievements and excitement, a few particularly stand out:

**DESERET NEWS,** *Dec. 2, 1990:* (Chicago Tribune) — Ty Detmer won it for Jim McMahon. And for Steve Young, Marc Wilson and Robbie Bosco.

Detmer won it for all those great Brigham Young quarterbacks who posted eye-popping numbers, yet were slighted because only a few ever saw them. If Brigham Young were situated in Notre Dame, Ind., the school probably would have two or three Heisman Trophies by now.

Saturday, Detmer picked up BYU's first, with a surprisingly easy win over the runner-up, Notre Dame's Raghib Ismail. With the coveted Heisman Trophy finally in the school's grasp, the latest in the line of great quarterbacks shared the award with his predecessors.

"They all had great seasons, and a couple of them should have won it. They set the tone here," said Detmer, a junior. "It would have been a devastating blow to BYU if we hadn't won it this year. Now we finally have it."

*April 22, 1995:* The University of Utah gymnastics team has reason to cheer after winning its 10th national title Friday at the NCAA Championships in Athens, Ga. The title is the team's second in a row and fourth in the 1990s. In one of the Utes' most astonishing wins ever (this was their ninth NCAA team championship), Utah came into the Super Six Night with the seventh-best score from Thursday's preliminary round, the

hardest start the sport has to offer (balance beam) and hurting so badly some of the Utes could hardly walk. The Utes finished with 196.65 points to Alabama's 196.425 total.

*Mar. 31, 1998:* Just like it had the previous two seasons, the Utah basketball season ended Monday night with another disappointing loss to the University of Kentucky.

This time it was just a little different, however.

This Ute loss came in the NCAA championship game in front of 40,509 fans at the Alamodome, with several hundred million people around the world watching on television. And this time the Utes came oh, so close to pulling off the greatest athletic accomplishment ever for a Utah team.

*Deseret News*

**BYU's Ty Detmer won the coveted Heisman Trophy in 1990. Below, Britton Johnsen shows emotion as the Utes make it to the NCAA finals in 1998.**

*Deseret News*

# Surviving I-15
## Or, get there if you can

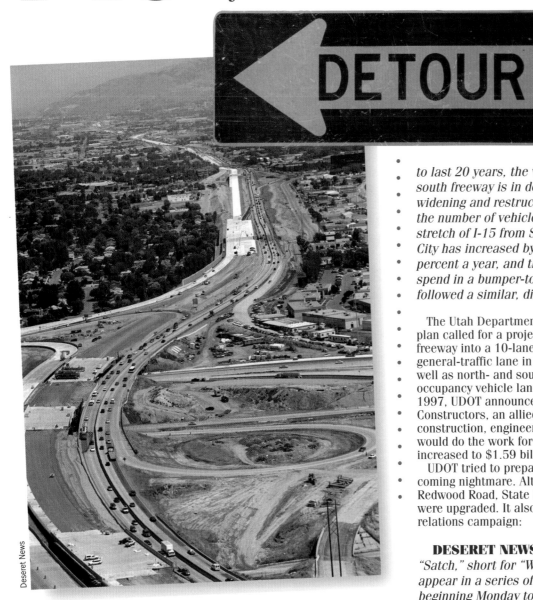

Deseret News

**Massive reconstruction projects added new dirt designs to the Salt Lake County landscape, while motorists chafed at detours and delays. This view looks north from the I-215 interchange.**

**Q** uestion: How do you completely rebuild and reconstruct a major highway system without disrupting the lives of everyone who drives on it?

Answer: You don't.

The only thing that made the massive I-15 project at all tolerable was that the alternatives were worse.

**DESERET NEWS,** *Dec. 26, 1995: Built to last 20 years, the valley's only north-south freeway is in desperate need of widening and restructuring. Since 1980, the number of vehicles on the 17-mile stretch of I-15 from Sandy to Salt Lake City has increased by an average of 7 percent a year, and the hours commuters spend in a bumper-to-bumper crawl has followed a similar, discouraging trend.*

The Utah Department of Transportation's plan called for a project that would turn the freeway into a 10-lane road, adding one general-traffic lane in each direction as well as north- and southbound high-occupancy vehicle lanes. On March 26, 1997, UDOT announced that Wasatch Constructors, an allied group of construction, engineering and supply firms, would do the work for $1.325 billion (later increased to $1.59 billion).

UDOT tried to prepare commuters for the coming nightmare. Alternate routes such as Redwood Road, State Street and 700 East were upgraded. It also began a public relations campaign:

**DESERET NEWS,** *Feb. 17, 1997: "Satch," short for "Wasatch,"… will appear in a series of television ads beginning Monday to help prepare Utahns for the $1.36 billion project…*

*The idea of the campaign is that Satch was in fact around in the 1960s when I-15 was built through the Salt Lake Valley.*

*He helped us survive that mess, although there was considerably less disruption to existing traffic flow then. UDOT assures us he'll be there for us again this time. His message: Relax and be patient.*

But this time around, Satch was a bust. Negative publicity proved too much of a distraction, and UDOT retired Satch in April.

Then the work began.

**DESERET NEWS,** *April 20, 1997: Drivers along the Wasatch Front will see the first signs of the Interstate 15 reconstruction starting this week. Survey crews will begin work, causing periodic one-lane closures.*

Major closures began with the 600 North interchange in June; reconstruction schedules became a regular part of the paper; the frustration level began to rise.

**DESERET NEWS,** *June 15, 1997: If you're struggling to cope with the fast-paced, ever-changing I-15 reconstruction schedule, you're no different than thousands of other motorists…*

*The first two months of the 4 1/2-year, $1.59 billion rebuild project have been characterized by frequent changes in the construction schedule, some so spontaneous that UDOT hasn't informed the media until lanes and ramps have already been shut down.*

*Aug. 10, 1997: A recent Deseret News opinion poll found that 82 percent of Utahns believe the $1.59 billion rebuild has been at least somewhat inconvenient during the first 3 1/2 months of work. Thirty-six percent said the project has been very inconvenient. Only 3 percent said they've noticed no inconvenience at all.*

With all the commotion on I-15, it was not surprising that another idea for minimizing traffic through the corridor was taking shape: light rail.

**DESERET NEWS,** *May 25, 1995: The Utah Transit Authority is proceeding with plans to build a 16-mile commuter rail line from suburban Sandy into downtown Salt Lake City despite claims the $294 million project might bankrupt the agency.*

*March 3, 1997: It will be known as the UTA Transit Express, but you can call it TRAX.*

*July 14, 1997: A giant machine called a pulverizer began chewing up and spitting out asphalt Monday to clear the way for light-rail trains to reach downtown Salt Lake City.*

Meanwhile, back on the freeway, as slow as it sometimes seemed, progress was being made:

**DESERET NEWS,** *Oct. 23, 1998: If you've had it up to your dashboard with freeway closures, Wasatch Constructors has some good news for you.*

*The first major interchange to be completely rebuilt as part of the $1.59 billion I-15 reconstruction effort will open this weekend… Wasatch, the I-15 contractor, plans to open the remaining three ramps of the 600 North interchange — and the 600 North viaduct above I-15 — about 4 p.m. Saturday.*

*Feb. 7, 1999: The I-15 reconstruction project is getting rave reviews from federal officials.*

*The inspector general's office of the U.S. Department of Transportation recently completed a report on the $1.59 billion project and concluded it is ahead of schedule and costing about what original estimates predicted.*

# Deseret News

---

Oct. 28, 1990

## Justice for fallout victims has been long time coming

WASHINGTON — Though it's been 32 years since the last U.S. atomic bomb was fired in the open air at the Nevada Test Site north of Las Vegas, the damage that radioactive fallout did to people downwind from that and many other tests has lingered on.

President Bush's signature on the downwinders act Oct. 15 finally ended more than a decade of efforts to apologize to those injured, and in some small way to compensate them or their heirs.

It's not possible to put an end to the fallout story — at least not yet. While many victims have long since gone to their graves, their friends and relatives still live with the results of government indifference. But the law does what was politically possible.

While it can never be definitively proved, former Utah Gov. Scott Matheson may have been one of the victims. Matheson lived in the fallout-stricken community of Parowan during the tests. He died this month of bone marrow cancer, a radiogenic disease.

Oct. 15, 1991

## Beautiful moment gave way to ugly spectacle

Clarence Thomas came to the nation's awareness in a heartwarming moment, in the sunshine, last July.

Fighting to control his emotions, far from his roots in dirt-poor coastal Georgia, he stood in the crisp splendor outside a president's ancestral vacation cottage at Kennebunkport, Maine.

"Only in America could this have been possible," he said, speaking slowly, stopping to regain composure. President Bush had just selected him for the Supreme Court, to become the second black ever to serve there.

Now swiftly, bewilderingly, Thomas' only-in-America dream has become an ugly never-before-in-America ordeal.

Never before had indecent language become the currency of congressional debate. Never has a Supreme Court contest turned on a question of pornography. Never have Senate aides spent the night

searching law libraries and popular novels for dirty words to prove a case in the next day's debate.

Jan. 13, 1992

## Dahmer pleads guilty but insane

MILWAUKEE (AP) — Jeffrey L. Dahmer pleaded guilty but insane Monday to the mutilation slayings of 15 young males, and now a jury must determine his mental state at the time of the killings.

"I want to emphasize that the decision to plead guilty is Mr. Dahmer's," defense attorney Gerald Boyle said during a hearing. "This case is about his mental condition."

Dahmer is accused of luring the victims to his apartment, then drugging, killing and dismembering them.

**Jeffrey L. Dahmer**

April 24, 1992

## Conviction of Watkins' killers is grim reminder to family

Sherwin and Karen Watkins celebrated the achievement of one son Thursday night while grieving the loss of their other son, who was fatally stabbed in a Manhattan subway station nearly two years ago.

Todd Watkins graduated from Brigham Young University on Thursday. Thugs prevented Brian Watkins from sharing the moment.

"Brian would have been there for sure. Todd and he were real close," Sherwin Watkins said. "We just did things as a family."

After two trials, seven men have been convicted of murder and robbery in the Sept. 2, 1990, slaying of Brian Watkins, 22. The four found guilty last December received 25 years to life in prison…

Oct. 6, 1992

## Hill says her loss in Thomas battle was no surprise

WASHINGTON — Anita Hill, the woman who accused Supreme Court Justice Clarence Thomas of sexual harassment a year ago and ignited a national debate on the issue, said Tuesday she was not

surprised that she had lost.

The Senate voted to confirm Thomas to the high court despite Hill's dramatic accusations that he had broken sexual harassment laws when she worked for him in a variety of government posts.

Oct. 12, 1992

## Starving families in Somalia are eating grass to survive

WAFDIAI, Somalia (AP) The huge international relief effort for Somalia's starving has bypassed Bashir Ibrahim Muktar and his family — they've been reduced to eating grass to survive.

They're far from alone.

Abdule Ibrahim Haidar, commissioner of the Acaba district, says thousands of people in the district's 376 villages are surviving on grass because the relief effort has targeted only the city of Bur Acaba.

Oct. 20, 1993

## Parents seek action against students who hazed son

A locker room hazing incident at Sky View High School has left a reserve quarterback without a team — and his parents demanding action against his attackers.

Brian Seamons, 16, said he was jumped by 10 teammates after stepping from the shower on Monday, Oct. 11. Seamons ran to an adjoining locker room to evade his attackers, many of whom he considered close friends, but could not escape. The mob restrained him, strapped him to a towel rack with athletic tape, and constricted his hands and legs. The group also placed tape across his chest, back and genitals. Once he was confined, his teammates brought in a female student who had been dating Seamons. When the girl realized what was happening she screamed and ran from the locker room.

**Anita Hill**

Feb. 6, 1994

## Wreckers begin tearing down the East High building

Demolition began Saturday on the second-oldest high school in the city: Salt Lake High School, East Campus, better-known as East High.

For those who grew up at the ancient and ailing school, there will soon only be memories…

"It's really a grand old building," said Joan Creer, the East Building Committee chairman. "We wish there was some way to preserve it, but ultimately, it was a safety issue."

The school has survived one major disaster, a 1972 fire that virtually gutted the building. Then, the decision was made to rebuild within the concrete-and-brick shell.

April 4, 1994

## Streisand concert tickets hit a high note: $1,500

When ticket brokers mention Barbra Streisand's rich voice, they're not talking tonal quality.

Brokers in Detroit are charging up to $1,500 per ticket for three concerts at The Palace of Auburn in Auburn Hills next month. The tickets sold out at prices of $50, $125 and $350 in less than an hour last week.

Scalping is illegal, but brokers skirt the law by selling someone a pen for several hundred dollars and throwing in the ticket, or getting buyers to say they joined a ticket club and pay extra for "services."

Oct. 3, 1995

## O.J. Simpson acquitted

**Associated Press**

LOS ANGELES (AP) — O.J. Simpson was acquitted Tuesday of murdering his ex-wife and her friend, a suspense-filled climax to the courtroom saga that obsessed the nation. With two words, "not guilty," the jury freed the fallen sports legend to try to rebuild a life thrown into disgrace.

Simpson looked toward the jury and mouthed, "Thank you," after the panel was dismissed.

Judge Lance Ito ordered him taken to the sheriff's

department and released forthwith.

Simpson, who stood facing the jury, raised his right hand and motioned to the jury. He then hugged his lead defense attorney, Johnnie Cochran Jr., and his friend and attorney Robert Kardashian.

In the audience, the sister of victim Ronald Goldman broke out in sobs. Her father sat back in his seat in disbelief, then embraced his daughter.

**[In 1997, Simpson lost a $33.5 million civil suit brought by the victims' families when the jury blamed him for the killings.]**

O.J. Simpson

## Oct. 6, 1995
## Crime pays? Trustee rips lenient deal

The Bonneville Pacific trustee has criticized federal prosecutors for cutting an easy deal with the richest Bonneville Pacific insider and urged a federal judge to impose a harsher sentence than the one recommended by prosecutors.

Carl Peterson took more than $15 million out of Bonneville Pacific, more than any other insider. That personal fortune was amassed by misleading investors, according to documents filed Thursday by trustee Roger Segal.

Yet prosecutors required only a $500,000 restitution and are recommending only a six- to 12-month sentence. Peterson has asked for home confinement, and prosecutors are supportive of that request.

## Oct. 7, 1995
## Hockey's back in Salt Lake — and it's as if it never left

ONCE THE PUCK dropped at center ice, it was as if hockey had never really left. The boards reverberated with the familiar grunts and grimaces brought on by serious body checks. The clattering of hockey sticks filled the air. The crowd oohed and ahhhed with every approach to the crease. The Zamboni squatted at the edge of the rink, ready to lap up any shavings that found their way onto the rink.

After 18 months of waiting, things were back to normal.

Hockey was back in town.

Once in town, the Grizzlies didn't waste any time making friends. On the opening night in their new locale, they pulled off a 4-2 victory...

## June 12, 1996
## Centennial census

It might have been Annie Christine Goodrich. Or maybe Mary Elizabeth Hutchinson or her twin sister, Amber Lynn, or maybe one of the other 27 babies born

over the past 24 hours at LDS Hospital. Somewhere this week, a baby will be born or a new resident will unload a U-Haul truck to become the state's 2 millionth resident, according to estimates released Wednesday by the Utah Population Estimates Committee.

"That sounds like an awful lot of people," said Annette Weed, who gave birth Tuesday to an as-yet unnamed daughter. "Pretty spectacular," added Shelley Hutchinson, the mother of twin daughters born late Tuesday.

## Nov. 1, 1996
## Enid cleared in her ex's activities

WASHINGTON — Prosecutors gave Rep. Enid Greene, R-Utah, a Halloween treat Thursday afternoon: an announcement that she won't be criminally prosecuted for any involvement with the illegal tricks of her ex-husband, confessed fraud artist Joe Waldholtz.

But prosecutors left her with one scary thought — the Federal Election Commission is continuing to investigate illegal activities by her 1992 and 1994 campaigns, and she could still face civil fines and penalties from it.

In a prepared statement Friday, Greene said she's relieved but not surprised by the U.S. attorney's announcement. "I'm relieved that this legal nightmare has finally ended and that my family's name has been cleared. This has been a torturous year and I'm thankful for the help and unending support from my family, friends, colleagues, staff and team."

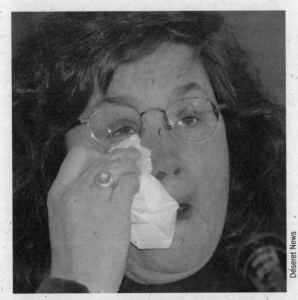

Rep. Enid Greene

## Sept. 19, 1996
## Conservationists cheer creation of monument

GRAND CANYON NATIONAL PARK — The euphoria of victory could be heard from Phoenix to Denver and Salt Lake City to Albuquerque.

Conservationists had won more than a battle. They had won a war between social and economic ideologies that had stalemated in southern Utah for three decades. The issue was decided when President Clinton sat near the edge of the Grand Canyon Wednesday afternoon and signed an executive order creating the Grand Staircase-Escalante National Monument — the largest national monument in the lower 48 states at 1.7 million acres...

Opponents to the designation were scarce, at least on the south side of the Grand Canyon. Elsewhere, members of Utah's congressional delegation continued to denounce the designation, as did elected officials in Arizona and Idaho...

[Interior Secretary Bruce] Babbitt also acknowledged he has an uphill battle to win the hearts of Utah's elected officials, who are angry Clinton would designate the park without their involvement. But Babbitt added that opposition to the new monument will be temporary, citing how people in Flagstaff were first opposed to the Grand Canyon but now support it.

## Dec. 12, 1996
## California condors get a desert home in Arizona

**Associated Press**

VERMILLION CLIFFS, ARIZ. — California condors soared above Arizona's reddish canyon walls Thursday, taking to the sky for the first time in decades with scientists' hopes flying with them.

For thousands of years, condors flew over these cliffs and fed on carcasses of woolly mammoths and saber-toothed tigers — before man pushed the huge birds to the brink of extinction.

Thursday morning, 72 years since a wild California condor was last seen in Arizona, six fledglings spread their 9-foot wings and took flight.

## Dec. 24, 1996
## 9 Tickle Me Elmo dolls fetch $9,000 at auction

Almost all the hard-to-find Tickle Me Elmo dolls up for auction in Utah Valley were sold.

The American Fork Police Department sold nine of the 12 red furry critters it received from Wal-Mart. The department raised $9,000 for the Alpine School District Foundation and the Dan Peterson School, a school for special-needs students. Police locked the Elmos in a holding cell until they were adopted. The three remaining dolls might be sold Tuesday.

Officer Rick Bockman said some of the buyers

promptly donated the stuffed toys to patients at Primary Children's Medical Center.

In Provo, the Greg Smith family was able to sell its Tickle Me Elmo for $1,000 Monday. The family will donate the money to the Food and Care Coalition of Utah Valley, said Becky Smith.

## Jan. 1, 1997
## Grim tally: '96 punctuated by number of random or bizarre killings

He was taking pictures of the moon at night. She was in her apartment waiting for her husband to come home.

He was working nights at a budget motel to put himself through school. She was trying to get the name of the driver who had hit her car.

These are some of the activities this year's murder victims were involved in when they were killed. There seemed to be an increase in the number of random or bizarre killings in 1996...

Police don't even know motives for 12 of the 67 homicides that occurred in Utah during 1996.

There were the usual drug killings, gang-related shootouts and child-abuse homicides. And as in years past, most victims were killed by someone they knew — sometimes by someone they loved.

## Aug. 31, 1997
## Car crash kills Princess Diana

PARIS (AP) — Britain's Princess Diana, who had been struggling to build a new public and private life after her turbulent divorce, was killed Sunday along with her companion, Dodi Fayed, in a car crash as their Mercedes was being pursued by photographers.

The 36-year-old princess died at 4 a.m. after going into cardiac arrest, doctors told a hospital news conference.

The crash happened shortly after midnight in a tunnel along the Seine River at the Pont de l'Alma bridge, less than a half mile north of the Eiffel Tower in central Paris. It came as paparazzi — the commercial photographers who constantly tail Diana — followed her car, police said...

Diana and Prince Charles, heir to the British throne, separated in 1992 after 11 years of marriage and divorced last year.

Princess Diana

# THE DESERET NEWS

**Feb. 24, 1997**

## Successful cloning of sheep in Britain raises ethical red flags

**New York Times News Service**

When a scientist whose goal is to turn animals into drug factories announced Saturday in Britain that his team had cloned a sheep, the last practical barrier in reproductive technology was breached, experts say, and with a speed that few if any scientists anticipated.

Now these experts say the public must come to grips with issues as grand as the possibility of making carbon copies of humans and as mundane, but important, as what will happen to the genetic diversity of livestock if breeders start to clone animals.

**Sept. 5, 1997**

## Mother Teresa, helper of the poor, dies at 87

ROME (AP) — Mother Teresa, the Roman Catholic nun whose very name became synonymous with charity for her work with "the poorest of the poor," has died. She was 87.

A nun at the Sisters of Charity in Rome disclosed her death Friday…

Mother Teresa created a global charity to care for the human castoffs the world wanted to forget.

For 50 years, she comforted the destitute dying in gutters, sheltered infants abandoned in trash heaps, soothed the putrid ulcers of lepers and gave succor to the insane.

**Mother Teresa**

**Nov. 20, 1997**

## 7 babies, 84 diapers, 35 outfits… a day

CEDAR RAPIDS, IOWA (AP) — Bobbi and Kenny McCaughey better be prepared to do a lot of counting. Seven babies can mean 84 diapers, 250 ounces of formula and 35 changes of clothes each day.

"As far as price goes, it's astronomical for one (baby)," said Michelle Waugh, the owner of the children's specialty store Once Upon a Child.

So for the McCaugheys of Carlisle the costs are multiplied — oh boy, are they multiplied! Formula? Depending on how much each baby drinks, that can cost $12 to $21 per day. That's roughly $360 to $630 each month or $4,300 to $7,500 per year.

And since some of that formula will no doubt end up on the infants' clothing, experts advise having five outfits on hand per child per day. At $10 per outfit, Waugh said, that translates into $350 worth of clothing to get each baby through a day.

**Nov. 21, 1998**

## Graham hails 'win' for states

Utah Attorney General Jan Graham Friday heralded a $206 billion settlement between 46 states and big tobacco as "a monumental win for each and every state."

Utah stands to recover $836 million — 6 1/2 times what it sued four major tobacco companies for in 1996. The settlement will be paid over 25 years, with the first payment of $10 million expected early in 1999. Thereafter, payments to Utah will be about $30 million a year.

[The historic tobacco settlement, aimed at giving states money to alleviate the costs of smoking-related health problems, triggered a fight between Graham and other state officials over how Utah's money should be spent. As of late 1999, debate continued over where the funds would go. No money had yet been received, but it was expected shortly after the turn of the century.]

**Feb. 5, 1999**

## Stones show up, play the part

The Rolling Stones — literally the granddaddy of rock 'n' roll — came to town last night. The hype surrounding the band these days preceded the show, which, unfortunately, didn't live up to it.

There were some pregnant pauses between songs, and the band seemed a bit off at times. The music was on, but the energy felt a little forced. And to some dismay, the core band members — guitarist Keith Richards, drummer Charlie Watts, guitarist Ron Wood and vocalist Mick Jagger — appeared to have become caricatures.

**April 20, 1999**

## Sheriff: 'Suicide mission' at school leaves 25 possibly dead

### One individual apprehended in Littleton

LITTLETON, Colo. (AP) — Three young men in fatigues and black trench coats opened fire at a suburban Denver high school Tuesday in what police called a suicide mission, and the sheriff said 25 people may have been killed. Two of the suspects were found dead in the library.

Several students said the killers were gunning for minorities and athletes.

The dead suspects, believed to be former students at Columbine High School, had devices on them that could be bombs.

A third young man was led away from the school in handcuffs more than four hours after the attack, which began at 11:30 a.m.

By early evening, FBI agents and police SWAT teams were still moving through the school, searching for victims and explosives.

At least 20 people were wounded at Columbine, which has 1,800 students. Shots ricocheted off lockers as the gunmen opened fire with what students said were automatic weapons and set off explosives. One girl was shot nine times in the chest.

[The number killed was 15, and only two shooters, both students, were involved.]

**Aug. 6, 1999**

## Even after 40 years, Barbie's still got 'it'

A Barbie model displays the 40th anniversary doll at a three-day National Barbie Convention in Pittsburgh, Pa. Collectors from across the country are displaying their wares and comparing prices with competitors. Barbie debuted in 1959 as a classic pin-up girl: spiked heels, black and white strapless bathing suit and powder blue eye shadow. After 40 years and numerous incarnations, Barbie dazzled fans at the convention by being unveiled wearing a gown inspired by her first outfit.

**Sept. 1, 1999**

## No more Beanie Babies? Panic grips parents

Beanie Babies are through. There will be no more.

The word swept the nation Tuesday as Ty Inc., the maker of Beanie Babies, announced via its Web site that it plans to retire all of the plush toys on Dec. 31, 1999.

The statement was brief… and tantalizingly vague.

Internet chat rooms spun into a frenzy. Online auction sites were buried under the weight of new bids for the pint-size stuffed animals. Panic and disbelief gripped parents, wondering how they would tell their Beanie-fanatic children…

Janell Johnson, Tooele, said she'll not be shedding any tears… Her daughter Bailee is 4 years old and has about 40 of the little critters… "My sister is the one who stands in line at 4 a.m. to get them. She has every single one of them, it seems, and she has all the books and magazines… her kids just worship them. I think they'll be very sad when they go."

**Sept. 11, 1999**

## S.L. jail delays opening doors due to Y2K worries

Good news for taxpayers and lawbreakers: The opening of the new Salt Lake County jail has been pushed back again.

Sheriff Aaron Kennard told county commissioners Sept. 7 that because of concerns about staff, security and Y2K, the $131 million jail will not be ready to receive prisoners until late in January.

This news, combined with previous delays, will save the county $5.6 million in operating costs this year.

**Sept. 11, 1999**

## Prepare for Y2K despite 9-9-99 bust

Are computer geeks feeling a bit like Chicken Little? 9-9-99 came and went without a hitch. The sky didn't fall, computers didn't lock up and the sun rose again in the east. What many had termed a rehearsal for Y2K didn't live up to the hype.

As the world creeps closer to Jan. 1, 2000, what's a rational human being to make of all the Y2K hoopla?

… No one can accurately predict the extent of problems and accompanying disruptions until Jan. 1, 2000. In the meantime, businesses, transportation firms, financial institutions, government agencies, utilities and health care providers and individuals would be wise to make necessary upgrades.

**Sept. 12, 1999**

## Monument instills healing at Mountain Meadows site

A hundred and forty-two years have passed since the Mountain Meadows Massacre. For a long time, it was something people tried to forget. But now, it has become something to remember — not with bitterness but with a spirit of compassion and understanding.

"All who knew firsthand about what occurred here are long since gone. Let the book of the past be closed. Let peace come into our hearts," said President Gordon B. Hinckley, president of The Church of Jesus Christ of Latter-day Saints, as he dedicated a gravesite memorial at the site of the massacre.

In the audience at the dedication Saturday morning were about a hundred descendants of children who had survived the massacre, people who had come from Arkansas, Oklahoma, Texas, New Mexico, Arizona and California.

As the century ends, the United States is to cede ownership of the Panama Canal, one of the century's major engineering feats, to Panama.

Aug. 31, 1999

# Turning over the canal

**The Panama Canal, pride of the United States at the beginning of the century, was a major news story to the end.**

## First woman president to take charge in Panama

**The Guardian**

Panama's first woman president, Mireya Moscoso, will be sworn in at Panama City's new national stadium Wednesday before a group of seven Latin American heads of state and a crowd of 25,000 supporters.

Few doubt that Moscoso, the opposition party leader who defeated the candidate of the majority Democratic Revolutionary party in the presidential election on May 2, has cause to celebrate. As the head of the populist Arnulfista party founded by her late husband — three times ousted strongman Arnulfo Arias — she will lead Panama into the new millennium at a key moment in its history.

A ceremony at noon on December 31 will mark the hand-over of the Panama Canal to Panamanian authorities and the final withdrawal of U.S. troops, in fulfillment of a treaty negotiated in 1977 by President Jimmy Carter of the United States and the then Panamanian military leader Gen. Omar Torrijos.

"The canal is pivotal for the development of the inter-oceanic region and the rest of the country," Moscoso told voters during campaigning, while promising to respect the strategic waterway's administrative autonomy after the U.S. withdrawal.

The controversial U.S. presence in Panama began in 1903 when President Theodore Roosevelt sent a gunboat to support Panamanian secession from Colombia. The new country's constitution granted U.S. control of the canal linking the Caribbean Sea and the Pacific Ocean, begun and then abandoned by the French in the 1880s, and the right to intervene "in any part of Panama to re-establish public peace and constitutional order."

U.S.-Panamanian relations reached their nadir in 1989 with the invasion to topple Gen. Manuel Noriega. An estimated 350 Panamanians and 18 U.S. servicemen were killed in Operation Just Cause, which was condemned by the Organization of American States. Noriega is serving a 40-year sentence in Miami for drug trafficking.

Gen. Manuel Noriega

Sept. 11, 1999

## Noriega's threat was viewed seriously

Former Panamanian ruler Gen. Manuel Noriega threatened to blow up the Panama Canal in 1978 if the Senate tried to amend an agreement to hand it over, former Sen. Howard Baker Jr. said.

Baker recalled how Noriega made the threat in a meeting with him during a trip Baker made to Panama City in 1978, while serving as the Republican leader in the Senate. The Senate was preparing to approve the treaty giving full control of the canal and the Canal Zone to Panama by the end of 1999.

## The world of the 1990s
### A TIMELINE

**1990**— Nelson Mandela, in prison for 27 years in South Africa, is freed.

**1990**— The Chunnel is completed under the English Channel, linking Britain and France by rail.

**1990**— Margaret Thatcher, known worldwide as the "Iron Lady," retires as Britain's prime minister.

**1990**— Boris Yeltsin elected president of Russia.

**1991**— The last apartheid laws are revoked in South Africa.

**1991**— A Serbian policy of ethnic cleansing in Bosnia shocks the world.

**1991**— Los Angeles is engulfed in riots after four white policemen are acquitted of beating Rodney King. The incident had been recorded on video.

**1991**— U.S. Marines are sent to Somalia, where warlords have forced thousands into starvation.

**1993**— New York's World Trade Center is hit by a massive bomb that is later traced to terrorists.

**1994**— Los Angeles is hit by a major earthquake that kills 34, levels freeway structures and causes $7 billion in damage.

**1995**— Horrific ethnic battles engulf Rwanda between Hutus and Tutsis. Some 100,000 are estimated killed in two weeks, and refugee camps spring up.

**1994**— Republicans take control of both houses of Congress for the first time in 40 years.

**1995**— Israeli Prime Minister Yitzhak Rabin is assassinated by a religious fanatic.

**1996**— A terrorist bomb attack in Saudi Arabia leaves 19 US troops dead and 300 injured.

**1996**— TWA Flight 800 crashes into the Atlantic Ocean, killing all 230 aboard.

**1996**— FBI agents arrest Theodore J. Kaczynski in his Montana cabin as the Unabomber who carried on a 17-year campaign of mail terror.

**1996**— The U.S. puts together a fragile peace in Bosnia.

**1997**— The stock market plunges 554 points in one day, then climbs back up again, rising 20 percent for the third straight year.

**1997**— Tobacco companies make their first agreement with states for $368 billion.

**1998**— Asian economies falter, hit hard by inflation, and the U.S. stock market plunges, only to regain its strength later.

**1998**— Two U.S. embassies are bombed — in the Sudan and in Kenya — by terrorist organizations. The U.S. retaliates against suspected bases.

**1999**— Hundreds of thousands of ethnic Albanians are driven from Kosovo by Serbs. NATO bombards Serbia, forcing Serb troops to withdraw from Kosovo.

**1999**— An earthquake in Turkey leaves at least 15,000 dead.

---

**THE FAR SIDE**    BY GARY LARSON

Suddenly, and to Rodney's horror, the police arrived with nerd-sniffing dogs.

"Tell it again, Gramps! The one about being caught in the shark frenzy off the Great Barrier Reef!"

**ZIGGY**    BY TOM WILSON

WELL, THANK YOU... YOU'RE LOOKING PRETTY SNAZZY YOURSELF!!

# The Olympics:
## boon and bane

A sea of celebrating Utahns looked like confetti in an aerial view when the news became official — Salt Lake would host the 2002 Winter Games.

**U**tahns had been talking about bringing the Olympic Games home for decades. In the late '80s, the talk turned serious. The city decided to go after the 1998 Games.

**DESERET NEWS,** *Dec. 2, 1988:* Aiming to make Salt Lake City not only the host of the 1998 Winter Olympics but also the "winter sports capital of the United States," the Salt Lake Organizing Committee met Friday to craft an Olympic bid.

The committee — composed of 56 government, business, education and sports leaders — must prepare a bid to present to the U.S. Olympic Committee, who will choose a U.S. city in June to bid internationally for the Games.

With the backing of the USOC, Salt Lake City made its presentation to the International Olympic Committee in June, 1991. But the 1998 Games went to Nagano, Japan.

**DESERET NEWS,** *Nov. 23, 1991:* Atlanta's success sealed Utah's doom in the game of who-gets-the-Olympics this past year.

Once again this was confirmed, this time by Mark Hodler, president of the International Ski Federation and executive board member for the International Olympic Committee.

"It was felt (by IOC members) that it would do nothing more than put oil on the fire if Salt Lake City had been selected," he said Friday at a press conference called prior to the opening of World Cup skiing in Park City.

"There was such a nasty campaign started after Atlanta. Many simply said we couldn't choose another site in the United States."

After Atlanta had been awarded the 1996 Summer Games, charges of payoffs and corruptions were leveled by several of the unsuccessful bidders at the IOC.

"We've looked into it and found some irregularities, but certainly not to the extent mentioned," Hodler said. "And we are looking at making changes, but I can't tell you when they will be made."…

Salt Lake's Olympic backers regrouped, took the lessons they had learned from the unsuccessful bid, and tried once more.

**DESERET NEWS,** *April 28, 1993:* Utah's corporate leaders need to dig

Suddenly, Olympic symbols were everywhere, including street signs.

deeper into their pockets — and the pockets of the out-of-state companies they do business with, according to the head of the board of trustees for the Salt Lake City Olympic Bid Committee.

Trustees voted Tuesday to spend more than $2 million in the budget year beginning July 1, an increase of about $1.3 million over the current budget of $772,000…

All of the money spent on the bid itself is raised privately. Taxpayers are picking up the tab for some $56 million in winter-sports facilities, including a ski-jumping facility that opened this winter near Park City.

*Nov. 21, 1993:* Utahns overwhelmingly favor Salt Lake City hosting the 2002 Winter Games, believing the Olympics will boost the state's image and economy without harming the environment.

A Deseret News-KSL poll of 605 Utahns found that 73 percent favor hosting the Games, while only 21 percent are opposed. And a whopping 90 percent believe the Olympics would have a positive effect on the state's image.

A record 10 cities competed for the 2002 Games, including three of the five that bid against Salt Lake City in 1991. Salt Lake's organizers were determined to show off what the city had to offer.

**DESERET NEWS,** *Feb. 5, 1994:* Backers of Utah's bid for the 2002 Winter Games are headed to Lillehammer, Norway, with enough round-trip airline tickets to bring every member of the International Olympic Committee to Salt Lake City at least once.

Delta Air Lines donated 150 tickets valued at $500,000 to the Salt Lake Olympic Bid Committee on Friday, as the state's delegation to the 1994 Winter Games was preparing to leave for Norway.

The money being spent on the IOC was beginning to rankle some Deseret News readers. In a letter to the editor, Travis Pearce noted:

After Salt Lake disclosures of wrongdoing, International Olympics president Juan Antonio Samaranch called for reform in the system for awarding the games.

Deseret News

Above, Nick Sullivan practices on the new luge course at the Winter Sports Park, where facilities were built to host the Olympics.

Deseret News

Mitt Romney

**DESERET NEWS,** *Mar. 4, 1994: In recent months there has been a great deal of criticism regarding gratuities showered upon politicians by lobbyists. But this practice pales in comparison to the financial and gift-giving our Utah Olympic delegation bestows upon the International Olympic Committee members...*

*IOC members are the consummate parasites of the world. They obviously have no pride. Why don't they just affix a price tag for hosting the Games and then take their cut from this amount? It would seem much more above board...*

- On Jan. 23, 1995, IOC narrowed the field down to four finalists. And to no one's surprise; Salt Lake was among them, joining Ostersund, Sweden; Sion, Switzerland, and Quebec.
- In June 1995, Salt Lake's delegation left for Budapest, Hungary, to make its presentation. And then came the moment everyone had been waiting for. IOC President Juan Antonio Samaranch stepped to the microphone and announced the winner: "the city of Salt Lake City."

Utah's delegation was ecstatic, and so were thousands of Salt Lakers who gathered on the grounds of the City-County

Building to await the announcement in what was billed as "the party of the century." Salt Lake hadn't just won, it had won big.

**DESERET NEWS,** *June 17, 1995: For the first time ever, a city bidding for the Olympic Winter Games beat its competition in the first round of balloting by the International Olympic Committee.*

*Tom Welch couldn't believe it. He stood on the stage of the Budapest Kongresszusi Kozport just after the 7:20 announcement Friday staring at a vote tally, too dazed to respond to the reporters asking if he was surprised.*

*"Yeah," he finally whispered...*

*Fifty-four of the first 92 votes cast Friday afternoon went to Salt Lake City.*

*Dec. 31, 1995: The image of tens of thousands of people on the grounds of the City-County Building spontaneously erupting with joy on news of the successful 2002 Winter Olympic bid will forever symbolize 1995 for many Utahns.*

Cautioned by the IOC not to coast toward 2002, the re-formed Salt Lake Organizing Committee moved ahead. In July 1997, Tom Welch stepped down as Olympics chief after personal problems erupted into headlines. But work moved on.

**DESERET NEWS,** *Sept. 12, 1997: The E Center of West Valley City, the new home of the Utah Grizzlies hockey team and future venue for a diverse lineup of entertainment and community events — not to mention the 2002 Olympics — will open its doors next weekend.*

*Dec. 13, 1997: The state's Olympic bobsled and luge track is not only fit for a king, a section of it is now named for a prince with the dedication Friday of Albert's Alley.*

*Prince Albert of Monaco, wearing a sweatsuit and sneakers, accepted the honor during a brief ceremony at the Utah Winter Sports Park Friday before he was scheduled to compete in the America's Cup bobsled race.*

*Feb. 23, 1998: NAGANO, Japan – Salt Lake Mayor Deedee Corradini took center stage during Sunday's closing ceremonies for the 1998 Winter Games, making history as the first woman to accept the Olympic flag.*

*Oct. 11, 1998: Olympic organizers are counting on signing up as many as 32,000 volunteers over the next four years, including up to 80 percent of the workers needed to put on the 2002 Winter Games.*

And then the hammer fell. Remember all that courting of the IOC? Maybe it hadn't been such a good thing, after all:

**DESERET NEWS,** *Nov. 25, 1998: Olympic organizers paid more than $10,000 for at least one relative of an International Olympic Committee member to attend college in the United States as part of the effort to win the 2002 Winter Games.*

*Dec. 6, 1998: It's no secret that backers of Salt Lake City's bid for the Winter Games spent a lot of money on everything from lavish meals to dental care for members of the International Olympic Committee.*

*Now it's an assistance program being described by the Salt Lake Organizing Committee as "humanitarian aid" that's focusing new attention on whether such expenditures amounted to an attempt at buying votes.*

The ensuing scandal reached international proportions. The USOC ordered a probe. The IOC ordered a probe. The U.S. Justice Department ordered a probe. Charges of ethical and moral — if not criminal — wrongdoing swirled. And

Deseret News

Tom Welch

the call for change was loud and clear.

**DESERET NEWS,** *Dec. 21, 1998: Once seen as a squeaky clean campaigner, Salt Lake City is now the catalyst to overhaul how the International Olympic Committee chooses where the Games will go.*

*"After this scandal, I believe that the IOC as a whole must accept that the system needs to change and that we can't continue like this," IOC President Juan Antonio Samaranch told a Swiss newspaper Sunday.*

In Utah, Frank Joklik and Dave Johnson resigned from their SLOC posts joining Tom Welch, who had resigned earlier after being charged in an unrelated scandal. The IOC itself backed its president but voted to oust six members who were seen as committing particularly egregious offenses. But the news came down: Games would not be taken from Salt Lake City.

Salt Lakers looked for a "white knight" to pick up the pieces and go on. They found him in Mitt Romney.

Polls showed that while support for the Games dropped somewhat, 60 percent of the state's residents still wanted to host the 2002 Winter Games. And there was work to be done.

**DESERET NEWS,** *May 16, 1999: There's a new face on the 2002 Winter Games — make that three new faces.*

*They belong to the bear, snowshoe hare and coyote selected as mascots for Salt Lake City's Olympics. The trio made their public debut during a downtown celebration that marks 1,000 days until the start of the Games...*

The pain of the scandal was fading and some of the old excitement was beginning to creep back in.

# A tornado? Here?

**Few meteorological events over the life of the newspaper hit with the force of an August 1999 tornado that whipped through downtown Salt Lake City, a few blocks from its offices. The daily deadline had just passed when the usual noon-time calm of the newsroom was shattered.**

L ights and computers blinked off as the tornado passed by. Reporters scattered in all directions to get the story. Editors organized to try to stay ahead of a dozen simultaneous events. They tried to cope with a power outage that closed down the presses for more than two hours. A late edition reached homes that night:

**DESERET NEWS,** Aug. 11, 1999: A powerful tornado touched down in Salt Lake City early Wednesday afternoon, reportedly killing at least one person, injuring scores of others, shattering windows, collapsing tents at the Outdoor Retailers Summer Market and ripping off sections of roof from the Delta Center and other buildings.

Rescuers and emergency management officials were still counting casualties at midafternoon...

As the dark tornado funnel — an uncommon sight in the Mountain West — crossed the I-15 corridor, motorists stopped in their tracks. Meteorologist Chris Young of the National Weather Service said the storm — classified as an F2 on a scale of 0-5 — then invaded the city's downtown areas and headed through the Capitol Hill and Avenues neighborhoods to the east, damaging houses but losing potency as it went...

The fickle storm wreaked significant damage in its swipe across the downtown area but spared many office buildings packed with people, the historic Salt Lake Temple and the State Capitol Building. Destruction in the Avenues was great.

Working overnight, the News staff by the next day offered readers insights into every aspect of the storm, including eyewitness reports, damage details, explanations of the odd weather phenomenon and advice on how to collect insurance, if necessary. Under the banner headline "Twister's terrible toll," the story was told.

**DESERET NEWS,** Aug. 12, 1999: Assessment teams converged on Salt Lake City Thursday to begin calculating the terrible toll of Wednesday's tornado.

The twister hit hard and fast, tearing apart buildings, shutting down power and scattering debris for miles.

One person was killed and at least 81 people were taken to area hospitals... At the Delta Center, one of the commercial buildings most badly damaged by the twister, Utah Jazz and Delta Center executives huddled, attempting to assess the damage and calculating whether the initial estimate of six weeks for repairs can be shortened.

The nearby Wyndham Hotel, 215 W. South Temple, was the next large structure in the tornado's northeastern path of destruction. Dozens of windows were shattered and bed linens and other items were sucked out into the street. The hotel was closed Wednesday evening and guests... were shuttled to other hotels in the area.

Approximately 300 homes were damaged, many in the historic Avenues neighborhood. Forty of those suffered severe damage, 80 had moderate damage ...

Corran Addison had lived his life like some big kahuna of adventurism, hanging tenuously to the edge of danger, surfing tidal waves of adrenalism.

But the world-class kayaker, who once plunged his craft over a 100-foot waterfall in France, never had a ride like Wednesday afternoon.

When the tornado hit downtown Salt Lake City, Addison was in one of the tented pavilions at the Outdoor Retailers Summer Market.

"My feet were straight out, 3 feet above my head," said Addison, 30, design and marketing director of Riot Kayaks of Montreal. "I'm just hanging on with my head down going, 'What's gonna hit me?'"

Grace Wilson and her daughters were watching "Big Valley" on TV when the big blow hit the Avenues Wednesday. They heard a ferocious wind, then looked out a window of their 16th Avenue home and saw lightning. A nearby power line exploded, so they cowered near the couch. They watched in horror as a tree crashed through the living room. And then the ceiling turned to sky...

The Wilsons' upper Avenues neighborhood was transformed Wednesday from a comfortable upper-class district to a trail of tears ...

When Farmington resident Wayne Klein left his office at the State Capitol Wednesday afternoon, he had no idea that it would take almost 3 1/2 hours to reach home.

Like many commuters, his fate became entwined in the aftermath of the twister that ripped through downtown earlier in the day...

Post mortems of the damaging storm went on much much longer than the storm itself. Although not unheard of in the Beehive State, tornados were rare. For Utahns, this was one for the record books.

Rubble that was once an outdoor retail show attested to the power of tornado that wreaked havoc in downtown Salt Lake City Aug. 11, 1999.

A funnel with winds whirling up to 115 per hour snapped a power pole, shattered windows and damaged the Delta Center's roof as it roared through.

# We were there

. . . . . . . . . . . . . . . . . . . . . . . . . . .

## THE STORY OF THE DESERET NEWS

**By Hal Knight**

**T**he first issue of the Deseret News was cranked out June 15, 1850, on a used, hand-operated press in an adobe shack on South Temple just east of Main Street. The unimpressive little paper had no real headlines, no pictures and no up-to-date information, but for the isolated settlers it was a promise of an open window into a left-behind world.

So starved were the pioneers for news in the early days that on rare occasions when Eastern newspapers were brought in by travelers, Brigham Young would call a "news conference" and the papers would be read to an assembled audience for more than an hour at a time.

While the appearance of a weekly Deseret News was warmly welcomed, it was soon clear that having a newspaper and having any news to print were quite different things. Salt Lake Valley was a remote and isolated place. There were no telephones, no telegraph, no railroad, no reliable mail system. Mountain passes were sometimes closed for months at a time in winter. And while far-flung missionaries served as sort of foreign correspondents, any information was irregular and colored by their religious duties. Even the communities in Utah were widely scattered and had little contact with each other. Just gathering items of local news was slow and tedious.

Most news items were weeks old by the time they reached print, yet the paper was read eagerly. Copies were shared with neighbors until they were illegible and falling apart. For every subscriber there were dozens of readers. Sometimes they were so anxious they wore out the paper passing it from hand to hand before the original subscriber had a chance to read it.

The first edition of the Deseret News contained eight pages, each slightly smaller than a sheet of today's typing paper. The metal type for the text was painstakingly set in place by hand, one letter at a time. Once the type was locked in the press, an energetic operator could produce about two pages a minute. By contrast, a modern press spews out a 50-page newspaper — with color — at the rate of 40,000 copies an hour.

The story of the Deseret News, as with papers everywhere, is partly one of evolving technology, but that wasn't an issue early on. Hand-operated printing presses were cheap; the Deseret News press cost just $61. Just about anyone could get into the business and did, but surviving was another matter. The challenges included a lack of paying customers plus a severe shortage of paper. More

Under the watchful eye of the copy chief, copy editors scan stories in their new offices on Richards Street in 1927.

*Deseret News files*

than 100 periodicals emerged and then died in Salt Lake City in the mid-to-late 1800s. The city was once described as a "newspaper cemetery."

Despite these early shaky times, the Deseret News weathered repeated adversity to eventually become a daily newspaper and celebrate 150 vigorous years as chronicler of Utah and the world for its readers.

## A society without cash

A subscription to the Deseret News supposedly was $2.50 for six months "in advance," but cash was scarce in the valley and the paper was willing to accept in-kind payments to support Editor Willard Richards and his three-man staff and help with publication costs. Early editions pleaded for food, wood, candles, animal skins and "every good thing." However, nearly everyone was living close to the bone in the infant Mormon communities, and paying for a newspaper was often a real sacrifice. Yet from an original 220 copies, the circulation grew to nearly 700 within a year.

Unfortunately, subscription payments hardly sustained life. Deseret News workers in 1853 were rationed to a half-pound of bread a day and became thin, frail and weak. But they survived and so did the growing paper, which reached a press run of 4,000 within six years. Nonetheless, the inconvenient use of barter for subscriptions and a portion of worker wages continued well into the 1870s. A printer once complained that after three weeks work

the cash portion of his salary amounted to 35 cents.

## No paper for the paper

After only a few months of publication, available supplies of newsprint were shrinking. The Deseret News began publishing only every other week. From time to time no Deseret News appeared at all because of a lack of paper; the vacant intervals lasted anywhere from three weeks to three months.

The pioneers had a typical answer for the problem: They would make their own paper. The Deseret News began writing appeals for rags to serve as pulp for homemade newsprint, and the first editions made with the new paper appeared in June 1854. The homemade paper, produced on Temple Square, was thick and gray but was accepted as "better than no paper." Readers could "almost see the buttonholes" from shirts that went into making of the newsprint.

Brigham Young purchased a paper-making machine in 1860 and installed it in a water-driven mill in Sugar House formerly used as a sugar factory. The quality of the newsprint improved slightly, although it still ranged from thick to thin and from brown to various shades of blue.

The desperate search for rags continued, and they were even accepted in lieu of church tithing. In 1861 George Goddard was called on a "rag mission" in which he ranged over much of Utah and within 20 months collected more than 100,000 pounds of rags.

By 1875 the Sugar House mill had become a steady source of paper, but it was too small. A new mill was built in Big Cottonwood Canyon in the early 1880s at enormous cost and produced five tons of paper a day, although quality was still a problem. Unfortunately, the mill was destroyed by fire about 10 years later. That ended local efforts to produce newsprint.

During World War II, the Deseret News, like all other newspapers, was limited to a certain quota of newsprint. The result was a thinner newspaper. After the war the rationing ended, but newsprint remained in short supply even while Deseret News circulation was growing rapidly. Unlike the early days when paper was purchased by the ream, it was now being bought by the ton.

When Deseret News officials heard that the Los Angeles Times was trying to get other papers to join in the purchase of a paper mill in Oregon, the News quickly made contact. The L.A. Times, the Deseret News and some Oregon business people bought the huge mill in 1947, scoring a major coup and assuring themselves of a large and steady supply of newsprint.

By 1949 the Deseret News was using some 700 tons of newsprint a month compared to less than 200 tons two years earlier. That compares to about 1,200 tons per month in 1999. The Deseret News eventually sold its one-quarter share in the Oregon paper mill to the Los Angeles Times, a move that LDS Church apostle and former Deseret News editor Mark E. Petersen said was "like selling one of my children."

## From a weekly to a daily

Although the Deseret News began as a struggling weekly, a looming Civil War and the arrival of the hard-riding Pony Express in 1860 caused the paper to issue extra editions known as the Pony Dispatch, a one-page publication with no headlines. War news was on one side and advertisements on the back. Telegraph lines arrived in 1861 and the Pony Express folded, but the name Pony Dispatch continued atop the extra editions. By the time they ended in 1864, the extras were appearing almost daily.

In October 1865, the Deseret News began appearing as a semi-weekly — one that would last for 57 years. But the weekly paper also continued as a separate publication. Two years later, despite crippling paper shortages, a daily edition was launched. It was named the Deseret Evening News and was published every day but Sunday and an occasional holiday.

Yet the weekly and semi-weekly both stayed on the scene as morning papers. The daily was for city readers and the others for rural areas where mail was delivered only once or twice a week. The weekly continued until 1898 and the semi-weekly until 1922.

The name, Deseret Evening News, was dropped in June 1920 and the original title, Deseret News, was reclaimed.

In 1948, in the midst of an aggressive post-war expansion that enlarged the staff and eventually more than doubled the paper's circulation to 100,000, the Deseret News began publishing a Sunday edition. Included on Sundays was a rotogravure magazine featuring color photographs, the first of its kind in the area. The magazine won many honors and was a boost to circulation. The section was edited by Ray McGuire and Olive Burt, who also was editor of the Deseret News children's section and a prolific author of children's books.

It was a heady year that saw an avalanche of increased advertising, as a colorful group of sales people pushed a major ad campaign. A youthful Thomas S. Monson, later to become an LDS Church apostle and a member of the First Presidency, joined the newspaper that year as a classified ad salesman. He remembers his colleagues as a talented and "individualistic" group. It included among others, Amos Jenkins, a charismatic advertising director; Susie Miller, who knew every real estate agent and auto dealer in Salt Lake City; Ralph Davison, a hard-pushing manager for national ads; and Kenneth Bourne, retail advertising manager who always wore a hat, indoors and out, hiding a lack of hair.

Along with a new Sunday paper, 1948 saw the introduction of a wide variety of new sections and columns, and the hiring of a host of talented young writers and editors.

Among the new features was Hi Tales, a popular column for teenagers, written by Elaine Cannon; a garden column by Hazel Moyle; a daily financial page and international political analysis by Vivian Meik, a piratical-looking Britisher, complete with eye-patch from a World War II wound. He had personally known both Hitler and Stalin and once had a price placed on his head by Mussolini as a result of Meik's writings for British papers during the war.

*In 1908, a crowds of young newsboys gathers at the News Development Room.*

Utah State Historical Society

Making an appearance in the paper was a new Family section, a children's section and a Midweek section. Teletype-equipped news bureaus expanded in Utah, Idaho, Nevada and Colorado. Some 50 part-time correspondents — known as "stringers" because they were paid by the inch of news copy they produced — were added to the 129 stringers already working in small communities around the Mountain West.

In a real sense, 1948 was an epochal year in which the Deseret News came of age as a thriving daily metropolitan newspaper.

## The NAC: A dramatic change

The exceptional Deseret News growth after 1948 came at a price. An aggressive but expensive circulation campaign reached homes all over the state and beyond, offering prizes to new subscribers. And despite the mounting expenses of an ever-larger paper, advertising rates remained lower than those of its fierce rival, the Salt Lake Tribune, which lost subscribers and ad revenue.

Faced with a serious financial drain, rising costs and troubled futures, the Deseret News and the Salt Lake Tribune in 1952 made a dramatic and startling move that changed much of Utah's newspaper landscape. The two papers worked out a 30-year arrangement known as a Joint Operating Agreement. This completely altered the way of doing business for both newspapers.

A jointly owned entity, the Newspaper Agency Corp., was created to handle the printing, delivery and advertising for both papers. One set of presses instead of two, one advertising department instead of two, one mechanical department instead of two, one circulation department instead of two — thus sharply reducing those operating expenses and guaranteeing the financial health of both publications.

Although both newspapers remained distinctly separate news operations, many people still confused the printing/circulation agency with joint newsrooms. "Aren't they the same?" was a puzzled query that took years to subside and still hasn't totally disappeared.

Yet the Deseret News and Tribune continue to take opposite editorial stands on many public issues. One memorable campaign between the papers in 1968 over allowing liquor to be sold by the drink in Utah lasted for the better part of a year before the Deseret News' view opposing the practice was backed by voters in a statewide election.

As part of the 1952 NAC agreement, the Salt Lake Telegram, an afternoon sister publication of the Tribune, was acquired by the Deseret News and ceased publication. The News also ended its own short-lived Sunday paper. Deseret News subscribers received the Sunday Tribune instead, which added to some people's confusion about who was doing what.

The operating agreement was renewed in 1982 for another 30 years — until the year 2012 — but with a significant difference: The Deseret News once again began publishing its own Sunday paper in January 1983.

## Newspaper wars

Newspapering in America was an emotional business in its early days. Editors engaged in personal attacks, name-calling and vicious partisanship. In return, editors occasionally were beaten, horse whipped, tarred and feathered, ridden out of town on a rail or even shot at. Salt Lake City generally avoided most of those violent practices, but newspapering still had its risks.

The last few decades of the 19th century were harsh, confrontational ones in Utah journalism. This was a reflection of the sometimes bitter emotional climate of the day in which divisions along religious and philosophical lines dominated life in Utah Territory.

Questions of local vs. federal control, statehood, polygamy, church influence, politics and economics were argued across a seeming chasm of enmity and prejudice. Facts were sometimes the first casualty.

The Deseret News naturally had the journalistic field to itself at the start, but in 1858 a Missouri newspaperman came to town and started the Valley Tan, which generally represented non-Mormon views and often attacked the LDS Church, even though the Deseret News had helped the Valley Tan get started with gifts of type and paper.

The Valley Tan went out of business two years later after Army troops stationed at Camp Floyd left for the Civil War. Other papers came and went in subsequent years, generally divided into Mormon and anti-Mormon camps.

Editors at the Deseret News mostly ignored jibes from local competitors and concentrated on answering articles published by critics of Mormonism in Eastern newspapers. The Salt Lake Tribune began in 1871 and soon launched an unrelenting campaign against the LDS Church, its politics, its doctrines, its practices, its leaders, its people and its very existence. The language became increasingly harsh, bitter and often downright slanderous.

In 1880, Charles W. Penrose became Deseret News editor and

gradually was drawn into the name-calling fray, wielding an often sarcastic and biting pen of his own. Feelings ran high. John Q. Cannon, a Deseret News writer, enraged over what he termed a "vile" story, once punched a Tribune reporter on the street and whipped him with a piece of rawhide.

Only after statehood and the disappearance of Mormon/non-Mormon political parties did the conflicts lose their substance. But not until the 20th century did antagonisms slowly fade, although the two papers competed fiercely in their coverage of the news.

## Inventions make a difference

Outside news was often difficult to get until the telegraph arrived in Salt Lake City in 1861. Suddenly, information across the country arrived in minutes instead of weeks and even months. The first weekly Deseret News containing telegraph dispatches was printed Oct. 22, 1861, and the office was mobbed by a news-hungry crowd. News columns for decades were simply headed "From the Telegraph," or even more colorfully as the "Latest by lightning."

When the Deseret News was founded, metal type was assembled by hand at the rate of about 10 words a minute. Another hand-operated press was added in 1851 and allowed individual pages of the newspaper to be enlarged. But a truly revolutionary change occurred in 1864 when the paper bought a steam-powered cylinder press capable of printing 1,800 newspapers an hour.

That was followed by a new Bullock press in 1890 that printed both sides of the newsprint at once and could produce 14,000 eight-page newspapers an hour. In 1897, linotype machines were installed with typewriter-like keyboards that could set molten metal into type five times faster than doing it by hand.

With these devices — linotype machines and high-speed presses — the basic production methods for the Deseret News were essentially established for the next 75 years.

Newsgathering itself got quicker when telephones were installed in 1878. Typewriters came in the 1870s, although many reporters still preferred scribbling out stories in pencil. Halftone photo engraving made it possible to print photographs in 1899.

Teletype machines were added in 1926. Essentially they were remote-controlled typewriters that reproduced information being written elsewhere. Clattering away day and night, the machines produced huge amounts of potential news copy. Finally, photos transmitted by wire started in 1935.

In 1972 a new revolution began, one that would alter the Deseret News more in its next two decades than in its first 120 years combined. First, the traditional hot metal type gave way to a photo composition process. The venerable linotype machines migrated into museums.

In 1983 word processing computers eliminated stories written on paper as well as the typewriters used to write them. Some old-timers stoutly resisted the new terminals, but it was a losing cause. Gone were the paste pots, editing with a pencil and other old-fashioned practices. National and international news was silently transmitted by satellite to Deseret News computers; the clattering teletype machines disappeared.

Artists who once busily turned out illustrations with pen and pencil or retouched photographs — the latter a constant job —

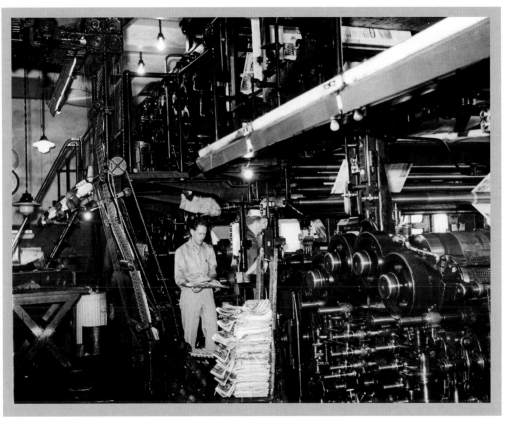

A pressman checks copies of the Deseret News as they come off the presses at Richards Street sometime around 1940.

*Deseret News files*

today hunch over a computer screen instead. Photographic prints themselves are largely gone, replaced by images on a screen.

In the 1990s, the Associated Press stopped sending copies of photos by wire. Instead they transmit photo images by satellite into a computer where the pictures are stored and retrieved as digital images.

The old Speed Graphic camera with flash attachment — a stereotypical symbol of a news photographer — is long gone. Increasingly, Deseret News photographers use digital cameras without any film at all in them. Those pictures exist as electronic signals on a computer disc. They can be transmitted by computer from a distant news site without having to rush film back to the photo lab darkroom.

For example, Deseret News photographer Jeff Allred was sent to cover the launch of hot air balloons at a Freedom Festival in Utah County, some 50 miles from the newspaper office. After taking a number of pictures, he hopped into a balloon with the pilot and clicked away from high in the air. While still aloft, he put a digital card into his laptop computer so he could look at what pictures he had taken, then hooked his laptop to his cell phone and transmitted the data to the Deseret News. Color photos were in the paper 30 minutes later.

In 1995 the paper took its first steps into the new computerized media with a Crossroads Information Network, a dial-up service that linked readers to Deseret News computers — free to Deseret News subscribers and at a monthly fee for others. Crossroads soon disappeared when the paper launched its popular Web site **(http://www.desnews.com).**

It now offers the day's editorial content in full, or any individual articles or pictures therefrom. Misplaced a recent newspaper or

article? Don't fret. It's still there online. One of the system's top features also allows related stories from past issues to be retrieved by topic.

The Deseret News Web site also offers access to constantly updated national news service stories and photos that didn't make it into print, plus expanded movie schedules and television logs. Within days, the complete texts of LDS conference talks are being read around the world. The newspaper's electronic archives dating back to 1988 and the Deseret News library's local, national and international sources are all available on the same Internet Web site.

The number of "hits" or contacts with items on the Deseret News Web site has grown steadily, reaching 350,000 to 400,000 a day by 1999 — as much as newspapers many times larger. The number of "page views" where someone turns to a Deseret News page online runs to more than 4 million a month from all over the world.

You can't line the bottom of the bird cage or wrap the garbage in an online newspaper, but on the other hand it has made the Deseret News a recognized worldwide name in the information business.

## Extra, extra, read all about it!

An enduring, old-fashioned image of early journalism is that of a newsboy peddling papers on the street, sometimes crying "extra" and shouting out the headlines. For more than 100 years that popular image was a reality for the Deseret News.

For a long time the paper had no home delivery. Papers were bought at the newspaper office or from a newsboy on downtown streets. Even after the advent of home delivery, street sales were a big item. There was little radio, no television, no malls, no suburbs, and in the 1920s, '30s and '40s downtown streets were crowded places full of customers.

During the '20s and '30s street sales became a regular battleground. About 50 newsboys sold papers on Salt Lake's streets. They were assigned certain corners but often tried to invade someone's more lucrative turf. Fistfights were common. Not until the approach of World War II did vendors work out a truce among themselves.

In those decades newsboys paid a nickel for three or four papers at the News office, taking 20 to 30 papers at a time and selling them for 5 cents apiece, perhaps making a profit of 75 cents or more on a really good day, plus occasional tips.

Big news doesn't always happen in tidy packages in tune with daily deadlines. In the days before radio and television — and even for many years after — major events often called for an "extra" edition to quickly get details before the public — morning, noon or night.

The biggest extra published by the Deseret News was on Aug. 16, 1935, telling of the death of humorist Will Rogers and famous pilot Wiley Post in a plane crash in Alaska. More than 30,000 newspapers were sold on the streets that morning. The last extra issued by the Deseret News reported details of the assassination of President John F. Kennedy on Nov. 22, 1963.

Coin-operated newspaper dispensers appeared in the city and elsewhere in 1960. A few newsboys continued to sell papers downtown during that decade, but they were all gone by 1970.

## Content, looks keep changing

The Deseret News in the early days was a somber journal, with narrow news columns topped by equally narrow and uninformative headlines. One page looked pretty much like another. There were no pictures on the news stories, but from the beginning many advertisements had woodcut illustrations.

When all ads were moved inside the paper in 1891, much of the eye appeal disappeared from the front pages, although columns were widened and the pages were more balanced. It was the first of many style changes over the years that would produce different looks, including headlines stretching over more than one column, a variety of type sizes, even wider news columns, "artistic" section heads, and a more horizontal makeup.

Want ads were published with the first Deseret News, but a regular classified ad section first appeared in the 1890s with only a handful of notices. Classified ads have grown steadily ever since and are now one of the more popular and successful parts of the paper, reaching up to 50 pages or more some days and containing thousands of ads.

The first illustration accompanying a news story was printed in April 1893, a three-column drawing of the Salt Lake Temple in connection with the temple dedication. The story also featured the biggest headlines to appear in the Deseret News up to that time. By 1897 drawings were being used lavishly in syndicated features.

A photograph first appeared in the Deseret News April 6, 1899, in an advertisement and created a sensation. (Early advertisers were always more daring than news editors, sometimes running their ads sideways or upside down to grab readers' attention.) Photos for the news columns began in 1900 with a picture of piled-up coffins after the Scofield mine disaster that killed 200.

An enormously popular photographic trend began in 1940 with the publication of pictures of 1-year-old babies. For more than 30 years, daily baby pictures were a staple in the paper, but the growing number of babies finally took so much space that the feature had to stop in 1972.

One-shot comic strips showed up in 1901, but the first regular strip with a standard title, "Just Kids," appeared in 1916. This was followed by the famous "Katzenjammer Kids." Others included a science-fiction type named "Radio Ray" and a family strip, "The Nebbs." The latter was so popular it ran for 30 years and often was printed at the top of the front page. By 1999, the Deseret News comic page carried 20 different strips and as many as five one-picture cartoons.

Articles especially for women began in 1892 as "Women and Home" and then as "In Woman's Sphere" subtitled, "By one of the sex," to make sure readers knew it was a woman author, a Mrs. Frances Richards. The items were a mixture of Dear Abby, Good Housekeeping, Miss Manners and Sunday School.

In one of her early columns, Mrs. Richards said it wasn't necessary to have meat at every meal and gave some alternatives. She followed that by explaining that women are not obliged to have the same political views as their husbands. They are, she declared, "free, independent, altogether untrammeled spirits" and can form

Deseret News files

A picture taken in 1941 has the staff gathered around the copy desk. Heavily-reinforced concrete pillars support the presses.

their own opinions "without consulting anybody's wishes."

Those early writings eventually gave rise to newspaper "society" pages featuring social events, weddings, fashions and recipes. Those evolved into more family-oriented features, and the name "society page" was dropped for more generic terms, like "Lifestyle" and "Today" sections.

The first Deseret News sports story was published in 1860, commenting on a boxing match near London between a British champion and an American challenger. The bare-knuckle bout was stopped in the 42nd round when "rowdies" broke up the event. Stories on cricket matches, which were big in the Mountain West, appeared from time to time. Although the winner was usually announced, sometimes in roundabout fashion, the score was often forgotten or added as a final afterthought.

The first actual sports page appeared April 23, 1898, under a banner announcing "The Sporting World." The page featured syndicated stories, with illustrations, on yachting and the preparing of boats, on the horse-racing season in New York and on the 50th birthday of W.G. Grace, a famous British cricket player; no games, no scores, no local sports.

A lack of material must have contributed to the title on the next week's sports page, which announced "The World of Sport and Drama." A lengthy illustrated story on wrestling and one on the Cincinnati baseball club shared space with stories of the theater and a drawing of a mature female star of the stage.

Soon after the turn of the century, however, daily sports pages became commonplace. They looked in many ways like today's sports sections, with much attention to local high school and college football games. Sports coverage grew from one page in 1919 to three and four pages within the next decade and for special emphasis was printed on pink paper.

One long-gone sports feature rated headlines for more than a

half-century: the LDS All-Church Basketball Tournament. The first games were in 1911, and the competition became a regular event in 1922. Until it was dissolved in 1972, the tournament drew church teams nationwide and received major coverage each year.

Except for major league baseball and local minor league teams, professional sports received little attention in the pages of the Deseret News for decades, a far cry from the flood of NFL and NBA coverage of today. Local boxing was big, starting with ex-Utahn Jack Dempsey becoming world heavyweight champion in 1919. Many Utah heroes, both individuals and college teams, made the national stage in golf, tennis, auto racing, boxing, the Olympics, basketball and football.

The era of major local professional sports franchises began in the early 1970s and gave an added dimension to sports news — particularly when the Utah Jazz gained national and even international esteem.

## Deseret News in private hands

Although the Deseret News has always been associated with the LDS Church, there was a time — October 1892 to September 1898 — when it was leased to a private firm in an effort to find a way out of heavy debt.

The new manager was the Deseret News Publishing Co., a private entity formed and owned chiefly by Abraham H. Cannon and John Q. Cannon. The Cannon family had a long association with the newspaper, and the Cannon name would continue to be a familiar one at the Deseret News for many decades.

John Q. Cannon had been a newsboy. He hauled rags to the paper mill and held a variety of jobs with the newspaper, from reporter to editorial writer. With the change in management he became editor. The Cannons brought dramatic changes to the appearance, content and mechanical operations of the Deseret News.

However, it remained a struggle to turn a profit, and the church took back the lease in 1898 and assumed all outstanding debt. Not until Horace G. Whitney became business manager in 1899 did a turnabout in profitability occur. In his 21 years on the job, the newspaper increased its circulation five-fold and continued to make innovative changes. When Whitney retired the Deseret News had a surplus in its bank account.

General authorities of the LDS Church have kept an eye on the newspaper. In fact, the first editor, Willard Richards, was a member of the First Presidency. Other apostles and general authorities held positions as editors and managers at the Deseret News from time to time.

But after 1932, when the paper was incorporated under the old title, Deseret News Publishing Co., some of them began to be appointed to an official new body — the board of directors. Sylvester Q. Cannon, presiding bishop of the church, was named first president of the newly incorporated company.

Albert E. Bowen, named to the board not long after being called as an apostle in 1937, eventually became president of the publishing company, serving until 1952.

Mark E. Petersen, who had been everything from cub reporter to editor in a distinguished 28-year career — and was an apostle during eight years of his editorship — became president in 1952. He served until 1963 when he was assigned as a mission president but returned as company president from 1966 to 1971. Annual writing awards at the newspaper are given in his memory.

Church President Gordon B. Hinckley, who among many other things is a prolific lifelong writer and a pioneer in adapting church materials for use in radio and television, originally planned on a journalism career. As a boy he was a paper carrier for the Deseret News. He joined the News board of directors in 1960 two years after being called as an assistant to the Twelve, and served as company president from 1971 to 1977.

Thomas S. Monson joined the advertising division of the Deseret News in 1948 and the subsequent Newspaper Agency Corp. Later he became sales manager and then general manager of the Deseret News Press, a post he held when he was called as an apostle in 1963. He was named to the News board of directors in 1965 and was its chairman from 1977 to 1996 — the year when all general authorities stopped serving on commercial boards.

L. Glen Snarr, a former Deseret News city editor and an advertising executive, has been chairman of the board since 1996.

## People make the big story

A newspaper is more than machines and type styles. From the half-starved writers and printers of the early days to the high-tech newsroom of the computer age, it still takes talented people to craft the stories and make the presses roll.

Bylines, featuring the name of the reporter who wrote the story, were first used in the Deseret News on sports pages in the 1920s, the so-called "golden era" of sports, but not until the 1930s were they used on stories in other parts of the paper. Recognized or not, many heroes helped the Deseret News write its way into history.

Any historical account of the Deseret News owes a major debt to Wendell J. Ashton, who in 1950 wrote "Voice in the West," a definitive 100-year detailed history of the newspaper and its people. Ashton had a stint at the Deseret News as managing editor and left for a high-powered career in advertising. He returned to the News to serve as publisher in 1978-1985.

The most prestigious award in journalism, the coveted Pulitzer Prize, was won by the Deseret News in 1961 for "local reporting under the pressure of deadline," thanks to the dogged work of reporter Robert D. Mullins.

An out-of-work miner tried to rob three tourists on a lonely road 250 miles from Salt Lake City. It escalated into murder, kidnapping, a manhunt and a dramatic suicide. In the holdup a woman tourist was killed, and her male companion was shot in the head and left for dead. The woman's 15-year-old daughter was kidnapped by the gunman and never seen again. When the FBI stopped the killer's car a few days later, the man shot himself, and the fate of the missing girl was never solved.

During the manhunt that followed the robbery-murder, Mullins scarcely slept over several days, drove 1,800 miles in desolate

In the 1920s, the newspaper's compositors were well-dressed despite working around heavy type and ink.

Deseret News files

country, often far from any phones, yet met every deadline with detailed stories. He scored several "firsts" even before law enforcement agencies knew about them.

Despite the Pulitzer Prize praise, Robert remained a quiet, self-effacing man who modestly gave fellow Deseret News staffers credit, saying the award really was a team effort.

One of the first illustrators at the Deseret News was Jack Sears, a young Salt Lake man who went to New York to study art. While there he did cartoons for a New York paper and on his return worked for the News after the turn of the century, when line drawings became commonly used on news stories. When no pictures were available of accident or crime victims, Sears was known to occasionally go to the morgue, prop up the corpse and do a quick portrait.

Later artists included James A. Bywater, who for more than 20 years ran a one-man department for both the newsroom and the advertising department. Charles A. Nickerson, a man of prodigious talent, became art director in 1947 and the art staff was greatly expanded, along with many other departments of the paper.

He helped plan and shape the changing appearance of the Deseret News, and for 37 years his drawings, carrying the signature "Chasnik," graced the pages of the newspaper with wit and style.

An 1861 writer, Scipio Africanus Kenner, fancied himself a Mark Twain-style humorist and even looked like the famous writer. Unfortunately he wasn't. He had such quick hands that he could compose stories by setting metal type as he went along. He probably started more newspapers in Utah than any other person,

but none of them survived. However, he began a somewhat erratic tradition of humor in the Deseret News.

One of the extremely funny people in more recent times was Harry Jones, a reporter and columnist who worked at the Deseret News from 1947 until his death in 1975 and was renowned for his quick wit. He wrote a humor column for nearly a decade and had a large following of faithful fans. His lament that his son graduated from Snow College and still couldn't shovel the sidewalks was typically wry Harry Jones.

Steve Hale, a former Deseret News columnist, tells of the time an irate reader called to complain about an editorial. Harry answered the phone. The caller became angrier as the conversation went on. Finally the man said, "I ought to come up and punch you in the nose. What's your name anyway?"

"Steve Hale," said Harry.

Other well-known personalities at the Deseret News over the years included Les Goates, a kindly, soft-spoken gentleman who became sports editor in 1919 just as the sports-crazy 1920s were about to explode. For 30 years he covered all the big stories and quietly worked to help many local athletes receive national recognition. He was a friend of legendary sports writers Grantland Rice and Walter Camp. His "Les Go" column was a familiar News fixture and at one time was the longest running column in any Western newspaper.

He was followed by Hack Miller, a prolific writer who churned out endless columns and stories for 45 years and served as sports editor for 30 years. He roamed the world and once was national president of the U.S. Basketball Writers Association. Hack made news as well as writing about it. As a young reporter, Hack covered University of Utah basketball games — after performing as a star forward in the games. And while writing about and taking part in an invitational golf tournament in Reno one year, he hit a hole-in-one to win a luxurious Ferrari auto.

But for all his years of sports writing, Hack made perhaps his biggest splash with another kind of story. In 1965 he toured Vietnam, using his military reserve rank of colonel to visit combat areas closed to most newsmen. He searched out Utah servicemen and wrote about them. Those daily stories made up one of the most avidly read series ever to appear in the Deseret News.

Another familiar face, Lee Benson, a former sports writer and editor in the 1970s and 1980s, won a national award as Utah Sportswriter of the Year an incredible 12 straight times. He now writes a general column for the paper.

Dignified Ted Cannon, who started at the Deseret News as a copy boy in 1917, was the public personification of journalism for many people during a 40-year career in which he held nearly every job on the newspaper, including sports writer, reporter and columnist to managing editor.

Theron C. Liddle, a hard-driving reporter who joined the News in 1936, later helped guide the news operation through some of its most tumultuous years of growth and change. He became city editor in 1944 and managing editor in 1949, a post he held for 22 years, one of the longest serving managing editors in Deseret News history.

Few Deseret News people were better known than Howard Pearson, who lived and breathed newspapering for 60 years, carrying an enormous work load and even sleeping at the office to cap 18-hour days.

Although he had been everything from a newsboy at age 7 to various kinds of writer and editor, Howard's most enduring legacy came from his work as entertainment editor. He loved the performing arts and personally knew or had interviewed just about everybody in the business. Although a discerning and careful critic, he never said mean things.

He was theater critic, the city's first movie editor and the town's first television critic. For more than 30 years he was "Mr. TV" in Utah and was highly respected throughout the entertainment industry. Howard owned one of the first television sets in Salt Lake Valley, and while many U.S. newspapers tried to ignore the new medium, he urged coverage of programs and in 1950 personally compiled and published the first local daily TV schedules in Utah.

Chris Hicks, a movie reviewer who followed Howard's pioneering work in the field, also became a prominent public personality. For 20 years, ending in 1998, he watched — and wrote about — as many as 200 films a year, the good, the bad and the ugly. Since there are more of the latter than the former, two decades worth is enough for anyone, including an enthusiastic fan like Chris. He has now turned to other kinds of writing and editing.

Another public figure at the Deseret News was Lavor K. Chaffin, who joined the paper in 1948 and subsequently was named as Utah's first full-time education writer. He became an authority on schools and won the trust and respect of parents, teachers, administrators and political leaders.

One sign of the quality of his work is the lengthy list of national and state awards given Lavor by education groups. In 1982 he received an honorary doctorate degree from Westminster College, an especially satisfying moment for someone who had never attended any college — except as a guest teacher.

In 1962, Lavor used his considerable prestige to win over reluctant and cautious Salt Lake educators for a new kind of program — suggested by writer Steve Hale — to honor high school seniors with "Academy Awards" type annual recognition for academic achievement. Lavor wrote many of the plan's details, and out of that effort came the now-heralded Sterling Scholar program. In 37 years — with the crucial involvement of promotion manager Keith West and his staff — it has spread to high schools all over the state, something Lavor called his "most satisfying achievement."

Gordon Eliot White, Deseret News Washington bureau chief for three decades until his retirement in 1991, made national waves in 1977-78 with his stories on the effects of 1950s atomic testing fallout on Utahns and others "downwind" from the Nevada test site. Federal officials for years had steadfastly denied any harm from the tests, but Gordon's stories uncovered the connection between the open-air tests and high rates of cancer among southern Utahns.

Gordon's work won him a whole collection of major national awards — everything except the Pulitzer Prize, and there were many who thought he should have received that as well. His honors included the 1980 Raymond Clapper Award from the White House Correspondents Association. It was presented in person by President Jimmy Carter.

The city desk area about 1959 shows reporters efficiently typing stories on double-carbon rolls of paper.

Lee Davidson succeeded Gordon in Washington and reaped seven major awards of his own during a decade in the nation's capital. They included some of the top honors from his peers at the National Press Club for his work in exploring Washington issues for hometown readers. He also received back-to-back first place honors in 1990 and 1991 for the quality of his work in general.

## Women at the News

Newspapering historically was mostly a man's world. Women were usually relegated — if they had any journalistic role at all — to the so-called "society pages." This was true at the Deseret News as well as papers across the country.

In the World War I era, about one of every 20 newspaper people nationally was a woman, usually writing for and about women. By 1968 this was down to one in five and many of them were general assignment reporters no longer doing just society, weddings, fashions and homemaking stories. By the end of the 20th century women made up half or more of all writers and editors at the Deseret News. The managing editor, looking around the newsroom one recent afternoon, noticed that of the various editors' desks, every single one was occupied at that moment by a woman.

But women also have been present at the Deseret News from its beginnings. Fourteen-year-old Ellen Richards, daughter of editor

Willard Richards, helped fold the pages of the first paper and later carried news copy from the editor to the printer, the very first copy girl.

In the 1870s, Brigham Young called women as typesetters at the paper in order for them to learn the business. They later set type for the Women's Exponent magazine. One of the early typesetters was Martha Hughes Cannon, who set type for five years to help pay her way through medical school. She later became one of Utah's first women physicians and its first female state senator.

Special features for women appeared in the Deseret News in the 1890s. In 1900 Josephine Spencer became society editor and introduced the detailed fashion and social chitchat that was to be the staple of society pages for the next 50 years. Question and answer columns — forerunners of Dear Abby — were carried in the 1890s, but not until the '20s and the writings of Kathleen Kaye and her "Heartitorium" did they become hugely popular. The quantity of mail that came across her desk was enormous.

Ramona Cannon, who wrote under the pen name Mary Marker, had an influential advice column for 26 years, starting in 1947. A highly educated woman, she was a teacher, a linguist, a writer of hundreds of articles for church magazines. Yet she started taking classes in marriage counseling, sociology and psychology at age 60 in order to function in her new role as Mary Marker. She finally laid down her pen at age 86.

Another well-known fixture on the women's page was Winifred Jardine, who joined the staff in 1948 as food editor, a post she held for 36 years. A whole generation was raised on her recipes and helpful kitchen hints. She, too, received an honorary degree, from Utah State University. Evelyn Sims Mazuran, a daughter of former Utah Gov. Henry H. Blood, became women's editor in 1947 and for 30 years ran a tight ship that saw a gradual evolution from "society" to more family related features.

No information exists on who was the very first female general assignment reporter at the Deseret News. But one of the early ones was Gladys Hobbs, who was at the paper in the '30s and '40s and did excellent work on a 1938 train-school bus crash that killed 23 Jordan District students.

World War II opened the gates for women reporters. During the war some 38 male Deseret News staffers entered the military, and many reporting positions were filled by women. Maxine Martz, an Iowa native, walked in and asked for a job in 1944. Fortunately they hired her because she turned out to be one of the best reporters who ever worked at the News. Her exemplary career spanned 42 years, mostly on the pressure-packed, deadline-driven rewrite desk and as a witty columnist.

Despite her excellent performance, Maxine labored in the early part of her career under the old prejudice about women. Once she complained to an editor about a new male reporter making more than she was. The editor replied, "Frankly, Max, if we had to pay you $400 a month, we'd rather have a man."

However, she persevered and a later city editor said if he had to trim his staff down to one person, he'd keep Maxine. Her work was once used at the University of Utah school of journalism as an example to would-be reporters on how to get the job done.

Also making a deep impression at the Deseret News was Twila Van Leer, who came to the newspaper as a quiet high school graduate from Pioche, Nev. She was hired as a copy girl in 1951 and through sheer hard work — and tremendous talent — became one of the most respected writers in the business.

In three stints at the Deseret News totaling 30 years — surrounding a couple of six-year interruptions to devote full time to her large family — Twila won more than 50 major journalism awards for her work as a medical writer and later as education writer.

Her retirement in 1995 was supposed to make a little room in a crowded life, but she hardly left the office, returning to do editing and to work as a consultant and writer for the newspaper on major history projects, including this book.

DeAnn Evans, who sandwiched two terms at the Deseret News around work in public relations at a Boston hospital, broke new ground when she was named the newspaper's managing editor in 1981. She was the first female managing editor of a daily newspaper in Utah, serving previously as associate city editor and in a variety of editing and reporting assignments. She left the Deseret News to acquire a doctorate in journalism and subsequently became a professor of communications at the University of Utah.

The first female city editor at the News is Angelyn N. Hutchinson, named to the post in December 1998. She joined the paper in 1983 after eight years as a medical writer for the Salt Lake Tribune. She juggled a young family around part-time work at the Deseret News until 1991, when she became a full-time staff writer. Angie was on her way to being an English teacher when a university journalism class unexpectedly diverted her career plans.

## Has anybody seen Swen?

In early 1937 a daily column began appearing in the Deseret News on the front page of the local section; a collection of newsy tidbits and chatty comments. The headline was always the same — "Dictated… But Not Read." The writer was one Swen Teresed.

Lots of Scandinavians lived in Utah, and many readers assumed the writer was one of that ethnic community. Only some perceptive people recognized Swen Teresed as Deseret News spelled backward. By 1939 the column carried a cursive art head "Swen Says" by Swen Teresed.

But no record remains about who Swen really was. An exhaustive search, including interviews with old-time newsmen, yielded no information. Earlier editors who would have known are no longer living.

In 1945 the mysterious Swen became a woman. A column titled "Scene Today" was written daily by Maxine Martz under Swen's name, but even she had no knowledge about the earlier Swen. One rookie reporter at the time is now embarrassed to admit that it took weeks for her to recognize the backward nature of Swen's name.

Swen was finally laid to rest in 1952, and Maxine in later years wrote a similar column under her own name. But the original

Offices on Richards Street, shown here about 1950, housed the newspaper for 42 years.

identity of Swen is one of those puzzles apparently lost in the mists of time — if one can say that about the 1930s.

## The Church News

From the beginning, the pages of the Deseret News naturally were loaded with stories, comments and sermons in connection with the LDS Church. Even into the 1880s, the front page frequently was given over entirely to a lengthy verbatim account of a sermon by a church general authority. Other stories contained detailed minutes of ward sacrament meetings.

But as efforts were made to put more emphasis on daily secular news, the church items were moved to inside pages in 1891, except for general conference and other major news events. Yet as early as the Civil War, editors had been thinking about a separate section carrying only church-related stories.

Finally, in April 1931, a weekly tabloid-size Church Section was published. At the time, the church had 672,000 members, and 678 missionaries were set apart that year. The new publication was such an immediate hit that it soon required a full-time editor. Henry A. Smith, a Deseret News reporter, was given the job. The original eight-page section grew over the years to as many as 24 pages.

The name changed in 1943 to the Church News, and it began using correspondents that year. In addition to being a supplement in the Saturday Deseret News, it was mailed independently to

people beyond the newspaper circulation area and soon had more readers than the daily. As of 1999, the Church News circulation was about 170,000 higher than the daily.

During World War II and beyond, the paper published an LDS serviceman's edition of the Church News. About the size of the palm of a hand, it was printed monthly and distributed free to men and women in the armed forces around the world from May 1944 to July 1948.

In 1948 a religion-based editorial essay began to appear each week on the back page of the Church News. Until his death in 1984, Elder Mark E. Petersen of the Council of the Twelve wrote virtually all of them.

After 37 years as editor, Henry Smith received another assignment in 1968. When J Malan Heslop, former chief photographer at the Deseret News, became editor the Church News featured more visual emphasis, and all covers were printed in color — a practice that continues today.

Heslop also sent staffers to cover church events worldwide. The paper — like the church itself — had long outgrown its original focus on the Wasatch Front when most stories featured detailed accounts of stake, ward and even quorum and class activities. A majority of Church News stories now carry datelines from other parts of the United States and other areas of the world where millions of members reside.

The Deseret News Church Almanac, a massive project currently approaching 600 pages, started in 1974, and a new version of the information-packed book is produced every two years by the Church News staff.

Dell Van Orden took the post as Church News editor in 1976 after eight years as assistant editor — a total tenure approaching Henry Smith-like numbers — before retiring in 1999.

## Deseret Press, a printing empire

You can do more things with a printing press than publish a newspaper. The Deseret Press was soon established as a commercial printing operation — in fact it began six months before the first Deseret News came out.

The first such work was theater handbills, perhaps because the printers were actors in the old Social Hall theater. Also produced was the first edition in 1851 of the annual Deseret Almanac. The press soon printed church books, including the first Utah edition of the Book of Mormon in 1871; local currency, and copies of the proposed constitution for the State of Deseret.

The Deseret Press had many different names over the years. It became known as the Deseret News Power Press Printing Establishment in 1867, evolved through several subsequent titles, including the Deseret News Book and Job Press in 1900 and then the Deseret News Press. Finally catching up to reality, the word "News" was dropped from the name and the printing plant became simply the Deseret Press in 1972.

The newspaper and job printing operation separated in 1900 when the Deseret News moved to a different building, although the two later shared quarters on Richards Street for 23 years. In 1948 the Deseret Press moved to a building acquired from the wartime Remington Arms Plant in an industrial area near 1700 South and Redwood Road. The printing plant became a completely

Dressed in their blazers, the Deseret News photo staff poses for its picture in 1955.

*Utah State Historical Society*

autonomous operation in 1967 with different management than the Deseret News.

It was one of the biggest printing operations in 11 Western states. The press had grown to include production of millions of copies of books, magazines and manuals for the LDS Church as well as a wide range of commercial printing. But work for a growing church was taking more and more of the plant's capacity.

In 1980 the Deseret Press abandoned all commercial work, gave up its historic name and became the Salt Lake Printing Center for the LDS Church. Wm. James Mortimer, vice president and general manager of Deseret Press, was with the press from 1959 to 1963 and again from 1979 to 1985, leading the transition from a commercial entity to a church operation before becoming Deseret News publisher in 1985.

## The Deseret News goes on the air

In 1920, an era when radio was pretty much confined to crystal set owners — who had to build their own — some people at the Deseret News began looking at the possibilities of radio. It was a hesitant beginning.

Horace G. (Bud) Whitney, the Deseret News' brilliant general manager and a far-sighted newspaper visionary, couldn't quite see the advantage of radio. The telegraph and wireless telegrams already offered fast communication; teletype machines gave a constant flow of information. He vetoed the idea.

Later the same year, others picked up the battle and in November the Deseret News announced plans for nightly "wireless news flashes" by Morse Code to some 100 members of the Deseret News Wireless Club, who would post bulletins in their local communities.

Several newspapers in the eastern United States were starting their own radio stations, which encouraged Deseret News enthusiasts. But efforts to set up a radio station were expensive and nearly killed the project before it started. American Telephone and Telegraph (AT&T) had a monopoly on most of the necessary equipment and wanted $25,000 for the tubes and condensers. Elias S. Woodruff, Deseret News business manager, was able to get

equipment for a few hundred dollars from sources back East who were fighting AT&T.

A radio license was acquired by the Deseret News April 21, 1922, and on May 6 the first broadcast of KZN took place in a one-room "studio" — a tin shack —atop the newspaper building. The daylong program reached for 1,000 miles and started with an inaugural talk by LDS Church President Heber J. Grant.

The newspaper and new radio station parted company later in 1922 when KZN was sold to its radio engineer. In 1924 it became KFTP and later that same year was purchased by Earl J. Glade, one of the early KZN employees and future Salt Lake mayor. The following year he obtained the call letters KSL from a radio station in Alaska.

The LDS Church in subsequent years reacquired the radio station, and it became the basis for today's large KSL Television and Radio operation.

## A bookseller, too

The newspaper began operating a bookstore after 1871, the year it issued an edition of the LDS hymnbook. The freshly printed hymnbooks were offered that year in exchange for clean cotton rags that could be used to manufacture newsprint for the paper-starved Deseret News.

In 1920 the newspaper's bookshop was merged with another church-owned entity — the Deseret Sunday School Union bookstore, which dealt generally in church instructional materials. The merger created Deseret Book, now grown to a retailing giant with more than 30 stores in 10 states.

## A sponsor of community events

As a good citizen in the community, the Deseret News has been more than just a provider of information. It also sponsors popular events that have become part of the community's fabric and tradition.

One of the most firmly entrenched is the annual Deseret News Ski School. Wilby Durham, who had been everything from reporter to assistant general manager, started the ski school in 1948 with legendary and influential Olympic skier Alf Engen, who ran the popular program for decades. It is considered by many to be the oldest free learn-to-ski program in the United States. More than 250,000 students were taught to ski in a tradition that has stretched across generations in some families. Graduates include several Olympic skiers.

Begun in 1962, the Deseret News/KSL-TV Sterling Scholar Awards offer academic recognition to high school seniors in 13 categories. The program operates in five regions across Utah. Fifty-two schools along the Wasatch Front participate in a program directly administered by the Deseret News. Over the years, some 25,000 students have been named Sterling Scholars. The honors are given in a prestigious television show.

The Deseret News marathon started in 1970 and the 10K race in 1983 — both run in connection with the July 24 pioneer parade. The marathon is considered one of the nation's toughest and currently draws an average of 800 participants each year. Another 2,500 run in the 10K event. Both attract world-class runners.

Since 1959 the Deseret News has sponsored an annual Salute to Youth symphony concert in which young musicians compete at the State Fair for the privilege of performing at a special program with

the Utah Symphony. Eight to 10 finalists are chosen each year, and over time hundreds of young artists have performed in an impressive display of talent.

In a commitment to education and literacy, the Deseret News Newspaper in Education (NIE) program reaches out to schools across the state, providing newspapers and curriculum materials to teachers and students. Most newspapers have similar programs, but none (in the 50,000 to 99,000 circulation range) has won more awards than the Deseret News. The News is famous for its No Books Day, which encourages teachers to put textbooks aside and teach from the newspaper. Carolyn Dickson and her NIE staff put approximately 300,000 copies of the Deseret News into classrooms each year.

A Goals for Utah program in the 1960s and 1970s involved editors and community leaders in an annual effort to identify and provide support for worthy state projects. One lasting legacy of that effort is the still-growing Jordan River Parkway. Deseret News Editor William B. Smart for several years spearheaded this effort and chaired an early community group seeking to design, promote and raise funds for the parkway. As executive editor and later editor, Smart was responsible for creation of many of the paper's community programs.

One unusual project in the mid-1940s was sponsorship — with J.R. Simplot, the Idaho potato magnate — of a basketball team known as the Simplot Deserets, featuring local collegiate players, plus a couple of imports. The outsiders included Laddie Gale, an all-American from Oregon, and Andy (Stretch) Duncan, from William and Mary who later played for the Boston Celtics. Gale and Duncan worked briefly for the Deseret News. Also on the team was All-American Arnie Ferrin, who didn't get out of the service in time to play for the University of Utah that year.

The team played in an Amateur Athletic Union league. AAU teams nationwide had corporate sponsors and the AAU tournament each year was the biggest basketball tournament in America. The AAU

*Deseret News files*

Picture from the 1980s shows the main newsroom, looking across the sports desk toward the city desk in the Regeant St. offices before they were demolished.

The First Presidency — Gordon B. Hinckley, center, Thomas S. Monson, left, and James E. Faust stand before the new Deseret News building before its dedication in 1997. All had been officers of the company.

*Deseret News files*

program in some respects was a predecessor of the National Basketball Association. The Deseret News co-sponsorship of the team only lasted for a year or two, but it was a hint of things to come, namely the Utah Jazz.

Other yearly events include a statewide spelling bee involving thousands of young students; a Fourth of July Cavalcade; Santa's Helping Hand (now merged with the Tribune's Sub for Santa); a Messiah sing-in; a newly revived art show; a Christmas I Remember Best story contest that has roots in the previous century, and a host of contests, concerts and competitions, to name just a few.

Many of these activities were started and/or supervised by Keith West, Deseret News promotion manager for 37 years until his retirement in 1993. Keith could juggle a variety of different programs at the same time and still win national awards for quality community projects.

## Oh, give me a home...

Despite being one of the first newspapers in the entire West and a fixture in Utah for 150 years, the Deseret News changed homes many times — doing business in a dozen different locations over the years.

The newspaper stayed in its first home, a tiny one-room adobe building, only a few months before moving into a nearby three-story adobe structure that served as a church store and post office, a site eventually occupied by the Hotel Utah. It was a constant battle to keep curious store customers from meddling with the press.

In 1854 the Deseret News found another home in the Tithing Office, an annex at the rear of the same church store. Two years later it moved into the Council House, a handsome public building on the southwest corner of South Temple and Main Street. But the paper was soon ordered to Fillmore because of the uncertainties of the Utah War. It returned to the Council House after five months.

This nomadic existence ended in 1862 when the newspaper moved back into cramped quarters at the church store where it stayed for the next 41 years.

The Deseret News in 1903 moved into new offices, a six-story building and eight-story annex on the site of the Council House, which burned down in 1883.

Because many of the new offices were occupied by the Union Pacific Railroad, the structure was commonly called the Union Pacific building despite bulletins from teletype machines being hung in the office windows so the latest news could be read by passers-by.

Some twenty-four years later, in 1926, the News found another long-lasting residence on Richards Street, across the street from the south entrance to Temple Square. The mammoth four-story concrete building with adjacent presses would be the newspaper's home for 42 years.

When the Joint Operating Agreement was signed with the Salt Lake Tribune in 1952, both papers began to be printed on presses on Regent Street a couple of blocks away, a frenetic experience for the Deseret News since all news copy had to be shuttled from the paper's Richards Street offices.

Because Deseret News offices on Richards Street were on the third floor of the building, messengers ran up and down stairs several dozen times a day. As a shortcut, news copy was lowered in a basket on a rope to the parking lot below. That didn't work too well; the papers tended to spill out or blow away. Staffers came up with an innovation — a breadbox. Tied on a rope, it was used to lower news copy to waiting messengers. Finally a metal chute was constructed with a tailor-made box. This high-tech movement of copy lasted 16 years.

In 1968, the Deseret News moved to remodeled offices on the 100 South corner of Regent Street, almost on top of the once-distant presses. In 1995, that building was torn down to make room for a new structure designed by the Deseret News. The newspaper offices were temporarily shifted to the other side of Regent Street under a parking terrace.

But on May 28, 1997, an attractive nine-story building opened at 30 E. 100 South, giving the Deseret News one of the most modern newspaper offices in the country. The building was paid for by the time of its completion — a tribute to the paper's soundness and those who guided its fortunes over the past century and a half.

## Facing the future

The Deseret News can look back with a great deal of satisfaction and pride on its 150-year history. Few commercial institutions in the United States can claim such a long, unbroken performance.

During a century-and-a-half, the newspaper has been more than a chronicler of events, large and small, although it has done that quite well. Those who read these pages will recognize that the Deseret News has preserved the past in vivid fashion.

But it also has done more than inform. It has touched the lives of hundreds of thousands of readers. It has helped them to cook and garden, to pursue hobbies, to solve personal problems, to raise their children, to learn new skills, to share interests, to gain honors and to help others.

The future clearly is going to be different from the past for the Deseret News. Change takes place faster than it once did and the result is more confusing. Like its readers, the newspaper will face new challenges, new ways of doing things and will have to find new answers.

Yet one thing will remain the same. The Deseret News will continue to inform, to explain, and try to make sense of an often confusing world. It will continue to help readers and to be a useful and improving presence in the community. Given the courage, hopes and dreams of the paper's very first editors, it can do no less.

## Deseret News editors, publishers

Willard Richards, first editor, 1850-54
Albert Carrington, 1854-59, 1863-67
Elias Smith, 1859-63
George Q. Cannon, 1867-73, 1877-79
David O. Calder, 1873-77
Charles W. Penrose, 1880-92, 1899-1907
John Q. Cannon, 1892-98, 1918-22, 1928-31
J.M. Sjodahl, 1898-99, 1907-14
E. LeRoy Bourne, 1914-17
Harold Goff, 1922-28
Alexander Buchanan, 1928
Joseph J. Cannon, 1931-34
James A. Langton, 1934-43
David A. Robinson, 1943-46
Mark E. Petersen, 1946-52
O. Preston Robinson, 1952-64
E. Earl Hawkes, 1964-72
William B. Smart, 1972-86
Wendell J. Ashton, publisher, 1978-85
Wm. James Mortimer, publisher-editor, 1985-1996; publisher 1997-
John Hughes, editor, 1997; editor and chief operating officer, 1999-

Hal Knight is a veteran Utah newsman who retired from the Deseret News in 1995 after 40 years of service. Before joining the newspaper in 1955 he worked for the Salt Lake Telegram and briefly for the Salt Lake Tribune between active military duty in the Korean War and a mission for the LDS Church. At the Deseret News he was a reporter, science editor for 20 years and editorial writer for 13 years.

# The century's biggest stories

April 15, 1999.

The Newseum in Arlington, Va., compiled this list of the century's 100 top news stories, based on a survey of prominent U.S. journalists and scholars.

**1.** United States drops atomic bombs on Hiroshima and Nagasaki, and Japan surrenders to end World War II. 1945.

**2.** American Neil Armstrong becomes the first human to walk on the moon. 1969.

**3.** Japan bombs Pearl Harbor; United States enters World War II. 1941.

**4.** Wilbur and Orville Wright fly the first powered airplane. 1903.

**5.** Women win the vote. 1920.

**6.** President John F. Kennedy assassinated in Dallas. 1963.

**7.** Horrors of Nazi Holocaust, concentration camps exposed. 1945.

**8.** World War I begins in Europe. 1914.

**9.** Brown vs. Board of Education ends "separate but equal" school segregation. 1954.

**10.** U.S. stock market crashes; the Great Depression sets in. 1929.

**11.** Alexander Fleming discovers the first antibiotic, penicillin. 1928.

**12.** Structure of DNA discovered. 1953.

**13.** USSR dissolves, Mikhail Gorbachev resigns, Boris Yeltsin takes over. 1991.

**14.** President Richard M. Nixon resigns after Watergate scandal. 1974.

**15.** Germany invades Poland; World War II begins in Europe. 1939.

**16.** Russian revolution ends; Communists take over. 1917.

**17.** Henry Ford organizes the first major assembly line to produce Model T cars. 1913.

**18.** Soviets launch Sputnik, first space satellite; space race begins. 1957.

**19.** Albert Einstein presents special theory of relativity; general relativity theory follows. 1905.

**20.** FDA approves birth control pill. 1960.

**21.** Dr. Jonas Salk's polio vaccine proven effective in University of Pittsburgh tests. 1953.

**22.** Adolf Hitler named chancellor of Germany; Nazi Party begins to seize power. 1933.

**23.** Civil rights leader Martin Luther King assassinated in Memphis, Tenn. 1968.

**24.** D-Day invasion marks the beginning of the end of World War II in Europe. 1944.

**25.** Deadly AIDS disease identified. 1981.

**26.** Congress passes landmark Civil Rights Act outlawing segregation. 1964.

**27.** Berlin Wall falls as East Germany lifts travel restrictions. 1989.

**28.** Television debuts in America at New York World's Fair. 1939.

**29.** Mao Tse-tung establishes People's Republic of China; Nationalists flee to Formosa (Taiwan). 1949.

**30.** Charles Lindbergh crosses the Atlantic in first solo flight. 1927.

**31.** First mass market personal computers launched. 1977.

**32.** World Wide Web revolutionizes the Internet. 1989.

**33.** Scientists at Bell Labs invent the transistor. 1948.

**34.** FDR launches "New Deal," sweeping federal economic, public works legislation to combat Depression. 1933.

**35.** Cuban missile crisis threatens World War III. 1962.

**36.** "Unsinkable" Titanic, largest man-made structure, sinks. 1912.

**37.** Germany surrenders: V.E. Day celebrated. 1945.

**38.** Roe vs. Wade decision legalizes abortion. 1973.

**39.** World War I ends with Germany's defeat. 1918.

**40.** First regular radio broadcasts begin in America. 1909.

**41.** Worldwide flu epidemic kills 20 million. 1918.

**42.** 'ENIAC' becomes world's first computer. 1946.

**43.** Regular TV broadcasting begins in the United States. 1941.

**44.** Jackie Robinson breaks baseball's color barrier. 1947.

**45.** Israel achieves statehood. 1948.

**46.** Plastic invented; revolutionizes products, packaging. 1909.

**47.** Montgomery, Ala., bus boycott begins after Rosa Parks refuses to give up her seat to a white person. 1955.

**48.** A-bomb tested in New Mexico. 1945.

**49.** Apartheid ends in South Africa; law to treat races equally. 1993.

**50.** Civil rights march converges on Washington, D.C.; Martin Luther King gives "I Have A Dream" speech. 1963.

**51.** American scientists patent the computer chip. 1959.

**52.** Marconi transmits radio signal across the Atlantic. 1901.

**53.** White House sex scandal leads to impeachment of President William Jefferson Clinton. 1998.

**54.** Secretary of State George Marshall proposes European recovery program (The Marshall Plan). 1947.

**55.** Presidential candidate Robert F. Kennedy assassinated in California. 1968.

**56.** U.S. Senate rejects Versailles Treaty, dooms League of Nations. 1920.

**57.** Rachel Carson's "Silent Spring" stimulates environmental movement. 1962.

**58.** British rock group The Beatles make debut on the "Ed Sullivan Show." 1964.

**59.** Congress passes Voting Rights Act, outlawing measures used to suppress minority votes. 1965.

**60.** Yuri Gagarin becomes first man in space. 1961.

**61.** First jet airplane takes flight. 1941.

**62.** U.S. combat troops arrive in South Vietnam; U.S. planes bomb North Vietnam. 1965.

**63.** North Vietnamese forces take over Saigon. 1975.

**64.** Manhattan Project begins secret work on atomic bomb; Fermi triggers first atomic chain reaction. 1942.

**65.** Congress passes GI Bill of Rights to help veterans. 1945.

**66.** Alan Shepard becomes first American in space. 1961.

**67.** Watergate scandal engulfs Nixon administration. 1973.

**68.** Earthquake hits San Francisco; "Paris of the West" burns. 1906.

**69.** United Nations officially established. 1945.

**70.** Communists build wall to divide East and West Berlin. 1961.

**71.** Mohandas Gandhi begins leading nonviolent reform movement in India. 1920.

**72.** Standard Oil loses Supreme Court antitrust suit; monopolies suffer blow. 1911.

**73.** United States withdraws last ground troops from Vietnam. 1973.

**74.** North Atlantic Treaty Organization established. 1949.

**75.** Joseph Stalin begins forced modernization of the Soviet Union; resulting famines claim 25 million. 1928.

**76.** Democrat Franklin D. Roosevelt beats incumbent President Herbert Hoover. 1932.

**77.** Mikhail Gorbachev becomes Soviet premier, begins era of "glasnost." 1985.

**78.** Max Planck proposes quantum theory of energy. 1900.

**79.** Scientists clone sheep in Britain. 1997.

**80.** Congress passes interstate highway bill. 1956.

**81.** Panama Canal opens, linking the Atlantic and Pacific oceans. 1914.

**82.** Betty Friedan's "The Feminine Mystique" inaugurates modern women's rights movement. 1963.

**83.** The space shuttle Challenger explodes, killing crew including schoolteacher Christa McAuliffe. 1986.

**84.** United States sends troops to defend South Korea. 1950.

**85.** Violence erupts at Democratic National Convention in Chicago. 1968.

**86.** Sigmund Freud publishes "The Interpretation of Dreams." 1900.

**87.** China begins "Great Leap Forward" modernization program: estimated 20 million die in ensuing famine. 1958.

**88.** United States enters World War I. 1917.

**89.** Babe Ruth hits 60 home runs — a record that would last for 34 years. 1927.

**90.** John Glenn becomes first American to orbit the Earth. 1962.

**91.** North Vietnamese boats reportedly attack U.S. ships; Congress passes Gulf of Tonkin resolution. 1964.

**92.** Pathfinder lands on Mars, sending back astonishing photos. 1997.

**93.** Hitler launches "Kristallnacht," ordering Nazis to commit acts of violence against German Jews. 1938.

**94.** Winston Churchill designated prime minister of Great Britain. 1940.

**95.** Louise Brown, first "test-tube baby," born healthy. 1978.

**96.** Soviets blockade West Berlin; Western allies respond with massive airlift. 1948.

**97.** Bill Gates and Paul Allen start Microsoft Corp. to develop software for Altair computer. 1975.

**98.** Chernobyl nuclear plant explosion results in deaths of an estimated 7,000. 1986.

**99.** Teacher John Scopes' trial pits creation against evolution in Tennessee. 1925.

**100.** The U.S. surgeon general warns about smoking-related health hazards. 1964.

---

## The Church News'
# Top 10
LDS stories of the century

**1.** The revelation on extending the priesthood to all worthy males.

**2.** A great increase in temple building worldwide.

**3.** The First Presidency's statements on God, the origin of man; proclamations to the world with the Quorum of Twelve, including on the Family.

**4.** Scriptures published, new editions; new sections to the Doctrine and Covenants.

**5.** Missionary work: more missionaries called, new training centers, standard discussions used.

**6.** Growth of the church to 10 million members, internationalization of the church.

**7.** Expansion of family history activity, worldwide microfilming of records.

**8.** Impact and use of technology, including radio, television, video and satellites to expand the reach of the church.

**9.** Creation of the Quorums of the Seventy and decentralization of many church administrative functions.

**10.** Priesthood correlation and development of the Correlation Committee, formalization of home teaching and family home evenings.

*This list was compiled from questionnaires sent to 900 randomly selected church leaders and members, 50 percent of which were returned. While not an official list, it is nevertheless an indication of how members perceive the growth of the LDS Church.*

# Newsmakers
## People we wrote about

### Beehive Hall of Fame

Maurice Abravanel, musician
Terrel H. Bell, educator
Lowell Bennion, humanitarian
Reva Beck Bosone, judge
Juanita Brooks, writer
John Browning, inventor
Martha Hughes Cannon, medicine
Billy Casper, golfer
Willam Farr Christensen, ballet director
Virginia Farr Cutler, home economics
Thomas D. Dee II, businessman
Jack Dempsey, boxer
Marriner S. Eccles, banker
Alf Engen, skier
Henry Eyring, scientist, educator
Philo T. Farnsworth, inventor
John Francis Fitzpatrick, publisher
Harvey Fletcher, inventor, educator
Gene Fullmer, boxer
Ken Day Garff, businessman
Robert H. Hinckley, engineering, aeronautics, broadcasting
Daniel Jackling, mining
David M. Kennedy, banking, ambassador
Willem Johan Kolff, scientist
J. Willard Marriott, businessman
David O. McKay, church leader
Mormon Tabernacle Choir, musicians
Merlin Olsen, football player
Esther E. Peterson, consumer leader
Alma W. Richards, Olympic athlete
George Romney, business, politics
Eliza R. Snow, poet and religious leader
Belle Spafford, religious leader
George Sutherland, U.S. Supreme Court Justice
N. Eldon Tanner, religious leader
Obert C. Tanner, businessman and philanthropist
Daniel Sylvester Tuttle, religious leader
John Wallace, banker
John A. Widtsoe, educator
Brigham Young, religious leader

*Sponsored by Fotheringham & Assoc., KUTV, Marriott Corporation and Utah State Historical Society*

### Utah Terrritorial governors

Brigham Young, 1850-1857
Alfred Cumming, 1857-1861
John W. Dawson, 1861
Stephen S. Harding, 1862-1863
James D. Doty, 1863-1865
Charles Durkee, 1865-1869
John W. Shaffer, 1870
Vernon H. Vaughan, 1870-1871
George L. Woods, 1871-1875
Samuel B. Axtell, 1875
George W. Emery, 1875-1880
Eli H. Murray, 1880-1886
Caleb W. West, 1886-1888; 1893-1896
Arthur L. Thomas, 1889-1893

### Utah State governors

Heber M. Wells (R) 1896-1905
John C. Cutler (R) 1905-1909
William Spry (R) 1909-1917
Simon Bamburger (D) 1917-1921
Charles R. Mabey (R) 1921-1925
George H. Dern (D) 1925-1933
Henry H. Blood (D) 1933-1941
Herbert B. Maw (D) 1941-1949
J. Bracken Lee (R) 1949-1957
George D. Clyde (R) 1957-1965
Calvin L. Rampton (D) 1965-1977
Scott M. Matheson (D) 1977-1985
Norman H. Bangerter (R) 1985-1993
Michael O. Leavitt (R) 1993-

### Presidents of The Church of Jesus Christ of Latter-day Saints

| President | Date set apart |
|---|---|
| Joseph Smith | April 6, 1830 |
| Brigham Young | Dec. 27, 1847 |
| John Taylor | Oct. 10, 1880 |
| Wilford Woodruff | April 7, 1889 |
| Lorenzo Snow | Sept. 13, 1898 |
| Joseph Fielding Smith | Oct. 17, 1901 |
| Heber J. Grant | Nov. 23, 1918 |
| George Albert Smith | May 21, 1945 |
| David O. McKay | April 9, 1951 |
| Joseph Fielding Smith | Jan. 23, 1970 |
| Harold B. Lee | July 7, 1972 |
| Spencer W. Kimball | Dec. 30, 1973 |
| Ezra Taft Benson | Nov. 10, 1985 |
| Howard W. Hunter | June 5, 1994 |
| Gordon B. Hinckley | March 12, 1995 |

*Source: Deseret News Church News Almanac*

# Acknowledgments

Through this book we came into contact with many friendly and helpful people. They include Bill Slaughter and Pauline Musig of the LDS Church Historical Department, who helped us find early photographs and provided back issues from their archives; Edith Menna at the International Society of the Daughters of Utah Pioneers who allowed us access to their collection of artifacts and photographs; Max Evans and his staff at the Utah State Historical Society for help in locating old photographs; and Ron Read of the LDS Church Museum of History and Art, who patiently combed through pictures of hundreds of paintings and photographs for us.

Here at the Deseret News we are indebted to Steve Handy, our marketing director; to Colleen Randall and her library staff and to Kari Morandi, Lisa Bowen and Jeannine Garrett who retyped many stories from blurry microfilm copies. Copy editors Susan Hermance and Anne Ferguson helped proofread the pages. John Clark located and scanned photographs, and Alex Nabaum made the corrections.

Lyle Mumford of Publishers Press, our printer, was very patient and tutored us in what we considered a complicated venture.

We appreciate and thank our publisher, Wm. James Mortimer, for his vision and encouragement, and our editor, John Hughes, for his great support and insights.

And, of course, we all are in debt to the great many talented staff members whose work since 1850 still seems as lively as the day they produced it.

— Don C. Woodward

This book was compiled from original microfilmed copies of the Deseret News. Each excerpt is dated. Those interested in reading the complete story or related ones can find copies of the microfilm at the Salt Lake City Public Library, Salt Lake County's Whitmore Library or at the Marriott Library at the University of Utah. Many books address Utah's history. We had guidance from the "Utah History Encyclopedia" edited by Allan Kent Powell; "Utah, the Right Place," the official centennial history by Thomas G. Alexander; and "Utah's Heritage" by S. George Ellsworth.

In 1851 the Deseret News moved into an adobe building on the northeast corner of South Temple and Main Streets known as the Deseret Store Building. The paper was produced there until 1854, and again from 1862 to 1903.

# Index